Mini Owners Workshop Manual

John S Mead

Models covered
All Mini Saloon, Estate, Van and Pick-up models including special and limited editions; 848 cc, 998 cc and 1098 cc
All Mini Clubman Saloon and Estate models; 998 cc & 1098 cc
Mini Cooper S Mk III; 1275 GT and Mini Cooper; 1275 cc

Does not cover ERA Mini Turbo

(646–12S13)

ABCDE
FGHIJ
KLMNO
PQRST
2

Haynes Publishing Group
Sparkford Nr Yeovil
Somerset BA22 7JJ England

Haynes Publications, Inc
861 Lawrence Drive
Newbury Park
California 91320 USA

Acknowledgements

Thanks are due to Rover Cars Limited for their assistance in the supply of technical information. Thanks are also due to the Champion Sparking Plug Company Limited who supplied the illustrations showing spark plug conditions, to Holt Lloyd Limited who supplied the illustrations showing bodywork repair, and to Duckhams Oils who provided lubrication data. Sykes-Pickavant provided some of the workshop tools. Finally, thanks are due to all those people at Sparkford who helped in the production of this manual.

A book in the **Haynes Owners Workshop Manual Series**

Printed by J. H. Haynes & Co. Ltd, Sparkford, Nr Yeovil, Somerset BA22 7JJ, England

ISBN 1 85010 718 1

British Library Cataloguing in Publication Data
Mead, John S. *1950–*
Mini '69 to '91 owners workshop manual.
1. Cars. Maintenance
I. Title
629.28722
ISBN 1-85010-718-1

Restoring and Preserving our Motoring Heritage

Few people can have had the luck to realise their dreams to quite the same extent and in such a remarkable fashion as John Haynes, Founder and Chairman of the Haynes Publishing Group.

Since 1965 his unique approach to workshop manual publishing has proved so successful that millions of Haynes Manuals are now sold every year throughout the world, covering literally thousands of different makes and models of cars, vans and motorcycles.

A continuing passion for cars and motoring led to the founding in 1985 of a Charitable Trust dedicated to the restoration and preservation of our motoring heritage. To inaugurate the new Museum, John Haynes donated virtually his entire private collection of 52 cars.

Now with an unrivalled international collection of over 210 veteran, vintage and classic cars and motorcycles, the Haynes Motor Museum in Somerset is well on the way to becoming one of the most interesting Motor Museums in the world.

A 70 seat video cinema, a cafe and an extensive motoring bookshop, together with a specially constructed one kilometre motor circuit, make a visit to the Haynes Motor Museum a truly unforgettable experience.

Every vehicle in the museum is preserved in as near as possible mint condition and each car is run every six months on the motor circuit.

Enjoy the picnic area set amongst the rolling Somerset hills. Peer through the William Morris workshop windows at cars being restored and browse through the extensive displays of fascinating motoring memorabilia.

From the 1903 Oldsmobile through such classics as an MG Midget to the mighty 'E' Type Jaguar, Lamborghini, Ferrari Berlinetta Boxer, and Graham Hill's Lola Cosworth, there is something for everyone, young and old alike, at this Somerset Museum.

Haynes Motor Museum

Situated mid-way between London and Penzance, the Haynes Moto Museum is located just off the A303 at Sparkford, Somerset (home o the Haynes Manual) and is open to the public 7 days a week all yea round, except Christmas Day and Boxing Day.

Contents

Mini 850 Saloon

Mini Clubman Saloon

Mini Clubman Estate

Mini 1275GT

General dimensions, weights and capacities

General dimensions

Overall length

Saloon	120.25 in (3054 mm)
Clubman Saloon	124.62 in (3165 mm)
Cooper (1990 on)	120.5 in (3061 mm)
Estate	134 in (3403 mm)
Van	129.87 in (3298 mm)
Pick-up	130.5 in (3314 mm)

Overall width

Except Cooper (1990 on)	55.5 in (1410 mm)
Cooper (1990 on) including mirrors	61.25 in (1560 mm)

Overall height

Saloon:	
Pre 1985 model	53 in (1346 mm)
1985 model on	53.25 in (1353 mm)
Cooper (1990 on)	52.4 in (1331 mm)
Estate, Van and Pick-up	53.5 in (1359 mm)

Wheelbase

Saloon	80.15 in (2036 mm)
Estate, Van and Pick-up	84 in (2134 mm)

Turning circle (kerb to kerb)

Saloon	342 in (8687 mm)
Estate, Van and Pick-up	348 in (8839 mm)

Weights

Kerb weight

Saloon (rubber cone suspension):	
Manual transmission	1406 lb (638 kg)
Automatic transmission	1450 lb (658 kg)
Saloon (Hydrolastic suspension):	
Manual transmission	1510 lb (679.5 kg)
Automatic transmission	1554 lb (699.3 kg)
Estate	1514 lb (686.7 kg)
Van	1369 lb (621.5 kg)
Pick-up	1371 lb (622.4 kg)

Maximum towing weights

Saloon	896 lb (404 kg)
Estate, Van and Pick-up	672 lb (303 kg)

Maximum towing hitch load .... 100 lb (45 kg)

Maximum roof rack load .... 90 lb (40 kg)

Capacities

Engine oil with filter change

Manual transmission	8.5 pints (10.2 US pints, 4.83 litres)
Automatic transmission	9 pints (11 US pints, 5 litres)

Engine oil without filter change (approximate)

Manual transmission	7.5 pints (9 US pints, 4.2 litres)
Automatic transmission	8 pints (9.6 US pints, 4.4 litres)

Cooling system .... 6.25 pints (7.5 US pints, 3.5 litres)

Fuel tank

Saloon and Clubman:	
Early models	5.5 gallons (6.6 US gallons, 25 litres)
Later models	7.5 gallons (8.7 US gallons, 33 litres)
Estate, Van and Pick-up	6 gallons (7.2 US gallons, 27 litres)
1275 GT	7.5 gallons (8.7 US gallons, 33 litres)
Cooper S Mk III	11 gallons (13 US gallons, 50 litres)

About this manual

Its aim

The aim of this manual is to help you get the best from your car. It can do so in several ways. It can help you decide what work must be done (even should you choose to get it done by a garage), provide information on routine maintenance and servicing, and give a logical course of action and diagnosis when random faults occur. However, it is hoped that you will use the manual by tackling the work yourself. On simpler jobs it may even be quicker than booking the car into a garage and going there twice to leave and collect it. Perhaps most important, a lot of money can be saved by avoiding the costs the garage must charge to cover its labour and overheads.

The manual has drawings and descriptions to show the function of the various components so that their layout can be understood. Then the tasks are described and photographed in a step-by-step sequence so that even a novice can do the work.

Its arrangement

The manual is divided into fourteen Chapters, each covering a logical sub-division of the vehicle. The Chapters are each divided into Sections, numbered with single figures, eg 5; and the Sections into paragraphs (or sub-sections), with decimal numbers following on from the Section they are in, eg 5.1. 5.2, 5.3 etc.

It is freely illustrated, especially in those parts where there is a detailed sequence of operations to be carried out. There are two forms of illustration: figures and photographs. The figures are numbered in sequence with decimal numbers, according to their position in the Chapter – Fig. 6.4 is the fourth drawing/illustration in Chapter 6. Photographs carry the same number (either individually or in related groups) as the Section or sub-section to which they relate.

There is an alphabetical index at the back of the manual as well as a contents list at the front. Each Chapter is also preceded by its own individual contents list.

References to the 'left' or 'right' of the vehicle are in the sense of a person in the driver's seat facing forwards.

Unless otherwise stated, nuts and bolts are removed by turning anti-clockwise, and tightened by turning clockwise.

Vehicle manufacturers continually make changes to specifications and recommendations, and these, when notified, are incorporated into our manuals at the earliest opportunity.

Whilst every care is taken to ensure that the information in this manual is correct, no liability can be accepted by the authors or publishers for loss, damage or injury caused by any errors in, or omissions, from the information given.

Introduction to the Mini

The brainchild of Sir Alec Issigonis, the Mini was first sold in Britain in August 1959. With its transverse engine and front wheel drive, it represented a radical departure from the traditional range of domestically produced small cars, and the fact that it is still selling well more than thirty years after its introduction is a tribute to the fundamental soundness of what appeared, at first, to be a somewhat unorthodox design.

Mini models covered by this manual are powered by the well proven A-series engine in 848 cc, 998 cc, 1098 cc and 1275 cc forms. Current 998 cc models also incorporate many of the components specially developed for the revised A-plus engine fitted to the Metro range. The engine crankcase is bolted directly to the transmission casing, which also serves as the sump since the two units share the same oil supply. The manual transmission is of the four-speed all-synchromesh type, with a four-speed automatic version being available as an option on 998 cc models.

Power to the driveshafts is transmitted via the differential, which is also housed in the transmission casing. The driveshafts have a universal joint at each end, the outer joints being of the Birfield constant velocity type, while at the inner end either a Hooke type or constant velocity type joint may be fitted.

The hydraulic braking system utilizes drum brakes on all wheels, with the exception of the high performance Cooper S and 1275 GT versions and late 1984-on models, which are equipped with disc brakes at the front. A dual circuit hydraulic system is used on all later models.

The rack-and-pinion steering gear and fully independent suspension provide the Mini with the safe, positive handling characteristics which have endeared this car to so many people since the first models were produced.

Tools and working facilities

Introduction

A selection of good tools is a fundamental requirement for anyone contemplating the maintenance and repair of a motor vehicle. For the owner who does not possess any, their purchase will prove a considerable expense, offsetting some of the savings made by doing-it-yourself. However, provided that the tools purchased meet the relevant national safety standards and are of good quality, they will last for many years and prove an extremely worthwhile investment.

To help the average owner to decide which tools are needed to carry out the various tasks detailed in this manual, we have compiled three lists of tools under the following headings: *Maintenance and minor repair, Repair and overhaul,* and *Special.* The newcomer to practical mechanics should start off with the *Maintenance and minor repair* tool kit and confine himself to the simpler jobs around the vehicle. Then, as his confidence and experience grow, he can undertake more difficult tasks, buying extra tools as, and when, they are needed. In this way, a *Maintenance and minor repair* tool kit can be built-up into a *Repair and overhaul* tool kit over a considerable period of time without any major cash outlays. The experienced do-it-yourselfer will have a tool kit good enough for most repair and overhaul procedures and will add tools from the *Special* category when he feels the expense is justified by the amount of use these tools will be put to.

It is obviously not possible to cover the subject of tools fully here. For those who wish to learn more about tools and their use there is a book entitled *How to Choose and Use Car Tools* available from the publishers of this manual.

Maintenance and minor repair tool kit

The tools given in this list should be considered as a minimum requirement if routine maintenance, servicing and minor repair operations are to be undertaken. We recommend the purchase of combination spanners (ring one end, open-ended the other); although more expensive than open-ended ones, they do give the advantages of both types of spanner.

Combination spanners - $\frac{5}{16}$, $\frac{3}{8}$, $\frac{7}{16}$, $\frac{1}{2}$, $\frac{9}{16}$, $\frac{5}{8}$, $\frac{11}{16}$, $\frac{3}{4}$ in AF
Adjustable spanner - 9 inch
Spark plug spanner (with rubber insert)
Spark plug gap adjustment tool
Set of feeler gauges
Brake adjuster spanner (where applicable)
Rear brake bleed screw spanner
Screwdriver - 4 in long x $\frac{1}{4}$ in dia (flat blade)
Screwdriver - 4 in long x $\frac{1}{4}$ in dia (cross blade)
Combination pliers - 6 inch
Hacksaw (junior)
Tyre pump
Tyre pressure gauge
Grease gun
Oil can
Fine emery cloth (1 sheet)
Wire brush (small)
Funnel (medium size)

Repair and overhaul tool kit

These tools are virtually essential for anyone undertaking any major repairs to a motor vehicle, and are additional to those given in the *Maintenance and minor repair* list. Included in this list is a comprehensive set of sockets. Although these are expensive they will be found invaluable as they are so versatile - particularly if various drives are included in the set. We recommend the $\frac{1}{2}$ in square-drive type, as this can be used with most proprietary torque spanners. If you cannot afford a socket set, even bought piecemeal, then inexpensive tubular box wrenches are a useful alternative.

The tools in this list will occasionally need to be supplemented by tools from the *Special* list.

Sockets (or box spanners) to cover range in previous list
Reversible ratchet drive (for use with sockets)
Extension piece, 10 inch (for use with sockets)
Universal joint (for use with sockets)
Torque wrench (for use with sockets)
Mole wrench - 8 inch
Ball pein hammer
Soft-faced hammer, plastic or rubber
Screwdriver - 6 in long x $\frac{5}{16}$ in dia (flat blade)
Screwdriver - 2 in long x $\frac{5}{16}$ in square (flat blade)
Screwdriver - $1\frac{1}{2}$ in long x $\frac{1}{4}$ in dia (cross blade)
Screwdriver - 3 in long x $\frac{1}{8}$ in dia (electricians)
Pliers - electricians side cutters
Pliers - needle nosed
Pliers - circlip (internal and external)
Cold chisel - $\frac{1}{2}$ inch
Scriber
Scraper
Centre punch
Pin punch
Hacksaw
Valve grinding tool
Steel rule/straight-edge
Allen keys
Selection of files
Wire brush (large)
Axle-stands
Jack (strong scissor or hydraulic type)

Special tools

The tools in this list are those which are not used regularly, are expensive to buy, or which need to be used in accordance with their manufacturers' instructions. Unless relatively difficult mechanical jobs are undertaken frequently, it will not be economic to buy many of these tools. Where this is the case, you could consider clubbing together with friends (or joining a motorists' club) to make a joint purchase, or borrowing the tools against a deposit from a local garage or tool hire specialist.

The following list contains only those tools and instruments freely available to the public, and not those special tools produced by the vehicle manufacturer specifically for its dealer network. You will find occasional references to these manufacturer's special tools in the text of this manual. Generally, an alternative method of doing the job without the vehicle manufacturers' special tool is given. However, sometimes, there is no alternative to using them. Where this is the case and the relevant tool cannot be bought or borrowed you will have to entrust the work to a franchised garage.

Valve spring compressor
Piston ring compressor
Balljoint separator
Universal hub/bearing puller
Impact screwdriver
Micrometer and/or vernier gauge
Dial gauge
Stroboscopic timing light
Dwell angle meter/tachometer
Universal electrical multi-meter
Cylinder compression gauge
Lifting tackle
Trolley jack
Light with extension lead

Buying tools

For practically all tools, a tool factor is the best source since he will have a very comprehensive range compared with the average garage or accessory shop. Having said that, accessory shops often offer excellent quality tools at discount prices, so it pays to shop around.

There are plenty of good tools around at reasonable prices, but always aim to purchase items which meet the relevant national safety standards. If in doubt, ask the proprietor or manager of the shop for advice before making a purchase.

Care and maintenance of tools

Having purchased a reasonable tool kit, it is necessary to keep the tools in a clean serviceable condition. After use, always wipe off any dirt, grease and metal particles using a clean, dry cloth, before putting the tools away. Never leave them lying around after they have been used. A simple tool rack on the garage or workshop wall, for items such as screwdrivers and pliers is a good idea. Store all normal spanners and sockets in a metal box. Any measuring instruments, gauges, meters, etc, must be carefully stored where they cannot be damaged or become rusty.

Take a little care when tools are used. Hammer heads inevitably become marked and screwdrivers lose the keen edge on their blades from time to time. A little timely attention with emery cloth or a file will soon restore items like this to a good serviceable finish.

Working facilities

Not to be forgotten when discussing tools, is the workshop itself. If anything more than routine maintenance is to be carried out, some form of suitable working area becomes essential.

It is appreciated that many an owner mechanic is forced by circumstances to remove an engine or similar item, without the benefit of a garage or workshop. Having done this, any repairs should always be done under the cover of a roof.

Wherever possible, any dismantling should be done on a clean flat workbench or table at a suitable working height.

Any workbench needs a vice: one with a jaw opening of 4 in (100 mm) is suitable for most jobs. As mentioned previously, some clean dry storage space is also required for tools, as well as the lubricants, cleaning fluids, touch-up paints and so on which become necessary.

Another item which may be required, and which has a much more general usage, is an electric drill with a chuck capacity of at least $\frac{5}{16}$ in (8 mm). This, together with a good range of twist drills, is virtually essential for fitting accessories such as wing mirrors and reversing lights.

Last, but not least, always keep a supply of old newspapers and clean, lint-free rags available, and try to keep any working area as clean as possible.

Spanner jaw gap comparison table

Jaw gap (in)	Spanner size
0.250	$\frac{1}{4}$ in AF
0.276	7 mm
0.313	$\frac{5}{16}$ in AF
0.315	8 mm
0.344	$\frac{11}{32}$ in AF; $\frac{1}{8}$ in Whitworth
0.354	9 mm
0.375	$\frac{3}{8}$ in AF
0.394	10 mm
0.433	11 mm
0.438	$\frac{7}{16}$ in AF
0.445	$\frac{3}{16}$ in Whitworth; $\frac{1}{4}$ in BSF
0.472	12 mm
0.500	$\frac{1}{2}$ in AF
0.512	13 mm
0.525	$\frac{1}{4}$ in Whitworth; $\frac{5}{16}$ in BSF
0.551	14 mm
0.563	$\frac{9}{16}$ in AF
0.591	15 mm
0.600	$\frac{5}{16}$ in Whitworth; $\frac{3}{8}$ in BSF
0.625	$\frac{5}{8}$ in AF
0.630	16 mm
0.669	17 mm
0.686	$\frac{11}{16}$ in AF
0.709	18 mm
0.710	$\frac{3}{8}$ in Whitworth, $\frac{7}{16}$ in BSF
0.748	19 mm
0.750	$\frac{3}{4}$ in AF
0.813	$\frac{13}{16}$ in AF
0.820	$\frac{7}{16}$ in Whitworth; $\frac{1}{2}$ in BSF
0.866	22 mm
0.875	$\frac{7}{8}$ in AF
0.920	$\frac{1}{2}$ in Whitworth; $\frac{9}{16}$ in BSF
0.938	$\frac{15}{16}$ in AF
0.945	24 mm
1.000	1 in AF
1.010	$\frac{9}{16}$ in Whitworth; $\frac{5}{8}$ in BSF
1.024	26 mm
1.063	$1\frac{1}{16}$ in AF; 27 mm
1.100	$\frac{5}{8}$ in Whitworth; $\frac{11}{16}$ in BSF
1.125	$1\frac{1}{8}$ in AF
1.181	30 mm
1.200	$\frac{11}{16}$ in Whitworth; $\frac{3}{4}$ in BSF
1.250	$1\frac{1}{4}$ in AF
1.260	32 mm
1.300	$\frac{3}{4}$ in Whitworth; $\frac{7}{8}$ in BSF
1.313	$1\frac{5}{16}$ in AF
1.390	$\frac{13}{16}$ in Whitworth; $\frac{15}{16}$ in BSF
1.417	36 mm
1.438	$1\frac{7}{16}$ in AF
1.480	$\frac{7}{8}$ in Whitworth; 1 in BSF
1.500	$1\frac{1}{2}$ in AF
1.575	40 mm; $\frac{15}{16}$ in Whitworth
1.614	41 mm
1.625	$1\frac{5}{8}$ in AF
1.670	1 in Whitworth; $1\frac{1}{8}$ in BSF
1.688	$1\frac{11}{16}$ in AF
1.811	46 mm
1.813	$1\frac{13}{16}$ in AF
1.860	$1\frac{1}{8}$ in Whitworth; $1\frac{1}{4}$ in BSF
1.875	$1\frac{7}{8}$ in AF
1.969	50 mm
2.000	2 in AF
2.050	$1\frac{1}{4}$ in Whitworth; $1\frac{3}{8}$ in BSF
2.165	55 mm
2.362	60 mm

Buying spare parts and vehicle identification numbers

Buying spare parts

Spare parts are available from many sources, for example: BL garages, other garages and accessory shops, and motor factors. Our advice regarding spare part sources is as follows:

Officially appointed BL garages – This is the best source of parts which are peculiar to your car and are otherwise not generally available (eg complete cylinder heads, internal gearbox components, badges, interior trim etc). It is also the only place at which you should buy parts if your car is still under warranty; non-BL components may invalidate the warranty. To be sure of obtaining the correct parts, it will always be necessary to give the storeman your car's engine and chassis number, and if possible, to take the old part along for positive identification. Remember that many parts are available on a factory exchange scheme – any parts returned should always be clean! It obviously makes good sense to go straight to the specialists on your car for this type of part for they are best equipped to supply you.

Other garages and accessory shops – These are often very good places to buy materials and components needed for the maintenance of your car (eg oil filters, spark plugs, bulbs, fanbelts, oils and greases, touch-up paint, filler paste etc). They also sell general accessories, usually have convenient opening hours, charge lower prices and can often be found not far from home.

Motor factors – Good factors will stock all of the more important components which wear out relatively quickly (eg clutch components, pistons, valves, exhaust systems, brake cylinders/pipes/hoses/seals/shoes and pads etc). Motor factors will often provide new or reconditioned components on a part exchange basis – this can save a considerable amount of money.

Vehicle identification numbers

When ordering spare parts it is essential to give full details of your car to the storeman. He will want to know the commission, car and engine numbers. When ordering parts for the transmission unit or body it is also necessary to quote the transmission casing and body numbers.

Commission number: Stamped on a plate fixed to the bonnet locking platform.

Car number: Located on a plate mounted adjacent to the commission number.

Engine number: Stamped on the cylinder block or on a metal plate fixed to the right-hand side of the cylinder block.

Transmission casing assembly: Stamped on a facing provided on the casting just below the starter motor.

Body number: Stamped on a metal plate fixed to the bonnet locking platform.

Jacking and Towing

Jacking

The jack supplied with Saloon models is intended to lift one side of the car at a time when engaged in one of the two jacking points. If the car bodywork is in poor condition, or if the jacking points are blocked or corroded, it will be necessary to use a scissor or pillar jack under an appropriate part of the subframe. The jack supplied with Estate, Van and Pick-Up models is designed to bear on the subframe.

Some owners jack the car up at the front by means of the engine/transmission casing. This is not a recognised means of lifting the car and cannot be recommended, but should it be necessary to raise the car in this way, place a block of wood between the sump and the jack to spread the load.

Whatever means of jacking is used, always chock the wheels remaining on the ground, apply the handbrake and engage first or reverse gear. Do not venture under the car whilst it is supported solely by a jack, but supplement the jack with axle stands or blocks.

Towing

When towing another vehicle, unless a towbar is fitted, attach the rope or chain to a central part of the rear subframe. Do not tow from the bumpers or from any of the suspension components. Cushion the tow rope if necessary to avoid damage to the body.

When being towed, similar advice applies, with the additional caution that the rope must not be attached to, or interfere with, any steering components. On models with automatic transmission, the engine/transmission oil level must be correct and the gear selector lever must be in the 'N' (neutral) position. The towing speed must not exceed 20 mph (30 kph) and the distance towed should not exceed 30 miles. If the above conditions cannot be met, or if transmission damage is suspected, the car must be towed with the front wheels off the ground.

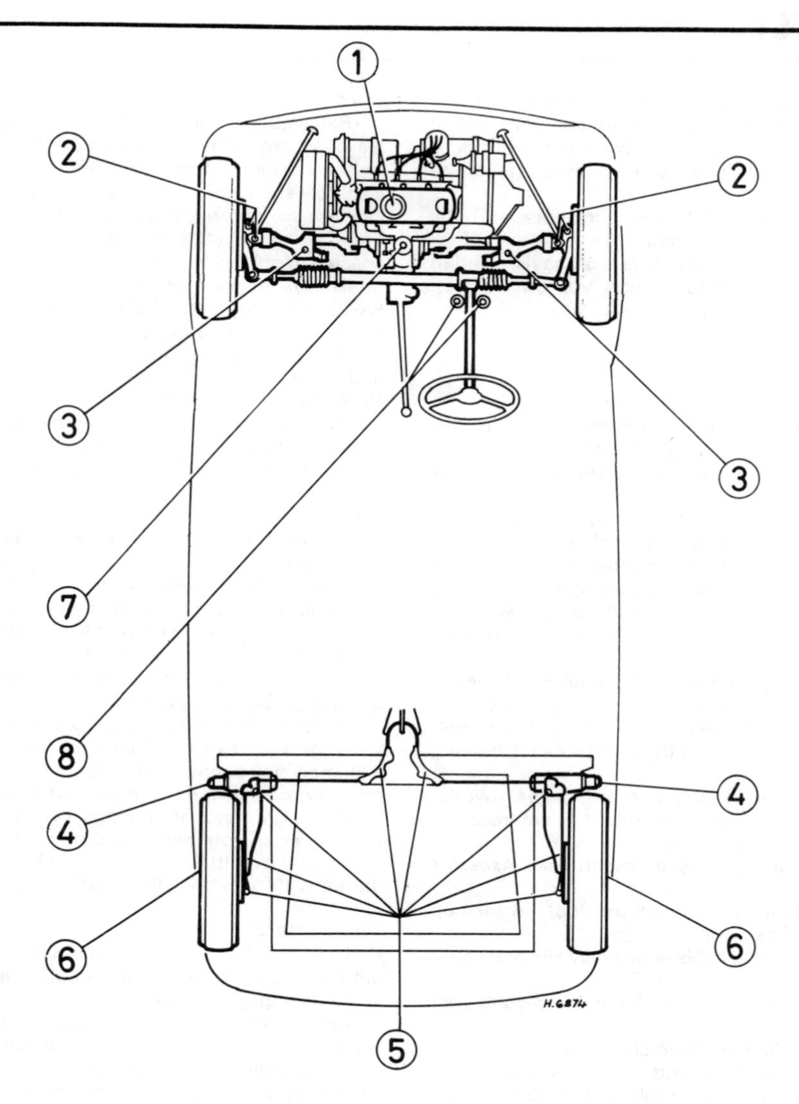

Recommended lubricants and fluids

Component or system	Lubricant type/specification	Duckhams recommendation
1 Engine/transmission*	Multigrade engine oil, viscosity SAE 20W/50, 10W/40 or 10W/30	Duckhams QXR, Hypergrade or 10W/40 Motor Oil
2 Steering swivel hub balljoints	General purpose lithium based grease	Duckhams LB 10
3 Upper front suspension arm swivel	General purpose lithium based grease	Duckhams LB 10
4 Rear radius arm pivots	General purpose lithium based grease	Duckhams LB 10
5 Handbrake cable guides, sectors and linkages	General purpose lithium based grease	Duckhams LB 10
6 Wheel bearings	General purpose lithium based grease	Duckhams LB 10
7 Carburettor dashpot(s)	Multigrade engine oil, viscosity SAE 20W/50, 10W/40, or 10W/30	Duckhams QXR, Hypergrade or 10W/40 Motor Oil
8 Brake and clutch fluid reservoirs	Hydraulic fluid to SAE J1703	Duckhams Universal Brake and Clutch Fluid

***Note:** *Austin Rover specify a 10W/40 oil to meet warranty requirements for models produced after August 1983. Duckhams QXR or 10W/40 Motor Oil are available to meet these requirements.*

Safety first!

Professional motor mechanics are trained in safe working procedures. However enthusiastic you may be about getting on with the job in hand, do take the time to ensure that your safety is not put at risk. A moment's lack of attention can result in an accident, as can failure to observe certain elementary precautions.

There will always be new ways of having accidents, and the following points do not pretend to be a comprehensive list of all dangers; they are intended rather to make you aware of the risks and to encourage a safety-conscious approach to all work you carry out on your vehicle.

Essential DOs and DON'Ts

DON'T rely on a single jack when working underneath the vehicle. Always use reliable additional means of support, such as axle stands, securely placed under a part of the vehicle that you know will not give way.

DON'T attempt to loosen or tighten high-torque nuts (e.g. wheel hub nuts) while the vehicle is on a jack; it may be pulled off.

DON'T start the engine without first ascertaining that the transmission is in neutral (or 'Park' where applicable) and the parking brake applied.

DON'T suddenly remove the filler cap from a hot cooling system – cover it with a cloth and release the pressure gradually first, or you may get scalded by escaping coolant.

DON'T attempt to drain oil until you are sure it has cooled sufficiently to avoid scalding you.

DON'T grasp any part of the engine, exhaust or catalytic converter without first ascertaining that it is sufficiently cool to avoid burning you.

DON'T allow brake fluid or antifreeze to contact vehicle paintwork.

DON'T syphon toxic liquids such as fuel, brake fluid or antifreeze by mouth, or allow them to remain on your skin.

DON'T inhale dust – it may be injurious to health (see *Asbestos* below).

DON'T allow any spilt oil or grease to remain on the floor – wipe it up straight away, before someone slips on it.

DON'T use ill-fitting spanners or other tools which may slip and cause injury.

DON'T attempt to lift a heavy component which may be beyond your capability – get assistance.

DON'T rush to finish a job, or take unverified short cuts.

DON'T allow children or animals in or around an unattended vehicle.

DO wear eye protection when using power tools such as drill, sander, bench grinder etc, and when working under the vehicle.

DO use a barrier cream on your hands prior to undertaking dirty jobs – it will protect your skin from infection as well as making the dirt easier to remove afterwards; but make sure your hands aren't left slippery. Note that long-term contact with used engine oil can be a health hazard.

DO keep loose clothing (cuffs, tie etc) and long hair well out of the way of moving mechanical parts.

DO remove rings, wristwatch etc, before working on the vehicle – especially the electrical system.

DO ensure that any lifting tackle used has a safe working load rating adequate for the job.

DO keep your work area tidy – it is only too easy to fall over articles left lying around.

DO get someone to check periodically that all is well, when working alone on the vehicle.

DO carry out work in a logical sequence and check that everything is correctly assembled and tightened afterwards.

DO remember that your vehicle's safety affects that of yourself and others. If in doubt on any point, get specialist advice.

IF, in spite of following these precautions, you are unfortunate enough to injure yourself, seek medical attention as soon as possible.

Asbestos

Certain friction, insulating, sealing, and other products – such as brake linings, brake bands, clutch linings, torque converters, gaskets, etc – contain asbestos. *Extreme care must be taken to avoid inhalation of dust from such products since it is hazardous to health.* If in doubt, assume that they *do* contain asbestos.

Fire

Remember at all times that petrol (gasoline) is highly flammable. Never smoke, or have any kind of naked flame around, when working on the vehicle. But the risk does not end there – a spark caused by an electrical short-circuit, by two metal surfaces contacting each other, by careless use of tools, or even by static electricity built up in your body under certain conditions, can ignite petrol vapour, which in a confined space is highly explosive.

Always disconnect the battery earth (ground) terminal before working on any part of the fuel or electrical system, and never risk spilling fuel on to a hot engine or exhaust.

It is recommended that a fire extinguisher of a type suitable for fuel and electrical fires is kept handy in the garage or workplace at all times. Never try to extinguish a fuel or electrical fire with water.

Note: *Any reference to a 'torch' appearing in this manual should always be taken to mean a hand-held battery-operated electric lamp or flashlight. It does NOT mean a welding/gas torch or blowlamp.*

Fumes

Certain fumes are highly toxic and can quickly cause unconsciousness and even death if inhaled to any extent. Petrol (gasoline) vapour comes into this category, as do the vapours from certain solvents such as trichloroethylene. Any draining or pouring of such volatile fluids should be done in a well ventilated area.

When using cleaning fluids and solvents, read the instructions carefully. Never use materials from unmarked containers – they may give off poisonous vapours.

Never run the engine of a motor vehicle in an enclosed space such as a garage. Exhaust fumes contain carbon monoxide which is extremely poisonous; if you need to run the engine, always do so in the open air or at least have the rear of the vehicle outside the workplace.

If you are fortunate enough to have the use of an inspection pit, never drain or pour petrol, and never run the engine, while the vehicle is standing over it; the fumes, being heavier than air, will concentrate in the pit with possibly lethal results.

The battery

Never cause a spark, or allow a naked light, near the vehicle's battery. It will normally be giving off a certain amount of hydrogen gas, which is highly explosive.

Always disconnect the battery earth (ground) terminal before working on the fuel or electrical systems.

If possible, loosen the filler plugs or cover when charging the battery from an external source. Do not charge at an excessive rate or the battery may burst.

Take care when topping up and when carrying the battery. The acid electrolyte, even when diluted, is very corrosive and should not be allowed to contact the eyes or skin.

If you ever need to prepare electrolyte yourself, always add the acid slowly to the water, and never the other way round. Protect against splashes by wearing rubber gloves and goggles.

When jump starting a car using a booster battery, for negative earth (ground) vehicles, connect the jump leads in the following sequence: First connect one jump lead between the positive (+) terminals of the two batteries. Then connect the other jump lead first to the negative (–) terminal of the booster battery, and then to a good earthing (ground) point on the vehicle to be started, at least 18 in (45 cm) from the battery if possible. Ensure that hands and jump leads are clear of any moving parts, and that the two vehicles do not touch. Disconnect the leads in the reverse order.

Mains electricity and electrical equipment

When using an electric power tool, inspection light etc, always ensure that the appliance is correctly connected to its plug and that, where necessary, it is properly earthed (grounded). Do not use such appliances in damp conditions and, again, beware of creating a spark or applying excessive heat in the vicinity of fuel or fuel vapour. Also ensure that the appliances meet the relevant national safety standards.

Ignition HT voltage

A severe electric shock can result from touching certain parts of the ignition system, such as the HT leads, when the engine is running or being cranked, particularly if components are damp or the insulation is defective. Where an electronic ignition system is fitted, the HT voltage is much higher and could prove fatal.

Routine maintenance

For modifications, and information applicable to later models, see Supplement at end of manual

The maintenance instructions listed below are basically those recommended by the manufacturer. They are supplemented by additional maintenance tasks which, through practical experience, the author recommends should be carried out at the intervals suggested.

The additional tasks are indicated by an asterisk and are primarily of a preventative nature, in that they will assist in eliminating the unexpected failure of a component due to fair wear and tear.

Weekly, before a long journey or every 250 miles (400 km)

Check oil level in engine/transmission unit and top up if necessary (photos).

Check battery electrolyte level and top up if necessary with distilled water (photo).

Check level of coolant in radiator and top up if necessary (photo).

Check level of water in windscreen washer reservoir and top up if necessary (photo).

Check tyre pressures and adjust as necessary (photo). Also check the depth of tread on the tyres (minimum 1 mm) and inspect for signs of damage to treads and sidewalls.

Check tightness of roadwheel nuts.

Check the level of fluid in the brake master cylinder reservoir and top up as necessary (photo).

Check the oil level in the engine/ transmission unit...

...and top up if necessary

Check the battery electrolyte level

Check and, if necessary, top up the radiator...

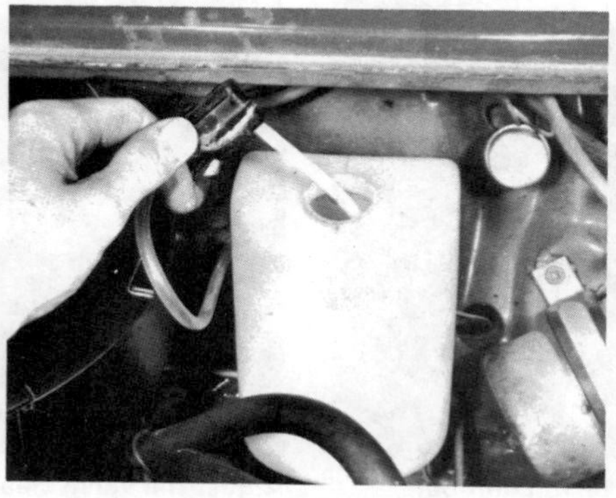

...and windscreen washer reservoir

Check the tyre pressures

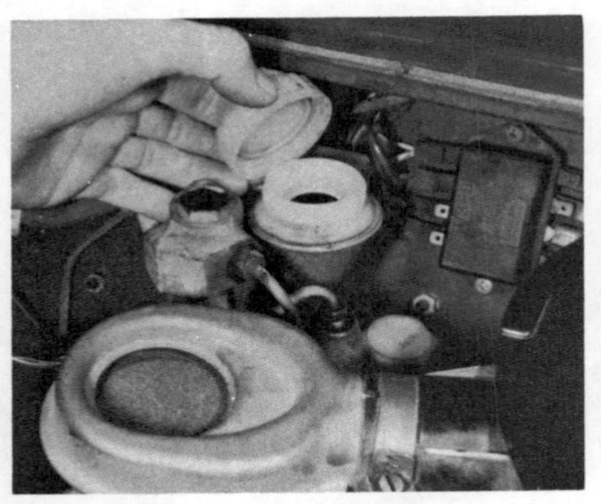

Check the fluid level in the brake...

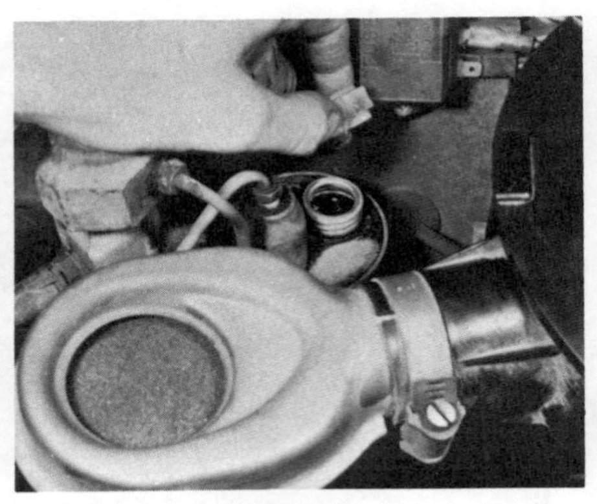

...and clutch reservoirs

Lubricate the swivel hub...

...upper suspension arm inner pivot...

...and rear radius arm pivot grease points

Engine/transmission unit drain plug

Renew the cartridge type...

...or canister type oil filter

Top up the carburettor piston damper

Adjust the valve clearances

Every 3000 miles (5000 km) or 3 months

Complete the service items in the weekly service check, plus the following additional items:

Check correct operation of horn, direction indicators, windscreen wipers/washers and all lights.
Check brake pedal travel and adjust if necessary; check operation of the handbrake.
Check condition and security of seats and seat belts.
Ensure that the rear view mirror and exterior mirrors are clean, undamaged and correctly adjusted.
Visually, check the condition of the brake, fuel and clutch pipes and unions for signs of chafing, leaks or corrosion.
Carefully inspect the exhaust system for leaks, and its mountings for security.
Check the condition and security of the steering gear, balljoints, and rubber boots.
Check for fluid leaks from the suspension system (Hydrolastic models).
Check and, if necessary, top up the brake and clutch fluid reservoirs (photos).
Check and, if necessary, renew the fanbelt or adjust its tension.
Check and, if necessary, renew the windscreen wiper blades.
Check and, if necessary, adjust the headlight aim.
If the tyres show signs of uneven wear, have the front wheel alignment checked by a BL garage.

Every 6000 miles (10 000 km) or 6 months

Carry out the 3000 mile service check, plus the following additional items:

Check the tightness of the steering column clamp bolt.
Inspect and, if necessary, renew the front brake pads or brake shoes; check the condition of the disc or drum.
Inspect and, if necessary, renew the rear brake shoes; check the condition of the drum.
Adjust the brakes and, if necessary, the handbrake.
Lubricate the following grease points:

(a) *Steering swivel hub; two nipples, one upper and one lower on each side (photo).*
(b) *Upper suspension arm inner pivot; one nipple on each arm (photo).*
(c) *Rear radius arm pivot; one nipple on each pivot (photo). Remove rubber blanking plug to expose nipple on early models.*
(d) *Handbrake cable and linkage; no nipple but grease cable guides on subframe and pack moving sectors to ensure smooth operation.*

Change engine/transmission oil (photo).
Renew engine oil filter (photos).
Top up carburettor piston damper(s) (photo).
Lubricate accelerator pedal, cable and linkage.
Clean and reset spark plugs.
Check and, if necessary, adjust clutch return stop.
Check cooling and heating system hoses for condition and leakage.
Check and, if necessary, clean or renew contact breaker points and reset gap.
Lubricate distributor.
Check ignition timing and automatic advance system, preferably using electronic equipment.
Lubricate dynamo rear bearing (early models).
Check carburettor settings and adjust if necessary.
Lubricate all hinges and locks (except steering lock).
*Check and, if necessary, adjust the position of the door striker plates and hinges.
Carry out a road test to ensure correct and smooth operation of all controls.
*Wax polish the body and the chromium plating; force wax into any joints in the bodywork to prevent rust formation.

Every 12 000 miles (20 000 km) or 12 months

Carry out the 6000 mile service check plus the following additional items:

Fit new air cleaner element.
Fit new rocker cover oil filler cap and filter assembly.
Check valve rocker clearances and adjust as necessary (photo).
Fit new spark plugs.
*Inspect the ignition HT leads for cracks and damage and renew as necessary.
*Examine the dynamo brushes; renew them if worn and clean the commutator; full details will be found in Chapter 10.
*Steam clean underside of body and clean the engine/transmission exterior, as well as the whole of the front compartment.
Clean and lubricate the battery terminals with petroleum jelly.
The following operations should also be carried out on engines fitted with emission control equipment:

Check the condition and security of air injection pipes and hoses.
Renew the fuel line filter.
Renew the charcoal absorption canister.
Check the operation of the gulp valve, air diverter valve and check valve; full information will be found in Chapter 3.

Every 24 000 miles (40 000 km) or 24 months

Carry out the 12 000 mile service check plus the following additional items.

*Examine the hub bearings for wear and renew as necessary; full information will be found in Chapter 11.
*Check the tightness of the battery earth lead on the bodywork.
*Renew the condenser in the distributor; see Chapter 4 for full information.
*Remove the starter motor, examine the brushes and renew as necessary; clean the commutator and starter drive as described in Chapter 10.
*Test the cylinder compressions, and if necessary remove the cylinder head, decarbonise, grind-in the valves and fit new valve springs; full information will be found in Chapter 1.
Completely drain the brake hydraulic fluid from the system. All seals and flexible hoses throughout the braking system should be examined, and preferably renewed. The working surfaces of the master cylinder, wheel and caliper cylinders (disc brakes) should be inspected for wear or scoring and new parts fitted as considered necessary. Refill the hydraulic system with new hydraulic fluid.
*Check and adjust any loose play in the rack-and-pinion steering gear. Full information will be found in Chapter 11.
*Examine all balljoints and hub bearings for wear and renew as necessary. Full information will be found in Chapter 11.
*Examine the driveshaft rubber couplings for wear and renew as necessary.

***Tasks additional to those specified by the manufacturer.**

Fault diagnosis

Introduction

The car owner who does his or her own maintenance according to the recommended schedules should not have to use this section of the manual very often. Modern component reliability is such that, provided those items subject to wear or deterioration are inspected or renewed at the specified intervals, sudden failure is comparatively rare. Faults do not usually just happen as a result of sudden failure, but develop over a period of time. Major mechanical failures in particular are usually preceded by characteristic symptoms over hundreds or even thousands of miles. Those components which do occasionally fail without warning are often small and easily carried in the car.

With any fault finding, the first step is to decide where to begin investigations. Sometimes this is obvious, but on other occasions a little detective work will be necessary. The owner who makes half a dozen haphazard adjustments or replacements may be successful in curing a fault (or its symptoms), but he will be none the wiser if the fault recurs and he may well have spent more time and money than was necessary. A calm and logical approach will be found to be more satisfactory in the long run. Always take into account any warning signs or abnormalities that may have been noticed in the period preceding the fault – power loss, high or low gauge readings, unusual noises or smells, etc – and remember that failure of components such as fuses or spark plugs may only be pointers to some underlying fault.

The pages which follow here are intended to help in cases of failure to start or breakdown on the road. There is also a Fault Diagnosis Section at the end of each Chapter which should be consulted if the preliminary checks prove unfruitful. Whatever the fault, certain basic principles apply. These are as follows:

Verify the fault. This is simply a matter of being sure that you know what the symptoms are before starting work. This is particularly important if you are investigating a fault for someone else who may not have described it very accurately.

Don't overlook the obvious. For example, if the car won't start, is there petrol in the tank? (Don't take anyone else's word on this particular point, and don't trust the fuel gauge either!) If an electrical fault is indicated, look for loose or broken wires before digging out the test gear.

Cure the disease, not the symptom. Substituting a flat battery with a fully charged one will get you off the hard shoulder, but if the underlying cause is not attended to, the new battery will go the same way. Similarly, changing oil-fouled spark plugs for a new set will get you moving again, but remember that the reason for the fouling (if it wasn't simply an incorrect grade of plug) will have to be established and corrected.

Don't take anything for granted. Particularly, don't forget that a 'new' component may itself be defective (especially if it's been rattling round in the boot for months), and don't leave components out of a fault diagnosis sequence just because they are new or recently fitted. When you do finally diagnose a difficult fault, you'll probably realise that all the evidence was there from the start.

Electrical faults

Electrical faults can be more puzzling than straightforward mechanical failures, but they are no less susceptible to logical analysis if the basic principles of operation are understood. Car electrical wiring exists in extremely unfavourable conditions – heat, vibration and chemical attack – and the first things to look for are loose or corroded connections and broken or chafed wires, especially where the wires pass through holes in the bodywork or are subject to vibration.

Carrying a few spares can save you a long walk!

All metal-bodied cars in current production have one pole of the battery 'earthed', ie connected to the car bodywork, and in nearly all modern cars it is the negative (–) terminal. The various electrical components' motors, bulb holders etc – are also connected to earth, either by means of a lead or directly by their mountings. Electric current flows through the component and then back to the battery via the car bodywork. If the component mounting is loose or corroded, or if a good path back to the battery is not available, the circuit will be incomplete and malfunction will result. The engine and/or gearbox are also earthed by means of flexible metal straps to the body or subframe; if these straps are loose or missing, starter motor, generator and ignition trouble may result.

Assuming the earth return to be satisfactory, electrical faults will be due either to component malfunction or to defects in the current supply. Individual components are dealt with in Chapter 10. If supply wires are broken or cracked internally this results in an open-circuit, and the easiest way to check for this is to bypass the suspect wire temporarily with a length of wire having a crocodile clip or suitable connector at each end. Alternatively, a 12V test lamp can be used to verify the presence of supply voltage at various points along the wire and the break can be thus isolated.

If a bare portion of a live wire touches the car bodywork or other earthed metal part, the electricity will take the low-resistance path thus formed back to the battery: this is known as a short-circuit. Hopefully a short-circuit will blow a fuse, but otherwise it may cause burning of the insulation (and possibly further short-circuits) or even a fire. This is why it is inadvisable to bypass persistently blowing fuses with silver foil or wire.

Spares and tool kit

Most cars are only supplied with sufficient tools for wheel changing; the *Maintenance and minor repair* tool kit detailed in *Tools and working facilities,* with the addition of a hammer, is probably sufficient for those repairs that most motorists would consider attempting at the roadside. In addition a few items which can be fitted without too much trouble in the event of a breakdown should be carried. Experience and available space will modify the list below, but the following may save having to call on professional assistance:

Spark plugs, clean and correctly gapped
HT lead and plug cap – long enough to reach the plug furthest from the distributor
Distributor rotor, condenser and contact breaker points
Drivebelt – emergency type may suffice
Spare fuses
Set of principal light bulbs
Tin of radiator sealer and hose bandage
Exhaust bandage
Roll of insulating tape
Length of soft iron wire
Length of electrical flex
Torch or inspection lamp (can double as test lamp)
Battery jump leads
Tow-rope
Ignition water dispersant aerosol
Litre of engine oil
Sealed can of hydraulic fluid
Emergency windscreen
Worm drive clips

If spare fuel is carried, a can designed for the purpose should be used to minimise risks of leakage and collision damage. A first aid kit and a warning triangle, whilst not at present compulsory in the UK, are obviously sensible items to carry in addition to the above.

When touring abroad it may be advisable to carry additional spares which, even if you cannot fit them yourself, could save having to wait while parts are obtained. The items below may be worth considering:

Throttle cables
Cylinder head gasket
Dynamo or alternator brushes
Fuel pump repair kit
Tyre valve core

One of the motoring organisations will be able to advise on availability of fuel etc in foreign countries.

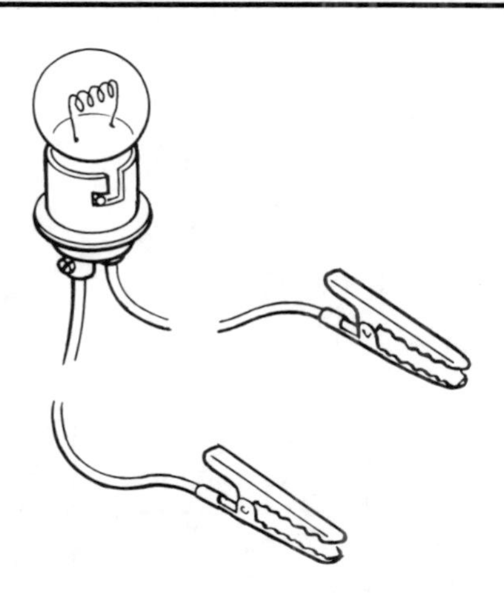

A simple test lamp is useful for tracing electrical faults

Engine will not start

Engine fails to turn when starter operated
Flat battery (recharge, use jump leads, or push start)
Battery terminals loose or corroded
Battery earth to body defective
Engine earth strap loose or broken
Starter motor (or solenoid) wiring loose or broken
Automatic transmission selector in wrong position, or inhibitor switch faulty
Ignition/starter switch faulty
Major mechanical failure (seizure) or long disuse (piston rings rusted to bores)
Starter or solenoid internal fault (see Chapter 10)

Starter motor turns engine slowly
Partially discharged battery (recharge, use jump leads, or push start)
Battery terminals loose or corroded
Battery earth to body defective
Engine earth strap loose
Starter motor (or solenoid) wiring loose
Starter motor internal fault (see Chapter 10)

Starter motor spins without turning engine
Flat battery
Starter motor pinion sticking on sleeve
Flywheel gear teeth damaged or worn
Starter motor mounting bolts loose

Engine turns normally but fails to start
Damp or dirty HT leads and distributor cap (crank engine and check for spark) (photo)
Dirty or incorrectly gapped CB points
No fuel in tank (check for delivery at carburettor)
Excessive choke (hot engine) or insufficient choke (cold engine)
Fouled or incorrectly gapped spark plugs (remove, clean and regap)
Other ignition system fault (see Chapter 4)
Other fuel system fault (see Chapter 3)
Poor compression (see Chapter 1)
Major mechanical failure (eg camshaft drive)

Engine fires but will not run
Insufficient choke (cold engine)
Air leaks at carburettor or inlet manifold
Fuel starvation (see Chapter 3)
Ballast resistor defective, or other ignition fault (see Chapters 4 and 14)

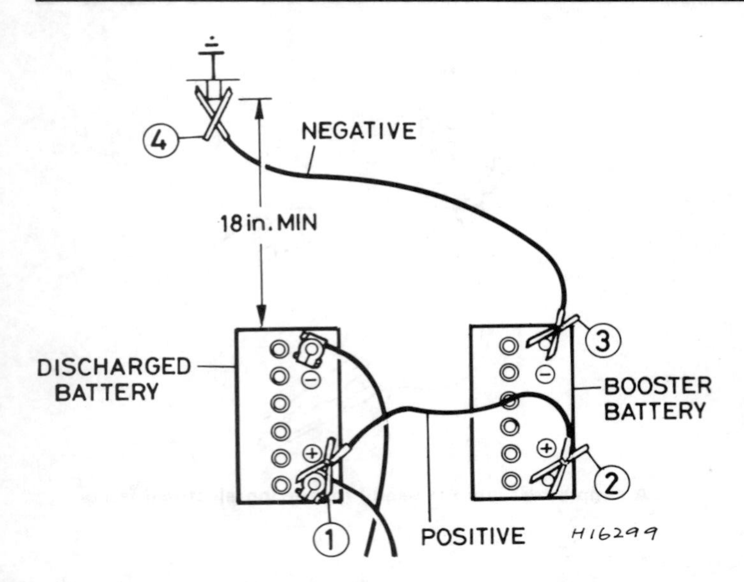

Jump start lead connections for negative earth vehicles – connect leads in order shown

Check for a spark at the HT lead

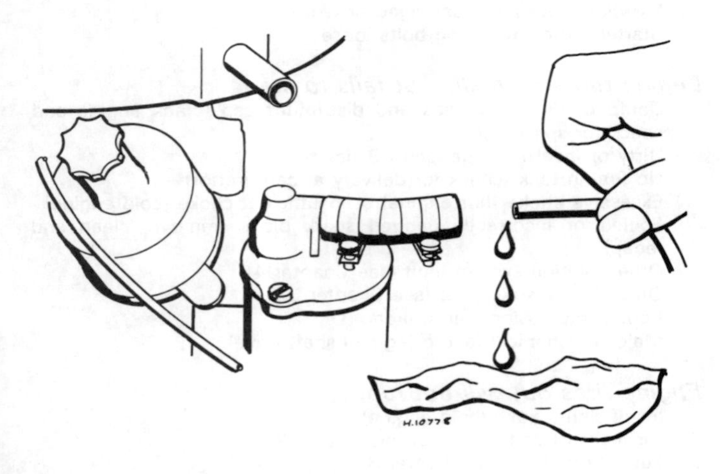

Remove fuel pipe from carburettor and check for fuel delivery

Engine cuts out and will not restart

Engine cuts out suddenly – ignition fault
- Loose or disconnected LT wires
- Wet HT leads or distributor cap (after transversing water splash)
- Coil or condenser failure (check for spark)
- Other ignition fault (see Chapter 4)

Engine misfires before cutting out – fuel fault
- Fuel tank empty
- Fuel pump defective or filter blocked (check for delivery)
- Fuel tank filler vent blocked (suction will be evident on releasing cap)
- Carburettor needle valve sticking
- Other fuel system fault (see Chapter 3)

Engine cuts out – other causes
- Serious overheating
- Major mechanical failure (eg camshaft drive)

Engine overheats

Ignition (no-charge) warning light illuminated
- Slack or broken drivebelt – retension or renew (Chapter 2)

Ignition warning light not illuminated
- Coolant loss due to internal or external leakage (see Chapter 2)
- Thermostat defective
- Low oil level
- Brakes binding
- Radiator clogged externally or internally
- Engine waterways clogged
- Ignition timing incorrect or automatic advance malfunctioning
- Mixture too weak

Note: *Do not add cold water to an overheated engine or damage may result*

Low engine oil pressure

Gauge reads low or warning light illuminated with engine running
- Oil level low or incorrect grade
- Defective gauge or sender unit
- Wire to sender unit earthed
- Engine overheating
- Oil filter clogged or bypass valve defective
- Oil pressure relief valve defective
- Oil pick-up strainer clogged
- Oil pump worn or mountings loose
- Worn main or big-end bearings

Note: *Low oil pressure in a high-mileage engine at tickover is not ncessarily a cause for concern. Sudden pressure loss at speed is far more significant. In any event, check the gauge or warning light sender before condemning the engine.*

Engine noises

Pre-ignition (pinking) on acceleration
- Incorrect grade of fuel
- Ignition timing incorrect
- Distributor faulty or worn
- Worn or maladjusted carburettor
- Excessive carbon build-up in engine

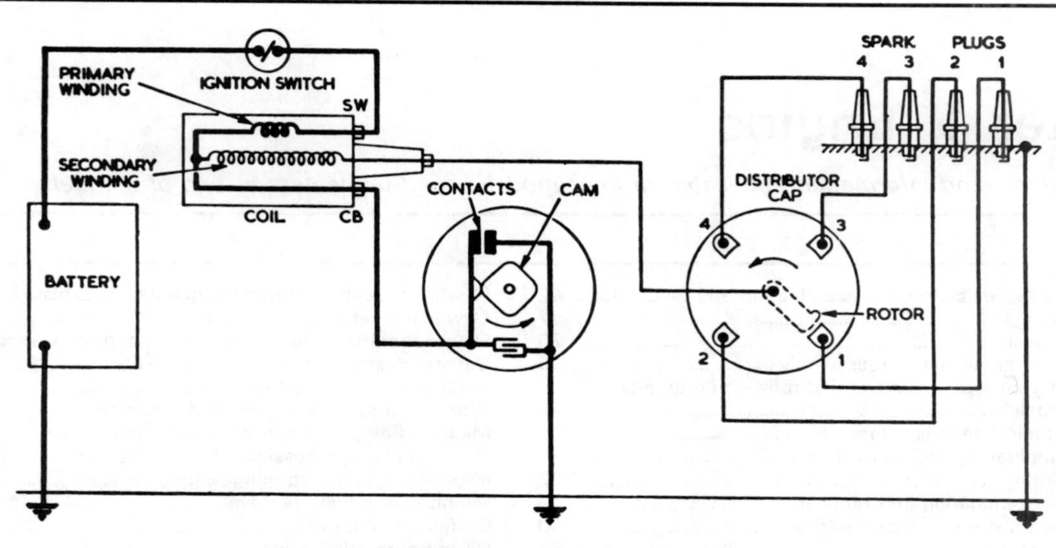

Ignition system circuit diagram (early models)

Whistling or wheezing noises
- Leaking vacuum hose
- Leaking carburettor or manifold gasket
- Blowing head gasket

Tapping or rattling
- Incorrect valve clearances
- Worn valve gear
- Worn timing chain
- Broken piston ring (ticking noise)

Knocking or thumping
- Unintentional mechanical contact (eg fan blades)
- Worn fanbelt
- Peripheral component fault (generator, water pump etc)
- Worn big-end bearings (regular heavy knocking, perhaps less under load)
- Worn main bearings (rumbling and knocking, perhaps worsening under load)
- Piston slap (most noticeable when cold)

Chapter 1 Engine

For modifications, and information applicable to later models, see Supplement at end of manual

Contents

Specifications

850 engine (manufacturer's type 85H)

Engine (general)

Type	4 cylinder, in-line, ohv
Bore	2.478 in (62.94 mm)
Stroke	2.687 in (68.25 mm)
Cubic capacity	51.7 cu in (848 cc)
Firing order	1 – 3 – 4 – 2 (No 1 cylinder next to radiator)
Compression ratio	8.3 : 1

Camshaft and camshaft bearings

Bearing type:	
Front	White-metal lined, steel backed
Centre and rear	Plain (running in block)
Camshaft journal diameter:	
Front	1.6655 to 1.6660 in (42.304 to 42.316 mm)
Centre	1.62275 to 1.62325 in (41.218 to 41.231 mm)
Rear	1.3727 to 1.3735 in (34.857 to 34.887 mm)

Bearing inside diameter (reamed after fitting):	
Front	1.6670 to 1.6675 in (42.342 to 42.355 mm)
Centre	1.6245 to 1.6255 in (41.262 to 41.288 mm)
Rear	1.3747 to 1.3755 in (34.908 to 34.938 mm)
Bearing running clearance:	
Front	0.0004 to 0.002 in (0.012 to 0.051 mm)
Centre and rear	0.00125 to 0.00275 in (0.0318 to 0.0699 mm)
Camshaft endfloat	0.003 to 0.007 in (0.076 to 0.178 mm)

Connecting rods and big-end bearings

Length between centres	5.75 in (146.05 mm)
Bearing side clearance	0.008 to 0.012 in (0.203 to 0.305 mm)
Bearing running clearance	0.001 to 0.0025 in (0.025 to 0.063 mm)

Crankshaft and main bearings

Main journal diameter	1.7505 to 1.7510 in (44.46 to 44.47 mm)
Minimum main journal regrind diameter	1.7105 in (43.45 mm)
Crankpin journal diameter	1.6254 to 1.6259 in (41.28 to 41.29 mm)
Minimum crankpin journal regrind diameter	1.5854 in (40.27 mm)
Crankshaft endfloat	0.001 to 0.005 in (0.025 to 0.127 mm)

Cylinder block and pistons

Maximum cylinder bore oversize (after reboring)	+0.040 in (+1.02 mm)
Piston-to-bore clearance:	
Top of skirt	0.0026 to 0.0036 in (0.066 to 0.81 mm)
Bottom of skirt	0.0006 to 0.0016 in (0.015 to 0.030 mm)
Piston oversizes available	+0.010 in (+0.254 mm), +0.020 in (+0.508 mm), +0.030 in (+0.762 mm), +0.040 in (+1.02 mm)
Piston ring type:	
Top compression ring	Plain, chrome faced
2nd and 3rd compression rings	Tapered, cast iron
Oil control ring	Slotted scraper
Piston ring gap	0.007 to 0.012 in (0.178 to 0.305 mm)
Ring-to-groove clearance	0.0015 to 0.0035 in (0.038 to 0.089 mm)

Gudgeon pins

Type	Semi-floating, held by clamp bolt
Fit in piston	Hand push fit at 68°F (20°C)

Valves and springs

Valve head diameter:	
Inlet	1.093 to 1.098 in (27.76 to 27.89 mm)
Exhaust	1.000 to 1.005 in (25.40 to 25.53 mm)
Valve stem diameter:	
Inlet	0.2793 to 0.2798 in (7.094 to 7.107 mm)
Exhaust	0.2788 to 0.2793 in (7.082 to 7.094 mm)
Valve stem-to-guide clearance:	
Inlet	0.0015 to 0.0025 in (0.038 to 0.064 mm)
Exhaust	0.002 to 0.003 in (0.051 to 0.076 mm)
Valve seat angle	45°
Valve lift	0.285 in (7.24 mm)
Valve clearance (inlet and exhaust)	0.012 in (0.305 mm)
Valve guide length	1.687 in (42.85 mm)
Valve guide diameter:	
Outside	0.470 to 0.471 in (11.94 to 11.97 mm)
Inside	0.2813 to 0.2818 in (7.145 to 7.157 mm)
Valve spring free length	1.75 in (44.45 mm)
Valve timing:	
Inlet opens	5° BTDC
Inlet closes	45° ABDC
Exhaust opens	40° BBDC
Exhaust closes	10° ATDC

Lubrication system

Oil type/specification*	Multigrade engine oil, viscosity SAE 20W/50, 10W/40 or 10W/30 (Duckhams QXR, Hypergrade or 10W/40 Motor Oil)
Oil filter type	Full-flow paper element Champion X101 (up to 1973) or Champion C103 canister (1974-on)
Oil pump shaft and rotor endfloat	0.005 in (0.127 mm)
Oil pump rotor lobe clearance	0.006 in (0.152 mm)
Oil pump rotor-to-body clearance	0.010 in (0.254 mm)
Oil pump relief pressure	60 lbf/in^2 (4.22 kgf/cm^2)
Oil pressure:	
Running	60 lbf/in^2 (4.22 kgf/cm^2)
Idling	15 lbf/in^2 (1.05 kgf/cm^2)

Pressure relief valve spring:	
Free length	2.859 in (72.63 mm)
Fitted length	2.156 in (54.77 mm)
Engine oil capacity (engine/manual transmission):	
Refill with filter change	8.5 pints (10.2 US pints, 4.83 litres)

***Note:** Austin Rover specify a 10W/40 oil to meet warranty requirements for models produced after August 1983. Duckhams QXR or 10W/40 Motor Oil are available to meet these requirements.*

1000 engine (manufacturer's type 99H)

The engine specification is identical to the 850 unit except for the differences listed below

Engine (general)

Bore	2.543 in (64.59 mm)
Stroke	3.0 in (76.2 mm)
Cubic capacity	60.96 cu in (998 cc)

Camshaft and camshaft bearings

Bearing type	All 3; white-metal lined, steel backed

Cylinder block and pistons

Piston-to-bore clearance:	
Top of skirt	0.0022 to 0.0033 in (0.060 to 0.085 mm)
Bottom of skirt	0.0004 to 0.0014 in (0.010 to 0.026 mm)

Gudgeon pins

Type	Fully floating with circlip retention

Lubrication system

Engine oil capacity (engine/automatic transmission):	
Total capacity	13 pints (16 US pints/7.38 litres)
Refill with filter change (approximately)	9 pints (11 US pints/5 litres)
Oil filter type	Champion X113 (Automatic only, otherwise same as for 850 cc models)

1100 engine (manufacturer's type 10H)

The engine specification is identical to the 850 unit except for the differences listed below

Engine (general)

Bore	2.543 in (64.59 mm)
Stroke	3.296 in (83.72 mm)
Cubic capacity	67.3 cu in (1098 cc)
Compression ratio	8.5 : 1

Camshaft and camshaft bearings

Bearing type	All 3; white-metal, steel backed
Bearing running clearance	0.001 to 0.002 in (0.025 to 0.051 mm)

Cylinder block and pistons

Maximum cylinder bore oversize (after reboring)	+0.020 in (+0.51 mm)
Piston-to-bore clearance:	
Top of skirt	0.0021 to 0.0033 in (0.05 to 0.08 mm)
Bottom of skirt	0.0005 to 0.0015 in (0.013 to 0.040 mm)
Piston oversizes available	+0.010 in (+0.254 mm), +0.020 in (+0.508 mm)
Piston ring type:	
Top compression ring	Plain, chrome faced
2nd and 3rd compression rings	Tapered, cast iron
Oil control ring	Duoflex 61
Piston ring gap:	
Compression rings	0.007 to 0.012 in (0.178 to 0.305 mm)
Oil control ring:	
Rails	0.012 to 0.028 in (0.305 to 0.711 mm)
Side springs	0.10 to 0.15 in (2.54 to 3.81 mm)
Ring-to-groove clearance (compression rings)	0.002 to 0.004 in (0.051 to 0.102 mm)

Gudgeon pins

Type	Fully floating with circlip retention

Valves and springs

Inlet valve head diameter	1.151 to 1.156 in (29.23 to 29.36 mm)
Valve guide length	1.531 in (38.89 mm)
Valve spring free length	1.96 in (49.7 mm)
Valve timing:	
Inlet opens	5° BTDC
Inlet closes	45° ABDC
Exhaust opens	51° BBDC
Exhaust closes	21° ATDC

1275 engine (manufacturer's type 12H)

The engine specification is identical to the 850 unit except for the differences listed below

Engine (general)

Bore	2.78 in (70.61 mm)
Stroke	3.2 in (81.28 mm)
Cubic capacity	77.8 cu in (1275 cc)
Compression ratio:	
1275 GT	8.8 : 1
Cooper S Mk III	9.75 : 1

Camshaft and camshaft bearings

Bearing type	All 3; white-metal, steel backed
Bearing running clearance	0.001 to 0.002 in (0.025 to 0.051 mm)

Crankshaft and main bearings

Main journal diameter:	
1275 GT	2.0012 to 2.0017 in (50.83 to 50.84 mm)
Cooper S Mk III	2.0005 to 2.0010 in (50.81 to 50.82 mm)
Minimum main journal regrind diameter:	
1275 GT	1.9605 in (49.78 mm)
Cooper S Mk III	1.9805 in (50.30 mm)
Crankpin journal diameter	1.7497 to 1.7504 in (44.44 to 44.46 mm)
Minimum crankpin journal regrind diameter	1.7102 in (43.44 mm)

Cylinder block and pistons

Maximum cylinder bore oversize (after reboring)	+0.020 in (+0.51 mm)
Piston-to-bore clearance:	
Top of skirt:	
1275 GT	0.0029 to 0.0045 in (0.070 to 0.114 mm)
Cooper S Mk III	0.0025 to 0.0028 in (0.063 to 0.072 mm)
Bottom of skirt:	
1275 GT	0.0012 to 0.0022 in (0.031 to 0.056 mm)
Cooper S Mk III	0.0019 to 0.0025 in (0.048 to 0.063 mm)
Piston oversizes available	+0.010 in (+0.254 mm), +0.020 in (+0.508 mm)
Piston ring type:	
Top compression ring:	
1275 GT	Internally chamfered chrome
Cooper S Mk III	Plain, chrome faced
2nd and 3rd compression rings	Tapered, cast iron
Oil control ring:	
1275 GT	Apex
Cooper S Mk III	Slotted scraper
Piston ring gap:	
Top compression ring:	
1275 GT	0.011 to 0.016 in (0.28 to 0.41 mm)
Cooper S Mk III	0.008 to 0.013 in (0.20 to 0.33 mm)
2nd and 3rd compression rings	0.008 to 0.013 in (0.20 to 0.33 mm)
Oil control ring:	
1275 GT	0.010 to 0.040 in (0.254 to 1.02 mm)
Cooper S Mk III	0.008 to 0.013 in (0.20 to 0.33 mm)
Ring-to-groove clearance	0.0015 to 0.0035 in (0.038 to 0.089 mm)

Gudgeon pins

Type	Interference fit in connecting rod

Valves and springs

Valve head diameter:	
Inlet:	
1275 GT	1.307 to 1.312 in (33.20 to 33.32 mm)
Cooper S Mk III	1.401 to 1.406 in (35.58 to 35.71 mm)
Exhaust:	
1275 GT	1.515 to 1.1565 in (29.24 to 29.37 mm)
Cooper S Mk III	1.214 to 1.219 in (30.83 to 30.96 mm)
Valve stem diameter:	
Inlet	0.2793 to 0.2798 in (7.094 to 7.107 mm)
Exhaust	0.2788 to 0.2793 in (7.082 to 7.094 mm)
Valve stem-to-guide clearance	0.0015 to 0.0025 in (0.040 to 0.080 mm)
Valve lift:	
1275 GT	0.285 in (7.24 mm)
Cooper S Mk III	0.318 in (8.08 mm)
Valve clearance (inlet and exhaust):	
Cooper S Mk III (competition only)	0.015 in (0.38 mm)
Valve guide length	1.531 in (38.89 mm)

Valve spring free length:	
1275 GT	1.96 in (49.70 mm)
Cooper S Mk III:	
Outer spring	1.740 in (44.19 mm)
Inner spring	1.705 in (43.31 mm)
Valve timing:	
Inlet opens	5° BTDC
Inlet closes	45° ABDC
Exhaust opens	51° BBDC
Exhaust closes	21° ATDC

Torque wrench settings	lbf ft	Nm
Cylinder head nuts	50	68
Cylinder head nuts (emission control engine)	40	54
Connecting rod big-end:		
Bolts	37	50
Nuts	33	45
Crankshaft pulley nut	75	102
Camshaft nut	65	88
Flywheel centre bolt	112	152
Flywheel housing nuts and bolts	18	25
Converter centre bolt	112	152
Converter (six central bolts)	21	29
Converter housing nuts and bolts	18	25
Gudgeon pin clamp bolt	24	32
Main bearing bolts	63	85
Timing cover and front plate:		
$\frac{1}{4}$ in UNF bolts	5	7
$\frac{5}{16}$ in UNF bolts	12	16
Rocker shaft pedestal nuts	24	32
Oil pump bolts	8	11
Oil filter housing nuts	14	19
Oil pipe banjo union	38	52
Oil pressure relief valve nut	43	59
Manifold-to-cylinder head nuts	14	19
Tappet side covers	3.5	4.7
Heater control valve	8	11
Rocker cover	3.5	4.7
Temperature gauge transmitter	16	22
Transmission casing to engine	6	8

1 General description

The Mini engine is a four-cylinder, water-cooled, overhead valve type of 848, 998, 1098, or 1275 cc displacement, depending on model and year of manufacture. The engine is bolted to the transmission assembly, which also forms the engine sump, and the complete power unit is supported, via rubber mountings, in the front subframe.

The cast iron cylinder head contains two valves per cylinder, mounted vertically and running in pressed-in valve guides. The valves are operated by rocker arms and pushrods via tubular cam followers from the camshaft, located in the left-hand side of the cylinder block.

The inlet and exhaust manifolds are attached to the left-hand side of the cylinder head and are linked to the valves via five inlet and exhaust ports of siamese configuration.

The pistons are of anodised aluminium alloy with either alloy or solid skirts depending on the model. Three compression rings and an oil control ring are fitted to all types. The gudgeon pin is retained in the small-end of the connecting rod by a pinch-bolt on 848 cc engines, by circlip on the 998 cc and 1098 cc engines and by an interference fit in the connecting rod small-end bore on 1275 cc engines. At the other end of the connecting rod, renewable white metal, lead-indium, or lead-tin big-end shell bearings are fitted.

At the front of the engine, a single row chain drives the camshaft via the camshaft and crankshaft sprockets. On 1275 cc Cooper S models a duplex timing chain is fitted. On the 848 cc engine, the camshaft is supported by three bearings, two being bored directly in the cylinder block while a white metal bearing (which is renewable) is fitted at the timing chain end. On the 998 cc, 1098 cc and 1275 cc units three steel-backed metal camshaft bearings are fitted.

The statically and dynamically balanced forged steel crankshaft is supported by three renewable shell type main bearings. Crankshaft endfloat is controlled by four semi-circular thrust washers located in pairs on either side of the centre main bearing.

The water pump and fan are driven together with the dynamo or alternator by a V-belt from the crankshaft pulley.

Both the distributor and oil pump are driven off the camshaft; the distributor via skew gears on the right-hand side, and the oil pump via a slotted drive or splined coupling from the rear.

2 Major operations possible with engine in car

The following operations can be carried out when the engine is in the car:

(a) Removal and refitting of the cylinder head and valve gear
(b) Removal and refitting of the timing chain and sprockets
(c) Removal and refitting of the clutch and flywheel
(d) Removal and refitting of the engine mountings

3 Major operations requiring engine removal

The following operations can only be carried out after removing the engine from the car:

(a) Removal and refitting of the main bearings
(b) Removal and refitting of the big-end bearings
(c) Removal and refitting of the piston/connecting rod assemblies
(d) Removal and refitting of the crankshaft
(e) Removal and refitting of the camshaft
(f) Removal and refitting of the oil pump

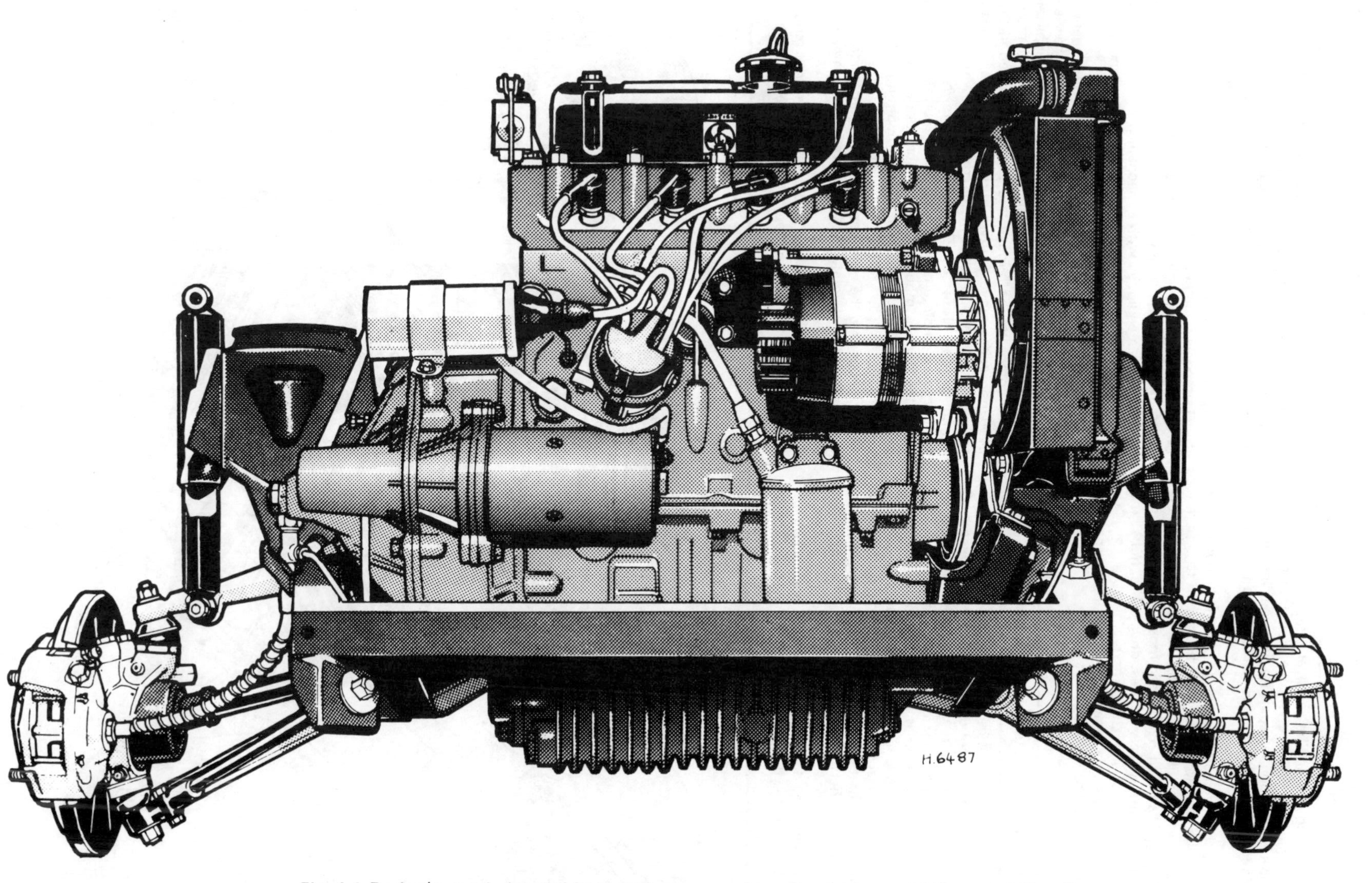

Fig. 1.1 Engine/transmission and front subframe assembly – disc brake model illustrated (Sec 1)

4 Methods of engine removal

There are two methods of engine removal. The engine can be removed from under the car, complete with subframe, or the engine can be lifted out through the bonnet aperture. In either instance the engine is removed complete with the transmission, and also the radiator.

It is easier to lift the engine/transmission assembly out of the engine compartment with the aid of a suitable hoist than to separate the subframe from the body, and lift the body up, using the rear wheels as a pivot. This is especially so with Hydrolastic models. The subframe comprises the frame itself, the wheels, brakes, driveshafts, hubs, and suspension, complete except for shock absorbers.

In either case, it is necessary to raise and support the front of the car so that it can be worked on from underneath.

5 Engine – removal (manual transmission models)

1 The engine/transmission unit can be removed without difficulty in about $4\frac{1}{2}$ hours (less with experience) using the procedure described below. The engine/transmission unit weighs approximately 330 lb (150 kg), so ensure that a sturdy hoist or crane is available.

2 The sequence of operations listed in this Section is not critical, as the position of the person undertaking the work or the tool in his hand, will determine to a certain extent the order in which the work is tackled. Obviously the power unit cannot be removed until everything is disconnected from it, and the following sequence will ensure that nothing is forgotten.

3 Drain the cooling system as described in Chapter 2 and then place a suitable container beneath the engine/gearbox oil drain plug. Remove the drain plug, allow the oil to drain out and then refit the plug.

4 Open the bonnet and, using a soft pencil, mark the outline position of both hinges at the bonnet to act as a datum for refitting.

5 With the help of an assistant, undo and remove the two nuts and washers securing each hinge to the bonnet. Lift off the bonnet and put it in a safe place where it will not be scratched.

6 From inside the car or luggage compartment disconnect the battery earth terminal.

7 On models equipped with an ignition shield mounted on the front of the engine, release the three retaining lugs and lift off the shield.

8 Refer to Chapter 3 and remove the air cleaner and carburettor(s).

9 On models equipped with a mechanical fuel pump, disconnect the fuel inlet hose and plug it with a suitable bolt or metal rod to prevent loss of fuel.

10 Slacken the retaining clips and remove the two heater hoses. Also slacken the two securing screws and withdraw the heater control cable from the valve on the cylinder head (where applicable).

11 If a fresh air heater/demister blower motor is mounted in the engine compartment, remove this unit as described in Chapter 12.

12 Undo and remove the two nuts and bolts on the clamp securing the exhaust front pipe to the manifold. Withdraw the two halves of the clamp (photo). **Note**: *On Cooper S models it will be necessary to remove the complete exhaust system as described in Chapter 3.*

13 If the horn is mounted on the front body panel, disconnect the electrical leads, undo and remove the mounting bolts and withdraw the horn

14 From beneath the right-hand front wing detach the heater fresh air ducting from the air intake. Now withdraw the air intake from the inner wing panel.

15 Undo the nut and washer and detach the starter motor cable from the stud at the rear of the motor. Undo and remove the starter motor

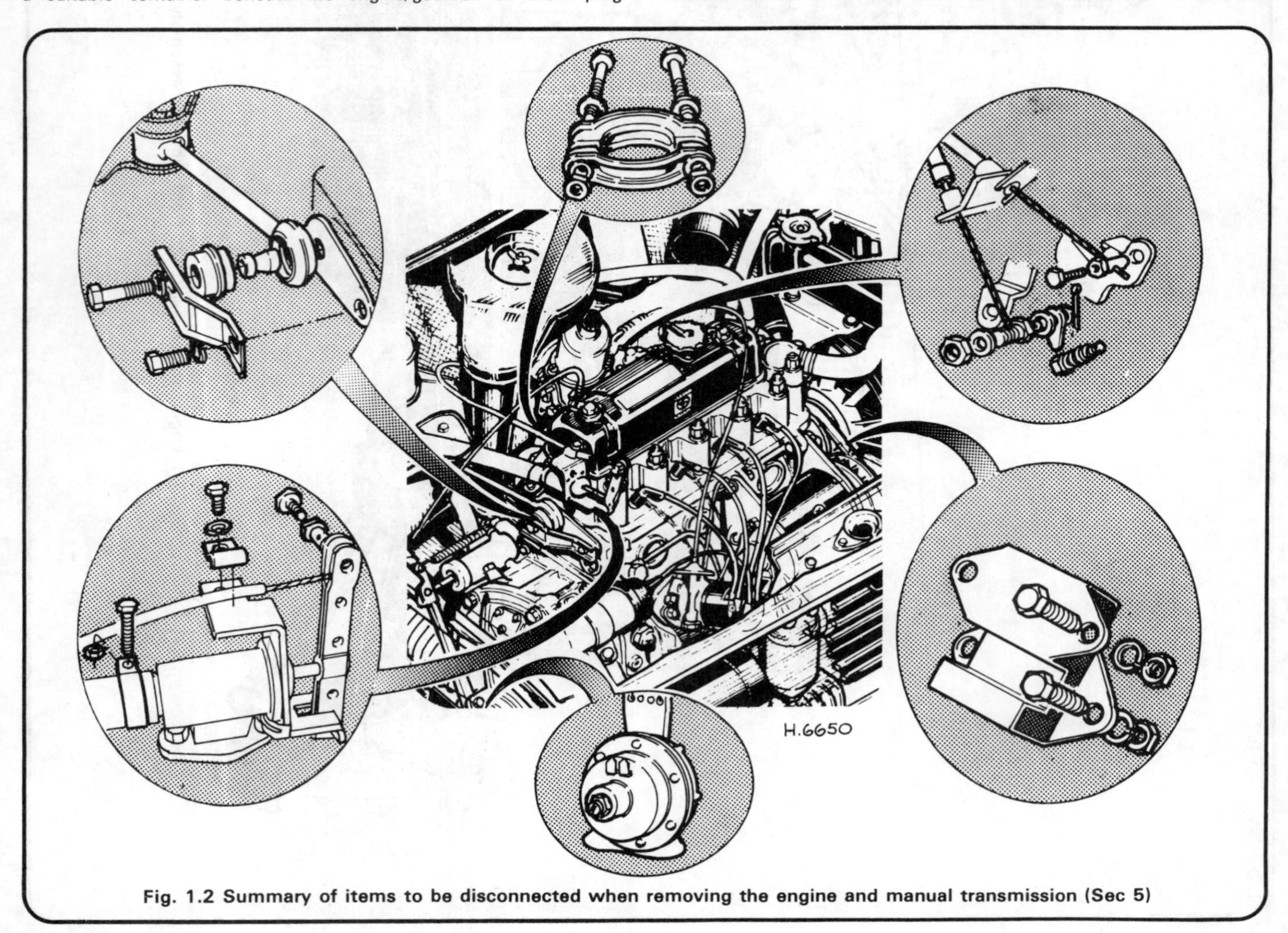

Fig. 1.2 Summary of items to be disconnected when removing the engine and manual transmission (Sec 5)

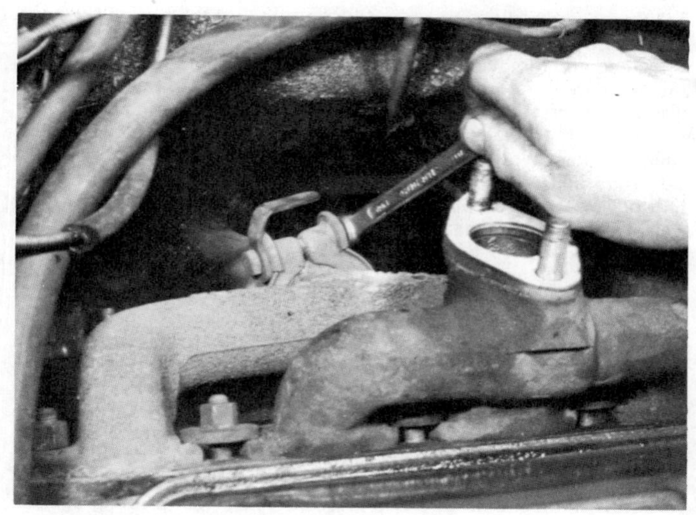
5.12 Removing the exhaust manifold clamp

5.22 Detaching the oil pressure gauge hose from the feed pipe

5.24 On early models the engine earth strap is secured to the flywheel housing

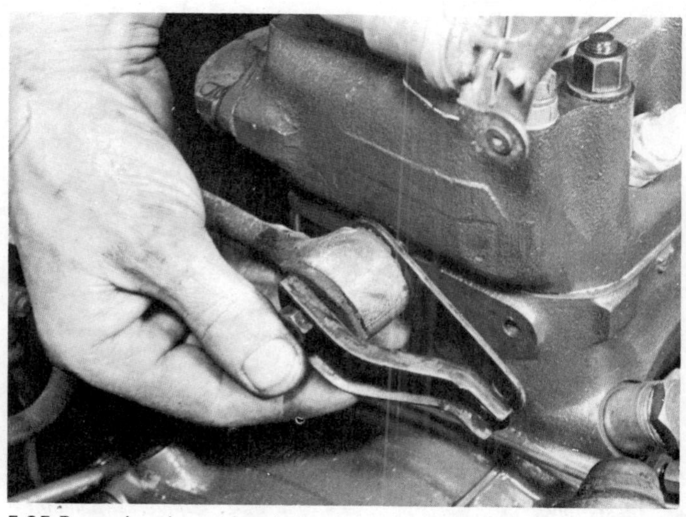
5.25 Removing the engine tie-bar from the cylinder block

mounting bolt securing the cable support bracket and lift away the cable.

16 Undo and remove the screws securing the starter solenoid to the inner wing panel and position the solenoid clear of the engine.

17 Disconnect the electrical leads from the temperature gauge transmitter and oil pressure switch where fitted.

18 Disconnect the two electrical leads from the rear of the dynamo or the plug from the rear of the alternator.

19 Make a note of the two LT electrical lead locations at the ignition coil and disconnect them. Now detach the HT cable from the centre of the coil.

20 Detach the HT leads from the spark plugs, spring back the distributor cap retaining clips, and remove the cap and leads. Remove the rotor arm from the distributor shaft.

21 Release the clutch slave cylinder return spring from the clutch operating lever. Undo and remove the two securing bolts and lift the slave cylinder off the flywheel housing. Tie the cylinder out of the way from a convenient place on the engine bulkhead.

22 If an oil pressure gauge is fitted, slacken the clamp screw and pull the rubber hose off the feed pipe at the rear of the engine (photo).

23 On models fitted with a vacuum servo unit mounted in the engine compartment, refer to Chapter 9 and remove the servo.

24 On early models undo and remove the bolt securing the engine strap to the flywheel housing (photo).

25 Undo and remove the bolt securing the engine tie-bar to the side of the cylinder block. Slacken the tie-bar bulkhead mounting and move the bar back out of the way (photo). Note that on later models the tie-bar retaining bolt also retains the engine earth strap.

26 On Cooper S models disconnect the oil cooler hose unions from

Fig. 1.3 The Cooper S oil cooler; note angled hose connection – arrowed (Sec 5)

the oil cooler and plug their ends to prevent dirt ingress. Now undo and remove the oil cooler retaining bolts and lift off the unit.

27 Working under the front wheel arch undo and remove the screw securing the upper suspension arm rebound rubber to the subframe and withdraw the rubber. Place a solid wooden wedge of approximately the same thickness in its place. Repeat this procedure on the other side of the car.

28 Jack up the front of the car and support it on axle stands positioned under the subframe. Withdraw the wheel trim and remove both front roadwheels.

29 Undo and remove the nut securing the steering tie-rod balljoint to the steering arm on each side of the car. Release the balljoint tapers using a universal separator. Alternatively, screw on the nut two turns to protect the threads and then strike the steering arms with a few sharp hammer blows to release the taper.

30 Undo and remove the nut securing the front suspension swivel hub balljoint to the upper suspension arm on each side of the car. Release the balljoint shanks from the upper suspension arms using the procedure described in the previous paragraph. Move the top of the two swivel hubs outwards and allow them to hang in this position. Take care not to strain the flexible brake hoses excessively.

31 On early models equipped with rubber couplings at the inner end of each driveshaft, undo and remove the two U-bolt locknuts securing each coupling to the differential driving flanges. Withdraw the two U-bolts from each side and move the driveshafts away from the differential.

32 On later models equipped with offset sphere joints at the inner end of each driveshaft, release the joints from the differential using BL special tool 18G1240. If this tool cannot be obtained, it is possible to withdraw the joints using a tyre lever or similar tool pivoting against the end cover retaining bolt directly below the joint. Once the joints have been released, move the driveshafts away from the differential as far as possible.

33 On Cooper S models undo and remove the four nuts securing each universal joint flange to the differential driving flanges. Move the driveshafts away from the differential to separate the flanges.

34 On models fitted with a direct engagement gear lever, undo and remove the retaining screws and lift off the interior rubber boot retaining plate. Now slide the rubber boot up the gear lever slightly. From under the car, undo and remove the two bolts securing the gear lever retaining plate to the rear of the differential housing. Withdraw the gear lever into the car and lift out the anti-rattle spring and plunger from the gear lever housing.

35 On models fitted with the early type remote control extension housing, undo and remove the four shouldered bolts securing the housing to the mounting on the rear of the differential assembly. Pull the front of the extension housing downwards to disengage the linkage and then support the front of the housing on a block of wood.

36 On models fitted with the later rod-change type remote control extension housing, drift out the roll pin securing the collar of the remote control extension rod to the selector shaft. Undo and remove the bolt securing the fork of the steady rod to the differential housing.

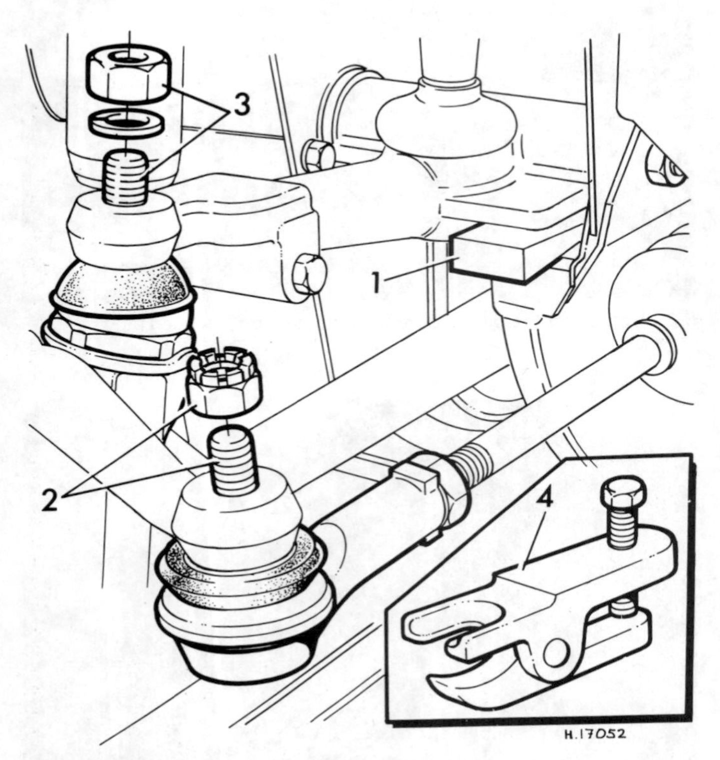

Fig. 1.4 Separation of the suspension and steering balljoint assemblies (Sec 5)

1 Packing wedge
2 Steering tie-rod balljoint assembly
3 Swivel hub balljoint assembly
4 Universal balljoint separator

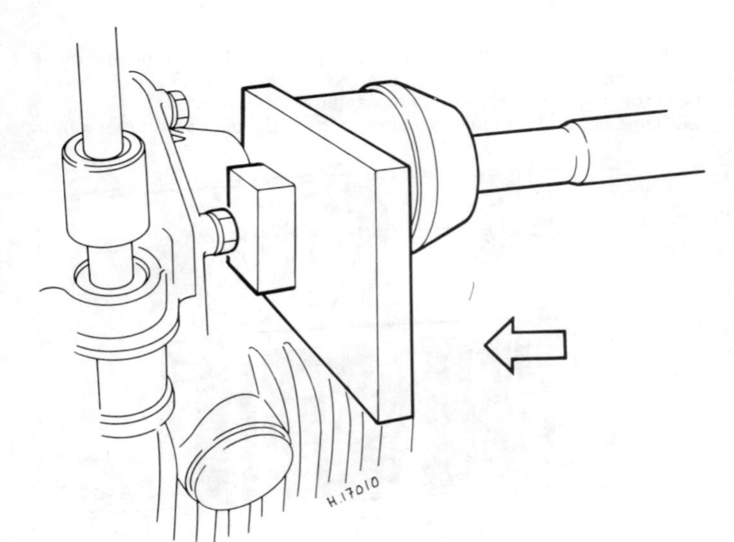

Fig. 1.5 Use of special tool 18G1240 to release offset sphere driveshaft joint (Sec 5)

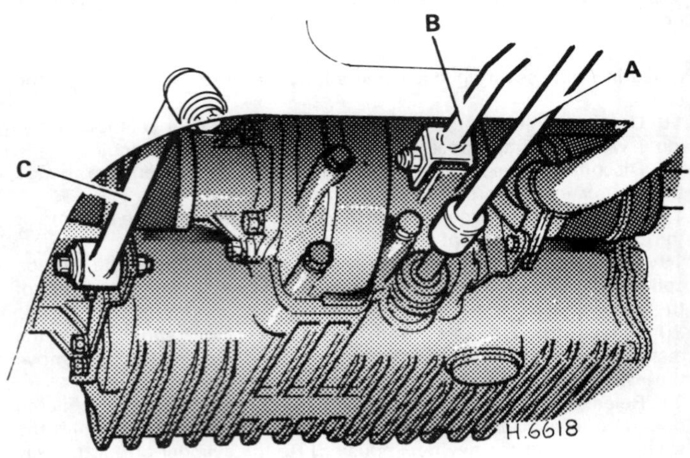

Fig. 1.6 Gear-change and lower tie-bar attachments on the rod – change type gearbox (Sec 5)

A Extension rod
B Steady rod
C Lower tie-bar

Release the extension rod and the steady rod from the rear of the transmission.
37 On all models undo and remove the nut and bolt securing the exhaust pipe strap to the bracket on the side of the differential housing.
38 Undo and remove the nut and bolt securing the lower engine tie-bar to the bracket on the gearbox casing. Slacken the nut and bolt securing the other end and remove the tie-bar clear of the transmission.
39 Position a crane or hoist over the engine and attach chains or ropes either to brackets bolted to the cylinder head or around each end of the transmission casing.
40 With the lifting gear in position, raise it slightly and just take the weight of the engine.
41 Undo and remove the two nuts and bolts securing the two engine mountings to the side of the front subframe (photo).
42 Make a final check that all cables, pipes and hoses have been disconnected and that all removed parts are clear of the engine.
43 The engine/transmission unit can now be lifted out. Tilt it backwards as it is lifted out to allow the differential to clear the rear of the subframe. When the unit is halfway out or when sufficient clearance exists, unscrew the speedometer cable knurled retaining nut and lift the cable off the housing (photos).
44 Now completely remove the power unit from the vehicle and position it on a bench or clean floor for dismantling (photo).

6 Engine – removal with subframe (manual transmission models)

Note: *After disconnecting all the relevant components, the body can be lifted up at the front by four strong people and wheeled away, or the body can be lifted by block and tackle and the engine/transmission and subframe assembly rolled out from underneath. When working on cars equipped with Hydrolastic suspension, it will be necessary to have the system depressurised by your local BL dealer before commencing the removal procedure (see Chapter 11, Section 2)*

1 Begin the removal sequence by carrying out paragraphs 2 to 26 inclusive of the previous Section, with the exception of paragraph 23.
2 Refer to Chapter 3 if necessary and remove the complete exhaust system from the car.
3 Refer to Chapter 6, and on models fitted with a direct engagement gear lever, remove the gear lever. On models equipped with a remote control gear lever and extension housing, remove the complete housing assembly.
4 Undo and remove the knurled nut securing the speedometer cable to its housing on the left-hand side of the gearbox. Withdraw the cable from the housing.
5 Remove the brake master cylinder filler cap and place a piece of polythene over the filler neck. Now securely refit the cap. This will help prevent loss of fluid when the hydraulic pipes are disconnected.

5.41 Location of the right-hand engine mounting-to-subframe retaining nuts

5.43a With the engine in this position...

5.43b ...detach the speedometer cable from its housing...

5.44 ...and then lift out the engine/transmission assembly

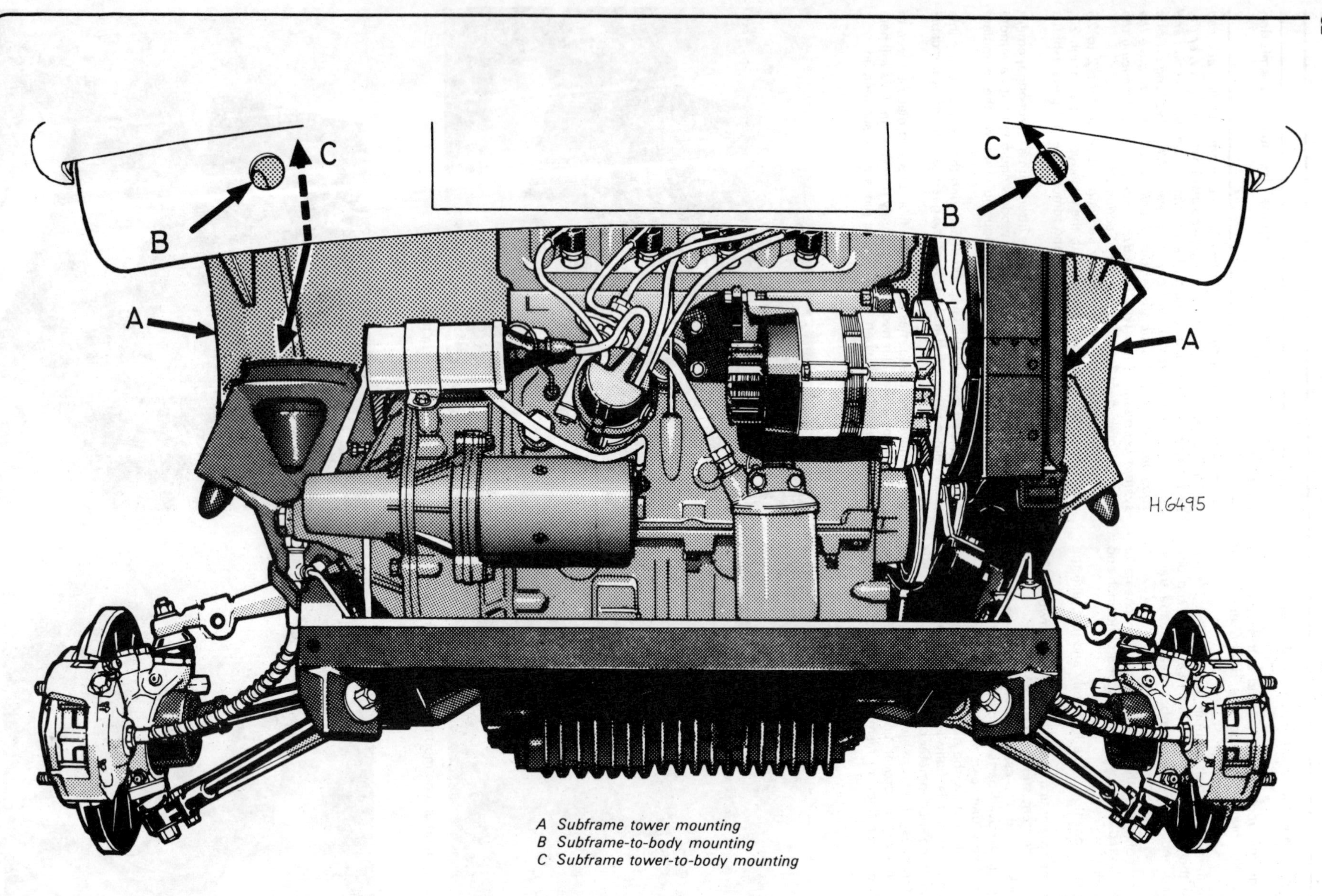

Fig. 1.7 Removal of engine and manual transmission with subframe – disc brake model shown (Sec 6)

6 On models equipped with a single line braking system undo and remove the brake hydraulic pipe to the front wheels at the three-way connector on the bulkhead. Where a dual line or split braking system is fitted, undo and remove the hydraulic pipes to the front wheels at the pressure differential warning actuator or the pressure reducing valve according to system type. In all cases plug or tape over the pipe ends after removal to prevent dirt ingress.
7 If the brake lights are operated by a hydraulic pressure switch, disconnect the electrical leads at the switch, which is located on the right-hand side of the subframe.
8 Slacken the clip and detach the brake servo vacuum hose (where fitted) at the union on the inlet manifold.
9 Undo and remove the nut securing each tie-rod outer balljoint to the steering arms. Separate the balljoint shanks from the steering arms by striking the ends of the arms with a few sharp blows from a medium hammer. Alternatively use a universal balljoint separator.
10 On models fitted with rubber cone suspension, remove the front shock absorber as described in Chapter 11.
11 On cars fitted with Hydrolastic suspension, undo and remove the displacer unit hoses at the transfer pipe unions.
12 Now refit the roadwheels and lower the car to the ground.
13 From inside the car lift up the carpets and undo and remove the two bolts each side securing the rear of the subframe or subframe mounting to the floor.
14 At the front of the car undo and remove the bolt that secures each side of the subframe or subframe mounting to the body.
15 On early models knock back the locking plate tabs from the two bolts (or nuts) on either side of the engine compartment which secure the subframe towers to the bulkhead crossmember.
16 Now undo and remove the bolts or nuts. On later models undo and remove the large hexagon-headed plug that is fitted in place of the early bolt or stud mounting.
17 Make a final check that all cables, pipes and hoses have been disconnected and that all removed parts are clear of the engine and subframe.
18 Support the front of the subframe and the rear of the gearbox casing with blocks of wood or jacks and lift the body at the front until it is clear of the engine. Take care that all components are clear when lifting the body and ensure that the radiator matrix is not damaged.
19 Now wheel the body away from the subframe or roll the subframe out from underneath, whichever is more convenient.

7 Engine – removal from subframe (manual transmission models)

1 Support the subframe securely on blocks or stands so that the wheels are clear of the ground. Remove both front roadwhels.
2 The remainder of the removal procedure is now the same as described in Section 5 paragraphs 30 to 33 and 38 to 43 inclusive.

8 Flywheel and flywheel housing – removal (manual transmission models)

Note: *To enable the engine to be removed from the gearbox it is first necessary to take off the flywheel and clutch as an assembly and then the flywheel housing*

1 Undo and remove the retaining bolts and lift off the flywheel housing cover and starter motor (photos).
2 Withdraw the wire retaining clips and lift away the clutch thrust plate from the centre of the diaphragm spring housing.
3 Rotate the flywheel until the timing marks on the flywheel periphery are at approximately the 3 o'clock position. This will prevent the primary gear retaining U-shaped washer from becoming dislodged as the flywheel is removed.
4 Using a punch or small chisel, knock back the lockwasher securing the large flywheel retaining bolt in the centre of the flywheel.
5 With a large socket and extension handle, undo and remove the flywheel retaining bolt. Insert a screwdriver between the flywheel ring gear teeth and housing to prevent the flywheel from turning while the bolt is removed. Also have an assistant support the engine, as this bolt will be tight requiring considerable leverage to remove it. When the bolt is removed, prise out the keyed locating washer from the end of the flywheel and crankshaft.
6 The flywheel is a taper fit on the end of the crankshaft and a special puller will be needed to remove it. This puller is BL special tool 18G304 and adaptor 18G304M. There are, however, a number of similar pullers readily obtainable from accessory shops or most local garages (photo).
7 Position the puller with the three studs or bolts inserted through the holes in the spring housing and screwed into the flywheel securely.

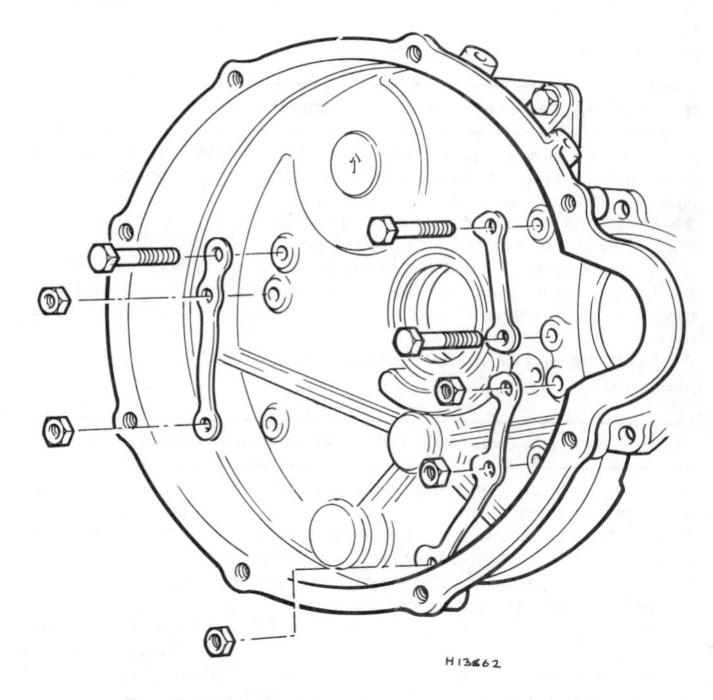

Fig. 1.8 Flywheel housing attachments (Sec 8)

8.1a Withdrawing the starter motor...

8.1b ...and the flywheel housing cover

8.6 Using a commercially available puller to remove the flywheel

Do not tighten the studs/bolts or the clutch disc may be damaged. Fit the thrust pad of the puller to the end of the crankshaft and then tighten the puller centre bolt. Prevent the flywheel from turning using a screwdriver inserted into the ring gear teeth.

8 Continue tightening the centre bolt of the puller until the flywheel breaks free from the taper. It is quite likely that the flywheel will be extremely tight requiring a great deal of effort to free it. If this is the case sharply strike the puller centre bolt with a medium hammer. This should 'shock' the flywheel off the taper. Take care when doing this as the flywheel may spring off and land on your feet!

9 Once the taper is released the complete clutch and flywheel assembly can be lifted off the end of the crankshaft.

10 With the flywheel and clutch removed the flywheel housing can be separated from the engine/transmission casing as follows.

11 If a breather is fitted to the top of the housing undo and remove the retaining bolts and lift off the breather assembly.

12 Knock back the tabs on the lockwashers inside the housing.

13 Undo and remove the nine nuts from the studs on the transmission casing.

14 Undo and remove the six bolts from the cylinder block. Note the positions from which the shorter bolts are removed.

15 The housing can now be carefully pulled off. The flywheel housing oil seal should always be renewed when the housing is removed. If for any reason this is not possible, then wrap tinfoil or adhesive tape round the primary gear splines before pulling off the housing, so that the splines do not damage the oil seal. Note that as the housing is withdrawn a small quantity of oil will be released so have some old rags or a small container handy.

9 Engine – removal from manual transmission

1 With the flywheel and flywheel housing removed as described in Section 8, undo and remove the flange nuts, bolts and spring washers securing the engine to the transmission.

2 Undo and remove the bolts securing the radiator lower mounting bracket to the engine mounting bracket.

3 Using a crane, or hoist and lifting slings, carefully lift the engine off the transmission casing. It may be necessary to tap the transmission casing downwards with a rubber or hide mallet to break the seal between the two mating faces.

4 With the engine removed, cover the top of the transmission to prevent dirt ingress.

10 Engine – removal (automatic transmission models)

1 The procedure for removing the engine/automatic transmission assembly is similar to that described for manual transmission models. Refer to Section 5 and carry out paragraphs 1 to 25 inclusive, with the exception of paragraph 21. Then proceed as follows.

2 Jack up the front of the car and support it on axle stands positioned under the subframe.

3 Working underneath the car, undo and remove the nut and bolt securing the exhaust pipe strap to the support bracket on the differential housing. Now undo and remove the retaining nuts and lift off the support bracket.

4 If the driveshafts are fitted with Hardy Spicer (Hooke's) universal joints at their inner ends, undo and remove the nuts securing the two universal joint flanges to the differential drive flanges.

5 If the driveshafts are fitted with offset sphere joints at their inner ends, remove the joints from the differential as described in Section 5 paragraphs 29, 30 and 32.

6 Undo and remove the two bolts securing the gear selector bellcrank cover plate to the right-hand end of the transmission casing. Lift off the cover plate.

7 Undo and remove the nut, washer and pivot bolt securing the selector cable fork to the bellcrank lever. On early models a clevis pin may be fitted in place of the bolt.

8 Slacken the fork retaining nut and unscrew the fork from the cable.

9 Unscrew the fork retaining nut and then slide off the two rubber ferrules.

10 Undo and remove the selector outer cable adjusting nut and then pull the cable out of the transmission casing bracket.

11 Attach suitable lifting slings around the transmission casing, or preferably to brackets bolted to the cylinder head. With a crane or hoist in position, raise it slightly and just take the weight of the power unit.

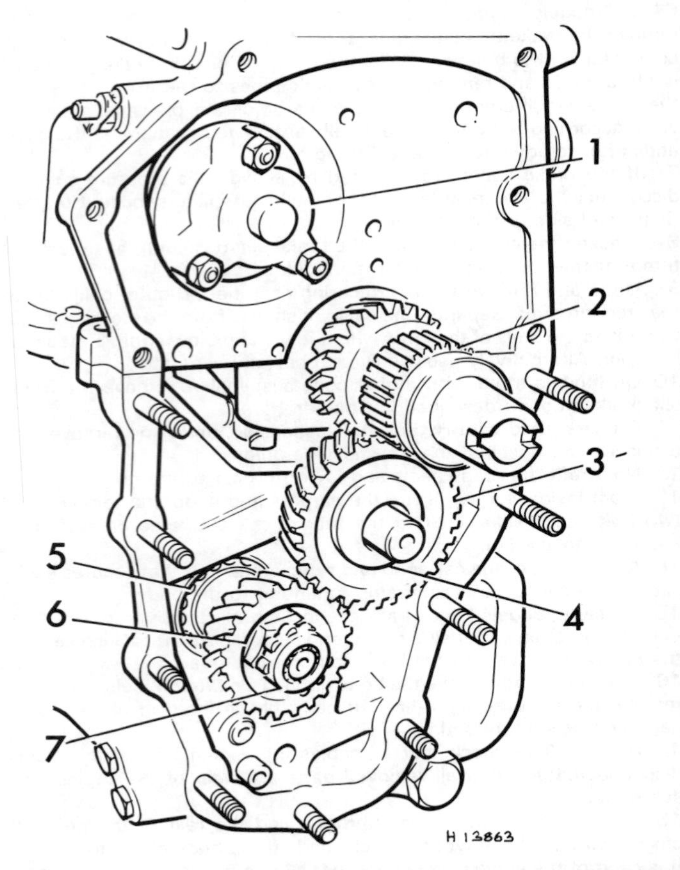

Fig. 1.9 End view of the transfer gears with the flywheel housing removed (Sec 8)

1 Oil pump
2 Crankshaft primary gear
3 Idler or transfer gear
4 Thrust washer
5 First motion shaft bearing
6 First motion shaft gearwheel
7 Roller bearing

12 Undo and remove the four nuts and bolts securing the engine mountings to the sides of the subframe.

13 Make a final check that all relevant components, cables and attachments have been removed, and lift the engine/transmission unit sufficiently to release the universal joint and differential drive flanges.

14 With the power unit halfway out, or when sufficient clearance exists, undo and remove the speedometer cable knurled nut and lift the speedometer cable off the transmission casing.

15 Now completely remove the power unit from the car and position it on a bench or clean floor for dismantling.

11 Engine – removal with subframe (automatic transmission models)

Note: *As with manual transmission models, after disconnecting the relevant components, the body may be lifted at the front off the subframe and then wheeled away, or the body can be lifted by block and tackle at the front and the subframe rolled out from beneath. If Hydrolastic suspension is fitted the system must first be depressurised by your local BL dealer before commencing the removal procedure (see Chapter 11, Section 2)*

1 Begin the removal procedure by referring to Section 5 and carrying out paragraphs 2 to 25 inclusive with the exception of paragraphs 21 and 23. Then proceed as follows.

2 Refer to Chapter 3 if necessary and remove the complete exhaust system from the car.

3 Remove the front wheels, undo and remove the steering tie-rod end balljoint locknuts, and then remove the balljoints from the steering arms using a universal separator. Alternatively strike the end of the

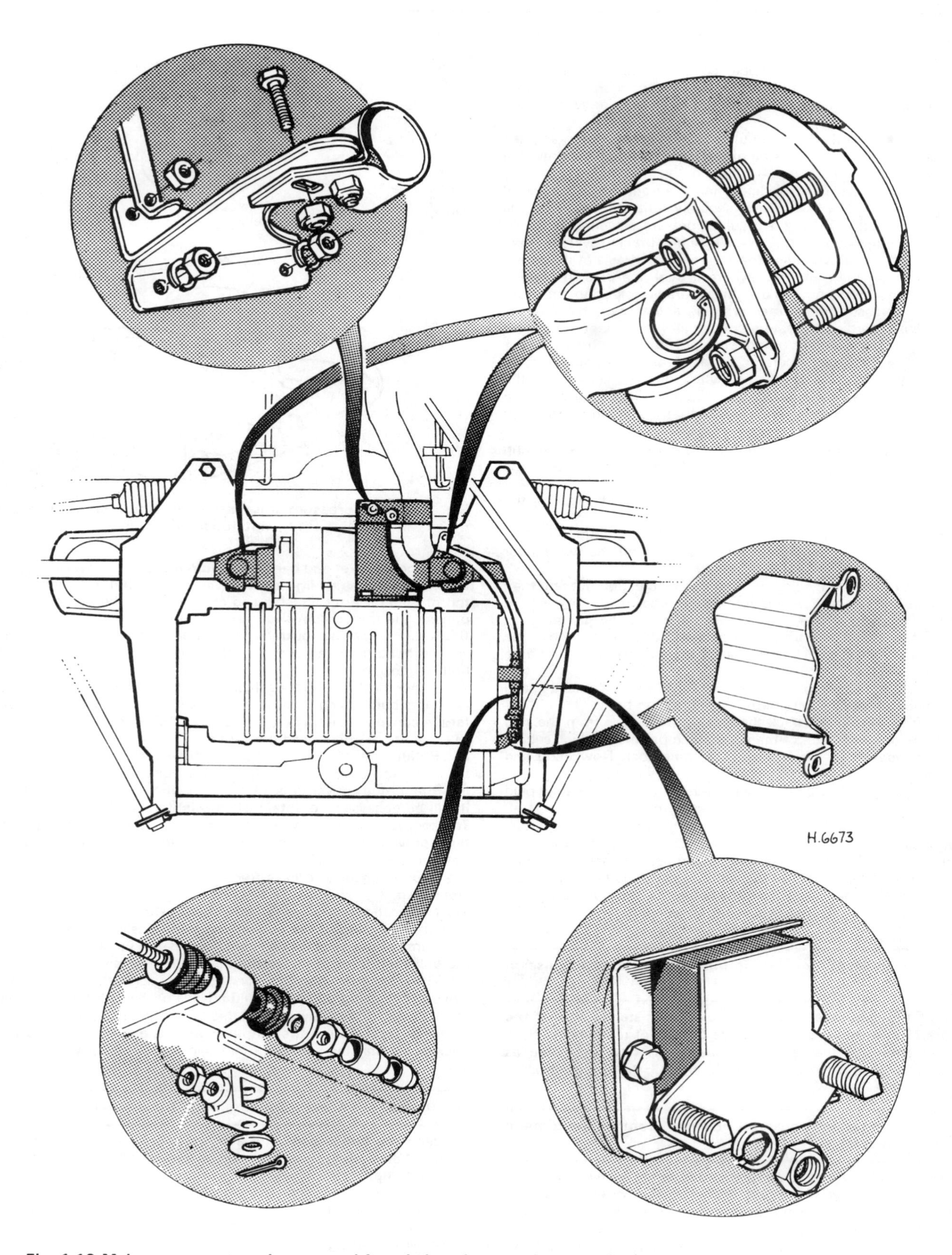

Fig. 1.10 Main components to be removed from below the car prior to engine/automatic transmission removal (Sec 10)

steering arms with a hammer to 'shock' the joints free. Now refit the roadwheels.
4 On models equipped with rubber cone suspension, remove the shock absorbers as described in Chapter 11. If Hydrolastic suspension is fitted, undo and remove the front displacer hose unions at the transfer pipes.
5 Undo and remove the knurled nut securing the speedometer cable to its housing on the left-hand side of the transmission. Withdraw the cable from the housing.
6 Remove the brake master cylinder filler cap and place a piece of polythene over the filler neck. Now securely refit the cap. This will prevent loss of fluid when the hydraulic pipes are disconnected.
7 On early models equipped with a single line braking system, undo and remove the brake hydraulic pipe to the front wheels at the three-way connector on the bulkhead. Where a dual line or split braking system is fitted, undo and remove the hydraulic pipes to the front wheels at the pressure differential warning actuator or the pressure reducing valve according to system type. In all cases plug or tape over the disconnected unions after removal to prevent dirt ingress.
8 If the brake lights are operated by a hydraulic pressure switch, disconnect the electrical leads at the switch, which is located on the right-hand side of the subframe. Slacken the retaining clip and remove the brake servo vacuum hose (where fitted) at the union on the inlet manifold.
9 Working under the car undo and remove the two bolts securing the gear selector bellcrank cover plate to the right-hand end of the transmission casing. Lift off the cover plate.
10 Undo and remove the nut, washer and pivot bolt securing the selector cable fork to the bellcrank lever.
11 Slacken the fork retaining nut and unscrew the fork from the cable.
12 Unscrew the fork retaining nut and then slide off the two rubber ferrules.
13 Undo and remove the selector outer cable adjusting nut and then pull the cable out of the transmission casing bracket.
14 Refit the front roadwheels and lower the car to the ground.
15 From inside the car lift up the carpets and undo and remove the two bolts each side securing the rear of the subframe or subframe mounting to the floor.
16 At the front of the car undo and remove the bolt that secures each side of the subframe or subframe mounting to the body.
17 On early models knock back the locking plate tabs from the two bolts (or nuts) on either side of the engine compartment which secure the subframe towers to the bulkhead crossmember. Now undo and remove the bolts or nuts.
18 On later models undo and remove the large hexagon-headed plug that is fitted in place of the early bolt or stud mounting.
19 Support the front of the subframe and the rear of the gearbox casing with blocks of wood or jacks, and lift the body at the front until it is clear of the engine. Take care that all components are clear when lifting the body and ensure that the radiator matrix is not damaged.
20 Now wheel the body away from the subframe or roll the subframe out from underneath, whichever is more convenient.

12 Engine – removal from subframe (automatic transmission models)

1 Support the subframe securely on blocks or stands so that the wheels are clear of the ground. Remove both front roadwheels.
2 The remainder of the removal procedure is now the same as described in Section 10 paragraphs 4, 5, and 11 to 15 inclusive.

13 Torque converter and converter housing – removal (automatic transmission models)

Note: *To enable the engine to be removed from the transmission, it is first necessary to take off the torque converter and converter housing*
1 If not done so already, remove the transmission oil drain plug and drain the oil into a suitable container. Refit the drain plug.
2 Undo and remove the retaining nuts and bolts and take off the converter housing cover.
3 Undo and remove the five retaining bolts and lift off the low pressure valve assembly from its location beneath the torque converter.
4 Undo and remove the two bolts and lift off the starter motor.

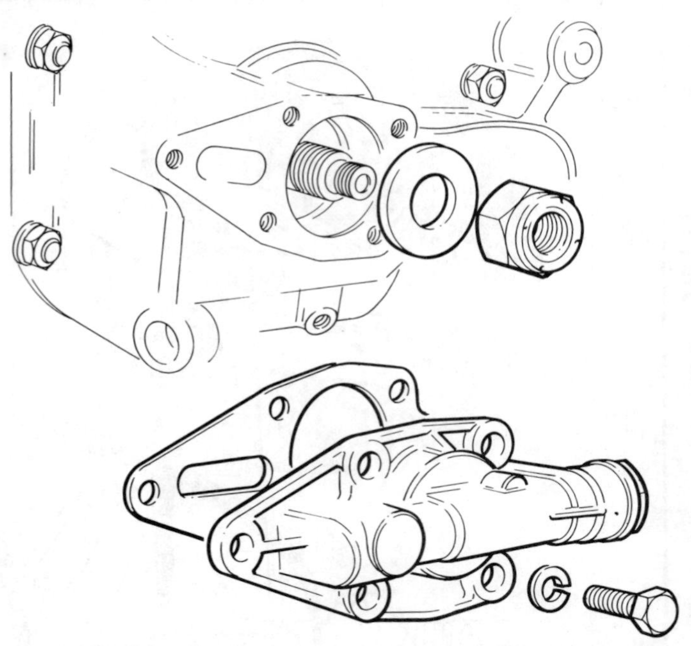

Fig. 1.11 Low pressure valve assembly and input gear retaining nut (Sec 13)

5 Using a socket and bar, undo and remove the converter input gear retaining nut. Use a large screwdriver inserted through the hole in the top of the converter housing and engaged with the ring gear teeth to prevent the torque converter from turning.
6 Knock back the locktabs, and undo and remove three equally-spaced bolts from the centre of the converter. Leave the other three bolts in position.
7 Knock back the lockwasher securing the large converter centre retaining bolt. Using a large socket and bar, undo and remove the torque converter centre bolt. Use a screwdriver as previously described to prevent the converter from turning.
8 Rotate the crankshaft until the timing marks on the converter periphery are at approximately the 3 o'clock position.
9 The torque converter is a taper fit on the end of the crankshaft and it will be necessary to obtain BL special tool 18G1086 to remove it. The tool is bolted to the torque converter through the holes of the three previously removed converter retaining bolts. With the adaptor in position on the end of the crankshaft, tighten the tool centre bolt until the torque converter breaks free of the taper, and then lift it off the crankshaft.
10 Undo and remove the nuts, bolts and washers securing the converter housing to the engine and transmission casing.
11 Remove the selector bellcrank lever clevis pin and nut, and lift off the bellcrank lever. Remove the bellcrank lever pivot.
12 The converter housing can now be carefully withdrawn. The converter housing oil seal should always be renewed when removing the housing. If for any reason this is not possible, wrap tin foil or adhesive tape around the output gear splines before pulling off the housing so that the splines do not damage the oil seal.

14 Engine – removal from automatic transmission

1 With the torque converter and housing removed as described in Section 13, carefully lever the main oil feed pipe from the transmission and oil pump.
2 Undo and remove the two retaining bolts and lift off the oil filter and housing assembly.
3 Unscrew the engine oil feed pipe union at the adaptor on the transmission casing.
4 Undo and remove the flange nuts, bolts and spring washers securing the engine to the transmission.
5 Undo and remove the bolts securing the radiator lower mounting bracket to the engine mounting adaptor.
6 Using a crane, or hoist and lifting slings, carefully lift the engine off

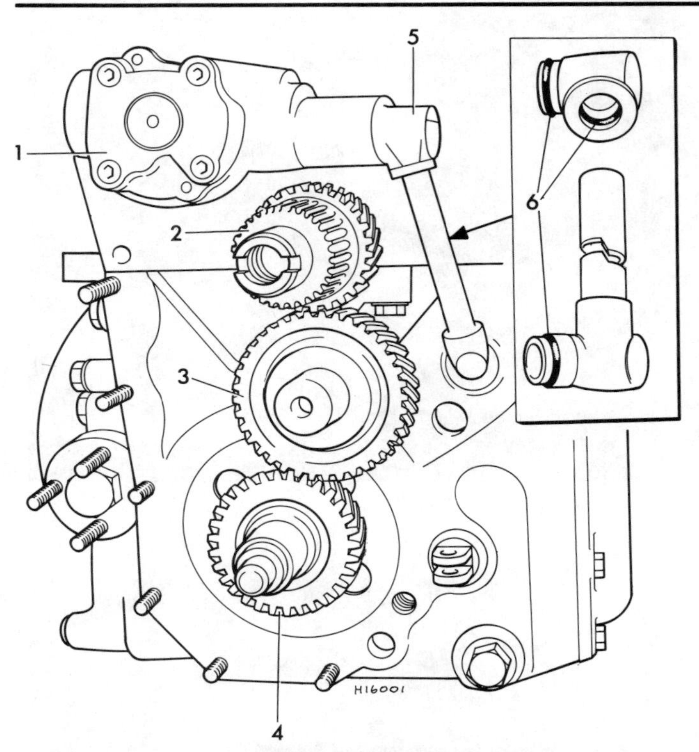

Fig. 1.12 End view of the transfer gears with the converter housing removed (Sec 13)

1 *Main oil pump*
2 *Converter output gear*
3 *Idler gear*
4 *Input gear*
5 *Oil feed pipe*
6 *Sealing rings*

the transmission casing. It may be necessary to tap the transmission casing downward with a rubber or hide mallet to break the seal between the two mating faces.

7 With the engine removed cover the top of the transmission completely to prevent dirt ingress.

15 Engine dismantling – general

During dismantling, the engine should be supported on blocks positioned under the crankcase flanges and placed either on a sturdy bench or at ground level. The greatest care should be taken to keep the exposed parts free from dirt and grit. As an aid to achieving this, clean the exterior of the engine thoroughly, removing all traces of oil and congealed dirt. A good water-soluble degreaser will make the job much easier. If the solvent has been applied and allowed to stand for a short while, a vigorous water jet will wash off all the solvent, dirt and grease. If the dirt is thick and deeply embedded, work the solvent into it with a stiff brush. Finally wipe down the exterior of the engine with a clean rag, and only then should the dismantling process begin.

As the engine is dismantled clean each part in a bath of paraffin or petrol. Never immerse parts with oilways in paraffin, (eg the crankshaft), but to clean wipe down carefully with a petrol-dampened rag. Oilways can be cleaned out with pipe cleaners. If an air line is present all parts can be blown dry and the oilways blown through as an added precaution.

A good way of cleaning greasy nuts, bolts, and washers, and similar small components, is to wash them in a special tin. Knock or drill a number of small holes in the bottom of a tin. Place the parts to be cleaned in the tin and then dip it into a paraffin filled container. Shake the tin around so as to allow the paraffin to clean the parts. When the parts are clean lift the tin out allowing the paraffin to drain. You will not have had to grope around at the bottom of the paraffin container and none of the parts will be lost.

Re-use of old engine gaskets is false economy and can give rise to oil and water leaks – if nothing worse. To avoid the possibility of trouble after the engine has been reassembled always use new gaskets throughout. Do not throw the old gaskets away as it sometimes happens that an immediate replacement cannot be found and the old gasket is then very useful as a template. Hang up the old gaskets, as they are removed, on a suitable hook or nail.

Wherever possible, refit nuts and bolts and washers finger-tight to the original stud, bolt, or hole from which they were removed. This helps avoid later loss and muddle. If they cannot be refitted then lay them out in such a fashion that it is clear from where they were removed, or keep them in clearly labelled boxes, tins or polythene bags.

16 Engine ancillary components – removal

1 Before starting a complete overhaul, or if the engine is being exchanged for a reconditioned unit, the following items should be removed:

Fuel system components:
Fuel pump (mechanical type)
Emission control equipment (where applicable)
Inlet and exhaust manifolds (photo)
Ignition system components:
Spark plugs
Distributor
Cooling system components:
Radiator and hoses
Fan and pulley
Water pump
Heater control valve (photo)
Thermostat housing and thermostat
Temperature gauge sender unit
Electrical system components:
Dynamo or alternator and mounting brackets

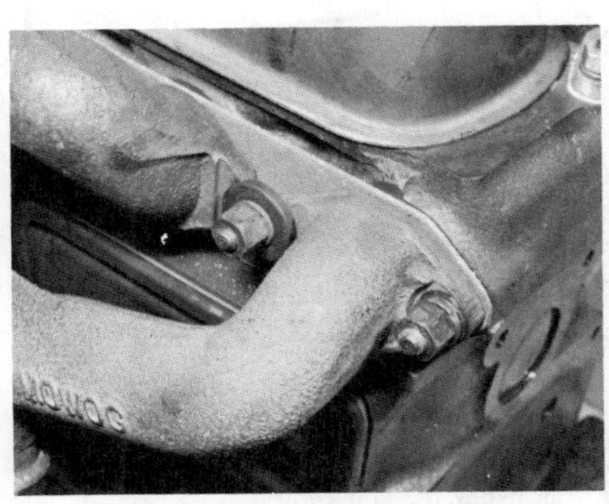

16.1a Inlet and exhaust manifold retaining nuts

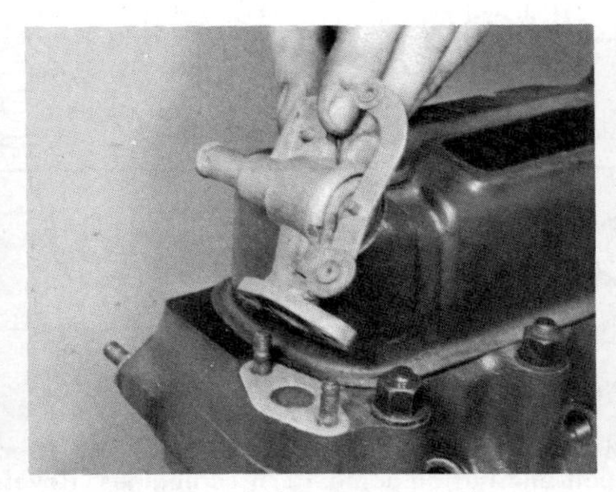

16.1b Removing the heater water valve

16.1c Location of the oil pressure gauge pipe union

16.1d Remove the oil feed pipe union at the engine...

16.1e ...and at the oil filter housing...

16.1f ...and then withdraw the housing

16.1g Removing the tappet block side covers

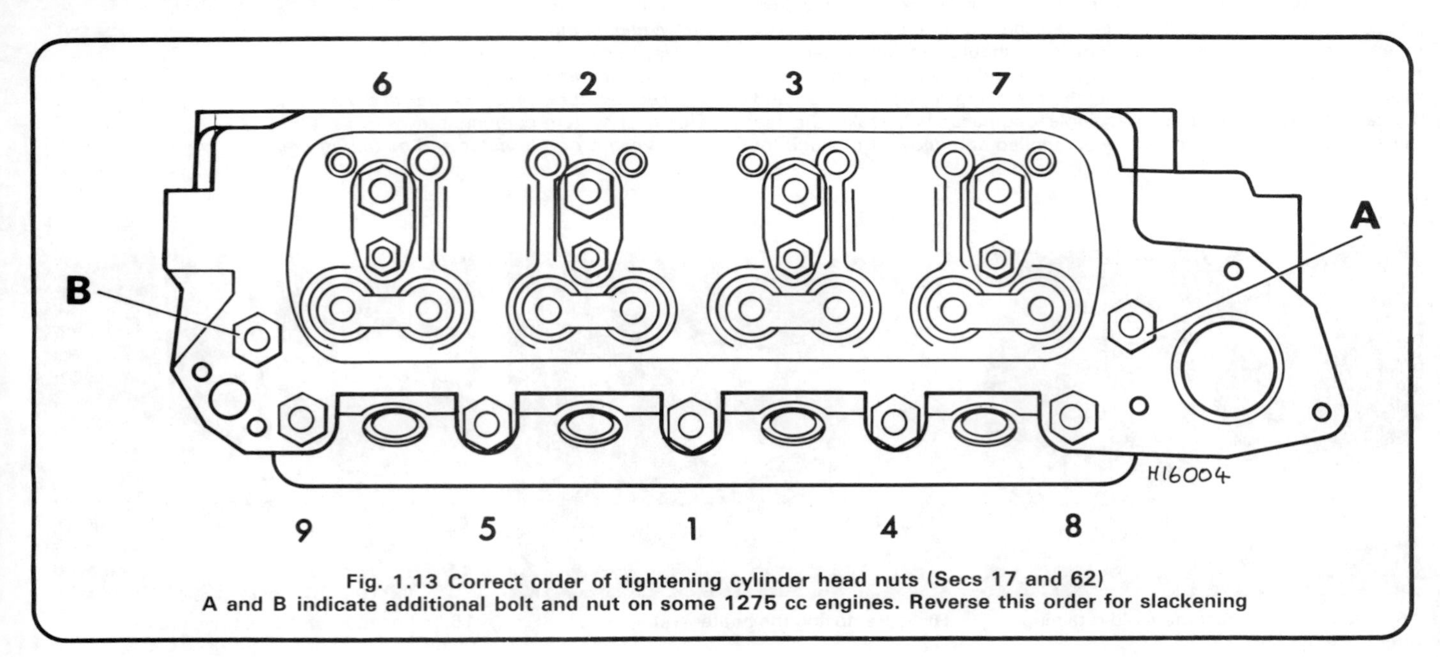

Fig. 1.13 Correct order of tightening cylinder head nuts (Secs 17 and 62)
A and B indicate additional bolt and nut on some 1275 cc engines. Reverse this order for slackening

Engine:

Oil pressure gauge pipe or sender unit (photo)
Oil feed pipe at cylinder block (photo)
Oil feed pipe at filter housing (photo)
Oil filter and housing
Dipstick
Tappet block side covers – where fitted (photo)

The removal of these components is quite straightforward; however, a more detailed removal sequence may be found in the relevant Chapters of this manual.

2 With the ancillary components removed, dismantling of the major engine assemblies can now be carried out as described in the following Sections.

17 Cylinder head – removal (engine in car)

Note: *If working on an engine fitted with emission control equipment, it will be necessary to first remove the diverter valve, air pump and associated hoses before proceeding with the removal sequence. Detailed removal procedures for these components will be found in Chapter 3*

1 Disconnect the battery earth terminal.

2 Slacken the clips securing the radiator top hose and remove the hose.

3 On models fitted with an ignition shield over the front of the engine, release the three retaining lugs and lift off the shield.

4 Make a note of the electrical connections at the ignition coil and disconnect them. Now undo and remove the nut securing the coil bracket to the cylinder head and lift away the coil.

5 Undo and remove the two nuts securing the radiator upper support bracket to the thermostat housing and the two bolts securing it to the radiator. Remove the bracket.

6 Refer to Chapter 3 and remove the air cleaner and carburettor(s).

7 Undo and remove the retaining nuts and bolts, and lift off the clamps securing the exhaust front pipe to the manifold. On Cooper S models, undo and remove the nuts and flat washers securing the inlet and exhaust manifolds to the cylinder head. Lift off the inlet manifold, ease the exhaust manifold back off the cylinder head studs and tie it securely in this position.

8 Slacken the water pump-to-cylinder head bypass hose retaining clips.

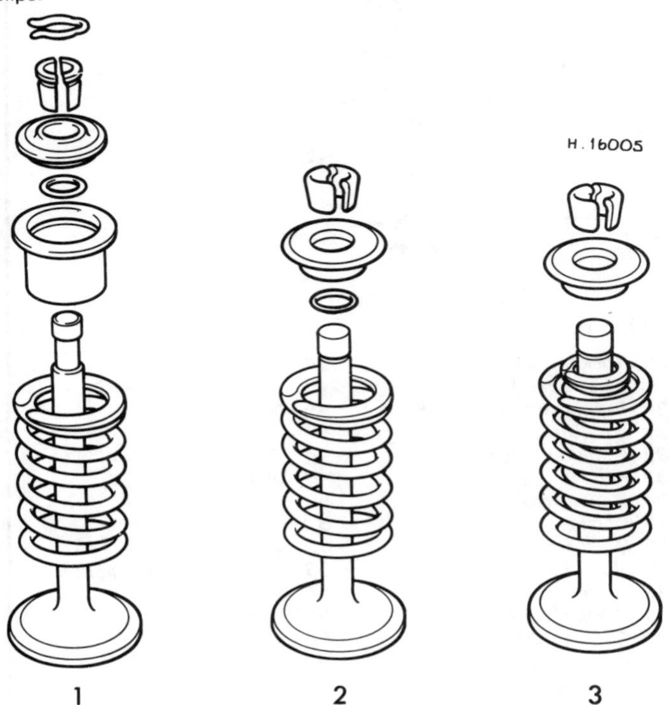

Fig. 1.14 Valve assembly components (Sec 19)

1 Early type 2 Later type 3 Cooper S type

9 Slacken the securing clip and remove the heater hose from the heater valve on the cylinder head. Now disconnect the control cable from the valve.

10 Make a note of their positions and then remove the HT leads from the spark plugs.

11 Detach the temperature gauge electrical lead from the sender unit.

12 Undo and remove the two bolts, and lift off the rocker cover and gasket.

13 Slacken the four rocker pedestal nuts and the nine main cylinder head nuts, half a turn at a time, in the reverse sequence to that shown in Fig. 1.13 to avoid distorting the cylinder head. On some 1275 cc engines an additional nut and bolt are located at the front and rear of the cylinder head, and these must be released first. When the tension is released from all the nuts, they may then be removed, one at a time, from their studs.

14 Now lift off the rocker assembly complete and place it to one side.

15 Lift out the pushrods, keeping them in the relative order in which they were removed. The easiest way to do this is to push them through a sheet of thick paper or thin card, numbered in the correct sequence.

16 The cylinder head can now be removed by lifting upwards. If the head is jammed, try to rock it to break the seal. Under no circumstances try to prise it apart from the block with a screwdriver or cold chisel, as damage may be done to the faces of the head or block. If the head will not free readily, turn the engine over by the flywheel, as the compression in the cylinders will often break the cylinder head joint. If this fails to work, strike the head sharply with a plastic or wooden headed hammer, or with a metal hammer with an interposed piece of wood to cushion the blows. Under no circumstances must you hit the head directly with a metal hammer, as this may cause the iron casting to fracture. Several sharp taps with the hammer, at the same time pulling upwards, should free the head. Lift the head off squarely and place it on one side.

18 Cylinder head – removal (engine on bench)

The procedure for removing the cylinder head with the engine on the bench is the same as for removal when the engine is in the car, with the exception of disconnecting the controls and services. Refer to the previous Section and follow the removal sequence given in paragraphs 12 to 16 inclusive.

19 Valves – removal

1 The valves can be removed from the cylinder head as follows. With a pair of pliers remove the spring clips (where fitted) holding the two halves of the split tapered collets together. Compress each spring in turn with a valve spring compressor until the two halves of the collets can be removed. Release the compressor and remove the spring(s) and cap (photos).

2 If, when the valve spring compressor is screwed down, the valve spring retaining cap refuses to free and expose the split collet, do not continue to screw down on the compressor as there is a likelihood of damaging it. Gently tap the top of the tool directly over the cap with a light hammer. This will free the cap. To prevent the compressor jumping off the valve spring retaining cap when it is tapped, hold the compressor firmly in position with one hand.

3 Slide the rubber oil seal off the valve stem and withdraw the valve through the combustion chamber. **Note:** *On 1275 cc engines the oil seal is positioned over the valve guide. On Cooper S models double valve springs are used.*

4 It is essential that the valves are kept in their correct sequence unless they are so badly worn that they are to be renewed. If they are going to be kept and used again, place them in a sheet of card having eight holes numbered 1 to 8 corresponding to the relative positions the valves were in when fitted. Also keep the valve springs, caps etc, in the correct order.

20 Valve guides – removal

If it is wished to remove the valve guides, they can be removed from the cylinder head in the following manner. Place the cylinder head with the gasket face on the bench and with a suitable hard steel punch, drift the guides out of the cylinder head.

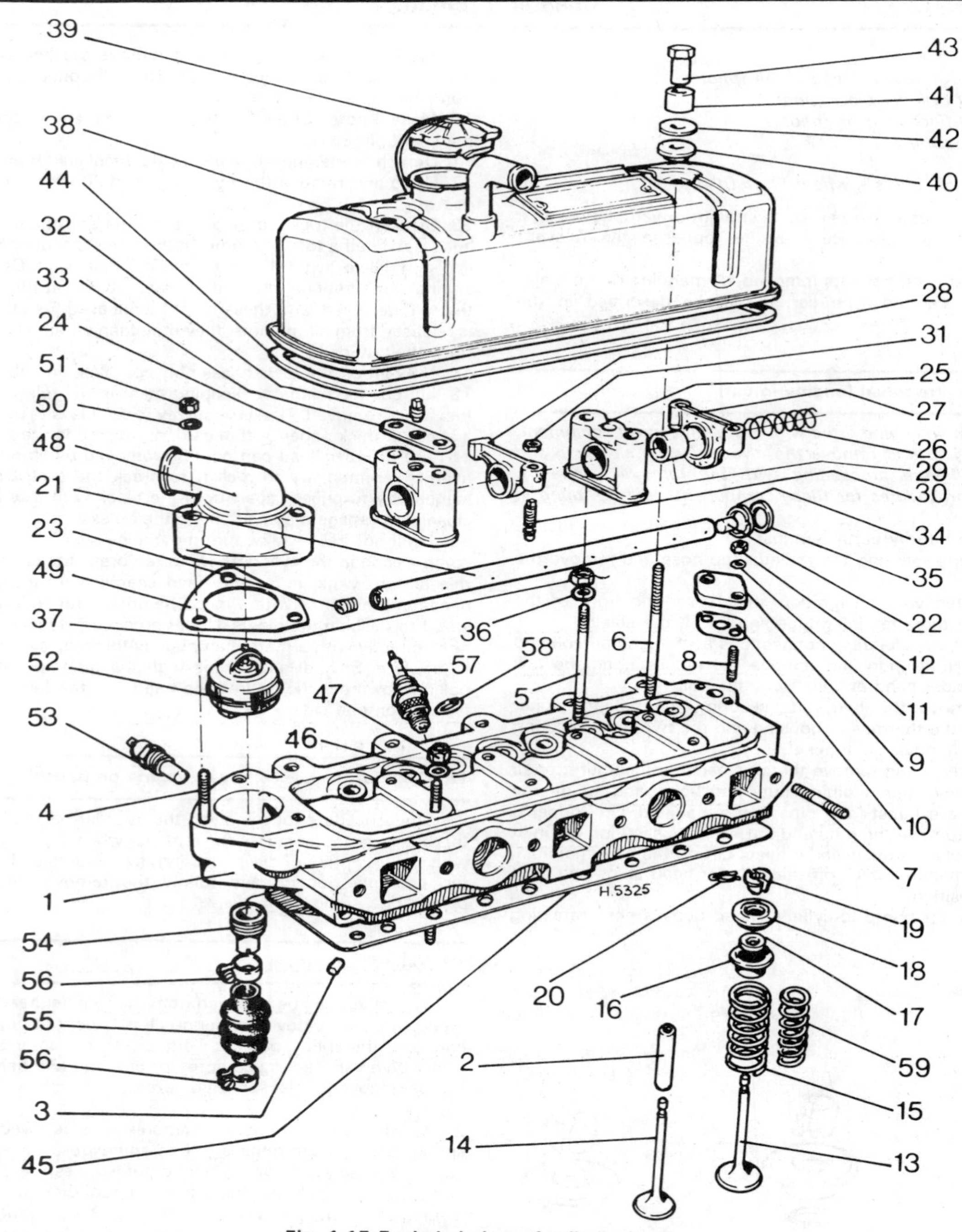

Fig. 1.15 Exploded view of cylinder head

1 Cylinder head
2 Valve guide
3 Plug
4 Water outlet elbow stud
5 Rocker pedestal stud (short)
6 Rocker pedestal stud (long)
7 Manifold stud
8 Stud
9 Cover plate
10 Cover gasket
11 Washer
12 Nut
13 Inlet valve
14 Exhaust valve
15 Valve spring
16 Guide shroud
17 Packing ring
18 Spring cup
19 Valve collets
20 Circlip
21 Rocker shaft
22 Rocker shaft plug
23 Rocker shaft plug (screwed)
24 Rocker pedestal
25 Rocker pedestal
26 Spacing spring
27 Valve rocker (pressed type)
28 Valve rocker (forged type)
29 Rocker bush (forged type rocker)
30 Tappet adjusting screw
31 Locknut
32 Locating screw
33 Pedestal plate
34 Double coil washer
35 Washer
36 Washer
37 Nut
38 Valve rocker cover
39 Oil filler cap
40 Rubber bush
41 Distance piece
42 Cup washer
43 Nut
44 Cover gasket
45 Cylinder head gasket
46 Washer
47 Nut
48 Water outlet elbow
49 Elbow gasket
50 Washer
51 Nut
52 Thermostat
53 Temperature transmitter
54 By-pass adaptor
55 By-pass hose
56 Clip
57 Spark plug
58 Washer
59 Inner spring – twin-carburettor application

19.1a Compress the valve springs with a spring compressor and lift off the collets...

19.1b ...then remove the compressor, valve cap and spring

21 Rocker gear – dismantling

To dismantle the rocker assembly, release the rocker shaft locating screw, remove the split pins, flat washers, and spring washers from each end of the shaft and slide from the shaft the pedestals, rocker arms, and rocker spacing springs.

22 Timing cover, gears and chain – removal

Note: *The timing cover, gears and chain can be removed with the engine in the car provided the radiator and fan are removed. (For radiator and fan removal see Chapter 2). The procedure for removing the timing cover, gears and chain is otherwise the same irrespective of whether the engine is in the car or on the bench, and is as follows:*

1 Bend back the locking tab of the crankshaft pulley locking washer under the crankshaft pulley retaining bolt, prising it back with a cold chisel or screwdriver through the radiator grille in the wing if the engine is still in the car. With a large spanner remove the bolt and locking washer. This bolt is sometimes very difficult to shift, and hitting the free end of the spanner with a heavy hammer is sometimes the only way to start it. If the engine is still in the car, put the car in top gear and apply the handbrake hard to prevent the engine from turning.

2 Placing two large screwdrivers behind the crankshaft pulley wheel at 180° to each other, carefully lever the wheel off. It is preferable to use a proper pulley extractor if this is available, but large screwdrivers or tyre levers are quite suitable, providing care is taken not to damage the pulley flange.

3 Remove the Woodruff key from the crankshaft nose with a pair of pliers and note how the channel in the pulley is designed to fit over it. Place the Woodruff key in a glass jam jar, as it is a very small part and can easily be mislaid.

4 Unscrew the bolts holding the timing cover to the block. **Note**: *Four of the bolts are larger than the others, and each bolt makes use of a large flat washer as well as a spring washer.*

5 Take off the timing cover and gasket. If fitted, detach the engine breather hose from the cover.

6 With the timing cover off, take off the oil thrower. **Note**: *The concave side faces forward.*

7 Bend back the locking tab on the washer under the camshaft retaining nut and unscrew the nut, noting how the locking washer locating tag fits in the camshaft gearwheel keyway.

8 To remove the camshaft and crankshaft timing wheels complete with chain, ease each wheel forward a little at a time, levering behind each gearwheel in turn with two large screwdrivers at 180° to each other. If the gearwheels are locked solid, it will be necessary to use a proper gearwheel and pulley extractor. With both gearwheels off, remove the Woodruff keys from the crankshaft and camshaft with a pair of pliers and place them in a jam jar for safe keeping. *Note the number of very thin packing washers behind the crankshaft gearwheel and remove them very carefully.*

23 Tappets (cam followers) – removal

1 With the rocker gear and pushrods removed, undo and remove the bolt securing each tappet block side cover to the rear of the cylinder block and lift off the covers (if still in place). **Note**: *On 1275 cc engines tappet block side covers are not fitted and the tappets can only be removed after removing the camshaft.*

2 Lift out each tappet from its location in the cylinder block and ensure that they are kept in the correct sequence in which they were removed.

24 Distributor drive – removal

Note: *To remove the distributor drive with the transmission casing still in position, it may first be necessary to remove one of the tappet cover bolts if fitted. With the distributor and the distributor clamp plate already removed, this is achieved as follows:*

1 Unscrew the single retaining bolt and lockwasher to release the distributor housing.

2 With the distributor housing removed, with the transmission casing still in position, screw into the end of the distributor driveshaft a $\frac{5}{16}$ in UNF bolt. A tappet cover bolt (where fitted) is ideal for this purpose. The driveshaft can then be lifted out, the shaft being turned slightly in the process to free the shaft skew gear from the camshaft skew gear.

3 If the gear casing has already been removed then it is a simple matter to push the driveshaft out from inside the crankcase.

25 Camshaft – removal

Note: *The camshaft can only be removed with the engine out of the car and on the bench. With the timing cover, gears and chain, fuel pump, distributor drivegear and tappets removed as previously described, proceed as follows:*

1 Undo and remove the three bolts and spring washers securing the camshaft locating plate to the cylinder block. Lift off the plate.

2 Carefully withdraw the camshaft from the cylinder block, taking care not to damage the camshaft bearings with the cam lobes as it is withdrawn. **Note**: *On 1275 cc engines position the engine on its side to prevent the tappets falling out as the camshaft is removed. Recover the oil pump drive coupling from the end of the camshaft after removal.*

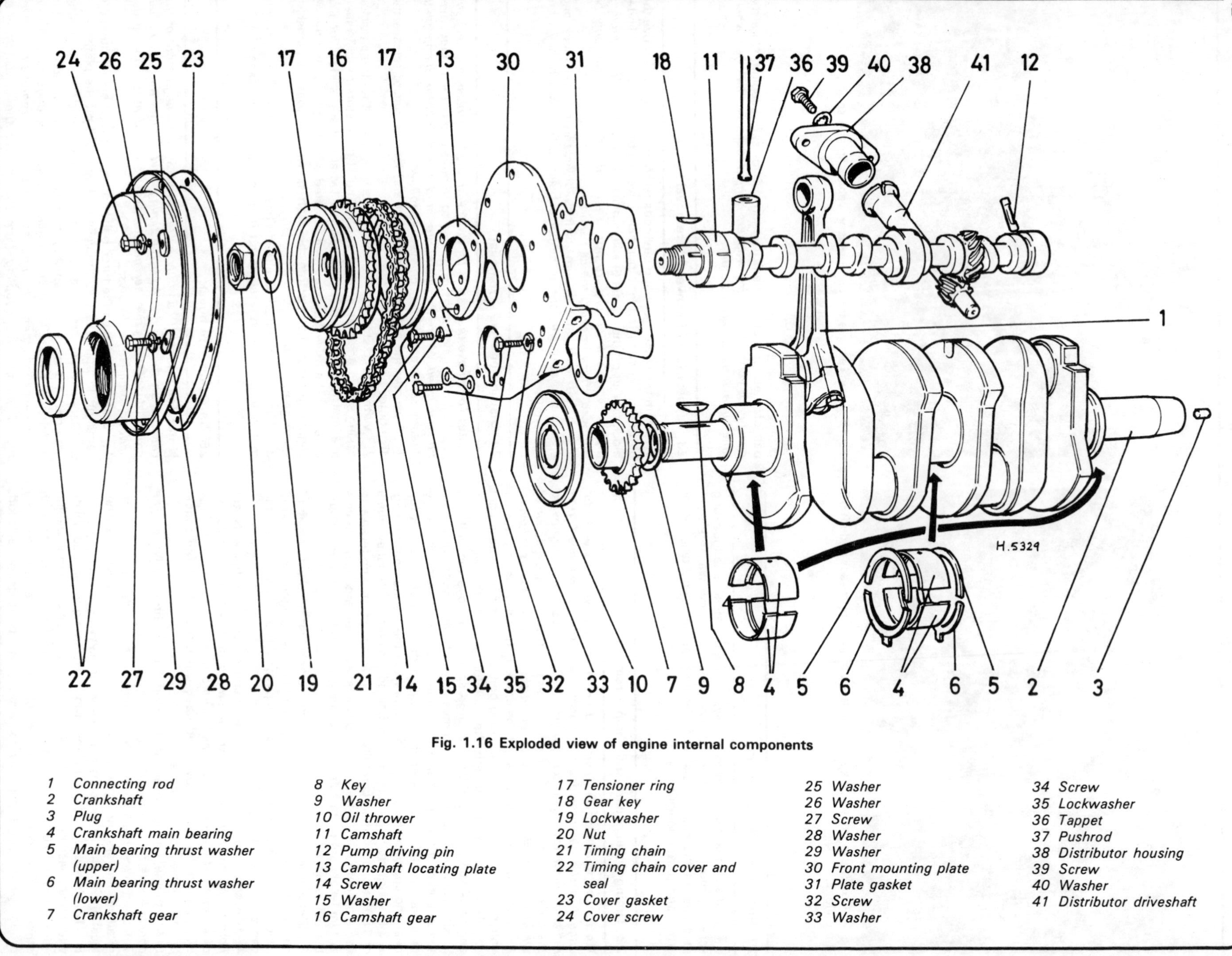

Fig. 1.16 Exploded view of engine internal components

1 Connecting rod
2 Crankshaft
3 Plug
4 Crankshaft main bearing
5 Main bearing thrust washer (upper)
6 Main bearing thrust washer (lower)
7 Crankshaft gear
8 Key
9 Washer
10 Oil thrower
11 Camshaft
12 Pump driving pin
13 Camshaft locating plate
14 Screw
15 Washer
16 Camshaft gear
17 Tensioner ring
18 Gear key
19 Lockwasher
20 Nut
21 Timing chain
22 Timing chain cover and seal
23 Cover gasket
24 Cover screw
25 Washer
26 Washer
27 Screw
28 Washer
29 Washer
30 Front mounting plate
31 Plate gasket
32 Screw
33 Washer
34 Screw
35 Lockwasher
36 Tappet
37 Pushrod
38 Distributor housing
39 Screw
40 Washer
41 Distributor driveshaft

26 Pistons, connecting rods and big-end bearings – removal

Note: *With the engine on the bench and the cylinder head removed, the piston and connecting rod assemblies can be withdrawn from the top of the cylinder bores using this procedure.*

1 Knock back with a cold chisel the locking tabs on the big-end retaining bolts, and remove the bolts and locking tabs. The 1275 cc engine does not have locking tabs and the big-end caps are retained by bolts and special multi-sided nuts.

2 Remove the big-end caps one at a time, taking care to keep them in the right order and the correct way round. Also ensure that the shell bearings are kept with their correct connecting rods and caps unless they are to be renewed. Normally, the numbers 1 to 4 are stamped on adjacent sides of the big-end caps and connecting rods, indicating which cap fits on which rod and which way round that cap fits. If no numbers or lines can be found then, with a sharp screwdriver, scratch mating marks across the joint from the rod to the cap. One line for connecting rod No 1, two for connecting rod No 2, and so on. This will ensure that there is no confusion later, as it is essential that the caps go back in the correct position on the connecting rods from which they were removed.

3 If the big-end caps are difficult to remove they may be gently tapped with a soft mallet.

4 To remove the shell bearings, press the bearing opposite the groove in both the connecting rod and the connecting rod caps, and the bearings will slide out easily.

5 Withdraw the pistons and connecting rods upwards and ensure that they are kept in the correct order for refitting in the same bore. Refit the connecting rod caps and bearings to the rods if the bearings do not require renewal, to minimise the risk of getting the caps and rods muddled.

27 Gudgeon pins – removal

1 Three different methods of gudgeon pin retention are employed, depending on the type and cubic capacity of the engine.

2 On the 848 cc engines the gudgeon pin is clamped firmly in place by a pinch-bolt located in the end of the connecting rod. To remove the piston from the connecting rod it is merely necessary to undo and remove the pinch-bolt and slide out the gudgeon pin. If it shows reluctance to move, do not force it as this may damage the piston. Immerse the piston in boiling water for a few minutes; the expansion of the aluminium should allow the pin to slide out easily.

3 On the 998 cc and 1098 cc engines fully floating gudgeon pins are used, these being retained in position by a circlip at each end of the gudgeon pin bore in the piston. To remove the gudgeon pin and piston, withdraw the circlip from one end and push the pin out, immersing it in boiling water if it appears reluctant to move.

4 On the 1275 cc engines the gudgeon pin is firmly held in the small-end of the connecting rod by an interference fit. Removal of the gudgeon pin calls for the use of BL special tool 18G1150. In view of the high performance of these engines it is essential that this job is done correctly and this tool *must* be used. It is thought best for the private owner to take his connecting rod/piston assemblies to a good BL agent, and to allow a factory-trained mechanic to withdraw the gudgeon pins. Use of the tool is fairly complex and it is easy to damage the piston if the work is done without previous experience.

28 Piston rings – removal

To remove the piston rings, slide them carefully over the top of the piston, taking care not to scratch the aluminium alloy. Never slide them off the bottom of the piston skirt. It is very easy to break the piston rings if they are pulled off roughly so this operation should be done with extreme caution. Special piston ring expanders are the best tools to use for the removal and refitting of piston rings; however, an old 0.020 in (0.5 mm) feeler gauge will do to assist with the removal of the rings if expanders are not readily available. Lift one end of the piston ring to be removed out of its groove and insert the end of the feeler gauge under it. Turn the feeler gauge slowly round the piston and as the ring comes out of its groove apply slight upward pressure so that it rests on the land above. It can then be eased off the piston, using the feeler gauge to stop it slipping into any empty grooves if it is any but the top piston ring that is being removed.

29 Crankshaft and main bearings – removal

Note: *Having first removed the timing cover, gears and chain, the cylinder head, the piston and connecting rod assemblies, proceed to remove the crankshaft and main bearings*

1 If identification marks are not present on the main bearing caps, mark them suitably so that they may be refitted in their original positions and the correct way round.

2 Release the locktabs from the six bolts which hold the three main bearing caps in place. Note that locktabs are not used on 1275 cc engines.

3 Unscrew the bolts and remove them together with the locktabs.

4 Remove the two bolts which hold the front main bearing cap against the engine front plate.

5 Remove the main bearing caps and the bottom half of each bearing shell, taking care to keep the bearing shells in the right caps.

6 When removing the centre bearing cap, *note the bottom semi-circular halves of the thrust washers – one half lying on each side of the main bearing.* Lay them with the centre bearing along the correct side.

7 Slightly rotate the crankshaft to free the upper halves of the bearing shells and thrust washers, which should now be extracted and placed over the correct bearing cap.

8 Remove the crankshaft by lifting it away from the crankcase.

30 Engine front plate – removal

The engine front plate is bolted to the cylinder block and front main bearing cap, and is also retained by the bolts that secure the camshaft retaining plate and timing cover. As most of the attachments will already have been removed as part of the dismantling process, undo and remove the remaining bolts and lift off the front plate.

31 Oil pump – removal

Note: *Oil pump removal can only be carried out with the engine/transmission unit out of the car. Prior to removing the pump, it will be necessary to remove the flywheel and flywheel housing, or torque converter and housing. The oil pump engages directly via a lip and slot or splined drive with the rear of the camshaft.*

1 Bend back the locking tabs on the securing bolts which hold the pump to the block.

2 Unscrew the bolts and remove them complete with washers.

3 Now lift off the oil pump assembly.

32 Lubrication system – general description

A forced feed system of lubrication is fitted, with oil circulated round the engine from the transmission casing/sump. The level of engine oil in the sump is indicated on the dipstick, which is fitted on the right-hand side of the engine. It is marked to indicate the optimum level, which is the maximum mark. The level of oil in the sump should not be above or below this line. Oil is replenished via the filler cap on the front of the rocker cover. The oil in the transmission casing/sump is also used to lubricate the gearbox and differential.

The oil pump is mounted at the end of the crankcase and is driven by the camshaft. Three different types of oil pump have been fitted at different times. These are the 'Burman' rotary vane type, or the 'Hobourn-Eaton' or 'Concentric (Engineering) Ltd' concentric rotor type. All are of the non-draining variety to allow rapid build-up when starting from cold.

Oil is drawn from the sump through a gauze screen in the oil strainer and is sucked up the pick-up pipe and drawn into the oil pump. From the oil pump it is forced under pressure along a gallery on the right-hand side of the engine, and through drillings to the big-end, main and camshaft bearings. A small hole in each connecting rod allows a jet of oil to lubricate the cylinder wall with each revolution.

From the camshaft front bearing, oil is fed through drilled passages in the cylinder block and head to the front rocker pedestal where it enters the hollow rocker shaft. Holes drilled in the shaft allow for the lubrication of the rocker arms, and the valve stems and pushrod ends. This oil is at a reduced pressure to the oil delivered to the crankshaft bearings. Oil from the front camshaft bearing also lubricates the timing chain. Oil returns to the sump by various passages, the tappets being lubricated by oil returning via the pushrod drillings in the block.

On all models a full-flow oil filter is fitted, and all oil passes through this filter before it reaches the main oil gallery. The oil is passed directly from the oil pump across the block to an external pipe on the right-hand side of the engine which feeds into the filter head. Cooper S models are fitted with an oil cooler.

33 Oil filter – renewal

The full-flow oil filter fitted to all engines is located underneath the dynamo or alternator on the forward-facing side of the engine. On early manual transmission models the filter is of the disposable cartridge type contained within an aluminium bowl. On later models a throwaway canister is used. All automatic transmission models utilize the cartridge type filter. To renew the filter proceed as follows.

Cartridge type

1 Place a suitable container beneath the filter bowl and then undo and remove the long centre bolt securing the bowl to the housing. On some models it may be advantageous to remove the grille panel, as space is rather limited.

2 With the bolts released, carefully lift away the filter bowl, which contains the filters and will also be full of oil.

3 Discard the old filter element but first make sure that the pressure plate has not stuck to it. Now thoroughly clean out the filter bowl, the bolt, and the parts associated with it, using petrol or paraffin. Dry with a lint free cloth (photo).

4 A rubber sealing ring is located in a groove round the head of the oil filter and forms an effective leak-proof joint between the filter head and the filter bowl. A new rubber sealing ring is supplied with each new filter element.

5 Carefully prise out the old sealing ring from the locating groove. If the ring has become hard and is difficult to move take great care not to damage the sides of the sealing ring groove.

6 With the old ring removed, fit the new ring in the groove at four equidistant points and press it home a segment at a time. Do not insert the ring at just one point and work round the groove pressing it home as, using this method, it is easy to stretch the ring and be left with a small loop of rubber which will not fit into the locating groove (photo).

7 Reassemble the oil filter assembly by first passing up the bolt through the hole in the bottom of the bowl, with a steel washer under the bolt's head and a rubber or felt washer on top of the steel washer and next to the filter bowl.

8 Slide the spring over the bolt followed by the other steel washer, the remaining rubber washer and finally the filter pressure plate concave face downwards.

9 After fitting the new element to the bowl, position the bowl on the rubber sealing ring (photo) then insert and hand tighten the bolt. Before finally tightening the centre bolt, ensure that the lip of the filter bowl is resting squarely on the rubber sealing ring and is not offset or seated off the ring. If the bowl is not seating properly, rotate it until it is. Run the engine and check the bowl for leaks.

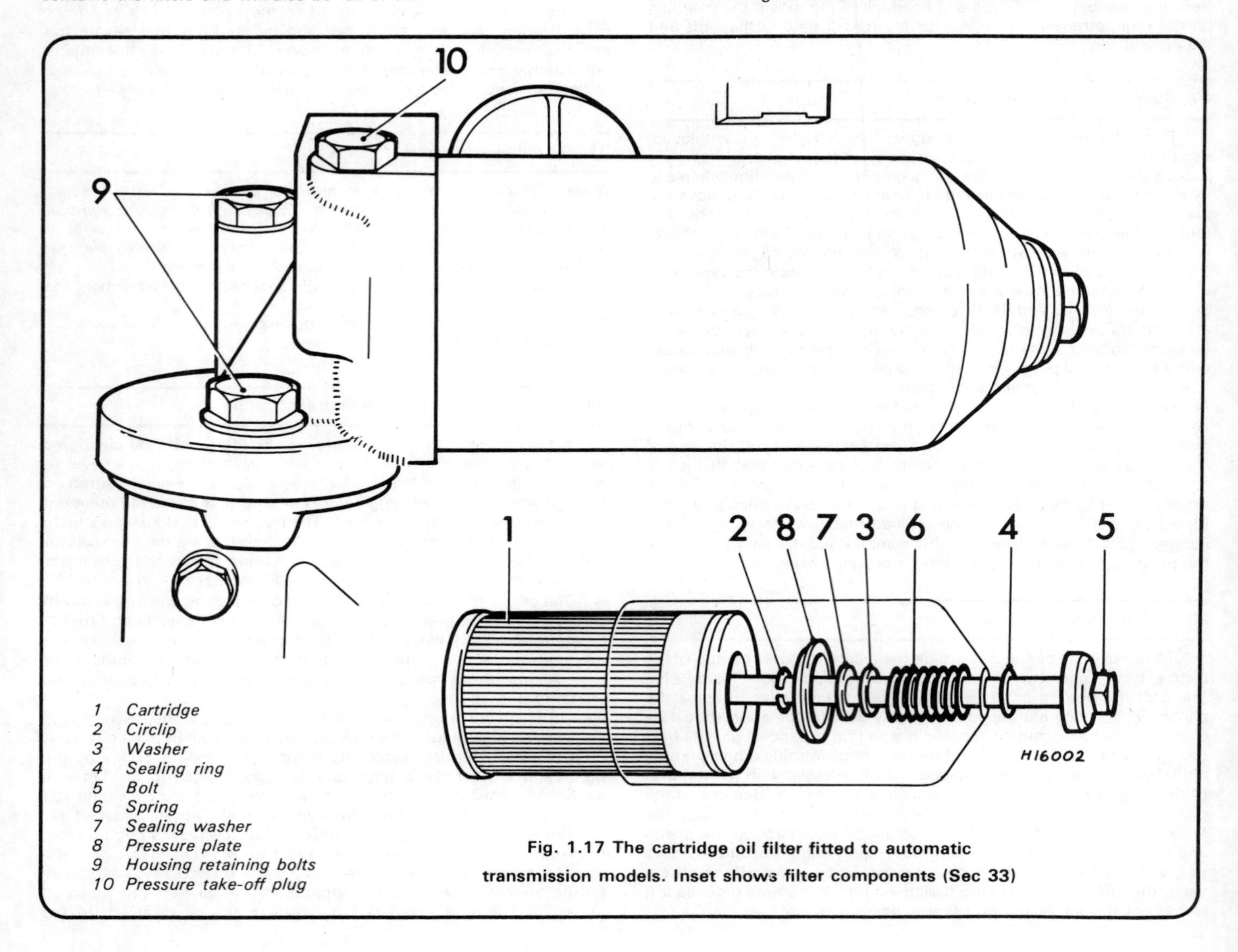

Fig. 1.17 The cartridge oil filter fitted to automatic transmission models. Inset shows filter components (Sec 33)

33.3 The cartridge type oil filter and associated parts

33.10 The canister type oil filter is accessible through the aperture in the front body panel

33.6 Refitting the cartridge type oil filter sealing ring

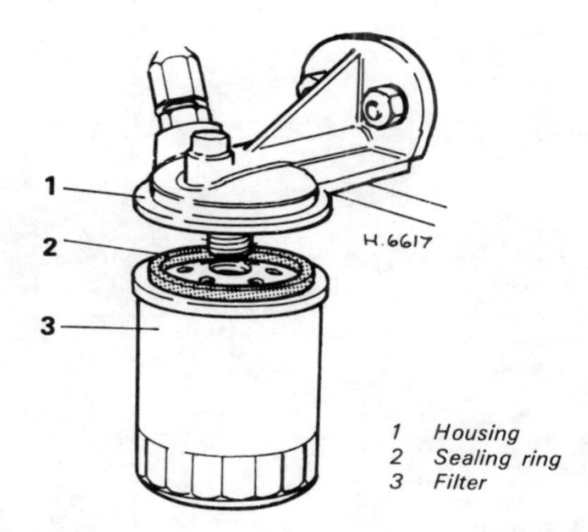

Fig. 1.18 The canister type oil filter fitted to later manual transmission models (Sec 33)

33.9 Refitting the assembled bowl and cartridge

Canister type

10 To renew the canister type filter place a suitable container beneath it and unscrew the complete canister from the housing (photo). If it is tight, pierce it with a screwdriver and tap it round, or preferably obtain a strap wrench or similar filter removing tool.
11 Discard the old canister and sealing ring and then smear the sealing ring of the new canister with clean engine oil.
12 Screw the canister onto the housing and tighten *by hand only.*
13 Run the engine and check for leaks.

34 Oil pressure relief valve – removal and refitting

1 To prevent excessive oil pressure – for example when the engine is cold – an oil pressure relief valve is built into the right-hand side of the engine just below the oil feed pipe union.
2 The relief valve is identified externally by a large domed hexagon nut. To dismantle the unit unscrew the nut and remove it, complete with the two fibre or copper sealing washers. The relief spring and the relief spring cup can then be easily extracted (photo).
3 In position, the metal cup fits over the opposite end of the relief valve spring resting in the dome of the hexagon nut, and bears against a machining in the block. When the oil pressure exceeds the specified

34.2 Withdrawing the oil pressure relief valve

35.14a The lower engine tie-bar may be fitted to the left-hand...

35.14b ...or right-hand side of the gearbox

pressure the cup is forced off its seat and the oil returns, via a drilling, directly to the sump.

4 Check the tension of the spring by measuring its free length. If it is shorter then the length shown in the Specifications it should be renewed. Reassembly of the relief valve unit is a reversal of the above procedure.

35 Engine mountings – removal and refitting

The engine/transmission unit is supported on two rubber mountings which are in turn bolted to the sides of the front subframe. One mounting is located under the radiator (left-hand mounting), and the other at the base of the flywheel or converter housing cover, to which it is attached (right-hand mounting). Fore-and-aft movement of the power unit is controlled by a tie-bar, one end of which is attached to the engine, and the other to a bracket on the bulkhead. Rubber bushes are used at each end to absorb vibration. On later models an additional lower tie-bar is used, one end of which is bolted to the subframe and the other to a bracket on the gearbox. A point worth noting is that the engine tie-bar rubber bushes are prone to wear and this is usually noticed as severe judder as the clutch is engaged, or excessive movement of the complete power unit when accelerating and decelerating. Should the engine mountings or tie-bar rubber bushes be worn or broken they can be renewed with the engine/transmission unit in the car, or on the bench.

Right-hand mounting

1 If the engine/transmission unit is in the car, remove the flywheel housing cover using the procedure described in Chapter 5, Section 9.

2 With the cover removed, undo the bolts securing the engine mounting and lift off the mounting.

3 Refitting is the reverse sequence to removal.

Left-hand mounting

4 To remove the mounting with the engine/transmission unit in the car first remove the radiator as described in Chapter 2.

5 Position a jack beneath the left-hand side of the transmission casing, and, using a block of wood to spread the load, *just* take the weight of the power unit.

6 Undo and remove the two nuts, bolt and spring washers securing the mounting to the subframe.

7 Raise the jack slightly and remove the bolts securing the mounting to the bracket on the gearbox casing. The engine mounting can now be withdrawn.

8 Refitting is the reverse sequence to removal.

Upper tie-bar and bushes

9 Undo and remove the two bolts securing the tie-bar and mounting bracket to the right-hand side of the engine. Move the tie-bar sideways and recover any spacing washers that may be fitted.

10 If the tie-bar is secured to its mounting bracket on the bulkhead by a through-bolt and locknut, remove the locknut and bolt and lift away the tie-bar.

11 If the tie-bar is secured by a stud with nuts and spring washers at each end, undo and remove the nuts and spring washers, then slacken the four nuts securing the clutch and brake master cylinder to the bulkhead. When sufficient clearance exists, lift up the tie-bar upper mounting bracket over the tie-bar stud, and withdraw the tie-bar.

12 With the tie-bar removed, slide out the rubber bushes and spacers and, if there is any sign of deterioration of the rubber, renew the bushes.

13 Refitting is the reverse sequence to removal.

Lower tie-bar and bushes

14 The lower tie-bar fitted to later models may be mounted in one of two positions; either bolted to a bracket on the left-hand side of the gearbox at one end and to the rear of the subframe at the other, or bolted to a bracket on the right-hand side of the gearbox at one end and to the front of the subframe at the other. The removal procedure is the same for both types (photos).

15 If the engine/transmission unit is in position, jack up the front of the car and support it on axle stands.

16 Undo and remove the bolts securing the tie-bar to the gearbox bracket and subframe, and withdraw the tie-bar.

17 To remove the bushes it will be necessary to draw them out using a tube of suitable diameter, a long bolt and nut, and packing washers. The new bushes are refitted in the same way but lubricate them with liquid detergent before fitting.
18 Refitting the tie-bar to the car is the reverse sequence to removal.

36 Engine components – examination for wear

When the engine has been stripped down and all parts properly cleaned, decisions have to be made as to what needs renewal. The following Sections tell the examiner what to look for. In any border-line case it is always best to decide in favour of a new part. Even if a part may still be serviceable its life will have been reduced by wear, and the degree of trouble needed to renew it in the future must be taken into consideration. However, these things are relative and it depends on whether a quick 'survival' job is being done, or whether the car as a whole is being regarded as having many thousands of miles of useful and economical life remaining.

37 Oil pump – dismantling, inspection and reassembly

Three types of oil pump have been fitted to Mini models covered by this manual; these are the Burman, Hobourn Eaton, and the Concentric (Engineering) pumps. The Burman and Hobourn Eaton pumps may be dismantled for inspection as described below; however the Concentric (Engineering) pump is a sealed unit which cannot be

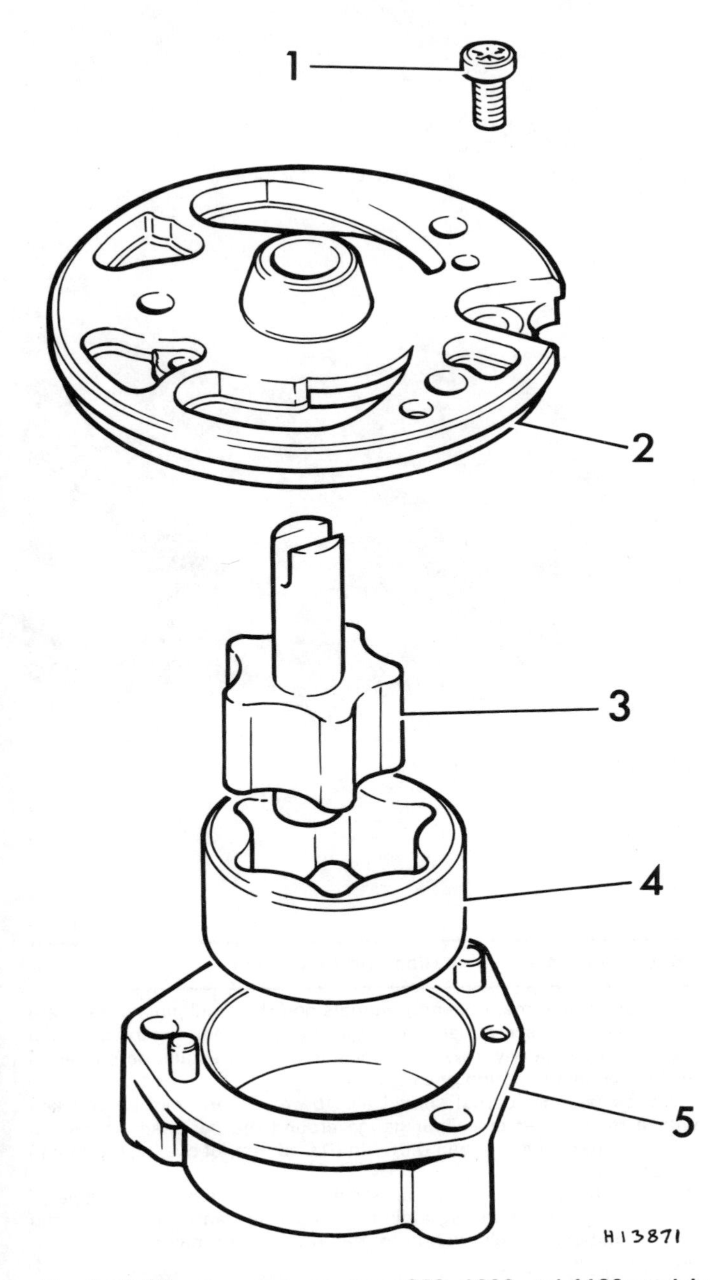

Fig. 1.19 Oil pump components – 850, 1000 and 1100 models (Sec 37)

1 *Screw*
2 *Cover*
3 *Inner rotor and shaft*
4 *Outer rotor*
5 *Body*

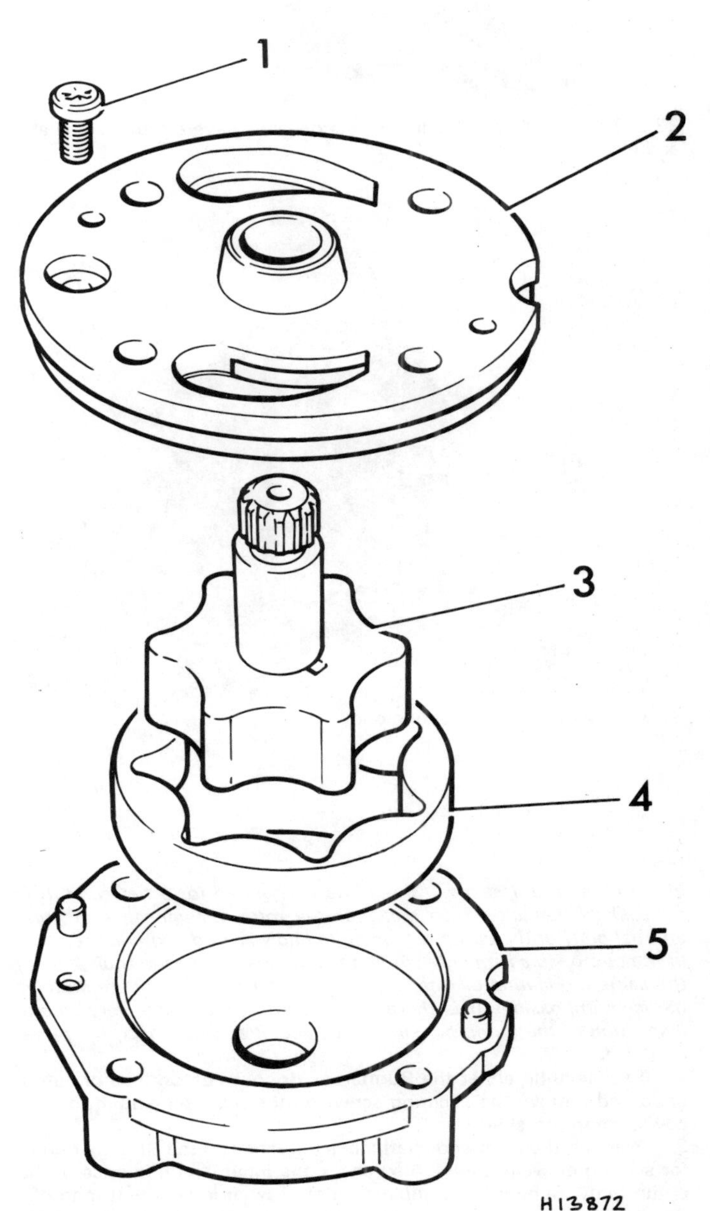

Fig. 1.20 Oil pump components – 1275 models (Sec 37)

1 *Screw*
2 *Cover*
3 *Inner rotor and shaft*
4 *Outer rotor*
5 *Body*

37.2 Oil pump dismantled for inspection. Note severe scoring of shaft and rotor

37.3a Measuring clearances between rotor lobes...

37.3b ...and between rotor and body

37.4 Reassembling the oil pump

dismantled, and if suspect should be exchanged for a new unit. It is quite likely that after high mileages the rotor, (or vanes), shaft, and internal body of the pump will be quite badly scored, requiring renewal of the pump. This is mainly due to the engine and transmission sharing the same lubricating oil, making thorough filtration of minute metallic particles impossible. It is therefore recommended that a very careful inspection of the pump be carried out and, if at all suspect, the pump renewed.

1 To dismantle either the Burman or Hobourn Eaton type of pump, undo and remove the securing screw on the rear face and lift off the cover, rotor and shaft.

2 Examine the rotor and shaft lobes (or vanes on the Burman pump) for scoring or wear ridges. Also check the inner circumference of the pump body. Renew the complete pump if wear is apparent (photo).

3 If the pump is in a satisfactory condition, measure the clearances between the shaft lobes and the side of the pump body (photos). If the clearances are outside the limits given in the Specifications the pump must be renewed.

4 Reassembly of the pump is the reverse sequence to dismantling (photo). Fill the assembled pump with clean engine oil before refitting to the engine.

38 Crankshaft – examination and renovation

1 Examine the main bearing journals and the crankpins; if there are any scratches or score marks then the shaft will need regrinding. Such conditions will nearly always be accompanied by similar deterioration in the matching bearing shells.

2 Each bearing journal should also be round and can be checked with a micrometer or caliper gauge around the periphery at several points. If there is more than 0.001 in (0.025 mm) of ovality, regrinding is necessary.

3 A main BL dealer or motor engineering specialist will be able to decide to what extent regrinding is necessary, and also supply the special undersize shell bearing to match whatever may need grinding off.

4 Before taking the crankshaft for regrinding, check also the cylinder bores and pistons as it may be advantageous to have the whole engine done at the same time.

5 The crankshaft oilways must be cleared. This can be done by probing with wire or by blowing through with an air line. Then insert the nozzle of an oil can into the respective oilways, each time blanking

off the previous hole, and squirt oil through the shaft. It should emerge through the next hole. Any oilway blockage must obviously be cleaned out prior to refitting the crankshaft.

39 Main and big-end bearings – examination and renovation

1 Big-end bearing failure is accompanied by a noisy knocking from the crankcase, and a slight drop in oil pressure. Main bearing failure is accompanied by vibration, which can be quite severe as the engine speed rises and falls, and a drop in oil pressure.

2 Bearings which have not broken up, but are badly worn, will give rise to low oil pressure and some vibration. Inspect the big-ends, main bearings, and thrust washers for signs of general wear, scoring, pitting, and scratches. The bearings should be matt grey in colour. With lead-indium bearings, should a trace of copper colour be noticed, the bearings are badly worn as the lead bearing material has worn away to expose the indium underlay. Renew the bearings if they are in this condition or if there is any sign of scoring or pitting.

3 Main bearings are not interchangeable between engine types as the main journals are of a different length. The undersizes available are designed to correspond with the regrind sizes; ie -0.010 bearings are correct for a crankshaft reground -0.010 undersize. The bearings are in fact, slightly more than the stated undersize as running clearances have been allowed for during their manufacture.

40 Cylinder bores – examination and renovation

1 The cylinder bores must be examined for taper, ovality, scoring and scratches. Start by carefully examining the top of the cylinder bores. If they are at all worn a very slight ridge will be found on the thrust side. This marks the top of the piston ring travel. The owner will have a good indication of the bore wear prior to dismantling the engine or removing the cylinder head. Excessive oil consumption accompanied by blue smoke from the exhaust is a sure sign of worn cylinder bores and piston rings.

2 Measure the bore diameter just under the ridge with a bore gauge (photo) and compare it with the diameter at the bottom of the bore, which is not subject to wear. If the difference between the two measurements is more than 0.006 in (0.152 mm) then it will be necessary to fit special piston rings or to have the cylinder rebored and fit oversize pistons and rings. If no such gauge is available, remove the rings from a piston and place the piston in each bore in turn about $\frac{3}{4}$ in (17 mm) below the top of the bore. If a 0.010 in feeler gauge can be slid between the piston and the cylinder wall on the thrust side of the bore, then remedial action must be taken. Oversize pistons are available dependent on the bore diameter, and the respective sizes available are given in the Specifications. These are accurately machined to just below these measurements so as to provide correct running clearances in bores bored out to the exact oversize dimensions.

40.2 Using a bore gauge to check cylinder bore wear

3 If the bores are slightly worn, but not so badly worn as to justify reboring, then special oil control rings can be fitted to the existing pistons which will restore compression and stop the engine burning oil. Several different types are available and the manufacturer's instructions concerning their fitting must be followed closely, but the piston must obviously be in good condition, and they may have to be machined to suit the oversize rings.

4 If new pistons and/or rings are to be fitted to cylinder bores that do not require reboring, then it will be necessary to remove the highly polished surface finish or 'glaze' of the cylinder bore. If this is not done the new rings will not bed-in and oil consumption will be excessive.

5 To remove the glaze, wrap a sheet of medium grade emery around a former and rub it up and down in the cylinder bore using a criss-cross action. Continue doing this until the shine is removed and the cylinder bore has a dull matt appearance. Repeat this procedure on the remaining three cylinders.

41 Pistons and piston rings – examination and renovation

1 If the old pistons are to be refitted, carefully remove the piston rings and then thoroughly clean them. Take particular care to clean out the piston ring grooves. Do not scratch the aluminium in any way. If new rings are to be fitted to the old pistons, then the top ring should be stepped, so as to clear the ridge left in the bore above the previous top ring. If a standard type oversize new ring is fitted it will hit the ridge and break, because the new ring will not have worn in the same way as the old.

2 Before fitting the rings on the pistons, each should be inserted approximately 3 in (75 mm) down the cylinder bore and the gap measured with a feeler gauge. This should be between the limits given in the Specifications at the beginning of this Chapter. It is essential that the gap is measured at the bottom of the ring travel, for if it is measured at the top of a worn bore and gives a perfect fit, it could easily seize at the bottom. If the ring gap is too small, rub down the ends of the ring with a very fine file until the gap is correct when fitted. To keep the rings square in the bore for measurement, line each one up in turn with an old piston in the bore upside down, and use the piston to push the ring down about 3 in (75 mm). Remove the piston and measure the piston ring gap.

3 When fitting new pistons and rings to a rebored engine the ring gap can be measured at the top of the bore, as the bore will now not taper. It is not necessary to measure the side clearance in the piston ring grooves with rings fitted, as the groove dimensions are accurately machined during manufacture. When fitting new oil control rings to the pistons it may be necessary to have the grooves widened by machining to accept the new rings. In this instance the manufacturer will make this quite clear and will supply the address to which the pistons must be sent for machining.

4 When new pistons are fitted, take great care to be sure to fit the exact size best suited to the particular bore of your engine. BL go one stage further than merely specifying one size piston for all standard bores. Because of very slight differences in cylinder machining during production, it is necessary to select just the right piston for the bore. A range of different sizes are available either from the piston manufacturer or from the local BL dealer.

5 Examination of the cylinder block face will show, adjacent to each bore, a small diamond-shaped box with a number stamped in the metal. Careful examination of the piston crown will show a matching diamond and number. These are the standard piston sizes and will be the same for all bores. If the standard pistons are to be refitted or standard low compression pistons changed to standard high compression pistons, then it is essential that only pistons with the same number in the diamond are used. With larger pistons, the amount of oversize is stamped in an ellipse on the piston crown.

6 On engines with tapered second and third compression rings, the top narrow side of the ring is marked with a 'T', or the word TOP. Always fit this side uppermost and carefully examine all rings for this mark before fitting (photo).

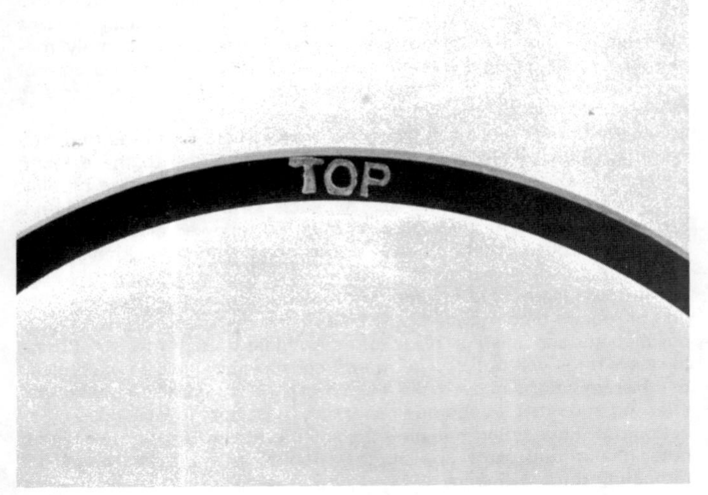

41.6 Piston ring identification markings

42 Camshaft and camshaft bearings – examination and renovation

1 Carefully examine the camshaft bearings for wear. **Note:** *On 848 cc engines, only the front camshaft bearing is renewable.* If the bearings are obviously worn or pitted or the metal underlay is showing through, then they must be renewed (where applicable). This is an operation for your local BL garage or the local engineering works as it demands the use of specialised equipment. The bearings are removed with a special drift, after which new bearings are pressed in, care being taken to ensure the oil holes in the bearings line up with those in the block. With a special tool the bearings are then reamed in position.
2 The camshaft itself should show no signs of wear, but if very slight scoring on the cams is noticed, the score marks can be removed by very gentle rubbing down with very fine emery cloth. The greatest care should be taken to keep the cam profiles smooth.

43 Valves, valve guides and valve seats – examination and renovation

1 Examine the heads of the valves for pitting and burning, especially the heads of the exhaust valves. The valve seats should be examined at the same time. If the pitting on valve and seat is very slight, the marks can be removed by grinding the seats and valves together with coarse, and then fine, valve grinding paste. Where bad pitting has occurred to the valve seats it will be necessary to recut them and fit new valves. If the valve seats are so worn that they cannot be recut, then it will be necessary to fit new valve seat inserts. These latter two jobs should be entrusted to the local BL garage or engineering works. In practice it is very seldom that the seats are so badly worn that they require renewal. Normally, it is the valve that is too badly worn for refitting and the owner can easily purchase a new set of valves and match them to the seats by valve grinding.
2 Examine the valve guides internally for wear. If the valves are a very loose fit in the guides and there is the slightest suspicion of lateral rocking, then new guides will have to be fitted.
3 When fitting new guides ensure that they are inserted into the cylinder head from above with the largest chamfer of the inlet guide at the top, and the counterbore of the exhaust guide at the bottom. Drive in the guides to the depth shown in Fig. 1.21. It will be necessary to have the valve seat recut to match the position of the new guides as described previously.
4 With the valves or guides renewed and the valve seats recut, where necessary, valve grinding can now be carried out as follows.
5 Place the cylinder head upside down on a bench, with a block of wood at each end to give clearance for the valve stems. Alternatively, place the head at 45° to a wall with the combustion chambers facing away from the wall.
6 Smear a trace of coarse carborundum paste on the seat face and apply a suction grinder tool to the valve head. With a semi-rotary motion, grind the valve head to its seat, lifting the valve occasionally to distribute the grinding paste. When a dull matt even surface finish

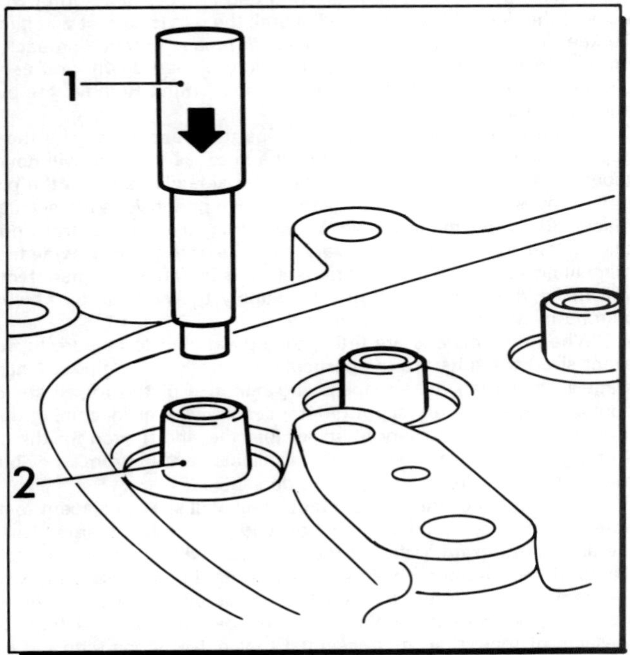

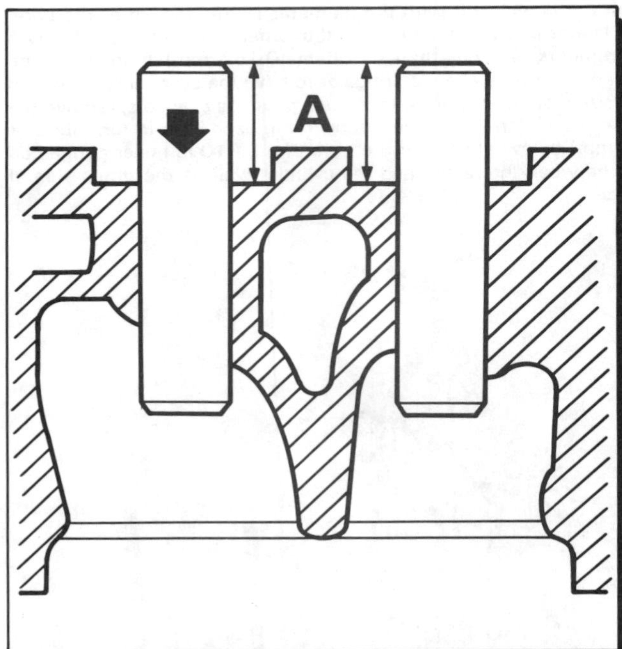

1 Shouldered drift
2 Guide correctly fitted

Dimension A = 0.593 in (15.08 mm)

Fig. 1.21 Refitting valve guides to cylinder head (Sec 43)

is produced, on both the valve seat and the valve, wipe off the paste and repeat the process with fine carborundum paste, lifting and turning the valve to re-distribute the paste as before. A light spring placed under the valve head will greatly ease this operation.

7 When a smooth unbroken ring of light great matt finish is produced, on both valve and valve seat faces, the grinding operation is completed.

8 Scrape away all carbon from the valve head and the valve stem. Carefully clean away every trace of grinding compound, taking great care not to leave any in the ports or in the valve guides. Clean the valves and valve seats with a paraffin soaked rag, then with a clean rag, and finally, if an air line is available, blow the valves, valve guides and valve ports clean.

44 Timing gear components – examination and renovation

1 Examine the teeth on both the crankshaft gearwheel and the camshaft gearwheel for wear. Each tooth forms an inverted 'V' with the gearwheel periphery, and if worn the side of each tooth under tension will be slightly concave in shape when compared with the other side of the tooth. If any sign of wear is present the gearwheels must be renewed.

2 Examine the links of the chain for side slackness and renew the chain if any slackness is noticeable when compared with a new chain. It is a sensible precaution to renew the chain at about 60 000 miles, and at a lesser mileage if the engine is stripped down for a major overhaul. The actual rollers on a very badly worn chain may be slightly grooved. Cooper S type engines use duplex chains.

3 Also check the rubber tension rings in the camshaft gearwheel where fitted. It is quite likely that the rubber will have become hard due to heat and oil contamination and it is advisable to renew them as a matter of course. The rings are simply prised out with a screwdriver and new rings stretched over the gearwheel flanges and into the grooves (photo). A spring-loaded rubber tensioning pad may be fitted to the timing cover on Cooper S type and later engines in place of the tensioning rings. If the rubber pad is grooved where it bears against the chain, it should also be renewed.

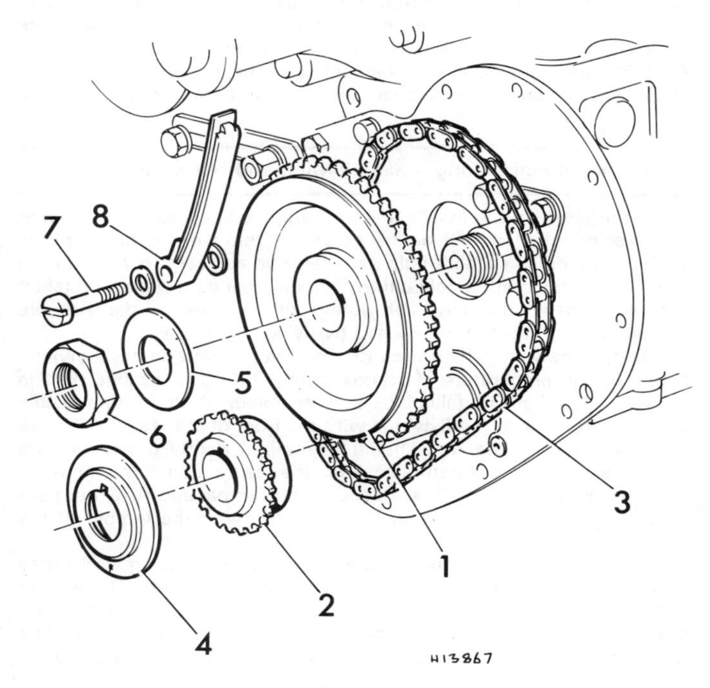

Fig. 1.22 Timing gear and chain assembly – later type (Sec 44)

1 Camshaft gear
2 Crankshaft gear
3 Timing chain
4 Oil thrower
5 Lockwasher
6 Nut
7 Tensioner retaining bolt
8 Tensioner

44.3 Fitting new timing chain tensioning rings to the camshaft gearwheel

44.4 Timing cover oil seal must be fitted with open side towards chain

4 It is advisable to renew the timing cover oil seal at this stage. Drive out the old seal and tap in the new one using the old seal to spread the load. Ensure that the open side of the seal faces inward, towards the chain (photo).

45 Valve rockers and rocker shaft – examination and renovation

1 Remove the threaded plug with a screwdriver from the end of the rocker shaft and thoroughly clean out the shaft. As it acts as the oil passage for the valve gear, clean out the oil holes and make sure they are quite clear. Check the shaft for straightness by rolling it on the bench. It is most unlikely that it will deviate from normal, but if it does, then a judicious attempt must be made to straighten it. If this is not successful, purchase a new shaft. The surface of the shaft should be free from any worn ridges caused by the rocker arms. If any wear is present, renew the shaft. Wear is only likely to have occurred if the rocker shaft oil holes have become blocked.

2 Check the rocker arms for wear of the rocker bushes, for wear at the rocker arm face which bears on the valve stem, and for wear of the adjusting ball-ended screws. Wear in the rocker arm bush can be checked by gripping the rocker arm tip and holding the rocker arm in place on the shaft, noting if there is any lateral rocker arm shake. If shake is present, and the arm is very loose on the shaft, remedial action must be taken. Pressed steel valve rockers cannot be renovated

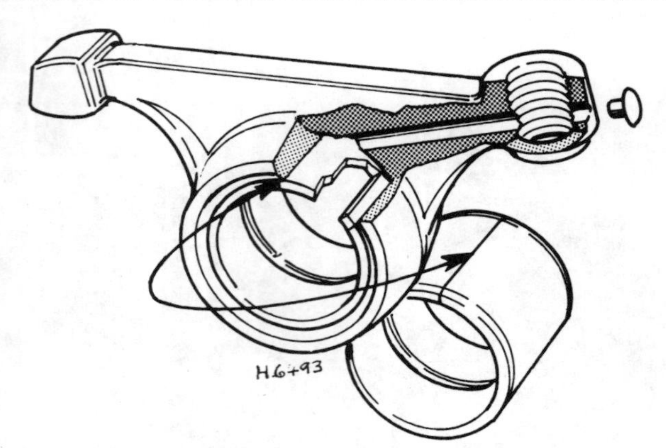

Fig. 1.23 Forged type valve rocker (Sec 45)

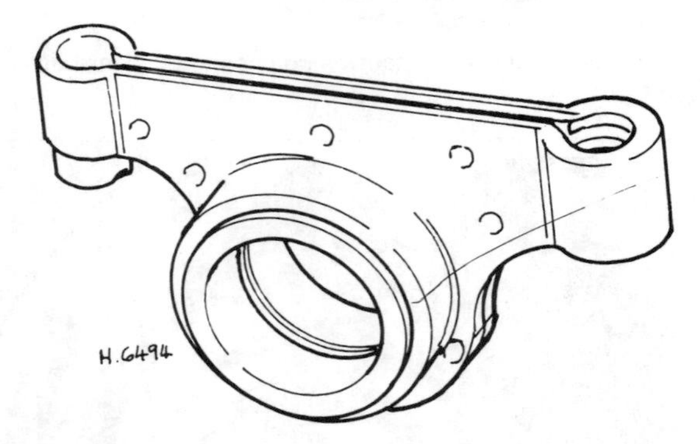

Fig. 1.24 Pressed steel type valve rocker (Sec 45)

by renewal of the rocker arm bush. It is necessary to fit new rocker arms. Forged rocker arms which have worn bushes may be taken to your local BL garage or engineering works to have the old bush drawn out and a new bush fitted. Forged rockers and pressed steel rockers are interchangeable in sets of eight, but, where one or two pressed steel rockers only require renewal, it is not advised to replace them with the forged type.

3 Check the tip of the rocker arm where it bears on the valve head for cracking or serious wear on the case hardening. If none is present, re-use the rocker arm. Check the lower half of the ball on the end of the rocker arm adjusting screw. On high performance mini engines, wear on the ball and top of the pushrod is easily noted by the unworn 'pip' which fits in the small central oil hole on the ball. The larger this 'pip' the more wear has taken place to both the ball and the pushrod. Check the pushrods for straightness by rolling them on the bench. Renew any that are bent.

46 Tappets (cam followers) – examination and renovation

Examine the bearing surface of the tappets (cam followers) which lie on the camshaft. Any indentation in this surface or any cracks indicate serious wear and the tappets should be renewed. Thoroughly clean them out, removing all traces of sludge. It is most unlikely that the sides of the tappets will prove worn, but, if they are a very loose fit in their bores and can readily be rocked, they should be exchanged for new units. It is very unusual to find any wear in the tappets, and any wear present is likely to occur only at very high mileages.

47 Flywheel housing oil seal – removal and refitting (manual transmission models)

1 It is recommended that this seal always be renewed whenever the flywheel housing is removed, as it is easily damaged and will allow oil to leak into the clutch components if it fails. The seal is simply removed from the housing using a screwdriver to prise it out.

47.2 Fitting a new flywheel housing oil seal

2 To fit a new seal, position it on the flywheel side of the flywheel housing with its flat face uppermost. Using the old seal to spread the load, gently tap it into position in the housing recess (photo).

48 Converter housing oil seal – removal and refitting (automatic transmission models)

1 Undo and remove the bolts securing the output gear oil seal housing to the inner face of the converter housing.

2 The output gear oil seal and converter oil seal can now be prised out of their respective housings using a stout screwdriver.

3 Use the old seals to assist the fitting of the new oil seals as in Section 47 and ensure that they enter their housings squarely. **Note:** *When refitting the converter oil seal, take care that it does not mask the oil drain hole in the housing when installed.*

4 With the new seals in position, refit the output gear oil seal housing to the converter housing and fully tighten the retaining bolts.

49 Flywheel starter ring – examination and renovation

1 If the teeth on the flywheel starter ring are badly worn, or if some are missing, then it will be necessary to remove the ring. This is achieved by drilling a pilot hole between two adjacent teeth and then splitting the ring with a cold chisel. The greatest care should be taken not to damage the flywheel during this process. Take suitable precautions to avoid injury caused by flying fragments.

2 To fit a new ring, heat it gently and evenly with an oxyacetylene flame until a temperature of approximately 350°C is reached. This is indicated by a light metallic blue surface colour. With the ring at this temperature, fit it to the flywheel with the front of the teeth facing the flywheel register. The ring should be tapped gently down onto its register and left to cool naturally, when the contraction of the metal on cooling will ensure that it is a secure and permanent fit. Great care must be taken not to overheat the ring, otherwise the temper of the ring will be lost.

3 Alternatively, your local BL garage or local engineering works may have a suitable oven in which the flywheel can be heated. The normal domestic oven will only give a temperature of about 250°C at the very most. Although it may just be possible to fit the ring at this temperature, it is unlikely, and excessive force should not be used.

50 Cylinder head and pistons – decarbonising

1 This can be carried out with the engine in or out of the car. With the cylinder head off, carefully remove (with a wire brush and blunt scraper) all traces of carbon deposits from the combustion spaces and

ports. The valve head and stems and valve guides should also be freed from any carbon deposits. Wash the combustion spaces and ports down with petrol and scrape the cylinder head surface free of any foreign matter with the side of a steel rule or similar article.

2 Clean the pistons and tops of the cylinder bores. If the pistons are still in the block, then it is essential that great care is taken to ensure that no carbon gets into the cylinder bores as this could scratch the cylinder walls or cause damage to the pistons and ring. To ensure this does not happen, first turn the crankshaft so that two of the pistons are at the top of their bores. Stuff rag into the other two bores or seal them off with paper and masking tape. The waterways should also be covered with small pieces of masking tape to prevent particles of carbon entering the cooling system and damaging the water pump.

3 Press a little grease into the gap between the cylinder walls and the two pistons which are to be worked on. With a blunt scraper carefully scrape away the carbon from the piston crown, taking great care not to scratch the aluminium. Also scrape away the carbon from the surrounding lip of the cylinder wall. When all carbon has been removed, scrape away the grease which will now be contaminated with carbon particles, taking care not to press any into the bores. To assist prevention of carbon build-up the piston crown can be polished with a proprietary metal polish. Remove the rags or masking tape from the other two cylinders and turn the crankshaft so that the pistons which were at the bottom are now at the top. Place rag or masking tape in the cylinders which have been decarbonised and proceed as before.

51 Engine reassembly – general

To ensure maximum life with minimum trouble from a rebuilt engine, not only must everything be correctly assembled, but everything must be spotlessly clean. All the oilways must be clear, locking washers and spring washers must always be fitted where indicated, and all bearing and other working surfaces must be thoroughly lubricated during assembly. Before assembly begins, renew any bolts or studs, the threads of which are in any way damaged, and whenever possible use new spring washers. Apart from your normal tools, a supply of clean rag, an oil can filled with engine oil, a new supply of assorted spring washers, a set of new gaskets, and a torque wrench, should be collected together.

52 Crankshaft – refitting

1 Ensure that the crankcase is thoroughly clean and that all oilways are clear. A thin twist-drill is useful for cleaning them out. If possible,

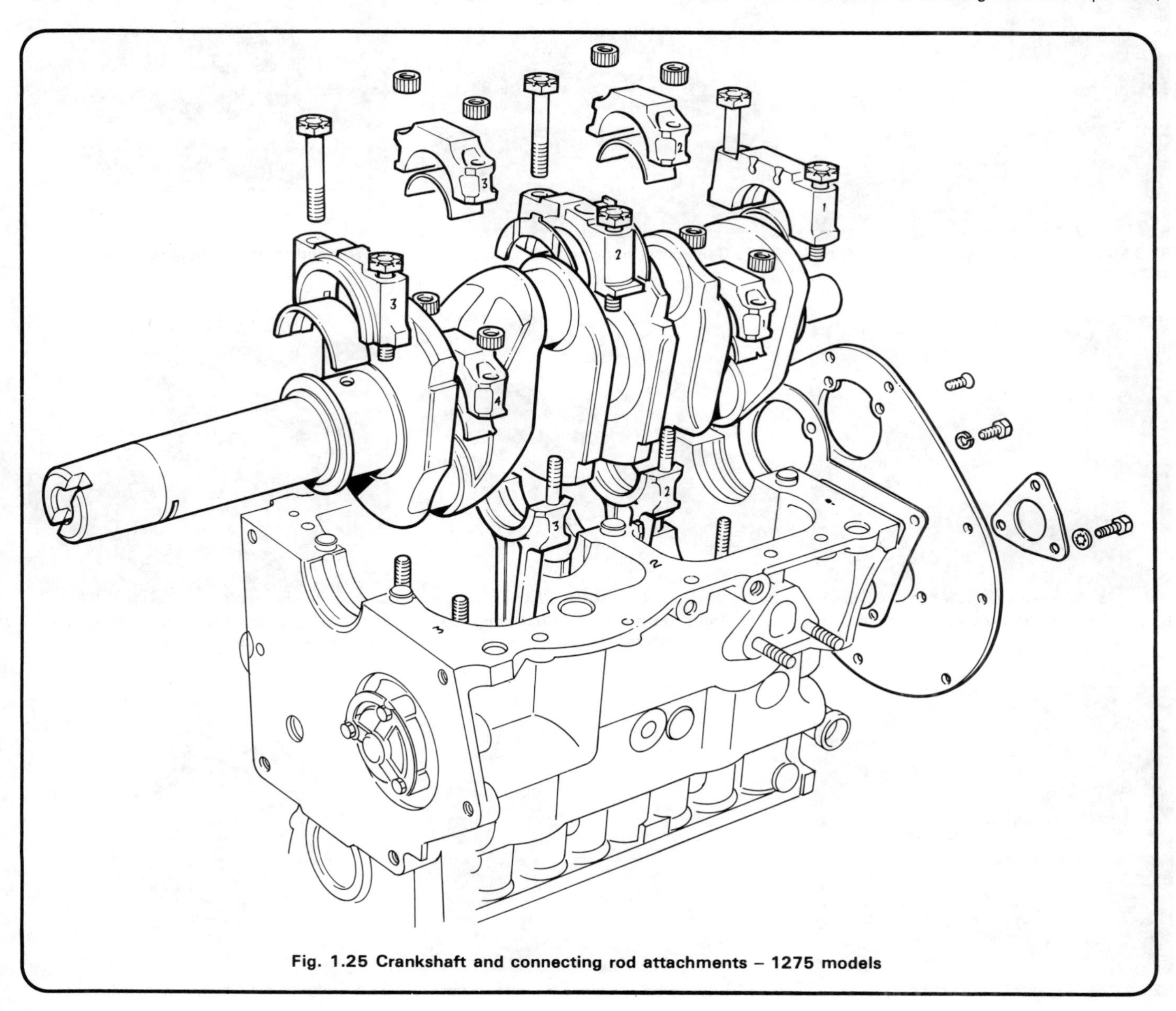

Fig. 1.25 Crankshaft and connecting rod attachments – 1275 models

blow them out with compressed air. Treat the crankshaft in the same fashion, and then inject engine oil into the crankshaft oilways.

2 Commence work on rebuilding the engine by refitting the crankshaft and main bearings as follows.

3 If the old main bearing shells are to be re-used (a false economy unless they are virtually as new), fit the three upper halves of the main bearing shells to their location in the crankcase, after wiping the locations clean (photo). **Note**: *At the back of each bearing is a tab which engages in locating grooves in either the crankcase or the main bearing cap housings.*

4 If new bearings are being fitted, carefully clean away all traces of the protective grease with which they are coated before fitting.

5 With the three upper bearing shells securely in place, wipe the lower bearing cap housings and fit the three lower shell bearings to their caps. Ensure that the right shell goes into the right cap if the old bearings are being refitted.

6 Wipe the recesses either side of the centre main bearings which locate the upper halves of the thrust washers.

7 Generously lubricate the crankshaft journals and the upper and lower main bearing shells and carefully place the crankshaft in position (photos).

8 Introduce the upper halves of the thrust washers (the halves without tabs) into their grooves on each side of the centre main bearing (photo), rotating the crankshaft in the direction towards the main bearing tabs (so that the main bearing shells do not slide out). At the same time feed the thrust washers into their locations with their oil grooves facing outwards away from the bearing.

9 Ensure that all six tubular locating dowels are firmly in place, one on each side of the upper halves of the three main bearings, and then fit the main bearing caps in position ensuring they locate properly on the dowels. The mating surfaces must be spotlessly clean or the caps will not seat properly.

10 When refitting the centre main bearing cap, ensure the thrust washers, generously lubricated, are fitted with their oil grooves facing outwards, and the locating tab of each washer is in the slot in the bearing cap (photo).

52.3 Main bearing shell upper half in position in the crankcase

52.7a Generously lubricate the bearing shells...

52.7b ...and carefully refit the crankshaft

52.8 Refitting the thrust washer upper halves

52.10 Refitting the centre main bearing cap with thrust washers in position

52.13 Using a torque wrench to tighten the main bearing cap retaining bolts

52.14 Checking crankshaft endfloat

53.1 Identification markings on piston crown

53.4 Gudgeon pin clamp bolt installed

11 Refit the one-piece locking tabs over the main bearing caps (where applicable) and refit the main bearing cap bolts, screwing them up finger-tight.
12 Test the crankshaft for freedom of rotation. Should it be very stiff to turn or possess high spots, a most careful inspection must be made, preferably by a qualified mechanic with a micrometer, to get to the root of the trouble. It is very seldom that any trouble of this nature will be experienced when fitting the crankshaft.
13 Tighten the main bearing bolts to the torque given in the Specifications and turn up the locking tabs (where applicable) with a cold chisel (photo).
14 Measure the crankshaft endfloat using feeler gauges, and ensure that it falls within the tolerance given in the Specifications (photo).

53 Pistons and connecting rods – reassembly

If the original pistons are being used, then they must be mated to the original connecting rod with the original gudgeon pin. If new pistons are being fitted, it does not matter which connecting rod they are used with, but the gudgeon pins should be fitted on the basis of selective assembly. This involves trying each of the pins in each of the pistons in turn, and fitting them to the ones they fit best, as described below.

The gudgeon pin may be a very tight fit in the piston when cold (particularly on pistons which have a small-end clamp bolt) but, because aluminium has a greater coefficient of expansion than steel, this fit will be much easier if the piston is heated in boiling water.

Lay the correct piston adjacent to its connecting rod and remember that the original rod and piston must go back into the original bore. If new pistons are being used, it is only necessary to ensure that the right connecting rod is placed in each bore.

Gudgeon pins retained by clamp bolts

1 Locate the small-end of the connecting rod in the piston with the marking 'FRONT' on the piston crown towards the front of the engine (photo) and the hole for the gudgeon pin bolt in the connecting rod towards the camshaft.
2 Note the indentation in the centre of the gudgeon pin, and insert the pin in the connecting rod, so that the indentation lines up with the clamp bolt hole in such a way that the bolt will pass through without touching the gudgeon pin.
3 For the gudgeon pin to fit correctly, it should slide in three-quarters of its travel quite freely and for the remaining quarter have to be tapped in with a plastic or wooden headed hammer. If the piston is heated in water then the pin will slide in the remaining quarter easily.
4 Fit a new spring washer under the head of the connecting rod bolt and secure it into position to the specified torque (photo).

Fully floating gudgeon pins

5 Fit a gudgeon pin circlip in position at one end of the gudgeon pin hole in the piston.
6 Locate the connecting rod in the piston with the marking 'FRONT' on the piston crown towards the front of the engine, and the connecting rod caps towards the camshaft side of the engine.
7 Slide the gudgeon pin in through the hole in the piston and through the connecting rod small-end until it rests against the previously fitted circlip. Note that the pin should be a push fit.
8 Fit the second circlip in position. Repeat this procedure for all four pistons and connecting rods.

Interference fit gudgeon pins

9 As stated previously, removal and refitting of the gudgeon pin on these engines is a delicate operation requiring the use of BL special tool 18G1150. It is therefore recommended that this task be entrusted to your nearest BL main dealer.

54 Piston rings – refitting

1 Check that the piston ring grooves and oilways are thoroughly clean and unblocked. Piston rings must always be fitted over the head of the piston and never from the bottom. If ring expanders are not available, the easiest method to use when fitting rings is to wrap a 0.020 in (0.5 mm) feeler gauge round the top of the piston and place the rings one at a time, starting with the bottom oil control ring, over the feeler gauge (photo).
2 The feeler gauge, complete with ring, can then be slid down the piston over the other piston ring grooves until the correct groove is reached. The piston ring is then slid gently off the feeler gauge into the groove (photo).
3 An alternative method is to fit the rings by holding them slightly open with the thumbs and both of your index fingers. This method requires a steady hand and great care as it is easy to open the ring too much and break it.

55 Pistons – refitting

The pistons, complete with connecting rods, can be fitted to the cylinder bores in the following sequence.

1 With a wad of clean rag, wipe the cylinder bores clean.
2 The pistons, complete with connecting rods, are fitted to their bores from above, but first lubricate the rubbing surfaces with engine oil.
3 As each piston is inserted into its bore, ensure that it is the correct piston/connecting rod assembly for that particular bore, that the

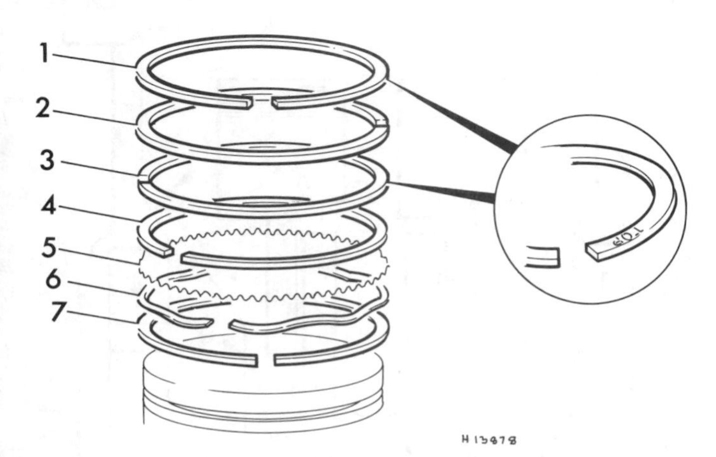

Fig. 1.26 Piston ring identification – 850, 1000 and 1100 models (Sec 54)

1 Chrome plated compression ring
2 Taper compression ring
3 Taper compression ring
4 Top rail
5 Expander
6 Side spring
7 Bottom rail

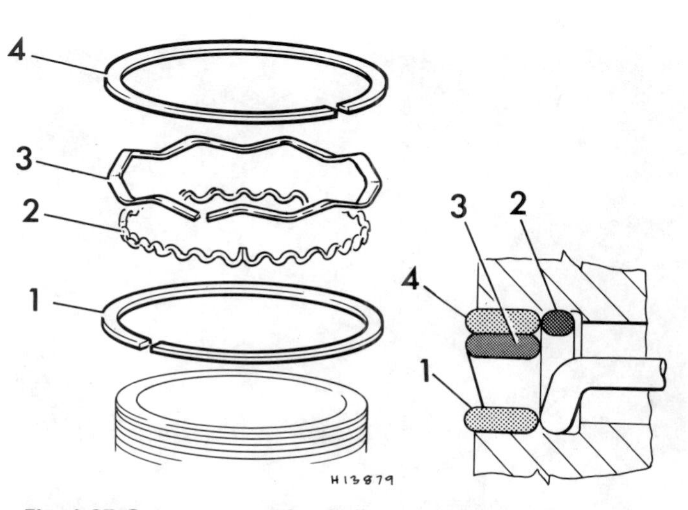

Fig. 1.27 Correct assembly of oil control ring – 1275 models (Sec 54)

1 Bottom rail
2 Expander
3 Oil control ring rail
4 Top rail

54.1 Assembling the oil control ring to the piston

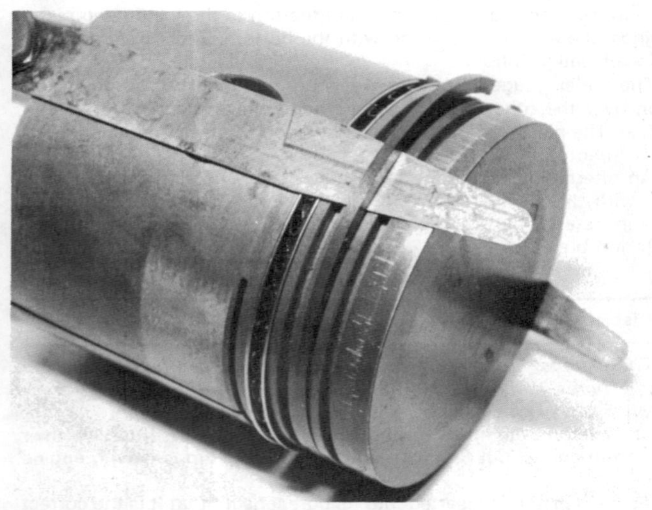
54.2 Using feeler gauges to slide the rings over the ring grooves

55.4 A piston ring clamp in position around the piston

connecting rod is the right way round, and that the front of the piston is towards the front of the engine.

4 The piston will only slide into the bore as far as the oil control ring. It is then necessary to compress the piston rings in a clamp and to gently tap the piston into the cylinder bore with a wooden or plastic hammer. If a proper piston ring clamp is not available then a suitable worm drive clip can be used provided that great care is taken (photo).

56 Connecting rods to crankshaft – reassembly

As the big-end bosses on the connecting rods are offset, it will be obvious if they have been inserted the wrong way round because they will not fit over the crankpin. The centre two rods must be fitted with their offset bosses facing away from the centre main bearing, and the connecting rods at each extremity of the engine must be fitted with their offset bosses facing inwards.

1 Wipe the connecting rod half of the big-end bearing cap and the underside of the shell bearing clean, and fit the shell bearing in position with its locating tongue engaged with the corresponding groove in the connecting rod.

2 If the old bearings are nearly new and are being refitted, ensure they are refitted in their correct locations on the correct rods.

3 Generously lubricate the crankpin journals with engine oil, and turn the crankshaft so that each crankpin is in the most advantageous position for the connecting rod to be drawn onto it.

4 Wipe the connecting rod bearing cap and back of the shell bearing clean and fit the shell bearing in position, ensuring that the locating tongue at the back of the bearing engages with the locating groove in the connecting rod cap.

5 Generously lubricate the shell bearing and offer up the connecting rod bearing cap to the connecting rod (photo).

6 Fit the connecting rod bolts with the one-piece locking tab under them (where applicable) and tighten the bolts with a torque wrench to the figure given in the Specifications (photo). On 1275 cc engines the arrangement is slightly different, the caps being retained by nuts.

7 When all the connecting rods have been fitted, rotate the crankshaft to check that everything is free, and that there are no high spots causing binding.

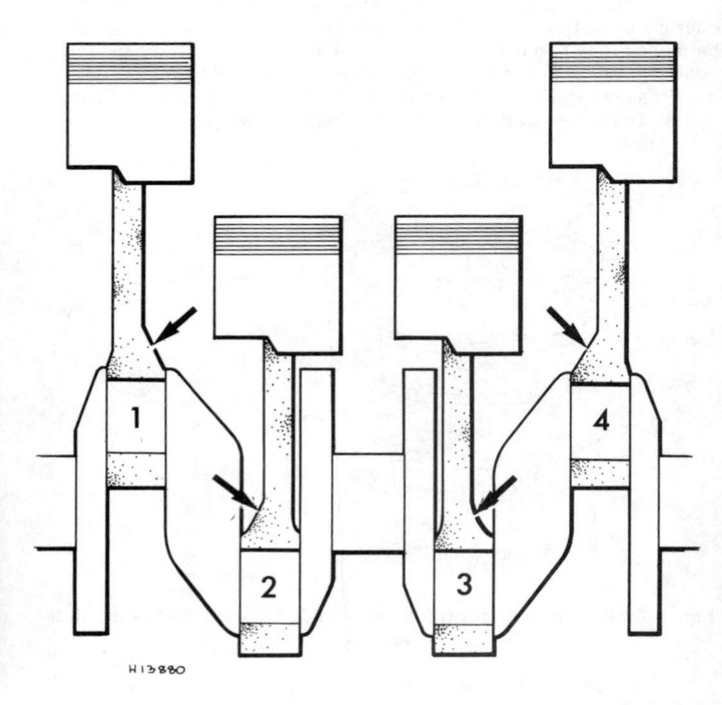

Fig. 1.28 The correct positions of the offsets on the connecting rod big-ends (Sec 56)

56.5 Refitting the cap to the connecting rod

57.2 Refitting the camshaft

56.6 Using a torque wrench to tighten the retaining bolts

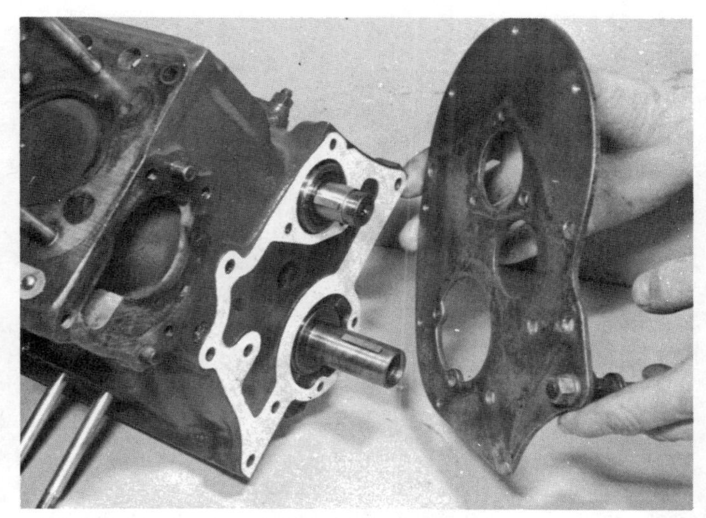
57.4 With a new gasket in place refit the front cover...

57 Camshaft – refitting

On 1275 cc engines the tappets (cam followers) must be refitted before installing the camshaft. Lay the engine on its side and slide each tappet into its correct bore, generously lubricating it as you do so. Now install the camshaft as described below:

1 Wipe the camshaft bearing journals clean and lubricate them generously with engine oil.

2 Insert the camshaft into the cylinder block, taking care not to damage the camshaft bearings with the sharp edges of the cam lobes (photo).

3 Push the camshaft back as far as it will go and, if the oil pump is in position, ensure that the camshaft flange has mated with the pump drive.

4 Place a new gasket in position and refit the front cover (if previously removed) (photo).

5 Now refit the camshaft locating plate and tighten the three retaining bolts (photo). Check the camshaft endfloat, referring to the figures given in the Specifications.

57.5 ...followed by the camshaft locating plate

58.2a Align the timing dots on the gearwheels...

58.2b ...then move the gears into mesh with the chain keeping the dots adjacent

58.5 Fitting the gearwheels and chain to the crankshaft and camshaft

58 Timing gears, chain and cover – refitting

Before reassembly begins check that the packing washers are in place on the crankshaft nose. If new gearwheels are being fitted it may be necessary to fit additional washers (see paragraph 6). These washers ensure that the crankshaft gearwheel lines up correctly with the camshaft gearwheel.

1 Refit the Woodruff keys in their respective slots in the crankshaft and camshaft, and ensure that they are fully seated. If their edges are burred they must be cleaned with a fine file.

2 Lay the two gearwheels on a clean surface so that the timing dots are adjacent to each other. Slip the timing chain over them and pull the gearwheels back into mesh with the chain so that the timing dots, although further apart are still adjacent to each other (photos).

3 Rotate the crankshaft so that the Woodruff key is at top dead centre (TDC).

4 Rotate the camshaft so that when viewed from the front the Woodruff key is at the two o'clock position.

5 Fit the timing chain and gearwheel assembly onto the camshaft and crankshaft, keeping the timing marks adjacent (photo). If the camshaft and crankshaft have been positioned accurately, it will be found that the keyways on the gearwheels will match the position of the keys, although it may be necessary to rotate the camshaft a fraction to ensure accurate lining-up of the camshaft gearwheel.

6 Press the gearwheels into position on the crankshaft and camshaft as far as they will go. **Note**: *If new gearwheels are being fitted they should be checked for alignment before being finally fitted to the engine. Place the gearwheels in position without the timing chain and place the straight edge of a steel ruler from the side of the camshaft gear teeth to the crankshaft gearwheel and measure the gap between*

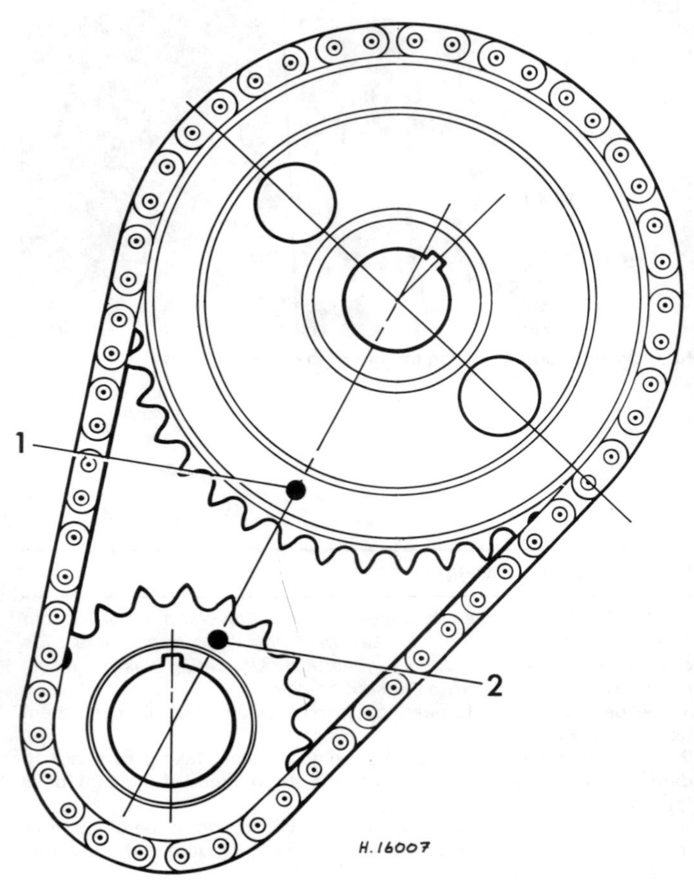

Fig. 1.29 Timing mark locations relative to keyways (Sec 58)

1 *Timing dot on camshaft sprocket*
2 *Timing dot on crankshaft sprocket*

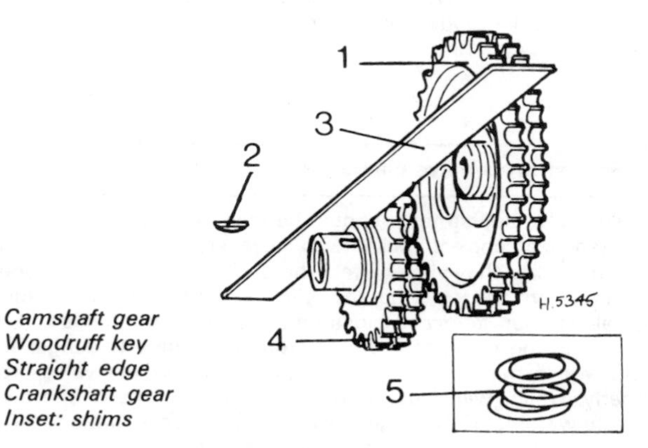

Fig. 1.30 Timing gear alignment – double row type shown (Sec 58)

Note that with single row type, it is important to align the sides of the teeth and not the raised hub of the sprocket

the steel rule and the gearwheel. If a gap exists a suitable number of packing washers must be placed on the crankshaft nose to bring the crankshaft gearwheel onto the same plane as the camshaft gearwheel.

7 Fit the oil thrower to the crankshaft with the concave side forward (photo).

8 Fit the locking washer to the camshaft gearwheel with its locating tab in the gearwheel keyway.

9 Screw on the camshaft gearwheel retaining nut and tighten securely (photo).

10 Bend up the locking tab of the locking washer to hold the camshaft retaining nut securely.

11 Generously oil the chain and gearwheels.

12 Ensure the interior of the timing cover and the timing cover flange is clean. Examine the condition of the timing cover oil seal and renew it if damaged or worn. Then, with a new gasket in position, fit the timing cover to the block (photo).

13 Screw in the timing cover retaining bolts with the flat washer next to the cover flange and under the spring washer. Tighten the respective bolts to the specified torque.

14 Fit the crankshaft pulley to the nose of the crankshaft, ensuring that the keyway engages with the Woodruff key.

15 Fit the crankshaft retaining bolt locking washer in position and screw in the crankshaft pulley retaining bolt. Tighten to the specified torque (photo).

59 Oil pump – refitting

1 Place a new gasket in position on the rear face of the engine block.

2 Ensure that the pump is filled with clean engine oil and then position it over the gasket, engaging the drive slot or coupling with the rear of the camshaft (photo).

3 Rotate the pump body until the offset holes in the pump, gasket and cylinder block are all in line, then refit the retaining bolts and locktabs.

4 Tighten the bolts to the specified torque and bend over the locktabs.

60 Valves and valve springs – reassembly

1 Rest the cylinder head on its side.

2 Fit each valve in turn, wiping down and lubricating each valve stem as it is inserted into the same valve guide from which it was removed (photo).

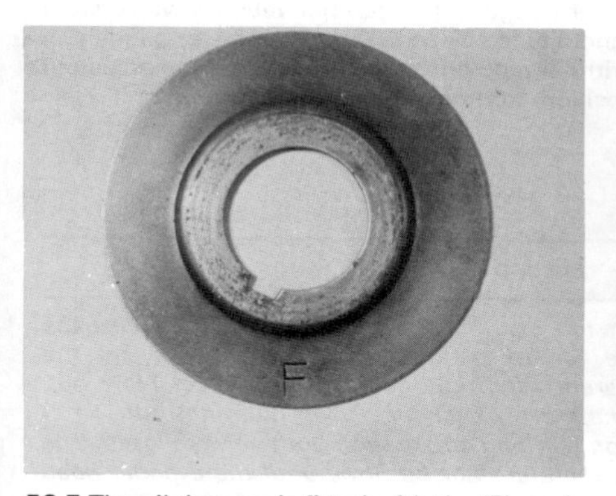

58.7 The oil thrower is fitted with the 'F' mark away from the chain

58.9 Refitting the camshaft retaining nut

58.12 The timing gears ready for cover refitting

58.15 Using a torque wrench to tighten the pulley retaining bolt

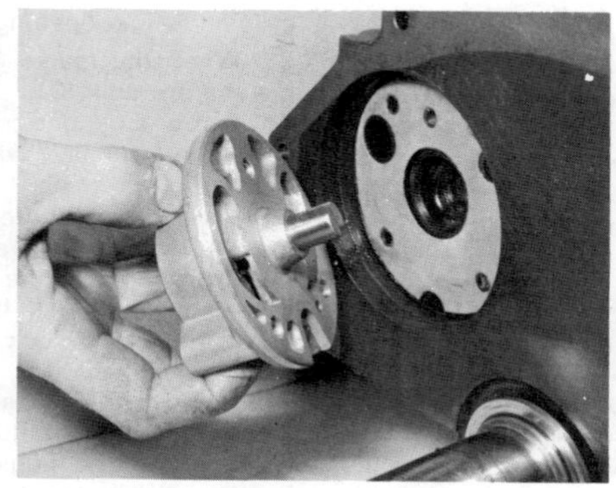

59.2 Refitting the oil pump

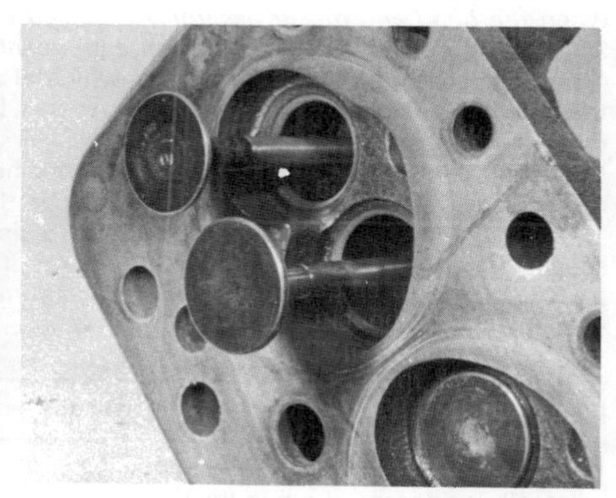

60.2 Refitting the valves to the cylinder head

3 As each valve is inserted, slip the oil control ring into place just under the bottom of the collet groove. A much larger oil seal is used on the 1275 cc engines. This should be fitted over the top of the valve guide.
4 For the next operation, it may be easier to lay the head with its cylinder block mating face downwards. Move the cylinder head towards the edge of the work bench if it is facing downwards and slide it partially over the edge of the bench so as to fit the bottom half of the valve spring compressor to the valve head.
5 Slip the valve spring(s) and cap over the valve stem.
6 With the base of the valve compressor on the valve head compress the valve spring(s) until the collets can be slipped into place in the valve grooves. Gently release the compressor and fit the circlip in position in the grooves in the collets (where applicable).
7 Repeat this procedure until all eight valves and valve springs are fitted.

61 Rocker gear – reassembly

1 To reassemble the rocker shaft fit the split pin, flat washer and spring washer at the rear end of the shaft and then slide on the rocker arms, rocker shaft pedestals, and spacing springs in the same order in which they were removed (photo).
2 With the front pedestal in position, screw in the rocker shaft locating screws and slip the locating plate into position. Finally, fit to the front of the shaft the spring washer, plain washer, and split pin, in that order.

62 Cylinder head – refitting

1 After checking that both the cylinder block and cylinder head mating faces are perfectly clean, generously lubricate each cylinder with engine oil.
2 Always use a new cylinder head gasket as the old gasket will be compressed and not capable of giving a good seal. It is also easier at this stage to refit the small bypass hose from the water pump to the cylinder head.
3 Never smear grease on the gasket, as when the engine heats up, the grease will melt and may allow compression leaks to develop. It should not be necessary to use gasket cement because a new gasket is used and the head and block faces are true.
4 The cylinder head gasket is marked 'FRONT' and 'TOP' and should be fitted in position according to the markings (photos).
5 With the gasket in position carefully lower the cylinder head onto the cylinder block (photos).
6 With the head in position fit the cylinder head nuts and washers finger tight to the five cylinder head holding-down studs, which remain outside the rocker cover. It is not possible to fit the remaining nuts to the studs inside the rocker cover until the rocker assembly is in position.
7 Fit the pushrods as detailed in the following section.
8 The rocker shaft assembly can now be lowered over its eight locating studs (photo). Take care that the rocker arms are the right way round. Lubricate the ball ends of the tappet adjusting screws and insert them in the pushrod cups. **Note:** *Failure to place the ball ends in the cups can result in them seating on the edge of a pushrod or outside it when the head and rocker assembly is pulled down tight.*
9 Fit the four rocker pedestal nuts and washers, and then the four cylinder head stud nuts and washers, which also serve to hold down the rocker pedestals. Pull the nuts down evenly, but without tightening them right up (photo).
10 When all is in position, the nine cylinder head nuts and the four rocker pedestal nuts can be tightened down in the order shown in Fig. 1.13. Turn the nuts a quarter of a turn at a time and tighten to the specified torque (photo).
Note: *On 1275 cc engines having an additional nut and bolt, these should be tightened last.*

63 Tappets (cam followers) and pushrods – refitting

1 Generously lubricate the tappets (cam followers) internally and externally, and insert them in the bores from which they were removed (photo).
2 With the cylinder head in position, fit the pushrods in the same order in which they were removed. Ensure that they locate properly in the stems of the tappets, and lubricate the pushrod ends before fitting (photos).

64 Rocker arms/valve clearances – adjustment

1 The valve adjustments should be made with the engine cold. The importance of correct rocker arm/valve stem clearances cannot be overstressed as they vitally affect the performance of the engine. If the clearances are set too wide, the efficiency of the engine is reduced as the valves open later and close earlier than was intended. If, on the other hand the clearances are set too close there is danger that the stems will expand upon heating and not allow the valves to close properly, which will cause burning of the valve head and seat, and possible warping. If the engine is in the car, access to the rockers is by removing the two large cap nuts from the rocker cover, and then lifting the rocker cover and gasket away.
2 It is important that the clearance is set when the tappet of the valve being adjusted is on the heel of the cam, (ie opposite the peak). This can be ensured by carrying out the adjustments in the following order (which also avoids turning the crankshaft more than necessary).

Valve fully open	Check and adjust
Valve No 8	Valve No 1
Valve No 6	Valve No 3
Valve No 4	Valve No 5
Valve No 7	Valve No 2
Valve No 1	Valve No 8
Valve No 3	Valve No 6
Valve No 5	Valve No 4
Valve No 2	Valve No 7

3 The correct valve clearance is obtained by slackening the hexagon locknut with a spanner while holding the adjusting screw against rotation with a screwdriver. Then, still pressing down with the screwdriver, insert a feeler gauge in the gap between the valve stem head and rocker arm, and adjust the screw until the feeler gauge will just move in and out without nipping. Then, still holding the adjusting screw in the correct position, tighten the locknut (photo).

65 Distributor drive – refitting

Note: *It is wise to set the distributor drive correctly, otherwise the ignition timing will be totally incorrect. It is possible to set the distributor drive in apparently the right position, but in fact 180° out, by omitting to select the correct cylinder, which must not only be at TDC but must also be on its firing stroke with both valves closed. The distributor drive should therefore not be fitted until the cylinder head is in position and the valves can be observed.*

1 Rotate the crankshaft so that No 1 piston is at TDC and on its firing stroke. When No 1 piston is at TDC the inlet valve on No 4 cylinder is just opening and the exhaust valve closing.
2 When the marks 1/4 on the flywheel are at TDC, Nos 1 and 4 pistons are at TDC.
3 Screw a tappet cover bolt into the head of the distributor drive (any $\frac{5}{16}$ in UNF bolt will do if it is not less than 3 in (76 mm) long) (photo).
4 Hold the distributor drive so that the slot is as shown in Fig. 1.31 inset A. Insert the drive into its housing. As the gear on the end of the drive meshes with the skew gear on the camshaft the drive will turn anti-clockwise. When it is fully home, the upper part of the slot should be in the two o'clock position, as shown in the inset B (Fig. 1.31) (photo).
5 Remove the tappet cover bolt from the driveshaft.
6 Refit the distributor housing and a new O-ring and lock it in position with the single bolt and lockwasher (photos).
7 The distributor can now be refitted and the ignition timing reset using the procedure described in Chapter 4.

61.1 Rocker shaft components laid out for assembly

62.4a The cylinder head gasket is marked FRONT...

62.4b ...and TOP to avoid confusion

62.5a With the gasket in position...

62.5b ...lower the cylinder head onto the block

62.8 Refitting the rocker shaft assembly

62.9 Fit the plate to the rocker pedestal, and then the retaining nuts

62.10 Tightening the cylinder head nuts with a torque wrench

63.1 Refit the cam followers...

63.2a ...and then the pushrods before fitting the rocker shaft assembly

63.2b Thoroughly lubricate the pushrods and tappets

64.3 Adjusting the rocker arm/valve clearances

65.3 Using a $\frac{5}{16}$ in bolt to refit the distributor drive

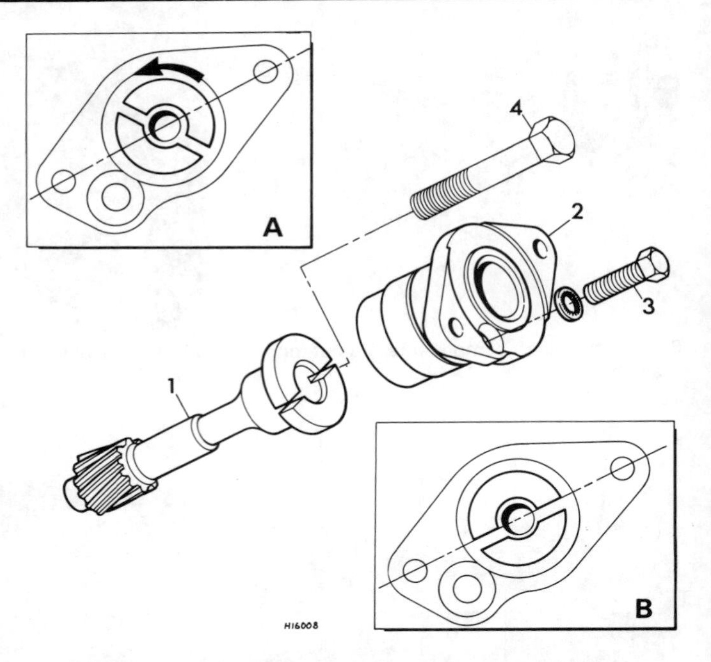

Fig. 1.31 Distributor driveshaft components (Sec 65)

Inset A shows the position of the slot ready for fitting
Inset B shows the shaft correctly installed

1 Driveshaft
2 Housing
3 Retaining screw
4 $\frac{5}{16}$ in UNF bolt (for removal and refitting of driveshaft)

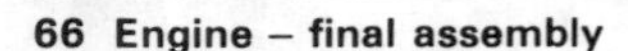

66 Engine – final assembly

1 The rocker cover can now be fitted, using a new gasket (photo); also refit the tappet block side covers (where applicable). The remainder of the ancillary components should also now be refitted using the reverse of the removal sequence described in Section 16. With these components all in position, the engine can be installed on the transmission as described in the following Section.

67 Engine – refitting to manual transmission

Note: *Before refitting the engine to the transmission, refer to Chapter 6 and adjust the endfloat of the transfer gears (primary gear and idler gear). Then proceed as described below.*
1 Carefully scrape away any remaining traces of old gasket from the engine/transmission mating faces and flywheel housing joint.
2 Lightly smear the upper sides of the engine/transmission joint gaskets with jointing compound and place them in position on the engine mating face.
3 Now place the front oil seal in position between the front main bearing cap and engine front plate (photo).
4 Locate the oil supply O-ring into its groove in the transmission casing face, and if necessary retain it in place with a trace of grease (photo).
5 Using suitable lifting gear and with the help of an assistant, carefully lower the engine onto the transmission casing. Have your assistant guide the engine, and lower it very slowly, as it is easy to dislodge the gaskets.
6 With the engine in position, refit and fully tighten the retaining nuts, bolts and spring washers, and refit the radiator lower mounting bolts.

68 Flywheel housing – refitting (manual transmission models)

1 Refit the primary gear thrust washer to the end of the crankshaft with its chamfered side toward the crankshaft flange (photo).
2 Slide on the primary gear (photo) and then turn the crankshaft until No 1 and 4 pistons are at TDC.
3 Refit the primary gear retaining ring and then secure the assembly in position with the C-shaped washer (photos).
4 Refit the idler gear to its bearings in the transmission casing, turning it slightly to mesh with the other two gears as it is installed. Ensure that both the thrust washers are in position, one each side of the idler gear; if the later type gear is being fitted, the longer boss goes toward the transmission casing.
5 Place a new joint gasket over the studs on the transmission casing.
6 Before fitting the flywheel housing, make sure that a new flywheel housing oil seal has been fitted, and cover the splines of the primary gear with the special thin sleeve of BL special tool 18G570. Alternatively, wrap tin foil or masking tape tightly over the splines to avoid damaging the seal. Lubricate the lip of the oil seal prior to fitting.
7 Carefully refit the flywheel housing, taking care that the rollers on the first motion shaft bearing enter their outer race squarely. On no account force the housing. If it does not easily push fully home, turn the bearing slightly and try again. Two or three attempts may be needed (photo).
8 Refit new locking tabs, followed by the housing retaining nuts and bolts to their correct locations. Tighten the fixings to the specified torque and bend over the locktabs (photo).

69 Flywheel – refitting

1 Turn the crankshaft so that cylinders 1 and 4 are at TDC and the grooves in the sides of the crankshaft are vertical.
2 Check that the curved portion of the C-washer which holds the primary gear in place is at the top of the crankshaft, and that the sides of the washer fit in the crankshaft grooves.
3 Carefully clean the mating tapers in the flywheel and on the end of the crankshaft, and make quite certain there are no traces of oil, grease, or dirt present.
4 Refit the flywheel on the end of the crankshaft with the 1/4 TDC markings at the top and then refit the driving washer which positively locates the flywheel.
5 Fit a new lockwasher under the head of the flywheel securing bolt. Insert the bolt in the centre of the flywheel and tighten it to the specified torque.
6 Tap down the side of the lockwasher against the driving plate, and tap up the other side of the washer against the retaining bolt head.
7 Refit the thrust plate and secure it in position with the circular retaining spring.
8 Now refit the flywheel housing cover and fully tighten the retaining bolts.

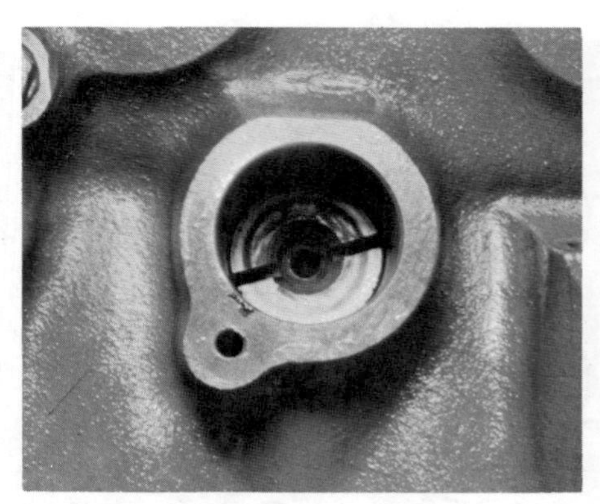

65.4 With the drive installed the slots must be in this position

65.6a Fit a new O-ring to the distributor housing...

65.6b ...and then refit the housing to the engine

66.1 Refitting the rocker cover

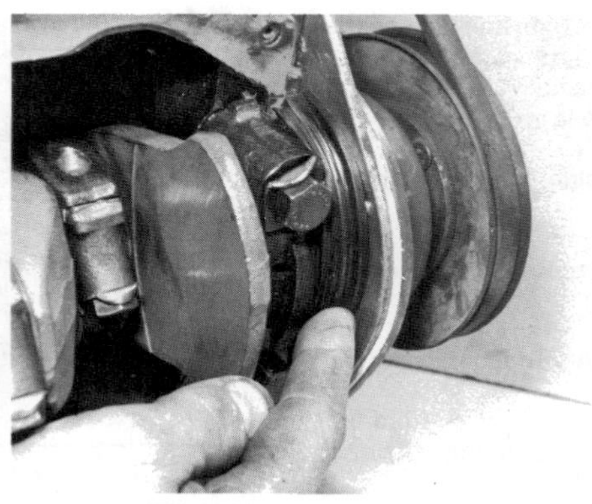

67.3 Fitting a new front oil seal to the crankcase...

67.4 ...and a new O-ring seal to the transmission casing joint face

68.1 Position the primary gear thrust washer on the crankshaft

68.2 Slide on the primary gear...

68.3a ...followed by the retaining ring...

68.3b ...and the C-shaped washer

68.7 Refit the flywheel housing...

68.8 ...and secure with the nuts and locktabs

70 Engine – refitting to automatic transmission

The procedure for refitting the engine to the automatic transmission is the same as described in Section 67 for models equipped with manual transmission.

71 Torque converter and converter housing – refitting (automatic transmission models)

1 Refit the engine oil feed pipe to the union on the transmission casing.
2 Place a new gasket in position and refit the oil filter assembly.
3 Using new O-rings where necessary, carefully push the oil feed pipe into engagement with the oil pump and transmission casing orifice.
4 Place the converter outlet gear thrust washer over the end of the crankshaft, with its chamfered face toward the crankshaft flange.
5 Now slide on the output gear. Turn the crankshaft until No 1 and 4 pistons are at TDC, and then refit the output gear retaining ring and C-shaped washer.
6 With the thrust washers located over each side of the idler gear, insert the gear into its needle roller bearing.
7 Ensure that the mating faces of the engine/transmission unit and converter housing are clean, and then position a new gasket over the studs on the transmission.
8 If available use the protective sleeve of BL special tool 18G1098 to cover the splines of the converter output gear. Alternatively wrap tin foil or adhesive tape tightly around the splines.
9 Now carefully refit the converter housing, pushing it squarely home over the transmission casting studs. Refit the retaining nuts and bolts, tightened to the specified torque.
10 Refit the selector bellcrank lever pivot, lever, clevis pin and nut.
11 Before fitting the torque converter, it will be first necessary to refit the three central bolts removed to allow the special converter removal tool to be used during dismantling. Then remove each pair of bolts in turn from the converter centre and fit new locking plates. Tighten the six bolts to the specified torque wrench setting and bend over the lock tabs. *On no account remove all six bolts at any one time.* Then, with No 1 and 4 pistons still at the TDC position, slide the torque converter onto the end of the crankshaft, with the timing marks uppermost. Refit the driving collar, a new lockwasher and the retaining bolt. Tighten the retaining bolt to the torque given in the Specifications, and then knock back the lockwasher.
12 Now refit and fully tighten the input gear retaining nut.
13 Position a new gasket on the transmission casing and refit the low pressure valve assembly.
14 Finally refit the converter housing cover and the starter motor.

72 Engine – refitting

Refitting the engine (with either manual gearbox or automatic transmission) to the car, or refitting the subframe complete with engine/transmission unit, is a straightforward reversal of the procedure used for removal. The following additional points should, however, be noted:

(a) Install the engine mountings and tie-bar mounting nuts and bolts finger-tight, and when all are fitted, tighten them fully to the specified torque
(b) On models fitted with automatic transmission, adjust the gear selector cable as described in Chapter 6 when installation is complete

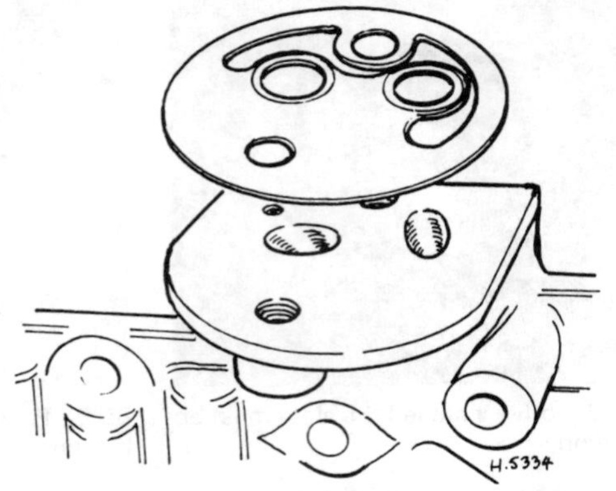

Fig. 1.32 Correct positioning of the automatic transmission oil filter housing gasket (Sec 71)

(c) If the power unit has been removed, complete with front subframe, it will be necessary to bleed the hydraulic system on completion as described in Chapter 9. Where Hydrolastic suspension is fitted it will be necessary to have the system repressurised by your nearest BL dealer
(d) When all connections, hoses and fittings are secure, refill the cooling system with coolant and the engine with the correct grade and quantity of oil

73 Engine – initial start-up after overhaul or major repair

1 Make sure that the battery is fully charged and that all lubricants, coolant and fuel are replenished.
2 Double check all fittings and electrical connections. Ensure that the distributor is correctly fitted and that the ignition timing static setting is correct. If in doubt refer to Chapter 4.
3 Remove the spark plugs and the (-) connection from the ignition coil. Turn the engine over on the starter motor until the oil pressure warning light is extinguished or until oil pressure is recorded on the gauge. This will ensure that the engine is not starved of oil during the critical few minutes of running after initial start-up. The fuel system will also be primed during this operation.
4 Reconnect the (-) connection on the ignition coil and refit the spark plugs and leads. Start the engine.
5 As soon as the engine fires and runs, keep it going at a fast idle only (no faster) and bring it up to normal working temperature.
6 As the engine warms up, there will be odd smells and some smoke from parts getting hot and burning off oil deposits. The signs to look for are leaks of water or oil, which will be obvious if serious. Check also the exhaust pipe and manifold connections as these do not always find their exact gas-tight position until the warmth and vibration have acted on them, and it is almost certain that they will need tightening further. This should be done, of course, with the engine stopped.
7 When normal running temperature has been reached, adjust the engine idle speed as described in Chapter 3.
8 Stop the engine and wait a few minutes to see if any lubricant or coolant is dripping out when the engine is stationary.
9 Road test the car to check that the timing is correct and that the engine is giving the necessary smoothness and power. Do not race the engine – if new bearings and/or pistons have been fitted, it should be treated as a new engine and run in at a reduced speed for the first 500 miles (800 km).

74 Fault diagnosis – engine

Symptom	Reason(s)
Engine fails to turn when starter operated	Flat battery Battery terminals loose or corroded Battery earth to body defective Starter motor, wiring or solenoid fault Starter motor pinion jammed Automatic transmission selector not in N, or inhibitor switch faulty Major mechanical failure (seizure) or long disuse (piston rings rusted to bores)
Engine turns but fails to start	Battery voltage insufficient for good spark, or terminals loose Ignition fault – see Chapter 4 No fuel in tank Excessive choke (hot engine) or insufficient choke (cold engine) Other fuel system fault – see Chapter 3 Major mechanical failure Valve timing incorrect (after rebuild)
Engine stalls and will not restart (starter motor operative)	Broken or disconnected ignition wiring No fuel in tank Ignition fault – see Chapter 4 Excessive/insufficient choke Other fuel system fault – see Chapter 3 Serious overheating Major mechanical failure
Engine misfires or idles unevenly	Engine earth strap loose Ignition fault – see Chapter 4 Air cleaner choked Carburettor(s) maladjusted or worn Other fuel system fault – see Chapter 3 Manifold or cylinder head gasket leaking Incorrect valve clearances Broken valve spring(s) Burnt, sticking or leaking valves Worn valve stems or guides Worn or damaged pistons, piston rings and bores
Engine lacks power	Ignition timing incorrect Worn or maladjusted carburettor(s) Worn or malfunctioning distributor Worn or maladjusted spark plugs Air cleaner choked Other fuel system fault – see Chapter 3 Carbon build-up in cylinder head Valve clearances incorrect Broken valve spring(s) Burnt, sticking or leaking valves Cylinder head gasket leaking Worn or damaged pistons, piston rings and bores Valve timing incorrect (after rebuild) Clutch slipping – see Chapter 5 Brakes binding – see Chapter 9 Torque converter malfunctioning – see Chapter 6 Overheating – see Chapter 2
Engine backfires	Carburettor maladjusted Other fuel system fault – see Chapter 3 Ignition timing incorrect Air leak in induction or exhaust manifold or silencer/exhaust pipe Incorrect valve clearances Burnt, sticking or leaking valves
Pre-ignition (pinking) on acceleration	Incorrect grade of fuel Ignition timing incorrect Distributor faulty or worn Worn or maladjusted carburettor Excessive carbon build-up in engine Incorrect valve timing (after rebuild)

Symptom	Reason(s)
Engine runs on after switching off	Carburettor maladjusted Excessive carbon build-up in cylinder head or on spark plugs Emission control fault (see Chapter 3) Overheating (see Chapter 2)
Low oil pressure (check sender or gauge before condemning engine)	Oil level low or incorrect grade Overheating Oil pressure relief valve defective Oil filter clogged or bypass valve defective Oil pick-up strainer clogged Oil pump worn or mountings loose Worn main or big-end bearings
Excessive oil consumption	Overfilling Leaking gaskets or drain plug washer Valve stem oil seals worn, damaged or missing after rebuild Valve stems and/or guides worn Piston rings and/or bores worn Piston oil return holes clogged
Oil contaminated with water	Leaking cylinder head gasket Cracked block or cylinder head
Unusual mechanical noises	Unintentional mechanical contact (eg fan blades) Worn valvegear (tapping noises from top of engine) or incorrect clearances Worn timing chain (rattling from front of engine) Peripheral component fault (generator, water pump etc) Worn big-end bearings (regular heavy knocking, perhaps less under load) Worn main bearings (rumbling and knocking, perhaps worsening under load) Small-end bushes or gudgeon pins worn (light metallic tapping) Piston clap (most noticeable when engine cold)

Note: *When investigating starting and uneven running faults do not be tempted into snap diagnosis. Start from the beginning of the check procedure and follow it through. It will take less time in the long run. Poor performance from an engine in terms of power and economy is not normally diagnosed quickly. In any event the ignition and fuel systems must be checked first before assuming any further investigation needs to be made.*

Chapter 2 Cooling system

For modifications and information applicable to later models, see Supplement at end of manual

Contents

Specifications

System type	Pressurized, water pump assisted, thermo-syphon
Thermostat	
Type	Wax
Opening temperatures:	
Up to 1976:	
Standard	180°F (82°C)
Hot climates	165°F (74°C)
Cold climates	188°F (88°C)
From 1976:	
Standard	188°F (88°C)
Radiator pressure cap	
Opening pressure:	
Up to 1974	13 lbf/in^2 (0.91 bar)
From 1974	15 lbf/in^2 (1.05 bar)
Water pump	
Type	Centrifugal
Drive	V-belt
Overhaul clearances:	
Bearing outer race to water seal seating	0.53 to 0.54 in (13.54 to 13.79 mm)
Impeller vane to pump body	0.020 to 0.030 in (0.51 to 0.76 mm)
Pulley hub face to pump joint face	3.71 to 3.73 in (94.3 to 94.8 mm)
Coolant capacity	
Less heater	5.25 pints (3 litres)
With heater	6.25 pints (3.55 litres)
Fanbelt tension	0.5 in (13 mm) deflection between crankshaft and dynamo or alternator pulleys

Torque wrench settings	**lbf ft**	**Nm**
Water pump	14 to 18	19 to 25
Thermostat housing	6 to 9	8 to 12
Temperature gauge transmitter	16	22

1 General description

The engine coolant is circulated by a thermo-syphon, water pump-assisted, and is pressurised. Pressurisation is necessary to allow the engine to operate at temperatures higher than the boiling point of the coolant. The pressure is controlled by the spring-loaded radiator cap which effectively seals off the cooling system from atmosphere. When the pressure in the system reaches the rated pressure of the radiator cap, the spring is overcome; the internal portion of the cap lifts off its seat allowing steam to escape down the overflow pipe, thus relieving the pressure. When the engine is stopped and the system is allowed to cool, a vacuum is created in the cooling system. To allow for this, a vacuum valve is incorporated in the cap which will open and allow excessive vacuum to vent to atmosphere.

The cooling system comprises the radiator, water pump, (mounted on the front of the engine, it carries the fan blades and is driven by the fanbelt), thermostat and associated hoses.

The system functions by circulating cold coolant from the bottom of the radiator, up the lower radiator hose to the water pump where it is pumped around the water passages in the cylinder block.

The coolant then travels up into the cylinder head and circulates around the combustion chambers and valve seats. When the engine is at its correct operating temperature, the coolant travels out of the cylinder head, past the open thermostat, into the hose and so into the top tank of the radiator. The coolant travels down the radiator where it is rapidly cooled by the rush of cold air through the radiator core. As the radiator is mounted in the wheel arch, the fan *pushes* cold air through the radiator matrix. The coolant, now cool, reaches the bottom of the radiator where the cycle is repeated.

When the engine is cold, the thermostat (which is simply a temperature sensitive valve), maintains the circulation of coolant in the engine by blocking the passage from the cylinder head to the radiator. The coolant is then forced to return to the cylinder block through the bypass hose. Only when the opening temperature of the thermostat has been reached, as shown in the Specifications, does the thermostat allow the coolant to return to the radiator.

2 Cooling system – draining

1 If the engine is cold, remove the filler cap from the radiator by turning anti-clockwise. If the engine is hot having just been run, then turn the filler cap very slightly until the pressure in the system has had time to disperse. Use a rag over the cap to protect your hand from escaping steam. If, with the engine very hot, the cap is released suddenly, the drop in pressure can result in coolant boiling. With the pressure released the cap can be removed.

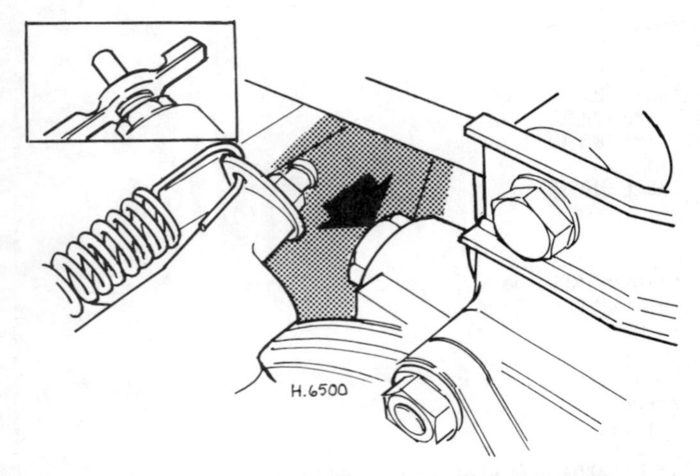

Fig. 2.1 The cylinder block drain tap or plug located beneath the engine tie-bar (Sec 2)

2.4 The radiator bottom hose connection is accessible from under the wheel arch

2 If there is anti-freeze in the system, place clean bowls beneath the radiator and at the rear of the engine to collect the coolant for re-use.

3 Undo and remove the radiator drain plug and cylinder block drain plug, and allow the coolant to drain. If fitted, the radiator drain plug is located at the bottom of the radiator nearest the grille, and the cylinder block drain plug (if fitted) can be found at the rear of the block, beneath the engine tie-bar.

4 On later models the radiator does not incorporate a drain plug, and it is therefore necessary to detach the bottom hose to drain the coolant. To do this slacken the bottom hose retaining clip and pull the hose off the radiator outlet. The hose clip is very inaccessible and a long thin screwdriver is quite useful here. If the hose proves difficult to remove from the radiator outlet, it is possible to gently push it off from the access hole under the wheel arch (photo).

5 When the coolant has stopped running, probe the orifices, particularly the cylinder block orifice, with a short piece of wire to dislodge any particles of rust or sediment which may be preventing the coolant from completely draining out.

3 Cooling system – flushing

1 With time, the cooling system may gradually lose its efficiency if the radiator core becomes choked with rust, scale deposits from the water, and other sediment.

2 To flush the system out first drain the coolant as described in the previous Section. Place a hose in the radiator filler cap neck and allow water to run through the system for ten to fifteen minutes.

3 In very bad cases the radiator should be reverse flushed. This can be done in the car but it is better if the radiator is removed as described in Section 5.

4 Invert the radiator (if removed from the car) and place a hose in the lower tank outlet, the gap between hose and outlet suitably padded with rags. Water under slight pressure is then forced through the radiator matrix, the reverse direction to normal flow, so loosening any scale, sediment etc and passing them out through the radiator top tank outlet.

5 With the hose then removed, and the radiator turned the right way up, fit the hose and padding to the top tank outlet and flush in the normal water flow direction.

6 If the radiator still appears to be partially blocked a proprietary radiator de-scaling compound may be used.

7 Once the radiator is clean, if removed, it should be refitted as described in Section 5.

4 Cooling system – filling

1 Refit the cylinder block and radiator drain plugs or bottom hose connection as applicable.

2 Set the heater control knob to the maximum heat position and then fill the cooling system slowly to prevent airlocks developing. The best type of water to use in the coolant mixture is rainwater, so use this whenever possible to avoid scale build-up in the system.

3 Do not fill the system higher than within 0.5 in (12 mm) of the filler orifice. Overfilling will merely result in coolant loss down the overflow pipe due to expansion.

4 Only use an antifreeze mixture with a glycerine or ethylene glycol base – see Section 12. **Note**: On models with no cylinder block drain plug, it is not possible to fully drain the coolant. To establish a suitable antifreeze concentration it will be necessary to pour adequate antifreeze directly into the radiator and then top-up with water. Subsequent topping-up should be done with an antifreeze/water mixture.

5 When the system is full, refit the filler cap and turn it firmly clockwise to lock it in position. Run the engine until normal operating temperature is reached, switch off and allow it to cool. Now recheck and if necessary top-up the coolant in the radiator.

5 Radiator – removal and refitting

1 Drain the cooling system as described in Section 2.

2 Refer to Chapter 12 and remove the bonnet.

3 Slacken the two retaining clips and completely remove the radiator top hose.

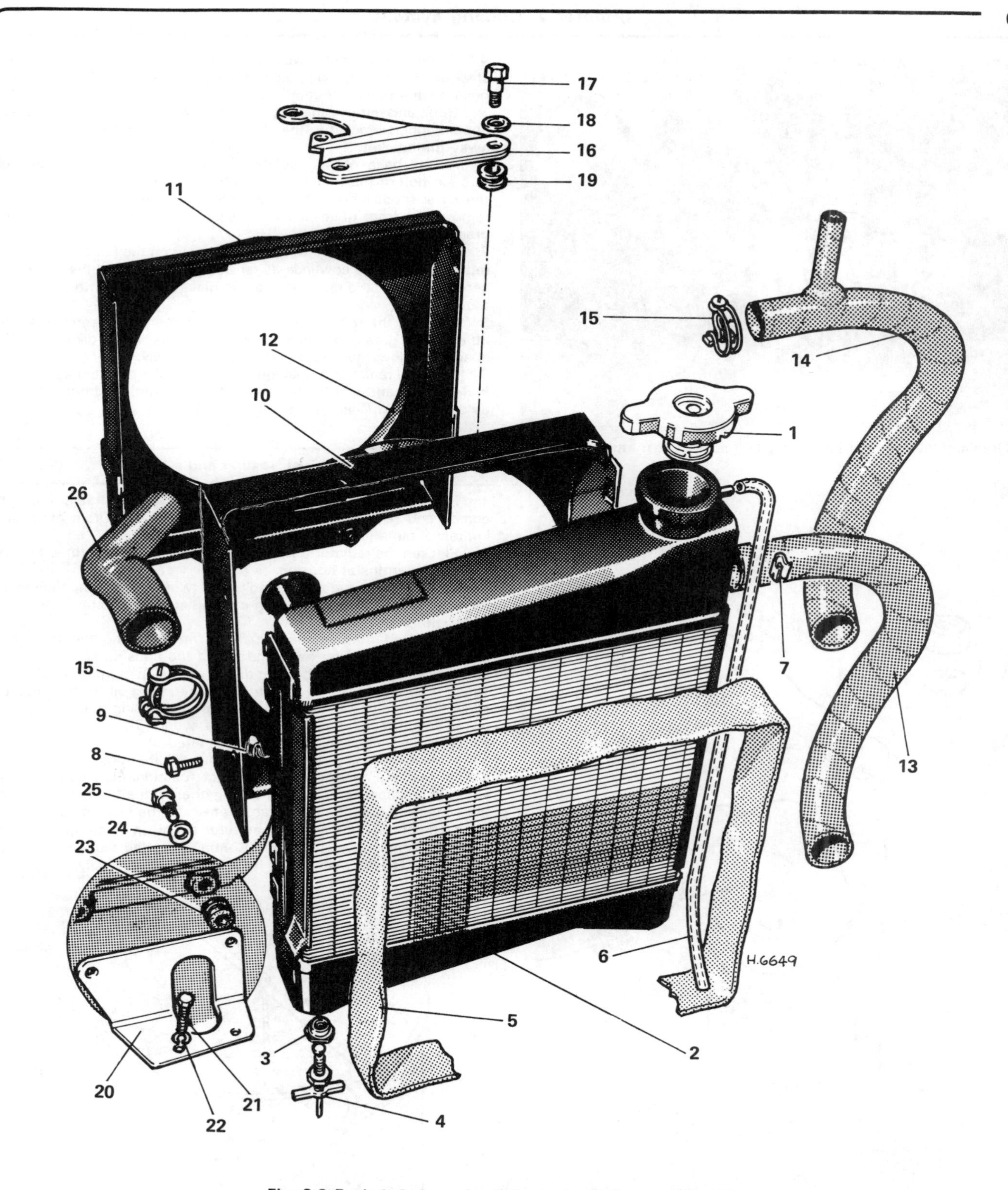

Fig. 2.2 Exploded view of radiator and attachments (Sec 5)

1 *Filler cap*
2 *Radiator*
3 *Drain tap adaptor*
4 *Drain tap or plug*
5 *Rubber surround*
6 *Overflow pipe*
7 *Retaining clip*
8 *Cowl fixing screw*
9 *Nut*
10 *Cowl (one piece type)*
11 *Cowl (upper – two piece type)*
12 *Cowl (lower – two piece type)*
13 *Bottom hose (non-heater type)*
14 *Bottom hose (heater type)*
15 *Hose clip*
16 *Upper mounting*
17 *Bolt*
18 *Washer*
19 *Rubber grommet*
20 *Lower mounting*
21 *Bolt*
22 *Washer*
23 *Rubber grommet*
24 *Washer*
25 *Bolt*
26 *Top hose*

5.6 Radiator lower support mounting bolt accessible through grille panel

4 If the bottom hose was not removed for draining (Section 2), slacken the retaining clip, using a long thin screwdriver, and pull the hose off the radiator outlet.
5 Undo and remove the two bolts and two nuts securing the radiator upper support bracket to the fan cowling and thermostat housing. Lift away the bracket.
6 At the base of the radiator undo and remove either the long through-bolt or the two short bolts (depending on model) that secure the lower support bracket to the engine mounting (photo). If necessary remove the front grille panel as described in Chapter 12 to provide greater access.
7 Finally undo and remove the bolts securing the fan cowlings to the radiator, move the cowlings as far as possible toward the engine and carefully lift out the radiator. If a two piece cowling is fitted, lift off the top half.
8 Refitting the radiator is the reverse sequence to removal. Apply a little rubber grease or liquid detergent to the inside diameter of the hoses, to allow them to be refitted more easily.
9 With the radiator in position, refill the cooling system as described in Section 4, and refit the bonnet and (if removed) the front grille panel as described in Chapter 12.

6 Thermostat – removal, testing and refitting

1 Remove the radiator filler cap, place a clean container under the engine and remove the cylinder block drain plug. Drain off approximately 2 pints (1 litre) and then refit the drain plug.
2 Slacken the radiator top hose retaining clip and withdraw the hose from the thermostat housing.
3 Undo and remove the two bolts and two nuts securing the radiator upper support bracket to the fan cowling and thermostat housing. Lift away the bracket.
4 Undo and remove the remaining nut securing the thermostat housing to the cylinder head and lift off the housing and gasket. The housing is likely to be quite tight due to corrosion of the three retaining studs. If so, apply liberal amounts of penetrating oil to the studs and allow time to soak. Now very gently tap the housing from side to side, using a soft-faced mallet or block of wood. This should ease the corrosion and allow the housing to be lifted off.
5 With the housing removed, take out the thermostat.
6 To test the thermostat for correct functioning, suspend it on a string in a saucepan of cold water together with a thermometer. Heat the water and note the temperature at which the thermostat begins to open. The correct opening temperatures are given in the Specifications at the beginning of this Chapter. Continue heating the water until the thermostat is fully open. Then let it cool down naturally.

Fig. 2.3 Exploded view of the thermostat and housing components (Sec 6)

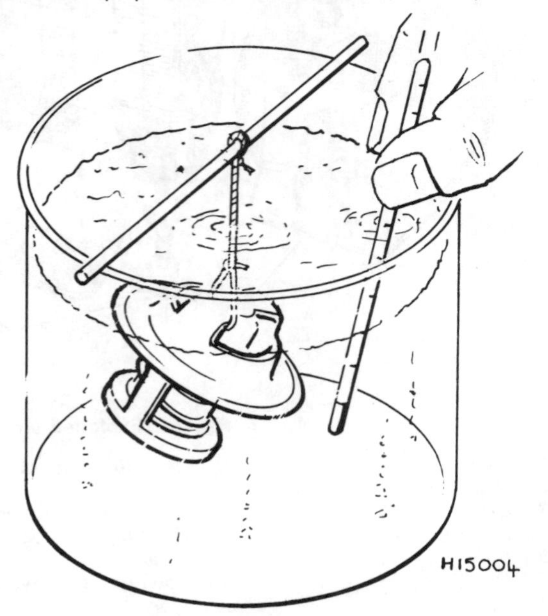

Fig. 2.4 Testing the thermostat (Sec 6)

7 If the thermostat does not fully open in boiling water, or does not close down as the water cools, then it must be discarded and a new one fitted. Should the thermostat be stuck open when cold, this will be apparent when removing it from the housing.
8 Refitting is the reverse sequence to removal. Always ensure that the thermostat housing and cylinder head mating faces are clean and flat. If the housing is badly corroded fit a new one. Always use a new gasket.

7 Water pump – removal and refitting

Note: *If the car is fitted with exhaust emission control equipment, it will be necessary to remove the air pump and drivebelt, as described in Chapter 3, to provide access to the water pump.*
1 Remove the radiator as described in Section 5.
2 Remove the fanbelt, referring to Section 10 if necessary; then undo and remove the two nuts, bolts and washers securing the dynamo or alternator to the mounting bracket and water pump flange. Move the dynamo or alternator away from the engine, pivoting it on the adjusting arm bolt, and allow the unit to rest against the body front panel.
3 Undo and remove the fan bolts securing the fan and fan pulley to the water pump hub. Lift off the fan and pulley, and where fitted recover the spacer. As a guide to reassembly, make a mark to indicate the outer face of the fan as it is quite easy to refit this component the wrong way round.
4 Slacken the hose clips and detach the radiator bottom hose from the water pump outlet and also from the heater take-off connection. Now slacken the clip that secures the bypass hose to the outlet on the top of the pump.
5 Undo and remove the four bolts securing the water pump to the cylinder block. Lift off the pump, and at the same time detach the bypass hose. Recover the water pump gasket (photo).
6 Before refitting the pump, clean off all traces of old gasket from the water pump and cylinder block mating faces, ensuring that the faces are smooth, clean and dry.
7 Refitting the water pump is the reverse sequence to removal, bearing in mind the following points:

(a) *Always use a new gasket, which should be lightly smeared on both sides with jointing compound*
(b) *The bypass hose should be renewed as a matter of course, because these hoses sometimes prove unreliable and are extremely difficult to renew when the water pump is installed*
(c) *On completion of refitting adjust the fanbelt tension as described in Section 11*

8 Water pump – dismantling and reassembly

Note: *Water pump failure is indicated by water leaking from the gland or front of the pump, or by rough and noisy operation. This is usually accompanied by excessive play of the pump spindle which can be checked by moving the fan blades from side to side. Water pumps are relatively inexpensive items and the simplest course of action is to fit a factory exchange unit. However, if you have access to a press or a wide opening vice, a selection of drifts and tubes of suitable diameter, it is possible to overhaul the pump. Make certain that new parts are available from your dealer before you start.*
1 First remove the water pump from the engine as described in Section 7.
2 Remove the front hub from the spindle using a press or suitable puller.
3 Support the pump body, carefully withdraw the bearing retaining wire (if fitted) and then press out the bearing spindle, impeller and seal as a complete assembly, from front to rear.
4 Preferably using a puller, withdraw the impeller off the rear of the bearing spindle.
5 Now remove the water seal from the spindle.
6 Examine all parts for wear or damage, and renew as necessary. The water seal should always be renewed as a matter of course.
7 To reassemble the pump, begin by pressing the bearing spindle assembly into the pump body until the distance from the bearing outer race to the water seal seating face in the pump body is as shown in the Specifications.

7.5 Removing the water pump (engine removed in this photo)

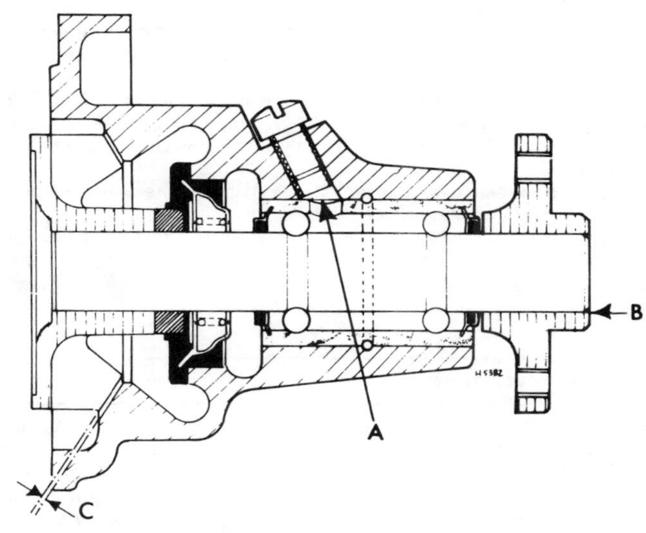

Fig. 2.5 Sectional view of the water pump (Sec 8)

A Pump bearing lubricating hole
B Pulley hub
C 0.020 to 0.030 in (0.51 to 0.76 mm)

8 Now refit the water seal to the spindle, seating it squarely in the pump body.
9 Lubricate the impeller sealing face with a silicone-based grease and press the impeller onto the spindle until the clearance between the vanes and pump body is as shown in the Specifications.
10 Press the front hub onto the spindle until the clearance between the hub face and pump body joint face is as specified.
11 Now place the bearing retaining wire in position (if fitted).
12 The assembled water pump can now be refitted to the car as described in Section 7.

9 Hoses – removal and refitting

1 The cooling system hoses should be regularly inspected, and if any external signs of cracking or deterioration are apparent, the hoses should be renewed. Pay particular attention to the bypass hose and radiator bottom hose. Due to the transverse layout of the Mini power unit, these hoses are particularly inaccessible and tend to be overlooked.
2 Removal and refitting of the hoses is generally straightforward because the hoses are simply withdrawn from their water outlets after

slackening the hose clips. When refitting, apply a little rubber grease or liquid detergent to the inside of the hose to help it slide easily over its outlet. Ensure also that the hose clips are in good condition, and are not damaged or corroded.

3 Renewal of the by-pass hose is an awkward and tedious task which often presents problems. The easiest way to refit a bypass hose is to first place both clips in position on the hose. Fit the bottom of the hose to the water pump, bend the hose in half and then place the flat faces of a knife or feeler blade over the top of the hose and outlet in the cylinder head. Push the hose into an upright position and withdraw the blade. The hose should now be in position over the outlet. Several attempts may be necessary befor the hose slides properly into position.

4 The radiator hose bottom outlet connection can also prove awkward. A very long thin screwdriver is needed to loosen the clip. If the hose is difficult to remove, it can usually be pushed off using a bar inserted through the gaps in the inner panel under the wheel arch.

10 Fanbelt – removal and refitting

Note: *If the fanbelt is stretched unduly, it should be renewed. The most common reason for renewal is that the belt has broken in service. It is therefore recommended that a spare belt is always carried. If the car is fitted with exhaust emission control equipment it will first be necessary to remove the air pump drivebelt as described in Chapter 3.*

1 To remove the fanbelt, slacken the two dynamo or alternator upper mountings and the nut on the adjusting arm below the water pump (photo).

2 Push the dynamo or alternator toward the engine and lift the old belt off the three pulleys. Feed the belt over each fan blade in turn and withdraw it from behind the fan cowling at the special gap just below the top hose.

3 Fit the new belt over the fan blades in the same way and then place it in position on the three pulleys.

4 Adjust the fanbelt tension as described in the following Section and then refit the air pump drivebelt, where applicable, as described in Chapter 3. **Note:** *After fitting a new fanbelt, check and if necessary readjust the tension after 250 miles (400 km).*

11 Fanbelt – adjustment

Note: *It is most important to keep the fanbelt correctly adjusted, and this should be carried out every 3000 miles (5000 km). If the belt is too loose it will slip and wear rapidly, resulting in inefficient operation of the water pump and dynamo or alternator. If it is too tight, it will impose excessive strain on the bearings of the water pump, dynamo or alternator causing premature failure of these components.*

1 The fanbelt tension is correct when there is 0.5 in (13 mm) of fanbelt deflection, using light finger pressure, at a point midway between the crankshaft and dynamo or alternator pulleys.

2 To adjust the fanbelt, slacken the mounting bolts of the dynamo or alternator, and also the nut on the adjusting arm located below the water pump. Now move the unit either in or out until the correct tension is obtained. It is easier if the adjusting arm nut is only slackened a little so it requires some force to move the dynamo or alternator. In this way the tension of the belt can be arrived at more quickly than by making frequent adjustments. If difficulty is experienced in moving the dynamo or alternator away from the engine, a long spanner or bar placed behind the unit and resting against the block serves as a very good lever and can be held in position while the adjusting and mounting bolts are fully tightened. When levering on an alternator, *only lever on the drive end* or damage may occur.

12 Antifreeze mixture

In circumstances where it is likely that the temperature will fall below freezing, it is essential that the cooling system is drained and refilled with the correct percentage of antifreeze in the coolant.

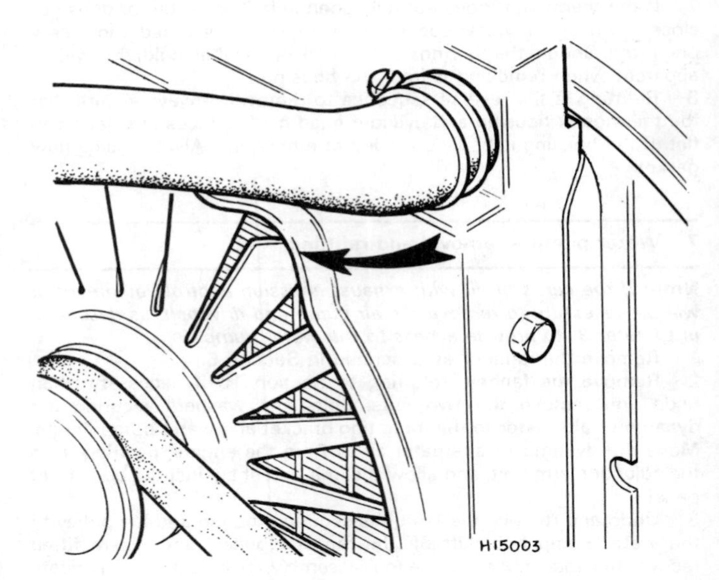

Fig. 2.6 The gap in the radiator shroud of early models (arrowed) to allow removal and refitting of the fanbelt (Sec 10)

10.1 Dynamo adjustment arm retaining bolts

An ethylene glycol antifreeze conforming to BS3151 or BS3152 should be used (Duckhams Universal Antifreeze and Summer Coolant). Alcohol-based antifreeze is not recommended due to its very high evaporation rate. Ethylene glycol antifreeze can be retained in the cooling system all the year round, for up to two years; however, it is advisable to have the specific gravity checked by your local garage every six months.

The table below gives the approximate antifreeze concentration and the degree of protection:

Antifreeze concentration	Commences to freeze	Frozen solid	Amount of antifreeze
%	*°C (°F)*	*°C (°F)*	*pt (l)*
25	–13 (9)	–26 (–15)	1.5 (0.85)
33	–19 (–2)	–36 (–33)	2.0 (1.2)
50	–36 (–33)	–48 (–53)	3.25 (1.8)

13 Fault diagnosis – cooling system

Symptom	Reason(s)
Overheating	Low coolant level (this may be the result of overheating for other reasons) Fanbelt slipping or broken Radiator blockage (internal or external), or grille restricted Thermostat defective Ignition timing incorrect or distributor defective (automatic advance inoperative) Carburettor maladjustment – see Chapter 3 Exhaust system partly blocked Water hose(s) collapsed Blown cylinder head gasket (combustion gases in coolant) Water pump defective Radiator pressure cap defective Brakes binding – see Chapter 9
Overcooling	Thermostat missing, defective or wrong heat range
Water loss – external	Loose hose clips Perished or cracked hoses Radiator core leaking Heater matrix leaking Radiator pressure cap leaking Boiling due to overheating Water pump, thermostat housing or bypass hose leaking Core plug leaking
Water loss – internal	Cylinder head gasket blown Cylinder head cracked or warped Cylinder block cracked
Corrosion	Infrequent draining and flushing Incorrect antifreeze mixture or inappropriate type Combustion gases contaminating coolant

Chapter 3
Fuel, exhaust and emission control systems

For modifications, and information applicable to later models, see Supplement at end of manual

Contents

Specifications

Air cleaner

Type .... Renewable paper element, with temperature control device on later models: Champion W131 (all models to 1973) or W125 (1974-on including Automatic from 1969)

Fuel pump

Type:
- Electric pump .... SU AUF 201
- Mechanical pump .... SU AUF 700 or AUF 800

Carburettor data

Mini 850 Saloon and variants, 848 cc

	1969-72	**1972-74**	**1974-76**	**1976 on**
Carburettor type	SU HS2	SU HS2	SU HS4	SU HS4
Piston spring	Red	Red	Red	Red
Jet size	0.090 in (3 mm)	0.090 in (3 mm)	0.090 in (3 mm)	0.090 in (3 mm)
Needle:				
Standard	EB	AAV	ABS	ADH
Rich	M	–	–	–
Weak	GG	–	–	–
Exhaust emission (%CO)	–	3.5 to 4.5	3.5 to 4.5	3 to 4.5
Idle speed	500 rpm	800 rpm	800 rpm	750 rpm
Fast idle speed	900 rpm	1200 rpm	1200 rpm	1200 rpm

Mini Clubman and Mini 1000 Saloon and variants, manual transmission, 998 cc, up to 1974

	1969-72	**1972-74**
Carburettor type	SU HS2	SU HS2
Piston spring	Red	Red
Jet size	0.090 in (3 mm)	0.090 in (3 mm)
Needle:		
Standard	GX	AAV
Rich	M	–
Weak	GG	–
Exhaust emission (%CO)	–	3.5 to 4.5
Idle speed	500 rpm	800 rpm
Fast idle speed	900 rpm	1200 rpm

Mini Clubman and Mini 1000 Saloon, automatic transmission, 998 cc, up to 1974

	1969-74
Carburettor type	SU HS4
Piston spring	Red
Jet size	0.090 in (3 mm)
Needle:	
Standard	AC
Rich	MI
Weak	HA
Idle speed	650 rpm
Fast idle speed	1050 rpm

Mini Clubman and Mini 1000 Saloon and variants, manual and automatic transmission, 998 cc, 1974 on

	1974-76	1976-78	1978 on
Carburettor type	SU HS4	SU HS4	SU HS4
Piston spring	Red	Red	Red
Jet size	0.090 in (3 mm)	0.090 in (3 mm)	0.090 in (3 mm)
Needle	ABX	ADE	ADE
Exhaust emission (%CO)	3.5 to 4.5	3 to 4.5	3
Idle speed	750 rpm	750 rpm	750 rpm
Fast idle speed	1200 rpm	1250 rpm	1250 rpm

Mini 1000 (Canada)

	1970-73	1973-77	1977 on
Carburettor type	SU HS4	SU HS4	SU HS4
Piston spring	Red	Red	Red
Jet size	0.090 in (3 mm)	0.090 in (3 mm)	0.090 in (3 mm)
Needle	AAG	ABJ	ADD
Exhaust emission (%CO)	4.5	4.5	4.5 to 5.5
Idle speed	800 rpm	850 rpm	750 to 850 rpm
Fast idle speed	1250 rpm	1250 rpm	1150 to 1350 rpm

Mini Clubman 1100, 1098 cc

	1974 on
Carburettor type	SU HS4
Piston spring	Red
Jet size	0.090 in (3 mm)
Needle	ABP
Exhaust emission (%CO)	3 to 4.5
Idle speed	750 rpm
Fast idle speed	1150 to 1300 rpm

Mini Cooper S Mk III, 1275 cc

	1969 on
Carburettor type	Twin SU HS2
Piston spring	Red
Jet size	0.090 in (3 mm)
Needle:	
Standard	M
Rich	AH2
Weak	EB
Idle speed	600 rpm
Fast idle speed	1000 rpm

Mini 1275 GT, 1275 cc

	1969-72	1972-76	1976-77	1978 on
Carburettor type	SU HS4	SU HS4	SU HS4	SU HS4
Piston spring	Red	Red	Red	Red
Jet size	0.090 in (3 mm)	0.090 in (3 mm)	0.090 in (3 mm)	0.090 in (3 mm)
Needle:				
Standard	AC	AAV	ABB	AAT
Rich	BQ	–	–	–
Weak	HA	–	–	–
Exhaust emission (%CO)	–	3.5 to 4.5	3 to 4.5	3 to 4
Idle speed	650 rpm	800 rpm	850 rpm	750 rpm
Fast idle speed	1050 rpm	1200 rpm	1300 rpm	1300 rpm

Carburettor dashpot (all models)

Oil type/specification	Multigrade engine oil, viscosity SAE 20W/50, 10W/40, or 10W/30 (Duckhams QXR, Hypergrade, or 10W/40 Motor Oil)
Oil level	0.5 in (13 mm) above piston rod

Fuel tank capacity

Saloon models except Cooper S Mk III and 1275 GT	5.5 gallons (25 litres) – 7.5 gallons (33 litres), later models
Estate, Van and Pick-up	6.0 gallons (27.3 litres)
Cooper S Mk III (twin fuel tanks)	11.0 gallons (50 litres)
1275 GT	7.5 gallons (34 litres)

1 General description

The fuel system comprises a fuel tank, an electric or mechanical fuel pump and a variable choke carburettor.

The fuel tank is located in the luggage compartment on Saloon models, and beneath the rear floor on the Estate, Van and Pick-up variants. On Cooper S versions twin fuel tanks are used, these being positioned on either side of the luggage compartment.

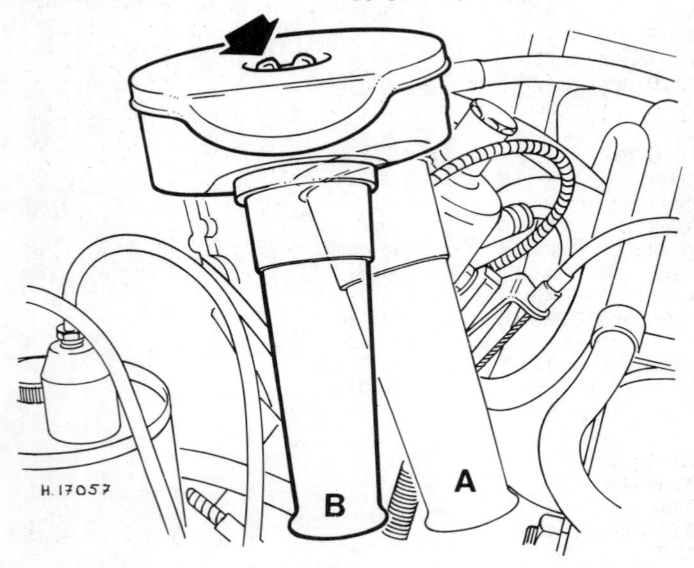

Fig. 3.1 The air cleaner fitted to early models (Sec 2)

A Winter position *Air cleaner retaining wing nut arrowed*
B Summer position

A number of the earlier vehicles covered by this manual are equipped with an SU electric fuel pump which is mounted on the left-hand member of the rear subframe. All later Mini models utilize a mechanical fuel pump bolted to the rear of the engine and operated by an eccentric on the camshaft.

A variable choke carburettor of SU manufacture is fitted to all models. Manual transmission versions manufactured up to 1974 utilize a single SU HS2 unit, the exception to this being the Cooper S model which incorporates a twin carburettor installation. Later manual and all automatic transmission vehicles are equipped with the larger SU HS4 carburettor.

Certain export models are fitted with emission control equipment to reduce the level of harmful emissions in the exhaust gases. A brief description will be found in Section 30.

2 Air cleaner – removal and refitting

All models except Cooper S

1 Undo and remove the single wing nut and washer on early models, or the twin wing bolts and washers on later models, securing the air cleaner to the carburettor (photos).

2 If the air cleaner is retained by a single wing nut lift off the air cleaner top cover. Detach the rocker cover hose, then lift the air cleaner body off the carburettor, tip it up at the front and slide it sideways until it is clear of the long retaining stud and can be lifted away. Recover the sealing ring (photos).

3 If the air cleaner is retained by two wing nuts, detach the hot air duct (where fitted) and then lift the air cleaner body off the carburettor (photos).

4 With the air cleaner removed from the engine, recover the rubber sealing ring if it stayed behind on the carburettor flange (photo).

5 Lift off the air cleaner cover and withdraw the paper element. On the later type moulded plastic air cleaners the cover is removed by prising it off with a screwdriver inserted in the slots on the periphery of the cover (photos).

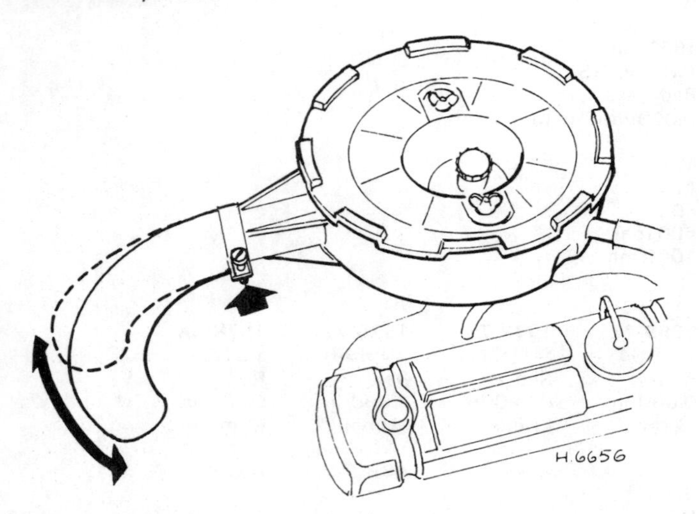

Fig. 3.2 The air cleaner fitted to automatic transmission and certain manual transmission models (Sec 2)

Adjustable intake spout clamp bolt arrowed

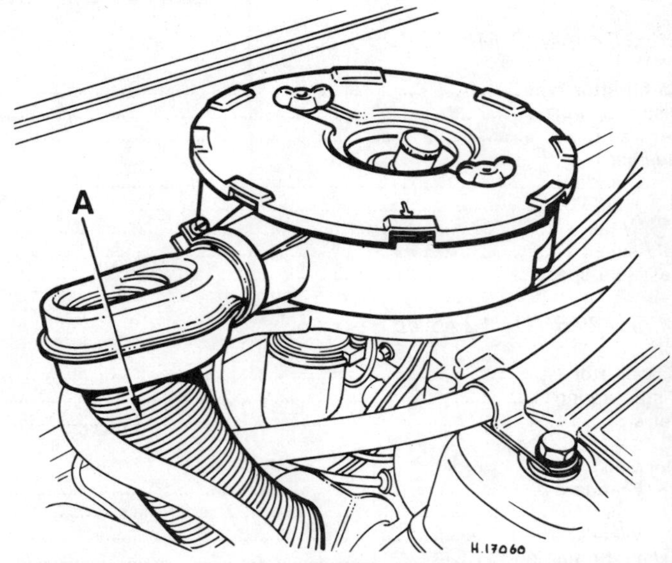

Fig. 3.3 The air cleaner fitted to all later models (Sec 2)

A Hot air intake duct

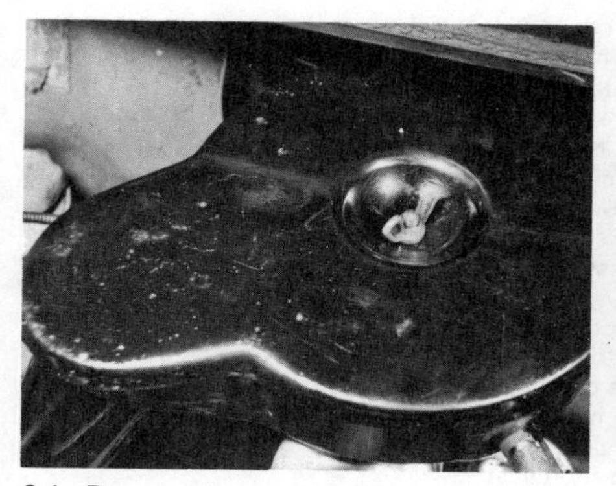
2.1a Remove the single wing nut on early models...

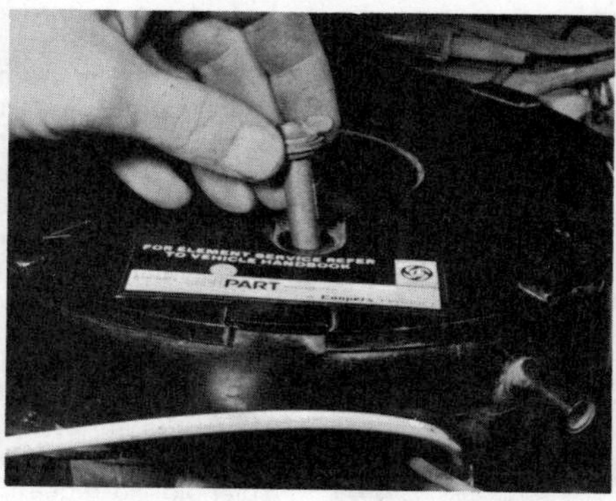
2.1b ...or the two wing bolts on later models

2.2a On early models lift off the top cover and withdraw the air cleaner body from the carburettor

2.2b Recover the sealing ring

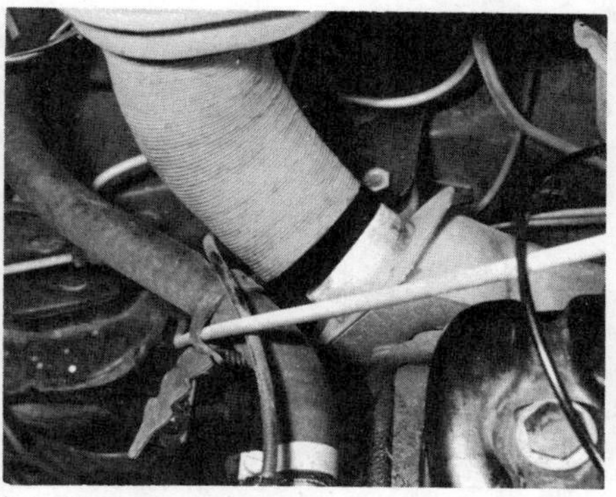
2.3a On later models detach the hot air duct...

2.3b ...lift off the air cleaner body...

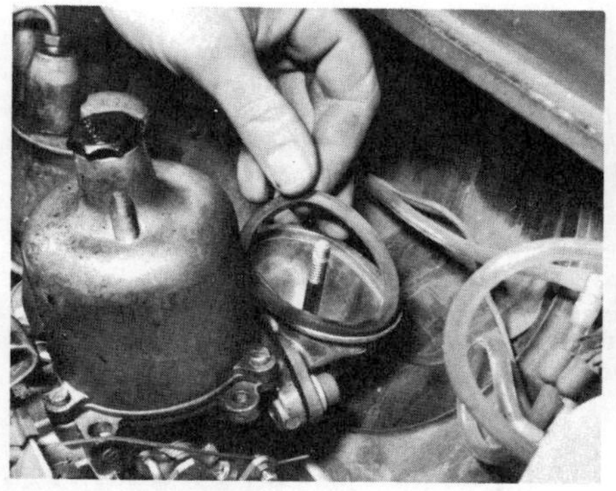
2.4 ...and recover the sealing ring

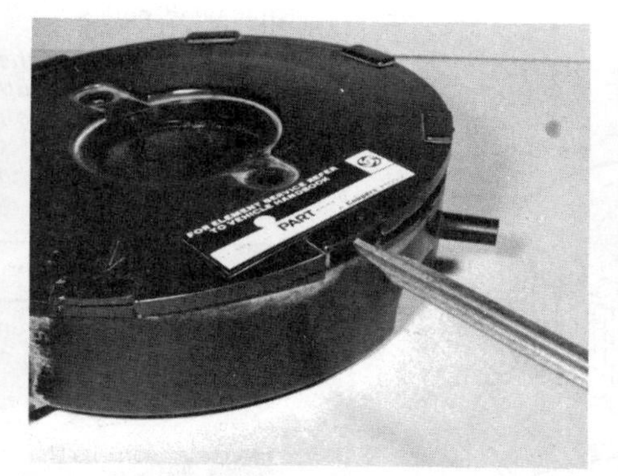
2.5a To remove the later type element, prise up the cover...

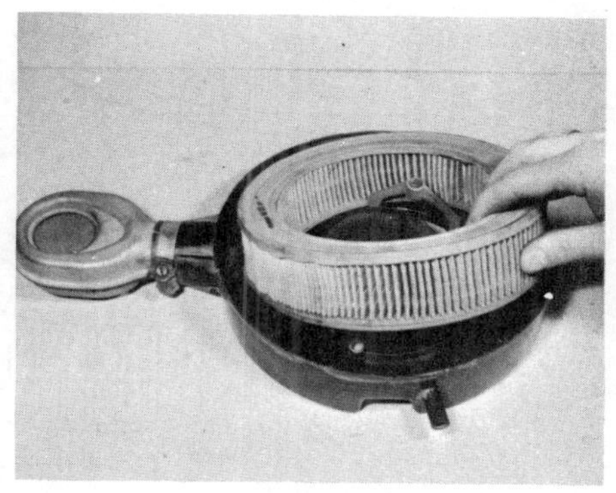
2.5b ...and lift the element out

6 Thoroughly clean the inside of the air cleaner body. Do not attempt to clean the paper element but renew it at the recommended service intervals.
7 Refitting the air cleaner is the reverse sequence to removal. Make sure that where an alignment arrow is stamped on the top cover, it is pointing toward the location lug on the air cleaner body (photo). Ensure also that the rubber sealing ring is in position before refitting the air cleaner.
8 If the air cleaner body incorporates an adjustable air intake spout, this should be positioned adjacent to the exhaust manifold in winter and away from it in summer.

Cooper S models

9 Undo and remove the two wing bolts and washers and lift off the air cleaner top cover. Lift out the paper elements and thoroughly clean the inside of the air cleaner body.
10 Do not attempt to clean the paper elements but renew them at the recommended service intervals.
11 The air cleaner body may be removed if necessary after disconnecting the engine breather pipe and the throttle return spring. Take care not to lose the two rubber sealing washers from the carburettor flanges.
12 Refitting the air cleaner and elements is the reverse of the removal procedure.

3 Electric fuel pump – general description

The SU electric fuel pump consists of a long outer body casing housing the diaphragm, armature and solenoid assembly, with at one end the contact breaker assembly protected by a bakelite cover, and at the other end a short casting containing the inlet and outlet ports, filter, valves, and pumping chamber. The joint between the bakelite cover and the body casing is protected with a rubber sheath.

The pump operates in the following manner. When the ignition is switched on current travels from the terminal on the outside of the

2.7 The top cover on the later type air cleaner is refitted with the alignment arrow toward the locating lug

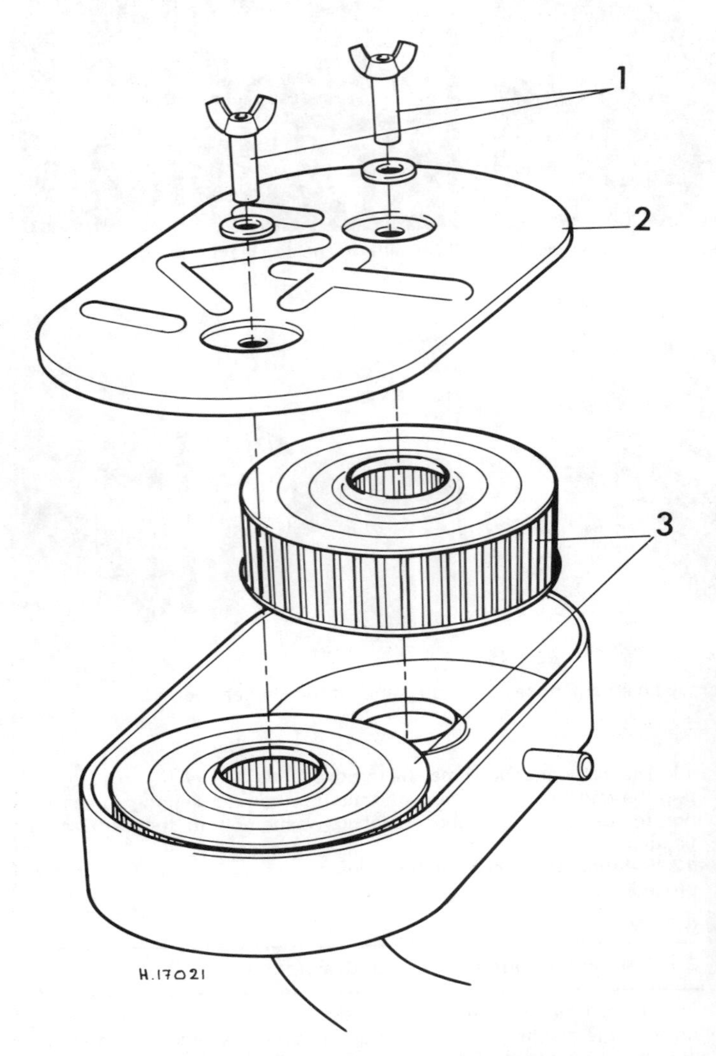

Fig. 3.4 The Cooper S air cleaner assembly (Sec 2)

1 *Wing bolts*
2 *Top cover*
3 *Elements*

bakelite cover, through the coil located round the solenoid core, which becomes energised. This acts like a magnet, drawing the armature towards it. The current then passes through the points to earth.

When the armature is drawn forward, it brings the diaphragm with it against the pressure of the diaphragm spring. This creates sufficient vacuum in the pump chamber to draw in fuel from the tank through the fuel filter and non-return inlet valve.

As the armature nears the end of its travel a 'throw-over' mechanism operates which separates the points so breaking the circuit.

The diaphragm return spring then pushes the diaphragm and armature forwards, into the pumping chamber, so forcing the fuel in the chamber out to the carburettor through the non-return outlet valve. When the armature is nearly fully forward the throw over mechanism again functions; this time closing the points and re-energising the solenoid, so repeating the cycle.

4 Electric fuel pump – removal and refitting

1 Jack up the rear of the car and support it on axle stands. Disconnect the battery earth terminal.
2 Working under the car, disconnect the earth lead and the electrical supply wire from their terminals on the pump body.
3 Prepare to squeeze the rubber portion of the petrol pipe leading from the tank with a self-gripping wrench or similar tool, to ensure that the minimum amount of fuel is lost when the inlet pipe is removed from the pump. Plug the end of the pipe with a bolt or metal rod of suitable diameter immediately it is disconnected.
4 Remove the inlet and outlet fuel pipes by undoing the retaining clip screws and easing the pipes off the pump nozzles (photo). Remove the vent pipe connector, if fitted, at this stage.
5 Undo and remove the two nuts, bolts and spring washers securing the pump bracket to the subframe and lift off the pump assembly, complete with bracket and clamp.
6 To separate the pump from the bracket, slacken the clamp bolt and slide the pump out of the clamp.
7 Refitting is the reverse sequence to removal, bearing in mind the following points:

(a) *Arrows on the pump body indicate the correct locations of the inlet and outlet pipes. Ensure that these are fitted correctly and that the pump is installed with the outlet pipe at the top*
(b) *Ensure that the electrical leads, particularly the earth, are clean and that a correct connection is made*

5 Electric fuel pump – dismantling

1 Prepare a clean uncluttered working surface and have some small jars or tins handy to store the small, easily-lost parts in.

4.4 Removing the fuel outlet pipe from the electric pump

2 Release the inlet and outlet nozzles, valves, sealing washers, and filter by unscrewing the two screws from the spring clamp plate which hold them all in place.

3 Mark the flanges adjacent to each other, and separate the housing holding the armature and solenoid assembly from the pumping chamber casting, by unscrewing the six screws holding both halves of the pump together. Take great care not to tear or damage the diaphragm, as it may stick to either of the flanges as they are separated.

4 The armature spindle, which is attached to the armature head and diaphragm, is unscrewed anti-clockwise from the trunnion at the contact breaker end of the pump body. Lift out the armature, spindle, and diaphragm, and remove the impact washer from under the head of the armature, (this washer quietens the noise of the armature head hitting the solenoid core), and the diaphragm return spring.

5 Slide off the protective rubber sheath and unscrew the terminal nut, connector (where fitted), and washer from the terminal screw, and remove the bakelite contact breaker cover.

6 Unscrew the screws which hold the contact spring blade in position and remove with the blade and screw washer.

7 Remove the cover retaining nut on the terminal screw, and cut through the lead washer under the nut on the terminal screw with a pocket knife.

8 Remove the two bakelite pedestal retaining screws, complete with

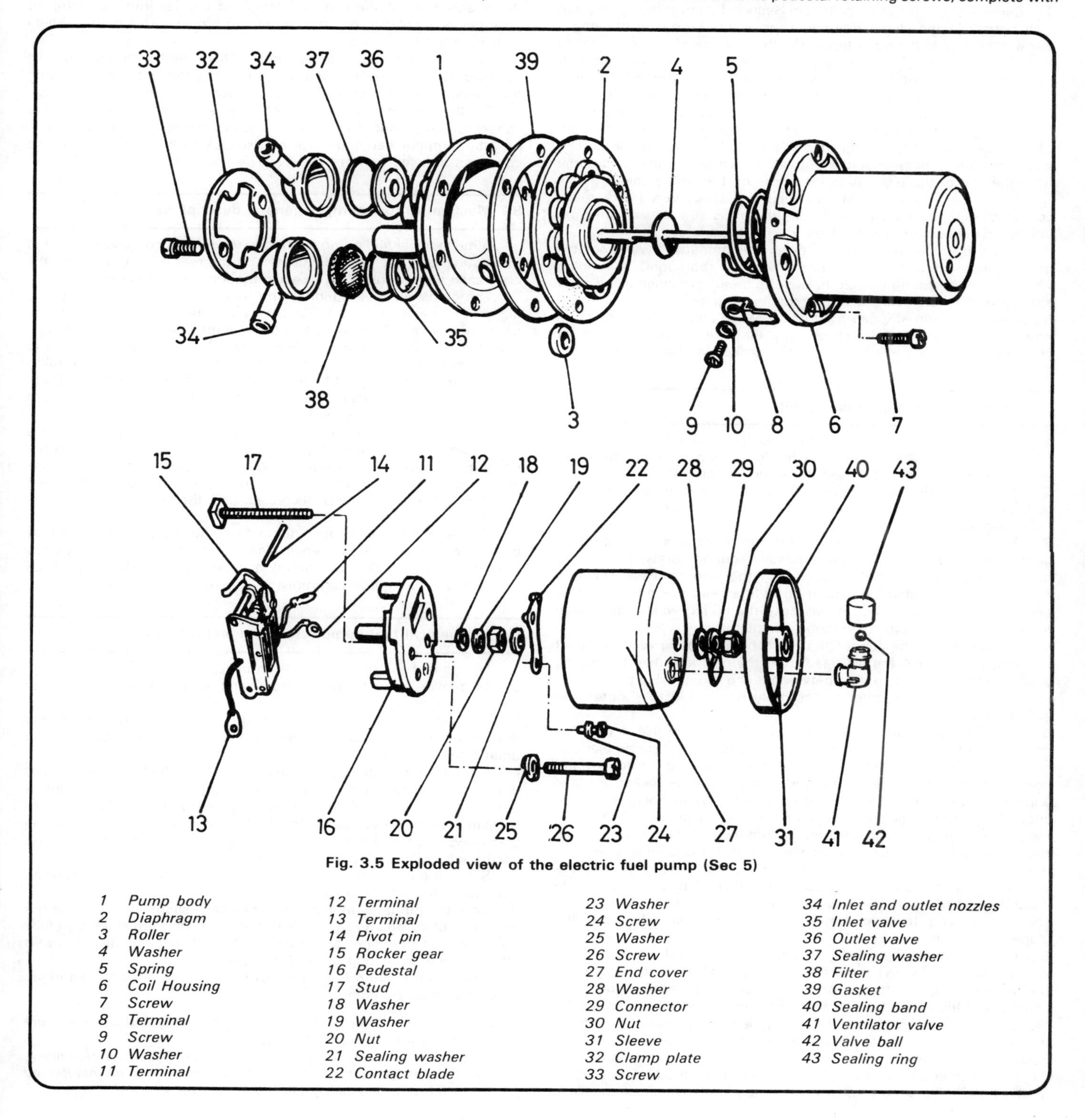

Fig. 3.5 Exploded view of the electric fuel pump (Sec 5)

1 Pump body
2 Diaphragm
3 Roller
4 Washer
5 Spring
6 Coil Housing
7 Screw
8 Terminal
9 Screw
10 Washer
11 Terminal
12 Terminal
13 Terminal
14 Pivot pin
15 Rocker gear
16 Pedestal
17 Stud
18 Washer
19 Washer
20 Nut
21 Sealing washer
22 Contact blade
23 Washer
24 Screw
25 Washer
26 Screw
27 End cover
28 Washer
29 Connector
30 Nut
31 Sleeve
32 Clamp plate
33 Screw
34 Inlet and outlet nozzles
35 Inlet valve
36 Outlet valve
37 Sealing washer
38 Filter
39 Gasket
40 Sealing band
41 Ventilator valve
42 Valve ball
43 Sealing ring

spring washers, which hold the pedestal to the solenoid housing. Remove the braided copper earth lead, and coil lead from the terminal screw.
9 Remove the pin on which the rockers pivot by pushing it out sideways, and remove the rocker assembly. The pump is now fully dismantled. It is not possible to remove the solenoid core and coil, and the rocker assembly must not be broken down, as it is only supplied on exchange as a complete assembly.

6 Electric fuel pump – inspection and servicing

1 Remove the filter as described in Section 5, and thoroughly clean it in petrol. At the same time clean the points by gently drawing a piece of thin card between them. Do this very carefully so as not to disturb the tension of the spring blade. If the points are burnt or pitted they must be renewed and a new blade and rocker assembly fitted.
2 Fuel starvation combined with rapid operation is indicative of an air leak on the suction side. To check whether this is so, undo the fuel line at the top of the carburettor float chamber, and immerse the end of the pipe in a jam jar half filled with petrol. With the ignition on and the pump functioning, should a regular stream of air bubbles emerge from the end of the pipe, air is leaking in on the suction side.
3 If the filter is coated with gum-like substance very like varnish, serious trouble can develop in the future unless all traces of this gum (formed by deposits from the fuel) are removed.
4 To do this soak the filter in a reasonable amount of water soluble paint stripper. Remove the filter and wash it thoroughly in running water. Dry with a non-fluffy cloth. Exercise great care when using paint stripper and follow the manufacturer's instructions.
5 With the pump stripped right down, wash and clean all the parts thoroughly in paraffin and renew any that are worn, damaged, or cracked. Pay particular attention to the gaskets and diaphragm.

7 Electric fuel pump – reassembly

1 Fit the rocker assembly to the bakelite pedestal and insert the rocker pivot pin. The pin is case hardened and wire or any other substitute should never be used if the pin is lost.
2 Place the spring washer, wiring tag from the short lead from the coil, a new lead washer, and the nut on the terminal screw, and tighten the nut down.
3 Attach the copper earth wire from the outer rocker immediately under the head of the nearest pedestal securing screw, and fit the pedestal to the solenoid housing with the two pedestal securing screws and lockwashers. It is unusual to fit an earth wire immediately under the screw head, but in this case the spring washer has been found not to be a particularly good conductor.
4 Fit the lockwasher under the head of the spring blade contact securing screw, then the last lead from the coil, and then the spring blade, so that there is nothing between it and the bakelite pedestal. It is important that this order of assembly is adhered to. Tighten the screw lightly.
5 The static position of the pump when it is not in use is with the contact points making firm contact, and this forces the spring blade to be bent slightly back. Move the outer rocker arm up and down and position the spring blade so that the contacts on the rocker or blade wipe over the centre line of the other points. When open, the blade should rest against the small ledge on the bakelite pedestal just below the points. The points should come into contact with each other when the rocker is halfway forward. To check that this is correct, press the middle of the blade gently so that it rests against the ridge with the points just having come into contact. It should now be possible to slide a 0.030 in (0.762 mm) feeler gauge between the rocker rollers and the solenoid housing. If the clearance is not correct bend the tip of the blade very carefully until it is.
6 Tighten down the blade retaining screw, and check that a considerable gap exists between the underside of the spring blade and the pedestal ledge, with the rocker contact bearing against the blade contact and the rocker fully forward in the normal static position. With the rocker arm down, ensure that the underside of the blade rests on the ledge of the pedestal. If not, remove the blade and very slightly bend it until it does.
7 Place the impact washer on the underside of the armature head, fit the diaphragm return spring with the wider portion of the coils against the solenoid body, place the brass rollers in position under the diaphragm and insert the armature spindle through the centre of the solenoid core, and screw the spindle into the rocker trunnion.
8 It will be appreciated that the amount the spindle is screwed into the rocker trunnion will vitally affect the functioning of the pump. To set the diaphragm correctly, turn the steel blade to one side, and screw the armature spindle into the trunnion until, if the spindle was screwed in a further sixth of a turn, the throw-over rocker would not operate the points-closed to points-open position. Now screw out the armature spindle four holes ($\frac{2}{3}$ of a turn) to ensure that wear in the points will not cause the pump to stop working. Turn the blade back into its normal position.
9 Reassembly of the valves, filters, and nozzles into the pumping chamber is a reversal of the dismantling process. Use new washers and gaskets throughout.
10 With the pumping chamber reassembled, refit it carefully on the solenoid housing, ensuring that the previously made mating marks on the flanges line up with each other. Screw the six screws in firmly.
11 Fit the bakelite cover and refit the shakeproof washer, Lucar connector, cover nut, and terminal knob to the terminal screw. Then, refit the terminal lead and cover nut, so locking the lead between the cover nut and the terminal nut.

8 Mechanical fuel pump – general description

A mechanical fuel pump is fitted to the majority of models covered by this manual. The pump is located on the rear left-hand side of the crankcase and is driven by an eccentric lobe on the camshaft.

The camshaft lobe operates the rocker lever, drawing the pump diaphragm downwards and thus creating suction on the fuel inlet pipe from the fuel tank. This draws fuel through the filter into the diaphragm chamber (upper body), via the two-way valve. The outer seat lifts to allow fuel to pass into the diaphragm chamber. The spring then takes over the return stroke and forces fuel back through the centre seat of the two-way valve (which now lifts) up through the central tube of the upper body through the outlet cover to the carburettor. When the carburettor float needle valve is closed against the pump delivery the diaphragm of the pump stays in the down position, line pressure holding the spring compressed. The rocker lever idles free in these instances. As soon as the needle valve opens, the pressure in the outlet line from the pump decreases and the normal fuel delivery continues.

The AUF 700 series fuel pump fitted to early models may be dismantled for overhaul or repair. The AUF 800 series pump fitted to later models is a sealed unit, and if its condition is suspect, it must be renewed as a complete assembly.

9 Mechanical fuel pump – removal and refitting

1 Disconnect the battery earth terminal.
2 To provide greater access, remove the air cleaner, referring to Section 2 if necessary.
3 Slacken the pipe clip screw on the outlet pipe connection and draw it off. Have a small container handy to collect what little fuel may drain from the pipe.
4 In all saloon models, if the tank is more than half full, the fuel will drain from the tank under gravity when the fuel pump inlet pipe is disconnected, so provide for this situation by fitting a suitable clip or bung in the pipe if necessary. On all other models the tank is below the pump level, so this problem will not occur. Slacken the pipe clip screw on the inlet pipe connection and draw it off.
5 Slacken the two nuts which hold the pump to the crankcase on two studs through the lower body.
6 Ease the pump away from the crankcase slightly and release the insulating block and its two sealing gaskets. If they are stuck, carefully prise them off the crankcase using a knife or thin screwdriver. Now lift off the pump, insulating block and gaskets.
7 Refitting the pump is the reverse sequence to removal bearing in mind the following points:

- *(a) Ensure that the mating faces of the pump and crankcase are thoroughly clean and dry*
- *(b) Use new sealing gaskets on either side of the insulating block, but make sure that the original thickness is maintained otherwise the pump operation may be affected*

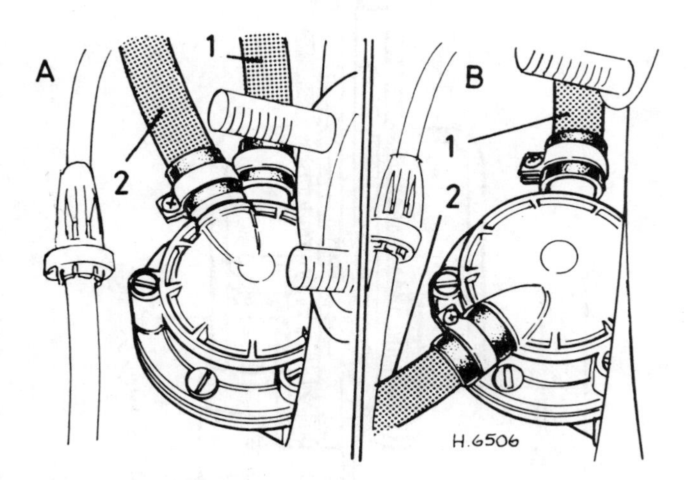

Fig. 3.6 AUF 700 mechanical fuel pump outlet pipe positions (Sec 9)

A 850, 1000 and 1100 models
B 1275 models
1 Inlet pipe
2 Outlet pipe

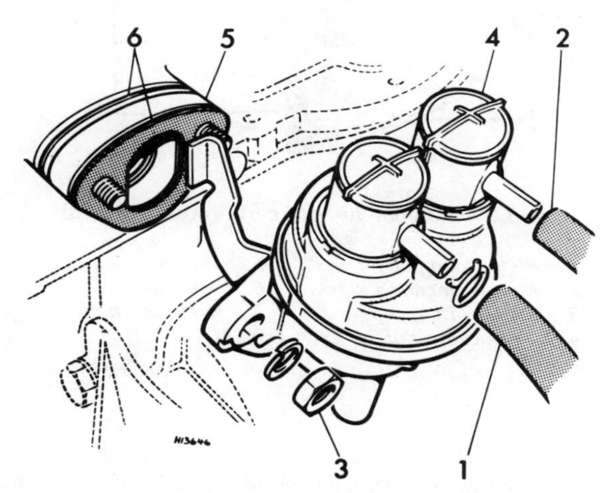

Fig. 3.7 AUF 800 fuel pump removal (Sec 9)

1 Inlet hose
2 Outlet hose
3 Nut
4 Pump body
5 Insulator
6 Gaskets

10 Mechanical fuel pump – dismantling

1 Clean any dirt off the whole of the assembly, and work on a bench covered with a clean sheet of paper.

2 Mark the relationship between the outlet cover, upper body and lower body, which must reassemble the same way.

3 Remove the three top cover retaining screws which clamp the lip of the cover.

4 The sealing ring should have come off with the outlet cover but if not, carefully lift it away from the upper body and remove the filter disc.

5 Remove the three screws holding the upper body to the lower body and lift it off.

6 Take out the inlet/outlet valve. This is a press fit and care is needed to avoid damage to the edge of the outer (inlet) seat.

7 To remove the diaphragm and spring, the rocker lever needs to be removed. Press the diaphragm and spring down sufficiently to take the pressure off the rocker lever pivot pin, which can be removed by a light tap with a long-nosed punch. Withdraw the lever from the diaphragm stirrup and watch for the spring flying out. Put a little oil on the diaphragm stirrup to prevent damage to the gland, and then carefully draw the diaphragm and spring from the lower body.

8 If the crankcase seal in the lower body requires renewal, it can be prised and hooked out. The seal will be damaged during removal so make sure that a new one is available before removing the old one.

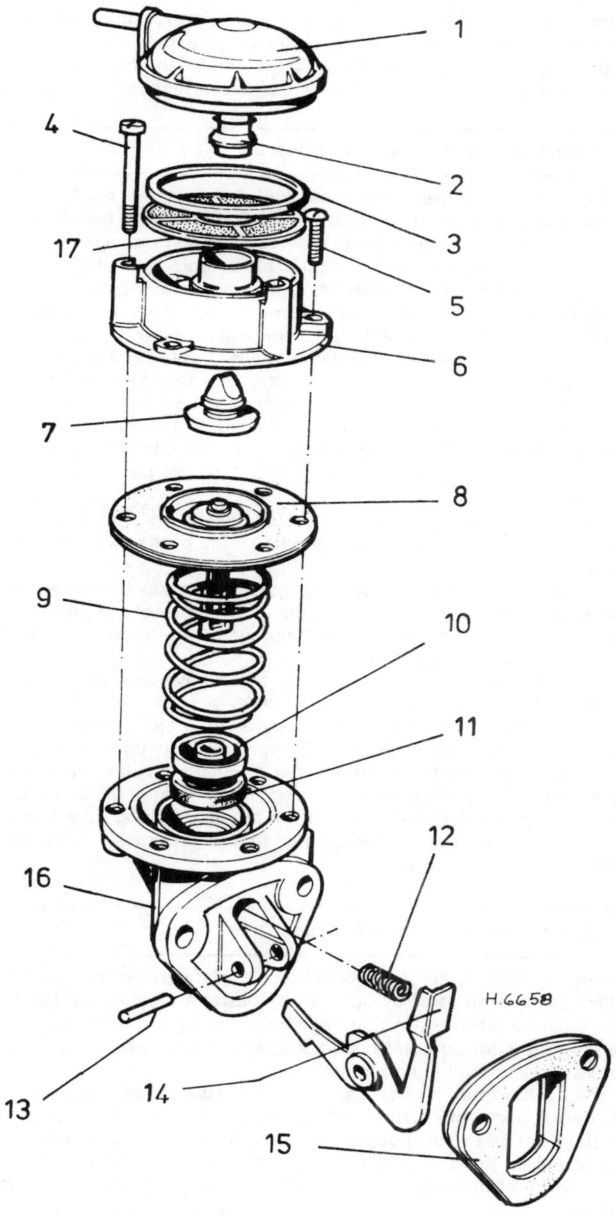

Fig. 3.8 Exploded view of the AUF 700 mechanical fuel pump (Sec 10)

1 Top cover
2 Outlet tube
3 Sealing ring
4 Screw
5 Screw
6 Upper body
7 Inlet/outlet valve
8 Diaphragm assembly
9 Diaphragm spring
10 Crankcase seal cup
11 Crankcase seal
12 Rocker lever return spring
13 Rocker lever pivot pin
14 Rocker lever
15 Insulating block
16 Lower body
17 Filter

11 Mechanical fuel pump – inspection and servicing

1 Ensure that the filter is clean and undamaged, check the diaphragm for signs of cracking and perforation and examine the seats of the inlet/outlet valve for chipping or wear on the seats. The sealing ring in the outlet cover is best renewed anyway, but does not have to be. If in doubt about any of these items, renew them.
2 Gum deposits should be cleaned off as described in Section 6.

12 Mechanical fuel pump – reassembly

1 Reassembly of the mechanical fuel pump is the reverse of the dismantling procedure but the following points should be noted.
2 If the crankcase seal is being renewed, press the seal carefully into the lower body using a drift or tube of suitable diameter. If a new diaphragm is being fitted, ensure that there are no sharp edges or burrs on the spindle or stirrup slot. Oil the spindle lightly and refit it with the stirrup slot positioned correctly for engagement with the rocker lever.
3 Refitting the rocker lever is best done with two pairs of hands. The diaphragm spring needs depressing sufficiently to introduce the end of the lever, and the lever in turn has to be positioned with its own return spring compressed. The pin is then installed. If another pair of hands is not available tie the diaphragm spring in the compressed position with a piece of string around the body, but do not put the string over the diaphragm.
4 Refit the inlet/outlet valve carefully ensuring that the groove registers in the housing and that the fine edge of the inlet valve seats evenly.
5 Place the upper body over the lower, lining up the screw holes with each other and the diaphragm, and replace the three short screws, holding the diaphragm flat by depressing the rocker lever. Do not tighten the short screws.
6 Refit the filter, sealing washer and outlet cover and the three long screws. Then tighten all six screws evenly.
7 To test the pump is functioning correctly, hold a finger over the inlet nozzle and operate the rocker lever through three full strokes, when suction should be heard and felt. Similarly for the outlet nozzle, one stroke of the rocker lever should give maintained pressure for 15 seconds. Never use compressed air for blowing through the pump as it is usually at a pressure far greater than the pump is designed to withstand.

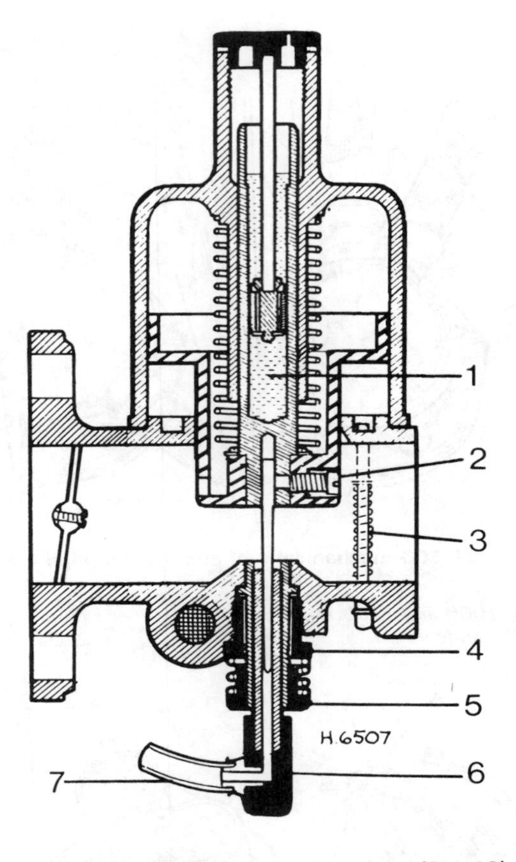

Fig. 3.9 Sectional view of carburettor (Sec 13)

1 Piston damper oil well
2 Needle securing screw
3 Piston lifting pin
4 Jet locking nut
5 Jet adjusting nut
6 Jet head
7 Fuel feed pipe

13 SU carburettor – general description

The variable choke SU carburettor is a relatively simple instrument and is basically the same irrespective of its size and type. It differs from most other carburettors in that, instead of having a number of various sized fixed jets for different conditions, only one variable jet is fitted to deal with all possible conditions.

The carburettor comprises four main assemblies; these are the carburettor body, the piston and dashpot assembly, the jet assembly and the float chamber. Fuel is carried from the float chamber to the base of the jet head by a nylon pipe, the float chamber being secured to the carburettor body by a horizontally positioned bolt and spacing washer.

The operation of the carburettor is as follows. Air passing rapidly through the carburettor creates a slight vacuum or depression over the jet, causing fuel to be drawn into the air stream, thus forming the fuel/air mixture. The amount of fuel drawn from the jet depends on the position of the tapered carburettor needle. This moves up or down the jet orifice according to engine load or throttle opening, thus effectively altering the size of the jet. This allows the right amount of fuel to be delivered for the prevailing road conditions.

The position of the tapered needle in the jet is determined by engine vacuum. The shank of the needle is held at its top end in a piston, which slides up and down the dashpot, in response to the degree of manifold vacuum. This is directly controlled by the throttle. The piston is necessary so that the depression over the jet needed to draw fuel into the air stream, can be kept approximately constant. At slow engine speeds, the air entering the carburettor would not be travelling fast enough to create sufficient vacuum to draw fuel from the jet. By allowing the piston to partially restrict the opening through the carburettor, the incoming air is speeded up, causing an adequate depression over the jet.

With the throttle fully open, the full effect of inlet manifold vacuum is felt by the piston, which has an air bleed into the carburettor venturi on the outside of the throttle. This causes the piston to rise fully, bringing the needle with it. With the throttle partially closed, only slight inlet manifold vacuum is felt by the piston (although on the engine side of the throttle, the vacuum is now greater), and the piston only rises slightly.

To prevent piston flutter, and to give a richer mixture when the accelerator is suddenly depressed, an oil damper and light spring are located inside the dashpot.

For cold starting, when fuel enrichment is necessary and very small amounts of air are drawn into the carburettor, actuation of the choke control causes the jet head to be lowered, thus effectively increasing the jet size.

The only portion of the piston assembly to come into contact with the piston chamber or dashpot is the actual central piston rod. All the other parts of the piston assembly, including the lower choke portion, have sufficient clearances to prevent any direct metal-to-metal contact, which is essential if the carburettor is to work properly.

The correct level of the petrol in the carburettor is determined by the level of the float in the float chamber. When the level is correct, the float rises, and by means of a lever resting on top of it, closes the needle valve in the cover of the float chamber. This closes off the supply of fuel from the pump. When the level in the float chamber drops, as fuel is used in the carburettor, the float sinks. As it does, the float needle comes away from its seat so allowing more fuel to enter the float chamber and restoring the correct level.

14 SU carburettor – removal and refitting

1 Remove the air cleaner from the carburettor as described in Section 2.
2 Disconnect the distributor vacuum advance pipe from the carburettor (where fitted).
3 Slacken the retaining clip screw and withdraw the fuel inlet pipe from the top of the float chamber. Plug the disconnected pipe with a bolt or metal rod of suitable diameter.
4 Disconnect the choke and accelerator cables from the carburettor linkages. Take care not to lose the small solderless nipple that retains the choke cable (photo).
5 Detach the throttle return spring from the bracket on the exhaust manifold clamp. On Cooper S models detach the throttle and throttle linkage return springs from the heat shield. On automatic transmission models detach the governor control rod fork end from the throttle lever.
6 Detach the engine breather hose from the carburettor (where fitted).
7 Undo and remove the two nuts which secure the carburettor(s) to the inlet manifold studs and recover the spring washers.
8 Lift the carburettor carefully off the inlet manifold (photo). If twin carburettors are being removed, lift off both carburettors together to avoid damaging the linkages that join the two carburettor spindles. These can be removed after the carburettors are lifted clear of the manifold studs.
9 Refitting the carburettor(s) is the reverse sequence to removal. Use new gaskets if necessary after ensuring that all traces of the old gasket are removed.
10 When refitting twin carburettors, ensure that the linkages joining the two spindles are in position, and that the operating forks are engaged in the slots on the carburettor spindles.

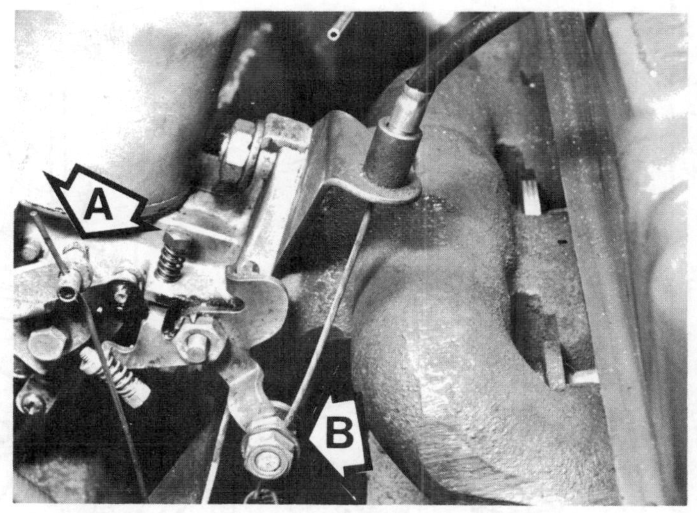

14.4 Choke cable (A) and accelerator cable (B) attachments at the carburettor linkage (early type)

14.8 Removing the carburettor from the manifold (early type)

15 SU carburettor – dismantling

1 The SU carburettor is a straightforward unit to dismantle and service, but at the same time it is a delicate unit and clumsy handling can cause damage. In particular, it is easy to knock the finely tapering needle out of true, and the greatest care should be taken to keep all the parts associated with the dashpot in a safe place and scrupulously clean. Prepare a clean and uncluttered working area before starting the dismantling, and have some small containers handy to store the small, easily-lost parts.
2 Begin by removing the carburettor(s) from the car as described in Section 14. Thoroughly clean the outside of the carburettor in petrol or paraffin and wipe dry with a non-fluffy cloth.
3 Unscrew the piston damper assembly and remove it from the top of the dashpot.
4 Mark the base of the dashpot and carburettor body to ensure that on reassembly the dashpot is refitted in the same position. Now undo and remove the securing screws and lift off the dashpot.
5 Next lift off the piston spring and then carefully withdraw the piston and needle assembly from the carburettor body. Undo the small sunken retaining screw in the side of the piston and lift out the needle. On later types equipped with a spring-loaded needle, recover the guide collar from the needle, and the spring from the piston, after removing the needle assembly.
6 Undo and remove the three retaining screws and lift off the float chamber cover and gasket. The float may be released from the cover by gently tapping out the float hinge pin. The fuel cut-off needle valve can now be withdrawn from its seat in the cover and the needle seat unscrewed if required.
7 Unscrew the union nut securing the nylon fuel pipe to the base of the float chamber and carefully withdraw the pipe. Note the position of the gland, ferrule and rubber sealing washer on the end of the pipe and make sure that the rubber washer has not been left behind in the float chamber as the pipe is withdrawn. If so, hook it out carefully with a small screwdriver.
8 If there is a tamperproof cap in position around the jet adjusting nut at the base of the carburettor, prise it apart with a screwdriver and discard it.
9 Release the jet link lever return spring from the cam lever on the linkage.

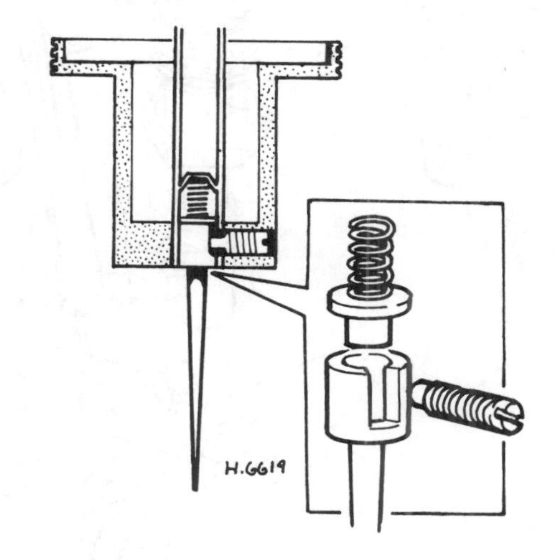

Fig. 3.10 The spring-loaded needle assembly fitted to the later SU HS4 carburettors (Sec 15)

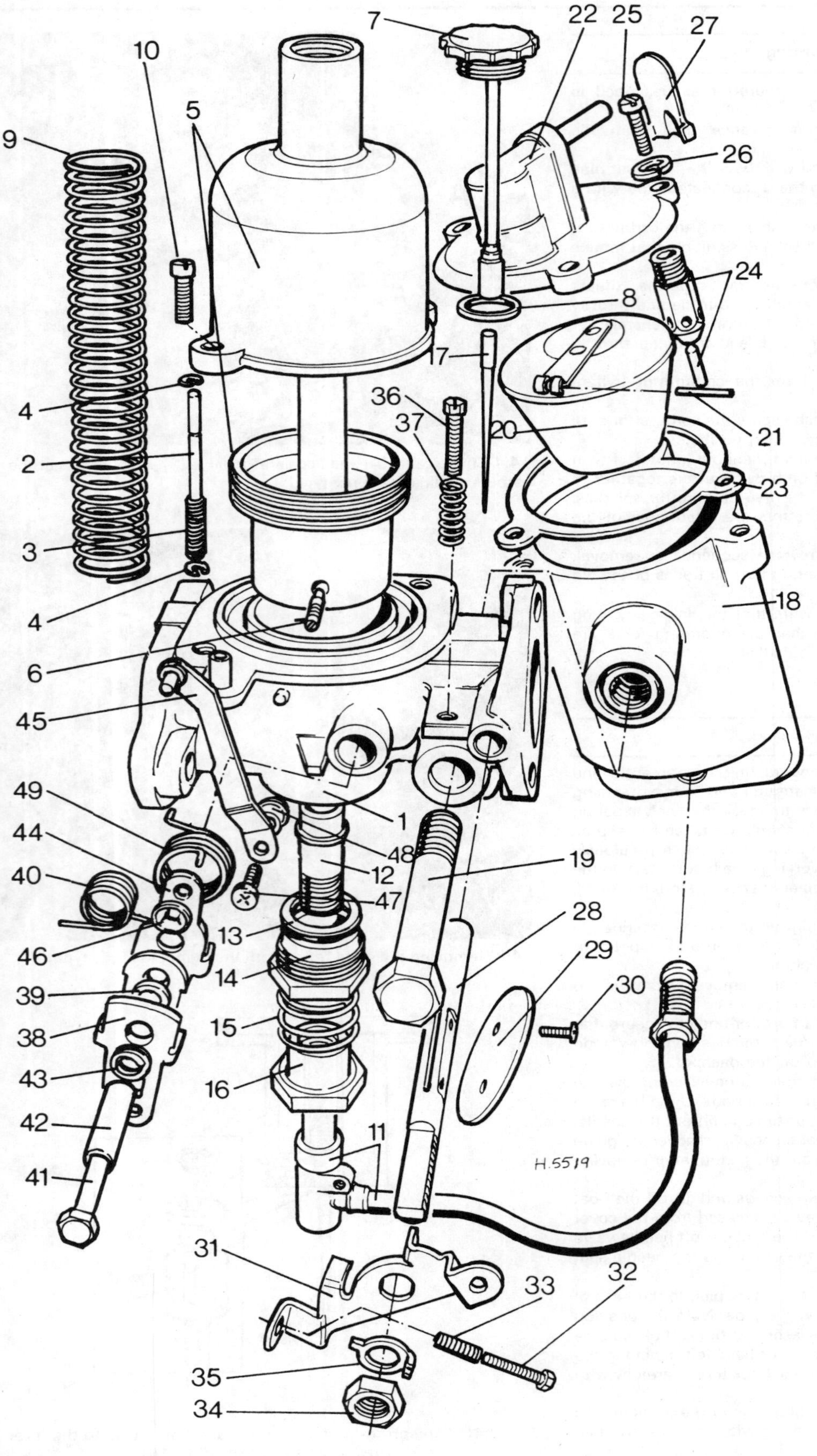

Fig. 3.11 Exploded view of the SU HS2 carburettor fitted to early manual transmission models (Sec 15)

1 *Body*
2 *Piston lifting pin*
3 *Spring*
4 *Circlip*
5 *Dashpot and piston assembly*
6 *Needle locking screw*
7 *Piston damper assembly*
8 *Washer for damper cap*
9 *Piston spring*
10 *Screw*
11 *Jet assembly*
12 *Jet bearing*
13 *Washer*
14 *Locknut for jet bearing*
15 *Lock spring*
16 *Jet adjusting nut*
17 *Jet needle*
18 *Float chamber body*
19 *Bolt*
20 *Float and lever assembly*
21 *Lever hinge pin*
22 *Float chamber lid assembly*
23 *Gasket*
24 *Needle and seat assembly*
25 *Screw*
26 *Spring washer*
27 *Baffle*
28 *Throttle spindle*
29 *Throttle disc*
30 *Screw*
31 *Throttle lever*
32 *Cam stop screw*
33 *Spring for stop screw*
34 *Throttle spindle nut*
35 *Tab washer*
36 *Idling stop screw*
37 *Spring for stop screw*
38 *Cam lever*
39 *Washer*
40 *Cam lever spring*
41 *Cam lever pivot bolt*
42 *Pivot bolt tube*
43 *Spring washer*
44 *Pick-up lever assembly*
45 *Jet link*
46 *Jet link retaining clip*
47 *Jet link securing screw*
48 *Bush*
49 *Spring for pick-up lever*

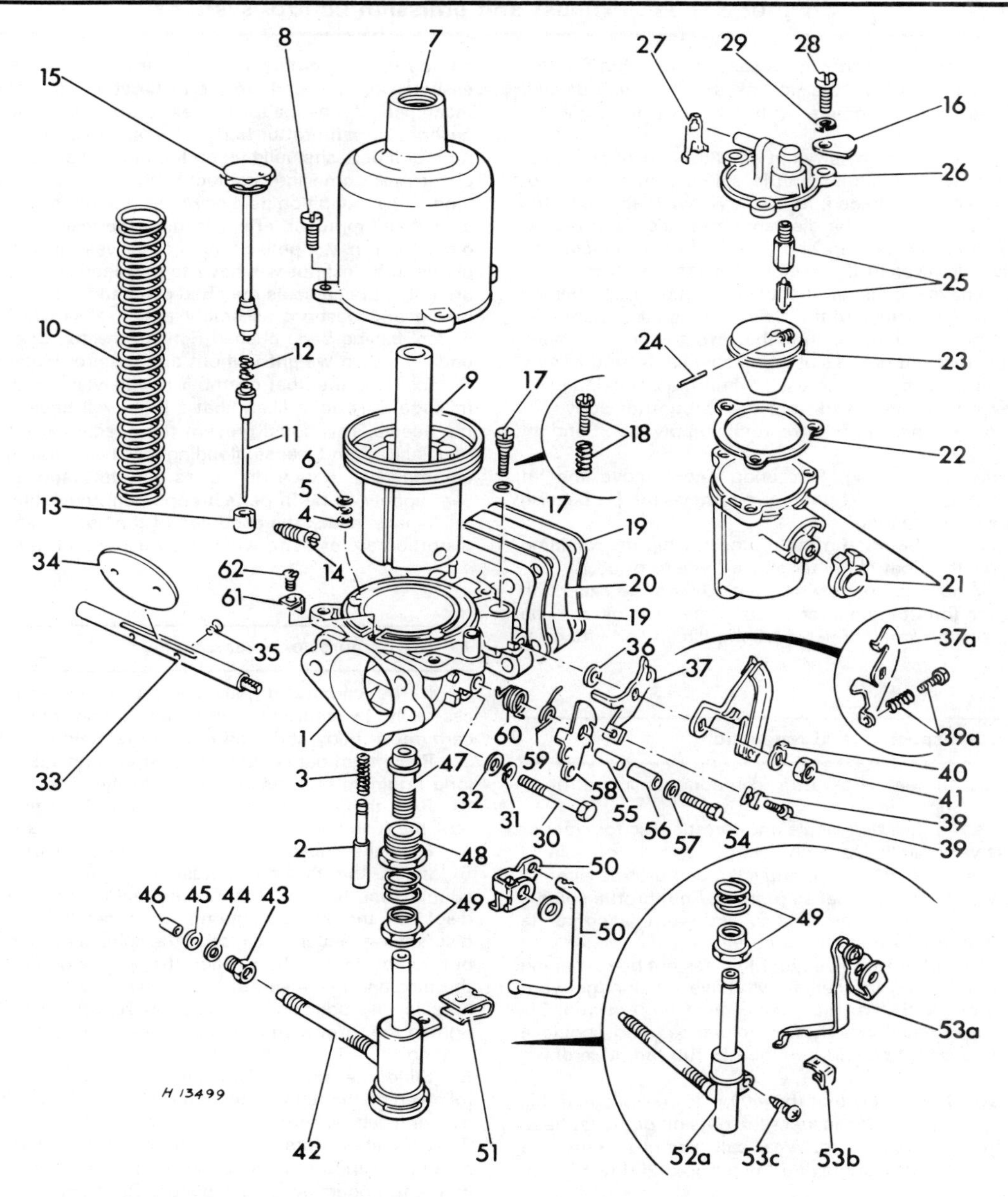

Fig. 3.12 Exploded view of the SU HS4 carburettor fitted to automatic transmission and later manual transmission models (Sec 15)

1 Body
2 Piston lifting pin
3 Spring
4 Sealing washer
5 Plain washer
6 Circlip
7 Dashpot
8 Screw
9 Piston
10 Spring
11 Needle
12 Needle tension spring
13 Needle guide collar
14 Locking screw
15 Piston damper
16 Identification tag
*17 Throttle adjusting screw and O-ring**
18 Throttle adjusting screw and spring
19 Gaskets
20 Insulator block
21 Float chamber and spacer
22 Gasket
23 Float
24 Hinge pin
25 Needle and seat
26 Float chamber cover
27 Baffle plate
28 Screw
29 Spring washer
30 Bolt
31 Spring washer
32 Plain washer
33 Throttle spindle
34 Throttle disc
35 Screw
36 Washer
*37 Throttle return lever**
37a Throttle return lever
38 Progressive throttle (snail cam)
*39 Fast idle screw**
39a Fast idle screw and spring
40 Lockwasher
41 Nut
42 Jet assembly – Capstat type
43 Sleeve nut
44 Washer
45 Gland
46 Ferrule
47 Jet bearing
48 Jet locating nut
49 Jet adjustment nut and spring
50 Rod link and pick-up lever
51 Spring clip
52a Jet assembly
53a Pick-up lever
53b Link
53c Screw
(52a–53c: non-Capstat type)
54 Pivot bolt
55 Pivot bolt tube – inner
56 Pivot bolt tube – outer
57 Distance washer
58 Cam lever
59 Cam lever spring
60 Pick-up lever spring
61 Piston guide
62 Screw
**Used with sealed adjustment carburettors*

10 Undo and remove the small screw or release the clip that secures the jet link arm to the jet. Move the jet link arm to one side and withdraw the jet assembly, complete with fuel pipe from the jet housing.
11 It is not normally necessary to carry out any further dismantling of the SU carburettor. However, if the throttle spindle, jet housing, or float chamber are worn, damaged, or in any way suspect, the remainder of the carburettor may be dismantled as described below.
12 Bend back the small tab washer and then undo and remove the nut securing the throttle lever to the spindle. Lift off the lever.
13 Straighten the splayed ends of the two throttle disc retaining screws and then mark the position of the disc in relation to the spindle. Undo and remove the two screws, turn the disc to the fully open position and slide the disc out of the slot in the spindle. Note that new throttle disc retaining screws must be used when reassembling.
14 The spindle can now be removed from the carburettor body.
15 To remove the choke linkage undo the retaining pivot bolt and lift it off complete with linkage.
16 To dismantle the jet housing, first undo and remove the jet adjusting nut and lock spring. Next undo and remove the jet bearing locknut and withdraw the bearing.
17 The float chamber can be lifted off after unscrewing the retaining through-bolt. Recover the float chamber spacer, where fitted.
18 The carburettor is now completely dismantled with the exception of the piston lifting pin (omitted on later carburettors). The pin may be removed by prising off the small upper retaining circlip and lifting off the pin and spring.

16 SU carburettor – inspection and renovation

1 Thoroughly clean all the carburettor components in petrol or paraffin and dry with a lint-free cloth.
2 Carefully examine the throttle spindle and throttle disc for wear or distortion. If excessive wear is apparent on the spindle or spindle bushes in the carburettor body, air will enter the carburettor, altering the mixture strength and causing uneven running. The throttle spindle is obtainable separately, but if the bushes are worn, a complete carburettor body will normally have to be obtained.
3 Closely inspect the carburettor needle. If this has not been running centrally in the jet orifice then the needle will have a tiny ridge worn on it. If a ridge can be seen then the needle must be renewed. SU carburettor needles are made to very fine tolerances and should a ridge be apparent no attempt should be made to rub the ridge down with emery paper.
4 If the needle is worn, it is likely that the jet will also be worn. If this is the case, also renew the jet. Also inspect the outside of the jet head where it bears against the jet bearing. Wear can take place here due to the action of the choke control moving the jet up and down in the jet bearing.
5 The most critical components of the SU carburettor are the piston and dashpot assembly. Free movement of the piston in the dashpot is essential for the carburettor to function satisfactorily. The piston is machined to very fine tolerances so that it will not touch the side of the dashpot or carburettor body. If wear takes place on the centre guide tube or if deposits build up on the internal surfaces of the dashpot, the piston will come into contact with the side of the dashpot and will bind. This condition is known as piston sticking. If this condition cannot be improved after cleaning the inside of the dashpot and the piston with metal polish (harsh abrasives must not be used), then the piston and dashpot will have to be renewed. These two components are only obtainable as matched pairs and cannot be interchanged. The piston and dashpot assembly are in a satisfactory condition if the piston, having been pushed right to the top of the dashpot, will drop under its own weight without any trace of binding.
6 Examine the float chamber needle valve and seat next. After high mileage, it is quite likely that a ridge will have formed on the face of the needle. This could prevent the needle valve from shutting off the fuel supply and cause flooding of the carburettor. This is quite a common occurrence on SU carburettors and unless the needle and seat appear to be in perfect condition, they should both be renewed.
7 Finally, check the condition of the float. If any signs of cracking or distortion are evident, which may allow fuel to enter, renew the float.

17 SU carburettor – reassembly

1 If the carburettor has been completely dismantled, begin re-assembly by refitting the piston lifting pin and spring into the carburettor body and then refit the retaining circlip.
2 Place the float chamber in position and secure it in place, with the long retaining bolt inserted through the side of the carburettor body.
3 Refit the jet bearing, washer and locknut finger-tight only. Do not refit the lock spring or jet adjusting nut at this stage.
4 Refit the choke linkage and retaining pivot bolt.
5 Insert the throttle spindle into the carburettor body with the countersunk holes in the spindle facing outwards. Insert the throttle disc into the spindle, noting the assembly markings made during dismantling. Secure the disc to the spindle using new retaining screws, but do not tighten them. Snap the spindle open and shut to centralise the disc and make sure that the disc does not bind in the carburettor bore in any position. If necessary reposition the disc slightly. Now tighten the screws and spread their ends enough to prevent them from turning.
6 Slide the spacing washer and throttle lever onto the spindle, followed by the tab washer and retaining nut. Tighten the nut and bend over the tab washer.
7 On carburettors with a fixed jet needle, insert the needle into the piston, ensuring that the shoulder on the shank of the needle is flush with the underside of the piston. Refit and fully tighten the sunken retaining screw (photos).

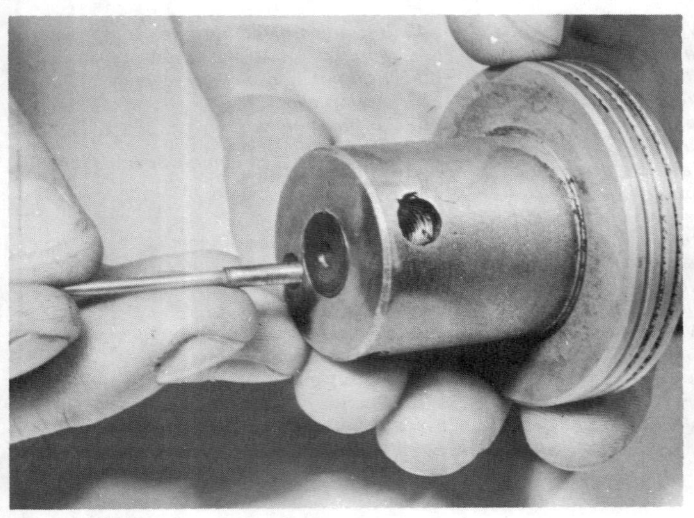

17.7a Refit the jet needle to the piston...

17.7b ...and secure with the retaining screw

8 On carburettors equipped with a spring-loaded needle, fit the spring and guide collar to the needle and insert this assembly into the piston. Position the guide collar so that it is flush with the underside of the piston and position the needle so that the small etch mark is between the two piston transfer holes. Secure the assembly with the sunken retaining screw.

9 If the jet housing has been removed, it will now be necessary to centralise the jet as follows.

10 With the jet bearing, washer and locknut in position as described in paragraph 3, refit the jet adjusting nut, without the lock spring, and screw it up as far as it will go. Now slide the jet assembly into the jet housing.

11 Carefully refit the piston and needle assembly to the carburettor body, followed by the spring and dashpot (photos). Align the previously made marks on the dashpot and carburettor body and then refit the securing screws.

12 Slacken the jet bearing locknut and hold the piston down using a pencil inserted through the damper opening. Now tighten the jet bearing locknut.

13 Lift the piston and allow it to fall under its own weight. A definite metallic click should be heard, as the piston falls and contacts the bridge in the carburettor body.

14 Now fully lower the adjusting nut and note whether the piston still falls freely. If not, slacken the jet bearing locknut and repeat the centering procedure. It may be necessary to carry out the centering operation several times, until the piston will fall freely with the adjusting nut at the top and bottom of its travel.

15 With the jet correctly centralised, slide out the jet assembly and unscrew the adjusting nut. Now place the lock spring in position and refit the adjusting nut and jet assembly (photo). Secure the jet link arm to the jet with the screw or retaining clip (photo).

16 The flexible jet fuel supply tube can now be refitted to the base of the float chamber. Ensure that the small rubber sealing washer, nut and gland are in position on the tube and that there is at least 0.18 in (5.0 mm) of pipe protruding through the washer. Push the tube into the float chamber and tighten the union nut (photo).

17 Refit the fuel cut-off needle and seat to the float chamber cover. Place the float in position and tap in the float hinge pin until equal

17.11a Refit the piston and needle assembly...

17.11b ...followed by the spring...

17.11c ...and dashpot

17.15a Refit the jet assembly...

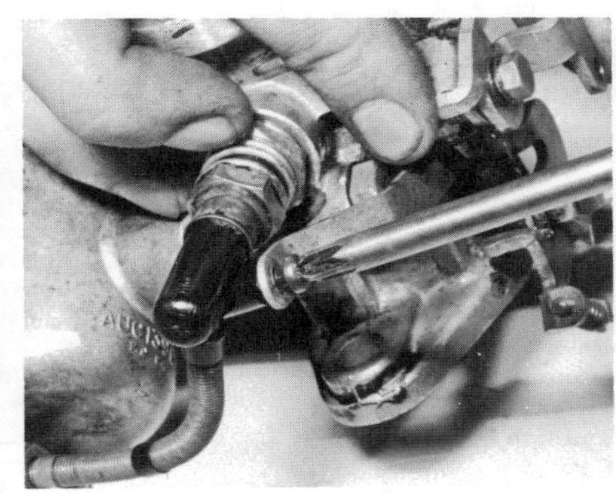

17.15b ...and connect the jet link arm

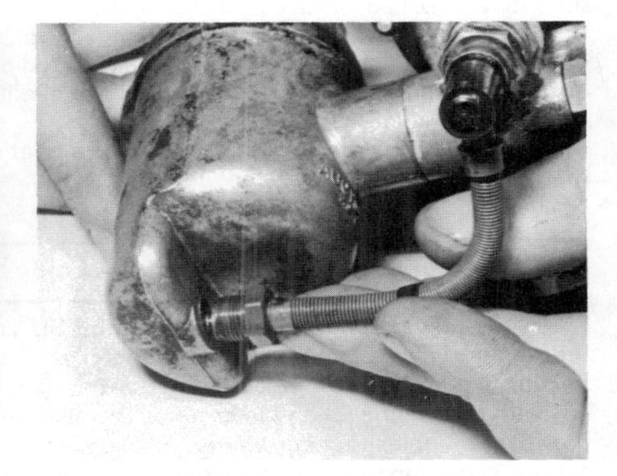

17.16 The other end of the feed tube is screwed into the float chamber

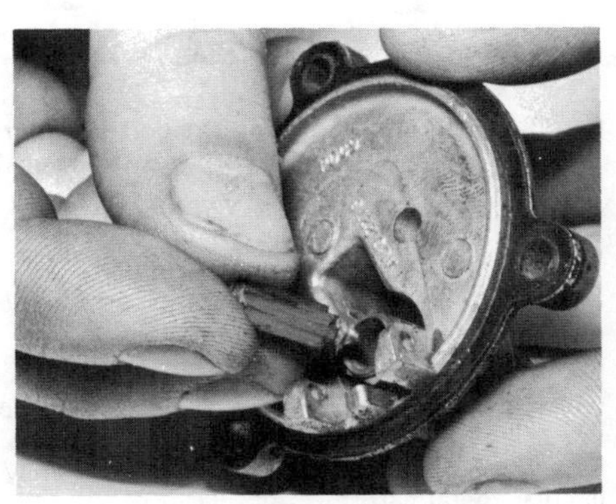

17.17a With the needle valve in place...

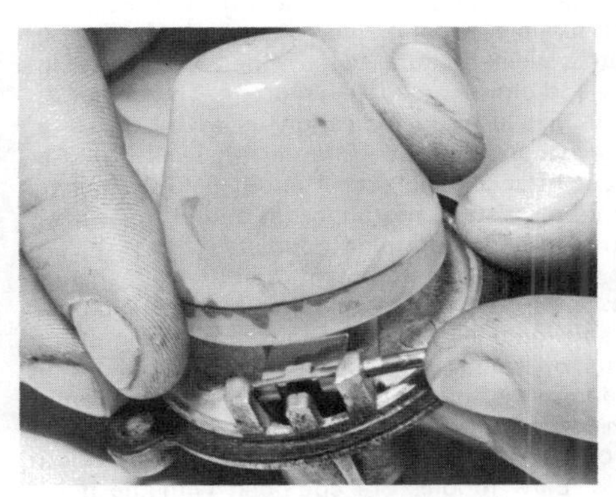

17.17b ...refit the float and hinge pin

amounts of the pin are protruding either side of the mounting lugs (photos).

18 Place a new gasket in position on the float chamber, refit the cover and secure it with the three retaining screws (photo).

19 Fill the carburettor piston damper with the correct grade of oil, until the level is 0.5 in (12.7 mm) above the top of the hollow piston rod. Now refit the damper plunger.

20 To obtain an initial jet setting and to allow the engine to be started, screw the jet adjusting nut up until the jet is flush with the bridge in the carburettor body. Now screw the nut down two complete turns on non-sealed carburettors and three complete turns on sealed units. **Note:** *The sealed type carburettors are identified by the throttle adjusting screw which is recessed within the carburettor body.*

21 The carburettor can now be refitted to the car as described in Section 14 and the slow running and mixture adjustments carried out as described in Section 19.

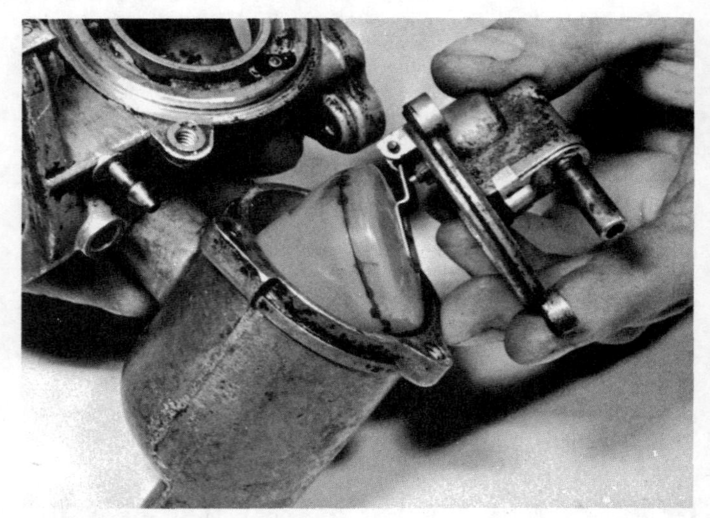

17.18 Refitting the float chamber cover

18 SU carburettor – float level adjustment

1 Refer to Section 2 and remove the air cleaner assembly.

2 Slacken the retaining clip screw and detach the fuel inlet pipe from the float chamber. Plug the pipe after removal.

3 Undo and remove the three securing screws and lift off the float chamber cover and gasket.

4 On early carburettors equipped with a brass float, invert the float chamber cover so that the needle valve is closed. It should now just be possible to place a $\frac{5}{16}$ in (8 mm) diameter bar parallel to the float hinge pin and in the centre of the float chamber cover, without fouling the float. If the bar lifts the float or if the float stands clear of the bar, bend the float lever very slightly until the clearance is correct.

5 Later carburettors fitted with plastic floats incorporate either a plain steel needle or a spring-loaded needle enclosed in a plastic sheath. The adjustment procedure for the plain steel needle type is the same as described in paragraph 4. Float level adjustment for spring-loaded needles is as follows.

6 Invert the float chamber cover so that the needle valve is closed but the spring is not compressed. The gap between the float and the flange on the float chamber cover, at the centre of the cover, should be between 0.125 in (3.18 mm) and 0.187 in (4.76 mm). If the gap is incorrect, bend the float lever slightly until the specified gap is obtained. In the case of floats having a moulded plastic hinge, increase or decrease the washer thickness under the needle seat to achieve the desired float level height.

7 When the float level is correct, refit the float chamber cover using the reverse sequence to removal.

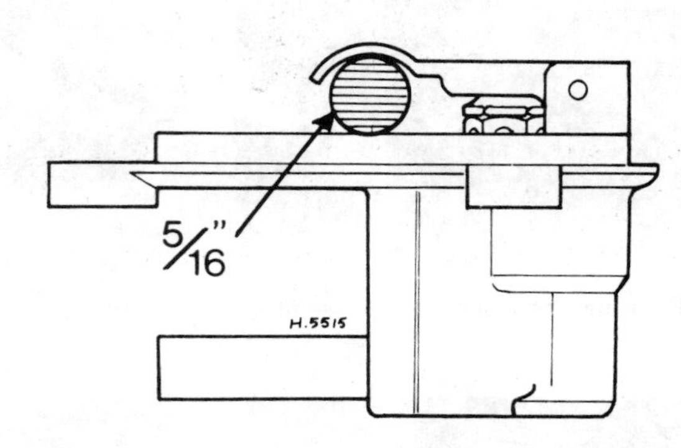

Fig. 3.13 Method of setting the correct clearance of the float lever – early carburettors (Sec 18)

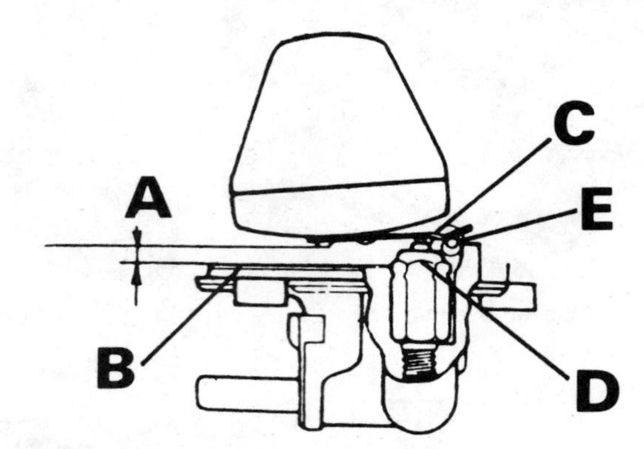

Fig. 3.14 Method of setting the correct clearance of the float lever – later carburettors (Sec 18)

A 0.125 to 0.187 in (3.18 to 4.76 mm)
B Machined lip
C Float lever adjustment point
D Float needle and seat assembly
E Lever hinge pin

19 SU carburettor – adjustments

Three adjustments are possible on the SU carburettor. These are the engine idling speed, fast idling speed and mixture strength. The mixture strength is particularly important as the initial setting, carried out with the engine idling, determines the mixture strength throughout the entire engine speed range. A good indication as to whether carburettor adjustment is necessary can be gained by checking the colour of the exhaust tailpipe and listening to the note of the exhaust at idling speed. If the tailpipe is black and the engine appears to be hunting, it is quite likely that the mixture is too rich. If the exhaust is light grey or white in appearance, accompanied by a rhythmic puffing sound, this would indicate a weak mixture. Ideally, the exhaust should be a medium grey colour and emit a steady even drone. The colour of the spark plugs will also give a good indication as to the mixture strength and general engine condition (see Chapter 4). These checks should only be carried out after a good run of about 5 to 10 miles. Idling in city traffic and stop/start motoring is bound to cause excessively dark exhaust pipe and spark plug deposits.

Before carrying out any adjustments to the carburettor, ensure that the ignition system is in good condition, that the spark plugs, contact breaker points and ignition timing settings are correct, and that the engine is at normal operating temperature. Check also that the carburettor dashpot oil damper is topped up to the correct level with the specified grade of oil.

Depending on year of manufacture either a sealed or non-sealed carburettor may be fitted. Early models are equipped with the non-sealed type, identified by the throttle and fast idle adjusting screws which are clearly visible and retained by a tension spring or locknut. On the sealed carburettors the throttle adjusting screw is located in a recessed hole in the carburettor body and may be covered by a small circular metal cap.

Carburettor adjustment is carried out as follows, according to type.

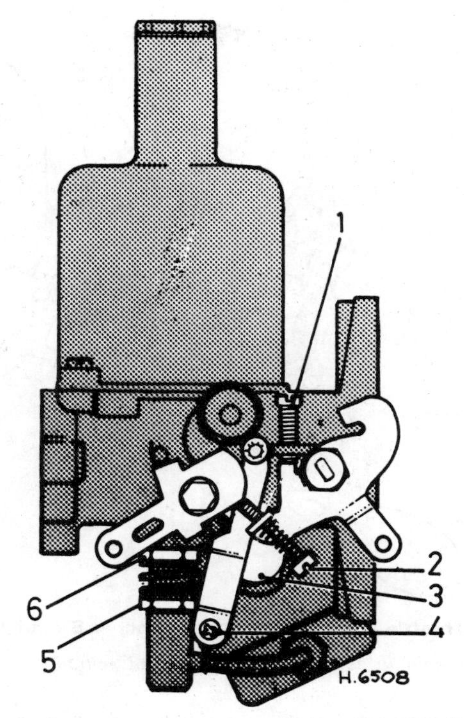

Fig. 3.15 Carburettor adjustment points – SU HS2 (Sec 19)

1 Throttle adjusting screw
2 Fast idle adjusting screw
3 Float chamber bolt
4 Jet link securing screw
5 Jet adjusting nut
6 Jet locknut

Fig. 3.16 Carburettor adjustment points – SU HS4 (Sec 19)

1 Fast idle adjusting screw
2 Jet adjusting nut
3 Governor control rod (automatic transmission)
4 Throttle adjusting screw

Single carburettor installations – non-sealed type

1 Remove the air cleaner as described in Section 2.

2 Set the engine idling speed by turning the throttle adjusting screw until the specified idling speed is obtained. **Note:** *If the throttle adjusting screw is secured by a locknut, slacken the locknut before turning the adjusting screw and leave it slackened until all the carburettor adjustments have been completed.*

3 To check the mixture strength, press the piston lifting pin on the side of the carburettor upwards, against light spring resistance, until it comes into contact with the piston. Now press it up a further $\frac{1}{32}$ in (1 mm) and listen to the engine speed. This will indicate one of the following:

(a) If the speed of the engine increases appreciably, the mixture is too rich
(b) If the engine speed immediately decreases or the engine stalls, the mixture is too weak
(c) If the engine speed remains constant or increases very slightly, the mixture is correct

4 To enrich the mixture, rotate the jet adjusting nut located at the base of the carburettor in an anti-clockwise direction viewed from below, ie downwards. To weaken the mixture, rotate the jet adjusting nut clockwise viewed from below, ie upwards, while at the same time pushing the jet assembly upwards against the nut. When altering the mixture strength, only turn the nut one flat at a time and check the mixture with the lifting pin each time.

5 It is quite likely that there will be a slight increase or decrease in engine rpm, after the mixture adjustment has been made. This should be corrected by turning the throttle adjusting screw, until the specified idling speed is again obtained.

6 With the engine idling at the specified speed and the mixture correctly adjusted, check the fast idle adjustment as follows.

7 Rotate the choke linkage on the side of the carburettor, to the point where the linkage just starts to lower the jet. Hold the linkage in this position and rotate the fast idle adjustment screw, until the specified engine fast idle speed is obtained.

8 When all adjustments are complete, refit the air cleaner and road test the car, carrying out any small adjustments that may be necessary, on the road.

Single carburettor installations – sealed type

9 Remove the air cleaner as described in Section 2.

10 If the tamperproof seals are still in position over the throttle adjusting screw and mixture adjusting nut, remove and discard them. The seal over the throttle adjusting screw can be hooked out of the recess using a small screwdriver. The seal on the jet adjusting nut can be removed by prising it open with a screwdriver and then lifting away the two halves.

11 Connect a tachometer to the engine (if one is not already fitted to the car), following the manufacturer's instructions. If your ears can attune to slight changes in engine rpm or to alterations of the exhaust note, then it is possible to carry out the adjustments without the use of a tachometer.

12 Set the engine idling speed, by turning the throttle adjusting screw until the specified idling speed is obtained.

13 Turn the jet adjusting nut located at the base of the carburettor in a clockwise or anti-clockwise direction, one flat at a time, until the fastest possible engine speed consistent with even running is obtained. Turning the nut clockwise viewed from below ie upward, weakens the mixture. Turning the nut anti-clockwise viewed from below, ie downward, enriches the mixture.

14 It is quite likely that there will be a slight increase or decrease in engine rpm after the mixture adjustment has been made. This should be corrected by turning the throttle adjusting screw until the specified idling speed is again obtained.

15 The remainder of the adjustment procedure is the same as described previously for non-sealed carburettors in paragraphs 6, 7 and 8.

Twin carburettor installations

16 Before adjusting the mixture strength on models fitted with twin carburettors, it is necessary to ensure that the volume of air passing through each carburettor is the same. This is done as follows.

17 Begin by removing the air cleaner assembly as described in Section 2.

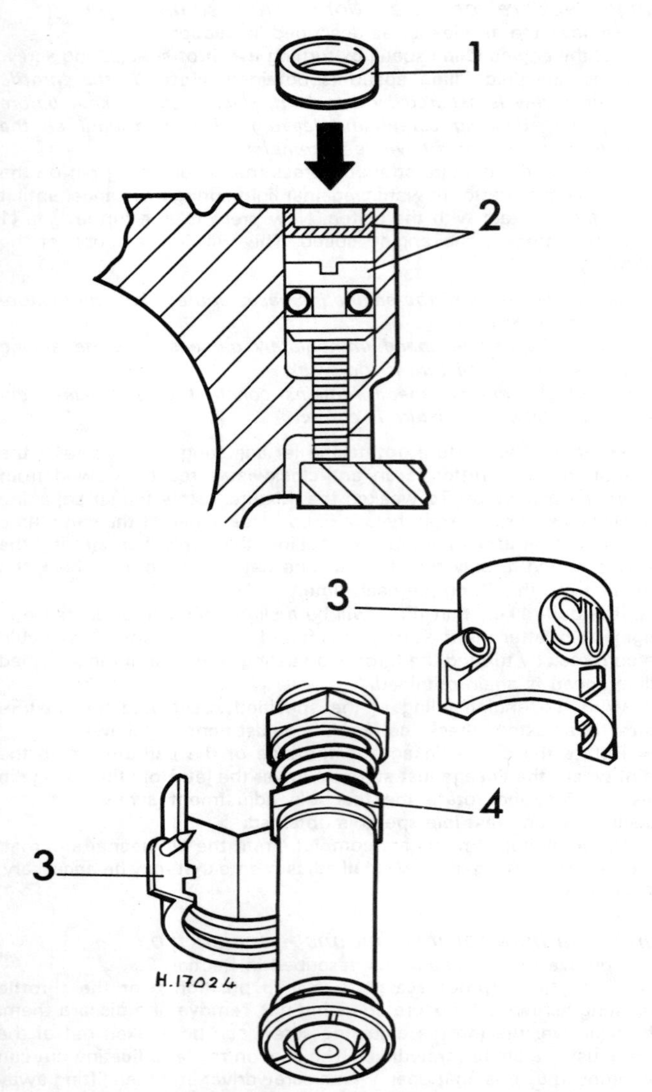

Fig. 3.17 The tamperproof caps fitted to the later type sealed carburettors (Sec 19)

1 *Throttle adjusting screw cap*
2 *Throttle adjusting screw showing cap in position*
3 *Jet adjusting nut seals*
4 *Jet adjusting nut*

18 Slacken the two clamp bolts on the throttle spindle operating arms and the two clamp bolts on the choke spindle operating arms.
19 Start the engine without depressing the accelerator and allow it to idle.
20 Using a proprietary balancing meter, in accordance with the manufacturer's instructions, balance the carburettor by altering the throttle adjusting screws until the airflow through both carburettors is the same.
21 Alternatively, use a length of small bore tubing, such as heater hose, approximately 18 in (457 mm) long, to compare the intensity of the intake hiss on both carburettors. Turn the throttle adjusting screws until the hiss sounds the same in both carburettors. It should be noted that this method is not really recommended, as it tends to be somewhat less accurate, and certainly more difficult, than using a balancing meter.
22 When the two carburettors are balanced, bring the engine idling speed back to the specified rpm by turning both throttle adjusting screws by equal amounts.

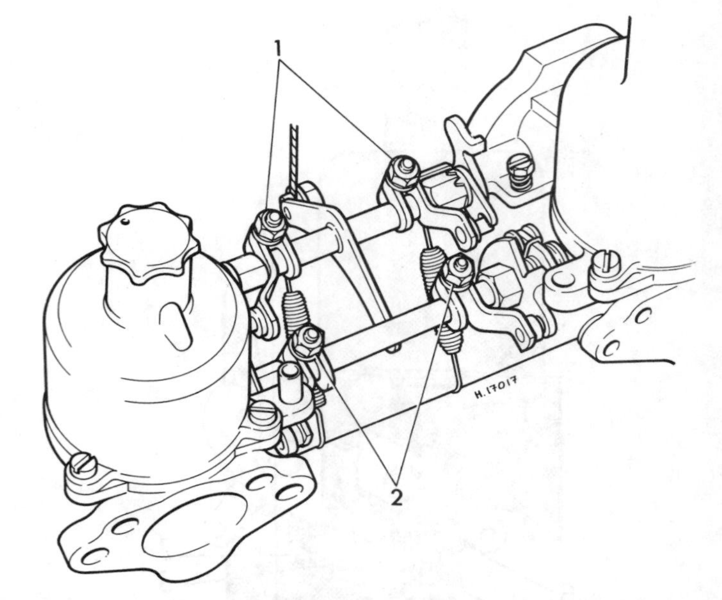

Fig. 3.18 Throttle and choke linkage – Cooper S models (Sec 19)

1 *Throttle spindle operating arms*
2 *Choke spindle operating arms*

23 Now tighten the two clamp bolts, on the throttle spindle operating arms, making sure that a slight clearance exists between the peg and the lower edge of the fork. Ensure also that the arms are positioned in such a way that both carburettor throttles open at the same time, when the accelerator pedal is depressed. If necessary, reposition one of the arms slightly to achieve this condition.
24 Now adjust the mixture strength for each carburettor using the procedure described in paragraphs 3 and 4.
25 If the idling speed requires adjustment after setting the mixture, turn both throttle adjusting screws by an equal amount in the desired direction.
26 The choke spindle operating arms can now be positioned and tightened using the method described previously for the throttle operating arms.
27 Finally, adjust the fast idle speed as follows.
28 Pull out the choke control knob or operate the linkage by hand, until the linkage just starts to lower the jet. Hold the linkage in this position and turn the fast idle adjusting screws, on both carburettors, until the specified fast idle speed is obtained and both carburettors are passing the same volume of air.
29 Adjustment of the carburettors is now complete. Refit the air cleaner and carry out a thorough road test.

20 Inlet manifold – removal and refitting

Note: *On vehicles fitted with emission control equipment it will be necessary to remove certain additional fittings, hoses and brackets to provide access to the inlet manifold. The items requiring removal will be obvious after a visual inspection, and full information regarding their removal will be found in the emission control Sections at the end of this Chapter.*

1 Refer to Section 14 and remove the carburettor(s) from the inlet manifold.
2 On models fitted with a brake servo, slacken the retaining clip screw and remove the vacuum hose from the union on the inlet manifold.
3 If working on Cooper S models, undo and remove the nuts, large flat washers and spring washers securing the manifold to the cylinder head. Lift off the manifold. On all other models proceed as follows.
4 Jack up the front of the car and support it on axle stands.
5 From underneath the car, undo and remove the nut and bolt securing the exhaust front pipe support strap to the gearbox bracket.

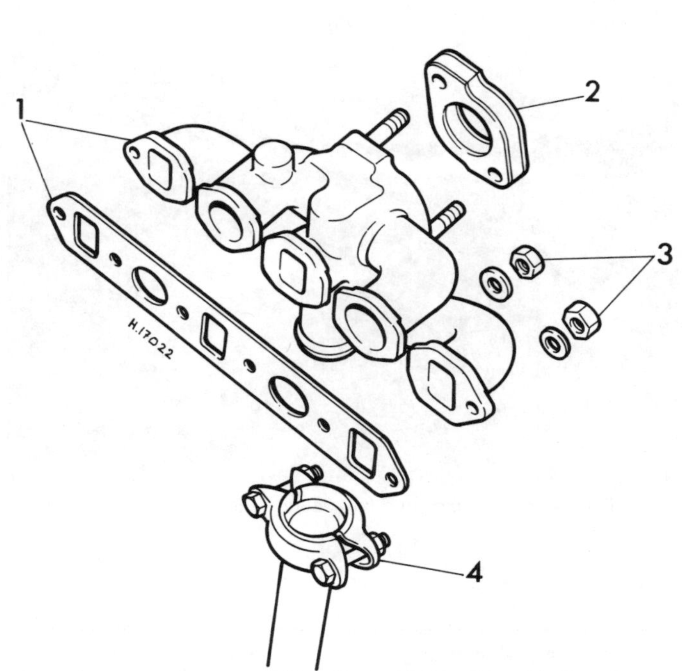

Fig. 3.19 Inlet and exhaust manifold assembly (Sec 20)

1 *Manifold and gasket*
2 *Carburettor insulating block*
3 *Retaining nuts*
4 *Manifold-to-front pipe clamp*

6 Undo and remove the two bolts and nuts securing the two halves of the exhaust manifold clamp to the front pipe. Lift away the clamp assembly.
7 Undo and remove the six nuts and flat washers securing the manifold to the cylinder head.
8 Lift off the hot air shroud, where fitted, and then slide the inlet and exhaust manifold assembly off the studs and withdraw it from the engine. Recover the manifold gasket.
9 Refitting is the reverse sequence to removal bearing in mind the following points:

(a) *Ensure that the mating surfaces of the manifold and cylinder head are clean, and use a new gasket*
(b) *Refit the exhaust manifold-to-front pipe clamp before tightening the front pipe support strap bolt*

21 Fuel tank – removal and refitting

Saloon models except Cooper S

1 Disconnect the battery earth lead and then remove the spare wheel from its location in the luggage compartment.
2 Remove the fuel gauge wires from their attachments to the sender unit located on the side of the tank (photo).
3 If the car is fitted with an electric fuel pump, slacken the clip and detach the fuel inlet hose from the pump inlet nozzle. Allow the fuel to drain into a suitable container. If a mechanical fuel pump is fitted it will be necessary to empty the tank by pumping or siphoning out all the fuel. **Note:** *A number of earlier models were fitted with a fuel tank incorporating a combined drain plug and tube. Access to this is from below the car, using a long box spanner.* In all cases carry out the draining or siphoning operation in a well ventilated area, never in a garage or over an inspection pit.
4 When the tank is empty, slacken the clip and detach the fuel hose from the front of the tank.
5 Detach the fuel tank breather pipe and remove the filler cap.
6 Undo and remove the tank securing strap bolt and carefully manoeuvre the fuel tank from the luggage compartment (photo).
7 Refitting is the reverse sequence to removal.

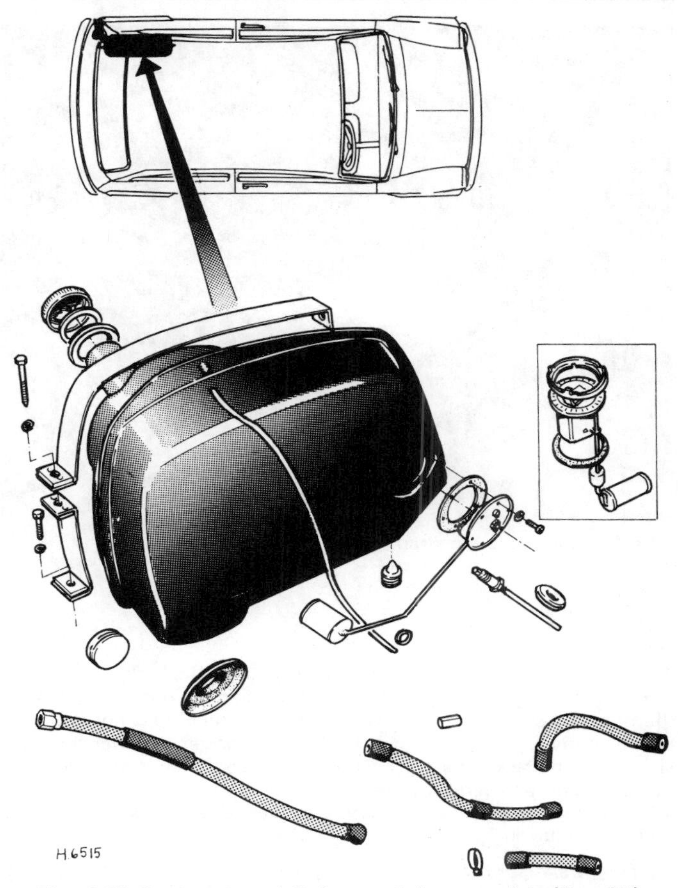

Fig. 3.20 Fuel tank and fittings – Saloon models (Sec 21)

21.2 Electrical leads at the fuel gauge sender unit on the side of the tank (Saloon models)

Estate, Van and Pick-up models

8 Jack up the rear of the car and support it on axle stands. Disconnect the battery earth terminal.
9 Remove the filler cap and from underneath the car, undo and remove the drain plug, allowing the fuel to drain into a suitable container. Do this in a well ventilated area, not in a garage or over an inspection pit. When drained, refit the drain plug and washer securely.
10 While still underneath the car, disconnect the fuel outlet pipe and the fuel gauge wires from their connections on the sender unit on the side of the tank (photo).

21.6 Fuel tank securing strap and bolt (Saloon models)

21.10 Fuel tank outlet pipe and fuel gauge sender unit (Estate, Van and Pick-up models)

11 Undo and remove the six screws which hold the tank in place and remove the tank. It is helpful if a jack is positioned under the tank as the retaining screws are removed so that the tank does not drop out under its own weight. It may also be found easier to lower the tank slightly on the jack before disconnecting the sender unit leads, as with the tank half removed they are more accessible.
12 Refitting the tank is the reverse sequence to removal bearing in mind the following points:

(a) *Make sure that the nylon spacers located at each retaining screw hole are in position before refitting the tank*
(b) *Ensure that the drain plug and washer are in place and securely tightened*
(c) *Ensure that the rubber ferrule beneath the filler cap makes an effective seal with the body*

Cooper S twin fuel tanks

13 Working in the rear luggage compartment remove the trimmed floor panel.
14 For safety reasons, disconnect the battery earth cable.
15 Lift out the spare wheel.
16 Remove the fuel filler caps.
17 Unscrew the left-hand fuel tank drain plug three turns and allow fuel to drain from both tanks.

Left-hand tank

18 Disconnect the electrical connectors from the sender unit.
19 Remove the tank strap securing bolt.
20 Detach the flexible pipe and the vent pipe from the fuel tank.
21 Carefully ease the fuel tank towards the centre of the luggage compartment and lift away from the rear of the car.

Right-hand tank

22 Completely remove the battery.
23 Remove the tank strap securing bolt.
24 Detach the flexible hose from the left-hand tank.
25 Move the tank slightly from its mountings, taking extreme care not to damage the flexible fuel pipes.
26 The fuel tank will still contain a small amount of petrol which should be drained into a small container when the flexible fuel pipe is disconnected.
27 Disconnect the flexible fuel pipe.
28 Finally detach the vent pipe from the tank and lift away the tank from the rear of the car.

Both tanks

29 Refitting the fuel tank is the reverse sequence to removal. Make sure that the seal around the drain plug housing is water-tight.

22 Fuel tank – cleaning

With time it is likely that sediment will collect in the bottom of the fuel tank. Condensation, resulting in rust and other impurities, will usually be found in the fuel tank of any car more than three or four years old.

When the tank is removed it should be vigorously flushed out and turned upside down, and if facilities are available, steam cleaned.

23 Fuel tank sender unit – removal and refitting

Saloon models

1 Disconnect the earth lead from the battery and remove the fuel gauge wires from their attachments to the sender unit mounted in the side of the tank.
2 *Early models:* Unscrew the screws which hold the gauge unit to the tank carefully, and lift the complete unit away, ensuring that the float lever is not bent or damaged in the process.
3 *Later models:* Using crossed screwdrivers remove the fuel gauge sender unit by turning the locking ring through 30° and lifting away. Carefully lift the unit from the tank, ensuring the float lever is not bent or damaged in the process.
4 Refitting the unit is a reversal of the above process. To ensure a fuel-tight joint, scrape both the tank and sender gauge mating flanges clean, and always use a new joint gasket and a suitable gasket cement.

Estate, Van and Pick-up models

5 Refer to Section 21 and remove the fuel tank from the car.
6 Removal and refitting of the sender unit now follows the procedure described for Saloon models.

24 Accelerator cable – removal and refitting

1 Working in the engine compartment, disconnect the throttle return spring(s) and undo the nut and washer securing the cable to the bolt on the throttle lever.
2 Pull the cable through the bolt and slide it out of the steady bracket on the rocker cover (if fitted).
3 From inside the car, depress the accelerator pedal and withdraw the ferrule on the cable from the slot in the top of the pedal arm.
4 The cable can now be withdrawn through the opening in the bulkhead and into the engine compartment.
5 To refit the cable, feed it through the bulkhead and engage the ferrule into the slot on the pedal arm.
6 Now feed the other end of the cable through the brackets on the

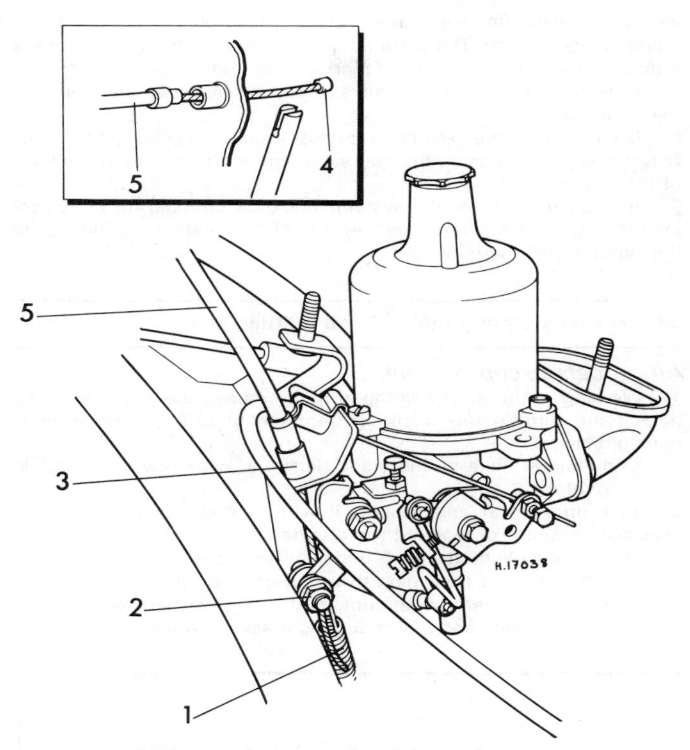

Fig. 3.21 Accelerator cable attachments (Sec 24)

1 Throttle return spring
2 Cable-to-throttle lever securing bolt
3 Cable support bracket
4 Cable ferrule – pedal end
5 Outer cable

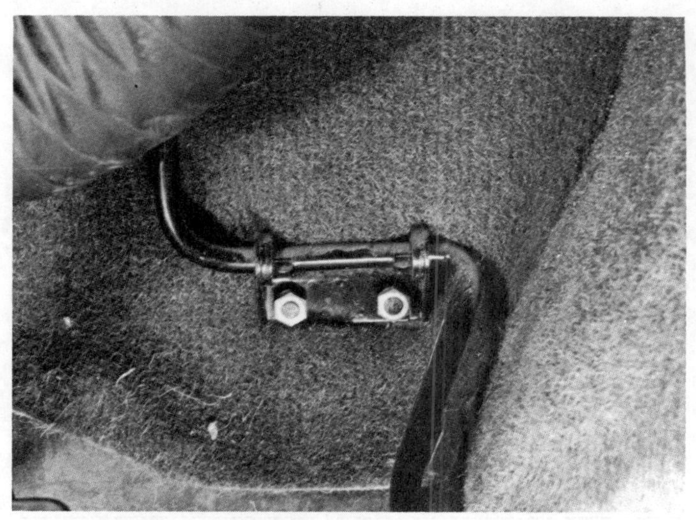

25.2 Accelerator pedal retaining nuts

rocker cover and carburettor, and then insert the inner cable into the slotted bolt on the throttle lever.

7 Pull the cable through the bolt to take up any slack and then refit the washer and nut.

8 Reconnect the return spring and check that a slight amount of free play exists between the pedal and cable.

9 Start the engine and check the operation of the cable.

25 Accelerator pedal – removal and refitting

1 Depress the accelerator pedal and detach the accelerator cable ferrule from the slot at the top of the pedal arm.

2 Undo and remove the two bolts securing the pedal assembly to the bulkhead and lift out the pedal (photo).

3 Refitting is the reverse sequence to removal.

26 Choke cable – removal and refitting

Note: *On models fitted with a centre console it will be necessary to remove the centre console and console glovebox retaining screws. This will allow the console to be moved slightly to provide access for the following operations.*

1 Disconnect the battery earth terminal.

2 Refer to Section 2 and remove the air cleaner assembly.

3 Working in the engine compartment, disconnect the choke inner cable from the trunnion screw on the choke linkage and the outer cable from the support bracket. Withdraw the complete cable from the carburettor.

4 From inside the car, undo and remove the two screws securing the heater assembly to the front of the parcel shelf. Now lower the heater slightly at the front.

5 Disconnect the heater switch wires from the switch.

6 Undo and remove the two nuts or screws which secure the auxiliary switch panel to the centre of the parcel shelf.

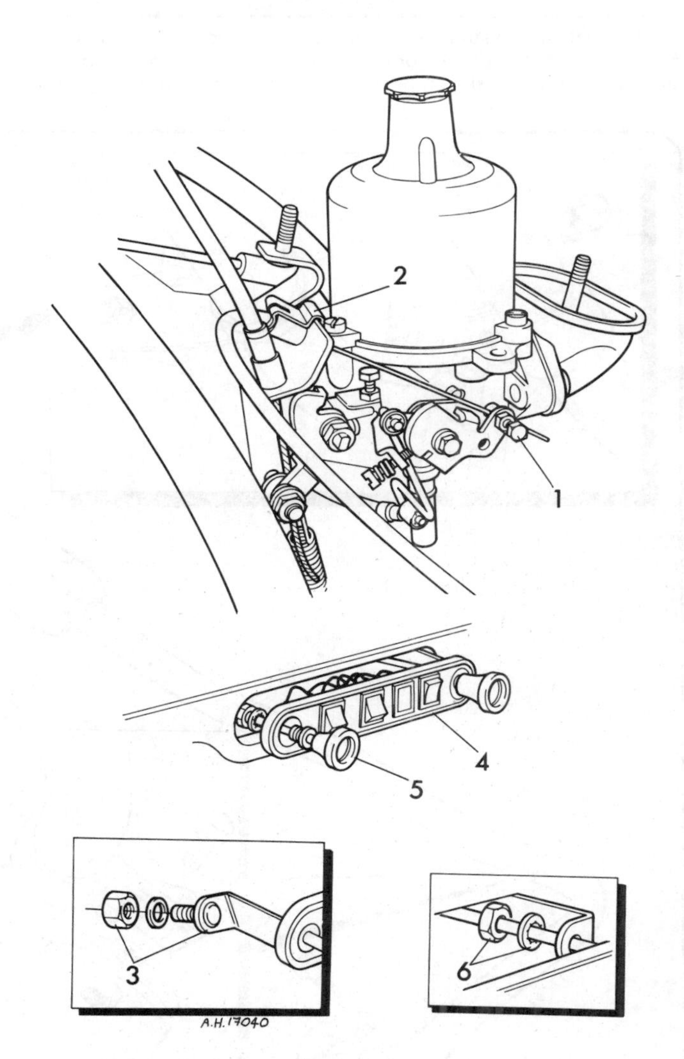

Fig. 3.22 Choke cable attachments (Sec 26)

1 Inner cable-to-linkage attachment
2 Outer cable support bracket
3 Switch panel retaining nuts
4 Switch panel
5 Choke cable
6 Cable retaining nut and washer

7 Draw the switch panel forward and unscrew the choke cable retaining nut from the rear of the panel.
8 Pull the complete cable through the bulkhead grommet and switch panel, into the passenger compartment. Recover the retaining nut and lockwasher from the end of the cable.
9 To refit the cable, slide it through the slot in the switch panel and then place the nut and washer over the cable.
10 Insert the cable through the bulkhead grommet and through to the engine compartment.
11 Screw on and fully tighten the choke cable retaining nut and then refit the switch panel, reconnect the heater switch leads and refit the heater securing screws.
12 Engage the other end of the cable into the support bracket and the inner cable into the trunnion on the choke linkage.
13 Ensure that the choke cable is pushed fully in, ie in the 'off' position, and then tighten the retaining screws on the support bracket and cable trunnion. Ensure that there is $\frac{1}{16}$ in (1.5 mm) of free play on the cable before the cable starts to operate the choke linkage.
14 Finally refit the air cleaner, reconnect the battery earth terminal and, where applicable, refit the centre console retaining screws.

27 Exhaust system – general description

The exhaust system fitted to all Mini models covered by this manual, except Cooper S, consists of a cast iron manifold and a one-piece tubular steel exhaust pipe. A single silencer is fitted to the rear section of early models; later versions incorporate an additional intermediate silencer. The system fitted to Cooper S models comprises a three branch manifold, a front pipe and separate tailpipe incorporating a silencer. Certain versions have a second silencer located beneath the floor pan.

On all models the exhaust system is flexibly attached to the car by two rubber mountings on the rear subframe and a bracket at the base of the transmission.

At regular intervals, the system should be checked for corrosion, joint leakage, the condition and security of the rubber mountings, and the tightness of the joints.

28 Exhaust system – removal and refitting

All models except Cooper S

1 Working in the engine compartment, remove the air cleaner and detach the throttle return spring from the bracket on the exhaust manifold clamp.
2 Undo and remove the nuts and bolts and withdraw the manifold clamp (photo).
3 Jack up the car and support it with axle stands to obtain the maximum amount of working room underneath.
4 From underneath the car, undo and remove the nut and bolt securing the exhaust front pipe to the gearbox or gearbox bracket.
5 Now undo and remove the nuts and spring washers securing the exhaust intermediate and rear mounting brackets to the rubber blocks

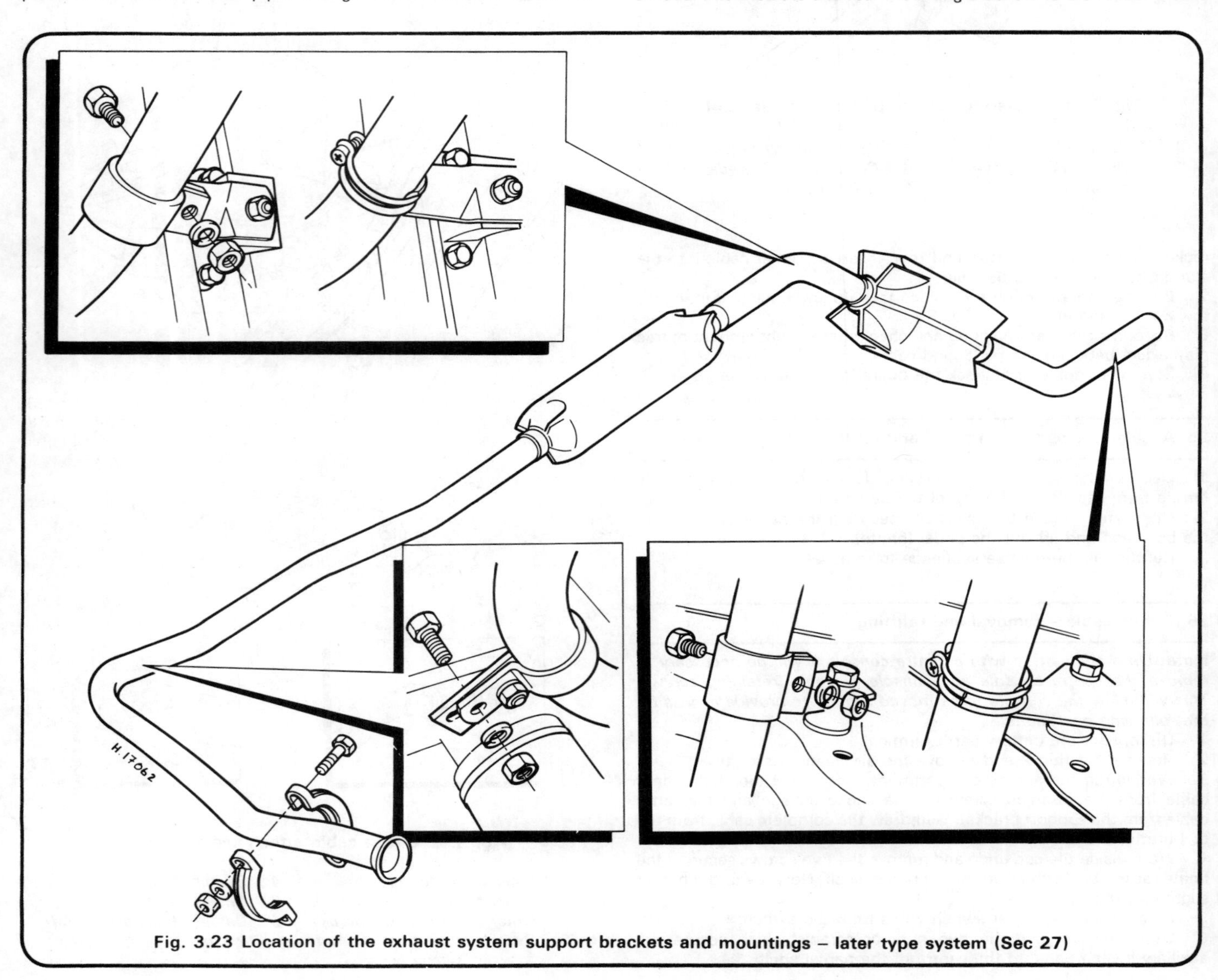

Fig. 3.23 Location of the exhaust system support brackets and mountings – later type system (Sec 27)

28.2 Exhaust front pipe-to-manifold clamp

28.5a Exhaust pipe intermediate...

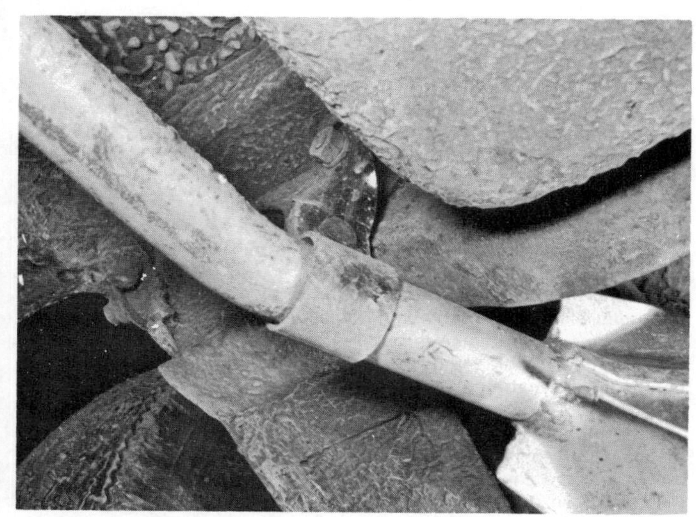

28.5b ...and rear mountings on subframe

on the rear subframe (photos). Slide the brackets off the studs on the rubber blocks and lower the complete system to the ground.
6 Carefully inspect the rubber mounting blocks, the exhaust system brackets and clamps for signs of deterioration, corrosion or damage and renew as necessary.
7 To refit the exhaust system, place it in position under the car and locate the brackets onto the rubber mounting blocks at the rear. Refit the nuts and spring washers but do not tighten at this stage.
8 With the help of an assistant or with the use of a jack, position the bellmouth on the front pipe squarely in position over the flange on the manifold. Hold the system in this position and refit the manifold clamp. Ensure that the pipe is square and that the clamp is seated properly over the pipe and manifold flanges otherwise leaks will occur at this joint.
9 Now fully tighten the manifold clamp securing bolts and refit the throttle return spring.
10 Check that the exhaust system is clear of the subframe and floor pan over its entire length and that it is not in tension. Now fully tighten the rear mountings.
11 Lower the car to the ground, refit the air cleaner, start the engine and check for leaks.

Cooper S models

12 Jack up the front and rear of the car, and support it on stands to obtain the maximum amount of working room underneath.
13 If the rear silencer and tailpipe only are to be removed, slacken the exhaust clamp securing the rear silencer to the front pipe and then remove the retaining clip securing the tailpipe to the rear mounting. Twist the rear silencer back and forth to separate the joint and then withdraw the tailpipe from under the car. Apply liberal amounts of releasing oil to the tailpipe-to-front pipe joint if it is reluctant to come free, and allow it time to soak in.
14 To remove the complete system, slacken the front pipe to exhaust manifold clamp, and undo and remove the bolts securing the rear mountings to the subframe. Twist the complete system back and forth to free the joint and lower it to the ground.
15 In all cases, refitting is the reverse sequence to removal.

29 Exhaust manifold – removal and refitting

All models except Cooper S

1 The exhaust manifold fitted to all engines except the 1275cc Cooper S units is removed as an assembly with the inlet manifold. Full details on this procedure will be found in Section 20.

Cooper S models

2 Begin by removing the inlet manifold as described in Section 20.
3 Remove the complete exhaust system as described in Section 28.
4 Undo and remove the nuts and flat washers securing the manifold to the cylinder head studs. Now ease the manifold off the studs and carefully manipulate it out of the engine compartment.
5 Refitting is the reverse sequence to removal, but use a new manifold gasket.

30 Emission control systems – general description

Certain models of the Mini, in particular those exported to the USA and Canada, are fitted with exhaust, crankcase, and fuel evaporative loss emission control systems. A brief description of the operation of the systems is given below. Note that testing, repair and overhaul of the emission control equipment requires specialist tools and knowledge, and no attempt should be made to dismantle any of the components. Should the system develop a fault it is recommended that you seek the advice of a BL dealer. The content of the following Sections is therefore limited to removal and refitting instructions for access to other engine components, and minor servicing and adjustments which can be carried out by the private owner.

Exhaust emission control system

The basis of this system is an air pump which supplies air under pressure to the cylinder head exhaust port of each cylinder, via an air injection manifold. A check valve is incorporated in the air delivery pipe to prevent a blow-back of exhaust gases from reaching the pump. Air from the pump is also supplied to the inlet manifold via a gulp valve

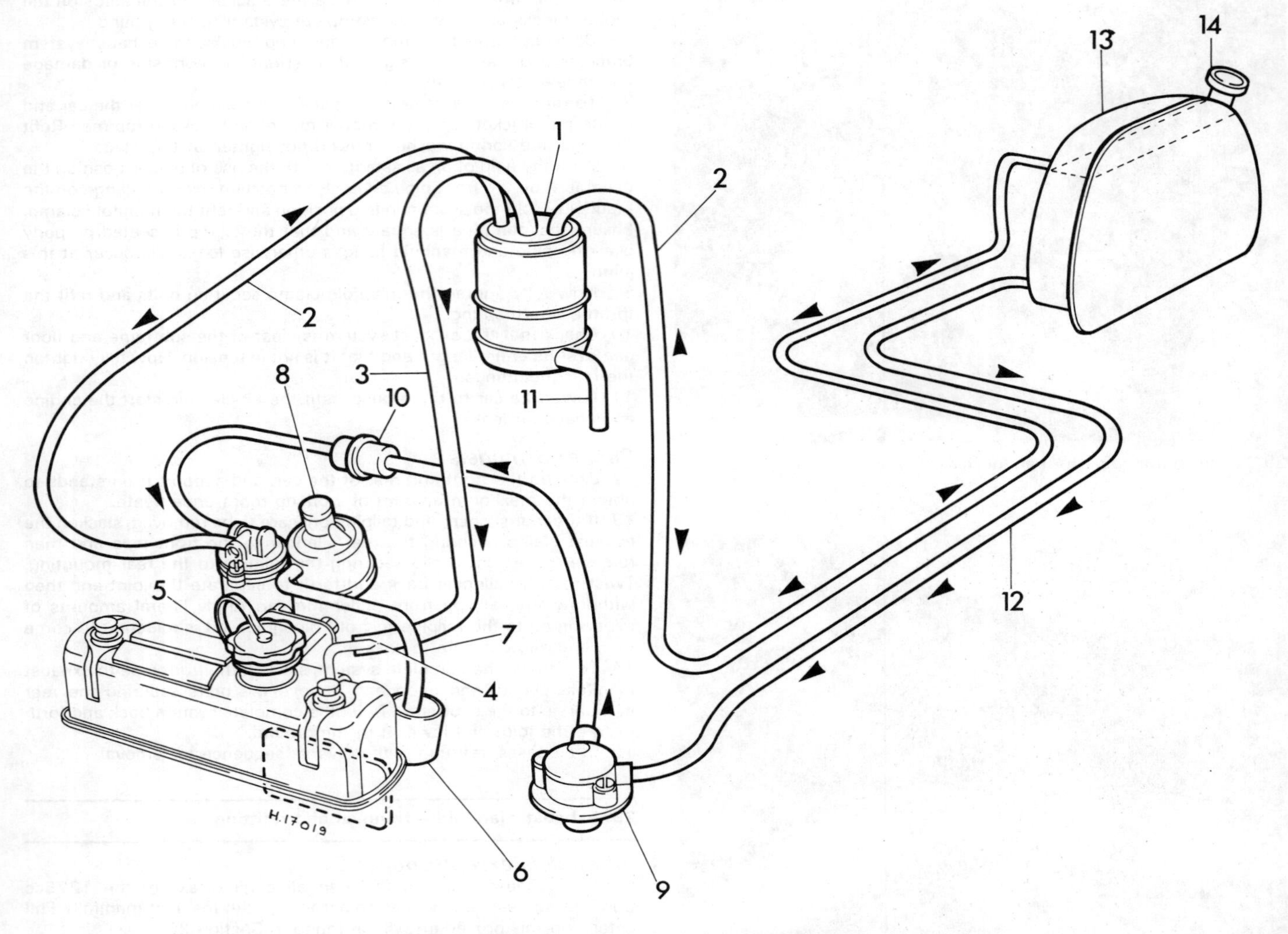

Fig. 3.24 General layout of the emission control systems (Sec 30)

1 Charcoal canister	*5 Oil filler cap*	*8 Carburettor*	*11 Vent hose*
2 Vapour pipes	*6 Flame trap*	*9 Fuel pump*	*12 Fuel pipe*
3 Purge hose	*7 Crankcase purge hose*	*10 Fuel filter*	*13 Fuel tank*
4 Breather restrictor			*14 Fuel filler cap*

to weaken the rich fuel/air mixture in the manifold during engine deceleration and overrun.

The air pump is of the rotary vane type and is mounted at the front of the cylinder head. Drive to the pump is by a V-belt from the water pump pulley. Air enters the pump through an extraction filter on early models, or through radial air intakes around the pulley on later versions. At high engine speeds, excess air is discharged to atmosphere through a relief valve.

A diverter valve is incorporated in the air delivery pipe between the air pump and check valve. The valve is operated by a cable on early models, or activated by a vacuum switch on later types, whenever the choke control is pulled out. During choke operation, air from the pump is cut off and diverted to atmosphere.

When the throttle is closed during deceleration or overrun, a rich fuel/air mixture is created in the inlet manifold. The gulp valve fitted between the air pump and manifold is activated by the depression also created in the manifold during these conditions, and opens to admit air from the air pump. The mixture is thus weakened preventing excessive exhaust emissions when the throttle is reopened. A restrictor is also fitted in the air feed to the gulp valve and prevents surging when the valve is in operation.

An SU HS4 carburettor is used on all engines equipped with an exhaust emission control system. The carburettor is manufactured to a special emission control specification and incorporates a spring-loaded jet metering needle to give a fine degree of mixture control.

Crankcase emission and fuel evaporative loss systems

Piston blow-by fumes are emitted through a flame trap breather outlet on the left-hand cylinder block side cover, which is connected to the depression chamber of the carburettor by a short hose. Additionally purged air from the charcoal canister of the fuel evaporative loss system enters the engine through an inlet on the valve rocker cover. These fumes combine with the incoming fuel/air mixture for combustion in the normal manner.

When the engine is stopped, vapours from the fuel tank vent, and on later models from the carburettor float chamber vent, are stored in the charcoal canister. When the engine is running the vapours are drawn into the engine via the rocker cover inlet, to be disposed of by the crankcase emission system. The design of the fuel tank ensures that only fuel vapour is allowed to reach the charcoal canister, and also that sufficient fuel tank volume remains after filling to allow for expansion of the fuel as a result of temperature rise.

31 Air pump drivebelt – removal and refitting

1 Release the three retaining lugs and remove the engine ignition shield, if fitted.
2 Undo and remove the two bolts securing the radiator upper mounting bracket to the radiator.
3 Unscrew the radiator filler cap and slacken the top hose securing clips. Carefully ease the radiator as far as possible toward the wing valance. Place a container beneath the engine to catch the small quantity of coolant that will be lost as the top hose is released.
4 Slacken the air pump pivot and adjusting link bolts, push the pump in toward the engine, and slip the drivebelt off the two pulleys.
5 Feed the belt between the fan blades and the radiator cowling at the top as the blades are rotated. Now pull the belt out from between the fan and radiator.
6 Refitting the drivebelt is the reverse sequence to removal. Adjust the tension of the drivebelt so that there is 0.5 in (12 mm) deflection of the belt, using thumb pressure, at a point midway between the two pulleys. Recheck to coolant level on completion.

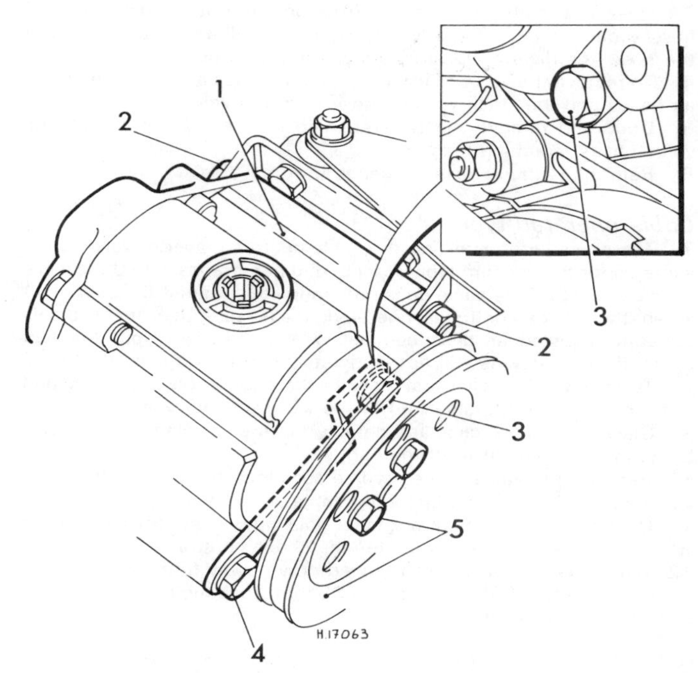

Fig. 3.25 Air pump drivebelt removal (Sec 31)

1 Air pump
2 Pump mounting pivot bolt and nut
3 Adjusting link inner retaining bolt
4 Adjusting link outer retaining bolt
5 Pulley and retaining bolts

32 Air pump – removal and refitting

1 Remove the drivebelt as described in the previous Section.
2 Slacken the clips and detach the outlet hoses from the pump adaptor.
3 Detach the HT lead and undo and remove No 1 cylinder spark plug.
4 Slacken the bolt securing the pump adjusting arm to the alternator pivot bolt.
5 Undo and remove the bolt securing the adjusting arm to the air pump.
6 Undo and remove the air pump pivot nut and bolt and lift off the pump.
7 Refitting is the reverse sequence to removal. Ensure that the drivebelt is correctly tensioned as described in the previous Section.

33 Air manifold – removal and refitting

1 Release the three retaining lugs and remove the engine ignition shield, if fitted.
2 Detach the HT lead from No 1 cylinder spark plug.
3 Undo and remove the four air manifold unions from the cylinder head.
4 Slacken the clip securing the check valve hose and lift away the air manifold complete with check valve.
5 Hold the air manifold union with a spanner and unscrew the check valve.
6 Refitting is the reverse sequence to removal.

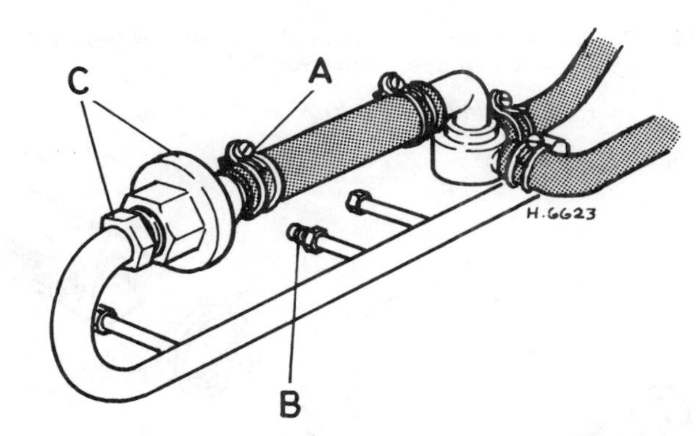

Fig. 3.26 Air manifold assembly (Sec 33)

A Check valve hose clip
B Air manifold unions
C Check valve and union nut

34 Check valve – removal, testing and refitting

1 Slacken the retaining clip and detach the hose from the check valve.
2 Hold the air manifold union to prevent it twisting and unscrew the check valve.
3 To test the valve gently blow into each end in turn. Air should pass through the valve from the air supply end only. If air will pass in both directions the valve is faulty and must be renewed. Do not use high pressure air or air from a tyre pump for this check or the valve will be damaged.
4 Refitting the check valve is the reverse sequence to removal.

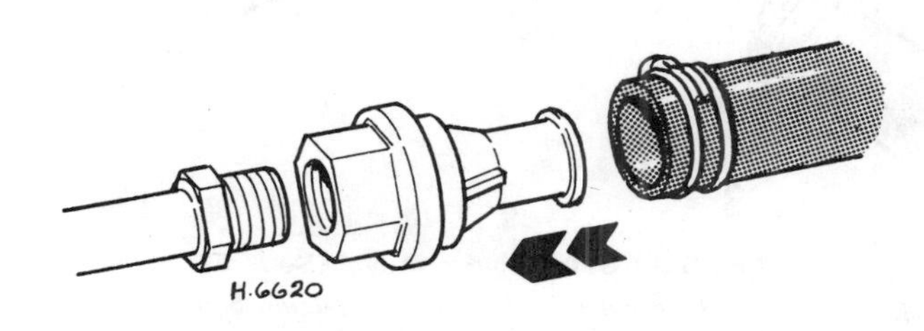

Fig. 3.27 Direction of airflow through check valve (Sec 34)

35 Diverter valve – removal, testing and refitting

Vacuum operated type

1 To test the operation of the valve, slacken the hose clip and detach the diverter valve-to-check valve hose at the check valve end.
2 Start the engine and allow it to idle. Air pressure should be felt at the end of the disconnected hose.

3 Operate the choke control, and air pressure at the disconnected hose should be cut off completely. If air can still be felt at the end of the hose, the diverter valve is faulty and should be renewed.
4 To remove the valve, slacken all the hose clips and detch the three air hoses and the small vacuum hose from the valve body.
5 Undo and remove the two retaining nuts and bolts and lift the valve off its mounting bracket.
6 Refitting is the reverse sequence to removal.

Cable operated type

7 The procedure for testing the cable operated diverter valve is the same as for the vacuum type described in paragraphs 1 to 3 inclusive of this Section. If the valve does not completely restrict the flow of air when the choke control is operated, make sure that the cable is correctly adjusted as described below and then carry out the test again. If the airflow is still not completely restricted renew the valve.
8 To remove the valve first slacken the cable retaining screw and slide the cable and retainer out of the valve operating lever.
9 Slacken the hose clips and detach the three hoses from the valve body; then lift the valve off the engine.
10 Refitting the valve is the reverse sequence to removal. With the valve installed adjust the operating cable as follows.
11 Observe the movement of the jet housing beneath the carburettor while an assistant slowly operates the choke control.
12 When the jet housing has moved down away from the adjusting nut by 0.010 to 0.015 in (0.25 to 0.38 mm), lock the choke control to hold it in this position.

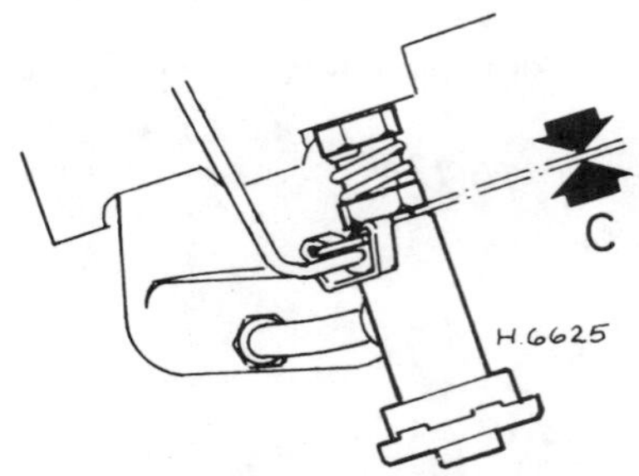

Fig. 3.28 Correct position of jet assembly when testing diverter valve operation (Sec 35)

C = 0.010 to 0.015 in (0.25 to 0.38 mm)

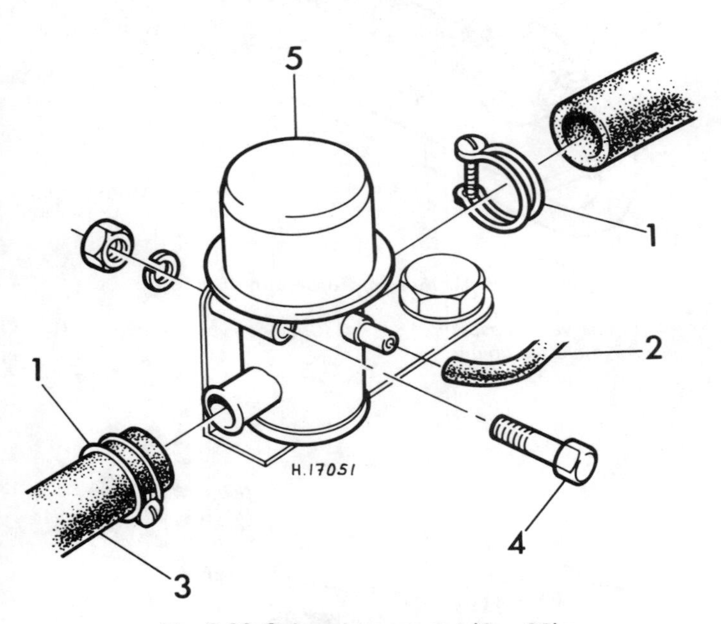

Fig. 3.30 Gulp valve removal (Sec 36)

1 Hose clips
2 Vacuum hose
3 Air hose
4 Retaining bolt
5 Gulp valve

13 The clearance between the diverter valve operating lever and the valve stem should now be 0.0015 to 0.003 in (0.04 to 0.08 mm). Adjust the position of the cable retainer to obtain this dimension.

36 Gulp valve – removal, testing and refitting

Note: *This component can only be tested satisfactorily using vacuum gauges. If the valve is suspect it is recommended that the testing is carried out by a BL dealer.*
1 To remove the gulp valve slacken all the hose clips, and detach the air hoses and the vacuum hose from the valve body.
2 Undo and remove the two retaining nuts and bolts and lift the valve off its mounting bracket.
3 Refitting is the reverse sequence to removal.

37 Fuel line filter – removal and refitting

1 Slacken the two retaining clips and detach the filter from the inlet and outlet hoses.
2 The filter cannot be dismantled for cleaning but must be renewed at the recommended service intervals.

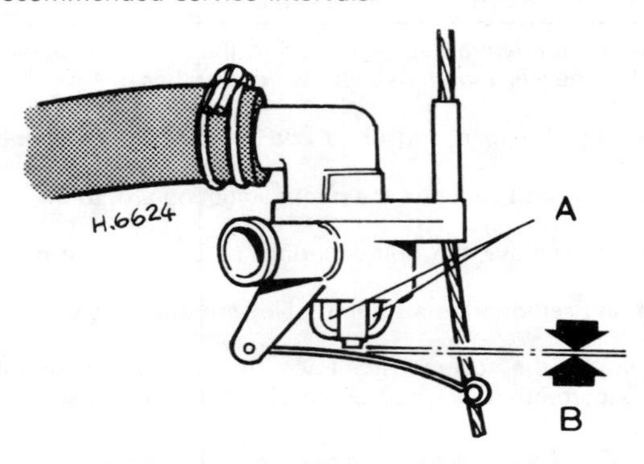

Fig. 3.29 Testing the diverter valve (Sec 35)

A Valve body
B = 0.0015 to 0.003 in (0.04 to 0.08 mm)

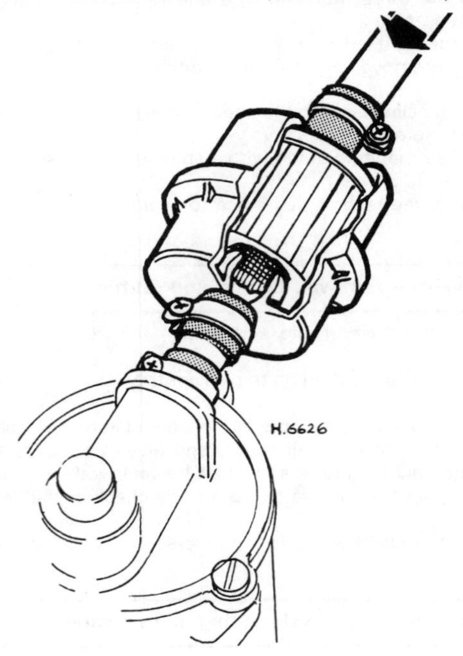

Fig. 3.31 Sectional view of the fuel line filter – arrow indicates direction of fuel flow (Sec 37)

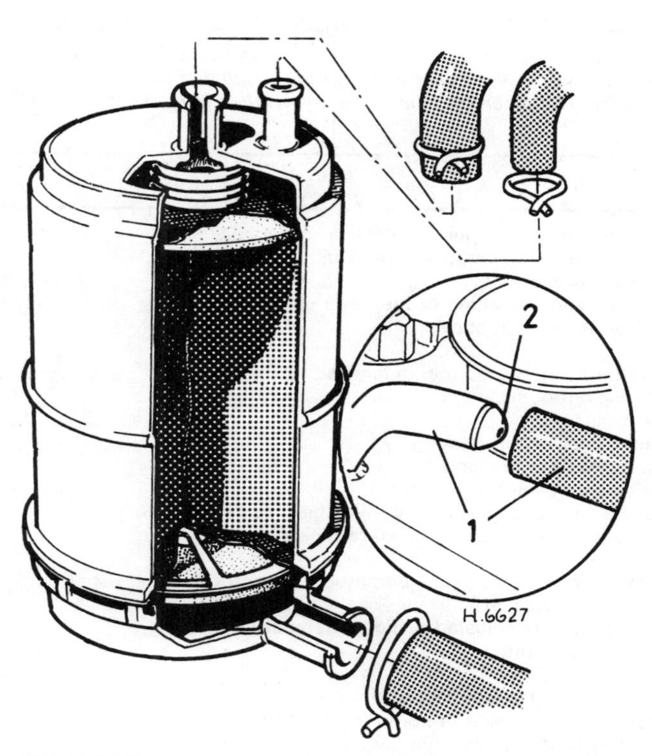

Fig. 3.32 Sectional view of the charcoal canister (Sec 38)

1 Purge hose connection at rocker cover
2 Restricted breather outlet

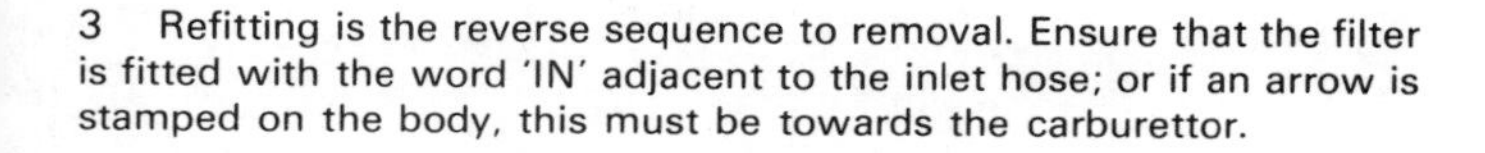
3 Refitting is the reverse sequence to removal. Ensure that the filter is fitted with the word 'IN' adjacent to the inlet hose; or if an arrow is stamped on the body, this must be towards the carburettor.

38 Charcoal canister – removal and refitting

1 Detach the air vent hose from the bottom of the canister, and the purge and vapour hoses from the top.
2 Undo and remove the retaining screw, open the retaining strap slightly and lift out the canister.
3 Do not attempt to open or clean the canister, but ensure that it is renewed at the recommended service intervals.
4 Refitting is the reverse sequence to removal. With the canister in place, detach the purge hose from the inlet elbow on the rocker cover. Clean the restrictor orifice with a short length of soft wire and then refit the hose.

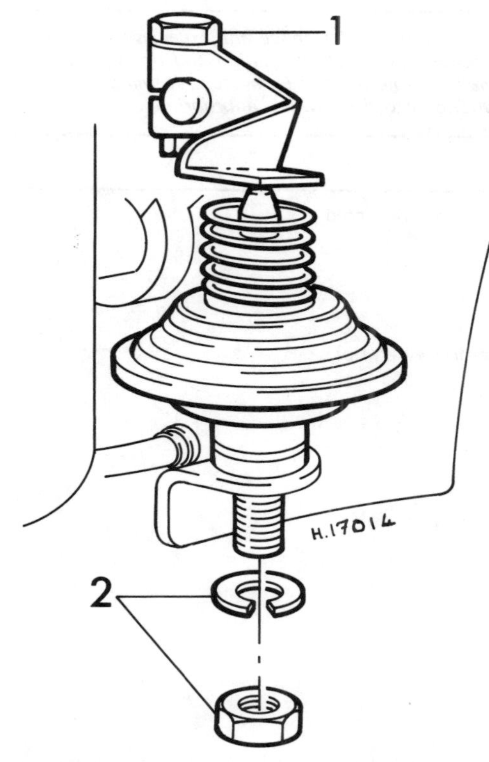

Fig. 3.33 Throttle damper assembly (Sec 39)

1 Contact lever retaining bolt
2 Damper retaining nut and washer

39 Throttle damper – removal and refitting

1 Remove the air cleaner assembly as described in Section 2.
2 Slacken the nut and bolt securing the damper contact lever to the carburettor spindle.
3 Undo and remove the nut and spring washer securing the throttle damper to the mounting bracket. Lift the damper upward and off the bracket.
4 To refit the damper, position it on the mounting bracket and secure with the nut and washer.
5 Insert a 0.080 in (2.03 mm) feeler gauge between the contact lever and the damper plunger.
6 Press the contact lever downward until the damper plunger is fully compressed. Hold the lever in this position and tighten the retaining nut and bolt. Release the lever and remove the feeler gauge.
7 Refit the air cleaner assembly.

see overleaf for 'Fault diagnosis – fuel system'

40 Fault diagnosis – fuel system

Unsatisfactory engine performance and excessive fuel consumption are not necessarily the fault of the fuel system or carburettor. In fact they more commonly occur as a result of ignition and timing faults. Before acting on the following, it is necessary to check the ignition system first. Even though a fault may lie in the fuel system, it will be difficult to trace unless the ignition is correct. The faults below, therefore, assume that this has been attended to first (where appropriate).

Symptom	Reason/s
Difficult starting when cold	Fuel tank empty or pump defective Choke control inoperative or maladjusted Air cleaner blocked Float chamber flooding or fuel level too low Carburettor piston sticking
Difficult starting when hot	Fuel tank empty or pump defective Choke control sticking on Air cleaner blocked Carburettor piston sticking Float chamber flooding Air cleaner blocked Vapour lock (especially in hot weather or at high altitude) Carburettor maladjusted (mixture too rich)
Excessive fuel consumption	Leakage from tank, pipes, pump or carburettor Blocked air cleaner Carburettor maladjusted or float chamber flooding Carburettor worn
Fuel starvation	Level in tank too low (especially on hills) Leak on suction side of pump (air bubbles in fuel line) Level in float chamber too low, or needle valve sticking Fuel tank breather restricted Pump or carburettor filters blocked Pump defective or electrical connection loose (if applicable)

Chapter 4 Ignition system

For modifications, and information applicable to later models, see Supplement at end of manual

Contents

Specifications

Spark plugs

Type:	
All models up to 1986	Champion N9YCC or N9YC
Electrode gap:	
Champion N9YCC	0.032 in (0.8 mm)
Champion N9YC	0.024 in (0.6 mm)

HT leads

HT leads	Champion CLS 2, boxed set

Ignition coil

Type:	
All models except Cooper S Mk III and later 1275 GT	Lucas LA12
Cooper S Mk III	Lucas HA12
1275 GT, 1978 on	Lucas 15C6
Primary resistance at 68°F (20°C):	
Lucas LA12 and 15C6	3.2 to 3.4 ohms (cold)
Lucas HA12	3.0 to 3.4 ohms (cold)
Consumption (ignition on)	3.9 amps

Distributor (general)

Type:	
All models except Cooper S Mk III:	
Early type	Lucas 25D4
Later type	Lucas 45D4 or Ducellier
Cooper S Mk III	Lucas 23D4
Diirection of rotor arm rotation	Anti-clockwise
Automatic advance	Centrifugal and vacuum (centrifugal only on Cooper S Mk III)
Contact breaker points gap	0.014 to 0.016 in (0.35 to 0.40 mm)
Dwell angle:	
Lucas 23D4 and 25D4	60° ± 3°
Lucas 45D4:	
Non-sliding contacts	51° ± 5°
Sliding contacts	57° ± 5°
Ducellier	57° ± 2°30′

Firing order

Firing order	1-3-4-2 (No 1 cylinder next to radiator)

Distributor serial numbers

(a) Mini 850 Saloon and Estate, 848 cc, 1969-72:	
Lucas 25D4	41026
Lucas 45D4	41411
(b) Mini 850 Van and Pick-up, 848cc, 1969-72:	
Lucas 25D4	41007
Lucas 45D4	41410
(c) Mini 1000 Saloon and Estate, 998 cc, 1969-72:	
Lucas 25D4	40931 or 41030
Lucas 45D4	41412
(d) Mini 1000 Van and Pick-up, 998 cc, 1969-72:	
Lucas 25D4	41007
Lucas 45D4	41410
(e) Mini 1000 Automatic, and Mini Clubman Automatic, 998 cc, 1969-74:	
Lucas 25D4	41134 or 41242
Lucas 45D4	41417

(f) Mini Cooper S Mk III, 1275 cc, 1969-72:	
Lucas 23D4	40819 or 41033
(g) Mini Clubman, 998 cc, 1969-72:	
Lucas 25D4	41030
Lucas 45D4	41412
(h) Mini 1275 GT, 1275 cc, 1969-72:	
Lucas 25D4	41257
Lucas 45D4	41419
(i) Mini 850 Saloon and variants, 848 cc, 1972-74:	
Lucas 25D4	41026 or 41569*
Lucas 45D£	41411 or 41570*
(j) Mini 1000 and Mini Clubman, Saloon and variants, 998 cc, 1972-74:	
Lucas 25D4	41254 or 41246*
Lucas 45D4	41212 or 41418*
(k) Mini 1275 GT, 1275 cc, 1972-76:	
Lucas 25D4	41257 or 41214
Lucas 45D4	41419
(l) Mini 850 Saloon and variants, 848 cc, 1974-76:	
Lucas 45D4	41570
(m) Mini 1000 and Mini Clubman, Saloon and variants, 998 cc, manual and automatic transmission, 1974-76:	
Lucas 45D4	41418
(n) Mini Clubman 1100, 1098 cc, 1974-76:	
Lucas 25D4	41246
Lucas 45D4	41418
(o) Mini 850 Saloon and variants, 848 cc, 1976 on:	
Lucas 45D4	41417 or 41767
(p) Mini 1000 and Mini Clubman, Saloon and variants, 998 cc, manual and automatic transmission, 1976-78:	
Lucas 45D4	41418 or 41793
(q) Mini Clubman 1100, 1098 cc, 1976 on:	
Lucas 45D4	41418 or 41793
(r) Mini 1275 GT, 1275 cc, 1976-77:	
Lucas 45D4	41419 or 41768
(s) Mini 1000 and Mini Clubman, Saloon and variants, 998 cc, manual and automatic transmission, 1978 on:	
Lucas 45D4	41406 or 41765
(t) Mini 1275 GT, 1275 cc, 1978 on:	
Lucas 45D4	41419 or 41768

* *Alternative distributor fitted to a limited number of 1974 models*

Ignition timing

Note: *the reference letter in the first column refers to the vehicle type as above. If a Ducellier distributor is fitted, the timing setting is the same as the equivalent Lucas distributor.*

Vehicle type	Static	Stroboscopic (vacuum pipe disconnected)
(a)	TDC	3° BTDC at 600 rpm
(b)	7° BTDC	10° BTDC at 600 rpm
(c)	5° BTDC	8° BTDC at 600 rpm
(d)	7° BTDC	10° BTDC at 600 rpm
(e)	4° BTDC	6° BTDC at 600 rpm
(f)	2° BTDC	4° BTDC at 600 rpm
(g)	5° BTDC	8° BTDC at 600 rpm
(h)	8° BTDC	10° BTDC at 600 rpm
(i)	TDC	19° BTDC at 1000 rpm
	9° BTDC*	14° BTDC at 1000 rpm*
(j)	5° BTDC	11° BTDC at 1000 rpm
	10° BTDC*	13° BTDC at 1000 rpm*
(k)	8° BTDC	13° BTDC at 1000 rpm
(l)	6° BTDC	11° BTDC at 1000 rpm
(m)	4° BTDC	7° BTDC at 1000 rpm
(n)	9° BTDC	12° BTDC at 1000 rpm
(O)	–	7° BTDC at 1000 rpm
(p)	–	7° BTDC at 1000 rpm
(q)	–	12° BTDC at 1000 rpm
(r)	–	13° BTDC at 1000 rpm
(s)	–	8° BTDC at 1000 rpm
(t)	–	13° BTDC at 1000 rpm

* *Alternative distributor*

Timing marks	Marks on flywheel, pointer on housing (marks on timing cover, notch on pulley – later models)

Torque wrench settings

	lbf ft	Nm
Spark plugs	18	25
Distributor clamp	5	6.8

1 General description

In order that the engine can run correctly, it is necessary for an electrical spark to ignite the fuel/air mixture in the combustion chamber at exactly the right moment in relation to engine speed and load. The ignition system is based on feeding low tension voltage from the battery to the coil, where it is converted to high tension voltage. The high tension voltage is powerful enough to jump the spark plug gap in the cylinders many times a second under high compression pressures, providing that the system is in good condition and that all adjustments are correct.

The ignition system is divided into two circuits: the low tension circuit and the high tension circuit.

The low tension (sometimes known as the primary) circuit consists of the battery, lead to the starter solenoid, lead to the ignition switch, lead from the ignition switch to the low tension or primary coil windings (terminal +), and the lead from the low tension coil windings (coil terminal –) to the contact breaker points and condenser in the distributor.

The high tension circuit consists of the high tension or secondary coil windings, the heavy ignition lead from the centre of the coil to the centre of the distributor cap, the rotor arm, and the spark plug leads and spark plugs.

The system functions in the following manner. Low tension voltage is changed in the coil into high tension voltage by the opening and closing of the contact breaker points in the low tension circuit. High tension voltage is then fed, via the carbon brush in the centre of the distributor cap, to the rotor arm of the distributor. The rotor arm revolves inside the distributor cap, and each time it comes in line with one of the four metal segments in the cap, which are connected to the spark plug leads, the opening and closing of the contact breaker points causes the high tension voltage to build up and jump the gap from the rotor arm to the appropriate metal segment. The voltage then passes, via the spark plug lead, to the spark plug, where it finally jumps the spark plug gap, before going to earth.

The ignition is advanced and retarded automatically. to ensure the spark occurs at just the right instant for the particular load at the prevailing engine speed. The ignition advance is controlled both mechanically and by a vacuum operated system on all but Cooper S models. Automatic advance is mechanical only on Cooper S models. The mechanical governor mechanism comprises two lead weights, which move out from the distributor shaft, due to centrifugal force, as the engine speed rises. As they move outwards they rotate the cam relative to the distributor shaft, and so advance the spark. The weights are held in position by two light springs, and it is the tension of the springs which is largely responsible for correct spark advancement. The vacuum control consists of a diaphragm, one side of which is connected, via a small bore tube, to the carburettor, and the other side to the contact breaker plate. Depression in the inlet manifold and carburettor, which varies with engine speed and throttle opening, causes the diaphragm to move, so moving the contact breaker plate, and advancing or retarding the spark.

2 Contact breaker points – adjustment

1 If an ignition shield is fitted over the front of the engine, release the three plastic retaining lugs and lift away the shield. Detach the two spring clips securing the distributor cap to the distributor body and lift off the cap (photo).

2 On models that have a distributor shield attached to the inner front panel, remove the ignition coil HT lead from the centre of the distributor cap. Now detach the two distributor cap securing spring clips. With careful manipulation it should be possible to withdraw the distributor cap upwards through the small space between the rotor arm and the distributor shield. If difficulty is experienced, undo and remove the retaining screws and lift out the shield.

3 With the distributor cap removed, clean it on the inside and outside with a dry cloth and then examine the four HT lead segments inside the cap. Scrape away any deposits that may have built up on the segments, using a knife or small screwdriver. If the segments appear badly burned or pitted, renew the cap.

4 Push in the carbon brush, located in the centre of the cap, and ensure that it moves freely. The brush should protrude by at least 0.1 in (3 mm). If it is worn it can be renewed separately.

5 Gently prise the contact breaker points open to examine the condition of their faces. If they are rough and pitted or dirty, it will be necessary to remove them for refacing, or preferably to enable new points to be fitted.

6 Assuming that the points are in a satisfactory condition, or that they have been refaced or renewed, the gap between the two faces should be measured using feeler gauges. To do this turn the engine

2.1 Removing the distributor cap

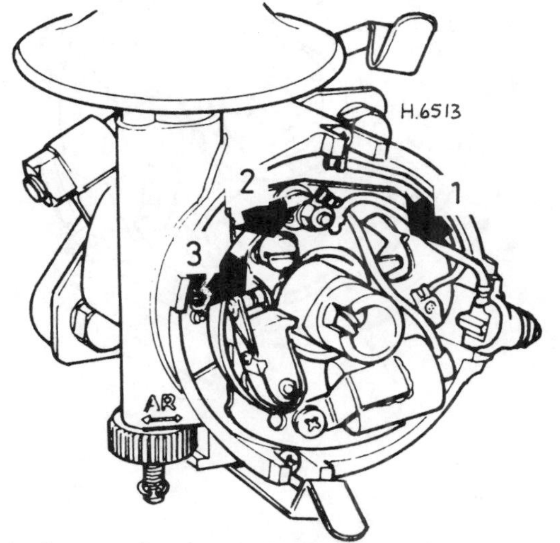

Fig. 4.1 Contact breaker points adjustment – Lucas 25D4 distributor (Sec 2)

1 Screwdriver slot for adjustment
2 Contact plate securing screw
3 Contact breaker points

over until the heel of the contact breaker arm is on the peak of one of the four cam lobes. On manual transmission models, the engine can be turned over quite easily by engaging top gear and moving the car backwards or forwards until the points are fully open. This should only be done on level ground; and make sure that the car cannot run away! An alternative method, and the method that should be used on automatic transmission models, is to press the fanbelt midway between the crankshaft pulley and dynamo or alternator pulley and then turn the fan blades. Removing the spark plugs will ease this operation. With the points fully open, a feeler gauge equal to the contact breaker points gap, as stated in the Specifications, should now just fit between the contact faces (photo).

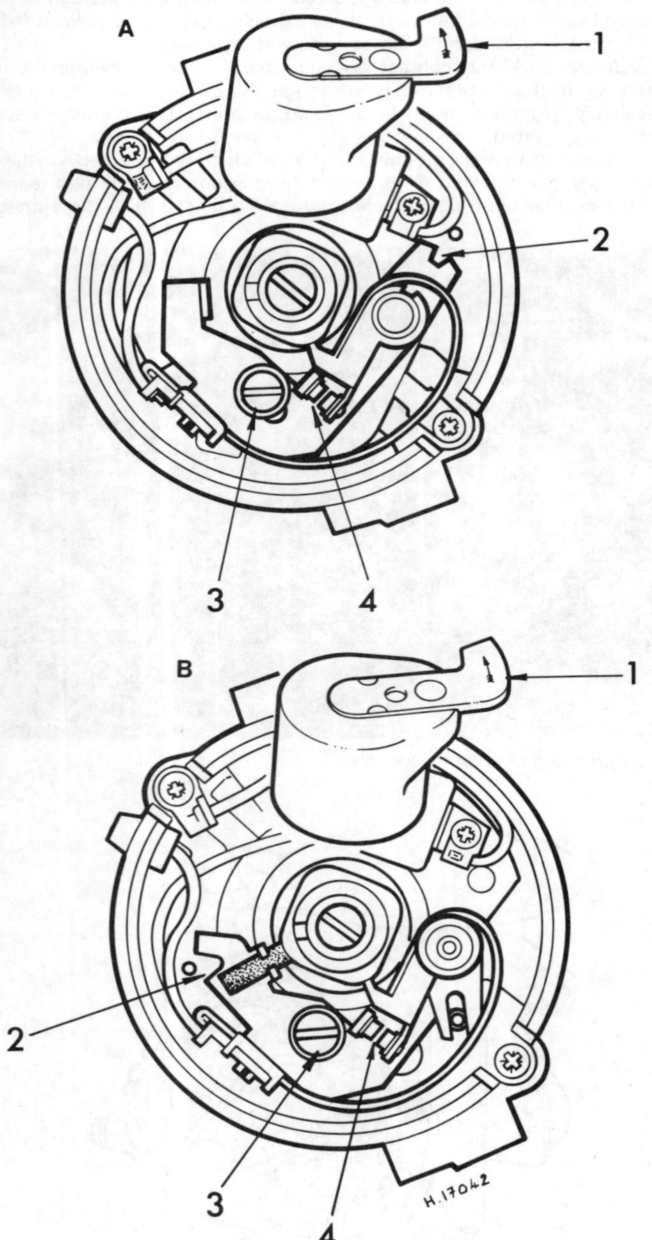

Fig. 4.2 Contact breaker points adjustment – Lucas 45D4 distributor (Sec 2)

A Non-sliding contact type *B Sliding contact type*

1 Rotor arm
2 Screwdriver slot for adjustment
3 Contact plate securing screw
4 Contact breaker points

7 If the gap is too large or too small, slacken the contact breaker securing screw slightly using a short screwdriver. Now insert the screwdriver into the slot on the side or at the rear of the contact breaker plate and move the plate in the desired direction to increase or decrease the gap (photo).
8 Tighten the securing screw and recheck the gap.
9 With the points correctly adjusted, refit the distributor cap and ignition shield or distributor shield if previously removed.
10 If a dwell meter is available, a far more accurate method of setting the contact breaker points gap is by measuring and setting the distributor dwell angle.
11 The dwell angle is the number of degrees of distributor cam rotation during which the contact breaker points are closed, ie the period from when the points close after being opened by one cam lobe until they are opened again by the next cam lobe. The advantages of setting the points by this method are that any wear of the distributor shaft or cam lobes is taken into account, and also the inaccuracies of using a feeler gauge are eliminated. In general, a dwell meter should be used in accordance with the manufacturer's instructions. However, the use of one type of meter is outlined as follows.
12 To set the dwell angle, remove the distributor cap and rotor arm, and connect one lead of the dwell meter to the + terminal on the coil, and the other lead to the – coil terminal.
13 Whilst an assistant turns on the ignition and operates the starter, observe the reading on the dwell meter scale. With the engine turning over on the starter the reading should be as stated in the Specification. **Note**: *Fluctuation of the dwell meter needle indicates that the engine is not turning over fast enough to give a steady reading. If this is the case, remove the spark plugs and repeat the checks.*
14 If the dwell angle is too small, the contact breaker point gap is too wide, and if the dwell angle is excessive, the gap is too small.
15 Adjust the contact breaker points gap, while the engine is cranking using the method described in paragraph 7, until the correct dwell angle is obtained.
16 When the dwell angle is satisfactory, disconnect the meter and refit the rotor arm, distributor cap and ignition or distributor shield.

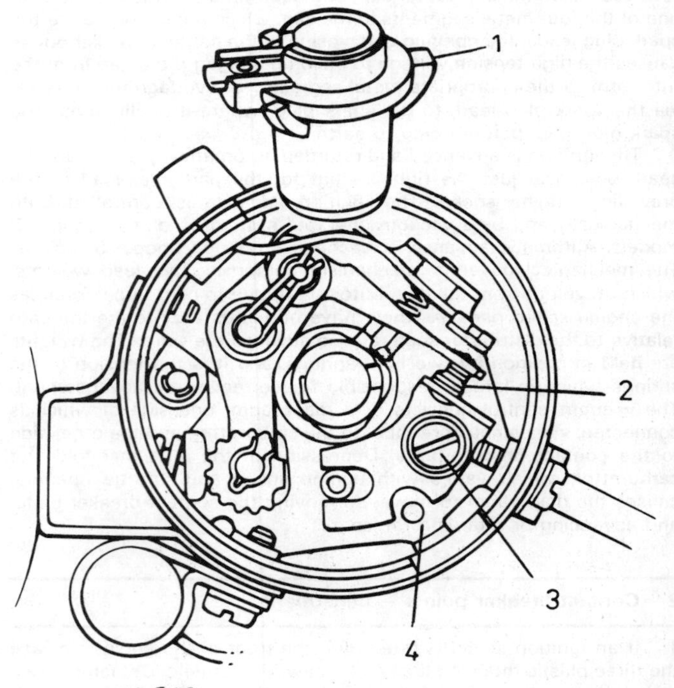

Fig. 4.3 Contact breaker point adjustment – Ducellier distributor (Sec 2)

1 Rotor arm
2 Contact breaker points
3 Contact plate securing screw
4 Screwdriver slot for adjustment

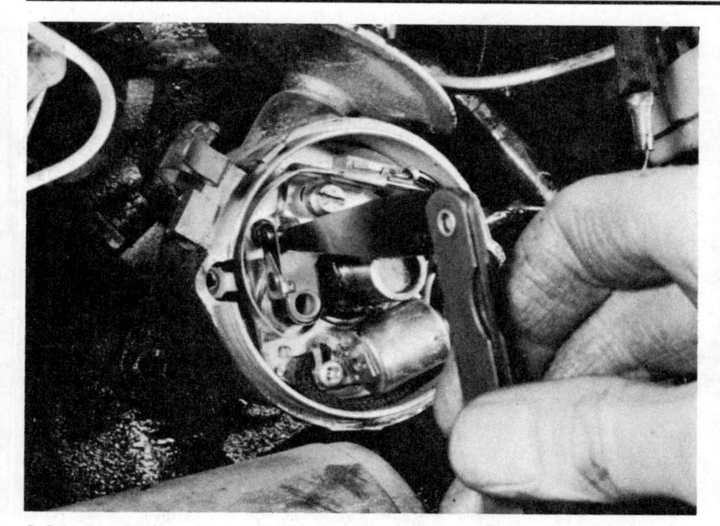

2.6 Using feeler gauges to check the contact breaker points gap

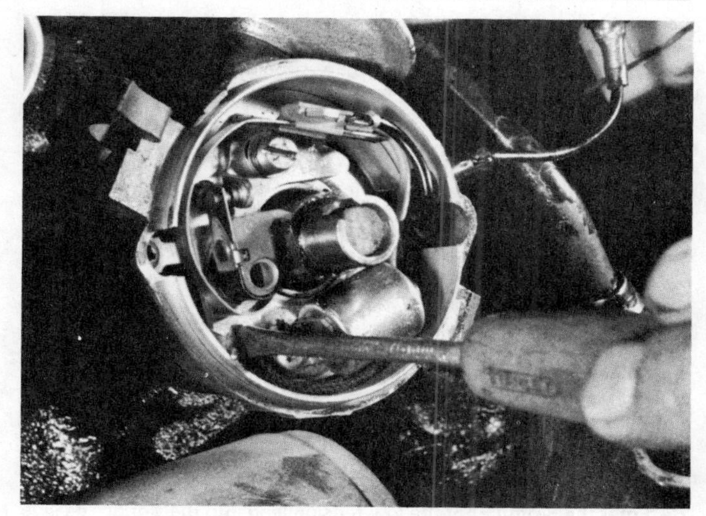

2.7 Adjusting the contact breaker points

3 Contact breaker points – removal and refitting

Note: *If the contact breaker points are burned, pitted, or badly worn, they must be removed to enable their faces to be filed smooth, or preferably they should be renewed. Mini models covered by this manual may be fitted with either a Lucas 23D4, 25D4, 45D4, or Ducellier distributor. Identify the unit being worked on by referring to the illustrations and then proceed as described below according to distributor type.*

Lucas 23D4 and 25D4

1 First remove the distributor cap as described in the previous Section and then withdraw the rotor arm from the distributor spindle.
2 Undo and remove the small terminal nut, together with the washer under its head, if fitted. Lift off the flanged nylon insulator, the condenser lead, and the low tension lead from the terminal post.
3 Using a short screwdriver, unscrew the single screw securing the adjustable contact breaker plate to the distributor baseplate. Lift off the screw and flat washer, taking care not to drop them inside the distributor. The contact breaker points can now be withdrawn.
4 To reface the points, rub each face on a fine carborundum stone or on fine emery paper. It is important that the faces are rubbed flat and parallel to each other, so that there will be a complete face-to-face contact when the points are closed. One of the points will be pitted and the other will have deposits on it. It is necessary to remove all the built-up deposits, but unnecessary to rub the pitted point right to the stage where all the pitting has disappeared. On completion, wipe the faces of the points using a cloth moistened with methylated spirit.
5 To refit the points, first position the adjustable contact breaker plate and secure it with the retaining screw and washer. Fit the fibre washer to the terminal post (and pivot post where applicable), and then place the contact breaker arm over it. Insert the flanged nylon insulator with the condenser lead immediately under its head, and the low tension lead under that, over the terminal post. Place the washer over the terminal post and finally the retaining nut.
6 If a one-piece contact breaker point assembly is being refitted, position the contact assembly on the distributor baseplate and refit the retaining screw and washer.
7 Place the condenser lead and low tension lead under the head of the upper nylon insulator, and then fit the insulator to the terminal post. Finally refit the washer and retaining nut.
8 The contact breaker points gap should now be adjusted as described in the previous Section.

Lucas 45D4

9 Remove the distributor cap as described in the previous Section and then withdraw the rotor arm from the distributor spindle (photo).
10 Using a short screwdriver, unscrew the single screw securing the adjustable contact breaker plate to the distributor baseplate. Lift off the screw and washer, taking care not to drop them inside the distributor.
11 Lift the contact assembly off the baseplate and detach the tensioning arm from the insulator. Release the terminal containing the condenser and low tension leads from the end of the arm and then lift away the contact breaker points (photos).
12 Refer to paragraph 4 of this Section if the points are to be refaced.
13 To refit the points first engage the terminal containing the condenser and low tension leads with the end of the tensioning arm. Make sure that the black lead is uppermost.

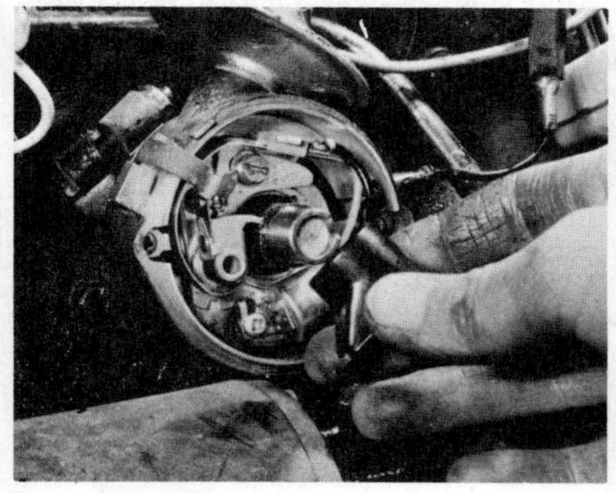

3.9 Lift off the rotor arm...

3.11a ...and with the retaining screw removed, lift the contact assembly off the baseplate

3.11b The LT terminal can then be detached from the tensioning arm

14 Position the tensioning arm in the insulator, place the contact assembly on the baseplate and refit the retaining screw and washer.
15 The contact breaker points gap should now be adjusted as described in the previous Section.

Ducellier

16 Remove the distributor cap as described in the previous Section and then withdraw the rotor arm from the distributor spindle.
17 Disconnect the contact breaker low tension lead at the connector.
18 Using a small screwdriver or pointed-nose pliers, carefully extract the circlip securing the moving contact arm to the pivot post. Remove the washer and lift off the moving contact arm and low tension lead assembly.
19 Unscrew the single screw securing the adjustable contact breaker plate to the baseplate. Lift off the screw and washer taking care not to drop them inside the distributor. Now lift away the breaker plate.
20 To refit the points first position the adjustable contact breaker plate on the baseplate and refit the retaining screw and washer.
22 Place the moving contact arm over the pivot post and engage the tensioning arm with the insulator. Refit the washer and circlip to the pivot post.
23 Enter the grommet of the low tension lead into the slot on the side of the distributor and reconnect the lead.
24 The contact breaker points gap should now be adjusted as described in the previous Section.

4 Condenser – removal, testing and refitting

1 The purpose of the condenser (sometimes known as a capacitor) is to prevent excessive arcing of the contact breaker points, and to ensure that a rapid collapse of the magnetic field, created in the coil, and necessary if a healthy spark is to be produced at the plugs, is allowed to occur.
2 The condenser is fitted in parallel with the contact breaker points. If it becomes faulty it will cause ignition failure, as the points will be prevented from cleanly interrupting the low tension circuit.
3 If the engine becomes very difficult to start, or begins to miss after several miles of running, and the contact breaker points show signs of excessive burning, then the condition of the condenser must be suspect. A further test can be made by separating the points by hand, with the ignition switched on. If this is accompanied by an excessively strong flash, it indicates that the condenser has failed.
4 Without special test equipment, the only reliable way to diagnose condenser trouble is to renew the suspect unit and note if there is any improvement in performance.
5 Removal and refitting of the condenser varies according to distributor type as follows.

Lucas 23D4 and 25D4

6 Remove the distributor cap and rotor arm, referring to Section 2 if necessary.
7 Undo and remove the nut and washer (if fitted) from the contact breaker terminal post. Withdraw the flanged nylon insulator and release the condenser lead.
8 Undo and remove the small screw securing the condenser to the distributor baseplate and lift the condenser away.
9 Refitting is simply a reverse of the removal sequence.

Lucas 45D4

10 Remove the distributor cap and rotor arm, referring to Section 2 if necessary.
11 Release the contact breaker points tensioning arm from the insulator and detach the condenser and low tension lead terminal from the end of the arm.
12 Undo and remove the small screw securing the condenser to the distributor baseplate.
13 Disconnect the distributor low tension lead at the connector, push the lead and grommet into the inside of the distributor body and lift away the condenser complete with low tension lead assembly.
14 Refitting is the reverse sequence to removal. Ensure that when the terminal is connected to the tensioning arm, the black lead is uppermost.

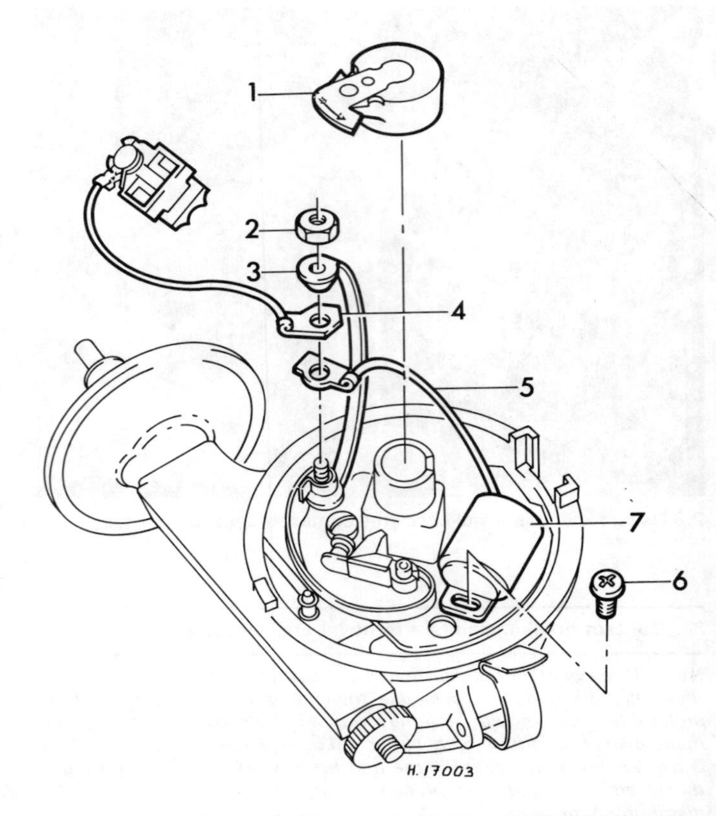

Fig. 4.4 Condenser removal – Lucas 25D4 distributor (Sec 4)

1 Rotor arm
2 Nut
3 Nylon bush
4 LT lead
5 Condenser lead
6 Screw
7 Condenser

Ducellier

15 On the Ducellier distributor the condenser is mounted externally and removal consists of simply disconnecting the lead and undoing the retaining screw.

5 Distributor – lubrication

1 It is important that the distributor cam is lightly lubricated with general purpose grease, and that the contact breaker arm, centrifugal advance weights and cam spindle are lubricated with engine oil once every 6000 miles (10000 km). In practice it will be found that lubrication every 3000 miles (5000 km) is preferable, although this is not specified by the manufacturers.
2 Great care should be taken not to use too much lubricant, as any excess that might find its way onto the contact breaker points could cause burning and misfiring.
3 To gain access to the cam spindle, lift away the rotor arm. Drop no more than two drops of engine oil onto the felt pad or screw head (photo). This will run down the spindle when the engine is hot and lubricate the bearings. The centrifugal advance weights can be lubricated by dropping two or three drops of engine oil through one of the holes or slots in the distributor baseplate. No more than one drop of oil should be applied to the contact breaker arm pivot post.

6 Distributor – removal and refitting

1 Release the three plastic retaining lugs and lift the ignition shield off the front of the engine. On models that have a distributor shield attached to the inner front panel, undo and remove the retaining screws and withdraw the shield.
2 Mark the spark plug high tension (HT) leads to ensure correct

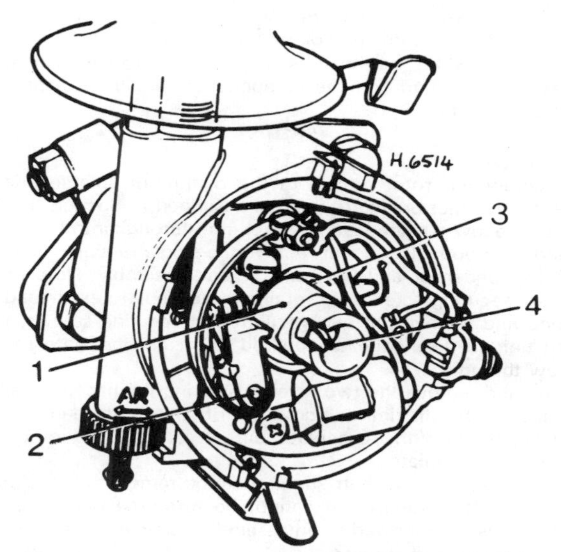

Fig. 4.5 Lubrication points for distributor (Sec 5)

1 Contact breaker cam
2 Contact breaker pivot post
3 Centrifugal weights lubrication point
4 Cam spindle

5.3 Lubricating the distributor cam spindle

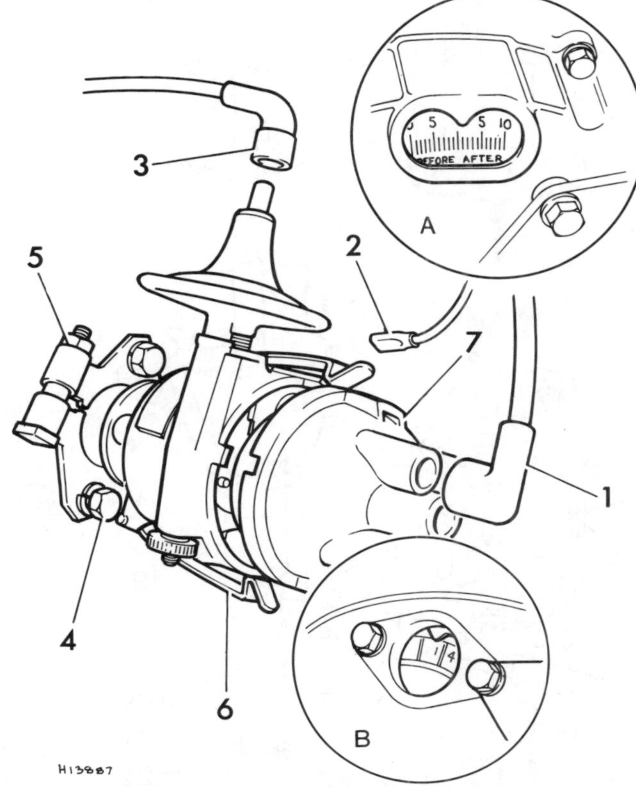

Fig. 4.6 Distributor removal (Sec 6)

1 HT lead
2 LT lead terminal connector
3 Vacuum pipe connection
4 Clamp securing bolts and spring washers
5 Clamp nut and bolt
6 Spring clip
7 Distributor cap
Inset: Timing marks:
A Automatic transmission
B Manual transmission

refitment, and then pull them off the ends of the spark plugs. Detach the HT lead from the ignition coil by sliding back the small rubber cap and pulling the lead out of the coil tower.

3 Spring back the two distributor cap retaining clips and lift away the cap complete with HT leads.

4 Detach the distributor vacuum advance pipe from the vacuum unit and then disconnect the low tension (LT) lead at the connector.

5 Using a dab of paint or a small file, make a mark between the distributor body and the clamping plate. This will ensure that the distributor is refitted in exactly the same position and that the timing is not lost.

6 If the distributor is retained by a clamping plate having a pinch bolt and nut, slacken one of the bolts securing the clamping plate to the cylinder block and then slacken the pinch bolt. If a C-shaped plate is used to retain the distributor, undo and remove the securing bolt and lift away the plate.

7 The distributor can now be withdrawn from the engine.

8 Refitting is a reverse of the removal sequence. When inserting the distributor into the engine aperture, press down lightly on the distributor body and at the same time rotate the distributor shaft. When the lug on the distributor driving dog aligns with the slot on the driveshaft, the distributor will move in toward the engine a further 0.25 in (6.3 mm). The previously made marks on the clamping plates can then be aligned and the retaining bolts tightened.

9 If a new distributor is being fitted, or if any of the engine internal components have been disturbed (ie after overhaul), then the ignition timing must be checked and, if necessary, reset as described in Section 10. It will be a wise precaution to check the ignition timing anyway.

7 Distributor – dismantling

Note: *As stated previously, Mini models covered by this manual may be fitted with a Lucas 23D4, 25D4, 45D4 or Ducellier distributor. Identify the unit being worked on and then proceed according to distributor type as described below.*

Lucas 23D4 and 25D4

1 Withdraw the rotor arm from the distributor spindle and then remove the contact breaker points as described in Section 3.

2 Undo and remove the single retaining screw and lift off the condenser.

3 Unhook the vacuum unit operating spring from the post on the distributor baseplate (not 23D4).

4 Undo and remove the two small screws and spring washers which secure the baseplate to the distributor body. Note that one of these screws also retains the baseplate earth lead.

5 Now carefully lift out the baseplate.

6 Make a note of the position of the rotor arm drive slot, in the

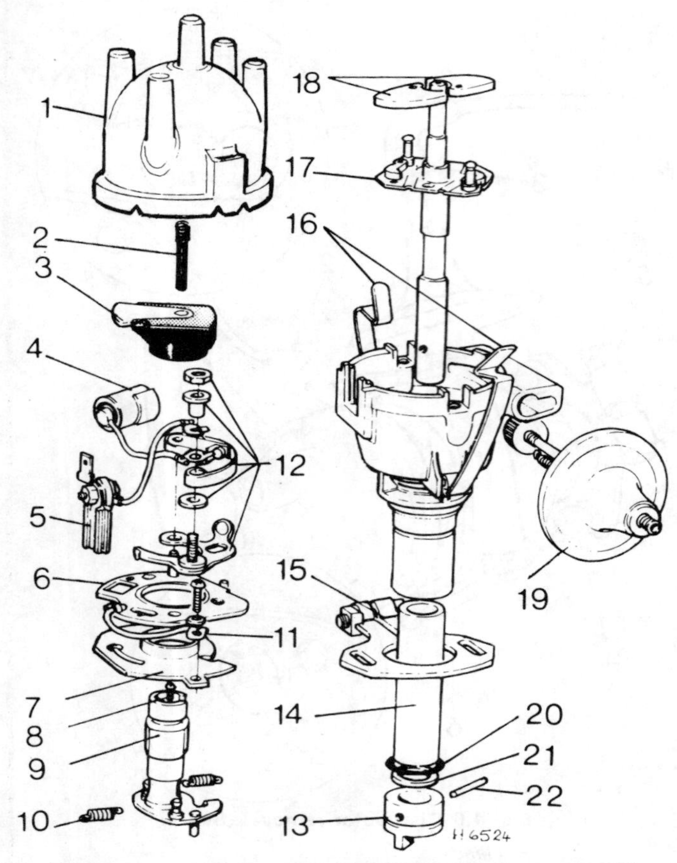

Fig. 4.7 Exploded view of Lucas 25D4 distributor (Sec 7)

1	*Distributor cap*	12	*Contact breaker points*
2	*Brush and spring*	13	*Driving dog*
3	*Rotor arm*	14	*Bush*
4	*Condenser*	15	*Clamp plate*
5	*Terminal and lead*	16	*Cap retaining clips*
6	*Moving baseplate*	17	*Shaft and action plate*
7	*Fixed baseplate*	18	*Bob weights*
8	*Cam screw*	19	*Vacuum unit*
9	*Cam*	20	*O-ring oil seal*
10	*Advance spring*	21	*Thrust washer*
11	*Earth lead*	22	*Taper pin*

spindle, in relation to the offset driving dog at the opposite end of the distributor. It is essential that this is reassembled correctly, otherwise the ignition timing will be 180° out.

7 Undo and remove the cam spindle retaining screw which is located in the centre of the rotor arm drive.

8 Remove the two centrifugal advance weight tension springs and then lift off the cam spindle. It is quite likely that the cam spindle will prove difficult to remove and will not slide readily off the shaft. If this is the case, apply liberal amounts of penetrating oil to the top of the spindle and rotate it back and forth while at the same time pulling upward. This should free the spindle and allow it to be removed from the shaft.

9 With the cam spindle removed, the centrifugal advance weights can now be lifted out.

10 To remove the vacuum unit, prise off the small circlip located behind the knurled adjustment wheel. Now unscrew the adjustment wheel until the vacuum unit is released and then withdraw the vacuum unit from the distributor body. **Note:** *A vacuum unit is not fitted to the 23D4 type.*

11 As the unit is withdrawn, retrieve the adjustment wheel together with the tension spring and spring plate. The spring plate is responsible for the clicks when the adjustment wheel is turned. This spring plate together with the circlip are small and easily lost so put them in a safe place.

12 It is only necessary to remove the distributor driveshaft if it is thought to be excessively worn. With a thin punch, drive out the retaining pin from the driving dog on the bottom end of the distributor driveshaft. The shaft can then be removed. The distributor is now completely dismantled and the components should be inspected as described in Section 8.

Lucas 45D4

13 Withdraw the rotor arm from the distributor spindle and then remove the contact breaker points as described in Section 3.

14 Push the low tension lead and grommet through into the inside of the distributor body. Undo and remove the single retaining screw and lift off the condenser and low tension lead assembly. Note that the condenser securing screw also retains the baseplate earth lead.

15 Undo and remove the two vacuum unit securing screws, tilt the vacuum unit to disengage the pullrod from the baspelate peg, and withdraw the unit.

16 Undo and remove the two screws securing the baseplate and the earth lead to the distributor body. Lift off the earth lead, lever the slotted segment of the baseplate out of its retaining groove and withdraw the baseplate.

17 The distributor driveshaft should only be removed if it is thought to be worn. After removal it cannot be further dismantled, and if necessary must be renewed as an assembly, complete with centrifugal advance weights and springs.

18 To remove the driveshaft, drift out the retaining pin from the driving dog using a thin punch. Remove the driving dog and thrust washer and then lift out the driveshaft assembly.

19 The distributor is now completely dismantled and the components should be inspected as described in Section 8.

Ducellier

20 Withdraw the rotor arm from the distributor spindle and then remove the contact breaker points as described in Section 3.

21 Undo and remove the two screws that secure the condenser, vacuum unit, and one of the distributor cap retaining clips to the distributor body. Lift away the condenser and clip.

22 Using a small screwdriver, extract the circlip securing the serrated eccentric cam to the D-post. Mark the position of the eccentric cam in relation to the spring seat of the vacuum unit operating link.

23 Detach the vacuum unit operating link and the eccentric cam from the D-post and lift off the vacuum unit. Store the eccentric cam and the small circlip safely, as they are easily lost.

24 Undo and remove the screw securing the other distributor cap retaining clip and take off the clip.

25 The distributor baseplace can now be removed, taking care not to allow the nylon pressure pad and spring to fly off as the baseplate is withdrawn.

26 This is the limit of dismantling that can be carried out on these units. If the driveshaft, centrifugal advance weights or springs are thought to be worn, it will be necessary to obtain a complete new distributor assembly. The components that have been dismantled should now be inspected as described in Section 8.

8 Distributor – inspection and repair

1 Thoroughly clean all the mechanical parts in paraffin or petrol and wipe dry, using a clean non-fluffy rag.

2 Examine the contact breaker points as described in Section 3 and reface or renew them if necessary.

3 Check the inside of the distributor cap for signs of tracking between the segments. This is indicated by a thin black wavy line between segments, or segment and centre carbon brush. Renew the cap if tracking is apparent. Also check the segments in the cap for scoring, burning, or a build up of white deposits on their faces. The deposits can be scraped off with a knife or small screwdriver, but if the segments are worn, the cap must be renewed.

4 Push in the carbon brush, located in the centre of the cap, several times to ensure that it moves freely. The brush should protrude by at least 0.1 in (3 mm).

5 Examine the rotor arm and check its fit on the spindle. If the metal portion of the rotor arm is badly burned or loose, or if the cam is a loose fit on the spindle it should be renewed. Slight burning of the metal contact portion may be cleaned with a fine file.

6 Check the vacuum unit for leaks of the internal diaphragm, by sucking on the advance pipe union connection and observing the

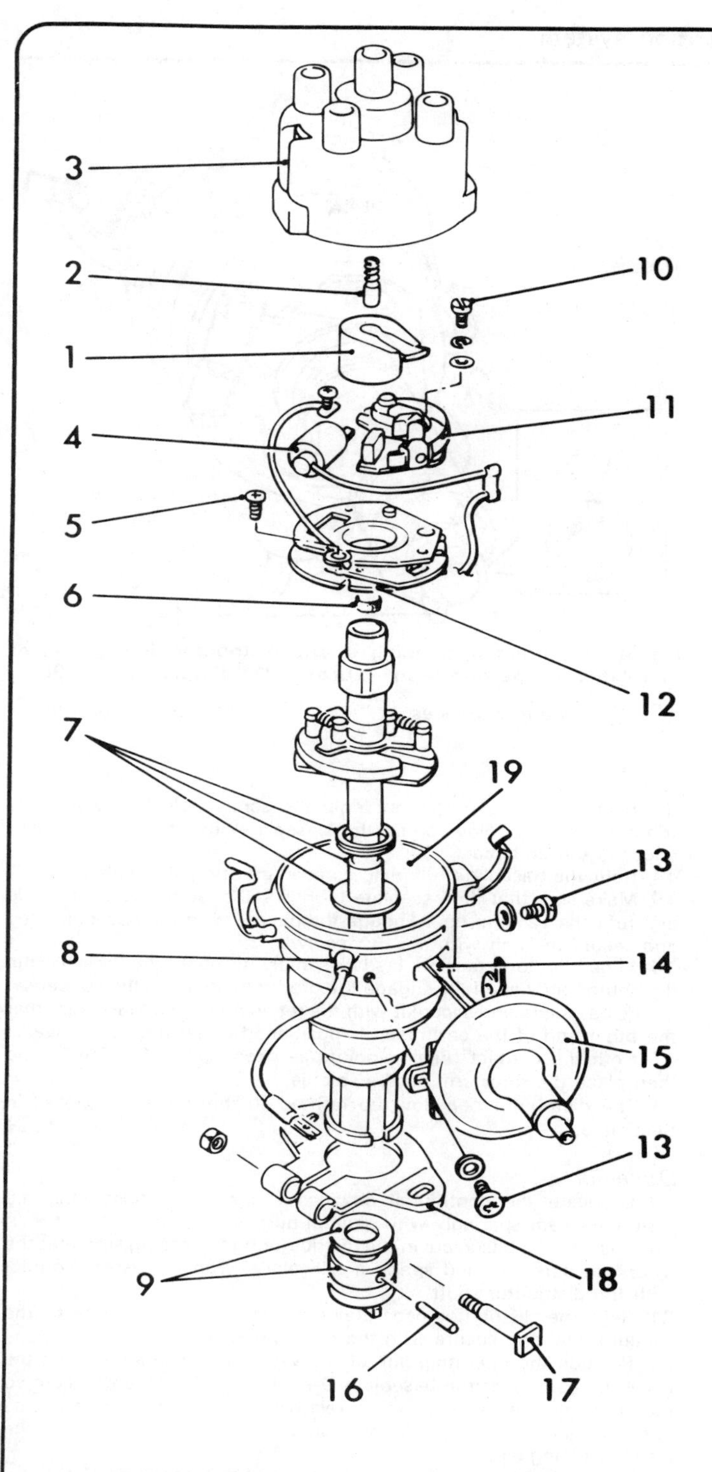

Fig. 4.8 Exploded view of Lucas 45D4 distributor (Sec 7)

1 *Rotor*
2 *Carbon brush and spring*
3 *Cap*
4 *Condenser (capacitor)*
5 *Baseplate securing screw*
6 *Felt pad*
7 *Shaft assembly with steel washer and spacer*
8 *Low tension lead and grommet*
9 *Drive dog and thrust washer*
10 *Contact set securing screw*
11 *Contact set*
12 *Baseplate*
13 *Vacuum unit retaining screws and washers*
14 *Vacuum unit link*
15 *Vacuum unit*
16 *Parallel pin*
17 *Pinch bolt and nut*
18 *Lockplate*
19 *Distributor body*

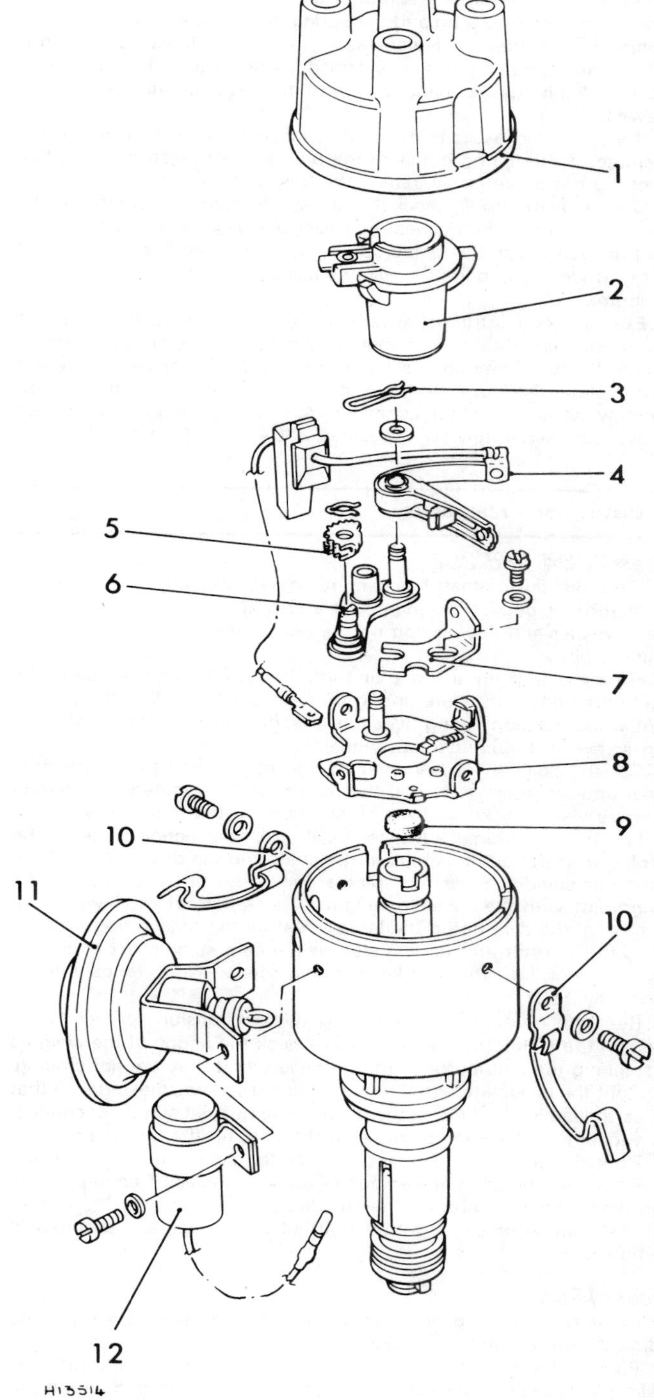

Fig. 4.9 Exploded view of Ducellier distributor (Sec 7)

1 *Cap*
2 *Rotor*
3 *Rocker arm clip*
4 *Moving contact assembly*
5 *Serrated cam*
6 *Eccentric D-post*
7 *Fixed contact*
8 *Baseplate*
9 *Felt pad*
10 *Cap retaining clips*
11 *Vacuum unit*
12 *Condenser*

movement of the operating spring or arm. If, when suction is applied, a firm resistance builds up and the spring or arm moves in toward the diaphragm then the unit is satisfactory. If no resistance to suction is felt, and the operating spring or arm does not move, then it is likely that the diaphragm is punctured and the vacuum unit should be renewed.

7 If working on a Lucas distributor, inspect the two halves of the baseplate. If the spring between the plates is damaged or if the two halves do not move freely, renew the baseplate.

8 On all distributors, check for excessive side movement of the distributor shaft in the bushes. Any excess side play here can greatly affect the acuracy of the ignition timing and the overall performance of the car. If wear is apparent it will be necessary to renew the complete distributor.

9 Examine the centrifugal advance weights and pivots for wear, and also check that the advance mechanism operates smoothly without binding. If these components are worn it will be necessary to renew the complete distributor in the case of the Ducellier unit, or the shaft assembly in the case of the Lucas 45D4. Advance weights and springs are available separately for the Lucas 23D4 and 25D4 distributors.

9 Distributor – reassembly

Lucas 23D4 and 25D4

1 If the distributor shaft has been removed, lubricate the bearings in the distributor body with engine oil and refit the shaft. Position the thrust washer and driving dog on the end of the shaft and tap in the retaining pin.

2 Slide the vacuum advance unit into its location on the side of the distributor body. Place the spring plate in position, slide the adjustment wheel tension spring over the threaded vacuum unit shaft, and then screw on the adjustment wheel.

3 Set the position of the vacuum unit by rotating the adjustment wheel until approximately half the marks on the vacuum unit vernier scale are visible. Now refit the small circlip to the end of the shaft.

4 Lay the centrifugal advance weights on the action plate of the distributor shaft. Lightly lubricate the shaft and the driving pins of the distributor spindle. Slide the spindle over the shaft and engage the driving pins with the advance weights. Check that when viewed from the base of the distributor, the large offset on the driving dog is to the left, with the rotor arm driving slot on the cam spindle uppermost. If this is correct, refit the spindle retaining screw. If not, reposition the spindle by 180°.

5 Refit the two centrifugal advance weight tension springs to the posts on the action plate and spindle. Check the action of the weights by spinning the distributor shaft and ensure that they are not binding.

6 Refit the baseplate and the two retaining screws, making sure that the earth lead is fitted under the head of the nearest screw. Reconnect the vacuum unit operating spring to the post on the baseplate.

7 Refit the condenser and secure with the single retaining screw.

8 Refit the contact breaker points as described in Section 3, and then place the rotor arm on the spindle.

9 The distributor can now be refittied to the car as described in Section 6.

Lucas 45D4

10 Begin reassembly by lubricating the distributor shaft assembly and sliding it into the distributor body.

11 Place the thrust washer and driving dog on the shaft, with the raised pips of the thrust washer toward the driving dog. Position the driving dog so that the tongues are parallel with the rotor arm electrode, and the offset is to the left of its centre line with the rotor arm pointing upward (Fig. 4.10).

12 Secure the driving dog with the retaining pin. If a new shaft is being fitted, it must be drilled through the hole in the driving dog to accept the retaining pin. The drill size will be either 0.125 in (3.175 mm) or 0.187 in (4.762 mm), depending on the type of driving dog fitted. When drilling, keep the shaft pressed down into the distributor body, and the driving dog tight against the body shank. After fitting the retaining pin, peen over the edges of the hole in the driving dog slightly to secure the pin. Make sure that there is a trace of endfloat of the shaft when the driving dog is fitted. If necessary, tap the end of the driving dog to flatten the thrust washer pips slightly and increase the endfloat.

13 Position the baseplate on the distributor body so that the two

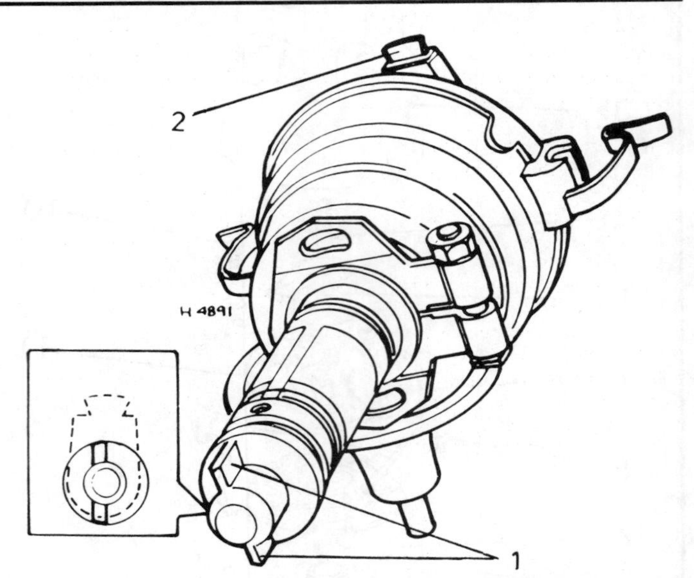

Fig. 4.10 Correct positioning of the distributor driving dog in relation to the rotor arm – Lucas 45D4 distributor (Sec 9)

1 Driving dog tongues 2 Rotor arm

downward pointing prongs straddle the screw hole below the distributor cap clip. Now press the baseplate into the body until it engages the undercut.

14 Refit the baseplate retaining screws and the earth lead.

15 Make sure that the baseplate prongs still straddle the screw hole and refit the vacuum unit. Engage the pullrod with the baseplate peg and secure the unit with the two screws.

16 Slide the low tension lead assembly through the hole in the distributor body and fully engage the grommet. Position the condenser on the baseplate and secure it with the retaining screw. Make sure that the other end of the earth lead is positioned under the screw head.

17 Refit the contact breaker points as described in Section 3, and then place the rotor arm on the spindle.

18 The distributor can now be refitted to the car as described in Section 6.

Ducellier

19 Lubricate the centrifugal advance weight pivot posts and the distributor cam sparingly with general purpose grease.

20 Position the baseplate in the distributor body, making sure that the nylon pressure pad and spring are in place, with the pad in contact with the distributor shaft.

21 Refit the distributor cap retaining clip, located opposite to the vacuum unit, and secure with the retaining screw.

22 Position the operating link of the vacuum unit together with the eccentric cam, over the baseplate D-post. Turn the eccentric cam so that it is in the same position relative to the spring seat of the operating link, as marked during dismantling. Now carefully refit the small retaining circlip.

23 Secure the vacuum unit, condenser, and the remaining distributor cap retaining clip to the distributor body, using the two screws.

24 Refit the contact breaker points as described in Section 3, and then place the rotor arm on the spindle.

25 The distributor can now be refitted to the car as described in Section 6.

10 Ignition timing

1 In order that the engine can run efficiently, it is necessary for a spark to occur ar the spark plug and ignite the fuel/air mixture at the instant just before the piston, on the compression stroke, reached the top of its travel. The precise instant at which the spark occurs is determined by the ignition timing, and this is quoted in degrees before top dead centre (BTDC). On pre-1976 models the ignition timing may

be checked with the engine stationary (this is the static ignition timing), or more accurately with the engine running, using a stroboscopic timing light. On post-1976 models a stroboscopic timing light *must* be used, as no static values are quoted.

2 If the distributor has been dismantled or renewed, or if its position on the engine has been altered, it will be necessary to reset the ignition timing using the following procedure.

3 First ensure that the contact breaker points are in good condition and that the gap is correctly set, as described in Section 2.

4 To obtain the static timing setting, remove the distributor cap and place it to one side. Undo and remove the two bolts securing the inspection plate to the top of the flywheel housing and lift off the plate. On models fitted with automatic transmission, withdraw the rubber grommet from the top of the converter housing.

5 The timing marks on the flywheel (or torque converter), and the pointer on the housing, can be viewed through the inspection aperture using a small mirror (photo). The 1/4 mark on the flywheel or torque converter indicates TDC, and the 5, 10 and 15 marks indicate 5°, 10°, and 15° of advance before TDC respectively.

Fig. 4.11 Ignition timing marks – manual transmission models (Sec 10)

1 Inspection cover
2 Timing marks
3 Pointer

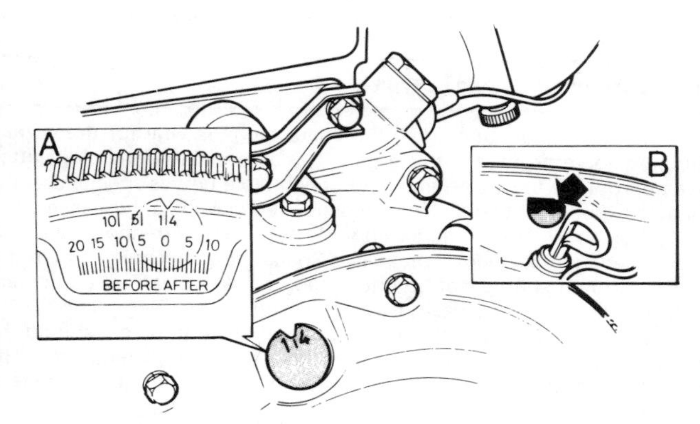

Fig. 4.12 Location of timing marks on torque converter – automatic transmission models (Sec 10)

A Detail showing alternative timing marks
B Insert screwdriver to turn converter

6 Refer to the Specifications at the beginning of this Chapter for the correct ignition timing static setting. The distributor number will be found stamped on the side of the distributor body, usually just below the vacuum unit (photo).

7 Having determined the correct setting, turn the engine over until No 1 piston is approaching TDC on the compression stroke. This can be checked by removing No 1 spark plug and feeling the pressure being developed in the cylinder as the piston rises, or by removing the rocker cover and noting when the valves of No 4 cylinder are rocking, ie the inlet valve just opening and the exhaust valve just closing. If this check is not made, it is all too easy to set the timing 180° out, as both No 1 and No 4 pistons approach TDC at the same time, but only one is on the compression stroke.

8 Continue turning the engine, in the correct direction of rotation, until the appropriate timing mark on the flywheel or torque converter is in line with the pointer on the housing.

9 The distributor rotor arm should now be pointing towards the No 1 spark plug HT lead segment in the distributor cap. Temporarily place the cap in position to verify this if necessary.

10 With the engine set in the correct position and the rotor arm pointing towards the appropriate segment, turn the knurled vernier adjustment wheel, on the distributor (where applicable), until approximately half the marks on the vacuum unit timing scale are visible.

11 Next slacken the distributor clamp plate pinch bolt and turn the

10.5 The timing marks on the flywheel can be viewed through the aperture in the housing using a mirror

10.6 The distributor number is stamped on the body below the vacuum unit

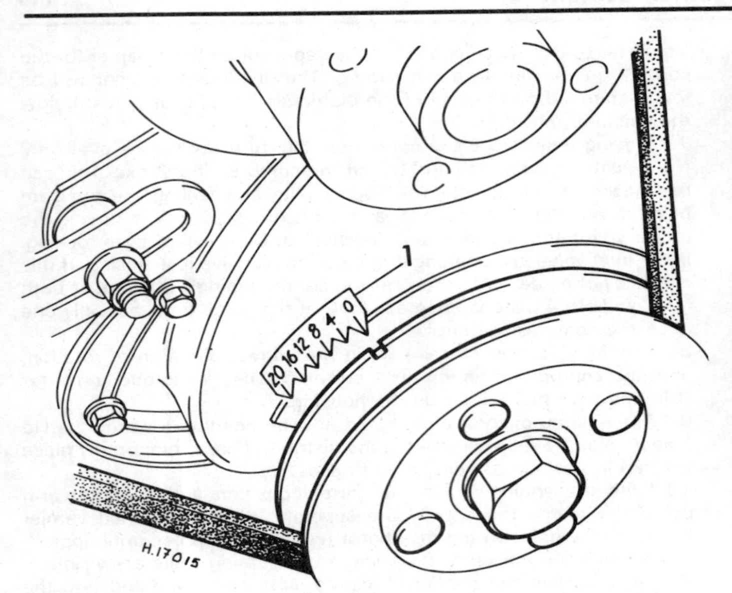

Fig. 4.13 The timing scale located on the timing cover of later models (Sec 10)

1 Timing scale

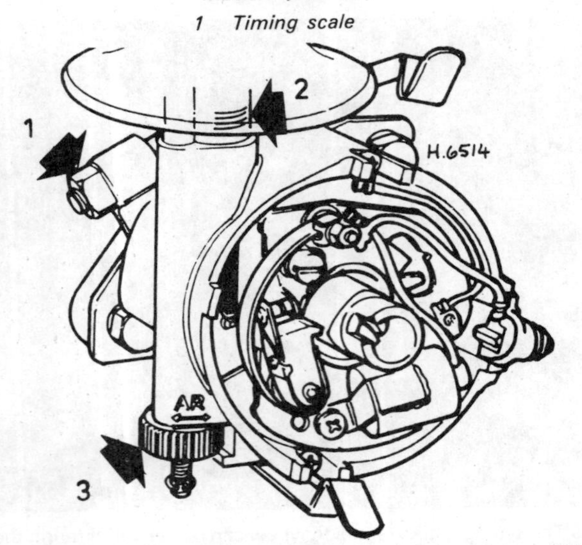

Fig. 4.14 Distributor timing adjustment points – Lucas 25D4 (Sec 10)

1 Distributor clamp pinch bolt *2 Vernier scale* *3 Knurled adjustment wheel*

distributor body clockwise until the points are *just* beginning to open. If they are already open, turn the distributor body anti-clockwise until they are fully closed, then turn it clockwise until they *just* begin to open. Now tighten the pinch bolt. If the distributor incorporates a knurled vernier adjustment wheel on the vacuum unit a very fine degree of accuracy can be obtained. Timing the wheel in the direction 'A' stamped on the vacuum unit advances the timing, and turning it towards 'R' retards it. Eleven clicks of the wheel represents 1° of timing movement and each graduation of the vernier scale is equal to approximately 5° of timing movement.

12 Difficulty will probably be experienced in determining exactly when the contact breaker points open, so the following method can be used. Connect a 12 volt bulb in parallel with the contact breaker points (one lead to earth and the other to the distributor (–) low tension terminal on the coil). With the ignition switch on the bulb will light as the points open. The distributor body should be turned as in paragraph 11 until the point is reached where the bulb *just* lights up.

13 To adjust the ignition timing using a stroboscopic timing light, first connect the light in accordance with the manufacturer's instructions. A typical method of connection is to attach one lead to No 1 spark plug, and attach the other lead to No 1 spark plug HT lead.

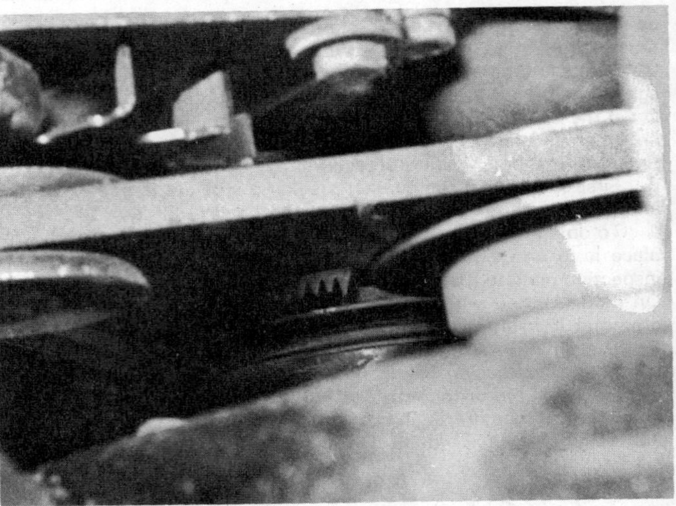

10.17 On later models there are additional timing marks at the front of the engine

14 Start the engine and allow it to reach normal running temperature.

15 Refer to the Specifications for the appropriate ignition timing setting and the corresponding engine speed.

16 Disconnect the vacuum advance pipe from the distributor and adjust the engine speed to that specified.

17 Remove the inspection cover from the flywheel or converter housing and shine the light beam into the aperture. Use a mirror to deflect the beam onto the flywheel or torque converter. On later models there is an additional and more easily visible timing scale on the timing cover, together with a notch or pointer on the crankshaft pulley (photo).

18 Turn the knurled adjustment wheel or slacken the distributor clamp or pinch bolt and rotate the distributor body until the timing marks and pointer appear stationary and directly in line with each other.

19 Tighten the clamp or pinch bolt, recheck that the timing is still correct, and then reconnect the vacuum pipe. After disconnecting the timing light, reset the engine idling speed to that specified (see Chapter 3).

20 Whichever method has been used to set the ignition timing, a thorough road test should be carried out to ensure that the engine performance is satisfactory under all engine load conditions. As a general guide, the timing is correct if very slight 'pinking' can be heard with the engine labouring (ie at the point where you would normally change to a lower gear). Any small corrections necessary can be made during the road test using the vernier adjustment wheel, or by turning the distributor body very slightly in the required direction.

11 Spark plugs and HT leads

1 The correct functioning of the spark plugs is vital for the correct running and efficiency of the engine. It is essential that the plugs fitted are appropriate for the engine, and the suitable type is specified at the beginning of this chapter. If this type is used and the engine is in good condition, the spark plugs should not need attention between scheduled replacement intervals. Spark plug cleaning is rarely necessary and should not be attempted unless specialised equipment is available as damage can easily be caused to the firing ends.

2 At intervals of 6000 miles (10 000 km) the plugs should be removed and examined, and if worn excessively, renewed. The condition of the spark plug will also tell much about the general condition of the engine.

3 If the insulator nose of the spark plug is clean and white, with no deposits, this is indicative of a weak mixture, or too hot a plug (a hot plug transfers heat away from the electrode slowly – a cold plug transfers heat away quickly). The plugs fitted as standard are detailed in the Specifications at the beginning of this Chapter.

4 If the top and insulator nose is covered with hard black-looking deposits, then this is indicative that the mixture is too rich. Should the plug be black and oily, then it is likely that the engine is fairly worn, as well as the mixture being too rich.

Are your plugs trying to tell you something?

Normal.
Grey-brown deposits, lightly coated core nose. Plugs ideally suited to engine, and engine in good condition.

Heavy Deposits.
A build up of crusty deposits, light-grey sandy colour in appearance.
Fault: Often caused by worn valve guides, excessive use of upper cylinder lubricant, or idling for long periods.

Lead Glazing.
Plug insulator firing tip appears yellow or green/yellow and shiny in appearance.
Fault: Often caused by incorrect carburation, excessive idling followed by sharp acceleration. Also check ignition timing.

Carbon fouling.
Dry, black, sooty deposits.
Fault: over-rich fuel mixture.
Check: carburettor mixture settings, float level, choke operation, air filter.

Oil fouling.
Wet, oily deposits. Fault: worn bores/piston rings or valve guides; sometimes occurs (temporarily) during running-in period.

Overheating.
Electrodes have glazed appearance, core nose very white – few deposits. Fault: plug overheating. Check: plug value, ignition timing, fuel octane rating (too low) and fuel mixture (too weak).

Electrode damage.
Electrodes burned away; core nose has burned, glazed appearance. Fault: pre-ignition. Check: for correct heat range and as for 'overheating'.

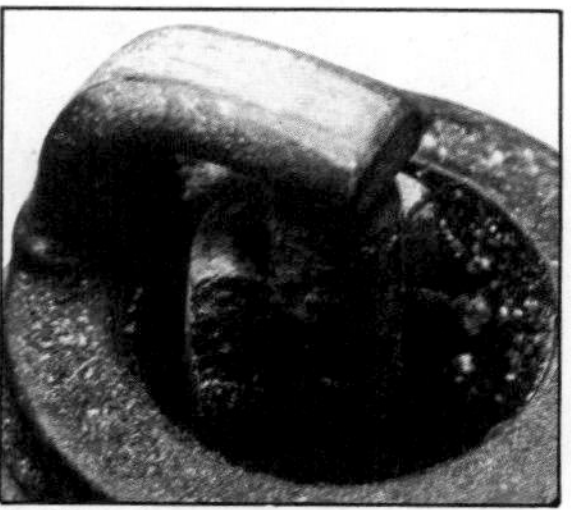

Split core nose.
(May appear initially as a crack). Fault: detonation or wrong gap-setting technique. Check: ignition timing, cooling system, fuel mixture (too weak).

WHY DOUBLE COPPER IS BETTER FOR YOUR ENGINE.

Champion Double Copper plugs are the first in the world to have copper core in both centre and earth electrode. This innovative design means that they run cooler by up to 100°C – giving greater efficiency and longer life. These double copper cores transfer heat away from the tip of the plug faster and more efficiently. Therefore, Double Copper runs at cooler temperatures than conventional plugs giving improved acceleration response and high speed performance with no fear of pre-ignition.

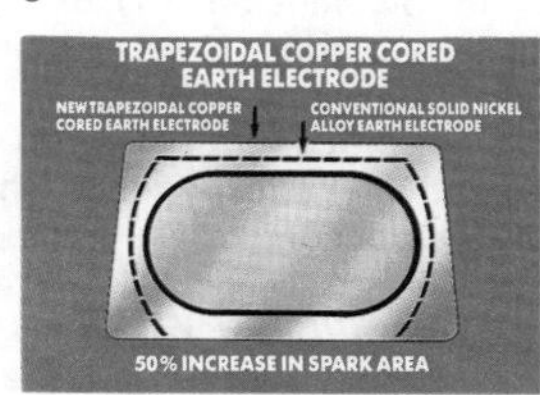

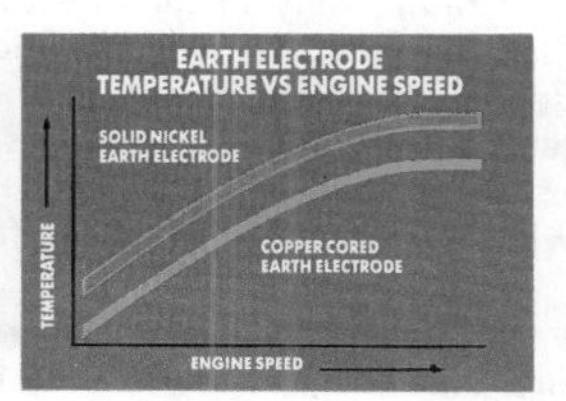

Champion Double Copper plugs also feature a unique trapezoidal earth electrode giving a 50% increase in spark area. This, together with the double copper cores, offers greatly reduced electrode wear, so the spark stays stronger for longer.

FASTER COLD STARTING

FOR UNLEADED OR LEADED FUEL

ELECTRODES UP TO 100°C COOLER

BETTER ACCELERATION RESPONSE

LOWER EMISSIONS

50% BIGGER SPARK AREA

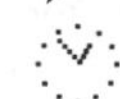
THE LONGER LIFE PLUG

Plug Tips/Hot and Cold.
Spark plugs must operate within well-defined temperature limits to avoid cold fouling at one extreme and overheating at the other.
Champion and the car manufacturers work out the best plugs for an engine to give optimum performance under all conditions, from freezing cold starts to sustained high speed motorway cruising.
Plugs are often referred to as hot or cold. With Champion, the higher the number on its body, the hotter the plug, and the lower the number the cooler the plug. For the correct plug for your car refer to the specifications at the beginning of this chapter.

Plug Cleaning
Modern plug design and materials mean that Champion no longer recommends periodic plug cleaning. Certainly don't clean your plugs with a wire brush as this can cause metal conductive paths across the nose of the insulator so impairing its performance and resulting in loss of acceleration and reduced m.p.g.
However, if plugs are removed, always carefully clean the area where the plug seats in the cylinder head as grit and dirt can sometimes cause gas leakage.
Also wipe any traces of oil or grease from plug leads as this may lead to arcing.

DOUBLE COPPER

5 If the insulator nose is covered with light tan to greyish brown deposits, then the mixture is correct, and it is likely that the engine is in good condition.

6 The spark plug gap is of considerable importance, because if it is either too large or too small the size of the spark and its efficiency will be seriously impaired. The spark plug gap should be set to the figures given in the Specifications.

7 To set it, measure the gap with a feeler gauge, and then bend open, or close, the outer plug electrode until the correct gap is achieved. The centre electrode should never be bent as this may crack the insulation and cause plug failure, if nothing worse.

8 When renewing the plugs, refit the leads from the distributor in the correct firing order, which is 1-3-4-2, cylinder No 1 being nearest the fan.

9 The HT leads require no routine maintenance other than being kept clean and wiped over regularly. At intervals of 6000 miles (10 000 km) however, pull each lead off a plug in turn and remove it from the distributor. Water can seep down these joints giving rise to a white corrosive deposit which must be carefully removed from the end of each cable.

12 Fault diagnosis – ignition system

1 Ignition faults may occur in either the low tension (LT) or high tension (HT) circuits. Regular attention to the contact breaker points and HT leads will minimise the chances of unexpected failure.

2 It may be instructive to carry out the test procedure below on an ignition system that is functioning correctly. The experience thus gained will be valuable if an actual fault does occur.

Engine will not start, or cuts out and will not restart

3 Ensure that the battery is fully charged, that the HT leads and distributor cap are clean and dry, that the points and plugs are in good condition and correctly gapped, and that all LT connections (including the battery terminals) are clean and tight.

4 Remove a spark plug cap from the end of an HT lead and hold the metal end of the lead about ¼ in (6 mm) away from the block. If the plug caps are not detachable, insert a nail or piece of stiff wire into the cap. Hold the lead with insulating material – eg a rubber glove, a dry cloth, or insulated pliers. With the ignition switched on, have an assistant crank the engine on the starter motor: a strong blue spark should be seen and heard to jump from the end of the lead to the block. If it does, this suggests that HT voltage is reaching the plugs, and that either the plugs themselves are defective, the ignition timing is grossly maladjusted, or the fault is not in the ignition system. If the spark is weak or absent, although the cranking speed is good, proceed with the checks below.

5 Remove the HT lead which enters the centre of the distributor cap. Hold the end near the block and repeat the check above. A good spark now, if there was none at the plug lead, indicates that HT voltage is not being transmitted to the plug leads. Check the carbon brush and the plug lead terminals inside the distributor cap. Check the inside of the cap itself for dampness, cracks or tracking marks (black lines formed where insulation defects allow voltage to pass to earth), and the rotor arm for cracks or tracking. If tracking is evident on the distributor cap or rotor arm, the component must be renewed. In an emergency it may be possible to interrupt the track by scraping or filing. If there is no spark at the HT lead from the coil, carry on to the next check.

6 The HT system has now been checked, with the exception of the HT lead from the coil to the distributor and the coil itself. The coil cannot easily be checked except by substitution. It is an expensive item to renew unnecessarily, so unless a spare coil is available, carry on to check the LT circuit, returning to the coil afterwards.

7 With the distributor cap and rotor arm removed, turn the engine over if necessary until the points are closed, then switch on the ignition and separate the points with an insulated screwdriver. A *strong* blue spark suggests condenser failure in the open circuit mode (a small spark is normal); fit a new one and the engine should run. No spark at all when the points are separated could be due to contamination or severe wear of the point faces. Clean them in methylated spirit or reface them and check again. If there is still no spark at the points, the fault is elsewhere in the LT system. For further checking a 12 volt test bulb or a voltmeter will be required.

8 Connect the test lamp or voltmeter between the coil contact breaker (CB) or (–) terminal and earth. Turn on the ignition and separate the points with a piece of cardboard. A reading suggests that the fault is either a broken or disconneted lead between the coil and distributor or an internal fault in the coil. No reading indicates a fault further up the line, or a short circuit to earth in the distributor. Disconnect the distributor-to-coil LT lead, leaving the test lamp or voltmeter still connected to the coil. A reading now where there was none before indicates a short circuit to earth somewhere between the lead and the fixed contact. Check the insulating washers on the moving contact pivot, the lead from the distributor LT terminal to the moving contact and the contact itself. No reading still means that further checking is required.

9 Connect the test lamp or voltmeter to the other coil LT terminal, marked (SW) or (+). Leave the distributor-to-coil LT lead disconnected and turn on the ignition. A reading here with none at the (CB) or (–) terminal confirms an internal fault in the coil which will have to be renewed. No reading indicates a break in supply from the battery to the coil via the ignition switch.

Engine misfires

10 Uneven running and misfiring should first be checked by seeing that all leads, particularly HT, are dry and connected properly. Ensure that they are not shorting to earth through broken or cracked insulation. If they are you should be able to see and hear it. If not, then check the plugs, contact breaker points and condenser just as you would in a case of total failure to start. A regular misfire can be isolated by removing each plug lead in turn, (taking precautions against electric shock). Removing a good lead will accentuate the misfire, whilst removing the defective lead will make no difference.

11 If misfiring occurs at high speed check the points gap, and the plugs. Check also that the spring tension on the points is not too light, thus causing them to bounce. This requires a special spring balance, so if in doubt it will be cheaper to buy a new set of contact breaker points rather than go to a garage and get them to check the tension. If the trouble is still not cured, then the fault lies in the carburation or engine itself.

12 If misfiring or stalling occurs only at low speeds the points gap is possibly too large. If not then the slow running and mixture settings on the carburettor may need attention.

Chapter 5 Clutch

For modifications, and information applicable to later models, see Supplement at end of manual

Contents

Specifications

Type	Borg and Beck single dry plate, diaphragm spring, hydraulically actuated
Clutch disc diameter	7.125 in (180.9 mm)
Master cylinder bore diameter	0.75 in (19.05 mm)
Slave cylinder bore diameter	0.875 in (22.2 mm)
Clutch return stop clearance	0.020 in (0.50 mm)
Clutch hydraulic fluid type/specification	Hydraulic fluid to SAE J1703 (Duckhams Universal Brake and Clutch Fluid)

Torque wrench settings	**lbf ft**	**Nm**
Flywheel centre bolt	112	152
Diaphragm spring housing to pressure plate	16	22
Driving strap to flywheel	16	22

1 General description

All manual transmission models covered by this book are equipped with a single dry plate diaphragm spring clutch. The design of the clutch is slightly unusual because there are major parts of the clutch assembly on both sides of the flywheel.

The main parts of the clutch assembly on the outside of the flywheel are the spring housing, the thrust plate, the release bearing, the diaphragm spring and the three dividing straps. Located on the inside of the flywheel are the clutch disc and the pressure plate.

The spring housing is firmly bolted to the pressure plate by bolts and spring washers. The spring housing is held to the flywheel by dividing straps which are held a little away from the outer clutch by spacing washers.

The clutch disc is free to slide along the splines of the primary gear which is fitted to the end of the crankshaft. Friction lining material is riveted to the clutch disc, which has a segmented hub to help absorb transmission shocks and to ensure a smooth take-off.

The clutch is actuated hydraulically. The pendant clutch pedal is connected to the clutch master cylinder and hydraulic fluid reservoir by a short pushrod. The master cylinder and hydraulic reservoir are mounted on the engine side of the bulkhead in front of the driver. Depressing the clutch pedal moves the piston in the master cylinder forwards, so forcing hydraulic fluid through the clutch hydraulic pipe to the slave cylinder. The piston in the slave cylinder moves forward on the entry of the fluid and actuates the clutch operating lever by means of a short pushrod. The opposite end of the operating lever slots, by means of a balljoint, into a throw-out plunger. As the pivoted operating lever moves backwards, it bears against the release bearing, pushing it forwards. This in turn bears against the clutch thrust plate, the spring housing, and the pressure plate which all move forward slightly, thus disengaging the pressure plate face from the clutch disc.

When the clutch pedal is released, the pressure plate springs force the pressure plate spring housing outwards, which, because it is attached to the pressure plate, brings the pressure plate into contact with the high friction linings on the clutch disc. At the same time the disc is forced firmly against the inner face of the flywheel and so the drive is taken up.

Although space is limited, removal of the clutch and flywheel assembly, for inspection or overhaul, can be carried out with the engine and transmission assembly still in position in the car.

2 Clutch – adjustments

Return stop – adjustment

Note: *As friction linings of the clutch disc wear, the distance between the clutch release bearing and the clutch thrust plate will decrease. The pressure plate will then move in closer to the clutch disc to compensate for wear. Unless the wear is taken up by adjustment of the stop located between the flywheel housing and the operating lever, the clutch will start to slip.*

1 To carry out the adjustment, first disconnect the clutch operating lever return spring.

2 Pull the operating lever away from the engine until all the free play is eliminated.

3 Hold the lever in this position and measure the gap between the lever and the head of the stop using feeler gauges (photo).

4 If necesary, slacken the locknut and adjust the stop bolt until the specified gap is achieved. Then tighten the locknut.

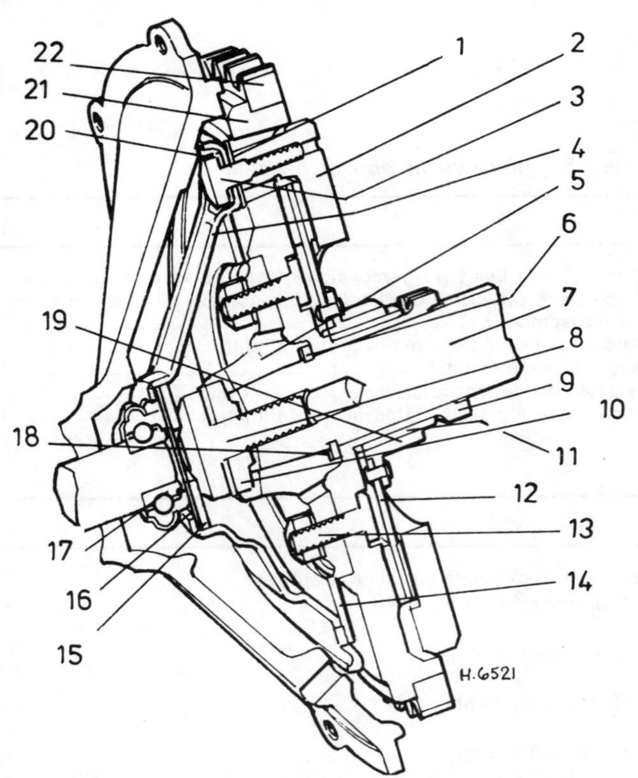

Fig. 5.1 Sectional view of the clutch and flywheel assembly (Sec 1)

1 Driving strap
2 Pressure plate
3 Driving bolt
4 Spring housing
5 Flywheel hub
6 C-washer
7 Crankshaft
8 Flywheel retaining bolt
9 Primary gear
10 Keyed washer
11 Primary gear bearing
12 Clutch disc
13 Driving bolt
14 Diaphragm spring
15 Thrust plate
16 Retaining spring clip
17 Release bearing
18 C-washer
19 Clutch disc hub
20 Lockwasher
21 Flywheel
22 Starter ring

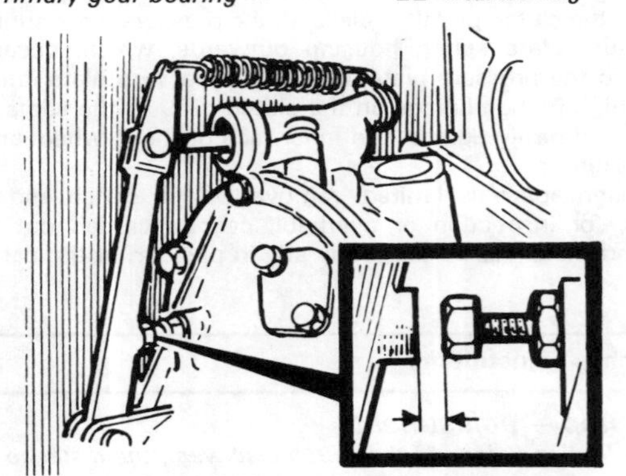

Fig. 5.2 Clutch lever adjustment (Sec 2)

Inset shows clearance measurement-point

Throw-out stop – adjustment

Note: *At the base of the clutch lever there is an adjustable collar and locknut threaded onto the end of the throw-out plunger. The position of this collar and locknut (known as the throw-out stop) determines the amount of travel of the operating lever when the clutch pedal is depressed. Throw-out stop adjustment is normally only necessary after clutch overhaul and is carried out as described below.*

5 Slacken the throw-out stop and locknut and unscrew them to the end of their travel.

2.3 Using feeler gauges to measure the clutch return stop clearance

6 Engage the help of an assistant to depress the clutch pedal several times and then hold it down.

7 Screw in the throw-out stop and locknut until the stop contacts the boss on the flywheel housing cover.

8 Release the pedal, screw in the throw-out stop one further flat and then tighten the locknut.

3 Clutch hydraulic system – bleeding

Note: *If any of the clutch hydraulic system components have been disconnected on removal, or if the fluid level in the master cylinder reservoir has fallen appreciably, air will have been introduced into the system. For the clutch to function correctly all air must be removed from the system, and this process is known as bleeding.*

1 To bleed the system first gather together a clean jar, a suitable length of rubber or clear plastic tubing, which is a tight fit over the bleed screw on the clutch slave cylinder, and a tin of the specified hydraulic fluid. The help of an assistant wil also be required. (If a one-man do-it-yourself bleeding kit for bleeding the brake hydraulic system is available, this can be used quite satisfactorily for the clutch also. Full information on the use of these kits may be found in Chapter 9 Section 3).

2 Remove the filler cap from the master cylinder reservoir, and if necessary top up the fluid. Keep the reservoir topped up during subsequent operations.

3 Wipe clean the area around the bleed screw on the slave cylinder and remove the dust cap (if fitted).

4 Connect one end of the bleed tube to the bleed screw, and insert the other end of the tube in the jar containing sufficient clean hydraulic fluid to keep the end of the tube submerged.

5 Open the bleed screw half a turn and have your assistant depress the clutch pedal and then slowly release it. Continue this procedure until clean hydraulic fluid, free from air bubbles, emerges from the tube. Now tighten the bleed screw at the end of a downstroke.

6 Check the operation of the clutch pedal. After a few strokes it should feel normal. Any sponginess would indicate air still present in the system.

7 On completion remove the bleed tube and refit the dust cover. Top up the master cylinder reservoir if necessary and refit the cap. Fluid expelled from the hydraulic system should now be discarded as it will be contaminated with moisture, air and dirt, making it unsuitable for further use.

4 Clutch slave cylinder – removal and refitting

1 Disconnect the clutch operating lever return spring from the lever and the tag on the slave cylinder bleed screw.

2 Clamp the flexible hydraulic hose with a suitable brake hose clamp or a self-gripping wrench with jaws protected. This will minimise hydraulic fluid loss when the hose is disconnected.
3 Wipe clean the area around the hose union on the slave cylinder and slacken the union half a turn.
4 Undo and remove the two bolts securing the slave cylinder to the top of the flywheel housing (photo).
5 Move the slave cylinder to the right to disengage the pushrod and then, while supporting the hydraulic hose, turn the slave cylinder anti-clockwise to unscrew it from the hose. Take care not to lose the copper sealing washer when the hose is undone.
6 Refitting the slave cylinder is the reverse sequence to removal. Take care not to kink the hose when refitting.
7 With the cylinder installed, bleed the clutch hydraulic system as described in Section 3.

5 Clutch slave cylinder – dismantling, inspection and reassembly

1 With the cylinder removed from the car, wipe off the exterior with a clean rag until it is free from dirt.
2 Lift off the dust cover, and then using circlip pliers, extract the circlip from the end of the cylinder bore.
3 Tap the cylinder on a block of wood until the piston emerges from the end of the cylinder. Now lift out the piston followed by the cup seal, cup filler and spring.
4 Thoroughly clean all the parts in clean hydraulic fluid and wipe dry with a non-fluffy rag.
5 Carefully examine the piston and cylinder bore for signs of scoring, pitting or wear ridges, and if apparent renew the complete cylinder assembly. If these parts are in a satisfactory condition a new set of seals in the form of a slave cylinder repair kit should be obtained as a matter of course. Old seals should not be re-used as they will have deteriorated with age even though this may not be apparent during visual inspection.
6 Immerse all the internal components in clean hydraulic fluid and assemble them wet.
7 Reassemble the spring into the cylinder bore first, followed by the cup filler and then the cup seal, with its lip or larger diameter away from the piston.
8 Now slide the piston into position and secure the assembly with the circlip.
9 Slip the dust cover over the end of the cylinder bore and then refit the assembled unit to the car as described in Section 4.

6 Clutch master cylinder – removal and refitting

1 Detach the flexible air intake ducting from the side of the heater unit and withdraw it sufficiently to provide access to the clutch pedal.
2 Extract the split pin and withdraw the clevis pin securing the master cylinder pushrod to the clutch pedal.
3 Working in the engine compartment, undo and remove the hydraulic pipe union from the top of the master cylinder and carefully lift out the pipe.
4 Undo and remove the two nuts securing the master cylinder mounting flange to the mounting bracket, and lift off the cylinder.
5 Refitting the master cylinder is the reverse sequence to removal. On completion, bleed the clutch hydraulic system as described in Section 3.

7 Clutch master cylinder – dismantling, inspection and re-assembly

1 Before dismantling the master cylinder, prepare a clean uncluttered working area on the bench.
2 Remove the filler cap from the master cylinder, and drain and discard the hydraulic fluid from the reservoir.
3 With the cylinder on the bench, withdraw the rubber dust cover and slide it off over the end of the pushrod.
4 Using circlip pliers, extract and lift off the pushrod and dished washer.
5 Tap the master cylinder body on a block of wood until the piston emerges from the end of the cylinder bore.

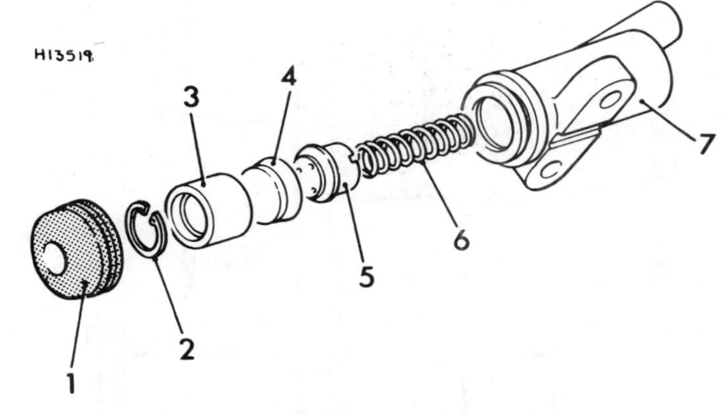

Fig. 5.3 Exploded view of clutch slave cylinder (Sec 5)

1	*Dust cover*	5	*Cup filler*
2	*Circlip*	6	*Spring*
3	*Piston*	7	*Cylinder body*
4	*Cup seal*		

4.4 Undoing the clutch slave cylinder bolts

6 Withdraw the piston from the cylinder followed by the piston washer, main cup seal, spring retainer and spring.
7 Lay the parts out in the order of removal and then very carefully remove the secondary cup seal by stretching it over the end of the piston.
8 Wash the components in clean hydraulic fluid and then dry with a lint-free cloth.
9 Examine the cylinder bore and piston carefully for signs of scoring or wear ridges. If these are apparent renew the complete master cylinder. If the condition of the components appears satisfactory, a new set of rubber seals must be obtained. Never re-use old seals as they will have deteriorated with age, even though this may not be evident during visual inspection.
10 Begin reassembly by thoroughly lubricating the internal components and the cylinder bore in the clean hydraulic fluid.
11 Using fingers only, place the secondary cup seal in position on the piston with the lip of the cup facing the opposite (drilled) end of the piston.
12 Position the spring retainer over the smaller diameter of the spring and place this assembly into the cylinder bore, larger diameter first.
13 Now insert the main cup seal into the cylinder bore, lip end first followed by the washers.
14 Insert the piston assembly into the cylinder bore, followed by the

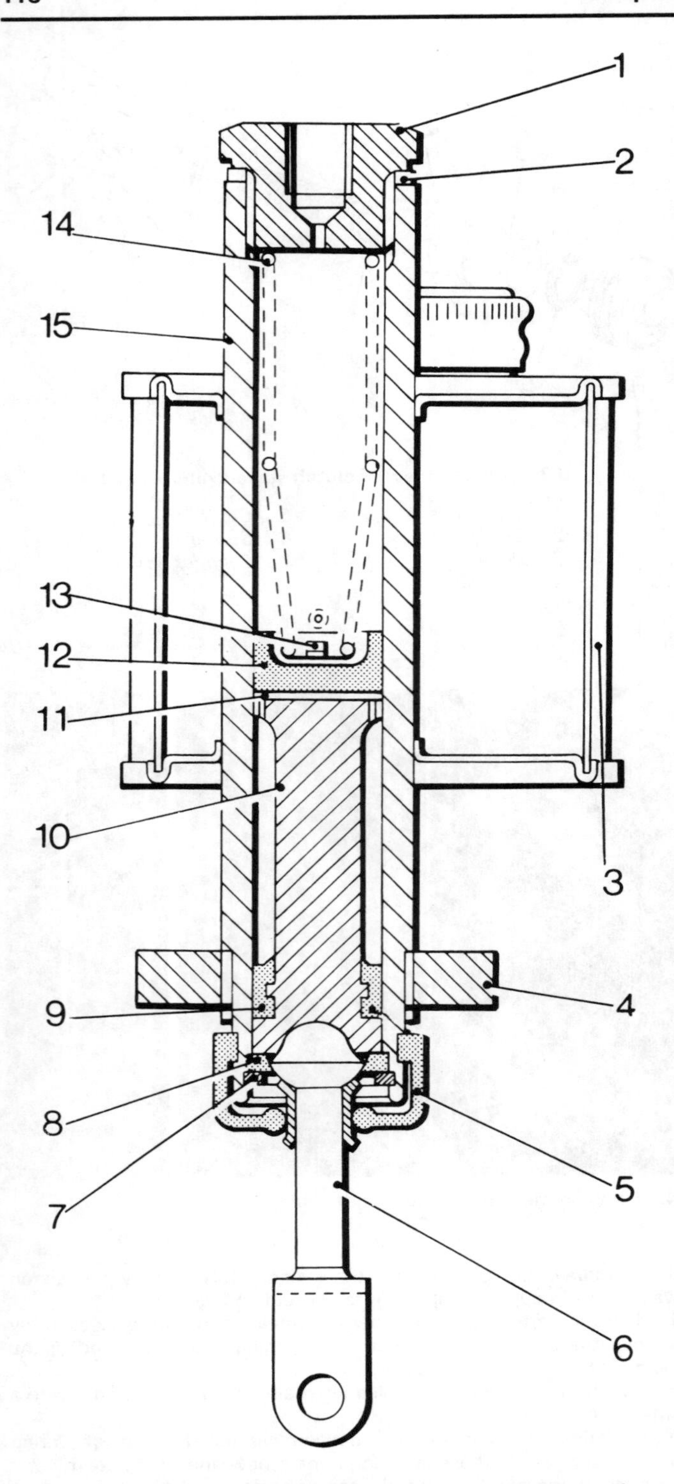

Fig. 5.4 Sectional view of clutch master cylinder (Sec 7)

1 End plug (early models only)
2 Washer (early models only)
3 Reservoir
4 Mounting flange
5 Rubber dust cover
6 Pushrod
7 Circlip
8 Stop washer
9 Secondary cup seal
10 Piston
11 Piston washer
12 Main cup seal
13 Spring retainer
14 Return spring
15 Cylinder body

pushrod, dished washer and circlip. Ensure that the circlip fully enters its groove.
15 Lubricate a new dust cover with rubber grease and stretch it over the pushrod and into position on the end of the cylinder.
16 The assembled master cylinder can now be refitted to the car as described in the previous Section.

8 Clutch pedal – removal and refitting

1 Detach the flexible air duct from the heater and from the air intake under the right-hand front wheel arch. Move the duct away from the heater sufficiently to provide access to the clutch and brake pedals.
2 Slacken the nut securing the rear of the heater unit to the mounting bracket.
3 Undo and remove the two screws securing the front of the heater to the parcel shelf and lower the unit to the floor.
4 Undo and remove the nut and washer securing the pedal cross-shaft to the pedal mounting bracket.
5 Extract the split pins and clevis pins securing the master cylinder pushrods to the clutch and brake pedals.
6 Slide the cross-shaft out of the mounting bracket, lift out the two pedals and detach the return spring.
7 Examine the pedal bushes and cross-shaft for wear and renew as necessary. The pedal bushes can be removed by drawing them out using a long bolt and nut, flat washers and a tube of suitable diameter. New bushes can be fitted in the same manner.
8 Refitting the pedals is the reverse sequence to removal. Lightly lubricate the pedal shaft and bushes with general purpose grease prior to refitting.

9 Clutch and flywheel assembly – removal and refitting

Note: *The clutch and flywheel assembly can be removed either with the engine/transmission unit in the car or on the bench. If the unit has been removed from the car, follow the instructions given in paragraphs 16 to 32 inclusive; otherwise proceed as follows.*
1 Jack up the front of the car and support it on axle stands positioned under the front subframe.
2 Disconnect the battery earth terminal.
3 To provide greater access remove the grille, referring to Chapter 12 if necessary.
4 Detach the heater air duct from the air intake under the right-hand front wing. Remove the air intake from the inner wing panel.
5 If an ignition shield is fitted over the front of the engine, release the three fasteners and lift away the shield.
6 Undo and remove the nut and spring washer securing the starter motor cable and lift off the cable. Now undo and remove the starter motor securing bolts and withdraw the starter.
7 Undo and remove the screws securing the starter solenoid to the inner wing panel. Lift off the solenoid and position it out of the way.
8 If the ignition coil is mounted on the flywheel housing, or on a bracket secured to one of the cylinder head studs, remove the coil and mounting bracket and position it well clear.
9 On later Mini 850 and 1000 models, remove the horn and place it to one side.
10 Disengage the return spring from the clutch operating lever and slave cylinder, and lift away the spring.
11 Undo and remove the two bolts securing the engine tie-bar and bracket to the side of the cylinder block. Note that on later models one of the bolts also retains the engine earth strap.
12 Undo and remove the two nuts and two bolts securing the radiator upper support bracket to the radiator and thermostat housing. Withdraw the bracket. **Note:** *It is not necessary to remove the support bracket if a large clearance exists between the radiator and left-hand inner wing panel, as is the case on later Mini 850 and 1000 models.*
13 Place a jack beneath the flywheel housing end of the gearbox casing and *just* take the weight of the power unit. Use a block of wood interposed between the gearbox casing and the jack to spread the load.
14 From beneath the car undo and remove the two nuts and bolts securing the right-hand engine mounting to the subframe side-members. The best way to do this is to engage the help of an assistant to hold the bolts from above while you undo the nuts from below. The bolt heads are tucked away beneath the flywheel housing and can only

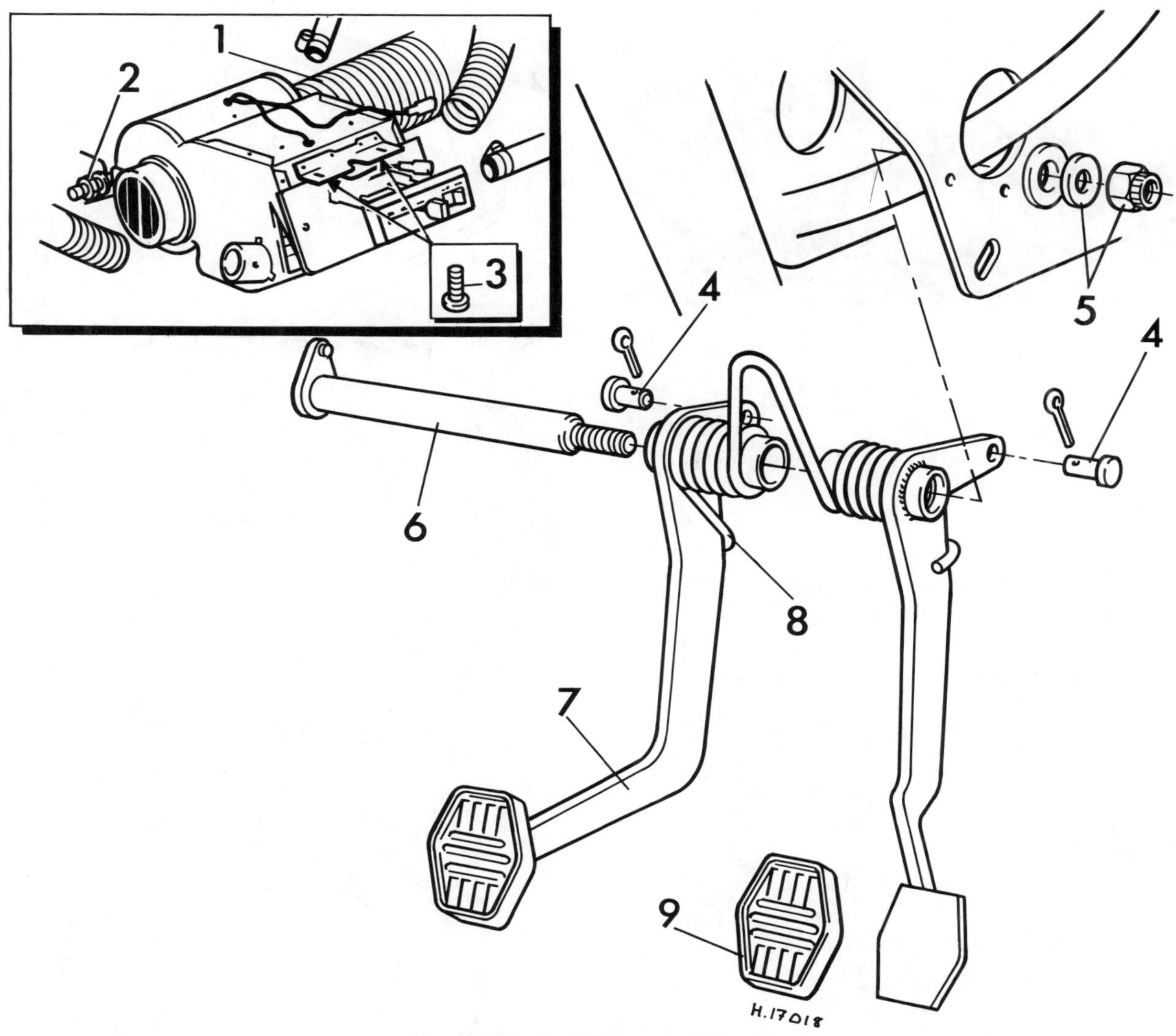

Fig. 5.5 Clutch pedal removal (Sec 8)

1 *Heater air duct*
2 *Heater rear securing nut*
3 *Heater front retaining screw*
4 *Clevis pins*
5 *Pedal shaft retaining nut*
6 *Pedal shaft*
7 *Clutch pedal*
8 *Pedal return spring*
9 *Pedal rubber*

be reached with a small open-ended spanner.

15 Having released the mounting, jack up the power unit sufficiently to enable the nine bolts securing the flywheel housing cover to be removed. Note that on early models one of the front bolts also retains the engine earth strap (photo). On all models the rear bolts are quite inaccessible, requiring a good deal of patience and a short spanner.

16 When all the bolts are undone, lift off the flywheel housing cover and at the same time disengage the clutch operating lever pushrod from the slave cylinder.

17 Undo and remove the three bolts securing the diaphragm spring housing to the driving straps and lift off the housing.

18 Tap back the locking washer securing the large flywheel central retaining bolt.

19 Rotate the crankshaft until the driving slot in the flywheel, located just behind the retaining bolt head, is horizontal. If this is not done the crankshaft primary gear C-shaped thrust washer may become dislodged, causing damage to the flywheel as it is removed.

20 Insert a large screwdriver through the starter motor aperture and engage the teeth of the ring gear to prevent the flywheel from turning.

21 Using a large socket and extension handle, undo and remove the flywheel retaining bolt and lift off the keyed washer.

22 The flywheel is retained on the crankshaft by means of a taper, and a puller is necessary to separate it. The puller is BL special tool No 186304 and adaptor 18G304N. There are, however, a number of similar pullers readily available from accessory shops or garages.

23 Position the puller over the three studs which are first screwed into the threaded holes in the flywheel. Do not tighten the studs or the clutch disc may be damaged. Fit the thrust pad to the end of the crankshaft and then secure the body of the puller to the studs using the three nuts.

24 Tighten the centre bolt on the puller until the flywheel is released from the taper. At the same time hold the ring gear with a screwdriver inserted into the starter motor aperture to prevent the flywheel from turning. It is quite likely that the flywheel will be extremely tight requiring a great deal of effort to free it. When it does free it will release with a 'bang' giving the impression that something has broken. This, however, is quite normal and nothing to be alarmed about.

25 Once the taper is released, lift the flywheel off the end of the crankshaft, slide the clutch disc off the primary gear splines and lift out the pressure plate.

26 Before commencing reassembly ensure that the flywheel and crankshaft tapers are clean and dry. Note also that the pressure plate and diaphragm spring housing are stamped with a balance mark 'A'

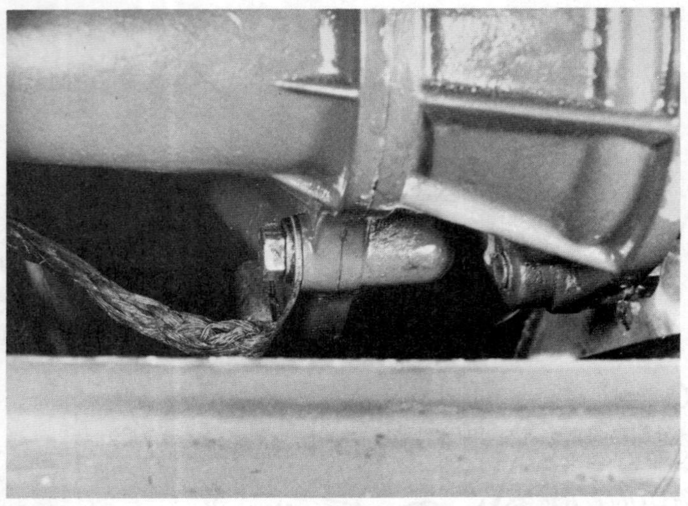

9.15 Engine earth strap location on flywheel housing cover bolts

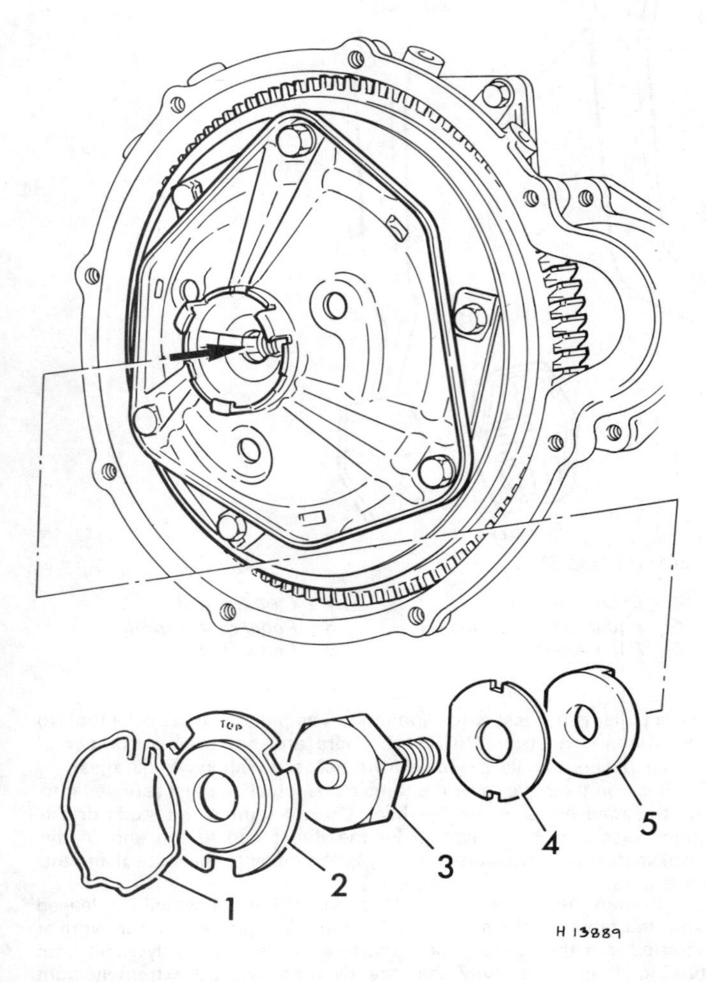

Fig. 5.6 Clutch thrust plate and flywheel securing bolt assemblies (Sec 9)

1 *Circlip*
2 *Release bearing thrust plate*
3 *Flywheel retaining bolt*
4 *Lockwasher*
5 *Keyed washer*

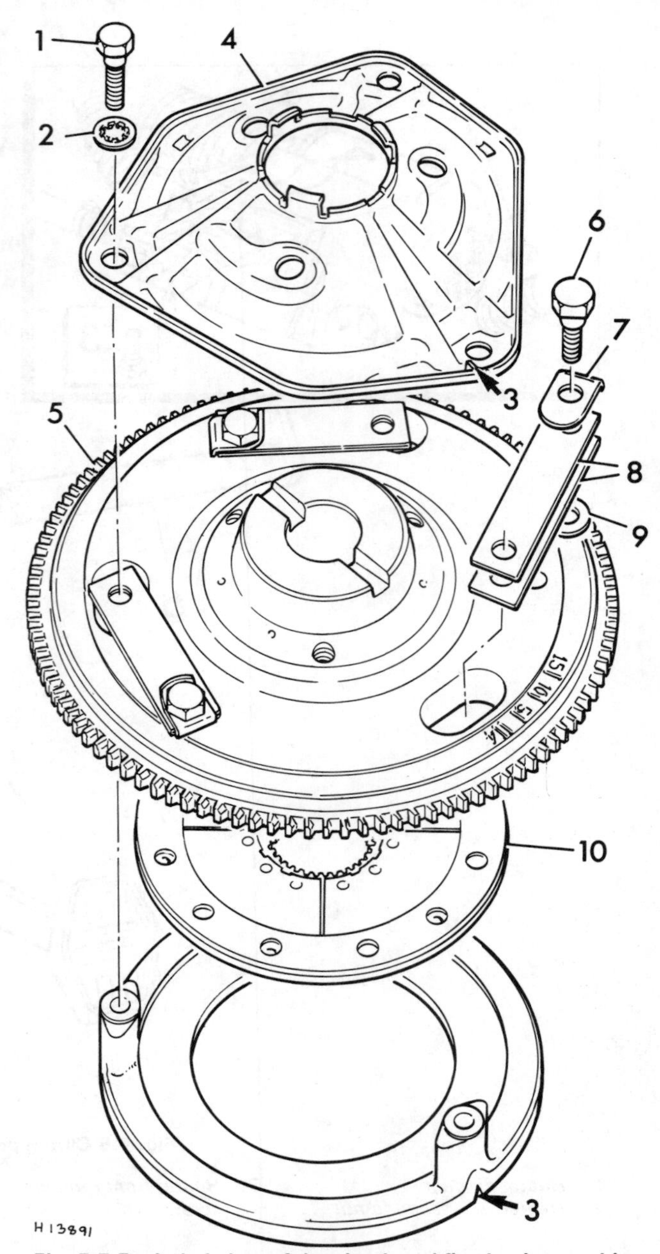

Fig. 5.7 Exploded view of the clutch and flywheel assembly (Sec 9)

1 *Driving bolt*
2 *Shakeproof washer*
3 *Alignment mark*
4 *Diaphragm*
5 *Flywheel*
6 *Driving bolt*
7 *Tab washer*
8 *Driving straps*
9 *Distance washer*
10 *Clutch disc*

adjacent to one of the bolt holes. These marks must be adjacent to each other when assembling, and aligned with the flywheel timing marks (photos).

27 Note the location of the balance mark 'A' on the pressure plate and position the plate in the flywheel housing.

28 Slide the clutch disc over the primary gear splines with the hub facing inwards and then centralise the pressure plate over the disc (photo).

29 Place the flywheel onto the crankshaft, ensuring that the lug of the pressure plate carrying the balance mark 'A' enters the flywheel opening adjacent to the timing marks (photo).

30 Refit the keyed washer, locking washer and retaining bolt. Tighten the bolt to the specified torque and then bend over the locking washer (photos).

31 Refit the diaphragm spring housing with the balance mark 'A'

9.26a Location of balance mark 'A' on pressure plate...

9.26b ...and diaphragm spring housing

9.28 Refitting the clutch disc

9.29 Refitting the flywheel

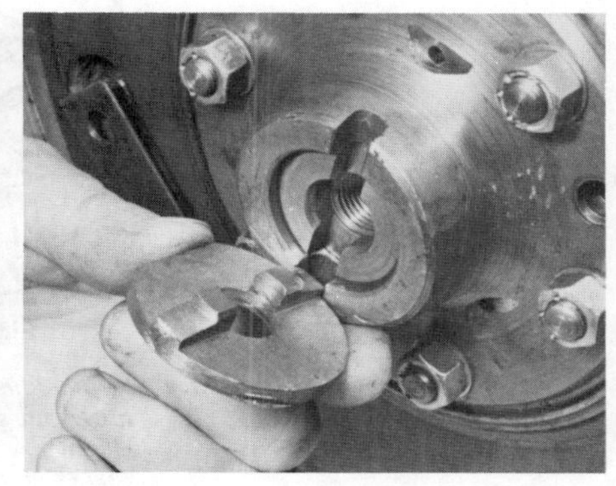

9.30a Refit the keyed washer and retaining bolt...

9.30b ...tighten the bolt to the specified torque...

9.30c ...and bend over the lockwasher

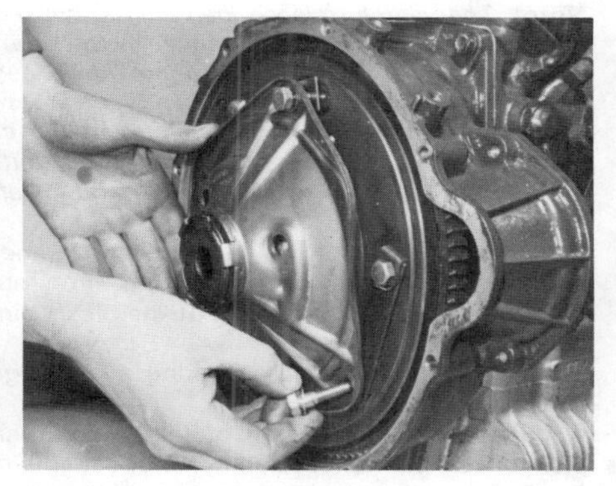

9.31 Refitting the diaphragm spring housing and retaining bolts

adjacent to the flywheel timing marks. Ensure that the retaining bolts pass squarely through each set of driving straps and then progressively tighten the bolts to the specified torque (photo).

32 The remainder of the reassembly procedure is a straightforward reverse of the removal sequence.

10 Clutch – inspection and renovation

1 Carefully inspect the clutch disc friction linings for wear and loose rivets, and the disc for rim distortion, cracks and worn splines. Renew the clutch disc if any of these conditions are apparent.

2 The disc should also be renewed if there is any sign of oil contamination of the friction linings. This is a common occurrence on Minis and can cause quite severe clutch judder or clutch slip. The cause of the contamination is oil leaking past the primary gear oil seal in the flywheel housing or up the centre of the gear between the bushes and the crankshaft. If this condition is evident it is recommended that the oil seal in the flywheel housing is renewed as described in Section 12. Also check that the endfloat of the primary gear is not excessive as this will encourage oil leakage through its centre. Full information regarding the primary gear running clearances will be found in Chapter 6.

3 Inspect the machined faces of the flywheel and pressure plate for scores or deep grooving; if apparent they should be machined until smooth. If the pressure plate is cracked or damaged it must be renewed.

4 Examine the diaphragm spring in the spring housing for cracks, and if evident renew the housing.

5 Finally, examine the holes in the spring housing and driving straps for elongation or distortion, and the retaining bolts for ridges or shoulders. Renew any worn items as complete sets to preserve the balanced conditions.

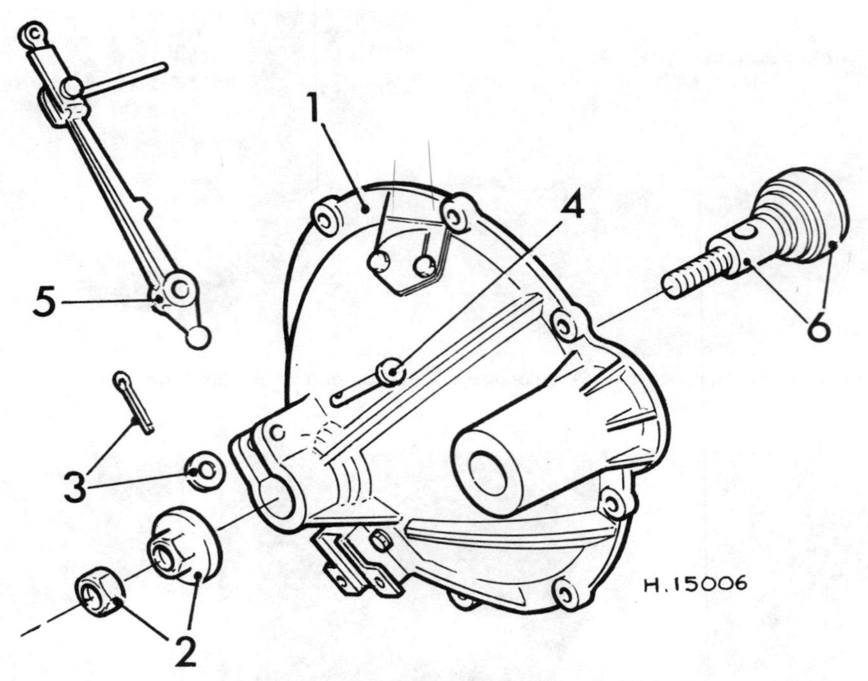

Fig. 5.8 Clutch release bearing components (Sec 11)

1 Flywheel housing cover
2 Throw-out stop and locknut
3 Washer and split pin
4 Clevis pin
5 Operating lever
6 Release bearing and plunger assembly

11 Clutch release bearing – removal, inspection and refitting

Note: *The clutch release bearing is housed within the flywheel housing cover and can be removed with the engine/transmission unit either in or out of the car. To provide access to the bearing, the flywheel housing cover must first be removed. If the engine/transmission unit is in position in the car, refer to Section 9 paragraphs 1 to 16 inclusive. If the power unit is out of the car, undo and remove the nine retaining bolts and lift off the flywheel housing cover.*

1 With the assembly on the bench, undo and remove the throw-out and locknut from the release bearing throw-out plunger.

2 Extract the split pin, tap out the clevis pin and lift off the clutch operating lever.

3 Now slide the release bearing and plunger out of the flywheel housing cover.

4 Support the underside of the release bearing and tap out the plunger using a hammer and drift of suitable diameter.

5 Examine the bearing for excess side-play or movement, and then spin the bearing and check for noisy operation or roughness. Renew the unit if any of these conditions are apparent.

6 To refit the bearing, place the plunger in position and then press the plunger into the bearing using a vice with protected jaws. Ensure that the bearing is pressed fully home until it is in contact with the shoulder of the plunger.

7 Later models are fitted with a self-aligning release bearing which is a loose fit on the plunger. This allows the bearing to move slightly when in operation and caters for any slight misalignment between the bearing and thrust plate. When refitting a bearing of this type always use a new locking ring, and ensure that when installed the ring has clamped the bearing firmly. Use a small diameter tube to push the locking ring fully into position.

8 Smear the plunger with a graphite-based grease and insert it into the flywheel housing cover.

9 Smear the ball-end of the operating lever with a graphite-based grease and position the lever on the cover, engaging the ball-end into the throw-out plunger.

10 Refit the clevis pin and washer then secure with a new split pin.

11 Refit the throw-out stop and locknut, but do not tighten at this stage.

12 The flywheel housing cover with release bearing installed can now be refitted using the reverse of the removal sequence. When installation is complete adjust the throw-out stop and return stop as described in Section 2.

12 Primary gear oil seal – removal and refitting

Note: *The majority of clutch faults experienced on Mini power units are caused by oil contamination of the clutch disc friction linings due to the failure of the primary gear oil seal. It is therefore recommended that the seal is renewed whenever problems of this nature are encountered. The oil seal can be renewed with the engine/transmission unit either in or out of the car. It will, however, be necessary to obtain BL special tools 18G1068B and 18G1043 if this operation is being carried out with the power unit installed in the car.*

1 First remove the flywheel and clutch assembly from the engine as described in Section 9.

2 The primary gear complete with oil seal can now be withdrawn from the crankshaft and flywheel housing as described below.

3 Lift off the C-shaped thrust washer and backing ring that retain the primary gear in position.

4 Now screw in the threaded centre bolt of special tool 18G1068B until the base of the tool abuts the oil seal. Pull the primary gear outwards as far as it will go and slide the two collets of 18G1068B between the groove at the rear of the primary gear splines and the base of the tool body.

5 Now slowly unscrew the threaded centre bolt of the tool while holding the tool body. This will cause the primary gear to be withdrawn from the flywheel housing, bringing the oil seal with it.

6 When the primary gear and oil seal are clear of the housing, lift them off the end of the crankshaft, remove the tool and slide the oil seal off the primary gear.

7 To fit a new oil seal first slide the primary gear onto the crankshaft and secure with the C-shaped washer and backing ring.

8 To avoid damage to the oil seal as it is fitted, place the protective sleeve, special tool 18G1043, over the primary gear, or if this tool is not available cover the primary gear splines and the stepped shoulder with masking tape.

9 Lubricate the lip of the oil seal, and very carefully slide it over the

primary gear and into position against the flywheel housing. The open part of the seal must be facing towards the engine.
10 Screw on the threaded centre bolt of special tool 18G1068B and, when the body of the tool contacts the seal, fully tighten the centre bolt, thus forcing the seal squarely into the housing. Remove the tool when the face of the seal is flush with the housing.
11 The flywheel and clutch assembly can now be refitted to the engine as described in Section 9.

13 Fault diagnosis – clutch

1 There are four main faults to which the clutch is subject: judder, drag, slip and squeal. These are dealt with separately below. There are also faults which are due to maladjustment or defects in the operating mechanism. It is important to ascertain whether the clutch itself ir its operating mechanism is at fault, since some of the symptoms are similar.

Clutch judder

2 Clutch judder when taking up the drive is apparent to some degree on all Minis, and several design changes have occurred over the years of production in attempts to improve matters. If judder is severe, first make sure that the engine mountings are sound and securely attached (Chapter 1). Pay particular attention to the engine tie-bar and its rubber bushes.
3 Oil contamination of the clutch disc friction linings can also cause judder. To ascertain this the clutch must be removed for inspection. If the clutch disc is contaminated it must be renewed and the source of contamination traced and rectified. The flywheel housing oil seal is a common cause of leakage (see Chapter 1). On early models it may be necessary to fit a modified type of primary gear (Chapter 6).

Clutch drag

4 Clutch drag is evident as difficulty in engaging or disengaging gears. Check the operating lever clearance and the hydraulic system before suspecting the clutch itself. Leaks in the hydraulic system or low fluid in the reservoir (probably due to leakage) will cause clutch drag. Failed seals in the master or slave cylinders may have the same effect without causing leakage.
5 If the fault is in the clutch itself it may be due to the friction linings sticking to the flywheel or pressure plate – perhaps due to contamination – or the clutch disc may not be sliding on its splines. This last condition may occur due to rust if the car has been standing for a long time. A temporary cure may be obtained by engaging fourth gear, depressing the clutch pedal and pushing the car backwards and forwards until the clutch frees. Ideally the clutch should be removed for inspection at the earliest opportunity.

Clutch slip

6 If the clutch is slipping, the engine speed will increase on acceleration without a corresponding increase in road speed. Slip is usually progressive, first being noticed on steep hills or when carrying heavy loads, eventually occurring under light acceleration on the flat.
7 First check that the operating lever is correctly adjusted. Neglecting to check the adjustment periodically will eventually cause slip.
8 If the fault persists after adjustment it may be due to wear or contamination of the clutch disc. The clutch must be removed and the disc examined. If wear is allowed to continue to the point where the rivets securing the friction linings are exposed, damage may be caused to the flywheel and pressure plate.

Clutch squeal

9 If a squealing or rumbling noise is heard when the clutch pedal is depressed, this indicates a worn clutch release bearing which will have to be renewed.

Spongy clutch pedal

10 A spongy clutch pedal usually indicates a fault in the clutch hydraulic system. The sponginess is due to air in the system which must be bled out. If the problem persists after bleeding and there are no obvious signs of leakage, remove the master and slave cylinders for examination.
11 If the pedal is firm after pressing it down halfway or more, check the clutch adjustment and correct if necessary.

Chapter 6
Manual gearbox and automatic transmission

For modifications, and information applicable to later models, see Supplement at end of manual

Contents

Specifications

Manual gearbox

Type .... Four forward and one reverse gear, synchromesh action on all forward gears

Clearances and adjustments

Laygear endfloat .... 0.002 to 0.006 in (0.05 to 0.15 mm)
Primary gear endfloat .... 0.0035 to 0.0065 in (0.089 to 0.165 mm)
Idler gear endfloat .... 0.003 to 0.008 in (0.076 to 0.203 mm)

Lubrication .... Engine/transmission lubrication system combined

Automatic transmission

Type .... Automotive products

Torque converter

Type .... Three-element
Multiplication .... 2.1 maximum

Lubrication .... Engine/transmission lubrication system combined (capacity 9 pints/5 litres)

Torque wrench settings	**lbf ft**	**Nm**
Manual gearbox		
Flywheel housing nuts and bolts	18	25
First motion shaft nut	150	207
Mainshaft (final drive pinion) nut	150	207
Mainshaft bearing retainer bolts	13	18
Engine to gearbox casing	6	8
Gearbox drain plug	25	35
Gearbox casing studs $\frac{3}{8}$ in UNC	8	11
Gearbox casing studs $\frac{5}{16}$ in UNC	6	8
Gearbox casing studs $\frac{3}{8}$ in UNF	25	35
Gearbox casing studs $\frac{5}{16}$ in UNF	18	25
Speedometer drive housing nuts	18	25

Automatic transmission

	lbf ft	Nm
Transmission drain plug	25	35
Converter centre bolt	112	152
Converter (six central bolts)	21	29
Converter drain plugs	20	27
Engine to transmission casing	12	16
Converter housing bolts	18	25
$\frac{5}{16}$ in UNF bolts	19	26
$\frac{3}{8}$ in UNF bolts	30	41

1 General description

The manual transmission fitted to all models covered by this manual comprises four forward and one reverse gear. All forward gears are engaged through baulk ring synchromesh units to obtain smooth silent gearchanges. The transmission is housed within an aluminium casing bolted to the lower face of the engine, and shares the engine lubricating oil. The differential assembly is contained within a separate housing bolted to the rear of the gearbox casing.

On early models movement of the gear lever is transmitted to the selector forks by a selector lever, two relay shafts and a ball-and-socket joint. The gear lever is mounted either on the rear of the differential casing or externally in a remote control housing, which is in turn bolted to the rear of the differential. In this case an additional shaft transmits movement of the gear lever to the relay shafts.

A revised gear selector mechanism with a simpler and more positive rod-change remote control linkage is incorporated in the later type gearboxes. Movement of the gearlever is transmitted to the selector forks by an external selector rod, a selector shaft, and a bellcrank lever assembly. The gear lever is mounted in a remote control housing attached to the vehicle floor via rubber mountings.

A four-speed automatic transmission is available on certain models as a factory option. Further information on the automatic transmission unit will be found in subsequent Sections of this Chapter.

2 Gearbox – removal and refitting

The gearbox is removed from the car together with the engine and differential assembly as described in Chapter 1. It is then necessary to separate the engine from the gearbox; full information on this procedure is also detailed in Chapter 1.

3 Gearbox (early type) – dismantling

1 Position the gearbox on a strong bench so that it is at comfortable working height and easily accessible from both sides. Alternatively place the gearbox on a clean floor, preferably covered with paper.

2 Begin dismantling by removing the differential assembly as described in Chapter 8.

3 Undo and remove the large hexagon-headed plug and washer from the front of the gearbox casing and then lift out the spring and reverse check plunger. **Note:** *On some models a reversing light switch may be fitted in place of the hexagon plug.*

4 Take off the idler gear from the side of the gearbox casing together with its thrust washers. Ensure that the thrustwashers are kept in their correct relative position either side of the gear.

5 Unscrew the clamp bolt and washer securing the selector lever to

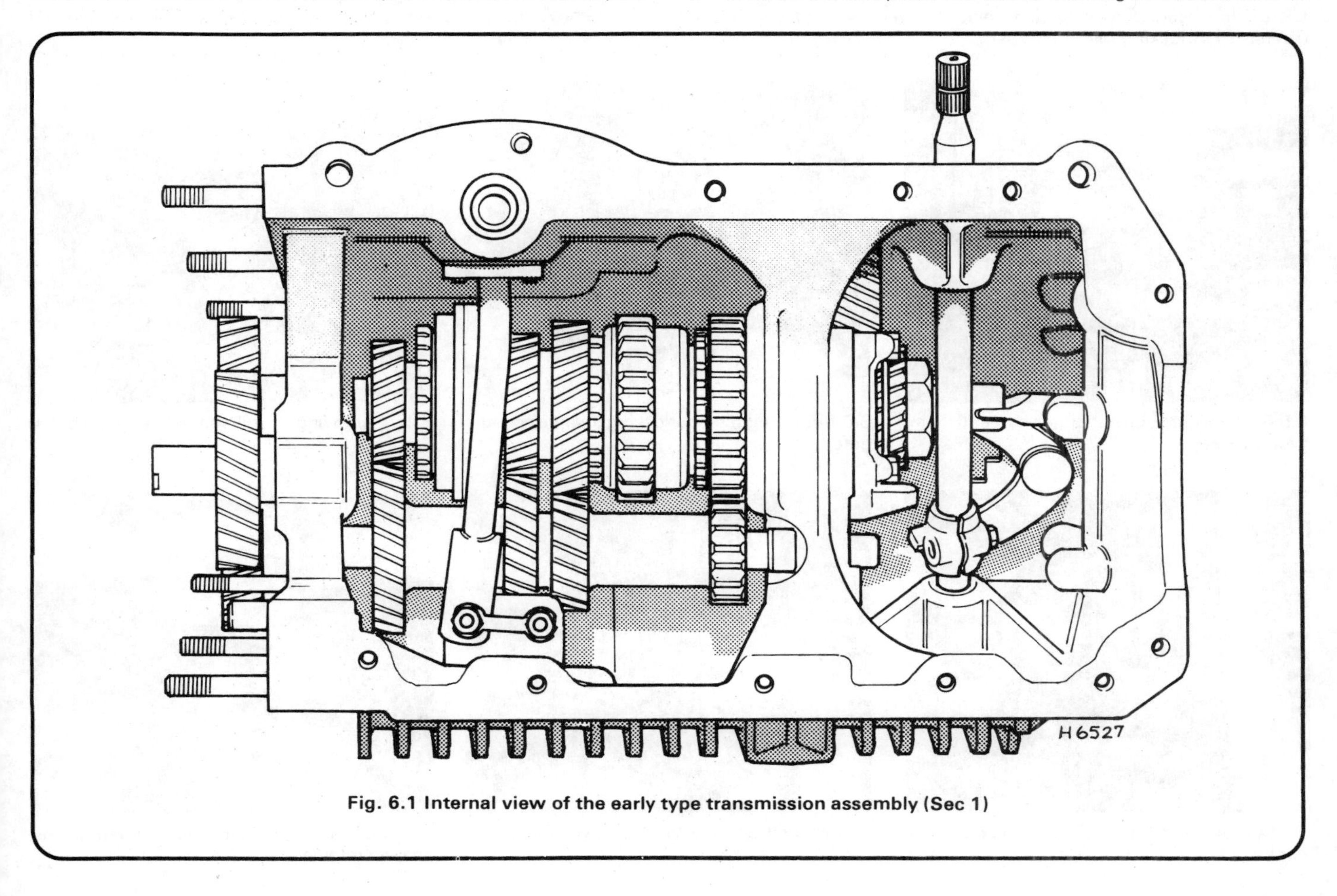

Fig. 6.1 Internal view of the early type transmission assembly (Sec 1)

the gearchange shaft. Slide the gearchange shaft off the selector lever and withdraw it from the casing. Take care not to lose the Woodruff key from the shaft (photo). Now lift out the selector lever and prise out the shaft oil seals if required.

6 Undo and remove the speedometer pinion housing cover retaining screw and lift off the cover and bush assembly. Now lift out the pinion.

7 Undo and remove the nuts and spring washers and lift off the engine mounting bracket and front cover.

8 Now lift out the interlocking change speed gate (photo).

9 Knock back the locktabs and undo and remove the two bolts securing the oil suction pipe blanking plate to the rear of the casing. Lift off the blanking plate and gasket.

10 Knock back the locktabs and undo and remove the two bolts securing the oil strainer and suction pipe support bracket to the lug on the gearbox casing. Pull the suction pipe out of the oil strainer and remove it from the gearbox (photo). The oil strainer cannot be removed at this stage.

11 From the flywheel housing side of the gearbox, extract the small circlip from the first motion shaft and then, using a puller or two screwdrivers, withdraw the small first motion shaft roller bearing from the end of the shaft.

12 Engage two gears simultaneously by moving two of the selector rods in or out. This will lock the mainshaft and prevent it from turning as the large retaining nuts are undone.

13 Tap back the lock washer and undo and remove the first motion shaft retaining nut from the flywheel housing side of the gearbox. This nut will be very tight and it may be necessary to place the gearbox on the floor and have an assistant stand on the casing as the nut is undone. Now slide the first motion shaft ear off the shaft.

14 Tap back the lockwasher and, using a socket and extension bar inserted through the open end of the casing, undo and remove the final drive pinion retaining nut. This will also be tight and your assistant may be required again. With the nut removed, slide off the final drive pinion (photos).

15 Knock back the locktabs and undo and remove the bolts securing the mainshaft bearing retainer to the centre web of the gearbox casing. Lift off the bearing retainer and shim followed by the layshaft and reverse shaft locking plate (photos).

16 Measure the endfloat of the leygear using feeler gauges. If the endfloat is outside the limits specified then new thrust washers must be fitted on reasssembly.

17 Unlock the two previously locked mainshaft gears by moving the selector rods back to the neutral position.

18 Using a brass drift, tap the layshaft out of the gearbox casing towards the flywheel housing side, and lift off the laygear together with the two thrust washers (photos).

19 Undo and remove the two plugs from the lower rear face of the gearbox and lift out the springs and interlocking plungers. Sludge in the bottom of the casing may prevent the plungers from being removed but this will not affect the dismantling procedure. Take care that they are not lost or dislodged when cleaning the casing after dismantling.

20 Extract the large circlip from the flywheel housing side of the gearbox which retains the first motion shaft bearing in position. Now very carefully, using a brass drift, tap out the first motion shaft and bearing from the casing (photos).

21 Using a brass drift or soft-faced mallet, tap the mainshaft toward the flywheel housing side of the gearbox until a gap of about 1 in (25 mm) exists between the bearing and first gear. Now, using extreme care, tap the outer race of the bearing away from the flywheel housing and out of the centre web of the casing. Tap each side of the bearing alternatively to prevent it from binding, and take care not to impose any load on the teeth of first gear. When the bearing is clear of the centre web slide it off the end of the mainshaft and withdraw it from the casing (photo).

22 Now carefully lift the complete mainshaft assembly up and out of the gearbox (photo).

23 Lift out the oil strainer assembly (photo).

24 Tap out the reverse gear shaft (photo) and withdraw the gear and selector fork.

25 Slacken the locknuts and then undo and remove the selector fork retaining locking screws (photo).

26 Slide the selector rods out of the forks and withdraw the rods and forks from the gearbox.

27 Remove the circlip from the reverse gear shift lever pivot pin and remove the lever (photo).

3.5 Removing the gearchange shaft and Woodruff key

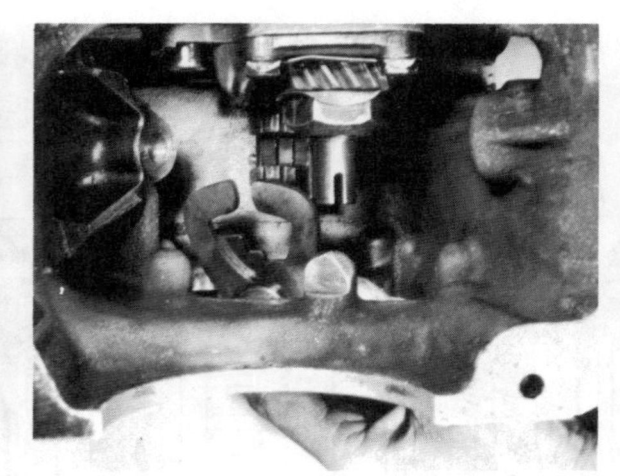
3.8 Removing the interlocking change speed gate

3.10 Removing the oil strainer retaining bolts

3.14a Unscrew the final drive pinion retaining nut...

3.14b ...and slide off the final drive pinion

3.15a Bend back the locktabs and remove the bearing retainer bolts...

3.15b ...followed by the bearing retainer...

3.15c ...shims and locking plate

3.18a Withdrawing the laygear...

3.18b ...and thrust washers

3.20a Extract the first motion shaft bearing circlip...

3.20b ...and remove the shaft and bearing assembly

3.21 With extreme care, tap the mainshaft bearing out of the casing

3.22 Lifting out the mainshaft assembly...

3.23 ...followed by the oil strainer

3.24 Removing the reverse gear shaft

3.25 Removing the selector fork locking screws

3.27 With the circlip removed, withdraw the reverse shift lever and pivot pin

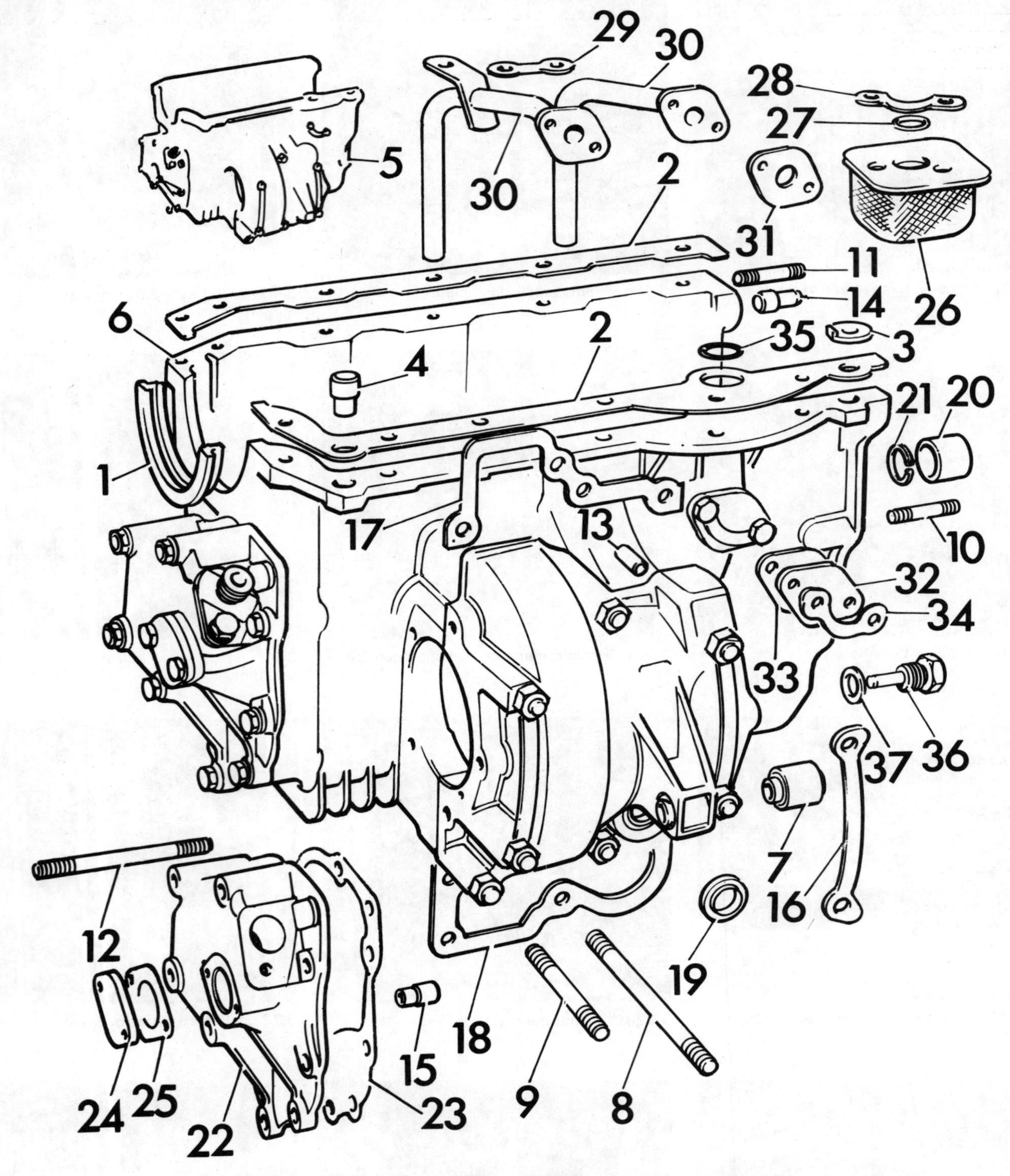

Fig. 6.2 Exploded view of the rod-change type transmission casing (Sec 4)

1 Oil seal
2 Gasket
3 Collar
4 Dowel
5 Transmission casing
6 Case assembly
7 Bush
8 Stud
9 Stud
10 Stud
11 Stud
12 Stud
13 Dowel
14 Dowel
15 Dowel
16 Lockwasher
17 Gasket
18 Gasket
19 Oil seal
20 Bearing
21 Circlip
22 Speedometer drive housing
23 Gasket
24 Cover plate
25 Gasket
26 Oil strainer
27 Sealing ring
28 Lockwasher
29 Lockwasher
30 Pick-up pipe (alternative type)
31 Gasket
32 Cover plate
33 Gasket
34 Lockwasher
35 Sealing ring
36 Drain plug
37 Washer

4 Gearbox (rod-change type) – dismantling

1 Position the gearbox on a strong bench so that it is at comfortable working height and easily accessible from both sides. Alternatively, place the gearbox on a clean floor, preferably covered with paper.
2 Begin dismantling by removing the differential assembly as described in Chapter 8.
3 Take off the idler gear from the side of the gearbox casing together with its thrust washers. Ensure that the thrust washers are kept in their correct relative positions on either side of the gear.
4 Undo and remove the speedometer pinion housing cover retaining screw and lift off the cover and bush assembly. Then lift out the pinion.
5 Undo and remove the nuts and spring washers and withddraw the engine mounting, adaptor, and front cover assembly.
6 Knock back the locktabs and undo and remove the two bolts securing the oil suction pipe blanking plate to the rear of the casing. Lift away the blanking plate and gasket.
7 Knock back the locktabs and undo and remove the two bolts securing the oil strainer and suction pipe support bracket to the lug on the gearbox casing. Pull the suction pipe out of the oil strainer and remove it from the gearbox. The oil strainer cannot be removed at this stage.
8 From the flywheel housing side of the gearbox, extract the small circlip from the first motion shaft and then, using a puller or two screwdrivers, withdraw the small first motion shaft roller bearing from the end of the shaft.
9 Turn the selector shaft anti-clockwise until the operating stub and the interlock spool are disengaged from the bellcrank levers.
10 Push the sliding collar of the third/ fourth synchro-hub toward the flywheel housing end of the gearbox to engage fourth gear. Now push the sliding collar of the first/second synchro-hub toward the gearbox centre web to engage first gear. This will lock the mainshaft and prevent it from turning as the large retaining nuts are undone.
11 Tap the lockwasher and undo and remove the first motion shaft retaining nut from the flywheel housing side of the gearbox. This nut will be very tight and it may be necessary to place the gearbox on the floor and have an assistant stand on the casing as the nut is undone. When the nut is removed, slide the first motion shaft gear and lockwasher off the shaft.
12 Tap back the lockwasher and, using a socket and extension bar inserted through the open end of the casing, undo and remove the final drive pinion retaining nut. This nut will also be tight and your assistant may be required again. With the nut removed slide off the final drive pinion and lockwasher.
13 Return the first and fourth gears to the neutral position.
14 Knock back the locktabs and undo and remove the bolts securing the mainshaft bearing retainer to the centre web of the gearbox casing. Lift off the bearing retainer and shim followed by the layshaft and reverse shaft locking plate.
15 Measure the endfloat of the laygear using feeler gauges. If the endfloat is outside the limits specified then new thrust washers must be fitted on reassembly.
16 Using a brass drift, tap the layshaft out of the gearbox casing towards the flywheel housing side, and lift out the laygear together with the two thrustwashers.
17 Extract the large circlip from the flywheel housing side of the gearbox which retains the first motion shaft bearing in position. Now, very carefully using a brass drift, tap out the first motion shaft and bearing from the casing.
18 Using a brass drift or soft-faced mallet, tap the mainshaft toward the flywheel housing side of the gearbox until a gap of about 1 in (25 mm) exists between the bearing and first gear. Take care that the sliding collar of the third/fourth synchro-hub does not become disengaged from the hub otherwise the detent balls and springs will be released.
19 Using extreme care tap the outer race of the bearing away from the flywheel housing end and out of the centre web of the casing. Tap each side of the bearing alternately to prevent it from binding, and take care not to impose any load on the teeth of first gear. As the bearing emerges it can be carefully levered the rest of the way out using a screwriver inserted between the casing and the bearing circlip.
20 When the bearing is clear of the centre web, slide it off the end of the mainshaft and withdraw it from the casing.
21 Carefully lift the complete mainshaft assembly up and out of the gearbox.
22 Remove the oil strainer assembly.

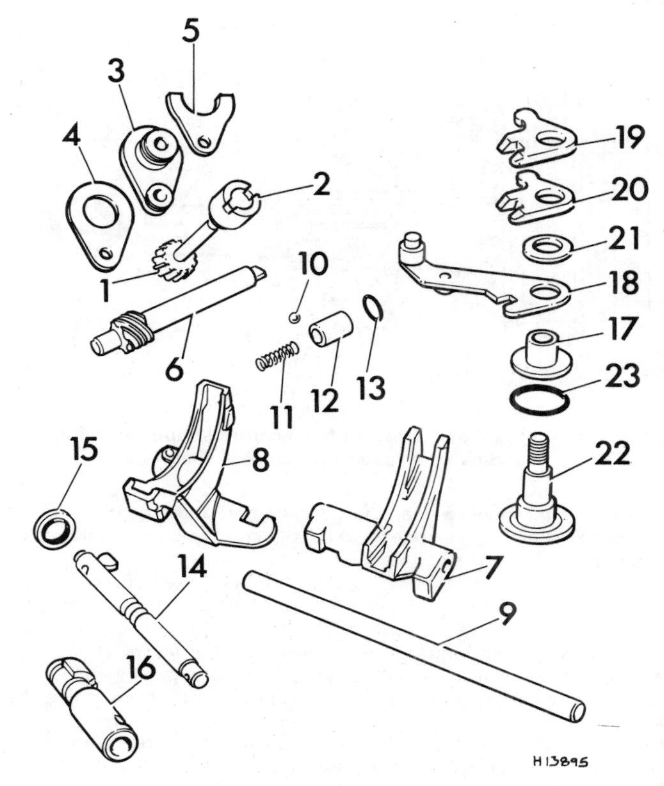

Fig. 6.3 The rod-change transmission selector mechanism (Sec 4)

1 *Speedometer pinion*
2 *Bush*
3 *Bush*
4 *Gasket*
5 *Retainer*
6 *Gear and spindle*
7 *1st and 2nd speed fork*
8 *3rd and 4th speed fork*
9 *Selector fork shaft*
10 *Detent ball*
11 *Detent spring*
12 *Detent sleeve*
13 *O-ring*
14 *Selector shaft*
15 *Oil seal*
16 *Interlock spool*
17 *Bush*
18 *Reverse lever*
19 *Upper bell crank lever*
20 *Centre bell crank lever*
21 *Spacer*
22 *Pivot pin*
23 *O-ring*

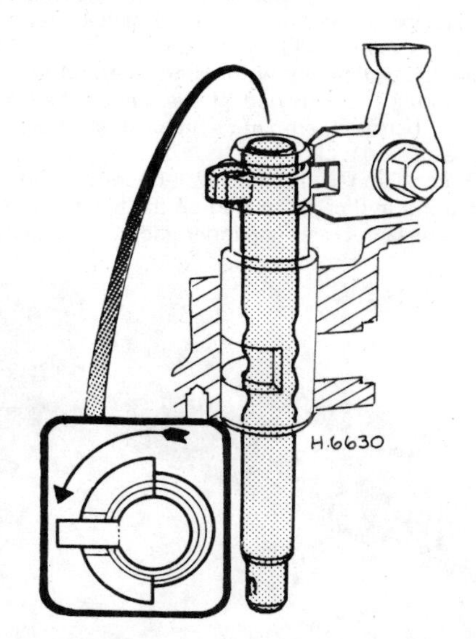

Fig. 6.4 Selector shaft turned anti-clockwise to disengage bellcrank levers (Sec 4)

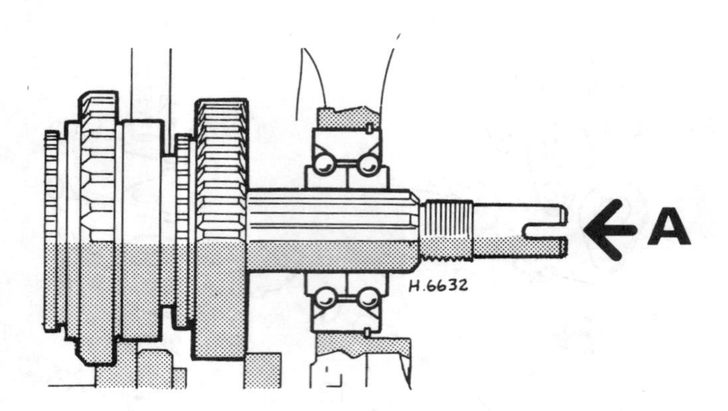

Fig. 6.5 Removal of mainshaft from centre support bearing – A indicates direction of removal (Sec 4)

23 Tap out the reverse gear shaft and withdraw the gear.
24 Using a small pin punch drift out the rollpin securing the third/fourth selector fork to its shaft.
25 Slide out the selector shaft and withdraw the two forks.
26 Undo and remove the bellcrank lever pivot post nut and washer.
27 Lift out the bellcrank levers, washers and pivot sleeve, noting the assembly sequence and the markings on the levers. Keep this assembly together to avoid confusion when refitting.
28 Wthdraw the interlock spool and selector shaft from inside the gearbox casing.
29 If necessary the bellcrank lever pivot post may be removed by drifting it downwards and out of the casing.

5 Gearbox – inspection

1 Thoroughly clean the interior and exterior of the gearbox casing. Check for any small parts that may have dropped into the gearbox during dismantling and recover them.
2 Examine the layshaft for signs of wear where the needle rollers bear. If a small ridge can be felt or if there is any deterioration of the surface hardening (photo), renew the layshaft. Also inspect the needle roller bearings (photo). If the shaft is worn the bearings will be worn and must be renewed. New thrust washers should be fitted as a matter or course, referring to the charts in Sections 8 and 9 for the correct size.
3 Examine the laygear, reverse idler gear and the gears on the mainshaft for excessive wear and chipping of the teeth.
4 Inspect the synchronising rings on the mainshaft for wear, distortion or cracks. If difficulty was experienced when changing gear then the rings should be renewed. If the vehicle had a tendency to jump out of gear then the complete synchro-hub of the relevant gear should be renewed.
5 Inspect the condition of the main ball-bearings, and also the small needle roller bearing and cage located on the front of the mainshaft. If there is any looseness between the inner and outer races, pitting of the balls or rollers, or roughness when the bearing is spun, then the bearing should be renewed. It is also advisable at this stage to check the condition of the idler gear bearings in the gearbox casing and flywheel housing. These bearings and the idler gear itself are notorious for wear and should be renewed if they show the slightest sign of such wear. Full information on these components will be found in Sections 11 and 12.
6 Examine the ends of the selector forks where they engage with the synchroniser-hubs. If possible compare the forks with new units to help determine the extent of the wear.
7 If it is necessary to renew the synchro-rings or the synchroniser-hubs or any of the mainshaft components, the mainshaft should now be dismantled as described in Section 7. If the first motion shaft or bearing require attention they should be dismantled as described below.

6 First motion shaft – dismantling and reassembly

1 To remove the bearing from the first motion shaft, slide the shaft between open vice jaws and support the outer race of the bearing on the top of the jaws.
2 Using a soft-faced mallet drive the first motion shaft down and out of the bearing inner race. The strain placed on the bearing does not matter, as the bearing would not be removed unless it was being renewed. Alternatively use a two-legged universal puller (photo).
3 To fit a new bearing slide it onto the first motion shaft with the shoulder of the bearing towards the front of the shaft.
4 Now support the inner race of the bearing on protected vice jaws, and using a drift of suitable diameter inserted into the bearing hole at the rear of the gear, drive the shaft pulley into the bearing.

7 Mainshaft – dismantling and reassembly

1 Place the mainshaft on a clean uncluttered working surface and begin dismantling by sliding off the third/fourth synchro-hub and baulk rings from the front of the shaft.
2 Using a thin screwdriver or thin piece of rod, press down the spring-loaded plunger and turn the splined thrust washer so that a spline holds the plunger down and the thrust washer is so positioned that it can now be slid off the front of the mainshaft.
3 Lift out the spring and plunger and then slide off the third speed gear and its caged needle roller bearing from the front of the mainshaft.
4 From the rear of the mainshaft withdraw the first speed gear and its caged needle roller bearing.
5 Using two screwdrivers carefully lever the first speed gear needle roller bearing journal rearwards and off the mainshaft.
6 Now slide off the first/second synchro-hub and the two baulk rings off the rear of the shaft.
7 The splined retaining thrust washer securing the second speed gear in position is retained with two spring-loaded plungers. To compress the plunger insert two small screwdrivers between the thrust washer and the edge of the gear. Now rotate the thrust washer so that the splines hold the plungers down and the thrust washer is so positioned that it can now be slid off the rear of the mainshaft.

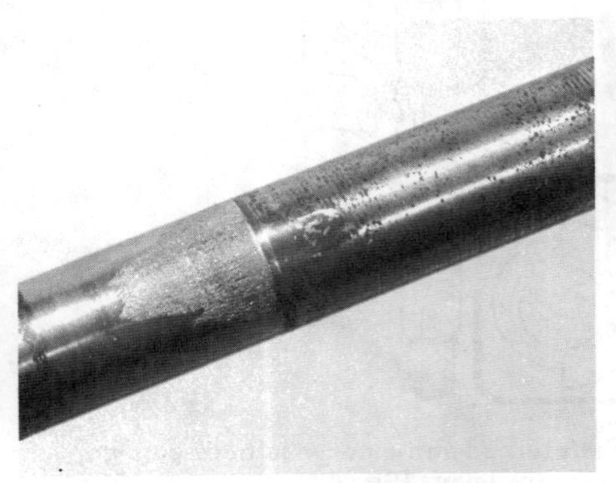

5.2a Deterioration of the layshaft surface hardening at the needle roller bearing journal...

5.2b ...will also cause wear on the bearings

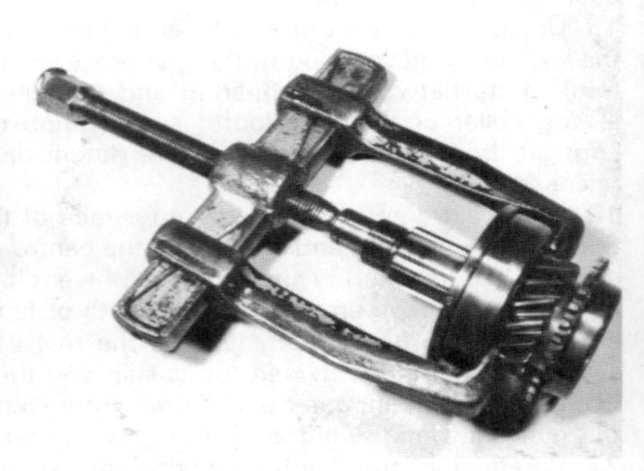

6.2 Using a puller to remove the first motion shaft bearing

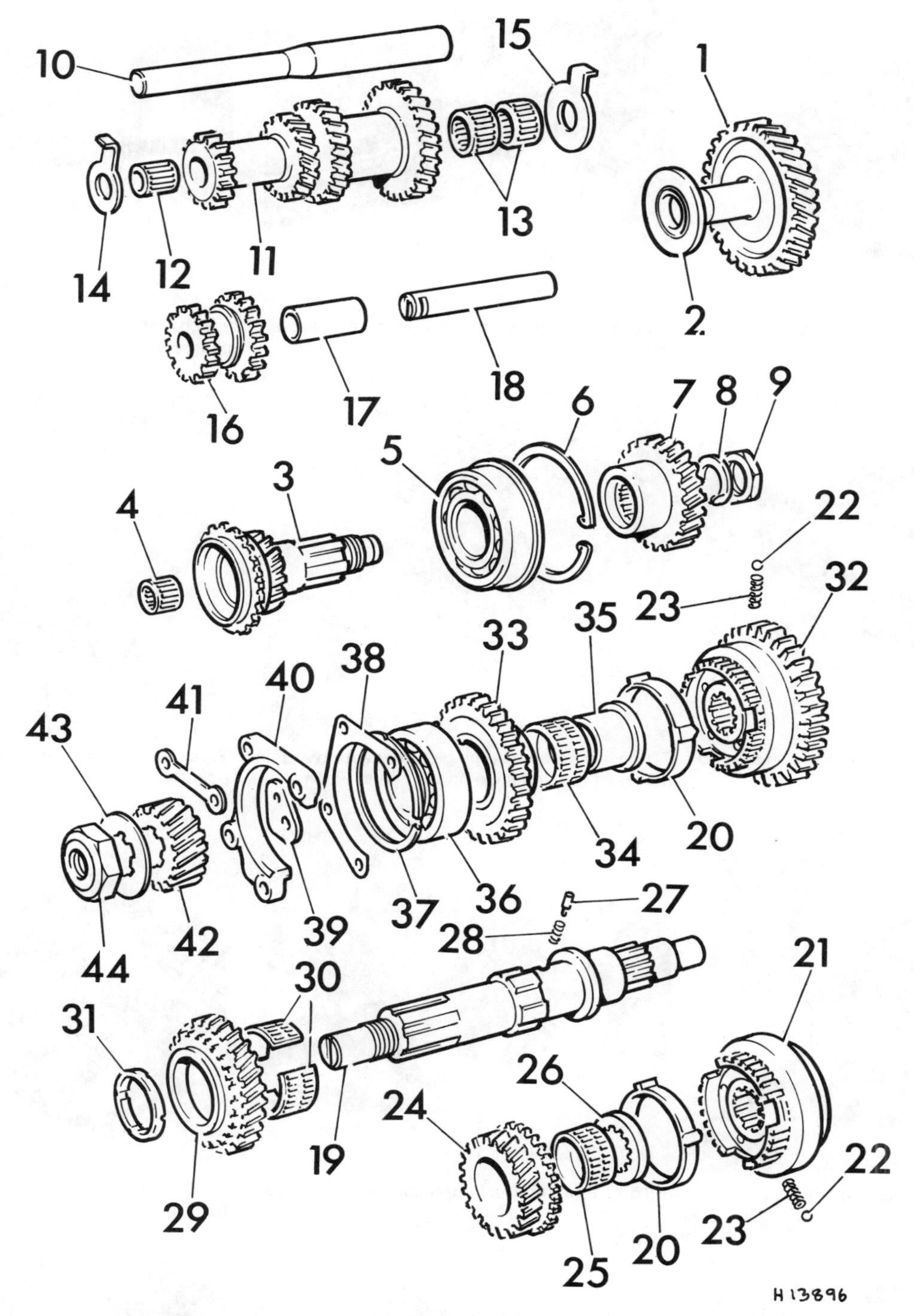

Fig. 6.6 Exploded view of the geartrain and related components (Sec 5)

1 Idler gear
2 Thrust washer
3 First motion shaft
4 Needle roller bearing
5 First motion shaft bearing
6 Circlip
7 First motion shaft drivegear
8 Tab washer
9 Nut
10 Layshaft
11 Laygear
12 Needle roller bearing
13 Needle roller bearing
14 Thrust washer (small)
15 Thrust washer (large)
16 Reverse idler assembly
17 Bush
18 Reverse idler shaft
19 Third motion shaft
20 Baulk ring
21 3rd and 4th speed synchroniser assembly
22 Ball
23 Spring
24 Third speed gear
25 Needle roller bearing
26 Thrust washer
27 Peg
28 Spring
29 Second speed gear
30 Needle roller bearing
31 Thrust washer
32 Reverse mainshaft gear and 1st & 2nd gear synchroniser
33 First speed gear
34 Needle roller bearing
35 First speed gear journal
36 Ball bearing
37 Circlip
38 Shim
39 Locating plate
40 Retainer (third motion shaft)
41 Lockwasher
42 Final drive pinion
43 Lockwasher
44 Pinion retaining nut

7.11 Synchro-hub balls and springs in position ready for assembly

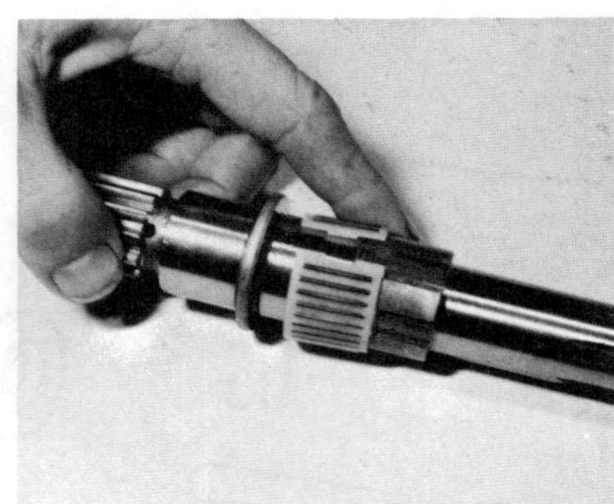

7.12a Place the two split halves of the needle roller bearing in position...

7.12b ...and then insert the spring and plungers

7.13 Depress the plungers and slide on second gear

7.14 Fully compress the plungers with two thin pieces of rod and slide on the thrust washer

7.15 Rotate the thrust washer to lock it in position

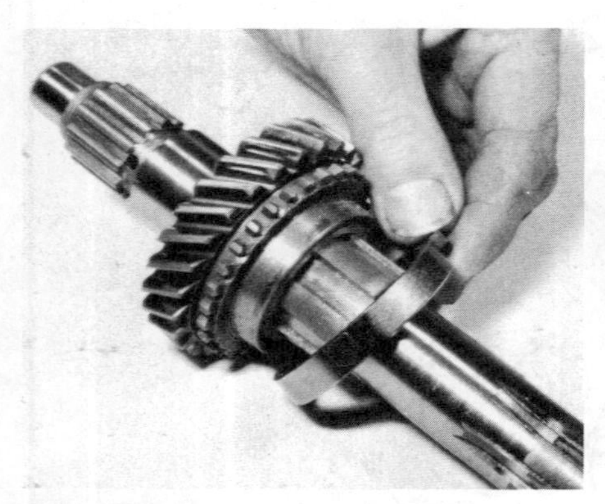

7.16a Place the baulk ring in position...

7.16b ...and refit the first/second synchro-hub

7.17 Fit the first gear needle roller bearing journal...

7.18a ...followed by the needle roller bearing

7.18b With the baulk ring in position, slide on first gear

7.19 At the other end of the mainshaft, assemble the third gear needle roller bearing

8 Insert two pieces of wire through the holes in the cone face of the second gear. Compress the two spring-loaded plungers and withdraw the gear from the rear of the mainshaft.
9 Finally lift out the spring and plunger and take off the second speed gear split caged needle roller bearing.
10 Should it be necessary to dismantle the synchro-hubs place a rag around the hub to catch the balls and springs that will be ejected and then slide the inner hub out of the collar. Now recover the balls and springs from the rag.
11 To reassemble the hubs, hold the balls against spring pressure with your fingers, and with the help of an assistant slide the hub into the collar (photo). Ensure that the spaces in the collar align with the cut-outs in the hub. Also ensure that the long boss on the collar and hub are on the same side when assembled.
12 Begin reassembly of the mainshaft by placing the two split halves of the second gear needle roller bearing in position, and then insert the spring and plungers into the drilling on the mainshaft (photos).
13 From the rear of the mainshaft slide on the second speed gear, flat face first, depress the plungers and slide the gear over the needle roller bearings (photos).
14 Support the mainshaft in a vice with suitable protected jaws and, using two thin pieces of rod inserted through the holes in the cone of the gear, compress the two plungers (photo).
15 Now slide the thrust washer into position and rotate it until the plungers can be heard to click into position and lock the thrust washer (photo).
16 Place the baulk ring in position on the second speed gear and then refit the first/second synchro-hub with the long boss towards the rear of the mainshaft (photos).
17 Fit the first speed gear needle roller bearing journal to the rear of the mainshaft (photo) and tap it fully home using a tube of suitable diameter.
18 Refit the first gear needle roller bearing, the baulk ring and then first gear with the flat side towards the rear of the mainshaft (photos).
19 From the front end of the mainshaft, assemble the third gear needle roller bearing and then place the spring and plunger into the drilling in the shaft (photo).
20 Slide on the third speed gear, flat side first, followed by the splined thrust washer (photos). Ensure that the notch at the rear of the thrust washer is adjacent to the plunger.
21 Depress the plunger and rotate the thrust washer until the plunger can be heard to click into place, and then lock the thrust washer (photos).
22 Refit the baulk ring to the third speed gear (photo) and then slide on the third/fourth synchro-hub ensuring that the large boss on the hub faces the front of the mainshaft (photo).
23 Finally refit the remaining baulk ring to the front of the third/fourth synchro-hub (photo).

7.20a With the spring and plunger in place refit third gear...

7.20b ...followed by the splined thrust washer

7.21a Depress the plunger and push the thrust washer fully home...

7.21b ...then turn it until it locks into position

7.22a Finally refit the third gear baulk ring...

7.22b ...the third/fourth synchro-hub...

7.23 ...and the remaining baulk ring

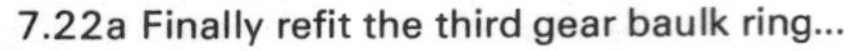

8 Gearbox (early type) – reassembly

Note: *Before reassembly commences ensure that the gearbox casing is thoroughly clean, with all traces of old gaskets removed. Also ensure that all the components are clean and dry and that a complete set of new gaskets is available.*

1 Press the reverse lever operating pin into its bore in the bottom of the casing with the groove in the pin uppermost.

2 Press the reverse operating lever into place on the operating pin and fit operating lever retaining circlip.

3 Refit the reverse fork into the hole in the operating lever, ensuring that the offset in the fork is towards the rear of the gearbox casing.

4 Place the reverse gear into the gearbox casing with the machined groove of the gear engaged with the selector fork. **Note:** *The gear must be positioned with the groove towards the right-hand side of the casing (photo).*

5 Lubricate the reverse gear shaft and pass it through the centre web of the casing, into reverse gear, and with the slotted end of the shaft facing upwards (photo).

6 Fit the reverse gear detent spring into the drilling in the rear of the casing and then slide in the reverse detent plunger, flat side first (photos).

7 Slide the reverse selector rod through the centre web of the casing and into the reverse selector fork (photo). Using a long screwdriver, push the detent plunger in against spring pressure, while at the same time pushing the reverse selector rod through into the end of the casing.

8 Place the third and fourth gear selector fork in the casing and push the third and fourth gear selector rod in from the left of the casing so the rod enters the lower hole in the fork (photo).

9 Place the first and second gear selector fork in the casing and push the first and second gear selector rod in from the left of the casing so the rod enters the locating hole in the first and second gear selector fork, and also passes through the clearance hole in the third and fourth gear selector fork (photo).

10 Line up the indentations in the rods with the holes in the forks and insert and tighten down the selector screws, lockwashers and locknuts. Make certain the locknuts are properly tightened down, and on no account omit the lockwashers. As the selectors lie in the bottom of the transmission casing, if one works loose the whole gearbox must be stripped to tighten it.

11 Place the oil strainer sealing ring in the recess in the oil strainer (photo) and lightly grease the ring to help the oil pipe pass through easily when it is fitted later. Attach the oil strainer bracket to the oil strainer, fit the lockwasher and insert and tighten the two bolts securely. Turn up the tabs on the lockwasher. Place the strainer in position in the bottom of the casing (photo). Do not yet insert the bolts which hold the bracket to the lugs on the casing.

12 Refit the mainshaft assembly with the forked end of the shaft toward the left of the gearbox casing and with the synchroniser hubs in place over the selector forks.

13 Ensure that the large circlip is in position in the retaining groove of the mainshaft bearing and refit the bearing, tapping it into the centre web of the casing with a tube of suitable diameter (photo).

14 Place the small caged needle roller bearing over the front of the mainshaft and then refit the first motion shaft and bearing assembly to the gearbox casing. Secure the bearing in position with the large circlip (photos).

15 Refit the first/second and third/fourth selector rod detent plungers to their drillings in the rear face of the gearbox casing. Refit the springs, plugs and sealing washers (photos).

16 Place the standard size laygear thrust washer into its location in the gearbox casing and retain it with a dab of grease on its rear face. **Note:** *The large thrust washer is of standard size and the smaller one selective.*

17 Carefully lower the laygear into the gearbox (photo), hold it against the thrust washer and, using feeler gauges, measure the clearance at the other end (photo).

8.4 Reverse gear in position over the selector fork

8.5 Refitting the reverse gear shaft

8.6a Place the reverse gear detent spring into the gearbox casing...

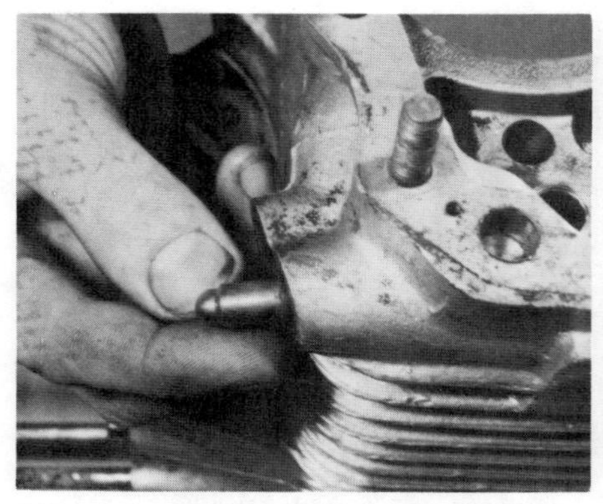
8.6b ...followed by the detent plunger

8.7 Refitting the reverse selector rod into the fork

8.8 Refit the third/fourth selector fork and rod...

8.9 ...followed by the first/second selector fork and rod

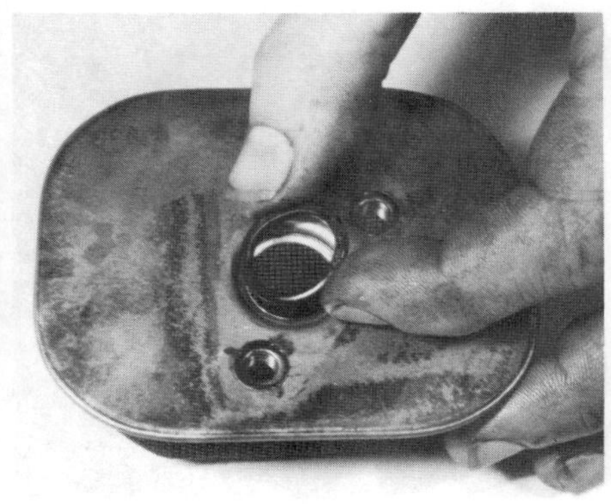
8.11a Fit a new oil seal to the oil strainer...

8.11b ...and with the bracket attached, place the strainer in the gearbox casing

8.13 With the mainshaft in place, tap in the bearing

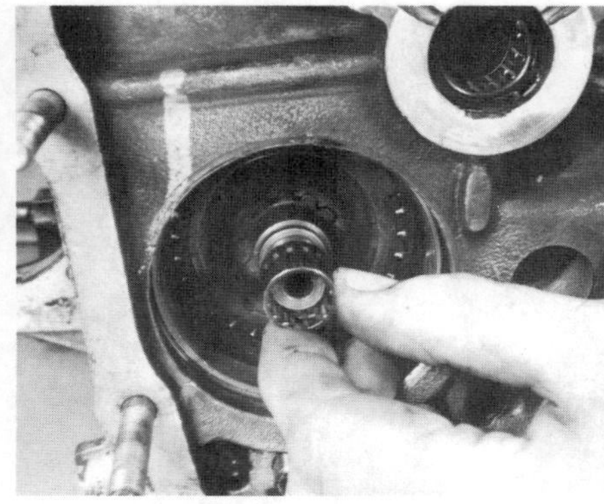
8.14a Position the small spigot bearing on the front of the mainshaft...

8.14b ...and then insert the first motion shaft assembly...

8.14c ...and secure with the circlip

8.15a Insert the detent plungers and springs...

8.15b ...and refit the plugs

8.17a Lower the laygear into the casing...

8.17b ...and with the standard size thrust washer fitted at the other end, measure the clearance

8.19a Now fit the appropriate thrust washers to the face of the gearbox casing...

8.19b ...and with the laygear held in position, insert the layshaft

8.21 Measuring the clearance between the mainshaft bearing retainer and casing

8.22a Fit the selected shims and the reverse/layshaft locking plate...

8.22b ...followed by the bearing retainer

8.23a The final drive pinion...

8.23b ...new lockwasher...

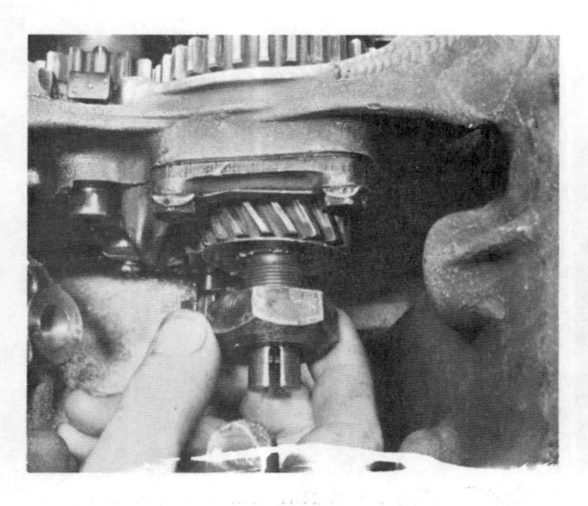

8.25 After tightening the nut bend over the lockwasher

8.26a Next refit the first motion shaft gear...

18 With the standard washer fitted and the gap between the end of the laygear and the casing measured, the selective washer can be decided upon. The table below gives the part numbers for the appropriate selective washers, based on the measured gap with the standard washer fitted.

Gap	Thrust washer
0.125 to 0.127 in (3.18 to 3.22 mm)	*22G 856*
0.128 to 0.130 in (3.25 to 3.30 mm)	*22G 857*
0.131 to 0.133 in (3.32 to 3.37 mm)	*22G 858*
0.134 in (3.41 mm)	*22G 859*

The correct endfloat with the laygear installed and the appropriate washer selected is given in the Specifications.

19 Now refit both thrust washers to the gearbox casing and place the needle roller bearings in the laygear (photo). Lower the laygear into the gearbox, and by judicious manipulation insert the layshaft from the right-hand side of the casing and into the thrust washers and laygear (photo). Note that when installed the slot in the layshaft must face downwards.

20 Now recheck the laygear endfloat which, if the correct thrust washers have been selected, should be within the specified limits.

21 Refit the mainshaft bearing retainer to the centre web of the gear casing, but do not fit any shims at this stage. Lightly tighten the retaining bolts and then measure the clearance between the retainer and the gearbox casing centre web using feeler gauges (photo). Refer to the table below for the correct thickness of shims required.

Measured gap	Fit shims totalling
0.005 to 0.006 in (0.127 to 0.152 mm)	*0.005 in (0.127 mm)*
0.006 to 0.008 in (0.152 to 0.203 mm)	*0.007 in (0.178 mm)*
0.008 to 0.010 in (0.203 to 0.254 mm)	*0.009 in (0.229 mm)*
0.010 to 0.012 in (0.254 to 0.304 mm)	*0.011 in (0.279 mm)*
0.012 to 0.014 in (0.304 to 0.356 mm)	*0.013 in (0.330 mm)*
0.014 to 0.015 in (0.356 to 0.381 mm)	*0.015 in (0.381 mm)*

22 Now remove the retainer and place the shims in position, followed by the reverse gear shaft and layshaft locking plate. Ensure that the plate engages with the slots in the two shafts and then refit the bearing retainer, bolts and locktabs. Tighten the bolts and bend over the locktabs (photos).

23 Fit the final drive pinion to the end of the mainshaft followed by a new lockwasher and the retaining nut (photos).

24 Engage two gears simultaneously by moving two of the selector rods in or out.

25 Tighten the final drive pinion retaining nut to the specified torque and then bend over the lockwasher (photo).

26 Place the first motion shaft gear over the splines of the first motion shaft and then fit a new lockwasher and the retaining nut. Tighten the nut to the specified torque and then bend over the lockwasher (photos).

27 Return the selector rods to the neutral position.

28 Refit the small roller bearing to the end of the first motion shaft, tapping it on using a tube of suitable diameter. Ensure that the bearing is positioned with the flat face of the roller cage facing the gear. Secure the bearing with the circlip (photo).

29 Lightly grease the end of the oil suction pipe and insert it into the hole in the centre of the oil strainer, taking care not to dislodge the rubber sealing ring.

30 The top flange on the bracket lies under the lug on the side of the gearbox casing. The oil pipe bracket lies on the top of the lug. Position the lockwasher and insert the two bolts through the two holes in the lug into the fixed nuts under the bracket flange. Place a new joint gasket between the pipe blanking plate and the flange on the outside of the casing, and a new gasket between the oil flange and the inside of the casing. Fit a new lockwasher and tighten up the two pairs of bolts. Turn up the tabs on both lockwashers (photos).

31 Refit the oil seal (photo) and partially insert the gearchange shaft into the transmission casing. Refit the Woodruff key (photo) to the shaft, position the selector lever in the casing, and push the gearchange shaft through the hole in the lever so the Woodruff key mates with the slot in the selector lever. Push the shaft right into its housing in the transmission case, and line up the cut out in the shaft with the hole for the clamp bolt in the lever. Insert and tighten the clamp bolt (photo) and turn up the tab on the lockwasher.

32 Refit the change speed gate (photo), fit a new front cover gasket

8.26b ...refit and tighten the retaining nut...

8.26c ...and bend over the lockwasher

8.28 Secure the first motion shaft bearing in place with the circlip

8.30a Place a new gasket on the oil feed pipe flange...

8.30b ...and refit the blanking plate from the other side

8.31a Fit a new gearchange shaft oil seal...

8.31b ...slide the shaft into the casing and refit the Woodruff key

8.31c Engage the shaft with the selector lever and refit the clamp bolt

8.32a Refit the change speed gate...

8.32b ...place a new gasket in position...

8.32c ...and refit the front cover

8.33a Finally refit the reverse check plunger and spring...

8.33b ...refit and tighten the spring plug

to the flange on the front of the casing; fit the front cover and insert and tighten up the bolts, nuts and springwashers as appropriate (photos).

33 Refit the reverse check plunger and the plunger spring in the hole in the casing; make sure the washer is under the head of the spring plug and tighten the plug securely (photos).

34 Insert the speedometer spindle and gear through the front cover so the spindle engages the slot in the end of the mainshaft, fit the joint gasket and endplate and tighten down the two securing bolts and lockwashers.

35 Refit the speedometer pinion to the front cover and then fit the bush, gasket and pinion housing cover. Secure the cover with the bolt and washer.

36 The differential assembly can now be refitted to the gearbox casing as described in Chapter 8. Before refitting the engine to the transmission refer to Section 11 regarding removal and refitting of the transfer gears.

9 Gearbox (rod-change type) – reassembly

Note: *Before reassembly commences, ensure that the gearbox is thoroughly clean with all trace of old gasket removed. Also ensure that all the components are clean and dry and that a complete set of new gaskets is available.*

1 Lightly lubricate a new O-ring oil seal and position it on the bellcrank lever pivot post. Drift the pivot post into the gearbox casing using a hammer and block of wood.

2 Refit the interlock spool to the selector shaft and insert this assembly into the gearbox casing. Position the operating stub of the selector shaft away from the bellcrank lever pivot post (photo).

3 Insert the bellcrank lever assembly onto the pivot post, ensuring that the sleeve, levers and washers are in their correct order as noted during dismantling (photo). Push the assembly fully home and refit the pivot post washer and locknut. **Note:** *Do not rotate the interlock spool*

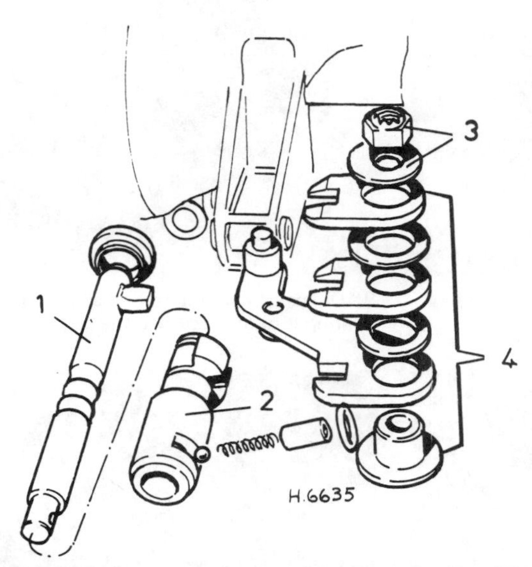

Fig. 6.7 Rod-change type gear selector mechanism (Sec 9)

1 Selector shaft
2 Interlock spool
3 Pivot post washer and locknut
4 Bellcrank lever assembly

and selector shaft into engagement with the bellcrank levers until the mainshaft and first motion shaft nuts have been refitted and fully tightened.

4 Place the third/fourth selector fork in the gearbox casing and engagement with the selector lever. Slide in the selector shaft until it just engages the fork (photo).

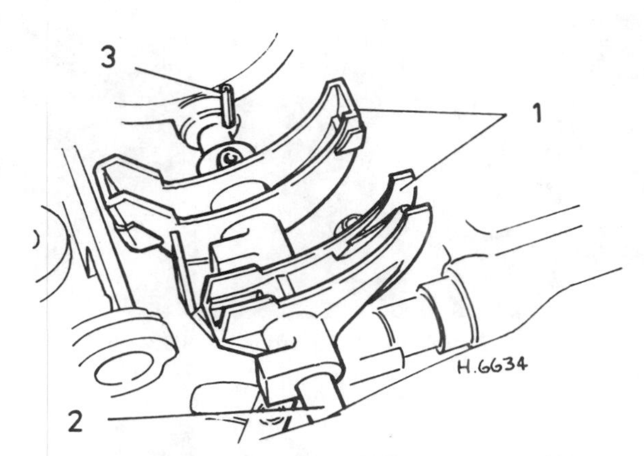

Fig. 6.8 Rod-change type selector fork assembly (Sec 9)

1 Selector forks
2 Selector shaft
3 Roll pin

5 Place the first/second selector fork in position and then slide the selector shaft fully home. Align the holes in the third/fourth selector fork and the selector shaft and drift in a new roll pin until it is flush with the fork boss (photos).

6 Lay the reverse idler gear in the casing, ensuring that the chamfer on the gear teeth faces the centre web of the gearbox casing, and that the gear is engaged with the pin on the reverse selector lever. Insert the reverse idler shaft through the gearbox centre web and into the gear. Rotate the shaft so that the slot faces upward (photo).

7 Lubricate the oil strainer sealing ring to help the oil pipe pass through easily when it is fitted later. Place the strainer in position in the bottom of the casing, but do not insert the bolts which hold the bracket to the lugs on the casing at this stage (photo).

9.2 Refitting the interlock spool and selector shaft assembly

9.3 Refitting the bellcrank lever assembly onto the pivot post

9.4 Position the third/fourth selector fork in the casing and insert the selector shaft

9.5a With the first/second selector fork in place push the selector shaft fully home...

9.5b ...align the holes and drift a new roll pin into the third/fourth fork

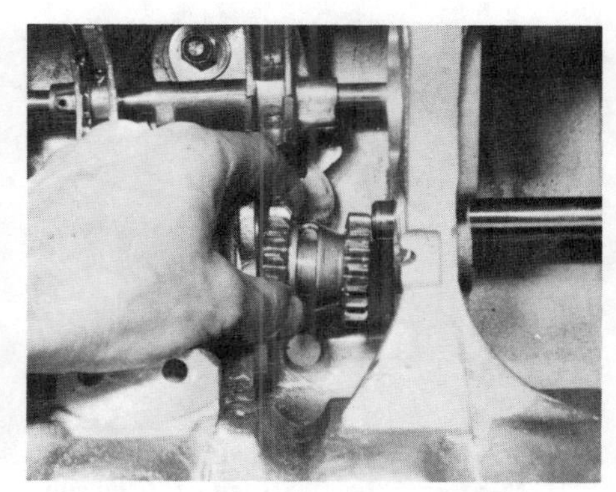

9.6 Lay the reverse idler in the casing and insert the reverse idler shaft

9.7 Positioning the oil strainer in the gearbox casing

9.9 With the mainshaft in place, refit the bearing

9.10a Insert the first motion shaft needle roller bearing into the recess in the gear...

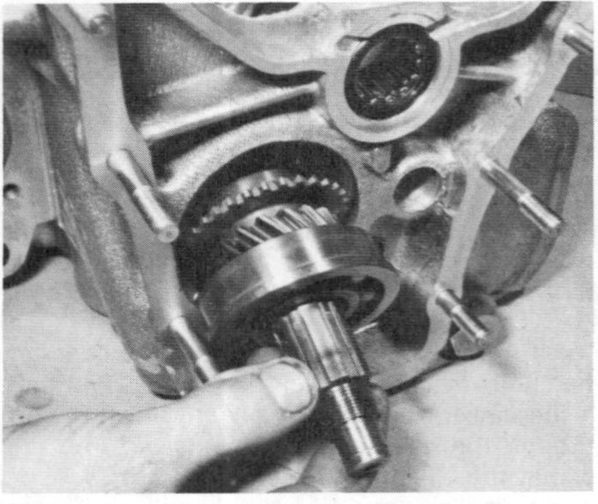

9.10b ...refit the first motion shaft assembly...

9.10c ...and secure it with the large circlip

9.11 With the large thrust washer in position...

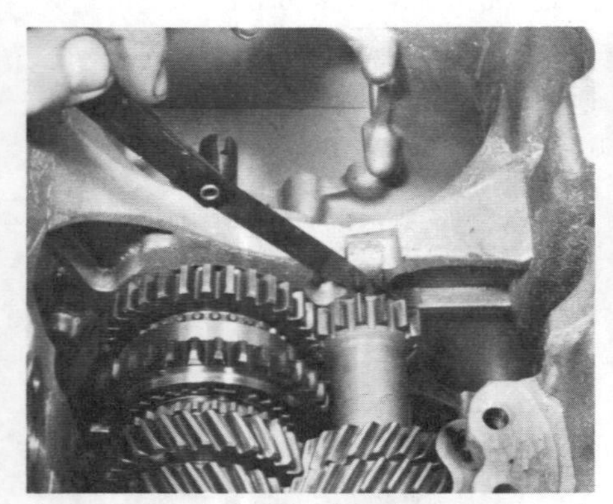

9.12 ...lower the laygear into the gearbox and measure the clearance at the other end

9.14a Refit the needle roller bearings to the laygear...

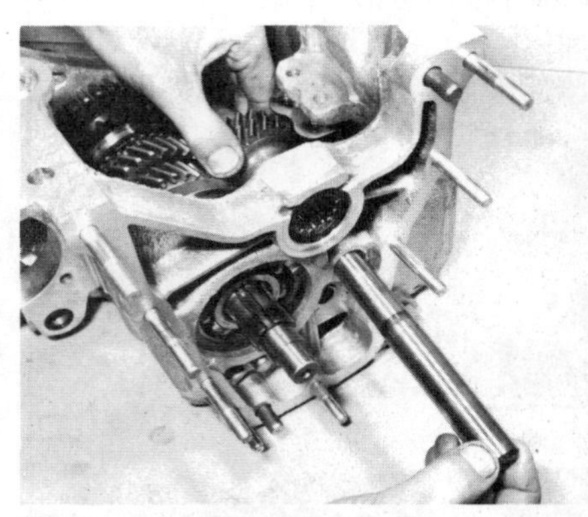

9.14b ...and with the thrust washer and laygear in place, insert the layshaft

9.16 Measuring the clearance between the bearing retainer and the casing

9.17 Place the selected shims and the reverse/layshaft locking plate in position, then refit the bearing retainer

9.18a Refit the final drive pinion...

8 Refit the mainshaft assembly with the forked end of the shaft toward the left of the gearbox casing and with the synchroniser hubs in place over the selector forks.
9 Ensure that the large circlip is in position in the retaining groove of the mainshaft bearing and refit the bearing, tapping it into the centre web of the casing with a tube of suitable diameter (photo).
10 Insert the small caged first motion shaft needle roller bearing into its location in the gear and then refit the first motion shaft and bearing assembly to the gearbox casing. Secure the bearing in position with the large circlip (photos).
11 Place the standard size laygear thrust washer into its location in the gearbox casing and retain it with a dab of grease on its rear face (photo). **Note:** *The large thrust washer is of standard size and the smaller one selective.*
12 Carefully lower the laygear into the gearbox, hold it against the thrust washer and, using feeler gauges, measure the clearance at the other end (photo).
13 With the standard thrust washer fitted and the gap between the end of the laygear and the casing measured, the selective washer can be decided upon. The washer required will have a thickness of the measured clearance minus the specified endfloat (see Specifications). The following table gives the part numbers for the appropriate selective thrust washers.

Washer thickness	Part number
0.123 to 0.124 in (3.12 to 3.14 mm)	*22G 856*
0.125 to 0.126 in (3.17 to 3.20 mm)	*22G 857*
0.127 to 0.128 in (3.22 to 3.25 mm)	*22G 858*
0.130 to 0.131 in (3.30 to 3.32 mm)	*22G 859*

14 Now refit both thrust washers to the gearbox casing and place the needle roller bearings in the laygear (photo). Lower the laygear into the gearbox, and by judicious manipulation insert the layshaft from the right-hand side of the casing and into the thrust washers and laygear (photo). When installed the slot on the end of the layshaft must face downward.
15 Recheck the laygear endfloat, which, if the correct thrust washers have been selected, should be within the specified limits.
16 Refit the mainshaft bearing retainer to the centre web of the gearbox casing, but do not fit any shims at this stage. Lightly tighten the retaining bolts and then measure the clearance between the retainer and the gearbox casing centre web using feeler gauges (photo). Refer to the following table for the correct thickness of shims required.

Measured gap	Fit shims totalling
0.005 to 0.006 in (0.127 to 0.152 mm)	*0.005 in (0.127 mm)*
0.006 to 0.008 in (0.152 to 0.203 mm)	*0.007 in (0.178 mm)*
0.008 to 0.010 in (0.203 to 0.254 mm)	*0.009 in (0.229 mm)*
0.010 to 0.012 in (0.254 to 0.304 mm)	*0.011 in (0.279 mm)*
0.012 to 0.014 in (0.304 to 0.356 mm)	*0.013 in (0.330 mm)*
0.014 to 0.015 in (0.356 to 0.381 mm)	*0.015 in (0.381 mm)*

17 Having selected the required shims, remove the retainer and place the shims in position, followed by the reverse gear shaft and layshaft locking plate (photo). Ensure that the locking plate engages with the slots in the two shafts and then refit the bearing retainer, bolts and shafts. Tighten the bolts and bend over the locktabs.
18 Fit the final drive pinion to the end of the mainshaft, followed by a new lockwasher and the retaining nut (photos).
19 Engage first and fourth gears, by moving the selector forks, to lock the mainshaft.
20 Tighten the final drive pinion nut to the specified torque and then bend over the lockwasher (photo).
21 Place the first motion shaft gear over the splines of the first motion shaft, and then fit a new lockwasher and the retaining nut. Tighten the nut to the specified torque and then bend over the lockwasher (photos).
22 Return the selector forks to the neutral position. Rotate the interlock spool and selector shaft into engagement with the bellcrank levers.

9.18b ...a new lockwasher...

9.20 ...and the retaining nut tightened to the specified torque

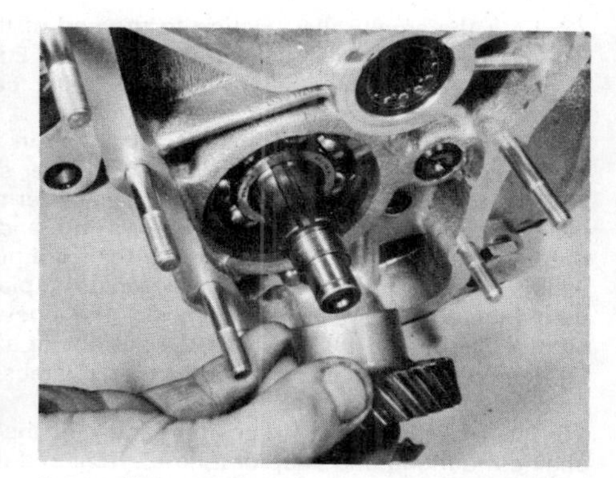
9.21a Slide the first motion shaft gear over the splines...

9.21b ...refit the lockwasher and retaining nut...

9.21c ...then tighten the nut to the specified torque

9.23a Drive the first motion shaft needle roller bearing onto the shaft...

9.23b ...and secure with the circlip

9.25a Place a new gasket on the oil pick-up pipe...

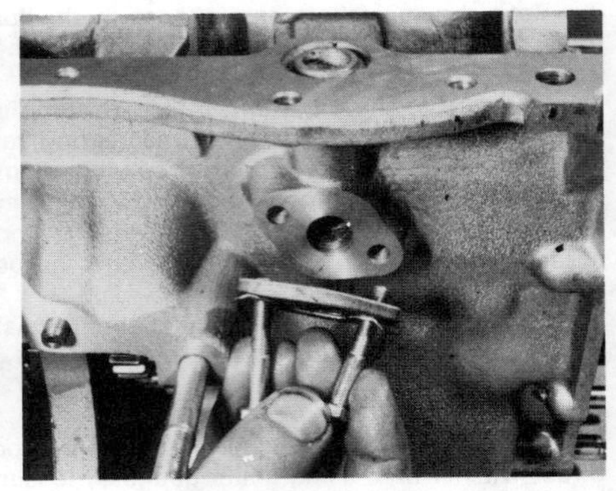

9.25b ...and on the blanking plate, then refit the bolts and lockwasher to the blanking plate...

9.25c ...and oil strainer, tightening both pairs of bolts fully

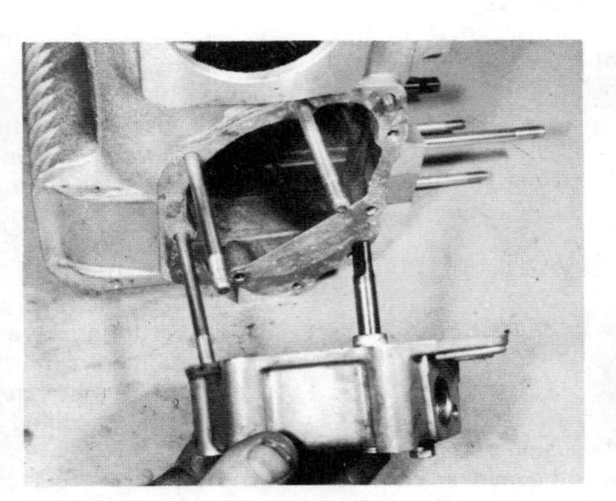

9.26 Refitting the gearbox front cover...

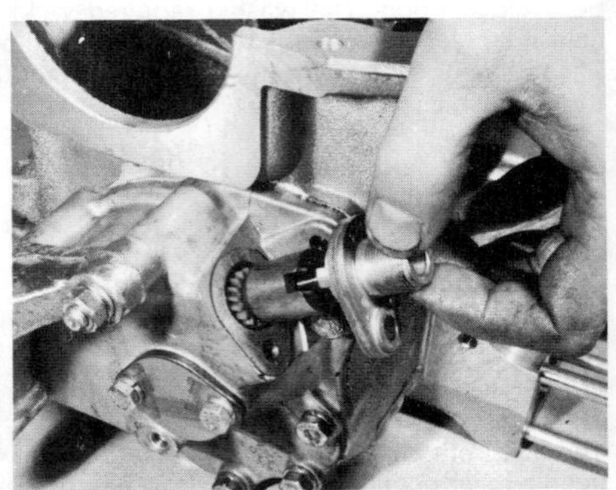

9.27 ...and the speedometer pinion and housing assembly

23 Refit the small roller bearing to the end of the first motion shaft, tapping it on using a tube of suitable diameter. Ensure that the bearing is positioned with the flat face of the roller cage facing the gear. Secure the bearing with the circlip (photos).
24 Insert the oil suction pipe into the hole in the centre of the oil strainer, taking care not to dislodge the rubber sealing ring.
25 The top flange on the oil strainer lies under the lug on the side of the gearbox casing. Position the lockwasher, and insert the two bolts through the two holes in the lug into the fixed nuts under the bracket flange. Place a new joint gasket between the pipe blanking plate and the flange on the outside of the casing, and a new gasket between the oil pipe flange and the inside of the casing. Fit a new lockwasher and tighten up the two pairs of bolts. Turn up the tabs on both lockwashers (photos).
26 Place a new gasket in position and refit the gearbox front cover, engine mounting and adaptor (photo). Refit and tighten the nuts, bolts and washers as appropriate.
27 Refit the speedometer pinion to the front cover and then fit the bush, gasket and pinion housing cover. Secure the cover with the bolt and washer (photo).
28 The differential assembly can now be refitted to the gearbox casing as described in Chapter 8. Before refitting the engine to the transmission, refer to Section 11 regarding removal and refitting of the transfer gears.

10 Transfer gears – description

Drive is transmitted from the clutch to the gearbox by means of three transfer gears. On the end of the crankshaft is the primary gear. When the clutch pedal is depressed the primary gear remains stationary while the crankshaft revolves inside it . On releasing the clutch pedal the drive is taken up and the primary gear revolves with the crankshaft at crankshaft speed.

Drive is taken from the primary gear, through an intermediate gear, to the first motion shaft drivegear, which is a splined fit on the nose of the first motion shaft.

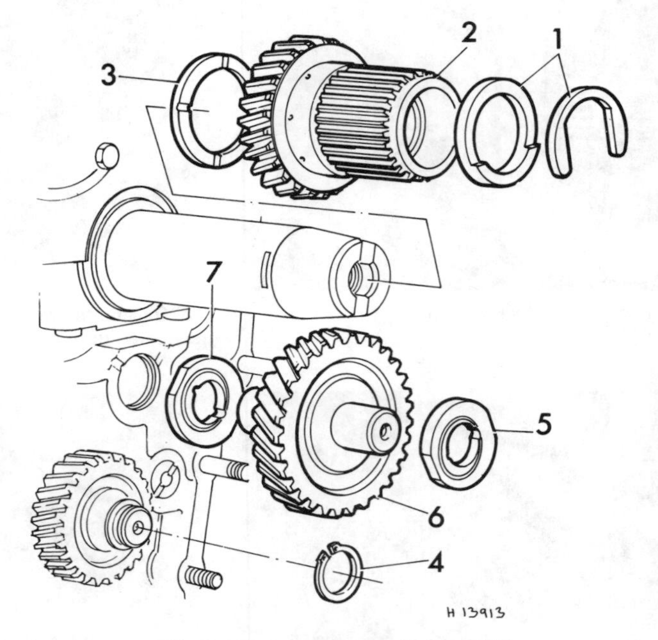

Fig. 6.9 Transfer geartrain (Sec 10)

1 *Retaining washer and U-ring*
2 *Primary gear*
3 *Thrust washer*
4 *Circlip*
5 *Thrust washer*
6 *Idler gear*
7 *Thrust washer*

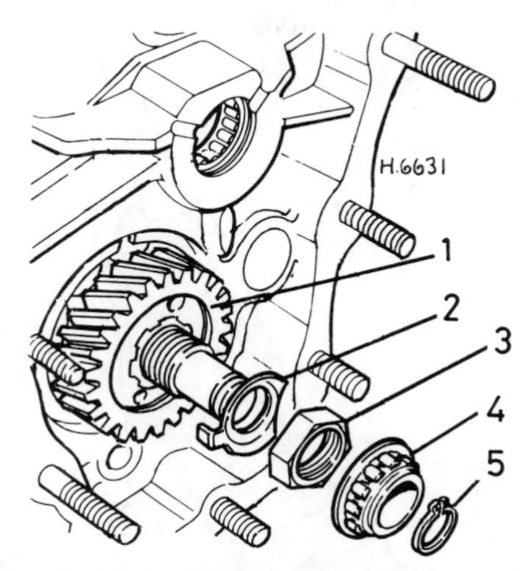

Fig. 6.10 First motion shaft gear and bearing assembly (Sec 11)

1 First motion shaft gear
2 Lockwasher
3 Retaining nut
4 Roller bearing
5 Circlip

11 Transfer gears – removal and refitting

Note: *To provide access to the transfer gears it will be necessary to remove the engine/transmission unit from the car as described in Chapter 1. The flywheel and flywheel housing must also be removed; full information on this procedure will also be found in Chapter 1.*

1 With the flywheel housing removed, the transfer gears are now exposed. The primary gear can be removed first by lifting off the U-shaped ring and retaining washer and sliding the gear off the end of the shaft. Now slide off the thrust washer.

2 Lift the idler gear out of its needle roller bearing in the transmission casing. Make sure that the thrust washers (one on each side) are kept in their correct relative positions.

3 To remove the first motion shaft gear, first extract the circlip and withdraw the roller bearing, using a puller or two screwdrivers, from the first motion shaft. Now bend back the lockwasher and undo and remove the nut. To prevent the first motion shaft from turning as the nut is undone, put the transmission in gear and then lock the drive flanges using blocks of wood between the flanges and gearbox casing. On later models BL tool 18G1088 may be needed.

4 Lift off the lockwasher and slide the gear off the first motion shaft.

5 Refitting the transfer gears is the reverse sequence to removal. However, the endfloat of the primary gear and idler gear must be checked, and if necessary adjusted, as described below before finally refitting the flywheel housing.

Primary gear

6 Refit the primary gear thrust washer with its chamfered bore against the crankshaft flange. Slide on the gear and secure with the retaining washer and U-shaped ring. Using feeler gauges measure the clearance between the end of the gear and the thrust washer (photo). The correct endfloat is given in the Specifications. If the measures endfloat is outside the specified limits, selective thrust washers are available from your BL dealer.

Idler gear

7 The endfloat of the idler gear can only be accurately measured with the engine removed from the transmission. If a new idler gear, thrust washers, transmission casing or flywheel housing are being fitted then this must be done to allow the endfloat to be accurately measured. If, however, the original components are being refitted, it can be assumed that the endfloat will be as before and therefore satisfactory.

8 To check the endfloat, refit the flywheel housing after making sure the mating faces are clean and a new gasket is in position. Tighten the retaining nuts to the specified torque and then, using feeler gauges, measure the clearance between the thrust washer and the side of the casing (photo). The endfloat should be as specified. Selective thrust washers are available from your BL dealer to correct any deficiency. The flywheel housing can now be removed, the engine positioned on the transmission and the transfer gears and housing finally refitted.

11.6 Using feeler gauges to measure the primary gear endfloat

11.8 Checking the endfloat of the idler gear

12 Transfer gear bearings – removal and refitting

Note: *If the idler gear bearings in the flywheel housing or gearbox casing on the first motion shaft support bearing outer race require renewal, proceed as follows.*

1 Remove the engine/transmission unit from the car and then remove the flywheel and flywheel housing as described in Chapter 1.

2 Heat the flywheel housing in boiling water. *On no account apply a direct flame to the housing.* If a receptacle large enough to hold the flywheel housing is not available, slowly pour boiling water over the area round the bearing.

3 Remove the reatining ring (where fitted) and carefully prise the bearing out of the casing, taking great care not to damage the bearing housing. If possible use BL service tool 18G581.

4 When fitting a new bearing carefully drift it into position (having previously heated the housing as described above) until it is just clear of the retaining ring recess (where fitted). *On no account press the bearing right into the recess in the housing,* as this would mask the bearing oil supply hole which is at the rear of the recess.

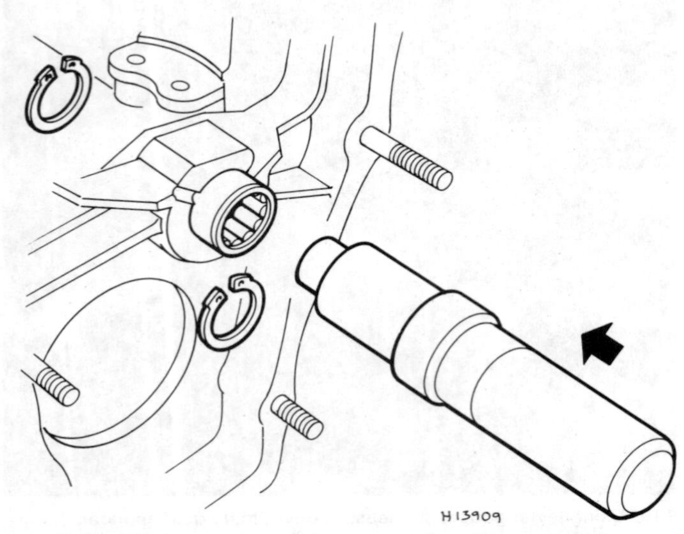

Fig. 6.11 Fitting a new idler gear bearing to the transmission casing (Sec 12)

13.3 Removing the gear lever retaining plate

Fig. 6.12 The remote control gear lever assembly used with the rod-change transmission (Sec 13)

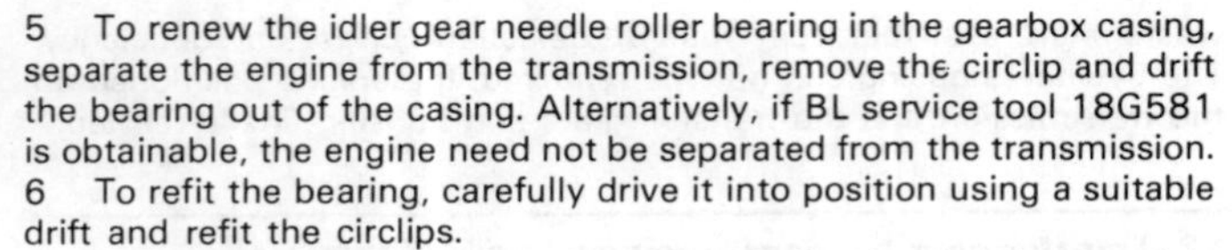
5 To renew the idler gear needle roller bearing in the gearbox casing, separate the engine from the transmission, remove the circlip and drift the bearing out of the casing. Alternatively, if BL service tool 18G581 is obtainable, the engine need not be separated from the transmission.
6 To refit the bearing, carefully drive it into position using a suitable drift and refit the circlips.
7 If the outer race of the first motion shaft roller bearing requires renewal, use the procedure described in paragraphs 2 and 3, or preferably obtain BL service tool 18G617A.

13 Gear lever – removal and refitting

Direct engagement lever

1 Jack up the rear of the car and support it on axle stands.
2 Lift up the front carpets and then undo and remove the screws securing the rubber boot retaining plate and rubber boot to the floor. Lift off the retaining plate and slide the boot up the gear lever slightly.
3 From underneath the car, undo and remove the two bolts and spring washers securing the gear lever retaining plate to the transmission casing (photo).
4 Lift the gear lever out of its location and remove it from inside the car. As the gear lever is removed take out the small anti-rattle spring and plunger from the drilling in the side of the gear lever seat.
5 Refitting the gear lever is the reverse sequence to removal. Lubricate the gear lever ball with general purpose grease before refitting.

Remote control lever (early type)

6 Working inside the car, lift up the carpets, undo and remove the screws securing the retaining plate and rubber boot to the floor.
7 Undo and remove the two screws and then lift off the gear lever complete with retainer, distance piece, spring and flange.
8 Refitting the gear lever is the reverse sequence to removal. Lubricate the gear lever ball with general purpose grease before refitting.

Remote contol lever (rod-change type)

9 Lift up the carpets, and then undo and remove the screws securing the retaining plate and rubber boot to the floor.
10 Slide the rubber boot up the lever then press down and turn the bayonet cap fixing to release the lever from the remote control housing.
11 Lift out the gear lever, rubber boot and retainer.
12 Refitting the gear lever is the reverse sequence to removal. Lubricate the gear lever ball with general purpose grease before refitting.

14 Gearchange remote control housing – removal and refitting

Early type

1 Jack up the front of the car and support it on axle stands.
2 Remove the gear lever as described in the previous Section.
3 From the rear of the housing, undo and remove the nut and washer securing the rubber mounting to the support bracket.
4 From the front of the housing, undo and remove the four shouldered bolts securing the front mounting to the housing.
5 Pull the housing down at the front to disengage the linkage, and then move it forward and out of the rear support bracket.
6 Refitting the remote control housing is the reverse sequence to removal. When engaging the front of the housing with the mounting it may be necessary to move the gear lever slightly to align the linkage and enable the front of the housing to be pushed fully home.

Rod-change type

7 Jack up the front of the car and support it on axle stands.
8 Remove the remote control lever as described in Section 13.
9 Working beneath the car, disconnect the reversing light switch wiring.
10 Unscrew the nut securing the rear of the steady rod to the remote control housing and remove the washer. There is no need to remove the steady rod from the differential housing on the gearbox except for examination of the rod. Furthermore, with the remote control housing fitted it may be difficult to remove the front rod bolt as it may foul the exhaust downpipe.
11 Using a parallel pin punch drift out the roll pin securing the collar to the gearchange extension rod or gearbox shaft. Note that although there is radial play between the collar and shaft/rod, the roll pin should be a tight fit in both components.
12 Unscrew and remove the nut and through-bolt securing the remote control housing to the mounting bracket, then withdraw the housing from the steady rod and remove from under the car.
13 Refitting is a reversal of removal.

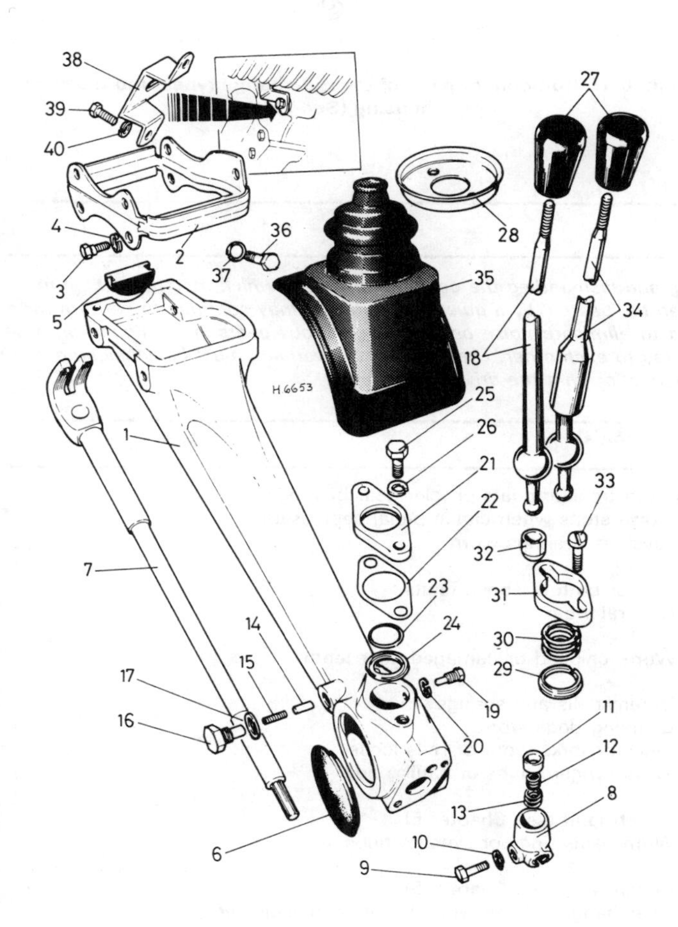

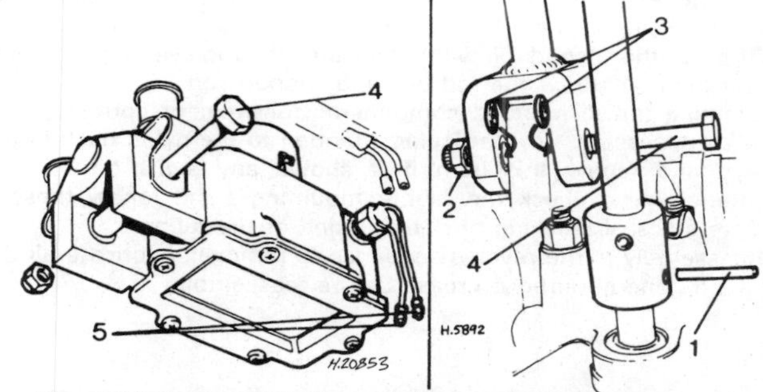

Fig. 6.13 Removal of the rod-change type remote control assembly from underside of car (Sec 14)

1 Roll pin
2 Nut
3 Plain washers
4 Bolt
5 Reversing light switch terminals

15 Gearchange remote control housing – dismantling and reassembly

Early type

1 Remove the remote control housing from the car as described in the previous Section.
2 Undo and remove the anti-rattle spring, plunger retaining nut and washer and take out the spring and plunger.
3 Prise off the large grommet from the side of the housing and then, using a socket, undo and remove the primary shaft pinch-bolt.
4 Slide the primary shaft forward to disengage the shaft lever and then lift out the shaft and lever.
5 Examine the primary shaft and the nylon bush in the shaft lever for wear and renew as necessary. The bush in the lever may be prised out with a screwdriver, and a new bush simply pushed into place. Check that the anti-rattle spring is not weak or broken as this will cause a sizzling noise to be emitted from the gear lever during hard accleration. Also inspect the front and rear mountings for deteioration of the rubber, and renew if suspect.
6 Lubricate all the components with general purpose grease and reassemble using the reverse of the dismantling procedure. Ensure that the machined groove in the end of the primary shaft is in line with the pinch-bolt hole in the shaft lever when reassembling these components.

Rod-change type

7 Remove the remote control housing from the car as described in the previous Section.
8 Undo and remove the six screws and lift off the bottom cover plate.
9 Undo and remove the locknut, washer and steady rod from the housing.
10 Using a parallel pin punch, drift out the roll pin securing the

Fig. 6.14 Exploded view of the early type remote control gearchange housing (Sec 15)

1 Remote control housing
2 Front mounting
3 Shouldered bolt
4 Washer
5 Grommet
6 Grommet
7 Primary shaft
8 Shaft lever
9 Bolt
10 Washer
11 Thrust button
12 Inner spring
13 Outer spring
14 Anti-rattle plunger
15 Anti-rattle spring
16 Nut
17 Washer
18 Gear lever
19 Locating pin
20 Washer
21 Retaining plate
22 Gasket
23 Ring
24 Flange
25 Bolt
26 Washer
27 Knob
28 Lever retainer
29 Nylon flange
30 Spring
31 Distance piece
32 Split bush
33 Retaining screw
34 Alternative gear lever
35 Rubber boot
36 Bolt
37 Washer
38 Exhaust bracket
39 Bolt
40 Washer

gearchange extension rod to the rod eye and then withdraw the extension rod.

11 Drift out the second roll pin that secures the rod eye to the support rod and then withdraw the rod eye and support rod.

12 Examine the dismantled components for wear or corrosion and renew as necessary. Pay particular attention to the nylon bush in the rod eye and renew this item if it shows any signs of wear or deformation. Also check the rubber mountings, and renew these if there are signs of cracking or deterioration of the rubber.

13 Reassembly is the reverse sequence to removal. Lubricate all the parts with general purpose grease before reassembly.

16 Gearchange selector shaft oil seal (rod-change gearbox) – removal and refitting

1 Jack up the front of the car and support it on axle stands.

2 Place a suitable container beneath the engine and drain the engine/transmission oil.

3 Using a parallel pin punch, drift out the roll pin securing the gearchange extension shaft collar to the selector shaft.

4 Undo and remove the nut and bolt securing the gearchange steady rod to the differential housing. Move the steady rod rearwards slightly and withdraw the extension rod collar off the selector shaft.

5 Withdraw the rubber gaiter (if fitted) and then hook out the oil seal with a screwdriver.

6 Before refitting a new seal wrap adhesive tape around the selector shaft to avoid damaging the seal lips as it is installed. If possible, obtain the protector sleeve, BL special tool No 18G1238 and place this over the selector shaft.

7 Lubricate the new seal in clean engine oil and slide it over the shaft with the open side of the seal toward the differential.

8 Tap the seal fully into position using a tube of suitable diameter.

9 Remove the adhesive tape or protector sleeve and then refit the gearchange extension shaft and the steady rod.

10 Lower the car to the ground and refill the engine/transmission with oil.

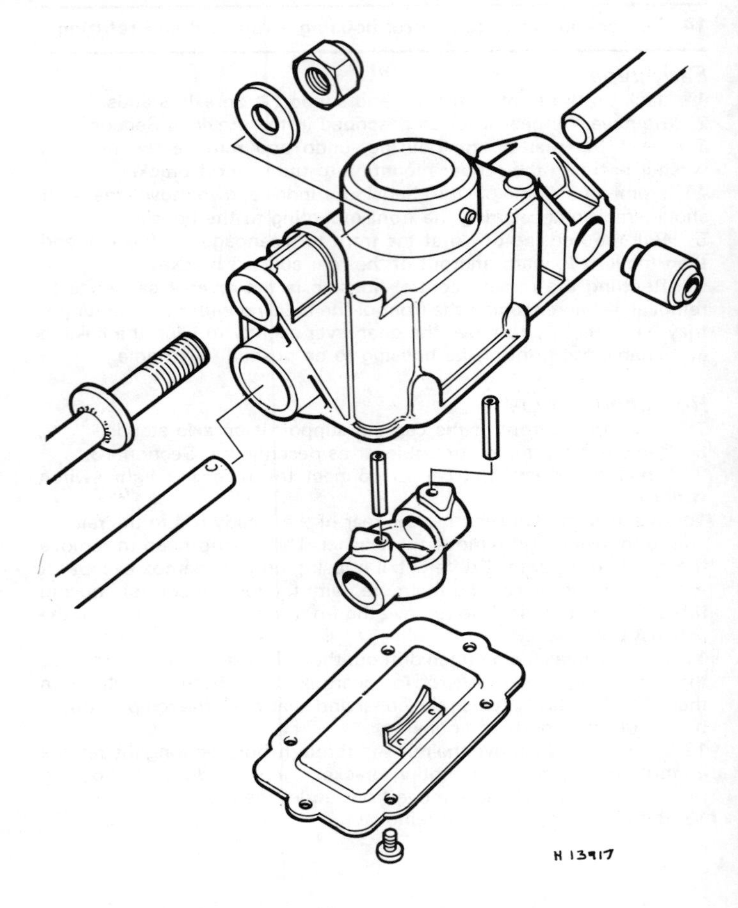

Fig. 6.15 Component parts of the rod-change type remote control housing (Sec 15)

17 Fault diagnosis – manual gearbox

Note: *It is sometimes difficult to decide whether it is worthwhile removing and dismantling the gearbox for a fault which may be nothing more than a minor irritant. Gearboxes which howl, or where the synchromesh can be 'beaten' by a quick gear change, may continue to perform for a long time in this state. A worn gearbox usually needs a complete rebuild to eliminate noise because the various gears, if re-aligned on new bearings, will continue to howl when different wearing surfaces are presented to each other. The decision to overhaul, must be considered with regard to time and money available, relative to the degree of noise or malfunction that the driver can tolerate.*

Symptom	Reason(s)
Gearbox noisy in neutral	Worn transfer gears or idler gear bearing (noise stops when clutch pedal depressed) Layshaft bearings worn
Gearbox noisy in all gears	One or both of above faults General wear
Gearbox noisy in one particular gear	Worn, chipped or damaged gear teeth
Gearbox jumps out of gear on drive or overrun	Detent balls and springs worn Coupling dogs worn Selector forks worn or rods loose Worn synchro hubs or baulk rings
Crunching or cracking when changing gear	Clutch fault (see Chapter 5) Worn baulk rings or synchro hubs
Difficulty in engaging gear	Clutch fault (see Chapter 5) Gearchange linkage worn, loose or maladjusted

18 Automatic transmission – general description

The automatic transmission fitted as an optional extra to Mini models incorporates a three element fluid torque convertor, with a maximum conversion of 2.1, coupled to a bevel geartrain assembly.

The final drive is transmitted from a drivegear to a conventional type differential unit, which in turn transmits engine torque through two flange type coupling driveshafts, employing constant velocity joints, to the roadwheels.

The complete geartrain assembly, including the reduction gears and differential units, runs parallel to, and below, the crankshaft and is housed in the transmission casing, which also serves as the engine sump.

The system is controlled by a selector lever within a gated quadrant marked with seven positions and mounted centrally on the floor of the car. The reverse, neutral, and drive positions are for normal automatic driving, with the first, second, third, and fourth positions used for manual operation or override as required. This allows the system to be used as a fully automatic four-speed transmission from rest to maximum speed, with the gears changing automatically according to throttle position and load. If a lower gear is required to obtain greater acceleration, an instant full throttle position (ie kick-down on the accelerator) immediately produces the change.

Complete manual control of all four forward gears by use of the selector lever provides rapid changes. However, it is very important that downward changes, are effected at the correct road speeds otherwise serious damage may result to the automatic transmission unit. The second, third and top gears provide engine braking whether driving in automatic or manual conditions. In first gear a freewheel condition exists when decelerating. Manual selection to third or second gear gives engine braking and also allows the driver to stay in a particular low gear to suit road conditions or when descending steep hills.

Due to complexity of the automatic transmission unit, if performance is not up to standard, or overhaul is necessary, it is imperative that this be left to the local main agents who will have the special equipment for fault diagnosis and rectification.

The content of the following Sections is therefore confined to supplying general information and any service information and instruction that can be used by the owner.

19 Automatic transmission – removal and refitting

The automatic transmission is removed from the car together with the engine and differential assembly as described in Chapter 1.

It will be necessary to separate the gearbox from the engine; again, full information will be found in Chapter 1.

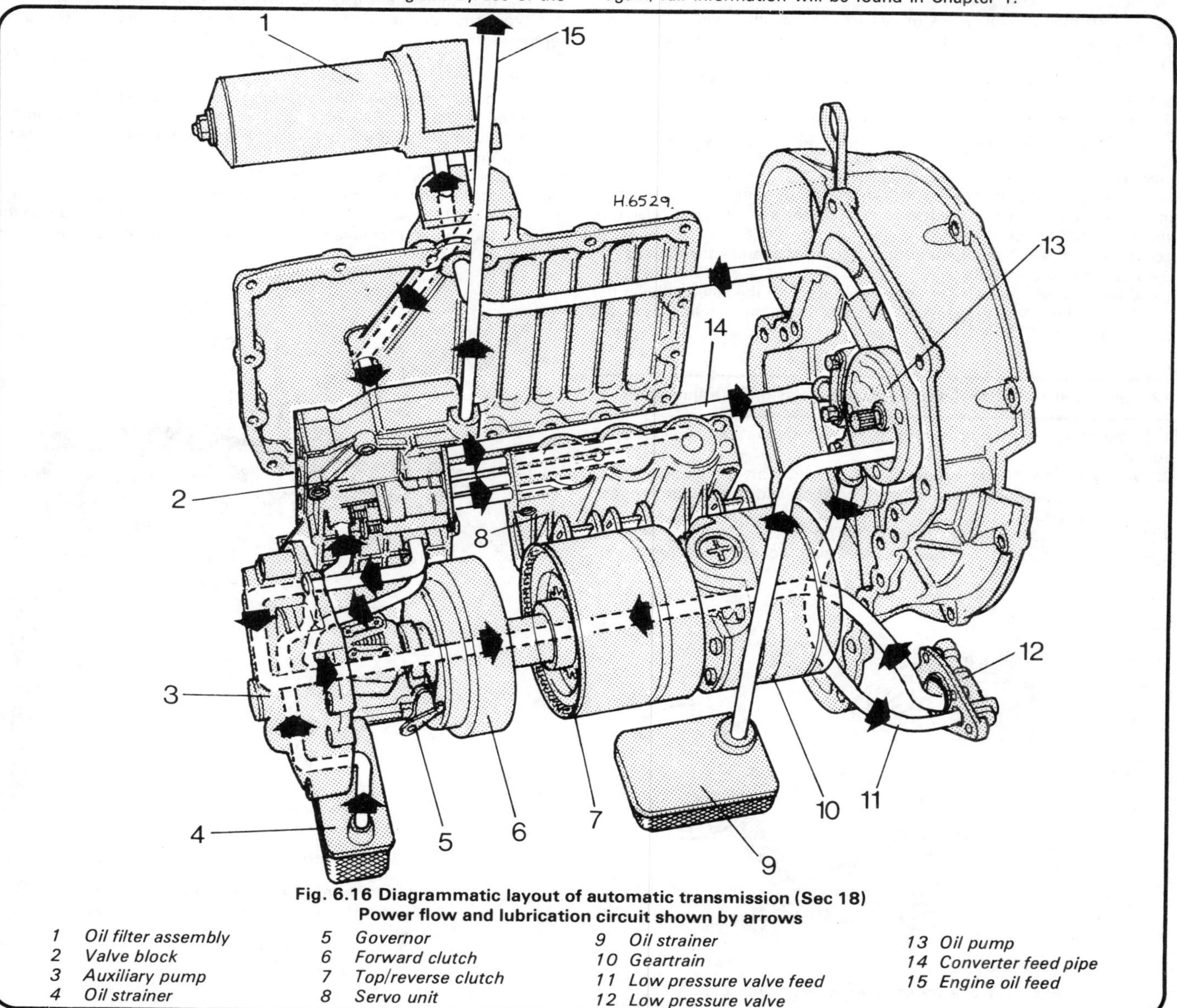

Fig. 6.16 Diagrammatic layout of automatic transmission (Sec 18)
Power flow and lubrication circuit shown by arrows

1 Oil filter assembly
2 Valve block
3 Auxiliary pump
4 Oil strainer
5 Governor
6 Forward clutch
7 Top/reverse clutch
8 Servo unit
9 Oil strainer
10 Geartrain
11 Low pressure valve feed
12 Low pressure valve
13 Oil pump
14 Converter feed pipe
15 Engine oil feed

20 Transfer gear (automatic transmission) – removal and refitting

1 The procedure for removing and refitting the transfer gear on vehicles equipped with automatic transmission is the same as described in Section 11 for manual gearbox models with the exception of the input (first motion shaft) gear which should not be disturbed.
2 To provide access to the transfer gears it will be necessary to remove the engine/transmission unit from the car and then remove the torque converter and converter housing as described in Chapter 1.

21 Starter inhibitor switch (automatic transmission) – adjustment

1 The starter inhibitor switch is located on the rear of the gear selector housing. Early switches have two terminals which are connected through the ignition/starter circuit. On later versions two additional terminals are used to actuate the reversing lights. The purpose of this is to ensure that the engine will only start when the gear selector lever is in the 'N' position.
2 The switch terminals marked '2' and '4' are used in the ignition/starter circuit and both the electrical leads are interchangeable to the '2' and '4' positions of the switch.
3 When the reversing light is fitted, terminals '1' and '3' are used for this light.
4 Before making any adjustments to the switch, ensure that the gearchange cable and selector rod adjustment is correct as described in Section 22.
5 To adjust the switch, just move the selector lever to the 'N' position.
6 Disconnect the electrical connections from the rear of the switch.
7 Slacken the locknut and screw out the switch as far as possible.
8 Connect a test light and battery across the switch terminals numbered '2' and '4'.
9 Screw the switch into the housing until the lamp *just* lights and then screw it in a further one half turn . Hold the switch in this position and tighten the locknut.
10 Remove the test equipment and reconnect the electrical leads to the appropriate terminals.
11 Check that the starter motor will operate with the selector lever in the 'N' position. When reversing lights are fitted check that they only come on when 'R' is selected.

22 Gear selector cable (automatic transmission) – adjustment

1 First check the cable setting as follows before carrying out any adjustment.
2 Apply the handbrake firmly, select 'N' and start the engine.
3 Move the selector lever to the 'R' position and check that reverse gear is engaged.
4 Move the lever slowly towards 'N' and check that reverse is disengaged just before or exactly as the lever locates the 'N' position.

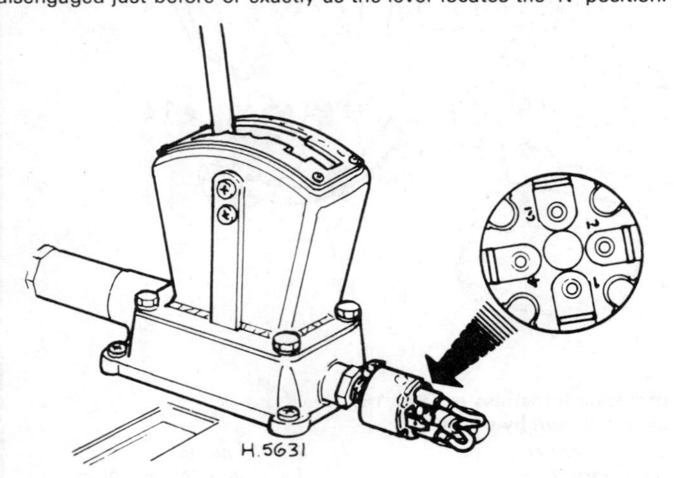

Fig. 6.17 Starter inhibitor switch (Sec 21)

5 Repeat the above procedure with the first gear '1' position.
6 If the checks show the cable to be in need of adjustment, proceed as follows.
7 Jack up the front of the car and support it on axle stands.
8 From underneath the car undo and remove the two bolts securing the bellcrank cover plate to the right-hand end of the transmission casing.
9 Undo and remove the nut and bolt securing the cable fork to the bellcrank lever.
10 Move the bellcrank lever to pull the transverse rod fully out and then move it back two detents.
11 From inside the car move the selector lever to the 'N' position.
12 Slacken the two selector cable adjusting nuts and position the cable so that the pivot bolt can be easily inserted through the cable fork and bellcrank lever.
13 Hold the cable in this position, tighten the adjusting nuts and check that the position of the cable has not altered.
14 Refit the pivot bolt and nut followed by the bellcrank cover plate.
15 Lower the car to the ground and recheck the cable setting as described in paragraphs 2 to 5 inclusive.

23 Governor control rod (automatic transmission) – adjustment

1 Fot this adjustment a tachometer is needed.
2 Start the engine and run it until it reaches normal operating temperature.
3 Refer to Chapter 3 and ensure that the carburettor settings are correct.
4 Disconnect the governor control rod at the carburettor.
5 Insert a 0.25 in (6.4 mm) diameter rod through the hole in the governor control rod bellcrank lever and into the hole in the transmission casing.
6 Slacken the locknut and adjust the length of the rod to suit the carburettor linkage in the tickover position.
7 Reconnect the governor control rod to the carburettor. Tighten the balljoint locknut and remove the checking rod from the bellcrank lever.

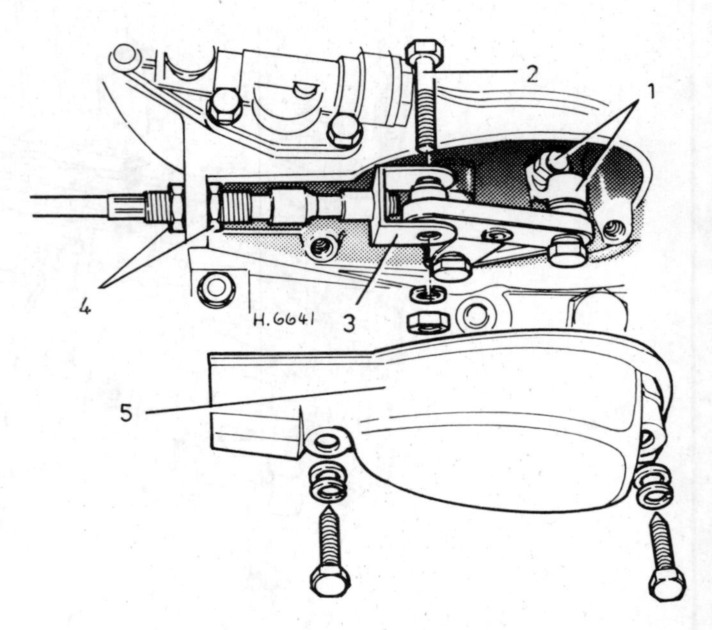

Fig. 6.18 Gear selector cable adjustment (Sec 22)

1 Transverse rod-to-bellcrank lever adaptor
2 Cable fork-to-bellcrank lever retaining bolt
3 Cable fork
4 Cable adjusting nuts
5 Bellcrank cover plate

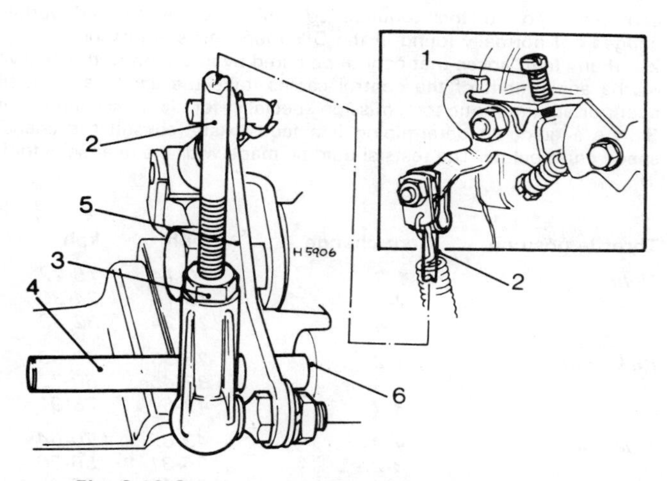

Fig. 6.19 Governor control rod adjustment (Sec 23)

1 *Throttle adjusting screw*
2 *Governor control rod*
3 *Locknut*
4 *0.25 in (6.4 mm) dia rod*
5 *Intermediate bellcrank lever*
6 *Transmission case hole*

24 Gear selector lever housing and cable (automatic transmission) – removal and refitting

1 Jack up the front of the car and support it on axle stands.
2 From underneath the car, undo and remove the two bolts securing the bellcrank cover plate to the right-hand end of the transmission casing.
3 Undo and remove the nut washer and pivot bolt securing the selector cable fork to the bellcrank lever.
4 Slacken the fork retaining nut and unscrew the fork from the cable.
5 Unscrew the fork retaining nut and then slide off the two rubber ferrules.
6 Undo and remove the outer cable adjusting nut and then pull the cable out of the transmission casing bracket.
7 Release the cable clip from the floor panel.
8 Working inside the car lift up the front floor covering.
9 Make a note of their relative positions, then disconnect the electrical leads from the starter inhibitor switch.
10 Undo and remove the four nuts and washers securing the selector lever housing to the floor panel, and withdraw the housing and cable from the car.
11 Refitting is the reverse sequence to removal. Adjust the cable as described in Section 22 and the inhibitor switch as described in Section 21 after refitting.

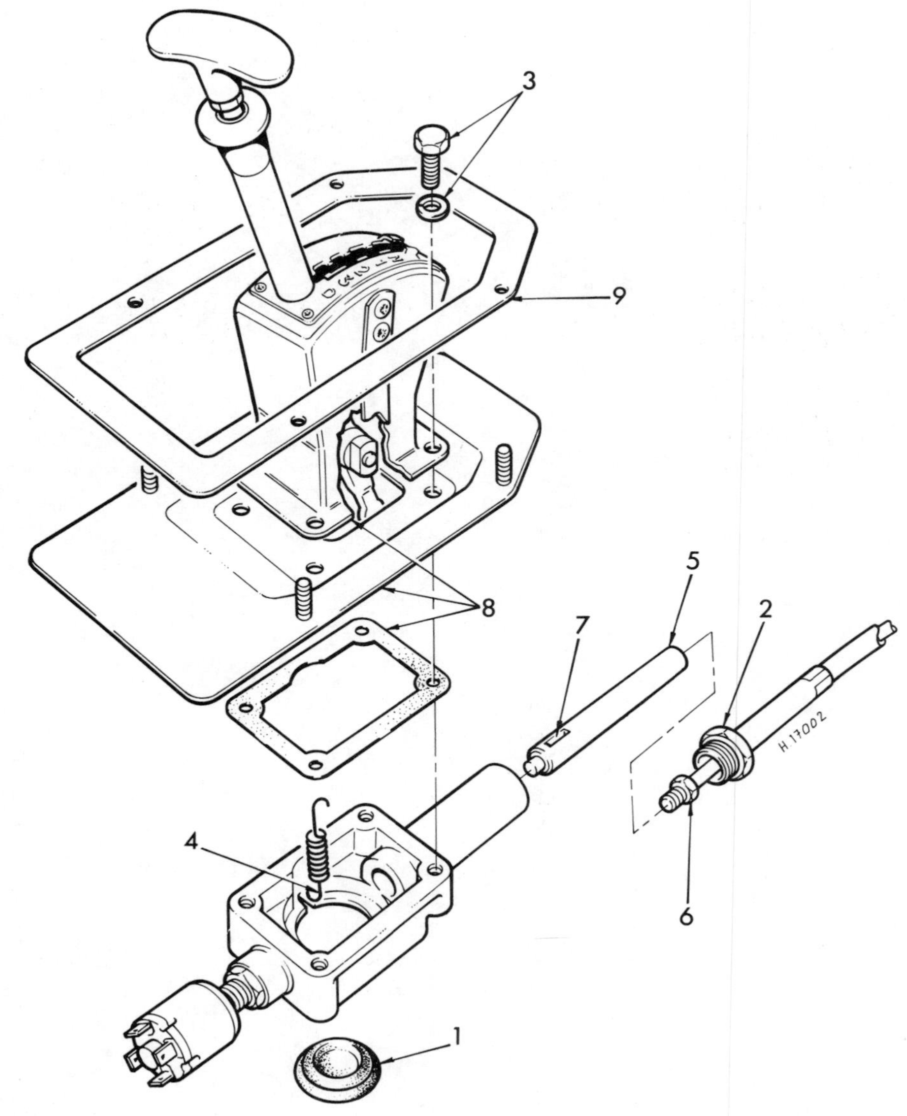

Fig. 6.20 Exploded view of gear selector lever housing (Sec 24)

1 *Grommet*
2 *Outer cable locknut*
3 *Quadrant securing bolts*
4 *Reverse return spring*
5 *Operating plunger*
6 *Inner cable locknut*
7 *Operating plunger slot*
8 *Quadrant, plate and gasket*
9 *Upper gasket*

25 Gear selector lever housing and cable (automatic transmission) – dismantling and reassembly

1 Remove the assembly as described in Section 24.
2 Prise out the rubber grommet at the base of the selector mechanism and then mount the assembly in a vice.
3 Slacken the nut securing the outer cable to the housing.
4 Undo and remove the four bolts securing the quadrant to the housing, release the reverse return spring and lift off the quadrant and lever.
5 Unscrew the outer cable and withdraw it from the housing.
6 Insert a screwdriver into the slot of the operating plunger to prevent it turning, and slacken the nut securing the cable to the plunger.
7 Finally, unscrew the plunger from the cable.
8 Inspect all the parts for wear and renew as necessary.
9 Reassembly is the reverse of the dismantling procedure. Lubricate all moving parts with general purpose grease before reassembling.

26 Fault diagnosis – automatic transmission

1 Before the automatic transmission is removed for repair of a suspected malfunction, it is imperative that the cause be traced and confirmed. To do this requires specialist experience and various gauges not normally found in the DIY mechanic's workshop.
2 If any fault arises that cannot be cured by attention to the oil level or the adjustment of the control cables, take the car to a BL main agent or an automatic transmission specialist for diagnosis and repair.
3 As a guide to determining if a fault exists, consult the change speed chart below. The tests should be made with the gear selector in 'D'.

Throttle position	Gear change	mph	kph
Light	*1-2*	*10-14*	*16-22*
	2-3	*15-19*	*24-30*
	3-4	*20-24*	*32-39*
Kickdown	*1-2*	*25-33*	*40-53*
	2-3	*37-45*	*60-72*
	3-4	*49-57*	*78-91*
Kickdown	*4-3*	*43-39*	*70-64*
	3-2	*35-31*	*56-50*
	2-1	*22-18*	*35-29*
Closed (roll out)	*4-3*	*20-16*	*32-26*
	3-2	*14-10*	*22-16*
	2-1	*8-4*	*12-6*

Chapter 7 Driveshafts and universal joints

For modifications, and information applicable to later models, see Supplement at end of manual

Contents

Specifications

Type .... Solid shaft reverse spline, with constant velocity outer joint and rubber coupling, Hardy-Spicer, or offset sphere type inner joint – depending on model and year of production

Torque wrench settings	**lbf ft**	**Nm**
Driveshaft retaining nut:		
All models except Cooper S and 1275 GT	60	83
Cooper S and 1275 GT	150	207
Rubber coupling U-bolts	10	14
Swivel hub balljoint nuts	38	52
Track rod end balljoint nut	22	30

1 General description

Drive is transmitted from the differential to the front wheels by means of two equal length driveshafts. A constant velocity joint is fitted to the outer end of each shaft to cater for steering and suspension movement. The constant velocity (CV) joint comprises a driving member (splined to the driveshaft), six caged steel balls, and a driven member (splined to the wheel hub flange). The driven member pivots freely on the steel balls, to any angle, thus allowing the drive to be smoothly transmitted to the front wheels throughout the full range of steering and suspension travel.

To allow for vertical movement of the driveshaft with the suspension, models equipped with manual transmission incorporate either a flexible rubber drive coupling or an offset sphere type joint, similar to a CV joint, at the inner end of each driveshaft. A Hardy-Spicer universal joint is used at each driveshaft inner end on Cooper S Mk III models and vehicles equipped with automatic transmission. On models fitted with offset sphere type inner joints, lateral movement of the driveshaft is catered for by the sliding components within the joint. On all other models each driveshaft incorporates a sliding spline at the inner end.

The CV joint, offset sphere joint and the driveshaft sliding spline are all protected by rubber boots. Other than a periodic inspection of the rubber boots, the driveshafts are maintenance-free.

2 Driveshaft assembly – tests for wear/fault diagnosis

1 The driveshaft assembly consists of the outer constant velocity joint, the inner sliding spline and rubber coupling on early models, the inner offset sphere joint on later models and the Hardy-Spicer universal joint on Cooper S Mk III and automatic transmission models. All of these components are subject to wear after high mileages, and the following tests can be used to isolate a suspect unit.

Constant velocity joint

2 This is a well publicised weak spot on Minis. Wear is easily recognised as a metallic clicking from the front of the car as it is driven slowly in a circle with the steering on full lock. The noise is caused by excessive clearance between the balls in the joint and the recesses in which they operate. If the noise is only slight it may be nothing more serious than a lack of grease in the joint due to a split or damaged rubber boot. The best course of action if a clicking noise is apparent is to remove the joint as described in Section 5 and carry out a visual inspection. If wear is excessive the joint must be renewed.

Inner sliding splines

3 To check for wear on these components it will be necessary to position the car over a ramp or pit, or to jack it up and support it on axle stands. Grasp the driveshaft with one hand and the inner flange with the other and attempt to turn them in opposite directions. If this is possible to any appreciable degree then wear has taken place and both the driveshaft and flange will need renewal. Also check the condition of the rubber boot; it damaged or split it should be renewed.

Inner rubber coupling

4 Wear in the rubber coupling can often be experienced on the road as a thumping, consistent with road speed and felt through the steering and body, usually on the overrun. A closer inspection can be carried out from beneath the vehicle with it over a ramp or pit, or jacked up and supported on axle stands. Check for swelling or deterioration of the rubber or for oil contamination. Place a flat bar or stout screwdriver between the flanges and apply gentle leverage. Appreciable movement indicates wear in the joint. In more advanced stages of wear the rubber may have worn to such an extent that the inner metal spider will be visible. If the rubber is swelling due to oil contamination, the joint will rub on the rear face of the gearbox casing, with the obvious disastrous results if this is allowed to continue.

Offset sphere joint

5 These joints are quite reliable and seldom give trouble. However, a vibration felt through the car, particularly during acceleration, may indicate wear in the joint. If the vibration is only slight it may be due to a lack of grease caused by a damaged rubber boot. If the joint is suspect it should be removed from the car and carefully inspected as described in Section 9. It is possible to renew the rubber boot separately, but if the internal components of the joint are worn it will

be necessary to renew the complete unit.

Hardy-Spicer universal joint

6 Wear in the needle roller bearings of these joints is characterised by vibration in the transmission, clonks on taking up the drive, and in extreme cases of lack of lubrication, metallic squeaking, and ultimately grating and shrieking as the bearings break up. With the car over a ramp or pit, or jacked up and supported on axle stands, attempt to turn the shaft with one hand while holding the inner drive flange with the other. If any movement exists this indicates considerable wear has taken place. Also try lifting the joint and noting if any movement takes place. If the joint is worn it may be overhauled using a repair kit consisting of a new spider, bearings, seals and circlips. This is described in detail in Section 7.

3 Driveshaft – removal and refitting

1 Remove the wheel trim and slacken the front roadwheel retaining nuts.
2 Extract the split pin and, using a large socket undo and remove the driveshaft retaining nut and washer (photos).
3 Working under the wheel arch, undo and remove the single retaining screw and lift out the upper suspension arm rebound rubber. Position a solid packing piece of approximately the same thickness in its place.
4 Jack up the front of the car and support it on axle stands placed under the subframe. Remove the front roadwheel.
5 The procedure now varies slightly according to the type of inner joint fitted to the driveshaft.

3.2a Removing the driveshaft retaining nut...

3.2b ...and thrust washer

Models with inner rubber coupling or Hardy-Spicer universal joint

6 From underneath the car, suitably mark the driveshaft flanges to ensure correct reassembly. Undo and remove the four outer locknuts from the U-bolts securing the driveshaft flange to the rubber coupling. On models fitted with Hardy-Spicer Universal joints, undo and remove the four locknuts securing the two flanges together.
7 Undo and remove the steering tie-rod balljoint retaining locknut and then release the balljoint tapered shank from the steering arm in the following manner.
8 If a universal balljoint separator is available, use the separator to release the tapered shank and then lift the balljoint off the steering arm. Alternatively refit the locknut to the balljoint and screw it on two or three turns. Using a medium hammer, sharply strike the end of the steering arm until the shock separates the taper (photo). Now remove the locknut and lift the joint off the arm.
9 Undo and remove the nuts and spring washers securing the upper and lower suspension arms to the swivel hub balljoints.
10 Using the method described in paragraph 8, separate the upper and lower suspension arms from the tapered shanks of the balljoints.
11 Support the swivel hub to avoid stretching the flexible brake hose. Tap the end of the driveshaft with a soft-faced mallet to free the shaft from the hub.
12 Slide the driveshaft fully out of the hub and then withdraw it from the car outwards through the aperture in the subframe. With the driveshaft removed refit the swivel hub balljoint to the upper suspension arm and screw on the retaining nut two or three turns.

Models wth offset sphere type inner joint

13 Release the driveshaft from the swivel hub, and the swivel hub from the suspension and steering arms, using the procedure described in paragraphs 7 to 11 inclusive.
14 Withdraw the swivel hub off the end of the driveshaft (photo) and then tie the hub assembly out of the way from a convenient place

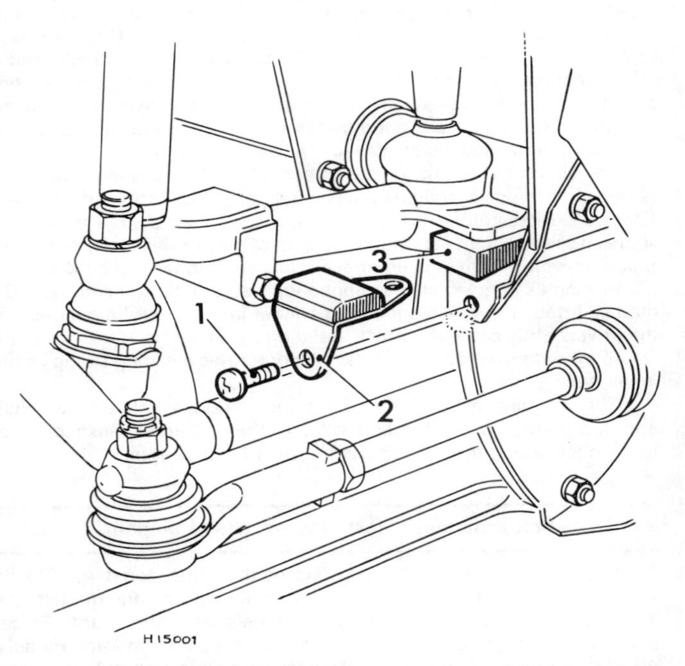

Fig. 7.1 Fitting a solid packing wedge in place of the suspension rebound rubber (Sec 3)

1 Screw
2 Rebound rubber
3 Packing piece

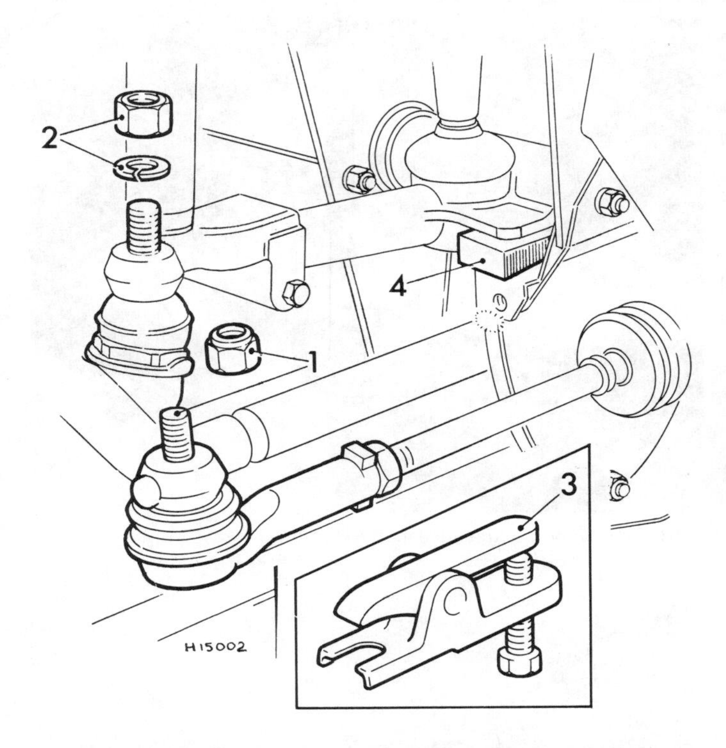

Fig. 7.2 Releasing the tie-rod and swivel hub balljoints (Sec 3)

1 *Tie-rod balljoint and nut*
2 *Swivel hub upper balljoint and nut*
3 *Universal balljoint separator*
4 *Solid packing piece*

3.8 Alternative method of releasing the balljoint taper

3.14 Withdraw the swivel hub from the end of the driveshaft...

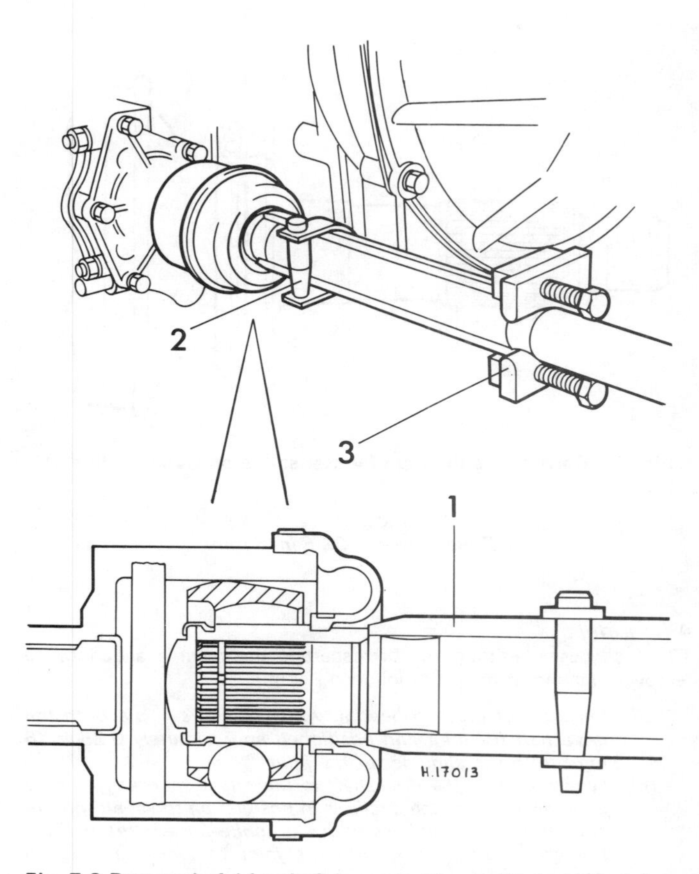

Fig. 7.3 Removal of driveshaft inner end from offset sphere joint (Sec 3)

1 *Special tool 18G1243*
2 *Tool in contact with joint flange*
3 *Tool plate engaged with driveshaft groove*

under the wheel arch. Avoid placing excessive strain on the flexible brake hose.

15 The inner end of the driveshaft must now be removed from the offset sphere joint. If BL special tool No 18G1243 can be obtained this will greatly simplify the task of removing the driveshaft from the joint. If this tool is not available the following procedure should be used.

16 Insert a flat metal bar or similar tool through the aperture in the subframe so that it rests on the driveshaft and is in contact with the flange of the joint (photo). Take care not to pinch the rubber boot with the bar as it is easily punctured.

17 Pull the driveshaft outwards approximately 1 in (25 mm) and firmly hold it in this position. The help of an assistant may be useful here.

18 Strike the end of the bar with a few sharp hammer blows. This will force the flange of the joint inwards and release it from the end of the driveshaft. The driveshaft can now be withdrawn from the car (photo).

3.16 ...release the inner end from the offset sphere joint...

3.18 ...and withdraw the driveshaft assembly

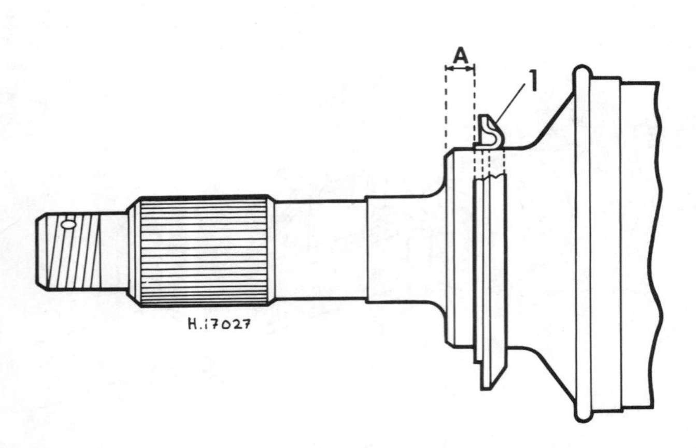

Fig. 7.4 Correct positioning of water shield on CV joint (Sec 3)

1 Water shield
Dimension A = 0.25 in (6 mm)

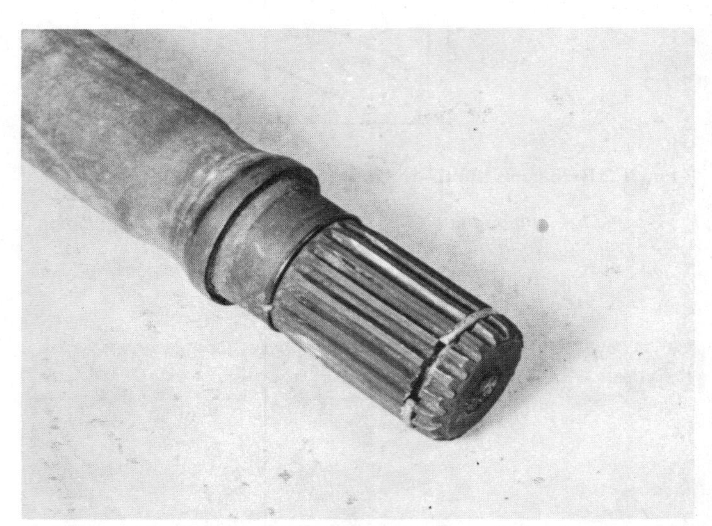

3.19 Ensure that the circlip is in position before refitting the driveshaft

All models

19 In all cases refitting the driveshaft is the reverse sequence to removal, bearing in mind the following points:

- (a) *Ensure that the hub bearing water shield is in place on the driveshaft CV joint and positioned approximately 0.25 in (6 mm) from the shoulder of the joint*
- (b) *When refitting the driveshaft to the offset sphere type inner joint, ensure that the circlip is in position on the shaft (photo) and lubricate the splines with a graphite-based grease. Push the driveshaft smartly into the joint to lock the shaft in position*
- (c) *Tighten all nuts and bolts to the specified torque*

4 Constant velocity joint rubber boot – removal and refitting

1 If a rubber boot on one of the CV joints has split or been damaged, it should be renewed as soon as possible otherwise water and grit will enter the joint, causing rapid wear.
2 To renew the rubber boot, begin by removing the driveshaft from the car as described in Section 3.
3 On models equipped with a rubber drive coupling or universal joint at the inner end of the driveshaft; remove the retaining clips or wire from the small inner rubber boot and then slide the flange and boot off the end of the driveshaft.
4 Now remove the retaining clips or wire from the constant velocity joint rubber boot. Slide the boot along the shaft and off the splined end.
5 Thoroughly clean all traces of rubber, old grease and dirt from the shaft and CV joint.
Note: *If the car has been operated for a considerable length of time with a defective rubber boot, or if the grease appears contaminated with grit, it is essential that the CV joint is thoroughly washed out with petrol or paraffin.*
6 New CV joint rubber boots are available in the form of a repair kit from your local dealer. The kit comprises the CV joint boot, the boot retaining clips and a tube of Duckhams Q5795 grease. It is most important that only this type of grease is used.
7 Thoroughly pack the CV joint using the grease supplied in the repair kit. Manipulate the joint from side to side and ensure that the grease is worked well into the balls and ball recesses.
8 Now slide the new CV joint boot over the splined end of the driveshaft and position it onto the joint. Ensure that the moulded lips of the boot fit into the shallow depressions machined in the outer circumference of the joint and on the driveshaft.
9 Place the larger retaining clip supplied in the repair kit over the CV joint with the end containing the tabs facing away from the forward

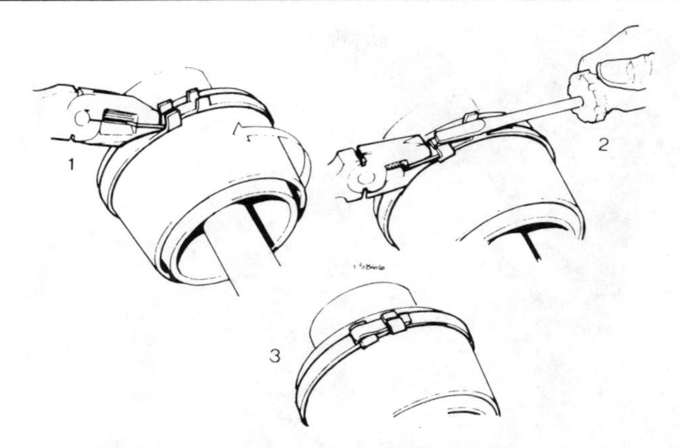

Fig. 7.5 When clips are used to secure rubber boot, pull clips tight and secure in order shown (Sec 4)
Arrow indicates forward rotation of shaft

direction of shaft rotation. Using pliers, pull the other end of the clip over the end containing the tabs and press down the first set of tabs using a screwdriver. Pull the free end tight and fold it over the compressed tabs. Now bend over the second set of tabs, trapping the free end of the clip underneath.

10 Alternatively secure the boot using two or three turns of soft iron wire. Twist the ends of the wire together and bend them over to face away from the forward direction of rotation of the shaft. Ensure that the wires are correctly located on the area of the boot directly over the shallow depressions in the joint.

11 Secure the smaller diameter of the CV joint boot to the driveshaft using the same method as described in paragraphs 9 and 10 above.

12 The remaining operations only apply to models fitted with a rubber drive coupling or universal joint at the inner end of the driveshaft.

13 Slide the smaller rubber boot over the splines until the moulded lip fits in the shallow depression on the shaft.

14 Liberally smear the splines on the driveshaft and the flange with the remains of the grease supplied in the repair kit.

15 Slide the flange onto the end of the shaft and pull the larger lip of the rubber boot over the end of the flange, engaging the lip into the shallow depression on the flange.

16 Secure the rubber boot using soft iron wire as described in paragraph 10.

17 The driveshaft can now be refitted to the car as described in Section 3.

5 Constant velocity joint – removal, inspection and refitting

1 Begin by removing the driveshaft from the car as described in Section 3, and the rubber boots from the driveshaft as described in Section 4.

2 Firmly grasp the driveshaft or support it in a vice. Using a hide or plastic mallet, sharply strike the outer edge of the joint and drive it off the shaft. The CV joint is retained on the driveshaft by an internal circular section circlip, and striking the joint in the manner described forces the circlip to contract into a groove, so allowing the joint to slide off.

3 With the CV joint removed from the driveshaft, thoroughly wash out the joint using petrol or paraffin and dry it, preferably using compressed air. Carry out a careful visual inspection of the CV joint, paying particular attention to the following areas.

4 Move the inner splined driving member from side to side to expose each ball in turn at the top of its track. Examine the balls for cracks, flat spots or signs of surface pitting.

5 Inspect the ball tracks on the inner and outer members. If the tracks have widened, the balls will no longer be a tight fit. At the same time check the ball cage windows for wear or for cracking between the balls. Wear in the balls, ball tracks and ball cage windows will lead to the characteristic clicking noise on full lock described previously.

6 It is no longer possible to obtain a CV joint overhaul kit consisting of a new ball cage and associated components. Therefore, if wear is apparent in the above mentioned areas, it will be necessary to renew

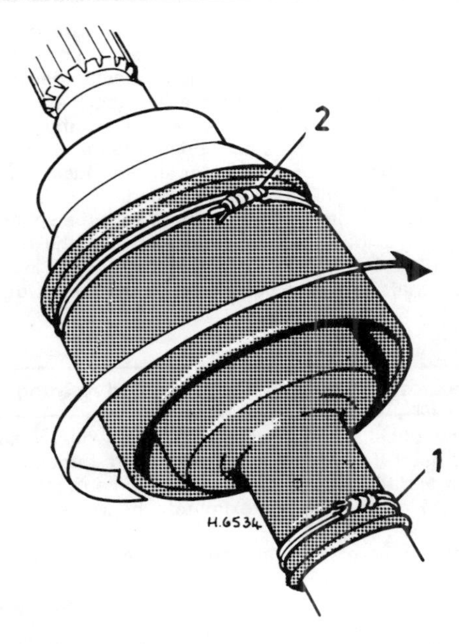

Fig. 7.6 When securing rubber boot with soft iron wire, ensure that the wire ends (1 and 2) are bent away from forward direction of rotation – arrowed (Sec 4)

the CV joint.

7 If a new joint has been obtained, or if the original joint was found to be in a satisfactory condition and is being refitted, a repair kit comprising a new CV joint rubber boot, boot retaining clips and a tube of Duckhams Q5795 grease should be obtained from your local dealer. Only use this type of grease in the CV joint.

8 The help of an assistant will be necessary whilst refitting the CV joint to the driveshaft. Ensure that the circlip is correctly located in its groove in the driveshaft. Position the CV joint over the splines on the end of the shaft until it abuts the circlip.

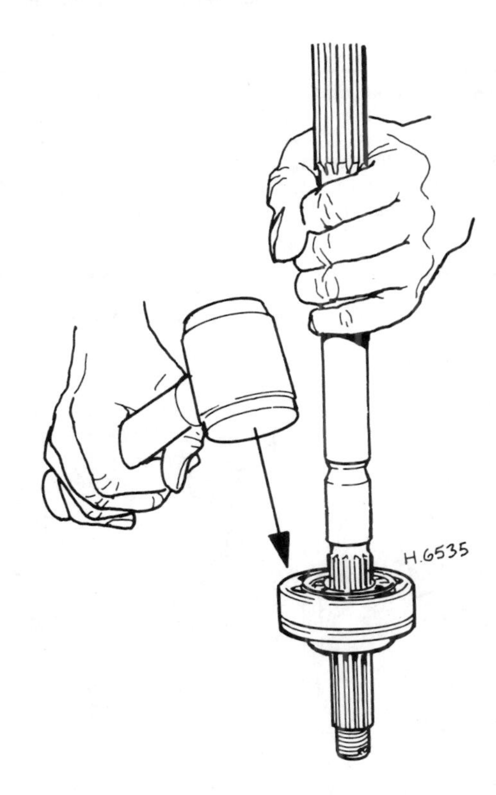

Fig. 7.7 Using a soft-faced mallet to remove CV joint (Sec 5)

9 Using two small screwdrivers placed either side of the circlip, compress the circlip and at the same time have your assistant firmly strike the end of the CV joint with a hide or plastic mallet.
10 The joint should slide over the compressed circlip and into position on the shaft. It will probably require several attempts before you achieve success. If the joint does not spring into place the moment it is struck, remove it, reposition the circlip and try again. Do not force the joint otherwise the circlip will be damaged.
11 With the CV joint in place and in contact with the spring collar on the shaft, the joint should now be lubricated and the rubber boots refitted as described in Section 4, paragraphs 7 to 16 inclusive. The assembled driveshaft can then be refitted to the car as described in Section 3.

6 Inner rubber drive coupling – removal and refitting

1 Remove the wheel trim and slacken the roadwheel retaining nuts.
2 Working under the wheel arch, undo and remove the single retaining screw and lift out the upper suspension arm rebound rubber. Place a solid packing piece of approximately the same thickness in its place.
3 Jack up the front of the car and place axle stands under the subframe. Remove the front roadwheel.
4 Undo and remove the nut and spring washer securing the upper suspension arm to the swivel hub balljoint.
5 If a universal balljoint separator is available, use the separator to release the tapered shank of the balljoint from the upper suspension arm. Alternatively, refit the nut to the balljoint and screw it on two or three turns. Using a medium hammer, sharply strike the end of the suspension arm until the shock separates the taper. Now remove the nut and detach the balljoint shank from the arm.
6 With the upper balljoint disconnected, pull the upper part of the hub assembly away from the car and allow it to hang in this position. Avoid placing undue strain on the flexible brake hose.
7 From underneath the car, undo and remove the eight locknuts securing the retaining U-bolts to the coupling flanges (photo).
8 Withdraw the U-bolts from the flanges, using a screwdriver to lever them out, and then lift off the rubber coupling.
9 Refitting the coupling is the reverse sequence to removal. Ensure that the U-bolt locknuts and swivel hub balljoint retaining nut are tightened to the specified torque.

6.7 Remove the rubber coupling U-bolt locknuts

7 Hardy-Spicer universal joint – dismantling, overhaul and reassembly

1 Remove the driveshaft from the car as described in Section 3.
2 Remove the retaining wire securing the sliding spline protective rubber boot to the yoke flange and slide the yoke off the end of the driveshaft.
3 Thoroughly clean the exterior of the universal joint and yoke in petrol or paraffin and dry with a lint-free cloth.
4 Using circlip pliers, remove the four circlips securing the universal joint bearing cups to the yokes. If the circlips are tight, tap the bearing cups downward to relieve the tension on the circlip using a hammer and brass drift.
5 Referring to Fig. 7.8 support the underside of the yoke on the top of a vice. Tap the outer circumference of the other yoke with a soft-faced mallet until the bearing cup emerges from the top of the yoke.
6 Turn the assembly over and grip the exposed bearing cup between protected vice jaws. Now tap the yoke upwards until the bearing cup is released.
7 Repeat paragraphs 5 and 6 on the opposite bearing cup and then lift the yoke off the spider.
8 Position the two exposed bearing trunnions on the spider over the top of the protected vice jaws. Tap the yoke downwards until the bearing cup emerges from the top of the yoke.
9 Turn the yoke over and grip the exposed bearing cup between the protected vice jaws. Tap the yoke upwards until the bearing cup is released.
10 Repeat paragraphs 8 and 9 on the opposite bearing cup and then lift the spider out of the yoke.
11 Inspect the needle roller bearings, spider and bearing cups for lack of lubrication, surface pitting or load markings. If wear is apparent a new universal joint must be fitted.

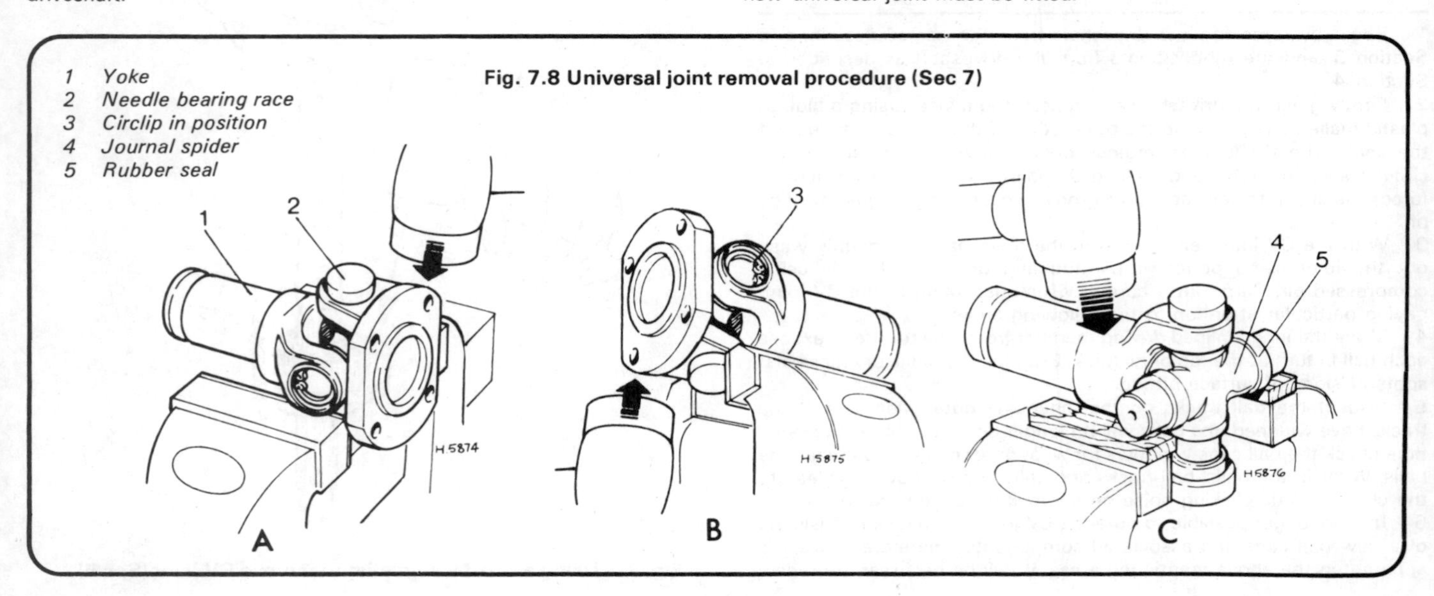

Fig. 7.8 Universal joint removal procedure (Sec 7)

1 Yoke
2 Needle bearing race
3 Circlip in position
4 Journal spider
5 Rubber seal

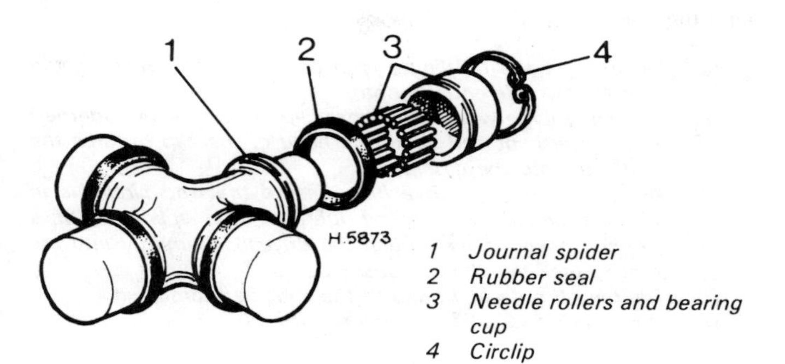

Fig. 7.9 Universal joint compound parts (Sec 7)

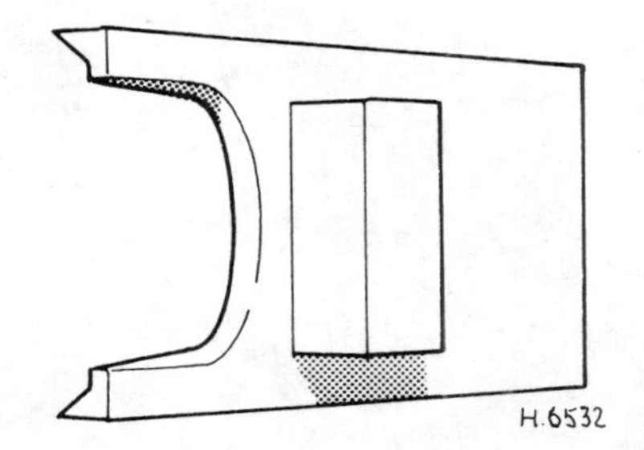

Fig. 7.10 Special tool 18G1240 for removing offset sphere joint (Sec 8)

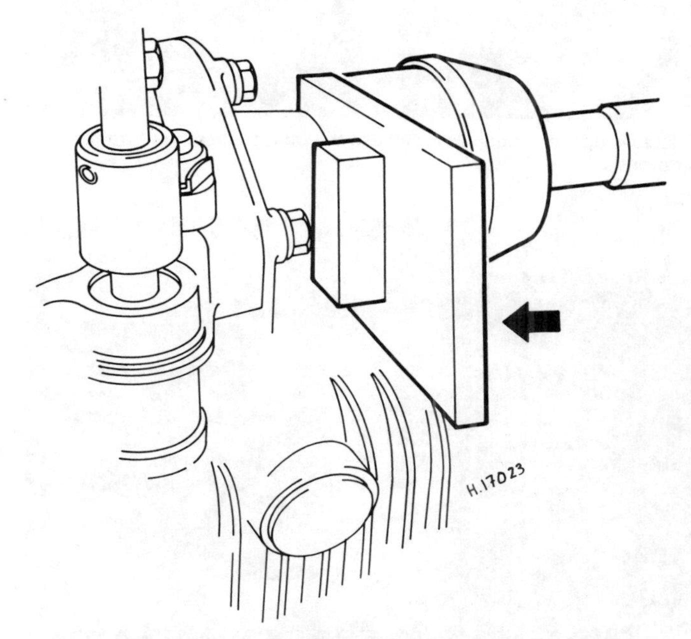

Fig. 7.11 Using the special tool to release the joint from the differential (Sec 8)

12 Before refitting the universal joint, ensure that each bearing cup contains a complete set of rollers and that the rubber seals are in position on the bearing cups. Smear the inside of each cup with general purpose grease to retain the needle roller bearings in position.
13 Check that the bearing cup apertures in the yokes are clean and dry, paying particular attention to the circlip grooves. Remove any burrs that may exist using a small file.
14 Insert one of the bearing cups into the yoke aperture and then place the spider in position pushing it up into the cup to hold the needle bearings in place.
15 Using a hammer and soft drift, tap the bearing cup fully into the yoke and then refit the circlip.
16 Place the bearing cup in the opposite side of the yoke in position and move the spider up slightly until it just engages the needles.
17 Now tap the bearing cup fully into the yoke and refit the circlip.
18 Repeat paragraphs 14 to 17 inclusive for the remaining two bearing cups.
19 If the assembled joint appears to bind, tap the top of the bearing cups lightly using the soft drift to relieve the pressure of the bearing cups on the spider.
20 Smear the splines on the driveshaft and yoke with grease, preferably Duckhams Q5795, and then refit the yoke to the driveshaft.
21 Engage the lip of the rubber boot over the yoke and secure with two or three turns of soft iron wire. Twist the ends of the wire together and then bend them down to face away from the forward direction of rotation of the driveshaft.
22 Refit the driveshaft to the car as described in Section 3.

8 Inner offset sphere joint – removal and refitting

1 Working under the wheel arch, undo and remove the single retaining screw and lift out the upper suspension arm rebound rubber. Position a solid packing piece of approximately the same thickness in its place.
2 Jack up the front of the car and support it on axle stands placed under the subframe. Remove the front roadwheel.
3 Undo and remove the steering tie-rod balljoint retaining locknut, and then release the balljoint tapered shank from the steering arm in the following manner.
4 If a universal balljoint separator is available, use the separator to release the tapered shank, and then lift the balljoint off the steering arm. Alternatively, refit the locknut to the balljoint and screw it on two or three turns. Using a medium hammer sharply strike the end of the steering arm until the shock separates the taper. Now remove the locknut and lift the joint off the arm.
5 Undo and remove the nut and spring washer securing the upper suspension arm to the swivel hub balljoint. Using the method described in the previous paragraph, separate the upper suspension arm from the tapered shank of the balljoint.
6 The inner end of the driveshaft must now be removed from the offset sphere joint. If BL special tool No 18G1240 can be obtained this will greatly simplify the task of removing the driveshaft from the joint. If this tool is not available the following procedure should be used.
7 Tip the swivel hub outwards slightly, pivoting it on the lower balljoint. Take care not to stretch the flexible brake hose. Have an assistant hold the hub and driveshaft in this position.
8 Insert a flat metal bar or similar tool through the aperture in the subframe so that it rests on the driveshaft and is in contact with the flange of the joint. Take care not to pinch the rubber boot with the bar, as it is easily damaged.
9 Strike the end of the bar with a few sharp hammer blows. This will force the flange of the joint inwards and release it from the end of the driveshaft.
10 Fully withdraw the driveshaft from the joint flange and temporarily position the end of the shaft over the differential housing out of the way.
11 Working underneath the car, remove the engine/transmission oil drain plug and allow the oil to drain into a suitable container. When the oil has drained, refit the drain plug.
12 Using BL special tool 18G1240, release the offset sphere joint from the differential. Alternatively, use a suitable cranked bar with a flattened end such as a tyre lever. Insert the flattened end of the bar between the joint inner face and the differential end cover. Pivot the bar against the end cover lower retaining bolt head. If the bar is not sufficiently cranked to reach the bolt head, use suitable spacers. *Do not lever against the end cover.* Strike the bottom of the bar with a few sharp hammer blows towards the centre of the car. This will release the joint from the retaining circlip on the differential shaft. Once the joint has moved outward slightly it can be removed the rest of the way by hand (photos).
13 With the offset sphere joint removed, recover the oil flinger, noting the direction of fitting.
14 Refitting the joint is the reverse sequence to removal, bearing in

8.12a Using a cranked bar to release the offset sphere joint from the differential

8.12b Once the joint is released it can be slid off by hand

8.14 Ensure that the oil flinger is in position before refitting

mind the following points:

(a) Ensure that the oil flinger is in position before refitting the joint to the differential (photo)
(b) Position a large worm drive hose clip (or two joined together) around the joint and strike the head of the clip to force the joint fully into the differential
(c) When refitting the driveshaft, ensure that the circlip is in position on the shaft, and lubricate the splines with a graphite-based grease. Push the driveshaft smartly into the joint to lock the shaft in position.
(d) Tighten all nuts and bolts to the specified torque
(e) Don't forget to refill the engine with oil

9 Inner offset sphere joint – dismantling and reassembly

1 With the joint removed from the car as described in the previous Section, remove and discard the two retaining rings and the rubber boot.

2 Withdraw the joint inner member and ball cage assembly from the outer members.

3 Using a screwdriver inserted between each ball in turn and the joint inner member, release the balls from the ball cage.

4 Turn the ball cage until the grooves on the inside of the cage are aligned with the lands on the inner member and then lift off the ballcage.

5 Wash off all the parts in petrol or paraffin and dry with a lint-free cloth.

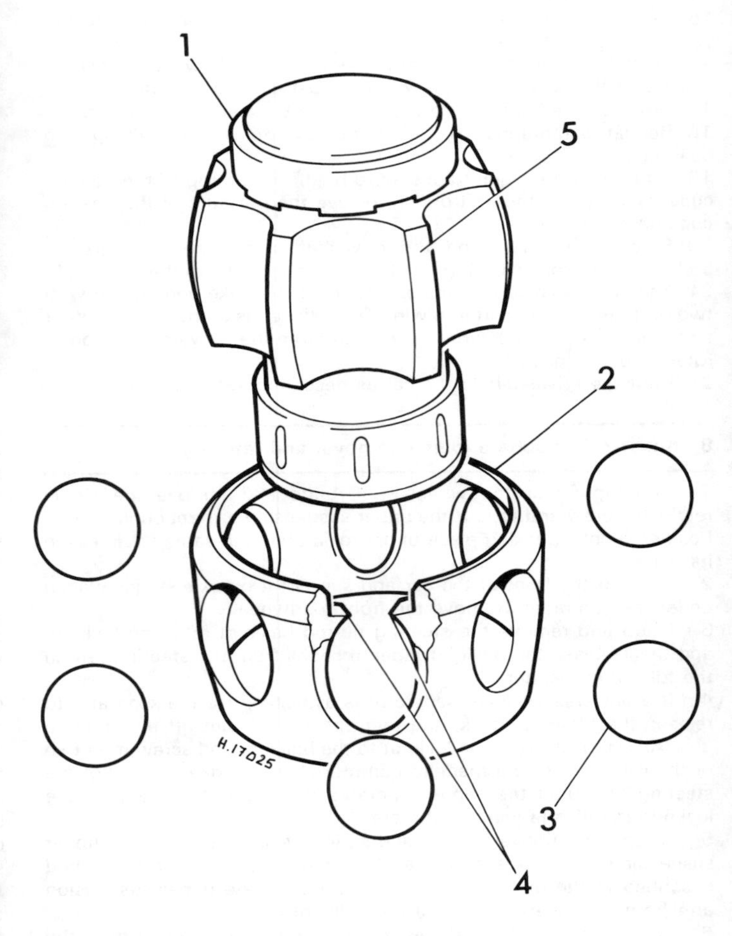

Fig. 7.12 Dismantling the offset sphere joint (Sec 9)

1 Inner member
2 Ball cage
3 Balls
4 Ball cage internal grooves
5 Inner member lands

6 Carefully inspect the balls and the inner and outer members for signs of pitting, scoring, wear ridges or breakdown of the surface hardening. Examine the ball cage for elongation of the ball locations. If any of the components are worn, it will be necessary to renew the complete joint, as the internal parts are not available separately. If the joint is in a satisfactory condition, obtain a new rubber boot, boot retaining clips and a tube of the special lubricant from your BL dealer.
7 Begin reassembly by refitting the balll cage to the inner member, noting that the long tapered end of the ball cage faces the driveshaft end of the inner member.
8 Press each of the balls in turn into the locations in the ball cage.
9 Slide the assembled inner member into the joint outer member.
10 Position a new retaining ring onto the inner neck of the rubber boot with the chamfered end of the ring toward the inside of the boot.
11 Fold back the boot and, using a tube of suitable diameter, push the boot onto the inner member.
12 Pack the assembled joint with the contents of the tube of special lubricant, working it well into the ball tracks and cage.
13 Position the larger diameter of the rubber boot over the joint outer member. Place the retaining clip over the boot with the end containing the tabs facing away from the forward direction of joint rotation. Using pliers, pull the other end of the clip over the end containing the tabs and press down the first set of tabs using a screwdriver. Pull the free end tight and fold it over the compressed tabs. Now bend over the second set of tabs, trapping the free end of the clip underneath.
14 The offset sphere joint can now be refitted to the car as described in the previous Section.

Chapter 8 Differential unit

For modifications, and information applicable to later models, see Supplement at end of manual

Contents

Specifications

Note: *The differential unit on all Mini variants with manual transmission is identical, with the exception of the final drive ratio which varies according to model. A different differential unit is fitted to models equipped with automatic transmission.*

Final drive ratio

848cc (all models)	3.76 : 1
998cc except Van and Pick-up:	
Manual	3.44 : 1
Automatic	3.27 : 1
998cc Van and Pick-up	3.76 : 1
1098cc (all models)	3.44 : 1
1275 Cooper S Mk III:	
Standard	3.65 : 1
Optional	3.93 : 1, 4.26 : 1, 4.35 : 1
1275 GT	3.44 : 1

Differential bearing preload

Early bearings	0.001 to 0.002 in (0.025 to 0.050 mm)
Later thrust bearings	0.004 in (0.10 mm)

Torque wrench settings

Torque wrench settings	lbf ft	Nm
End cover bolts	18	25
Driveshaft flange nut	70	96
Driveshaft flange bolt	40	55
Differential case to drivegear bolts	60	83
Retaining stud nuts $\frac{5}{16}$ in UNF	18	25
Retaining stud nuts $\frac{3}{8}$ in UNF	25	34
Kickdown linkage retaining bolts	5	7
Rubber coupling U-bolts	10	14
Swivel hub balljoint nut	38	52

1 General description

The differential unit is of the two-pinion design and is contained within a housing bolted to the rear of the transmission casing. The differential gears are located in the differential case, which is bolted to the spur-type drivegear. The drivegear pinion is mounted on the end of the mainshaft in the gearbox.

Repair or overhaul of the differential unit can only be carried out after first removing the engine/transmission unit from the car. If it is wished to attend to the drivegear pinion, it will be necessary to separate the engine from the transmission. This is not recommended on vehicles equipped with automatic transmission as considerable dismantling is necessary to provide access to the pinion. As this work requires specialist knowledge and equipment, it is best left to your BL main dealer.

2 Differential unit – removal and refitting (manual transmission models)

Note: *The design of the differential housing varies slightly according to model year and the type of gearchange mechanism fitted. The removal procedure is basically the same for all models; however, if working on the latest rod change type transmission, omit paragraphs 2, 3 and 4.*

1 Remove the engine/transmission assembly as described in Chapter 1.

2 On models not fitted with a remote control gearchange, undo and remove the four bolts securing the cover plate to the underside of the gearchange extension and lift off the plate.

3 Undo and remove the pinch-bolt securing the shaft lever to the remote control shaft and then withdraw the shaft downwards and out

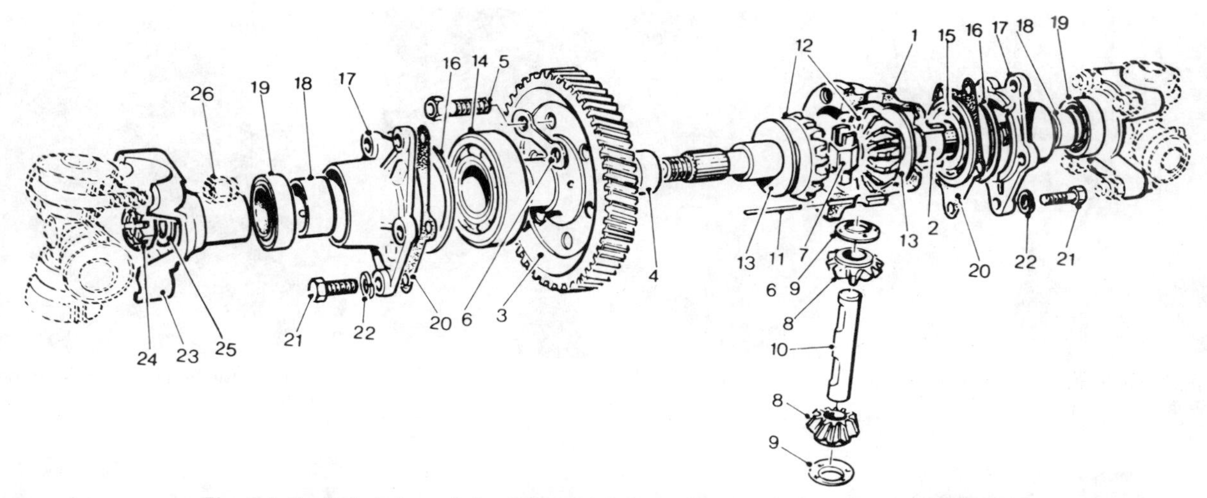

Fig. 8.1 Exploded view of the differential assembly – manual transmission (Sec 1)

1 Differential case
2 Case bush
3 Drivegear
4 Gear bush
5 Gear bolt
6 Lockwasher
7 Thrust block
8 Differential pinion
9 Pinion thrust washer
10 Centre pin
11 Pin peg
12 Differential gear
13 Thrust washer
14 Drivegear bearing
15 Case bearing
16 Bearing shim
17 End cover
18 Cover bush
19 Oil seal
20 Cover joint
21 End cover bolt
22 Washer
23 Driving flange
24 Flange nut
25 Washer
26 Locknut

of the differential housing (photo).

4 Extract the split pins and then undo and remove the two driveshaft flange castellated retaining nuts. The flanges can be prevented from turning during this operation by wedging a block of wood between the flange and gearbox casing (Note that on Cooper S models, bolts instead of nuts are used to retain the driveshaft flanges). Now slide the flanges off the gearshafts.

5 Undo and remove the five bolts and spring washers which secure the two end covers to the sides of the differential housing (photo). Lift off the two end covers together with their gaskets, and recover the shim fitted behind the end cover furthest away from the flywheel housing (photo). On later models lift out the selector shaft detent sleeve, spring and ball (photos).

6 Tap back the locktabs and undo and remove the nuts securing the differential housing to the gearbox casing.

7 Carefully withdraw the differential housing and differential assembly rearwards and off the mounting studs (photo).

8 Before refitting the differential, scrape away all traces of old gaskets and ensure that the mating faces of all the components are scrupulously clean and dry.

9 Begin assembly by placing the differential assembly into the gearbox casing, biased slightly towards the flywheel side (photo).

10 Lightly smear both sides of the differential housing gaskets with jointing compound and place them in position over the mounting studs (photo).

11 Refit the differential housing (photo) and secure it in position with the retaining nuts and washers. Tighten the nuts sufficiently to hold the differential bearings and yet still allow sideways movement of the complete assembly.

12 Refit the selector shaft detent spring, sleeve and ball (later models), lightly smear a new gasket on both sides with jointing compound, and position it on the flywheel side end cover. Position the cover on the differential housing and refit the retaining bolts. Progressively and evenly tighten the bolts, to displace the differential assembly away from the flywheel side, finally tightening to the specified torque.

13 Now fit the left-hand side end cover *without* the gasket or shims. Tighten the cover bolts evenly until the register just contacts the differential bearing outer race. Do not overtighten the bolts as this could distort the end cover.

14 Measure the gap between the end cover and the differential housing in several places, using feeler gauges, to ensure that the end cover is seating squarely on the differential assembly (photo). Variations in measurement indicate that the cover bolts have not been tightened evenly. If this is the case adjust the tightness of the end cover bolts to give a uniform gap.

2.3 Remove the remote control shaft lever pinch-bolt

2.5a With the driving flanges removed, undo the end cover retaining bolts...

2.5b ...and recover the shims

2.5c On later models lift out the selector shaft detent sleeve...

2.5d ...spring and ball

2.7 Lift off the housing and differential assembly

2.9 Refit the differential biased toward the flywheel side

2.10 Place a new gasket in position...

2.11 ...and lower the housing into place

15 The required bearing preload on earlier models is as shown in the Specifications and the compressed thickness of the gasket when installed is 0.007 in (0.18 mm). Therefore the clearance now being measured, without the gasket, must be between 0.008 and 0.009 in (0.20 and 0.23 mm). Any deviation from this figure must be rectified by fitting the appropriate sized shims between the end cover register and the bearing outer race in accordance with the table below:

Measured gap (No gasket) – see lower table for shim thickness	
(a) Zero to 0.001 in	*(Zero to 0.0254 mm)*
(b) 0.001 to 0.002 in	*(0.0254 to 0.0508 mm)*
(c) 0.002 to 0.003 in	*(0.0508 to 0.0762 mm)*
(d) 0.003 to 0.004 in	*(0.0762 to 0.1016 mm)*
(e) 0.004 to 0.005 in	*(0.1016 to 0.1270 mm)*
(f) 0.006 to 0.007 in	*(0.1524 to 0.1778 mm)*
(g) 0.007 to 0.008 in	*(0.1778 to 0.2032 mm)*
(h) 0.008 to 0.009 in	*(0.2032 to 0.2286 mm)*

Shim thickness	
(a) 0.008 in	*(0.2032 mm)*
(b) 0.006 to 0.007 in	*(0.1524 to 0.1778 mm)*
(c) 0.005 to 0.006 in	*(0.1270 to 0.1524 mm)*
(d) 0.004 to 0.005 in	*(0.1016 to 0.1270 mm)*
(e) 0.003 to 0.004 in	*(0.0762 to 0.1016 mm)*
(f) 0.002 to 0.003 in	*(0.0508 to 0.0762 mm)*
(g) 0.001 to 0.002 in	*(0.0254 to 0.0508 mm)*
(h) None necessary	

Note: *On later differential assemblies having the word THRUST stamped on the bearing outer race, the bearing preload is increased (see Specifications) and therefore the measured clearance without the gasket must be 0.011 in (0.28 mm).*

16 When the correct gap has been obtained, remove the end cover, lightly smear the gasket with jointing compound and refit the cover, gasket and retaining bolts. Tighten the bolts to the specified torque (photos).

17 Now fully tighten the differential housing retaining nuts and tap over the lockwashers (photo).

18 Refit the two driveshaft flanges, washers and castellated nuts or bolts. Tighten the nuts or bolts to the specified torque, and in the case of the castellated nuts, continue tightening until the split pin hole is in line with the next castellation and then fit a new split pin (photos).

19 Refit the remote control shaft (photo), the shaft lever and the extension cover plate (where fitted).

20 The engine/transmission unit can now be refitted to the car as described in Chapter 1.

3 Differential unit – dismantling, examination and reassembly (manual transmission models)

1 With the aid of a bearing extractor or universal puller, pull off the two bearings from the right and left-hand gearshafts. The bearings on some models are marked THRUST on the outside face.

2 Mark the differential case and the drivegear so that they can be reassembled in their original positions.

3 Knock back the tabs of the three lockwashers and unscrew the six set bolts which hold the drivegear to the differential case.

4 Remove the drivegear complete with the left gearshaft. Pull the drivegear off the shaft together with the thrust washer.

5 Gently tap out the tapered peg roll pin which holds the centre pin in place.

6 Remove the centre pin and the component parts of the differential case. The differential case can now be removed from the right gearshaft.

7 Check the bearings for side play and the rollers and races for general wear. Examine the centre pin, the thrust block, and the thrust washers for score marks, and pitting, and renew these components as necessary.

8 Examine the differential pinion gear for pitting, score marks, chipping and general wear. If wear is evident on any of the gears, they must all be renewed as a complete set. Similarly inspect the drivegear; if its condition is suspect, it must be renewed as a matched assembly with the drive pinion. If necessary renew the end cover oil seals (photo).

2.14 Measure the end cover clearance...

2.16a ...and then fit the selected shims and end cover

2.16b Tighten the end cover bolts...

2.17 ...and with the housing bolts fully tightened, tap over the lockwashers

2.18a Refit the driving flanges...

2.18b ...castellated nuts...

2.18c ...and new split pins

2.19 Finally refit the remote control shaft

9 Reassembly is a straight reversal of the above sequence. Tighten all nuts and bolts to the specified torque. **Note**: *When refitting the differential gear thrust washers, ensure that the slightly chamfered bores are facing the machined faces of the differential gears, and that all components are refitting in their original positions.*

4 Final drive pinion – removal and refitting (manual transmission models)

Note: *The following procedure applies to the early type transmission, having either a direct engagement gearchange lever, or remote control gearchange and extension housing. If working on the latest rod-change type transmission, refer to paragraphs 12 to 20 inclusive. In all cases, if the final drive pinion is to be renewed, it will also be necessary to renew the differential drive gear as a matched assembly.*

Early type transmission

1 Refer to Chapter 1 and remove the engine/transmission unit from the car, and then separate the engine from the transmission.

2 Remove the differential assembly from the transmission as described in Section 2 of this Chapter.

3 Undo and remove the large hexagonal plug from the front left-hand side of the transmission casing. This plug holds the change speed reverse detent plunger in place. With the plug removed, lift out the spring and plunger.

4 Undo and remove the clamp bolt from the gearchange operating shaft selector lever. Slide the shaft up and out of the lever, withdraw the Woodruff key, and remove the shaft from the transmission casing.

5 Undo and remove the retaining bolt and lift out the speedometer pinion.

6 Undo and remove the nuts and bolts securing the engine mounting bracket and speedometer drive housing to the left-side of

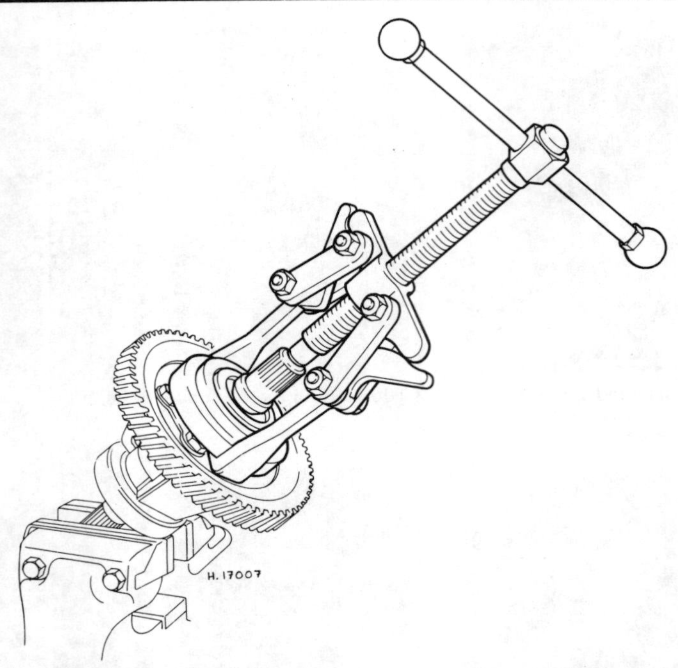

Fig. 8.2 Using a universal puller to remove differential bearing (Sec 3)

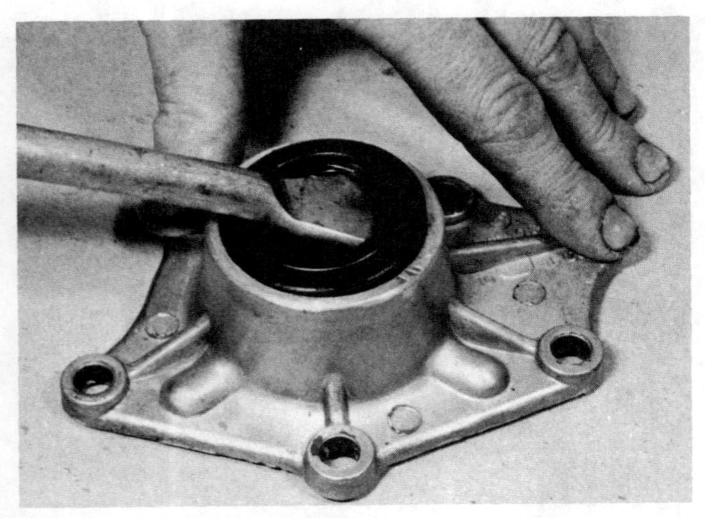

3.8 Removing an end cover oil seal

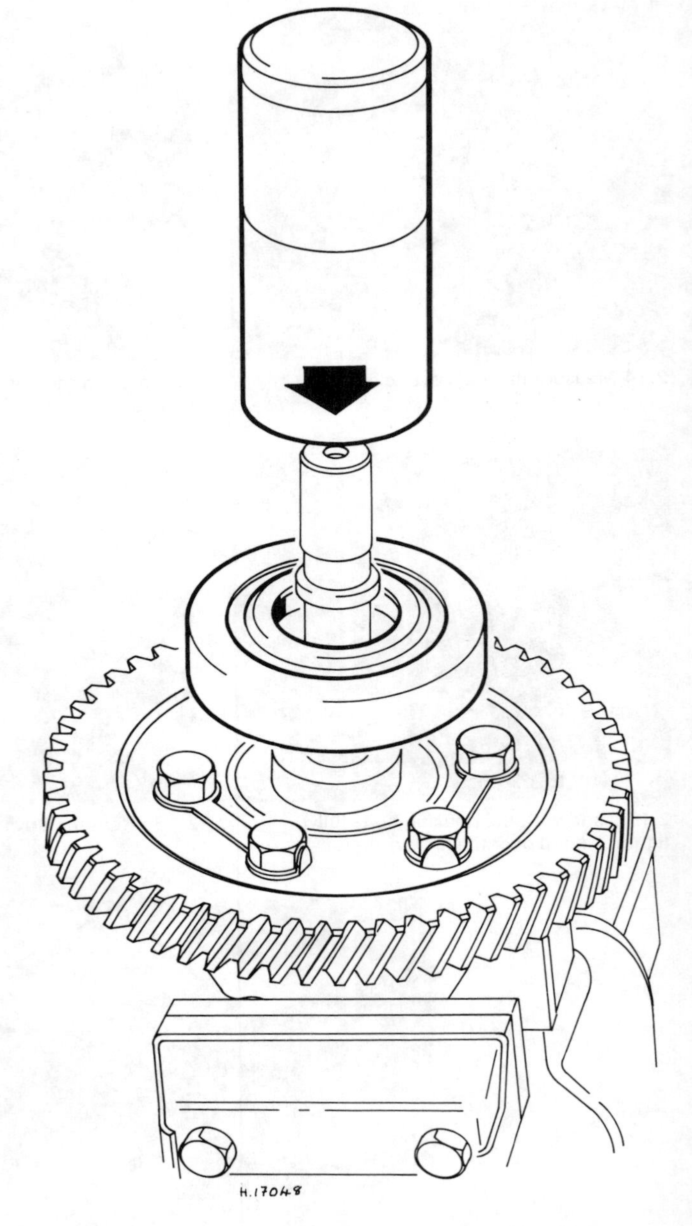

Fig. 8.3 Fitting a differential bearing (Sec 3)

the transmission casing. Lift off the bracket and housing, taking care not to damage the gasket if possible.

7 Lift out the gear selector interlocking plate from its location at the base of the transmission casing.

8 Engage two gears simultaneously by means of the selector rods to prevent the mainshaft from turning as the final drive pinion retaining nut is undone.

9 Bend back the locktab and, using a large socket and long extension bar, undo and remove the final drive pinion retaining nut.

10 Now lift off the locktab and slide the final drive pinion off the end of the mainshaft.

11 Refitting the final drive pinion is the reverse sequence to removal. Tighten all nuts and bolts to the specified torque.

Later type transmission

12 Refer to Chapter 1 and remove the engine/transmission unit from the car, and then separate the engine from the transmission.

13 Remove the differential assembly from the transmission as described in Section 2 of this Chapter.

14 Undo and remove the retaining bolt and clamp plate and lift out the speedometer pinion.

15 Undo and remove the retaining nuts and bolts, and lift off the engine mounting bracket and adaptor bracket from the speedometer drive housing. Undo and remove the remaining bolts and carefully slide the drive housing off the side of the transmission casing.

16 Using a small chisel or screwdriver, knock back the lockwasher tab securing the final drive gear pinion nut.

17 To enable the pinion nut to be undone the gearbox must be locked in two gears at once, to prevent the mainshaft from turning, as follows.

18 Rotate the selector shaft anti-clockwise to disengage the operating stub and the interlock spool from the bellcrank levers. Carefully lever the 1st/2nd gear selector fork towards the gearbox casing centre web. This will engage first gear. Carefully drift the centre bellcrank lever inwards using a screwdriver. This will engage fourth gear and lock the gearbox.

19 Using a large socket, undo and remove the final drive gear pinion retaining nut. Withdraw the lockwasher and the gear.

20 Refitting the final drive pinion is the reverse sequence to removal, ensuring that all nuts and bolts are tightened to the specified torque.

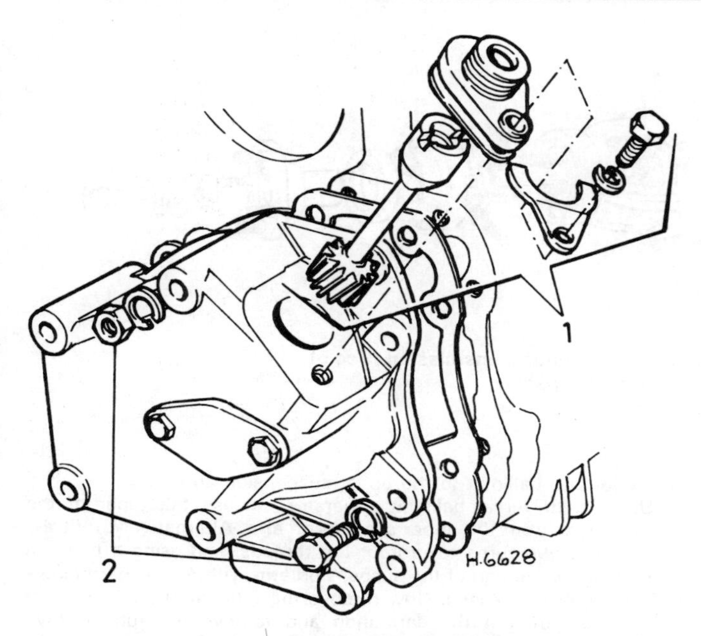

Fig. 8.4 Removing the speedometer drive housing (Sec 4)

1 *Speedometer pinion assembly*
2 *Retaining bolts and nuts*

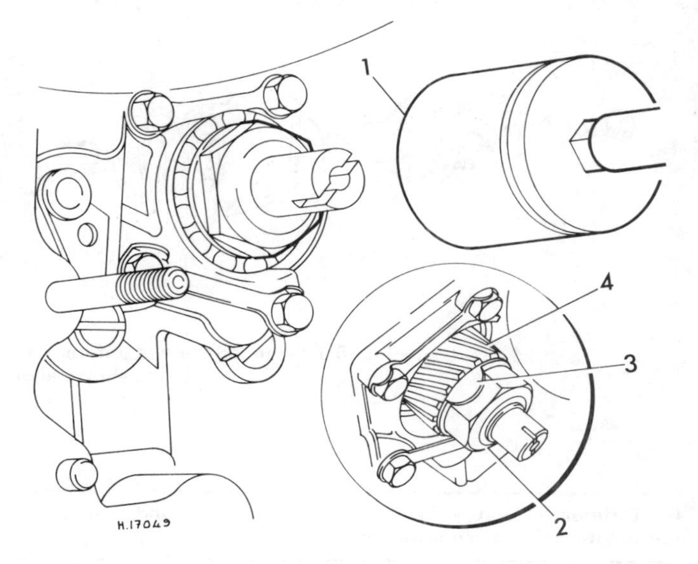

Fig. 8.5 Use of a large socket to undo the final drive pinion retaining nut (Sec 4)

1 *Socket*
2 *Nut*
3 *Lockwasher*
4 *Final drive pinion*

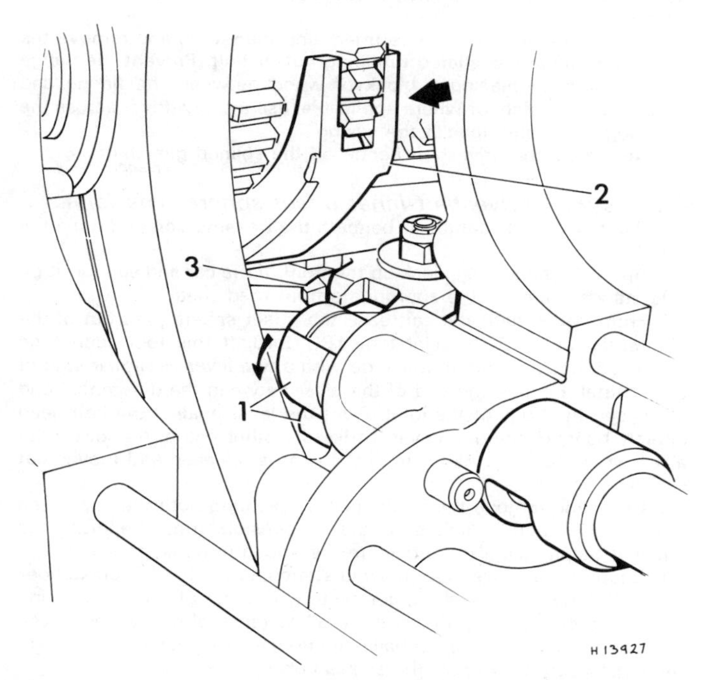

Fig. 8.6 Positioning of selector shaft – rod-change transmission (Sec 4)

1 *Rotation of selector shaft to disengage operating stub and interlock spool from bellcrank levers*
2 *First/second selector fork*
3 *Centre bellcrank lever*

5 Differential unit – removal and refitting (automatic transmission models)

1 Remove the engine/automatic transmission assembly from the car as described in Chapter 1.
2 Thoroughly clean the exterior of the transmission casing, paying particular attention to the area around the differential unit. Absolute cleanliness is essential when working on any components associated with the automatic transmission assembly.
3 Undo and remove the two driveshaft flange retaining bolts and washers. Prevent the flanges from turning by using a screwdriver, placed across two of the flange retaining studs. Now withdraw the flanges from the splined shafts.
4 Bend back the locktabs and undo and remove the differential unit retaining nuts.
5 Undo and remove the two retaining bolts and position the kickdown linkage clear of the transmission casing.
6 Undo and remove the four retaining screws and lift off the end cover and gasket from the left-hand side of the transmission casing. Recover the shims fitted behind the end cover.
7 Carefully lift off the differential housing and differential assembly from the transmission casing.
8 Before refitting the differential, clean off all traces of old gaskets and ensure that the mating faces of all components are scrupulously clean and dry.
9 Place the differential assembly into the transmission casing and slide it sideways towards the converter. Ensure that the slot in the spacer is in line with the dowel in the transmission casing.
10 Smear both sides of the differential housing gasket lightly with jointing compound and place them in position over the mounting studs.
11 Refit the differential housing, ensuring that the oil seal is squarely seated against the spacer as the housing is installed. Secure the housing with the nuts and locktabs, but only tighten the nuts sufficiently to hold the differential bearings and yet still allowing sideways movement of the complete assembly.
12 Refit the end cover but *without* the shims or the gasket. Tighten the cover bolts evenly until the register just contacts the shims and the bearing outer race. Do not overtighten the bolts as this could distort the end cover.
13 Now adjust the differential bearing preload using the procedure given in Section 2, paragraphs 14 to 17 inclusive.
14 Refit the driveshaft flanges ensuring that the split collets are correctly positioned inside the flanges. Place new rubber seals over the retaining bolts and refit the bolts and washers, tightening to the specified torque.
15 Refit the kickdown linkage to the transmission casing, ensuring that the linkage is positioned correctly. Refer to Chapter 6 for details.
16 The engine/automatic transmission assembly can now be reassembled and refitted to the car as described in Chapter 1.

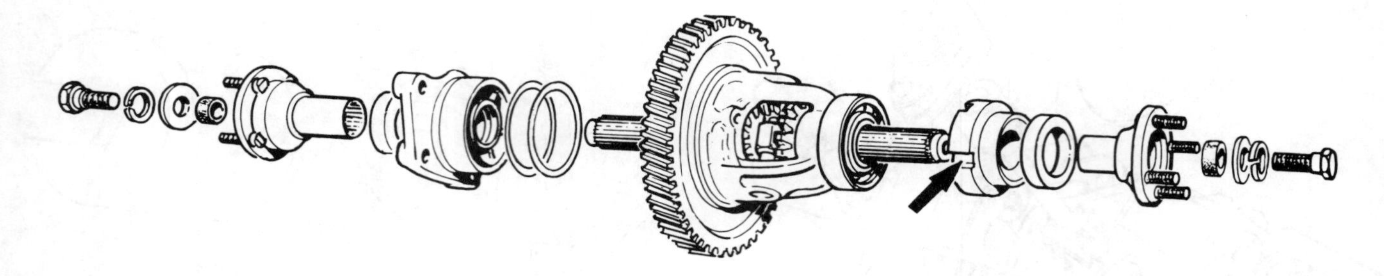

Fig. 8.7 Exploded view of differential assembly – automatic transmission (Sec 5)
Arrow shows alignment slot in the spacer

6 Differential unit – dismantling, examination and reassembly (automatic transmission models)

1 With the differential unit on the bench, first withdraw the spacer and then, using a bearing extractor or universal puller, pull off the two bearings from the right and left-hand gearshafts. Note that on later units the bearings are marked THRUST on the outside face.
2 Mark the differential case and drivegear so that they can be reassembled in their original positions.
3 Knock back the locktabs and undo and remove the bolts securing the drivegear to the differential case.
4 Separate the drivegear and case and lift out the left-hand gearshaft and thrust washer from the drivegear.
5 Gently tap out the tapered peg roll pin which secures the centre pin in position in the differential case.
6 Withdraw the centre pin, both pinions and their thrust washers and the pinion spacer. Slide out the right-hand gearshaft from the differential case.
7 Check the bearings for side play and the rollers and races for general wear. Examine the centre pin, pinion spacer and the thrust washers for score marks and pitting, and renew these components as necessary.
8 Examine the pinion gears for pitting, score marks, chipping and general wear. If wear is evident on any of these gears, they must all be renewed as a complete set. Similarly inspect the drivegear; if its condition is suspect it must be renewed as a matched assembly with the final drive pinion. As removal of the final drive pinion requires considerable dismantling of the automatic transmission assembly, it is recommended that if renewal of these gears is necessary, the work should be entrusted to your BL main dealer who will have the necessary special tools and equipment to dismantle the automatic transmission.
9 Inspect the two oil seals and renew them if necessary.
10 Reassembly is a straightforward reversal of the above sequence. Tighten all nuts and bolts to the specified torque. **Note:** *When refitting the differential gear thrustwashers, ensure that the slightly chamfered bores are facing the machined faces of the differential gears. Also ensure that all components are refitted in their original positions.*

7 Driveshaft flange oil seals – removal and refitting(manual transmission models)

Note: *The driveshaft flange oil seals, located in the differential end covers, can be renewed with the engine/transmission assembly installed in the car as described below.*

Models with driveshaft inner rubber coupling or Hardy-Spicer universal joint

1 Place a suitable container beneath the transmission and drain the oil.
2 Apply the handbrake, jack up the front of the car and support it on axle stands.
3 Withdraw the wheel trim and remove the appropriate front wheel.
4 Undo and remove the retaining nut and spring washer securing the swivel hub balljoint to the upper suspension arm.
5 Using a universal balljoint separator, release the taper of the balljoint shank from the upper suspension arm. Alternatively, refit the retaining nut two turns to protect the threads, and using a medium hammer, strike the end of the suspension arm with a few sharp blows until the taper is released. Now remove the retaining nut.
6 From underneath the car, undo and remove the rubber drive coupling retaining U-bolts and locknuts then lift off the coupling. On Cooper S models, undo and remove the universal joint flange retaining nuts and separate the flanges.
7 Move the driveshaft as far as possible away from the differential to provide sufficient clearance to enable the driveshaft flanges to be removed.
8 Extract the split pin, where fitted, and then undo and remove the driveshaft flange castellated retaining nut or bolt. Prevent the flange from turning by placing a block of wood between the flange and transmission casing, or where applicable, use a screwdriver across the retaining studs and against the casing.
9 Now slide the driveshaft flange off the splined gearshaft.

Models with driveshaft inner offset sphere type joint

10 Place a suitable container beneath the transmission and drain the oil.
11 Apply the handbrake, jack up the front of the car and support it on axle stands. Remove the appropriate front roadwheel.
12 From underneath the car, ease the offset sphere joint out of the differential using BL special tool 18G1240. If this tool cannot be borrowed, it is possible to make do with a tyre lever or similar strip of thick metal. Engage the end of the lever between the differential end cover and the body of the joint. Pivot the lever against the bolt head directly beneath the end cover. Strike the other end of the lever with a few sharp hammer blows until the joint is released and moves out slightly.
13 Undo and remove the retaining nuts securing both the upper and lower swivel hub balljoints to the suspension arms. Separate the balljoint tapers using the procedure described in paragraph 5.
14 Support the swivel hub to avoid stretching the flexible brake hose and withdraw the driveshaft, complete with inner offset sphere joint, out of the differential sufficiently to allow removal of the end cover. Temporarily locate the upper balljoint into the suspension arm and refit the nut loosely to support the swivel hub.

All models

15 Undo and remove the appropriate end cover retaining bolts and lift off the cover. **Note:** *If working on the right-hand side end cover of the later rod-change type transmission, take care not to lose the selector shaft detent spring which will be released as the cover is withdrawn.*
16 Using a drift or tube of suitable diameter, tap out the oil seal from the end cover. Carefully press in a new seal or tap it in using a flat block of wood to distribute the load. Ensure that the seal enters the end cover squarely and that the open side of the seal faces inwards.
17 Clean off all traces of old gasket from the mating faces of the end cover and differential housing, and ensure that the faces are clean and dry.
18 Refitting is the reverse sequence to removal, bearing in mind the following points:

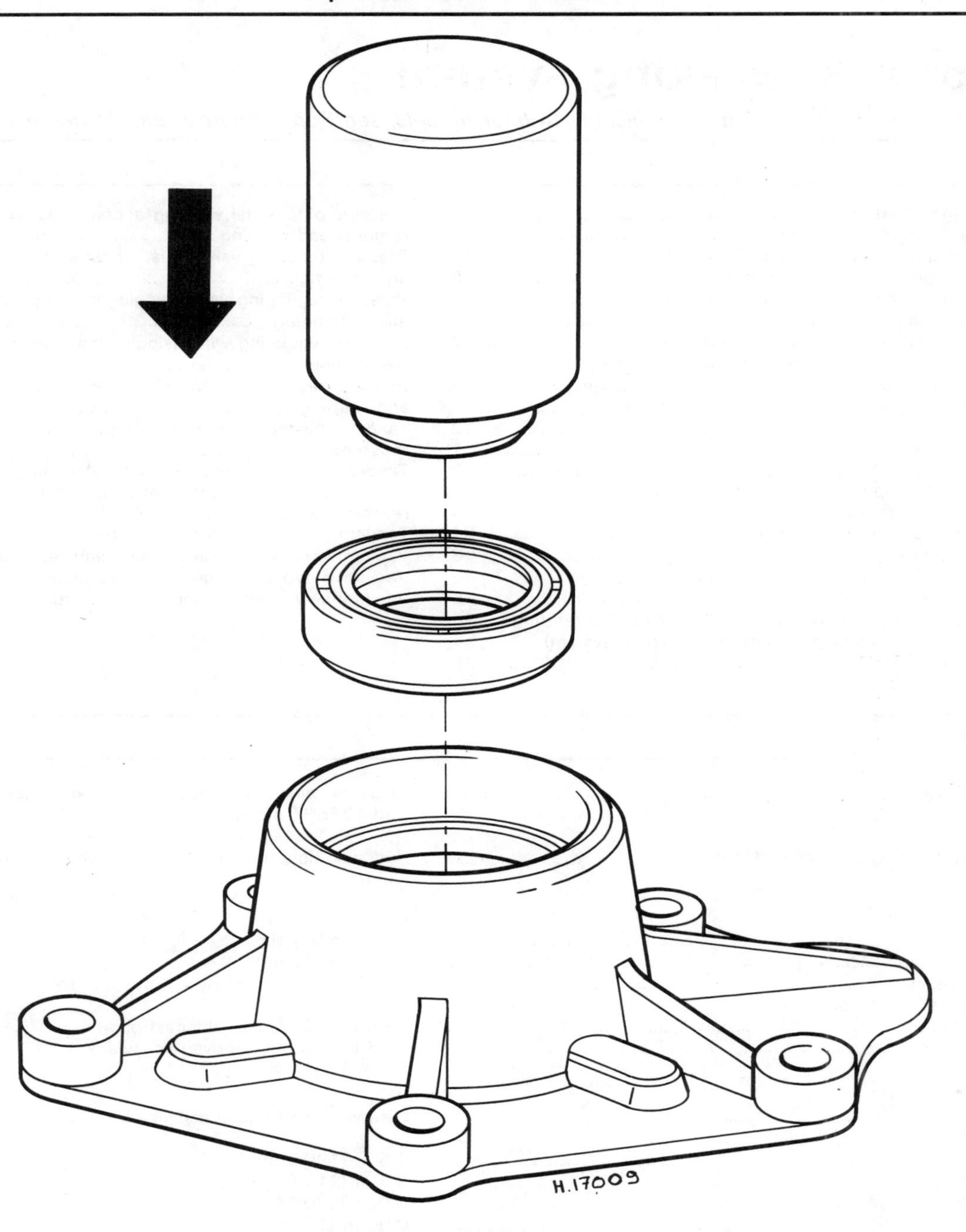

Fig. 8.8 Fitting a new oil seal to the differential end cover (Sec 7)

(a) Use a new gasket lightly smeared on both sides with jointing compound
(b) Tighten all nuts and bolts to the specified torque, and in the case of the castellated nuts, align the next split pin hole
(c) When refitting an offset sphere driveshaft joint, ensure that the joint is fully engaged on the differential gearshaft. If necessary wrap a long jubilee clip around the joint and tap the head of the clip with a mallet until the joint is fully home
(d) Remember to refill the engine with oil on completion of the reassembly

8 Fault diagnosis – differential unit

Because of the position of the differential unit, it is not practical to attempt fault diagnosis with the unit in situ. Clonks on acceleration or deceleration may be attributable to the driveshafts or their joints; noise when cornering may be due to defective wheel bearings. The DIY mechanic is advised to leave the differential alone unless definite evidence of malfunction has been obtained, or other dismantling renders the unit accessible.

Chapter 9 Braking system

For modifications, and information applicable to later models, see Supplement at end of manual

Contents

Specifications

System type

Lockheed single or dual circuit hydraulic, servo assisted on Cooper S and 1275GT models

Brake fluid type/specification

Hydraulic fluid to SAE J1703 (Duckhams Universal Brake and Clutch Fluid)

Front drum brakes

Type	Twin leading shoe
Drum diameter	7.0 in (178 mm)
Lining dimensions	6.75 in (171.4 mm) by 1.5 in (38.1 mm)
Minimum lining thickness:	
Bonded type	0.06 in (1.5 mm) at thinnest point
Riveted type	0.06 in (1.5 mm) above rivet heads

Front disc brakes

Type	Disc with twin piston caliper
Disc diameter:	
Cooper S	7.5 in (190.5 mm)
1275GT	8.4 in (213.4 mm)
Maximum disc run-out	0.002 in (0.05 mm)
Minimum pad thickness	0.06 in (1.5 mm)

Rear brakes

Type	Single leading shoe drum
Drum diameter	7.0 in (178 mm)
Lining dimensions	6.75 in (171.4 mm) by 1.25 in (31.7 mm)
Minimum lining thickness:	
Bonded type	0.06 in (1.5 mm) at thinnest point
Riveted type	0.06 in (1.5 mm) above rivet heads

Torque wrench settings

	lbf ft	Nm
Caliper retaining bolts	38	52
Disc to hub flange	42	57
Backplate retaining bolts	20	28
Master cylinder reservoir flange screws	5	7
Master cylinder body outlet plugs	28	39
Master cylinder pressure differential piston end plug	33	45
Pressure differential warning actuator end plug	26	35
Pressure differential warning actuator failure switch	14	19
Vacuum servo shell retaining bolts	17	23

1 General description

Drum brakes are fitted to the front and rear wheels on all models except Cooper S and 1275 GT versions, which have disc brakes at the front. The braking system is operated hydraulically by a master cylinder, which is actuated by the brake pedal. Disc brake models are servo assisted by a vacuum servo unit mounted in the engine compartment.

The hydraulic system on early models is of the single circuit type, whereby both the front and rear brakes are operated by the same hydraulic system from the master cylinder. On later models a dual circuit system is used, whereby the brakes at each pair of wheels are operated by a separate hydraulic system from a tandem master cylinder. In the event of hydraulic failure in one circuit, full braking force will still be available at two wheels. On early dual circuit systems a diagonal split is used, each circuit supplying one front and one diagonally opposite rear brake. Later versions employ a front-to-rear split whereby both front and both rear brakes are operated by a separate hydraulic circuit. A pressure differential warning actuator informs the driver of a hydraulic circuit failure via an illuminated warning light, and also restricts the flow of hydraulic fluid into the failed circuit. This unit is either mounted separately on the engine compartment bulkhead on early versions, or incorporated in the master cylinder on later types. On single circuit and certain dual circuit systems, a pressure reducing valve is incorporated in the rear brake circuit. This valve reduces hydraulic fluid pressure to the rear brakes and prevents rear wheel lock-up due to forward weight transfer under heavy braking. On models that are not equipped with a pressure reducing valve, the same effect is achieved by reducing the rear wheel cylinder piston diameters.

On models fitted with front drum brakes, the brake shoes are operated by two single piston wheel cylinders at each wheel. At the rear on all models one twin piston wheel cylinder operates the leading and trailing brake shoe at each wheel. When the brake pedal is depressed, hydraulic fluid under pressure is transmitted to the wheel cylinders by a system of metal and flexible pipes. The pressure moves the pistons outwards, so pushing the shoe linings into contact with the inside circumference of the brake drum, and slowing down its rotational speed.

On Cooper S and 1275GT models the front disc is secured to the hub flange, and the caliper is mounted on the swivel hub, so that the disc is able to rotate between the two halves of the caliper. Inside each half of the caliper is a hydraulic cylinder, this being interconnected by a drilling which allows hydraulic fluid under pressure to be transmitted to both halves. A piston operates in each cylinder and is in contact with the rear face of the brake pad. By depressing the brake pedal, hydraulic fluid under pressure is transmitted to the caliper by a system of metal and flexible pipes. The pistons are thus moved outwards, so pushing the pads onto the face of the disc and slowing down its rotational speed.

The handbrake provides an independent mechanical means of rear brake shoe application.

Adjustment of the drum brakes is provided by two adjusters on each front brake and a single adjuster on each rear brake. Periodic adjustment is necessary to compensate for wear on the brake shoe friction linings. The front disc brakes do not require adjustment, as the pistons in the caliper automatically compensate for brake pad wear. An independent means of handbrake adjustment is provided on the cable(s).

2 Drum brakes – adjustment

1 As wear takes place on the brake shoe friction material, the clearance between the friction material and the inner circumference of the brake drum will increase, resulting in excessive brake pedal travel before the brakes are applied. To compensate for this, adjusters are provided at the rear of each brake backplate, enabling the clearance between the brake shoe and drum to be kept to a minimum.
2 At the rear a single adjuster is located at the top of each brake backplate. At the front two adjusters are fitted to each brake backplate.
3 If, when attempting to adjust the brakes, the square-headed adjuster is reluctant to turn, it is quite likely that it has become seized in its housing. If this is the case do not force it, or you will probably break off the square head, necessitating renewal of the complete backplate assembly. Apply liberal amounts of penetrating oil to the rear of the adjuster and allow it to soak in. Now turn the adjuster back and forth slightly, using gentle force if necessary, increasing the movement each time. When the adjuster turns easily apply a multi-purpose grease to the exposed portion of the adjuster at the rear of the backplate and then turn it through its entire travel. Preferably do this with the brake drum removed. With the adjusters free to turn and the drums in position, adjustment of the brakes can be carried out as follows.

Rear brakes

4 Jack up the rear of the car and support it on axle stands. Chock the front wheels and ensure that the handbrake is off.
5 Using a brake adjusting spanner, turn the square-headed adjuster in a clockwise direction (viewed from the rear of the backplate) until the wheel is locked (photo).
6 Now turn the adjuster back a quarter of a turn at a time until the wheel turns freely without binding. A slight rubbing may be felt when the wheel is turned slowly, indicating a high spot on the drum or dust on the linings. This is acceptable providing the drum does not bind.
7 Repeat this procedure for the other rear brake, and then lower the car to the ground.

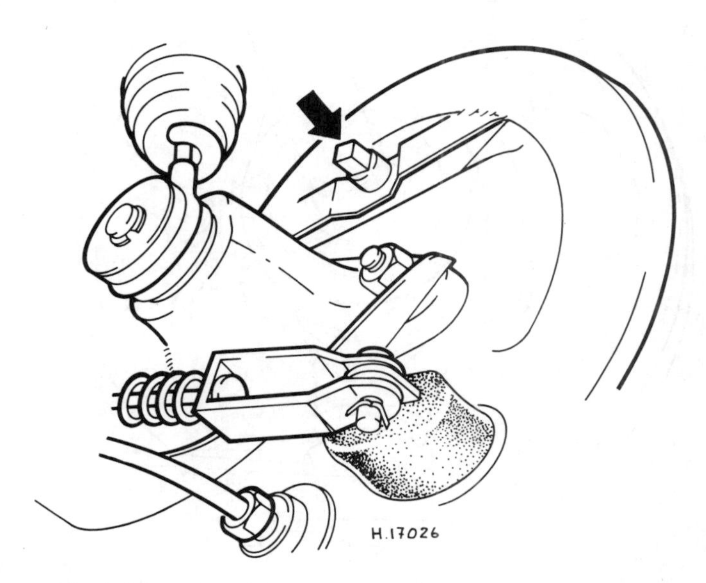

Fig. 9.1 Location of the rear brake adjuster – arrowed (Sec 2)

2.5 Using a square-headed brake adjusting spanner to adjust the rear brakes...

Front brakes

8 Each front brake has two adjusters of the eccentric cam type, accessible from the rear of each brake backplate. One of these adjusters is located behind the steering arm and insufficient clearance exists to enable an ordinary brake adjusting spanner to be used. Providing the adjuster is not excessively tight or partially seized in the backplate, a $\frac{5}{16}$ in AF open-ended spanner can be used quite successfully to turn the adjuster.

9 Begin by turning one of the adjusters in the forward direction of wheel rotation until the wheel is locked (photo). Now back it off slightly, until the wheel turns freely. The brake drum may rub slightly in one or two places as the wheel is turned. This is acceptable providing the wheel does not bind.

10 Turn the second adjuster also in the direction of forward wheel rotation until the drum locks again. Now back the adjuster off until the wheel turns freely once more.

11 Repeat this procedure for the other front wheel and then lower the car to the ground.

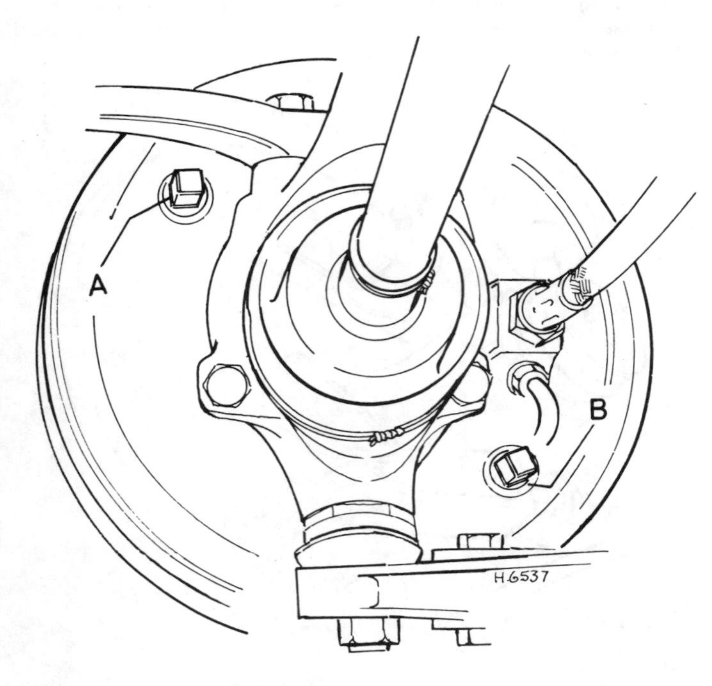

Fig. 9.2 Location of the two front brake adjusters – A and B (Sec 2)

3 Hydraulic system – bleeding

1 If any of the hydraulic components in the braking system have been removed or disconnected, or if the fluid level in the master cylinder has been allowed to fall appreciably, it is inevitable that air will have been introduced into the system. The removal of all the air from the hydraulic system is essential if the brakes are to function correctly, and the process of removing this air is known as bleeding.

2 There are a number of one-man, do-it-yourself, brake bleeding kits currently available from motor accessory shops. It is recommended that one of these kits should be used wherever possible, as they greatly simplify the bleeding operation, and they also reduce the risk of expelled air being drawn back into the system.

3 If one of these kits is not available, then it will be necessary to gather together a clean jam jar, a suitable length of clear plastic tubing which is a tight fit over the bleed screw, and also to engage the help of an assistant.

4 Before commencing the bleeding operation, check that all rigid pipes and flexible hoses are in good condition and that all hydraulic unions are tight. Take great care not to allow hydraulic fluid to come into contact with the paintwork, otherwise the finish will be seriously affected. Wash off any spilled fluid immediately with cold water.

5 If hydraulic fluid has been lost from the master cylinder due to a leak in the system, ensure that the cause is traced and rectified before proceeding further, otherwise a serious malfunction of the braking system may occur.

6 The procedure for bleeding varies according to whether the car is equipped with a single or dual circuit braking system, and also with dual circuit systems, the type of master cylinder that is fitted. Identify the type of system being worked on by referring to the illustrations and then proceed according to type.

Single circuit system

7 To bleed the system, clean the area around the bleed screw of the wheel to be bled. If the hydraulic system has only been partially disconnected, and suitable precautions were taken to prevent further loss of fluid, it should only be necessary to bleed that part of the system. However, if the entire system is to be bled, refer to Fig. 9.3 and proceed in the sequence ABCD for right-hand drive cars, and BADC for left-hand drive vehicles.

8 Remove the master cylinder filler cap and top up the reservoir. Periodically check the fluid level during the bleeding operation and top up as necessary.

9 If a one-man brake bleeding kit is being used, connect the outlet tube to the bleed screw (photo) and then open the screw $\frac{3}{4}$ of a turn. Position the unit so that it can be viewed from the car and then depress the brake pedal to the floor and rapidly release it. The one-way valve in the kit will prevent expelled air from returning to the system at the end of each stroke. Repeat this operation until clean hydraulic fluid, free from air bubbles, can be seen coming through the tube. Then

2.9 ...and the front brakes

3.9 The one-man brake bleeding kit connected to the front bleed screw

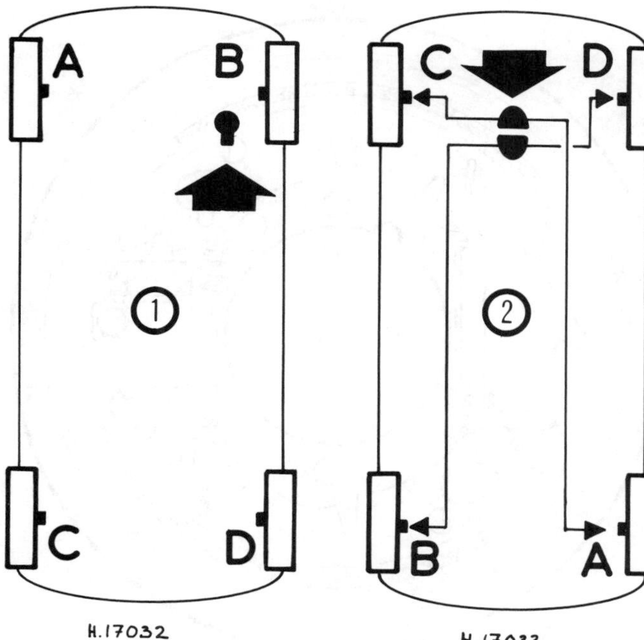

Fig. 9.3 Bleeding sequence for single circuit braking systems – see text (Sec 3)

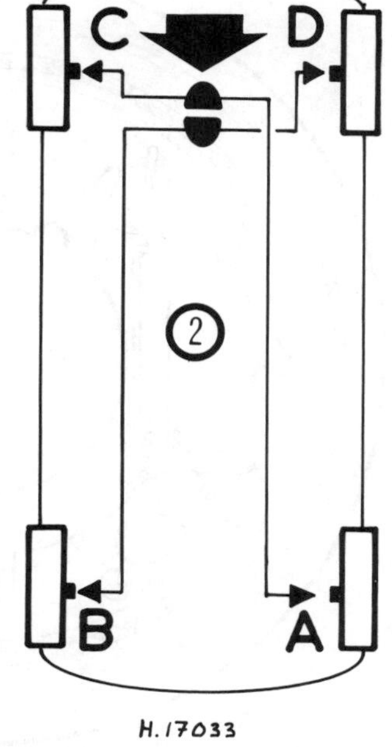

Fig. 9.4 Bleeding sequence for early dual circuit braking systems with separate pressure differential warning actuator – see text (Sec 3)

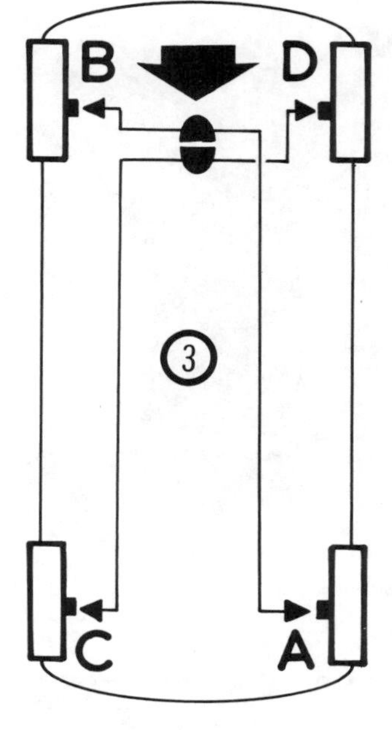

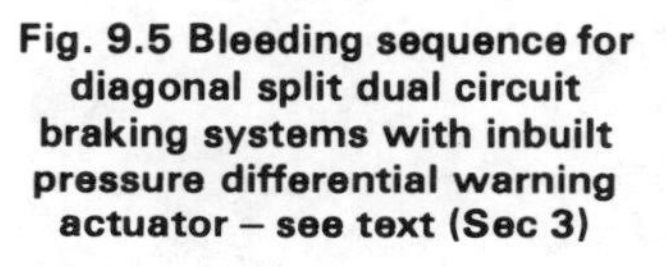

Fig. 9.5 Bleeding sequence for diagonal split dual circuit braking systems with inbuilt pressure differential warning actuator – see text (Sec 3)

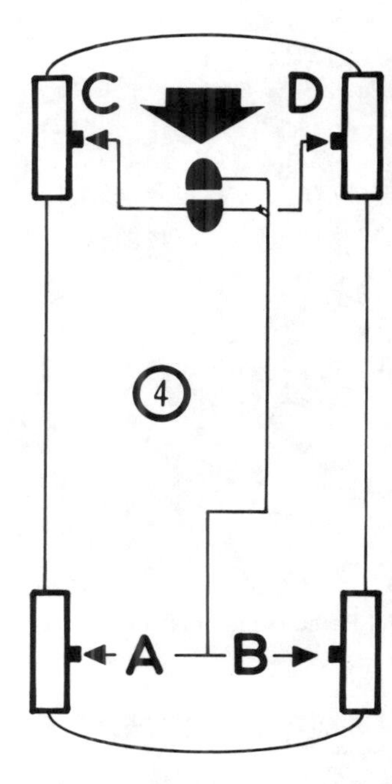

Fig. 9.6 Bleeding sequence for front-to-rear split dual circuit braking systems with inbuilt pressure differential warning actuator – see text (Sec 3)

tighten the bleed screw and remove the outlet tube.

10 If a one-man brake bleeding kit is not available, connect one end of the plastic tubing to the bleed screw and immerse the other end in the jam jar containing sufficient clean hydraulic fluid to keep the end of the tube submerged.

11 Open the bleed screw ¾ of a turn and have your assistant depress the brake pedal to the floor, and then rapidly release it. Tighten the bleed screw at the end of each downstroke to prevent expelled air from being drawn back into the system.

12 Repeat this operation until clean hydraulic fluid, free from air bubbles, can be seen coming through the tube. Then tighten the bleed screw on a downstroke and remove the plastic tube.

13 If the entire system is being bled the procedures described previously should now be repeated at each wheel in the correct sequence.

14 When completed, check the fluid level in the master cylinder, top up if necessary, and refit the cap. Check the feel of the brake pedal, which should be firm and free from any sponginess; this would indicate air still present in the system.

15 Discard any used hydraulic fluid, as the minute air bubbles and contamination which will be present in the fluid make it unsuitable for further use in the hydraulic system.

Dual circuit system (early type with separate pressure differential warning actuator)

16 To bleed the system, clean the area around the bleed screws of the wheels to be bled. If only half of the hydraulic system has been disconnected, it should only be necessary to bleed that half, provided no air has entered the other half. However, if the entire system is to be bled, refer to Fig. 9.4 and proceed in the sequence ABCD for right-hand drive cars and BADC for left-hand drive vehicles.

17 The procedure is now the same as described in paragraphs 8 to 15 for the single circuit system, except that the brake pedal should be depressd rapidly, held down for three seconds and then released slowly. A delay of fifteen seconds should then be allowed before repeating.

18 When bleeding is complete, check the operation of the pressure differential warning actuator as described in Section 25.

Dual circuit system (later type with pressure differential warning actuator incorporated in master cylinder)

19 Before commencing the bleeding operation, remove the brake failure pressure switch from the side of the master cylinder body. (No fluid loss will occur unless there is internal pressure differential piston seal failure).

Note: *If the system is being bled following renewal of the master cylinder, check whether a plastic spacer is fitted between the pressure switch and master cylinder body. If a spacer is present, leave it in position during the bleeding operation and then discard it.*

20 To bleed the system, clean the area around the bleed screws of the wheels to be bled. If only half of the hydraulic system has been disconnected, it should only be necessary to bleed that half, provided no air has entered the other half. However, if the entire system is to be bled, it must be done in the following sequence.

21 For diagonally split systems, refer to Fig. 9.5 and proceed in the order ABCD for right-hand drive cars, and CDAB for left-hand drive vehicles.

22 For front-to-rear split systems refer to Fig. 9.6 and proceed in the order ABCD, irrespective of driving position.

23 The procedure is now the same as described in paragraphs 8 to 15 for the single circuit system, except that the brake pedal should be depressed rapidly, held down for three seconds, and then released slowly. A delay of fifteen seconds should then be allowed before repeating.

24 Refit the brake failure pressure switch after completing the bleeding operation.

4 Drum brake shoes – inspection, removal and refitting

1 After high mileages the friction linings on the brake shoes will have worn, and it will therefore be necessary to fit replacement shoes with new linings.

2 To inspect the brake shoes, jack up the front or rear of the car and support it on axle stands. If the rear is being jacked up, chock the front wheels and release the handbrake.

3 Withdraw the wheel trim and then remove the roadwheel.

4 Slacken off the brake shoe adjuster(s) from behind the backplate,

4.4 Remove the brake drum retaining screws...

4.5 ...and withdraw the drum

and then undo and remove the two brake drum retaining screws (photo).

5 Remove the brake drum from the wheel hub (photo). If the drum is tight, gently tap its circumference with a soft-faced mallet.

6 Using a clean dry paint brush and lint-free cloth, brush and wipe away all traces of asbestos dust from the brake shoes, wheel cylinders and backplate, and also from the inner circumference of the brake drum. **Note:** *Asbestos dust can be harmful if inhaled. Wipe away the dust carefully in a well-ventilated area if possible. Do not use compressed air and do not inhale the dust.*

7 A careful inspection of the brake shoes and brake components can now be carried out. Inspect the friction material and renew the brake shoes if they have worn down to less than the specified minimum thickness.

8 The brake shoes must also be renewed if there is any sign of hydraulic fluid contamination of the linings due to a leaking brake wheel cylinder. If this is the case, the cause of the leak must be traced and rectified before fitting new brake shoes.

9 Brake shoes should always be renewed as complete front or rear sets (four shoes to a set), otherwise uneven braking and pulling to one side may occur.

10 It is advisable to check that the brake wheel cylinders are operating correctly before proceeding further. To do this hold the brake shoes in position using two screwdrivers while an assistant very slowly

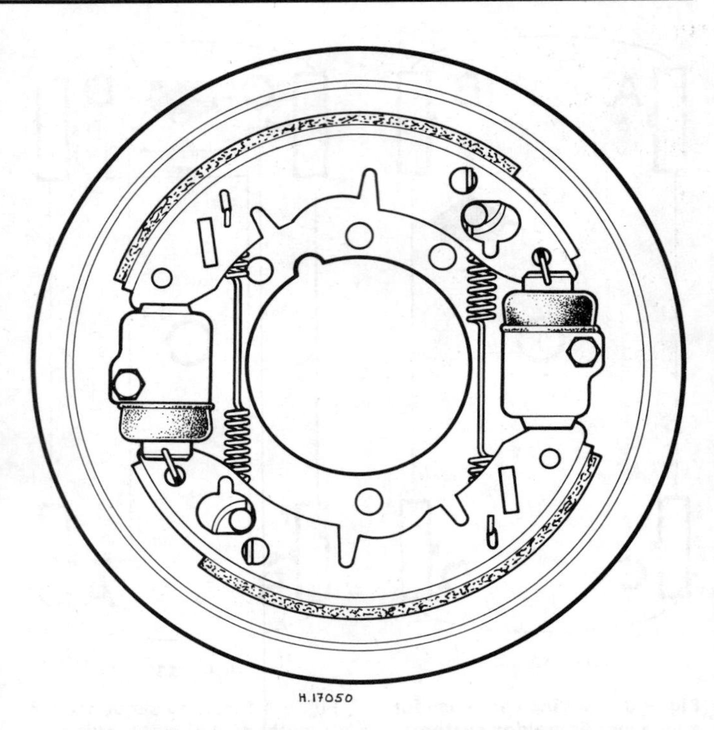

Fig. 9.7 Correct fitting of front brake shoes and return springs – left-hand side shown (Sec 4)

depresses the brake pedal slightly. Check that the wheel cylinder pistons move out as the pedal is depressed, and return when the pedal is released. If this is not the case, it is quite likely that one of the wheel cylinder pistons is seized and the cylinder should therefore be renewed as described in Section 5.

11 Also check the condition of the brake drum. If it is deeply scored on its inner circumference it must be skimmed at your local machine shop, or preferably renewed.

12 Before removing the brake shoes, make a note of the positions of the shoes and the return springs and then remove the brake shoes as follows.

Front brakes

13 First release the small hook springs (where fitted) securing the brake shoes to the wheel cylinder pistons. Now lift the end of each shoe off the pivot side of each wheel cylinder, and then the other end off the wheel cylinder pistons. Detach the return springs and withdraw the shoes (photos).

Rear brakes

14 Lift the top of both shoes off the brake adjuster pivots and detach the top brake shoe return spring. Now lift the bottom of the front shoe off the wheel cylinder piston and disengage the handbrake operating lever (photos). Repeat this for the rear shoe and lift away both shoes and lower return spring.

15 Refitting the brake shoes is the reverse sequence to removal, bearing in mind the following points:

- (a) *Before refitting the shoes, smear a trace of high melting point brake grease to the pivot areas of the wheel cylinder, brake adjuster and backplate (photos)*
- (b) *Do not allow any grease or hydraulic fluid to come into contact with the brake shoe linings*
- (c) *Ensure that the shoes are refitted correctly and the return springs are in their correct holes (photo). Ensure that the lower rear return spring does not rub on the wheel hub when refitted*
- (d) *With the brake shoes assembled and drum refitted, adjust the brakes as described in Section 2*

4.13a Remove the front brake shoes from the wheel cylinder pivot end first...

4.13b ...and then from the piston end

4.14a Withdraw the rear brake shoes from the brake adjuster pivots, detach the return spring ...

4.14b ... then lift off the front ...

4.14 c ... and rear shoe from the handbrake lever and wheel cylinder pistons

4.15a Before refitting the brake shoes, apply a trace of high melting point grease to the areas arrowed...

4.15b ...and ensure that the adjusting plungers are well lubricated

4.15c Rear brake shoes and return spring correctly fitted

5 Drum brake wheel cylinder – removal and refitting

1 If the wheel cylinder pistons are seized, or if hydraulic fluid is leaking from the wheel cylinder, the cylinder must be removed for overhaul or renewal as follows.
2 Begin by removing the brake shoes from the relevant wheel as described in the previous Section.
3 The wheel cylinders can now be removed as described below.

Front wheel cylinder

4 Thoroughly clean the rear of the backplate in the area around the wheel cylinder.
5 Clamp the flexible brake hose leading to the wheel cylinder with a proprietary brake hose clamp, or a self-gripping wrench with their jaws suitably protected. This will minimise hydraulic fluid loss when the hose or pipe is disconnected.
6 Disconnect the interconnecting brake pipe from the rear of the two wheel cylinders.
7 Undo and remove the two bolts securing each cylinder to the backplate.
8 If removing the cylinder containing the bleed screw, undo and remove the screw and lift off the cylinder.
9 If removing the cylinder containing the flexible brake hose, slacken the hose union at the wheel cylinder half a turn. Withdraw the wheel cylinder from the backplate and when it is clear, turn the cylinder anti-clockwise to unscrew it from the hose, taking care not to lose the copper sealing washer.
10 If the hose has not been clamped, suitably plug its end to prevent fluid loss and dirt ingress.

Rear wheel cylinder

11 Thoroughly clean the rear of the backplate in the area around the wheel cylinder.
12 Clamp the flexible hose located at the front of the rear suspension arm with a proprietary brake hose clamp, or a self-gripping wrench

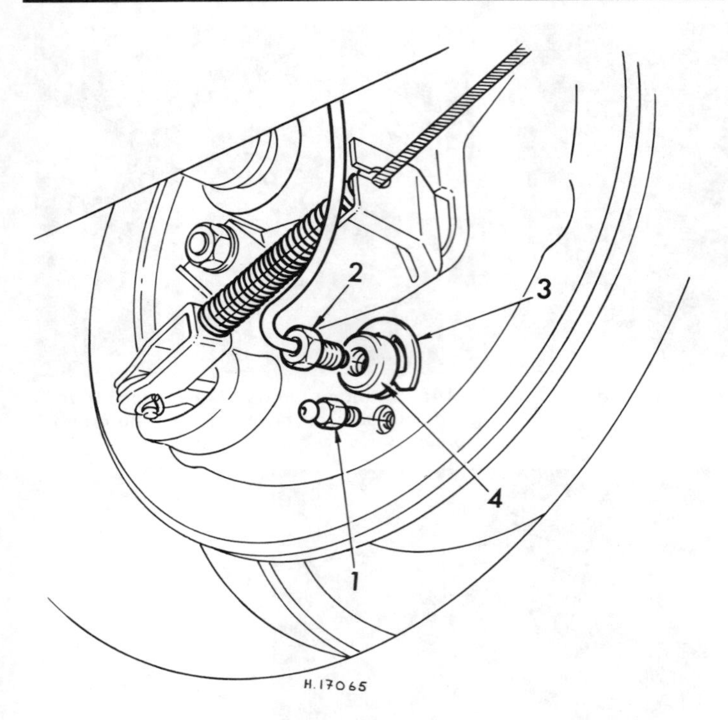

Fig. 9.8 Rear wheel cylinder removal (Sec 5)

1 Bleed screw
2 Hydraulic pipe union
3 Retaining circlip
4 Wheel cylinder

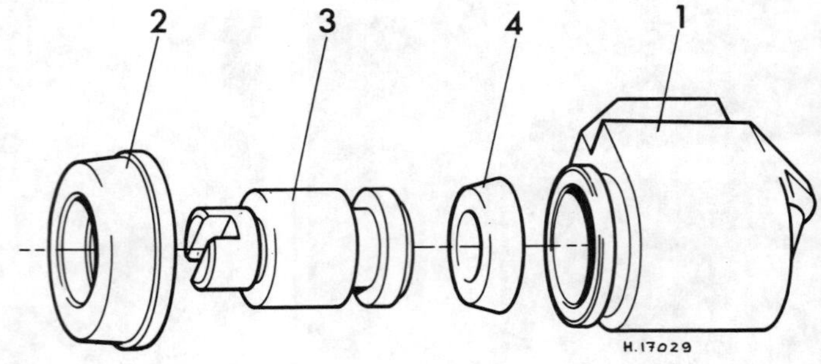

Fig. 9.9 Exploded view of a front wheel cylinder (Sec 6)

1 Cylinder body
2 Dust cover
3 Piston
4 Rubber seal

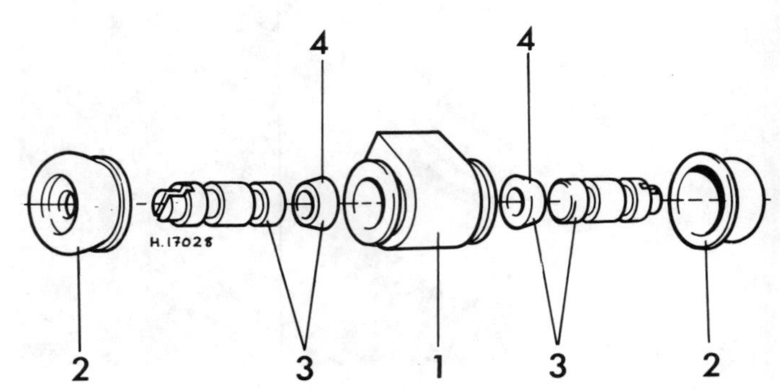

Fig. 9.10 Exploded view of a rear wheel cylinder (Sec 6)

1 Cylinder body
2 Dust covers
3 Piston assemblies
4 Rubber seals

with its jaws suitably protected. This will minimise hydraulic fluid loss when the hydraulic pipe is disconnected.

13 Undo and remove the brake bleed screw and the hydraulic pipe union from the rear of the wheel cylinder. Suitably protect the end of the brake pipe against dirt ingress.

14 Using a screwdriver, prise off the retaining circlip from the rear of the cylinder and then withdraw the wheel cylinder from the backplate.

15 Refitting the wheel cylinders is in all cases a reverse sequence to removal, bearing in mind the following points:

(a) Where a wheel cylinder has been unscrewed from a flexible hose, ensure that the hose is not kinked when the cylinder is refitted

(b) Ensure that the retaining spring circlips are correctly located in their grooves in the wheel cylinder body

(c) After fitting the wheel cylinder and refitting the brake shoes and drum, bleed the hydraulic system as described in Section 3. Providing the hoses were clamped as instructed, it should only be necessary to bleed the relevant wheel and not the entire system

6 Drum brake wheel cylinder – dismantling and reassembly

1 With the wheel cylinder removed from the car as described in the previous Section, thoroughly clean off the exterior of the cylinder and then prepare a clean working area on the bench.

2 Lift off the rubber dust cover(s) from the end of the wheel cylinder and then withdraw the piston(s) and rubber seal(s), noting their precise location in relation to each other.

3 Thoroughly wash the components in clean hydraulic fluid and dry with a lint-free cloth.

4 Carefully inspect the surface of the piston(s) and the internal bore of the cylinder body for scoring, pitting or other signs of wear. If any of these conditions are apparent the cylinder must be renewed.

5 If the wheel cylinder is in a satisfactory condition, a new set of rubber seals should be obtained from your local dealer or brake and clutch stockist. Never re-use old seals as their condition is bound to be suspect.

6 To reassemble the wheel cylinder, immerse the piston and the new internal rubber seals in clean hydraulic fluid.

7 Carefully fit the seal(s) to the piston(s) with their lip or larger diameter facing away from the main part of the piston(s) as noted previously (paragraph 2) – see Fig. 9.9 or 9.10.

8 Now slide the piston into the cylinder bore and then refit the dust cover(s) after first lubricating with the rubber grease supplied in the kit.

9 The wheel cylinder may now be refitted to the car as described in the previous Section.

7 Drum brake backplate – removal and refitting

Front

1 Withdraw the wheel trim, extract the large split pin and slacken the front hub securing nut.

2 Jack up the front of the car and support it on axle stands placed under the subframe.

3 Remove the roadwheel, hub securing nut and the brake drum. Withdraw the hub flange from the driveshaft using a suitable puller if necessary.

4 Remove the brake shoes as described in Section 4 and the wheel cylinders as described in Section 5.

5 Undo and remove the four bolts securing the backplate to the swivel hub and lift away the backplate.

6 Refitting is the reverse sequence to removal. Fully tighten the hub securing nut to the specified torque when the car has been lowered to the ground.

Rear

7 Jack up the rear of the car and support it on axle stands. Remove the wheel trim and the rear roadwheel.

8 Referring to Chapter 11, Section 15 remove the rear hub.

9 Remove the rear brake shoes and wheel cylinder as described in Sections 4 and 5 respectively.

10 From beneath the car extract the split pin and withdraw the clevis pin securing the handbrake cable to the operating lever at the rear of the backplate. Now disengage the cable and its tension spring from the bracket on the suspension arm.
11 Pull the operating lever through the rubber dust cover and lift it off the backplate.
12 Undo and remove the four nuts, bolts and spring washers securing the backplate to the suspension arm. Note that the two lower bolts also secure the handbrake cable abutment bracket and that there is a flat washer fitted between the suspension arm and bracket on each bolt.
13 The backplate can now be lifted off.
14 Refitting the backplate is the reverse sequence to removal. Apply a jointing compound to the backplate and suspension arm mating surfaces.

8 Disc brake friction pads – removal and refitting

1 Jack up the front of the car and place axle stands beneath the front subframe.
2 Withdraw the wheel trim and remove the front roadwheel.
3 Extract the two friction pad retaining split pins from the brake caliper.
4 Lift away the pad retaining spring plates and then, using a pair of pliers, carefully withdraw the two friction pads and their anti-rattle shims from the front of the caliper.
5 Carefully inspect the pads and renew them if the friction material has worn down to less than the minimum specified thickness.
6 Thoroughly clean the recesses in the caliper, in which the friction pads lie, and the exposed face of each piston, from all traces of dirt and dust.
7 If new friction pads are being fitted it will be necessary to move the pistons back into the caliper as far as they will go to accommodate the new pads.
8 Remove the filler cap from the hydraulic fluid reservoir on the master cylinder and place a large rag beneath the reservoir. Using a flat bar or large screwdriver, lever the piston in each half of the caliper, back into its cylinder as far as it will go. This will cause a quantity of hydraulic fluid to be returned to the master cylinder, causing the fluid level to rise and overflow onto the protective rag.
9 Check that the cutaway face of each piston is facing upwards and then place the anti-rattle shims in position.
10 Now slide in the friction pads and refit the pad retaining spring plate, and then secure the assembly using new split pins.
11 Depress the brake pedal several times (it will probably go right to the floor on the first stroke), to centralise the pads, and then check that the disc turns reasonably freely with the pedal released.
12 Refit the roadwheel and trim and lower the car to the ground.

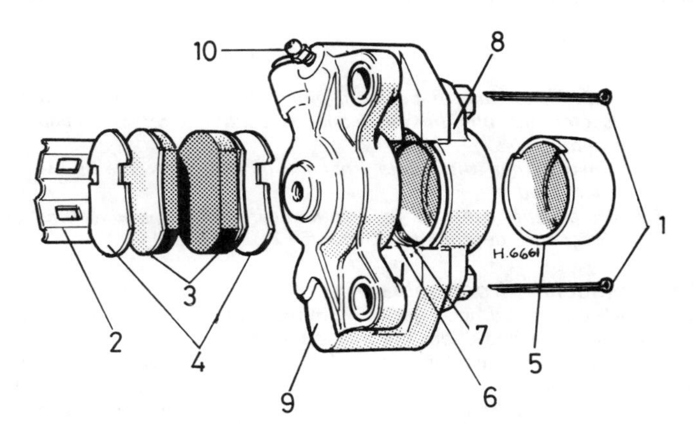

Fig. 9.11 Exploded view of the front disc brake caliper and friction pads (Sec 8)

1 Retaining split pins
2 Pad retaining spring plate
3 Friction pads
4 Anti-rattle shims
5 Piston
6 Dust seal
7 Fluid seal
8 Caliper body – rim half
9 Caliper body – mounting half
10 Bleed screw

9 Disc brake caliper – removal and refitting

1 Remove the disc brake friction pads first, as described in Section 8.
2 If the caliper is being removed for overhaul, slowly depress the brake pedal to bring the caliper pistons into contact with the brake disc. This will assist subsequent removal of the pistons.
3 Using a proprietary brake hose clamp, or a self-gripping wrench with its jaws suitably protected, clamp the flexible brake hose leading to the caliper. This will eliminate any hydraulic fluid loss when the hose is disconnected.
4 Slacken the flexible hose union on the side of the caliper half a turn.
5 Undo and remove the two bolts securing the caliper to the swivel hub, and then withdraw the caliper forward and off the hub.
6 With the caliper clear of the hub and brake disc, support the flexible hose and turn the caliper anti-clockwise to unscrew it. With the hose disconnected, recover the copper sealing washer and plug its end to prevent dirt ingress.
7 Refitting the brake caliper is the reverse sequence to removal, bearing in mind the following points:

(a) Ensure that with the caliper in position the flexible hose is not kinked or twisted
(b) Tighten the caliper retaining bolts to the specified torque
(c) Refit the friction pads as described in Section 8 and then bleed the hydraulic system as described in Section 3. If the flexible hose was clamped as described, it should not be necessary to bleed the entire system

10 Disc brake caliper – dismantling and reassembly

1 Begin by removing the caliper from the car using the procedure described in the previous Section.
2 Carefully withdraw the two pistons one at a time from the caliper body. Do not attempt to separate the caliper halves.
3 Taking great care not to scratch the cylinder walls of the caliper, hook out the dust seal and piston seal from each caliper cylinder.
4 Thoroughly clean the caliper and pistons in clean hydraulic fluid and dry with a lint-free cloth.
5 Inspect the pistons and caliper bores in the caliper for wear, score marks or surface pitting, and if evident renew the complete caliper assembly.
6 If the caliper and pistons are in a satisfactory condition, a new set of seals should be obtained from your local dealer or brake and clutch stockist. *Never re-use old seals.*
7 Lubricate the pistons, seals and the cylinder bores in the caliper with clean hydraulic fluid.
8 Insert the piston seal into the groove in the caliper and then insert the piston with the cutaway facing upwards.
9 Push the piston into its cylinder until 0.32 in (8 mm) remains protruding.
10 Now carefully insert the dust seal into the outer groove in the caliper and push it squarely into place.
11 Repeat paragraphs 8, 9 and 10 for the other piston.
12 The assembled caliper can now be refitted to the car as described in the previous Section.

11 Brake disc – removal and refitting

1 Remove the wheel trim, extract the split pin and then slacken the front hub retaining nut.
2 Jack up the front of the car and support it on axle stands. Remove the roadwheel.
3 Undo and remove the two bolts securing the brake caliper to the swivel hub.
4 Withdraw the caliper, with pads still in position and flexible hose still attached, and tie it out of the way from a convenient place under the wheel arch. Take care not to stretch the flexible hose.

5 Undo and remove the front hub retaining nut and lift out the thrust collar.
6 Now withdraw the front hub flange and brake disc off the driveshaft.
7 To separate the disc from the hub flange, first mark the two components to ensure that they are refitted in the same position.
8 Undo and remove the bolts securing the hub flange to the disc and lift away the disc.
9 Thoroughly clean the disc and inspect it for signs of deep scoring or excessive corrosion. If these are evident the disc should be skimmed at your local machine shop, or preferably renewed.
10 Refitting the disc is the reverse sequence to removal. Ensure that the mating surfaces between disc and hub flange are thoroughly clean before refitting the retaining bolts.
11 When reassembly is complete, check the run-out of the disc by inserting feeler blades between the disc and edge of the caliper and recording the maximum and minimum clearance. The difference between the readings is the run-out. Excessive clearance can lead to judder during braking and in severe cases rapid wear of the friction pads and suspension components.
12 If the brake disc run-out is excessive the condition can often be improved by removing the retaining bolts and repositioning the disc on the hub flange. In most cases, however, excessive run-out is caused by distortion of the disc and renewal is the only satisfactory cure.

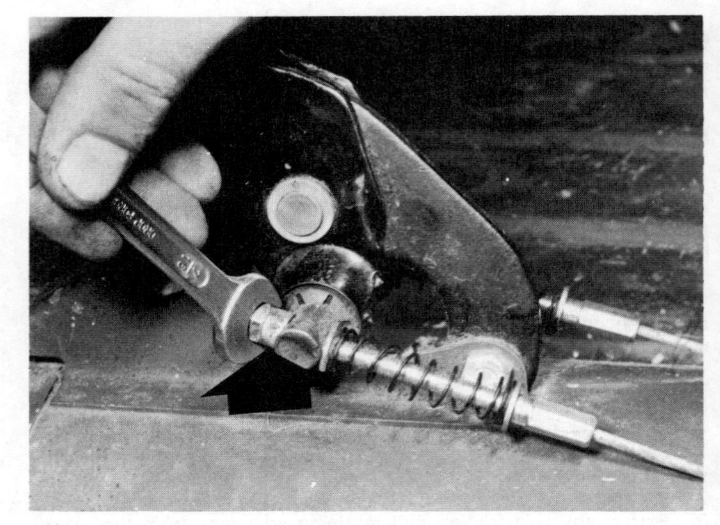
12.5a Handbrake cable adjusting nuts on twin cable...

12 Handbrake cable – adjustment

1 Adjustment of the handbrake cables is usually only necessary after high mileages when a slight stretching of the cables will have taken place, or if the cables have been removed.
2 Before adjusting the handbrake check that the footbrake is correctly adjusted as described in Section 2. If the handbrake lever travel is still excessive proceed as follows.
3 Jack up the rear of the car and support it on axle stands placed under the subframe.
4 Apply the handbrake to the third click of the ratchet.
5 Tilt the front seats forward, and on models having twin cables, tighten the cable adjusting nuts at the base of the lever until the rear wheels can only just be turned by heavy hand pressure. On models having a single front cable, slacken the locknut and rotate the cable adjusting nut. When the wheels can only just be turned by heavy hand pressure, tighten the locknut (photos).
6 Release the handbrake lever and ensure that the wheels rotate freely. If satisfactory lower the car to the ground.

12.5b ...and single cable models

13 Handbrake cable – removal and refitting

Early models

1 Chock the front wheels, jack up the rear of the car and support it on axle stands placed under the rear subframe. Remove the rear roadwheel.
2 From inside the car, undo and remove the cable adjusting nut at the lever, and then pull the cable out of the trunnion. Now slide the two washers and tension spring off the threaded end of the cable.
3 Lift up the carpets to expose the cable guide plates located at the point where the cable passes through the floor.
4 Engage the help of an assistant to hold the two nuts from underneath the car while the two cable guide retaining screws are removed from above. Lift off the guide and sealing pad.
5 From beneath the car, pull the end of the cable through the opening in the floor and out of the passenger compartment.
6 Bend back the tags slightly on the guide channel located on the forward crossmember of the rear subframe. Lift the cable out of the guide channel.
7 Similarly bend up the pinched ends of the moving sector (photo) located at the front of the rear suspension arm. Lift the cable and the locating peg out of the sector, and then pull the disconnected end of the cable through the opening in the side of the subframe.
8 At the other end of the cable, extract the split pin and withdraw the clevis pin securing the cable end to the handbrake operating arm.
9 Release the cable from the abutment bracket at the rear of the brake backplate and lift the cable off the car.
10 Refitting the cable is the reverse sequence to removal, bearing in mind the following points:

(a) With the cable in position, pinch the ends of the moving sector and subframe guide channel slightly to retain the cable (photo)
(b) Ensure that the guide channel in the subframe is well lubricated
(c) When the cable is in position carry out the adjustment procedure described in Section 12

Later models – front cable

11 Chock the front wheels, jack up the rear of the car and support it on axle stands placed under the rear subframe.
12 Tilt the front seats forward and lift up the carpet around the handbrake lever.
13 Slacken the locknut, and then unscrew the cable adjusting nut until the cable can be withdrawn from the lever assembly.
14 Undo and remove the screws securing the cable guide plate to the floor. Have an assistant hold the two nuts from under the car as the screws are undone.
15 Lift off the guide plate and pass the cable through the hole in the floor.
16 Pull the cable rearwards and remove it from the compensator on the rear cable (photo).
17 Refitting is the reverse sequence to removal. Adjust the cable as described in Section 12 after refitting.

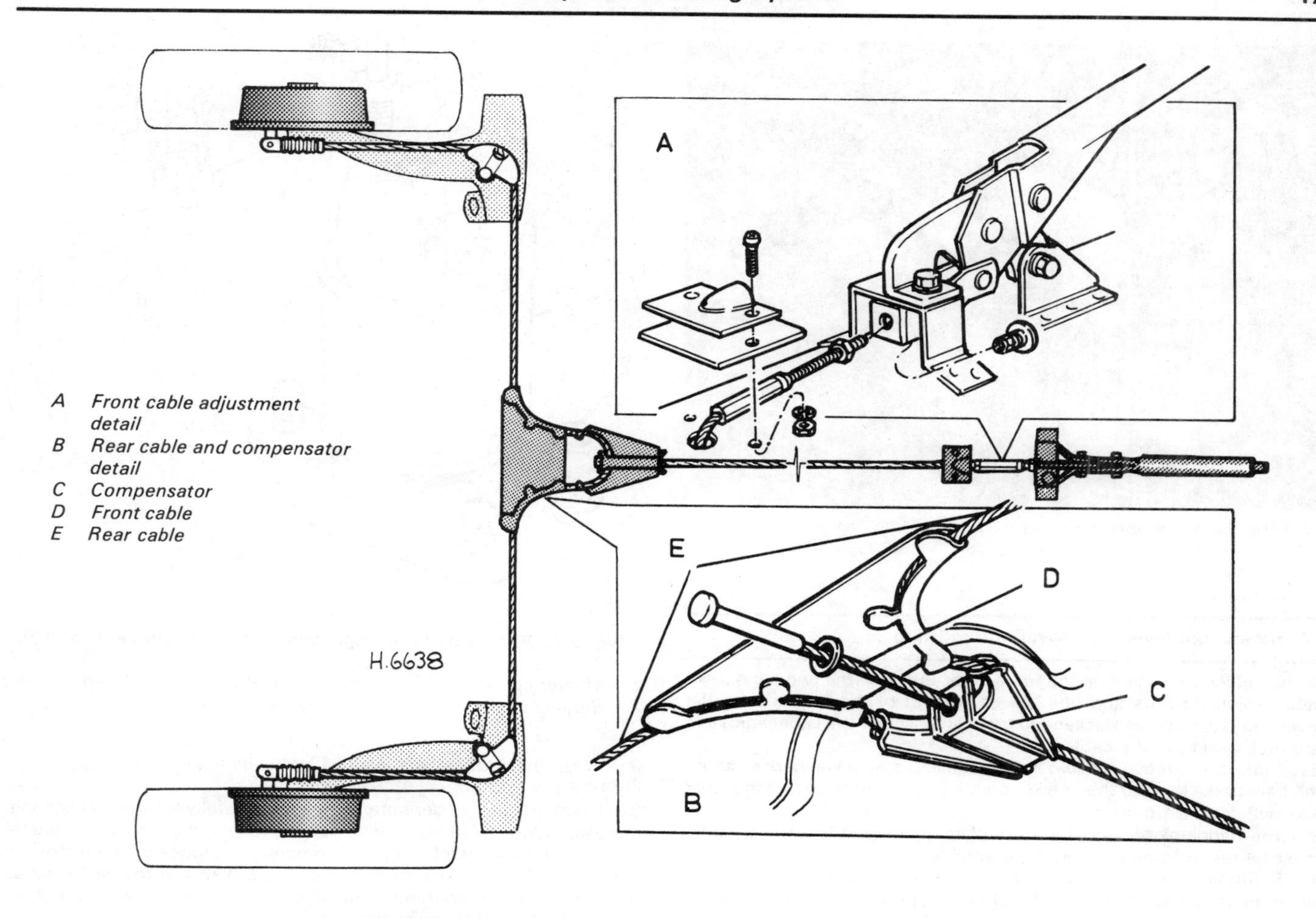

Fig. 9.12 The handbrake cables and lever assembly fitted to later models (Sec 13)

13.7 Removing the handbrake cable from the moving sector

13.10 Pinching the ends of the moving sector to retain the handbrake cable

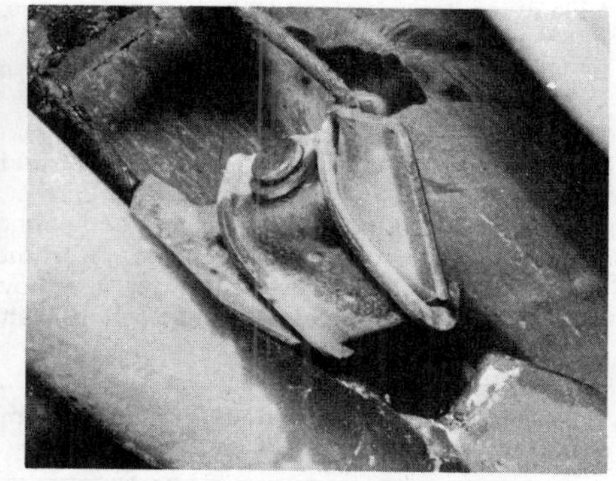

13.16 Handbrake rear cable compensator

Later models – rear cable

18 Remove the front cable as described previously.

19 Extract the split pins and withdraw the clevis pins securing the cable ends to the handbrake operating arms at the rear of each brake backplate. Release the cable and tension springs from the abutment brackets on the backplate.

20 Bend back the tags slightly on the guide channels located on the forward crossmember of the rear subframe.

21 Similarly bend up the pinched ends of the moving sectors located at the front of each rear suspension arm. Lift the cable and locating pegs out of the sectors, pull the disconnected ends of the cable through the openings in the side of the subframe, and lift away the cable complete with compensator.

22 Refitting the rear cable is the reverse sequence to removal bearing in mind the following points.

(a) *With the cable in position pinch the ends of the moving sectors and subframe guide channels slightly to retain the cable*

(b) *Ensure that the guide channels in the subframe are well lubricated*

14.2 Handbrake lever retaining nuts and bolts

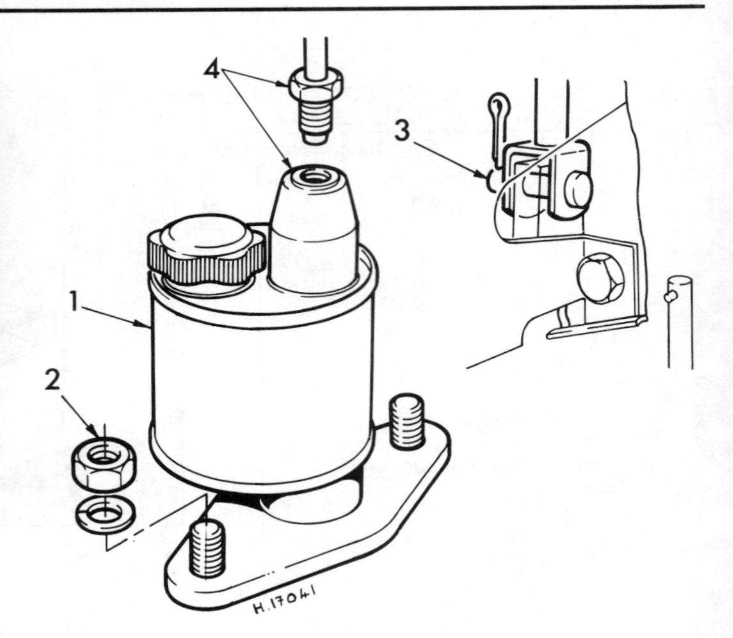

Fig. 9.13 Removal of the single circuit master cylinder (Sec 15)

1 Master cylinder
2 Retaining nuts
3 Pushrod-to-brake pedal attachment
4 Hydraulic pipe union

14 Handbrake lever – removal and refitting

1 On early models lift up the front seats, unscrew the two handbrake cable adjusting nuts and pull the cables out of the trunnion on the lever. On later models slacken the locknut, unscrew the cable adjusting nut and withdraw the cable.
2 Undo and remove the two nuts, bolts and spring washers securing the handbrake lever to the bracket on the floor (photo). Lift off the lever and withdraw it from the car.
3 The handbrake lever cannot be dismantled, and if worn or faulty must be renewed as a complete assembly.
4 Refitting is the reverse sequence to removal. Adjust the handbrake cable as described in Section 12 after refitting.

15 Master cylinder (single circuit system) – removal and refitting

1 From inside the car release the heater air intake ducting from the side of the heater unit and wheel arch. Remove the ducting from under the parcel shelf.
2 Extract the split pin and withdraw the clevis pin securing the master cylinder pushrod to the brake pedal.
3 Working in the engine compartment, unscrew the brake pipe union from the top of the master cylinder and carefully pull the pipe clear.
4 Undo and remove the two nuts and spring washers securing the master cylinder to the bulkhead and lift off the cylinder.
5 Refitting is the reverse sequence to removal. Bleed the complete hydraulic system as described in Section 3 after refitting.

16 Master cylinder (single circuit system) – dismantling and reassembly

1 Before dismantling the master cylinder, prepare a clean uncluttered working area on the bench.
2 Remove the filler cap from the master cylinder, and drain and discard the hydraulic fluid from the reservoir.
3 With the cylinder on the bench, withdraw the rubber dust cover and slide it off over the end of the pushrod.
4 Using circlip pliers, extract the circlip and lift off the pushrod and dished washer.
5 Tap the master cylinder body on a block of wood until the piston emerges from the end of the cylinder bore.
6 Withdraw the piston from the cylinder, followed by the piston washer, main cup seal, spring retainer, spring and non-return valve.
7 Lay the parts out in the order of removal, and then very carefully remove the secondary cup seal from the piston by sretching it over the end of the piston.
8 Wash the components in clean hydraulic fluid and then dry with a lint-free rag.
9 Examine the cylinder bore and piston carefully for signs of scoring, or wear ridges. If these are apparent, renew the complete master cylinder. If the condition of the components appears satisfactory, a new set of rubber seals must be obtained. *Never re-use old seals* as they will have deteriorated with age even though this may not be evident during visual inspection.
10 Begin reassembly by thoroughly lubricating the internal components and the cylinder bore in clean hydraulic fluid.
11 Using fingers only, place the secondary cup seal in position on the piston with the lip of the cup facing the opposite (drilled) end of the piston.
12 Position the non-return valve over the larger diameter of the spring and the spring retainer over the smaller diameter, and place this assembly into the cylinder bore, larger diameter first.
13 Now insert the main cup seal into the cylinder bore, lip end first followed by the washer.
14 Insert the piston assembly into the cylinder bore followed by the pushrod, dished washer and circlip. Ensure that the circlip fully enters its groove.
15 Lubricate a new dust cover with rubber grease and stretch it over the pushrod and into position on the end of the cylinder.
16 The master cylinder can now be refitted to the car as described in the previous Section.

17 Tandem master cylinder (early type) – removal and refitting

1 Unscrew the hydraulic pipe unions from the master cylinder and carefully pull the pipes clear.
2 Undo and remove the two nuts and spring washers securing the master cylinder to the bulkhead. Lift off the master cylinder, leaving the pushrod attached to the brake pedal.
3 Refitting is the reverse sequence to removal. Bleed the hydraulic system as described in Section 3 after refitting.

18 Tandem master cylinder (early type) – dismantling and reassembly

1 Before dismantling the master cylinder, prepare a clean uncluttered working area on the bench.

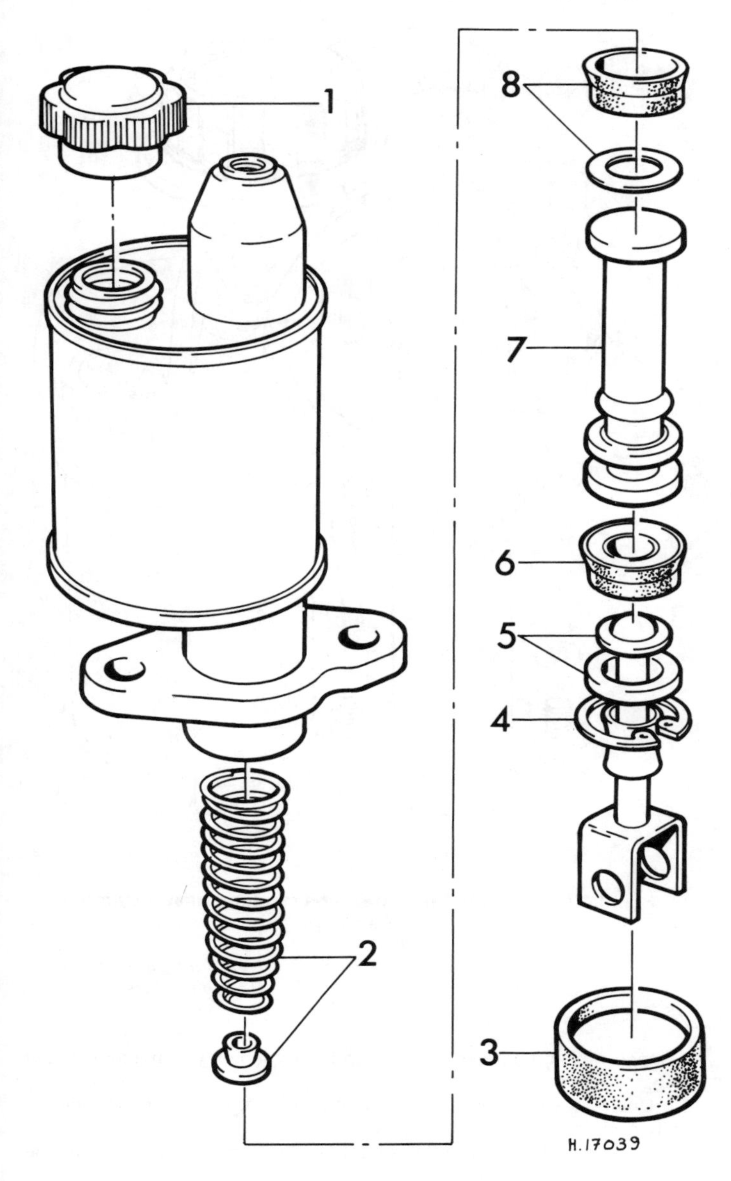

Fig. 9.14 Exploded view of single circuit master cylinder (Sec 16)

1 Filler cap
2 Spring and spring retainer
3 Dust cover
4 Circlip
5 Pushrod and stop washer
6 Secondary cup seal
7 Piston
8 Piston washer and main cup seal

2 Remove the filler cap from the master cylinder, drain and discard the hydraulic fluid from the reservoir.
3 Mount the master cylinder in a vice with protected jaws, so that the mouth of the cylinder bore is uppermost.
4 Slide off the rubber boot, compress the return spring and, using a small screwdriver, remove the Spirolex ring from its groove in the primary piston. Take care not to distort the coils of the ring or score the bore of the cylinder.
5 Using a pair of circlip pliers, remove the piston retaining circlip.
6 Carefully move the piston up and down in the bore so as to free the nylon guide bearing and cap seal. Lift away the guide bearing seal.
7 Lift away the plain washer.
8 Using a pair of circlip pliers, remove the inner circlip.
9 The primary and secondary piston assembly, complete with the stop washer, may now be withdrawn from the cylinder bore.

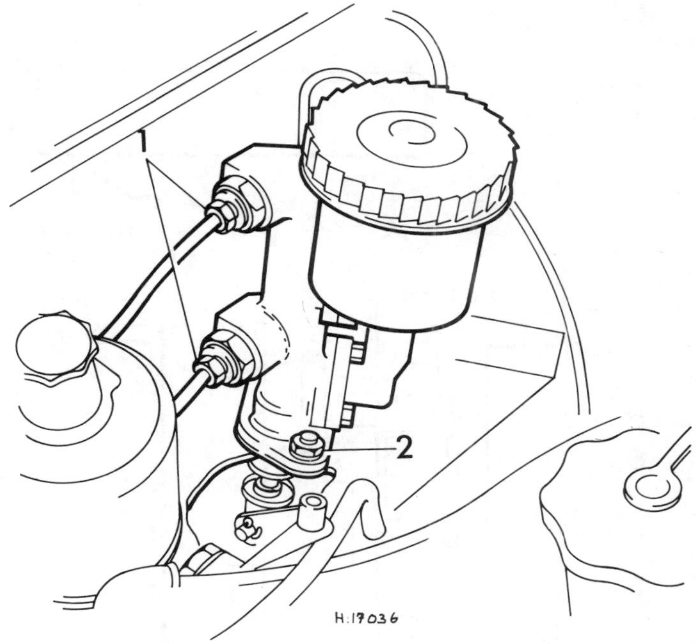

Fig. 9.15 Removal of the early type tandem master cylinder (Sec 17)

1 Hydraulic pipe unions
2 Retaining nuts

10 Lift away the stop washer.
11 Compress the spring that separates the two pistons and then, using a small diameter parallel pin punch, drive out the roll pin that retains the piston link.
12 Inspect and note the location of the rubber cups (look for the moulded indentations) and then remove the cups and washers from the pistons.
13 Undo and remove the four bolts that secure the plastic reservoir to the body and lift away the reservoir.
14 Recover the two reservoir sealing rings.
15 Unscrew and remove the hydraulic pipe connection adaptors, discard the copper gaskets and then recover the spring and trap valves.
16 Wash all parts in clean hydraulic fluid or methylated spirits and wipe dry.
17 Examine the bore of the cylinder carefully for any signs of scores or ridges. If this is found to be smooth all over, new seals can be fitted. If, however, there is any doubt of the condition of the bore, then a new cylinder must be obtained and fitted.
Never re-use old seals as they will have deteriorated with age even though this may not be evident during visual inspection.
18 Reassembly of the master cylinder is the reverse sequence to removal, but the following additional points should be noted.

(a) All components should be assembled wet by dipping in clean brake fluid
(b) Locate the piston washer over the head of the secondary piston, convex surface first, and then carefully ease the secondary cup over the piston and seat it with its flat surface against the washer
(c) Fit new copper gaskets to the connection adaptors
(d) The master cylinder can now be refitted to the car as described in the previous Section

19 Tandem master cylinder (later type) – removal and refitting

1 From inside the car, release the heater air intake ducting from the side of the heater unit and wheel arch. Remove the ducting from under the parcel shelf.
2 Extract the split pin and withdraw the clevis pin securing the master cylinder pushrod to the brake pedal.
3 Working in the engine compartment, disconnect the wiring

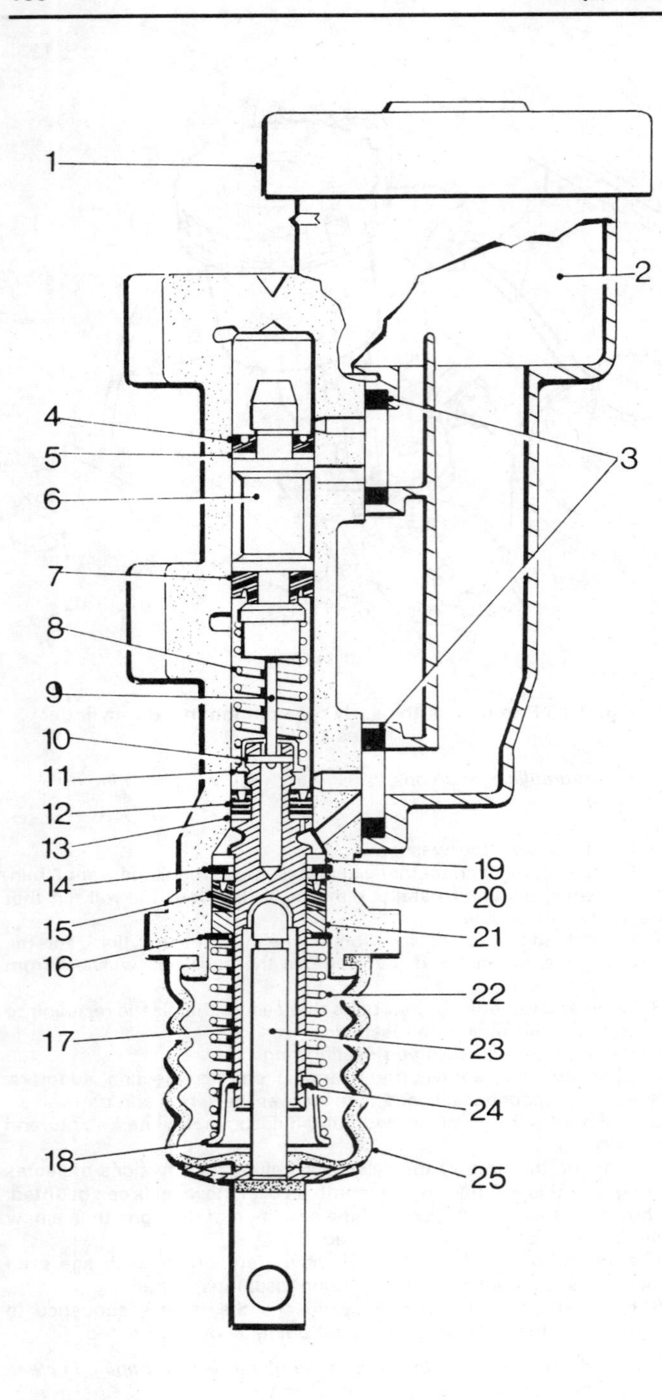

Fig. 9.16 Cross-sectional view of early type tandem master cylinder (Sec 18)

1	*Filler cap*	*14*	*Circlip*
2	*Plastic reservoir*	*15*	*Cup*
3	*Reservoir seals*	*16*	*Circlip*
4	*Main cup*	*17*	*Piston*
5	*Piston washer*	*18*	*Spring retainer*
6	*Piston*	*19*	*Stop washer*
7	*Main cup*	*20*	*Washer*
8	*Spring*	*21*	*Bearing*
9	*Piston link*	*22*	*Spring*
10	*Pin*	*23*	*Pushrod*
11	*Pin retainer*	*24*	*Spirolex ring*
12	*Main cup*	*25*	*Rubber boot*
13	*Piston washer*		

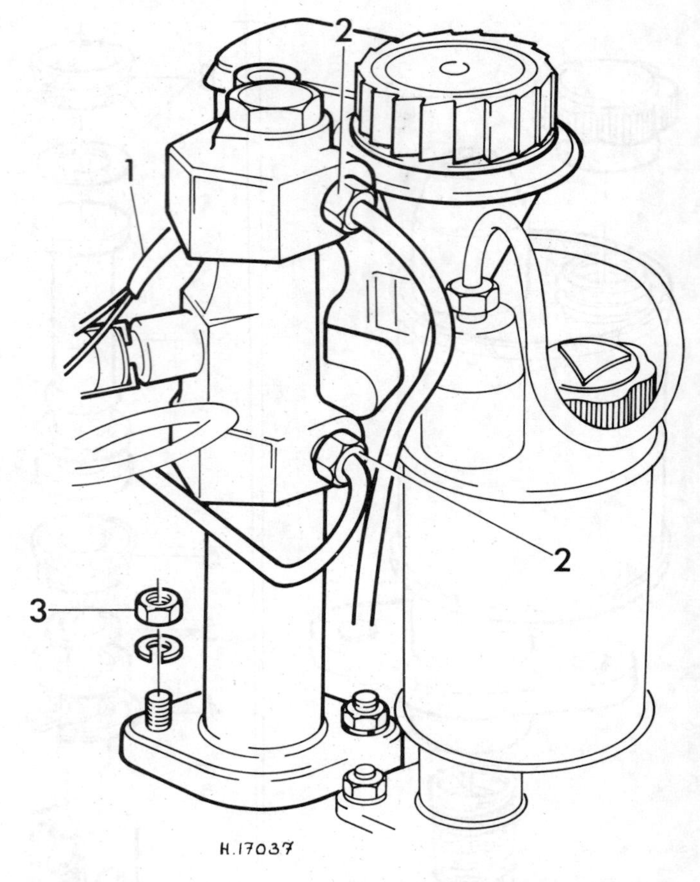

Fig. 9.17 Removal of the later type tandem master cylinder (Sec 19)

1 Electrical wiring to failure switch
2 Hydraulic pipe unions
3 Retaining nuts

connector from the brake failure warning switch on the master cylinder body.

4 Unscrew the hydraulic pipe unions from the side of the cylinder body and carefully pull the pipes clear. .

5 Unscrew the two nuts securing the master cylinder to the bulkhead and lift the unit off.

6 Refitting is the reverse sequence to removal. Bleed the complete hydraulic system as described in Section 3 after refitting.

20 Tandem master cylinder (later type) – dismantling and reassembly

1 Before dismantling the master cylinder, prepare a clean uncluttered working area on the bench.

2 Remove the filler cap from the master cylinder, and drain and discard the hydraulic fluid from the reservoir.

3 Mount the cylinder in a vice with protected jaws, so that the reservoir is uppermost.

4 Unscrew the two reservoir retaining screws and lift the reservoir off the master cylinder body. Carefully withdraw the two reservoir sealing washers from the outlets.

5 Push in the pushrod as far as possible, and using pliers, extract the secondary piston stop pin from its recess.

6 Release the pushrod rubber boot from the end of the cylinder, push the pushrod in and extract the retaining circlip. Now lift away the pushrod assembly.

7 Remove the master cylinder from the vice, tap it on a block of wood and withdraw the primary and secondary piston assemblies from the cylinder bore.

8 Unscrew the brake failure switch from the cylinder body.

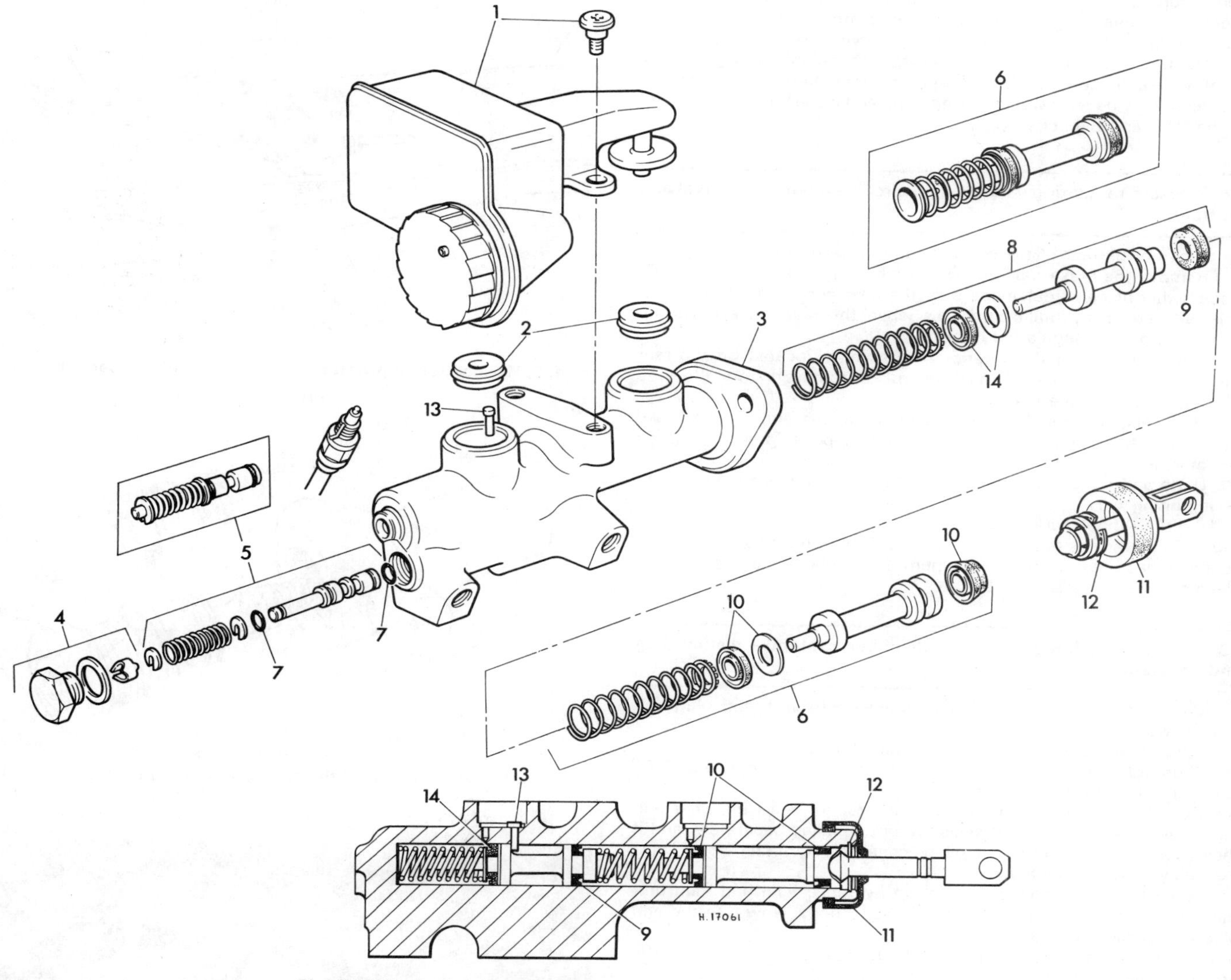

Fig. 9.18 Exploded view of later type tandem master cylinder (Sec 19)

1 *Reservoir and retaining screw*
2 *Reservoir sealing washers*
3 *Master cylinder body*
4 *End plug assembly*
5 *Pressure differential piston (insert shows alternative assembly)*
6 *Primary piston and spring (inset shows alternative assembly)*
7 *Piston rubber seals*
8 *Secondary piston and spring*
9 *Secondary piston seals*
10 *Primary piston seals*
11 *Dust cover*
12 *Circlip*
13 *Stop pin*
14 *Secondary piston seals*

9 Unscrew the end plug and washer, then remove the distance piece and pressure differential piston assembly.

10 Note the position and direction of fitting of the rubber seals on the piston assemblies, and then carefully remove them.

11 Wash all the parts in clean hydraulic fluid and dry with a lint-free cloth.

12 Examine the bore of the master cylinder carefully for any signs of scores or ridges. If this is found to be smooth all over, new seals can be fitted. If, however, there is any doubt about the condition of the bore, then a new cylinder must be obtained and fitted. Never re-use old seals, as they will have deteriorated with age even though this may not be evident during visual inspection.

13 Reassembly of the master cylinder is the reverse sequence to removal, but the following additional points should be noted:

(a) *Thoroughly lubricate all components in clean hydraulic fluid and assemble them wet*
(b) *Refit the seals onto the pistons using fingers only, and ensure that they are fitted the correct way round*
(c) *When refitting the secondary piston assembly, push the piston down the bore using a soft metal rod and insert the stop pin. The primary piston and remaining components can then be fitted*
(d) *On completion, refit the master cylinder to the car as described in the previous Section*

21 Pressure regulating valve (single circuit system) – general description

All models with single circuit braking systems incorporate a pressure regulating valve in the rear brake hydraulic circuit. The valve regulates the hydraulic pressure available at the rear wheels, and therefore prevents the rear brakes from locking due to forward weight transfer under heavy braking.

The action of the valve is as follows: Under normal braking conditions hydraulic fluid under pressure passes through the valve and out to the rear brake wheel cylinders. As line pressure increases with heavier application of the footbrake, the piston in the valve is moved against the pressure of a spring until it closes off the outlet ports to the rear wheel cylinders. This prevents further operation of the rear brakes and all further braking effort is transmitted to the front wheels only. As pressure is released the spring forces the piston off its seat thus re-opening the outlet ports to the rear wheel cylinders once more.

The pressure regulating valve is extremely reliable, and gives very little trouble in service. If, however, the condition of the valve is suspect it may be removed for dismantling and inspection as described in the following Sections.

22 Pressure regulating valve (single circuit system) – removal and refitting

1 Jack up the rear of the car and support it on axle stands.
2 Remove the brake master cylinder filler cap, top up the reservoir, place a thin piece of polythene over the filler neck and refit the cap. This will reduce hydraulic fluid loss when the rear brake pipes are removed from the regulating valve.
3 Thoroughly clean the exterior of the valve, located on the rear subframe, ensuring that all dirt and grit is removed from the area around the brake pipe unions.
4 Undo and remove the three hydraulic unions and lift the brake pipes out of the valve. Protect the ends of the pipes to prevent possible dirt ingress.
5 Undo and remove the retaining nut and bolt and lift the valve off its mounting.
6 Refitting the valve is the reverse sequence to removal. Bleed the hydraulic system as described in Section 3 after refitting. If hydraulic fluid loss has been kept to a minimum it should only be necessary to bleed the rear brakes.

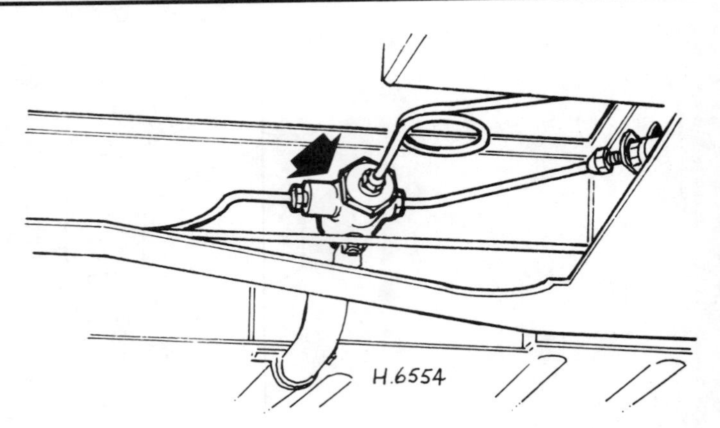

Fig. 9.19 Location of pressure regulating valve on rear subframe (Sec 22)

23 Pressure regulating valve (single circuit system) – dismantling and reassembly

1 Clamp the valve in a vice and remove the large end plug and sealing washer.
2 Lift out the valve assembly and return spring.
3 Thoroughly clean the components in clean hydraulic fluid and dry with a lint-free cloth.
4 Examine the valve, cylinder bore and rubber seals for wear and renew as necessary. Rubber seals are not supplied separately, and if they appear swollen or worn it will be necessary to obtain a new valve assembly complete with seals.
5 Lubricate the components in clean hydraulic fluid and then refit the spring and valve assembly into the valve body. Now refit the end plug and sealing washer.
6 The valve can now be refitted to the car as described in the previous Section.

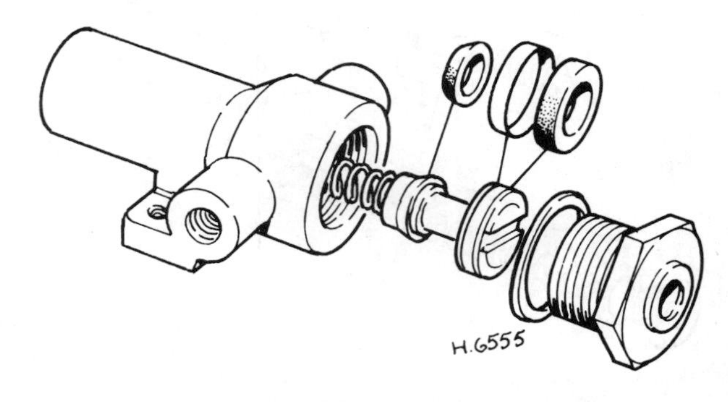

Fig. 9.20 Exploded view of the pressure regulating valve (Sec 23)

24 Pressure reducing valve (dual circuit system) – removal and refitting

Note: *On certain models fitted with dual circuit braking systems a pressure reducing valve is used to limit the braking force at the rear wheels. The operation of the valve is similar to the pressure regulating valve used on single circuit systems.*
1 Remove the brake master cylinder filler cap, top up the reservoir, place a thin piece of polythene over the filler neck and refit the cap. This will reduce hydraulic fluid loss when the brake pipes are disconnected from the valve.
2 Unscrew the four pipe unions from the reducing valve and carefully lift out the pipes. Protect the disconnected unions to prevent possible dirt ingress (photo).
3 Undo and remove the retaining bolt and lift off the valve.
4 The pressure reducing valve is a sealed unit and cannot be dismantled. If the valve is faulty it must be renewed as a complete assembly.
5 Refitting is the reverse sequence to removal. Bleed the hydraulic system as described in Section 3 after refitting.

24.2 Pressure reducing valve hydraulic pipe unions

25 Pressure differential warning actuator (dual circuit system) – removal and refitting

Note: *On early type dual circuit braking systems, a separate pressure differential warning actuator, located on the engine compartment bulkhead, informs the driver of failure of one of the braking hydraulic circuits. On later systems the warning actuator is incorporated in the master cylinder.*
1 Unscrew the brake master cylinder filler cap, place a piece of polythene over the filler neck and refit the cap. This will reduce hydraulic fluid loss when the brake pipes are disconnected.
2 Detach the electrical connector from the side of the warning actuator body.
3 Unscrew the hydraulic pipe unions and carefully remove the pipes.

Protect the disconnected unions from possible dirt ingress.
4 Undo and remove the retaining bolt and lift off the unit.
5 Refitting is the reverse sequence to removal. Bleed the hydraulic system as described in Section 3 after refitting.
6 After bleeding the braking system, switch on the ignition and observe the brake failure warning light. If the light is illuminated, press the brake pedal hard; the light should go out and stay out when the pedal is released. If the light fails to go out, the pressure in the braking system is unbalanced or there is a fault in the warning actuator or its switch. Bleed the braking system again, and if this fails to cure the trouble, investigate the warning actuator and the switch.
7 If the brake failure warning light is not illuminated when the brake pedal is depressed, but does come on when the test-push on the switch is operated, then the system is functioning satisfactorily.

26 Pressure differential warning actuator (dual circuit system) – dismantling and reassembly

1 Clean off the exterior of the unit and make sure it is free from dirt and grit.
2 Undo and remove the end plug and discard the copper washer.
3 Unscrew the warning light switch.
4 Tap the warning actuator body on a block of wood to release the shuttle valve piston assembly and withdraw it from the bore.
5 Remove the two rubber seals from the piston.
6 Wash the components in clean hydraulic fluid and dry with a lint-free cloth.
7 Carefully inspect the piston and the casing bore for scoring and damage. If the bore and piston are not in perfect condition, renew the complete pressure differential warning actuator. If the components are in a satisfactory condition obtain new seals and a new copper sealing washer. *Do not re-use the old seals.*
8 Reassembly of the unit is the reverse of the dismantling sequence. Lubricate all the parts with clean hydraulic fluid and assemble them wet. Observe the specified torque wrench settings when refitting the end plug and warning light switch.
9 Refit the assembled pressure differential warning actuator to the car as described in Section 25.

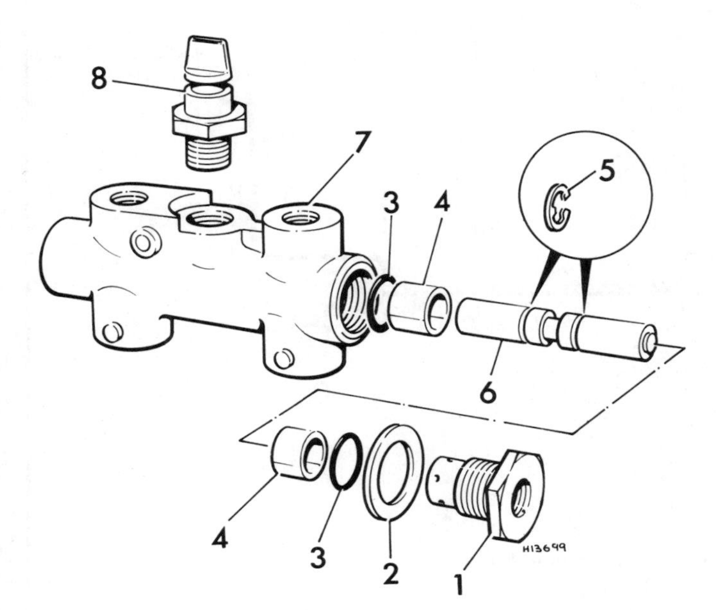

Fig. 9.21 Exploded view of the pressure differential warning actuator (Sec 26)

1 End adaptor
2 Copper washer
3 O-ring
4 Sleeve
5 Circlip
6 Piston
7 Body
8 Switch

27 Vacuum servo unit – general description

Mini Cooper S and 1275GT models are fitted with a vacuum servo unit incorporated in the brake hydraulic circuit. The servo unit provides assistance to the driver when the brake pedal is depressed and reduces the effort required to stop the car under all braking conditions.

The servo unit consists of three main assemblies: the vacuum chamber, the air valve assembly and the slave cylinder. The slave cylinder is connected in series with the main hydraulic circuit between the master cylinder and the brake wheel cylinders and calipers.

When the brake pedal is depressed gently, hydraulic fluid passes directly to the wheels through the hollow centre of the slave piston. Under these conditions no servo assistance is obtained. As pressure on the brake pedal increases fluid pressure acts on the air valve piston which closes the diaphragm. The two chambers, one either side of the main servo diaphragm, are now isolated from each other. Further movement of the air valve piston opens the air valve, allowing atmospheric pressure to enter the chamber behind the diaphragm and destroy the vacuum. A vacuum now exists on one side of the diaphragm only, causing it to move toward the slave cylinder. As it does so the central rod is pushed into the hollow centre of the slave piston, sealing it off and forcing the piston down the bore. The fluid pressure at the wheel cylinders and calipers is therefore increased.

When the brake pedal is released the hydraulic fluid pressure beneath the air valve piston decreases, the diaphragm re-opens and the air valve closes. A suspended vacuum is recreated around both sides of the main diaphragm via the non-return valve. The return spring moves the main diaphragm, pushrod and slave piston back to their original positions and the pressure at the wheel cylinder and brake calipers is lost.

28 Vacuum servo unit – removal and refitting

1 Unscrew the brake master cylinder filler cap, place a piece of polythene over the filler neck and refit the cap. This will minimise hydraulic fluid loss when the servo is removed.
2 From under the right-hand front wing detach the intake ducting from the intake unit and then withdraw the intake unit from inside the engine compartment.
3 Disconnect the vacuum pipe from the one-way valve on the servo unit.
4 Remove the securing bracket from the end of the servo unit.
5 Unscrew the hydraulic pipe unions and carefully withdraw them from the servo. Protect the disconnected unions against possible dirt ingress.
6 Undo and remove the nuts securing the servo to its mounting bracket and lift away the unit.
7 Refitting is the reverse sequence to removal. Bleed the hydraulic system as described in Section 3 after refitting.

29 Vacuum servo unit – dismantling and reassembly

1 Grip the servo unit in a well padded vice by the slave cylinder body, with the air valve uppermost.
2 Remove the rubber pipe from the end cover connection.
3 Undo the screws securing the plastic air valve cover and lift off the cover assembly complete, which comprises the filter and valve. If the air valve is suspect, a new assembly which is part of the complete repair kit will have to be obtained – individual parts cannot be obtained separately. The dome containing these items is a snap fit into the air valve cover.
4 Remove the rubber diaphragm and its plastic support, and the three valve housing securing screws will then be revealed. Undo these and take off the housing and joint washer.
5 To get the air control valve piston out of its cylinder will require a low pressure inside the slave cylinder. This can be done by blocking one of the two hydraulic fluid unions on the slave cylinder with a finger and applying air pressure from a foot pump to the other. When it is out, remove the rubber cup from the piston.
6 The non-return valve, which is mounted in a rubber grommet, can be pushed out by thumb pressure. Remove the grommet also.
7 It is now necessary to remove the end cover from the main servo shell. This is a twist fit bayonet type of connection and to remove it

calls for an anti-clockwise twist as far as the stops in the cover will permit, when it will come off. Although there is a special tool for this (C2030) one can achieve the same result by remounting the servo on the car mounting bracket by the three end cover studs and gripping the shell and twisting it anti-clockwise. The end cover can be left on the mounting bracket.

8 Put the unit back into the vice as before. To remove the diaphragm it is not necessary to free the retaining key from the pushrod. Turn the diaphragm support so that the retaining key points downwards. Then supply light fluctuating pressure to the backplate against the main return spring and the retaining key will drop out.

9 Hold on to the diaphragm support and take it and the diaphragm and the return spring from the servo shell.

10 The bolts holding the servo shell to the slave cylinder are now exposed. Bend back the locking plate table from the bolt heads and remove the bolts, locking plate and abutment plate.

11 The shell can now be taken from the slave cylinder. Retrieve the washer between the two.

12 The pushrod can now be drawn from the slave cylinder together with piston assembly.

13 Slide the bearing, cup and spacer off the pushrod, noting the order and position in which they came off.

14 Prise the rubber seal off the slave piston.

15 If the rod is to be detached from the piston, the following action will be required, but a new retaining clip will be needed. It should not normally be necessary to separate them. Open up the retaining clip by twisting a small screwdriver in the join, and this will expose the connection pin which can be pushed out. This disconnects the slave piston from the connection rod. This unit is now completely dismantled.

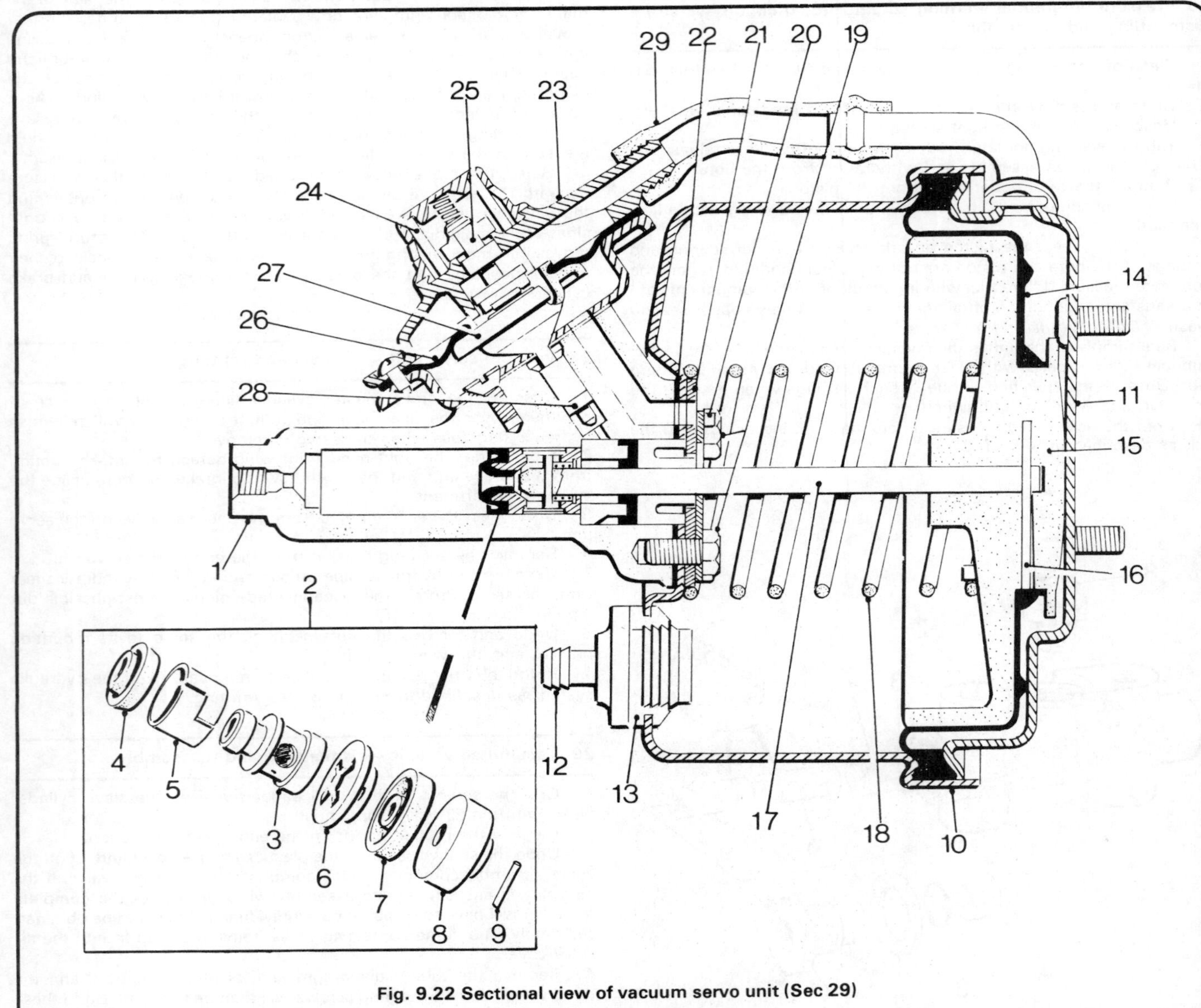

Fig. 9.22 Sectional view of vacuum servo unit (Sec 29)

1 Slave cylinder
2 Slave piston assembly
3 Slave piston
4 Seal
5 Retaining clip
6 Spacer
7 Cup
8 Bearing
9 Pin
10 Servo shell
11 End cover
12 Non-return valve
13 Rubber mounting
14 Main servo diaphragm
15 Diaphragm support
16 Retaining key
17 Pushrod
18 Main return spring
19 Servo shell retaining bolts
20 Locking plate
21 Abutment plate
22 Gasket
23 Air valve cover
24 Filter
25 Air valve
26 Air valve diaphragm
27 Diaphragm support
28 Air valve piston
29 Rubber pipe

16 Examine all rubber cups and seals for wear and renew as necessary. If the air valve unit is in good condition and it is only necessary to clean the filter, blow it through with a tyre foot pump. Do not use any cleaning fluids or lubricants on the filter.
17 Wash all slave cylinder components in clean hydraulic fluid, and remove any deposits from the slave cylinder walls in the same way. If the slave cylinder is scored then it must be replaced.
18 Reassembly must be done in very clean conditions as a single speck of grit in the wrong place can cause total malfunction. It is best to wash your hands, get new clean cloths and lay out all the components on a sheet of clean white paper. Five minutes extra attention now could save you another complete dismantling operation later.
19 Use clean hydraulic fluid as a lubricant when reassembling the hydraulic components.
20 If the piston and pushrod were separated, push the rod into the rear of the piston against the spring until the connection pin hole is open. Fit the pin followed by the retaining clip. It is important to ensure that the clip fits snugly in its groove. Any protrusions will score the cylinder wall.
21 Refit the rubber seal to the slave piston using only the fingers, ensuring that the lips of the seal face away from the pushrod.
22 Lubricate (with hydraulic fluid only) the cylinder bore and insert the piston. Then refit in correct order, over the pushrod the spacer, cup, and bearing, into the mouth of the slave cylinder. Ensure that each item placed into the cylinder has its sealing lips neither bent nor turned back, and that each is bedded individually in turn.
23 The servo shell is now refitted in the reverse order as given in paragraph 10. If the locking plate has been used more than once before (ie if the servo has already been twice dismantled) a new one should be fitted. Tighten the bolts evenly to the specified torque and tap up the locking plate tabs.
24 To refit the diaphragm, support and spring trap, pull out the pushrod as far as possible. Fit the spring and diaphragm support ensuring that the spring ends are correctly located over the abutment plate and the diaphragm support boss.
25 Press the diaphragm support over the pushrod with the key slot facing upwards, and when the groove in the pushrod and the slot in the diaphragm are lined up insert the key.
26 Ensuring that the support and diaphragm are quite clean and dry, fit the diaphragm to the support, gently stretching the inner edge to ensure that it seats properly in the groove of the support.
27 Smear the outer edge of the diaphragm with disc brake lubricant (not grease or hydraulic fluid). This prevents it from binding when the lid cover is refitted to the servo shell.
28 If no service tool is available, fix the end cover onto the vehicle mounting bracket, (if you did not leave it there when taking it off) using the normal mounting units. Offer up the servo unit to the end cover so that when twisted clockwise the pipe will line up with the elbow on the end cover when the turn is completely up to the stops.
29 With the unit back on the bench, refit the non-return valve and its mounting grommet.
30 To refit the air valve assembly, first fit the rubber piston cup to the spigot of the piston, ensuring that the lips face away from the spigot shoulder. Lubricate the cup with a little hydraulic fluid and insert it into the slave cylinder, taking care that the lips do not get bent back.
31 Fit the joint washer and valve housing to the slave cylinder using the three securing screws.
32 Fit the diaphragm support into the diaphragm and make sure that the inner ring fits snugly into the groove in the support. Then place the spigot of the support into the hole in the air valve piston. Use no lubricants.
33 Line up the screw holes in the diaphragm and the valve housing.
34 If the air filter and dome have been removed, now is the time to snap the complete assembly back into the air valve cover.
35 Place the valve cover over the diaphragm so that the projection in the cover engages the slots in the diaphragm. Refit all five securing screws finger tight. Tighten them down firmly, but not overtight, in a progressive and diagonal manner. This tightening sequence is important as the air valve must seat evenly and precisely. Any leak renders the whole servo inoperative.
36 Refit the rubber pipe from the valve cover port to the end cover elbow.

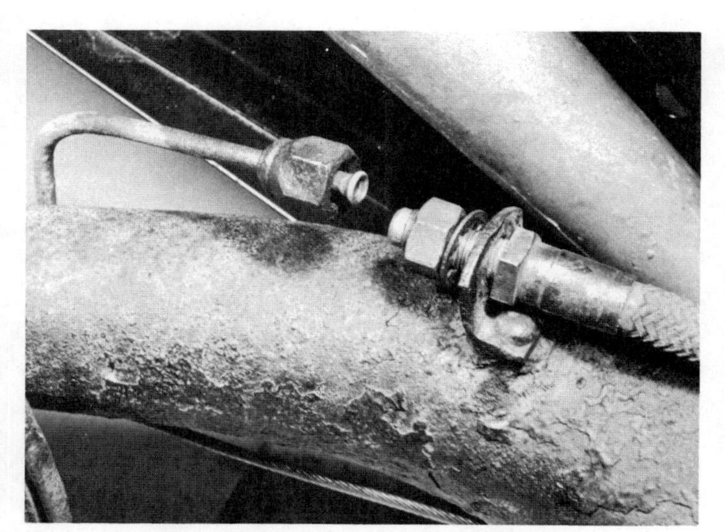
31.7 Removal of a rear flexible hose from the suspension arm

30 Brake pedal – removal and refitting

The brake pedal is removed together with the clutch pedal, and full information on the removal and refitting procedure will be found in Chapter 5.

31 Hydraulic pipes and hoses – general

1 Carefully examine all brake pipes/hoses, pipe hose connections and unions periodically.
2 First examine for signs of leakage where the pipe unions occur. Then examine the flexible hoses for signs of chafing and fraying and, of course, leakage. This is only a preliminary part of the flexible hose inspection, as exterior condition does not necessarily indicate the interior condition, which will be considered later.
3 The steel pipes must be examined carefully and methodically. They must be cleaned off and examined for any signs of dents, corrosion or other damage. Corrosion should be scraped off and, if the depth of pitting is significant, the pipes renewed. This is particularly likely in those areas underneath the vehicle body where the pipes are exposed and unprotected.
4 If any section of pipe is to be taken off, first wipe and then remove the fluid reservoir cap and place a piece of polythene over the reservoir neck. Refit the cap; this will help to prevent fluid loss during subsequent operations.
5 Rigid pipe removal is usually quite straightforward. The unions at each end are undone, the pipe and union pulled out, and the centre sections of the pipe removed from the body clips. Where the pipes are exposed to the full force of road and weather they can sometimes be very tight. As one can only use an open-ended spanner and the unions are not large, burring of the flats is not uncommon when attempting to undo them. For this reason a self-locking wrench is often the only way to remove a stubborn union.
6 To remove a flexible hose, wipe the unions and bracket free from dust and undo the union nut from the metal pipe end.
7 Next undo and remove the hose securing nut and washer and lift the end of the hose out of its mounting bracket (photo).
8 If a front hose is being removed it can now be unscrewed from the brake wheel cylinder. Take care not to lose the copper sealing washer from the end of the hose.
9 With the flexible hose removed, examine the internal bore. If it is blown through first, it should be possible to see through it. Any specks of rubber which come out, or signs of restriction in the bore, mean that the rubber lining is breaking up and the pipe must be renewed.
10 Rigid pipes which need renewing can usually be purchased at any garage where they have the pipe, unions and special tools to make them up. All they need to know is the total length of the pipe, the type of flare at each end with the union, and the length and thread of the union.
11 Refitment of the pipe is a straightforward reversal of the removal procedure. If the rigid pipes have been made up, it is best to get all the

sets (bends) in them before trying to install them. Also, if there are any acute bends, ask your supplier to put these in for you on a special tube bender, otherwise you may kink the pipe and thereby decrease the bore area and fluid flow.

12 With the pipes refitted, remove the polythene from the reservoir cap and bleed the system as described in Section 3.

32 Fault diagnosis – braking system

Symptom	Reason(s)
Excessive pedal travel	Adjustment needed Fluid level low (check for leaks or damaged pipes or hoses) Master cylinder seals defective
Brake pedal feels spongy	Air in system (check fluid level, inspect for leaks or damaged pipes or hoses) Master cylinder seals defective or mountings loose
Judder felt through brake pedal or steering wheel when braking	Brake drum(s) out of round or (if fitted) excessive disc run-out Brake backplate or disc caliper loose Brake linings or pads worn Steering or suspension components worn or loose – see Chapter 11
Excessive pedal pressure required to stop car	Brake linings or pads worn or contaminated Wheel cylinder(s) or caliper piston seized Servo defective or hoses disconnected (where applicable) Brake shoes incorrectly fitted New linings or pads not yet bedded in Incorrect grade of linings or pads fitted
Brakes pull to one side	Linings contaminated or badly worn Adjustment incorrect Linings renewed on one side only, or different grades on each side Wheel cylinder or caliper piston seized Tyre pressures incorrect Wheel alignment incorrect Steering or suspension damage
Brakes binding	Adjustment incorrect Master cylinder vent hole blocked Wheel cylinder or caliper piston seized Handbrake linkage seized Master cylinder defective

Chapter 10 Electrical system

For modifications, and information applicable to later models, see Supplement at end of manual

Contents

Specifications

Battery

Type	12 volt, negative earth
Capacity	30 to 50 amp hour at 20 hour rate

Dynamo

Type	Lucas C40/1
Maximum output	22 amps at 2250 rpm
Cut-in speed	1450 rpm at 13.5 volts
Field resistance	6.0 ohms
Minimum brush length	0.5 in (12.7 mm)
Brush spring tension	18 oz (510 g)

Control box

Type	Lucas RB106/2
Regulator:	
Open circuit setting at 3000 rpm (dynamo speed) at 68°F (20°C)	16.0 to 16.6 volts, decreasing by 1 volt for every increase of 18°F (10°C) above 68°F (20°C)
Cut-out:	
Cut-in voltage	12.7 to 13.3 volts
Drop-off voltage	8.5 to 11 volts
Reverse current	5.0 amps (maximum)

Alternator

Type	Lucas 11AC or 16ACR
Maximum output:	
11AC	43 amps
16ACR	34 amps
Minimum brush length:	
11AC	0.15 in (3.9 mm)
16ACR	0.3 in (7.5 mm)

Starter motor

Type	Lucas M35G or M35J
Number or brushes	4
Brush spring tension:	
M35G	15 to 25 oz (425 to 710 g)
M35J	28 oz (794 g)
Minimum brush length	0.3 in (8.0 mm)
Minimum commutator diameter (M35G)	1.2 in (30.4 mm)
Minimum commutator thickness (M35J)	0.08 in (2.03 mm)

Windscreen wiper motor

Type	Lucas 14W
Light running current (rack disconnected)	1.5 amps (normal speed), 2.0 amps (fast speed)
Brush spring pressure	5 to 7 oz (140 to 200g)
Minimum brush length	0.2 in (4.8 mm)
Armature endfloat	0.002 to 0.008 in (0.05 to 0.02 mm)
Maximum pull to move rack in guide tubes	6 lb (2.7 kg)

Wiper blades

Champion C-2901 (1973-on) or CS 26-01 (1969 to 1973)

Bulbs

	Wattage	Type
Headlights, LHD (except Europe – dip right)	50/40	415
Headlights, Europe (except France – dip vertical)	45/40	410
Headlights, France – dip vertical	45/40	411
Sidelights (bayonet type)	5	989
Sidelights (capless type)	5	501
Sidelights and front direction indicators	21/5	380
Direction indicators – front (UK only)	21	382
Direction indicators – rear	21	382
Direction indicator repeaters	4	233
Side marker lights, Canada only	4	222
Number plate light (Saloon)	6	254
Number plate light (Estate, Van and Pick-up)	5	989
Number plate light, Canada only	6	254
Panel and warning lights	2.2	987
Stop/tail lights	21/5	380
Reversing lights (where fitted)	21	382
Interior light	6	254
Illuminated switches	0.75	284
Seat belt warning light, Canada only	2	281
Heater panel illumination, Canada only	2	281
Sealed beam light units:		
Sealed beam with sidelights, dip left (UK only)	60/45	104
Sealed beam without sidelight, dip left (not UK)	60/54	101

1 General description

The electrical system is of the 12 volt negative earth type. The major components comprise a 12 volt battery, a voltage regulator and cut-out, a dynamo or alternator, a starter motor and various electrical accessories.

The battery supplies a steady current for the ignition, lighting and other electrical circuits, and provides a reserve of electricity when the current consumed by the electrical equipment exceeds that being produced by the dynamo or alternator.

The dynamo is of the two-brush type and works in conjunction with the voltage regulator and cut-out. It is cooled by a multi-bladed fan mounted behind the dynamo pulley, which blows air through cooling holes in the dynamo end brackets. The output of the dynamo is controlled by the voltage regulator; this ensures a high output if the battery is in a low state of charge or the demand from the electrical system is high, and a low output if the battery is fully charged and there is little demand from the electrical equipment.

Later Minis are fitted with an alternator, and further information on this unit will be found in subsequent Sections of this Chapter.

When fitting electrical accessories it is important (if they contain silicon diodes or transistors) that they are connected correctly, otherwise serious damage may result to the component concerned. Items such as radios, tape players and electronic tachometers, should all be checked for correct polarity before fitment.

For safety reasons, when carrying out any work on the electrical system, always disconnect the battery earth terminal. When removing the battery, disconnect the earth terminal first, and when refitting reconnect it last. If jumper cables are used to start the car, they must be connected correctly – positive to positive and negative to negative.

2 Battery – removal and refitting

1 The battery is located in a recess in the right-hand side of the luggage compartment floor on Saloon models, beneath the rear seat on Estate models, and behind the passenger seat on the Van and Pick-up.

2 Disconnect the negative and then the positive leads from the battery after first removing the retaining screws or nuts and bolts from the terminal posts (photo).

3 Remove the battery clamp and carefully lift the battery out of its compartment. Hold the battery upright to ensure that none of the electrolyte is spilled.

4 Refitting is a direct reversal of this procedure. **Note:** *Refit the*

2.2 Removing the battery earth terminal (Saloon model shown)

positive lead before the negative lead and smear the terminals with petroleum jelly. Never use an ordinary grease.

3 Battery – maintenance and inspection

1 Normal weekly battery maintenance consists of checking the electrolyte level of each cell to ensure that the separators are covered by $\frac{1}{4}$ in (6 mm) of electrolyte. If the level has fallen, top up the battery using distilled water only. Do not overfill. If a battery is overfilled or any electrolyte is spilled, immediately wipe away the excess as electrolyte attacks and corrodes any metal it comes into contact with very rapidly.
2 As well as keeping the terminals clean and covered with petroleum jelly, the top of the battery, and especially the top of the cells, should be kept clean and dry. This helps prevent corrosion and ensures that the battery does not become partially discharged by leakage through dampness and dirt.
3 Once every three months remove the battery and inspect the battery securing bolts, the battery clamp plate, tray and battery leads for corrosion (white fluffy deposits on the metal which are brittle to touch). If any corrosion is found clean off the deposit with ammonia and paint over the clean metal with an anti-rust/anti-acid paint.

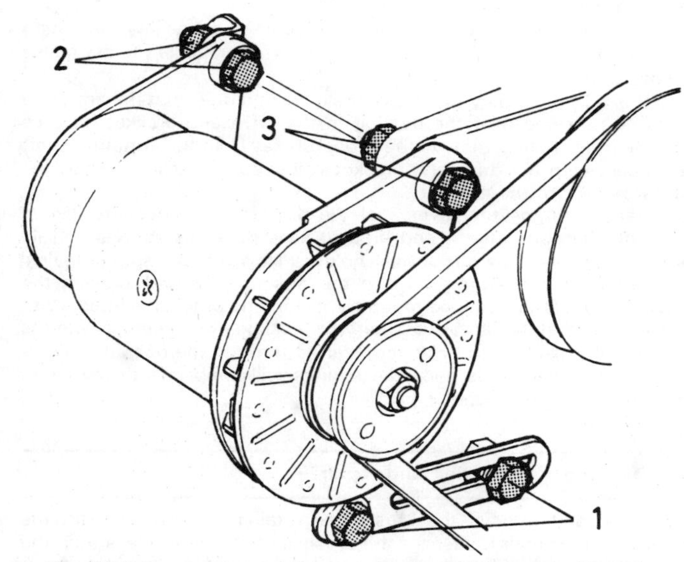

Fig. 10.1 Dynamo mountings and adjustment points (Sec 6)

1 Adjustment arm retaining nuts
2 Securing nut and bolt (rear)
3 Securing nut and bolt (front)

4 At the same time inspect the battery case for cracks. Cracks are frequently caused to the top of the battery case by pouring in distilled water in the middle of winter *after* instead of *before* a run. This gives the water no chance to mix with the electrolyte and so the former freezes and splits the battery case.
5 If topping up the battery becomes excessive and the case has been inspected for cracks that could cause leakage, but none are found, the battery is being overcharged.
6 With the battery on the bench at the three monthly interval check, measure the specific gravity with a hydrometer to determine the state of charge and condition of the electrolyte. There should be very little variation between the different cells, and if a variation in excess of 0.025 percent is present it will be due to either:

(a) Loss of electrolyte from the battery at some time caused by spillage or a leak, resulting in a drop in the specific gravity of the electrolyte when the deficiency was made up with distilled water instead of fresh electrolyte
(b) An internal short circuit caused by buckling of the plates or similar malady, pointing to the likelihood of total battery failure in the near future.

7 The specific gravity of the electrolyre for fully charged and discharged conditions, at the electrolyte temperature indicated, is listed in the table below.

Temperature	Specific gravity fully charged	Specific gravity fully discharged
100°F (38°)	*1.268*	*1.098*
90°F(32°C)	*1.272*	*1.102*
80°F(27°C)	*1.276*	*1.106*
70°F(21°C	*1.280*	*1.110*
60°F(16°C)	*1.284*	*1.114*
50°F(10°C)	*1.288*	*1.118*
40°F(4°C)	*1.292*	*1.22*
30°F(–1.5°C)	*1.296*	*1.126*

4 Battery – electrolyte replenishment

1 If the battery is in a fully charged state and one of the cells maintains a specific gravity reading which is 0.025 or more lower than the others, then it is likely that electrolyte has been lost from the cell at some time.
2 Top up the cell with a solution of 1 part sulphuric acid to 2.5 parts of water by volume, obtainable ready mixed from your local garage. If the cell is already fully topped-up, draw off some of the electrolyte with a pipette.

5 Battery – charging

1 In winter time when heavy demand is placed upon the battery, such as when starting from cold and much electrical equipment is continually in use, it is a good idea to occasionally have the battery fully charged from an external source at the rate of 3.5 to 4 amps.
2 Continue to charge the battery at this rate until no further rise in specific gravity is noted over a four hour period.
3 Alternatively, a trickle charger charging at the rate of 1.5 amps can be safely used overnight.
4 Special rapid boost charges which are claimed to restore the power of the battery in 1 to 2 hours are not recommended as they can cause serious damage to the battery plates, note that the temperature of the electrolyte should never exceed 100°F (37.8°C).

6 Dynamo – maintenance

1 Routine maintenance consists of checking the fanbelt condition and tension every 3000 miles (5000 km) and adding a few drops of engine oil to the dynamo rear bearing lubricating hole every 6000 miles (10 000 km).
2 The fanbelt should be tight enough to ensure that there is no

slip between the belt and the dynamo pulley. If a shrieking noise is heard from the engine when the unit is accelerated rapidly, then it is likely that the fanbelt is slipping. On the other hand, the belt must not be *too* tight otherwise the bearings will wear rapidly, causing dynamo failure or bearing seizure. Ideally 0.5 in (12 mm) of fanbelt deflection should be felt using light finger pressure at a point midway between the dynamo and crankshaft pulleys.
3 To adjust the fanbelt tension, slacken the two dynamo upper retaining bolts and lower retaining nut on the adjustment arm slightly and move the bottom of the dynamo outwards to increase the tension and inwards to decrease it. If the fanbelt tension is bing increased, use a large screwdriver or flat bar placed between the dynamo and cylinder block to lever the dynamo outwards and hold it in position until the retaining nut is tightened.

7 Dynamo – testing in position

1 If the ignition warning light fails to go out with the engine running, or if the battery does not appear to be receiving a charge, the dynamo may be at fault and should be tested while still in position on the engine as follows.
2 First check the fanbelt condition and adjust the tension if necessary.
3 Check the leads from the dynamo to the control box (D and F), ensuring that they are firmly attached and that one has not come loose from its terminal.
4 To test the dynamo, first ensure that all electrical equipment is switched off and then pull the leads off the two dynamo terminals. Now join the two dynamo terminals together using a short length of non-insulated wire.
5 Attach to the centre of this short length of wire the positive clip of a 0 to 20 volt voltmeter. Connect the negative clip of the voltmeter to a good earth on the dynamo yoke.
6 Start the engine and allow it to run at a fast idle. A reading of approximately 15 volts should now be indicated on the voltmeter. If no reading is recorded, it is quite likely that the dynamo brushes or brush connections are at fault. If a very low reading of approximately 1 volt is observed then the field winding may be suspect. If a reading between 4 and 6 volts is recorded it is quite likely that the armature winding is faulty.
7 If any of the above voltmeter readings are recorded, the dynamo should be removed from the car for inspection and repair as described in the following Sections.
8 If the voltmeter readings are satisfactory, switch off the engine and disconnect the voltmeter. With the temporary link still in position, reconnect the two leads to the dynamo terminals and then disconnect the D and F terminals at the control box. Connect the positive clip of the voltmeter to the D lead and the negative clip to earth. Start the engine and allow it to run at a fast idle. The reading on the voltmeter should be identical to that recorded at the dynamo. If no voltage is recorded there is a break in the wire. If the voltage is less than previously recorded check the terminals for corrosion and the wire for chafing. Test the F lead in a similar fashion. If both readings are the same as recorded at the dynamo, then it will be necessary to test the control box as described in Sections 14 and 15.
9 On completion of the tests remove the temporary link from the dynamo terminals and reconnect the leads to the dynamo and control box.

8 Dynamo – removal and refitting

1 Slacken the two dynamo upper retaining bolts and the nut on the adjustment arm. Move the dynamo towards the engine and lift the fanbelt off the pulley.
2 Disconnect the two leads from the dynamo terminals. **Note** *If the ignition coil is mounted on the dynamo, slide back the rubber cover and disconnect the high tension lead from the centre of the coil. Release the two low tension leads (photo).*
3 Undo and remove the lower bolt securing the adjustment arm to the dynamo and remove the two upper retaining bolts, nuts and washers. The dynamo can now be lifted off the engine.
4 Refitting the dynamo is the reverse sequence to removal, ensuring that the fanbelt is correctly tensioned as described in Section 6 before fully tightening the retaining bolts.

8.2 Remove the coil leads

5 If a new or exchange dynamo is being fitted, ensure that the unit is correctly polarised as described below before installing.
6 In order for the dynamo to function it must be correctly polarised to suit the electrical installation to which it is being fitted. To polarise the dynamo to suit a negative earth system, connect a suitable length of wire from the battery earth terminal to the dynamo yoke or end bracket. Now connect another length of wire to the battery positive terminal and flick the other end of the wire several times on the dynamo F (small) terminal. This will induce a magnetism of the correct polarity into the dynamo field windings.
7 The correctly polarised dynamo can now be fitted to the car.

9 Dynamo – dismantling and reassembly

1 If the ignition coil is mounted on the dynamo, undo and remove the clamp retaining bolts and lift off the coil.
2 Undo and remove the two long screws from the rear of the dynamo and lift off the commutator end bracket.
3 Now lift out the armature complete with drive end bracket and pulley from the dynamo yoke.
4 Support the armature between well-protected vice jaws and undo and remove the pulley retaining nut and washer. Slide off the pulley followed by the fan.
5 It is only necessary to remove the drive end bracket if the armature is to be renewed or if the bearing in the drive end bracket requires attention. To do this, remove the Woodruff key from the armature shaft and then, with the drive end bracket will supported, tap or press the armature out of the bearing.
6 Reassembly is the reverse of the dismantling procedure. When refitting the commutator end bracket ease back the springs and lift the brushes half way out of their holders. Now rest the spring against the side of the brush to hold it in this position. This will prevent the brushes from fouling the commutator as the end bracket is fitted. With the end bracket in place, push the brushes down into contact with the commutator using a screwdriver inserted through the openings in the end bracket. As this is done the springs will jump into their correct position over the brushes.

10 Dynamo – inspection and repair

1 Undo and remove the brush lead retaining screws and lift the brushes out of their holders. If the brushes have worn to less than the minimum specified length, they must be renewed.
2 Check that the brushes slide freely and easily in their holders. If either of the brushes has a tendency to stick, clean the brushes with a petrol moistened rag, and if still stiff, lightly polish the sides of the brush with a very fine file until the brush moves quite freely and easily in its holder.

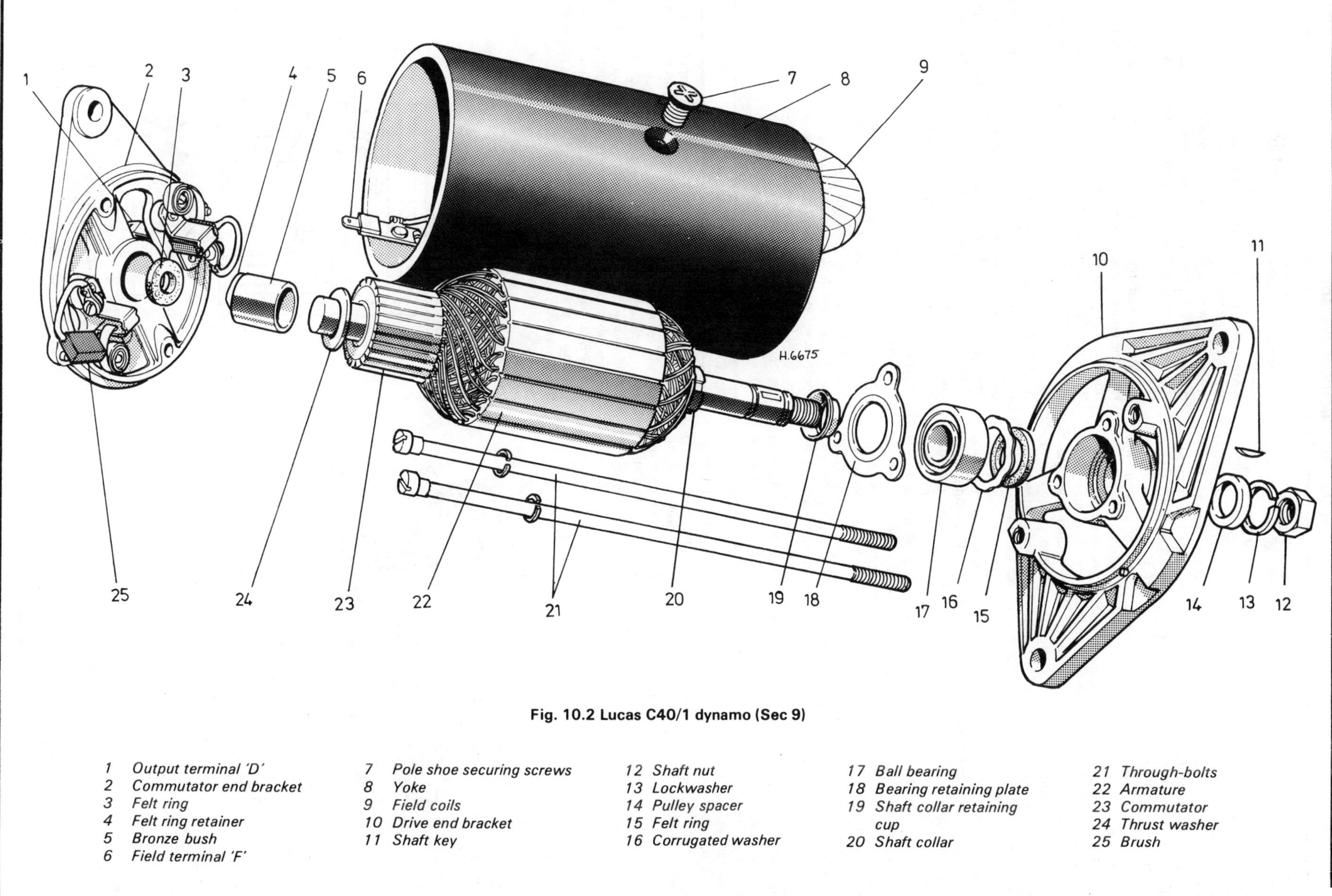

Fig. 10.2 Lucas C40/1 dynamo (Sec 9)

1 Output terminal 'D'
2 Commutator end bracket
3 Felt ring
4 Felt ring retainer
5 Bronze bush
6 Field terminal 'F'
7 Pole shoe securing screws
8 Yoke
9 Field coils
10 Drive end bracket
11 Shaft key
12 Shaft nut
13 Lockwasher
14 Pulley spacer
15 Felt ring
16 Corrugated washer
17 Ball bearing
18 Bearing retaining plate
19 Shaft collar retaining cup
20 Shaft collar
21 Through-bolts
22 Armature
23 Commutator
24 Thrust washer
25 Brush

3 If the brushes are in a satisfactory condition and are to be re-used, ensure that they are refitted in the same holders from which they were removed. Check the tension of the brush springs using a small spring balance. If the tension is insufficient, renew the springs.
4 Check the condition of the commutator. If the surface is dirty or blackened, clean it with a petrol dampened rag. If the commutator is in good condition, the surface will be smooth and quite free from pits or burnt areas, and the insulated segments clearly defined.
5 If, after the commutator has been cleaned, pits and burnt spots are still present, then wrap a strip of glass paper round the commutator and rotate the armature.
6 In extreme cases of wear the commutator can be mounted in a lathe and with the lathe turning at high speed, a very fine cut may be taken off the commutator. Then polish the commutator with glass paper. If the commutator has worn so that the insulators between the segments are level with the top of the segments, then undercut the insulators to a depth of 0.03 in (0.79 mm). Th best tool to use for this purpose is half a hacksaw blade ground to the thickness of the insulator, and with the handle end of the blade covered in insulating tape to make it comfortable to hold. On later models using commutators of the moulded type, the commutator should not be undercut more than 0.020 in (0.508 mm) deep, or 0.040 in (1.016 mm) wide.
7 Check the armature for open or short circuited windings. It is a good indication of an open circuited armature when the commutator segments are burnt. If th armature has short circuited, the commutator segments will be very badly burnt, and the overheated armature windings badly discoloured. If open or short circuits are suspected, then test by substituting the suspect armature for a new one.
8 Check the resistance of the field coils. To do this, connect an ohmmeter between the field terminal and the yoke, and note the reading on the ohmmeter. If the ohmmeter reading is infinity, this indicates an open circuit in the field winding. If the ohmmeter reading is below 5 ohms, this indicates that one of the field coils is faulty and must be renewed.
9 Field coil renewal involves the use of a wheel-operated screwdriver, a soldering iron, caulking and riveting and this operation is considered to be beyond the scope of most owners. Therefore, if the field coils are at fault, either purchase a rebuilt dynamo, or take the casing to a reputable electrical engineering works for new field coils to be fitted.

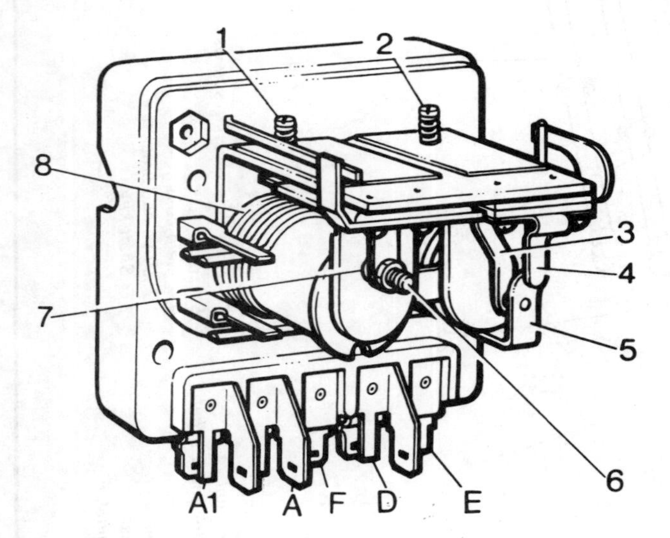

Fig. 10.3 Control box components (Sec 14)

1 *Regulator adjusting screw*
2 *Cut-out adjusting screw*
3 *Fixed contact blade*
4 *Stop arm*
5 *Armature tongue and moving contact*
6 *Regulator fixed contact screw*
7 *Regulator moving contact*
8 *Regulator series windings*

11 Dynamo bearings – removal and refitting

Note: *With the dynamo partially dismantled, check the condition of the bearings. They must be renewed when wear has reached such a state that they allow visible side movement of the armature shaft. A bush bearing is fitted to the commutator end bracket and a ball bearing to the drive end bracket. To renew the bush bearing proceed as follows.*

1 With a suitable extractor, pull out the old bush from the commutator end bracket. Alternatively screw a $\frac{5}{8}$ in (7.9 mm) tap into the bush and pull out the bush together with the tap.
2 Note that the bush bearing is of the porous bronze type, and it is essential that it is allowed to stand in engine oil for at least 24 hours before fitting.
3 Carefully fit the new bush into the endplate, pressing it in until the end of the bearing is flush with the inner side of the endplate. If available press the bush in with a smooth shouldered mandrel the same diameter as the armature shaft. To renew the ball bearing fitted to the drive end bracket, remove the armature from the end bracket, as detailed in Section 9 and then proceed as follows.
4 Drill out the rivets which hold the bearing retainer plate to the end bracket and lift off the plate.
5 Press out the bearing from the end bracket and remove the corrugated washer and felt washer from the bearing housing.
6 Thoroughly clean the bearing housing and the new bearing and pack with high melting-point grease.
7 Place the felt washer and corugated washer, in that order, in the end bracket bearing housing, and then press in the new bearing.
8 Refit the plate and fit new rivets opening out the rivet ends to hold the plate securely in position.

12 Control box – general description

The control box comprises the voltage regulator and the cut-out. The voltage regulator controls the output from the dynamo depending on the state of the battery and the demands of the electrical equipment, and ensures that the battery is not over-charged. The cut-out is really an automatic switch and connects the dynamo to the battery when the dynamo is turning fast enough to produce a charge. Similarly it disconnects the battery from the dynamo when the engine is idling or stationary so that the battery does not discharge through the dynamo.

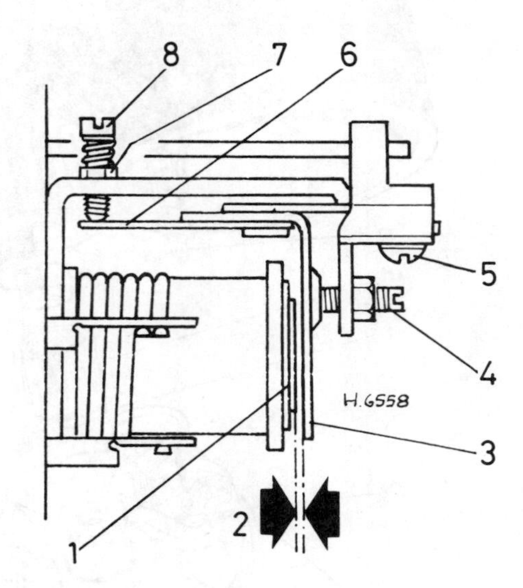

Fig. 10.4 Mechanical setting of regulator (Sec 14)

1 *Core face and shim*
2 *0.021 in (0.533 mm)*
3 *Armature*
4 *Fixed contact adjustment screw*
5 *Armature securing screws*
6 *Armature tension spring*
7 *Locknut*
8 *Voltage adjusting screw*

13 Cut-out and voltage regulator contacts – maintenance

1 Every 12 000 miles (20 000 km) check the cut-out and regulator contacts. If they are dirty or rough or burnt, place a piece of fine glasspaper (do not use emery paper or carborundum paper) between the cut-out contacts, close them manually, and draw the glasspaper through several times.
2 Clean the regulator contacts in exactly the same way, but use emery or carborundum paper *and not glasspaper.* Carefully clean both sets of contacts from all traces of dust with a rag moistened in methylated spirit.

14 Voltage regulator – adjustment

1 If the battery and dynamo are in sound condition but the operation of the charging circuit is still suspect, then the voltage regulator and cut-out in the control box should be checked, and if necessary adjusted.
2 Check the regulator settings by removing the leads A and A1 from the control box and joining them together using a short length of wire. Connect the positive clip of a 0 to 20 volt voltmeter to the D terminal of the control box, and the negative clip to a good earth.
3 Start the engine and slowly increase its speed until the voltmeter needle flicks and then steadies. This should occur at about 2000 rpm.
4 If the voltage at which the needle steadies is outside the limits listed in the table, switch off the engine, remove the control box cover and turn the regulator adjusting screw a fraction of a turn at a time, clockwise to increase the setting and anti-clockwise to decrease it. Recheck the voltage reading after each adjustment.

Air temperature	Open circuit voltage
10°C or 50°F	*16.1 to 16.7*
20°C or 68°F	*16.0 to 16.6*
30°C or 86°F	*15.9 to 16.5*
40°C or 104°F	*15.8 to 16.4*

It is essential that the adjustments be completed within 30 seconds of starting the engine otherwise the heat from the shunt coil will affect the readings.

15 Cutout – adjustment

1 With the control box A and A1 leads joined together, and the voltmeter connected as described in the previous Section, the cut-in voltage can be checked, and if necessary adjusted, as follows.
2 Switch on the headlights to provide an electrical load, start the engine and slowly increase its speed. The voltage reading will rise steadily, drop back and then rise again. The point reached just before the drop back should be between 12.7 and 13.3 volts.
3 If the reading obtained is outside these limits, switch off the engine and turn the cut-out adjusting screw a fraction of a turn at a time clockwise to raise the voltage and anti-clockwise to lower it. Recheck the voltage reading after each adjustment. As with the voltage regulator, it is essential that the adjustments be completed within 30 seconds of starting the engine, otherwise the heat from the shunt coil will affect the readings.
4 After completing the adjustments remove the voltmeter, disconnect the control box leads and refit the cover.

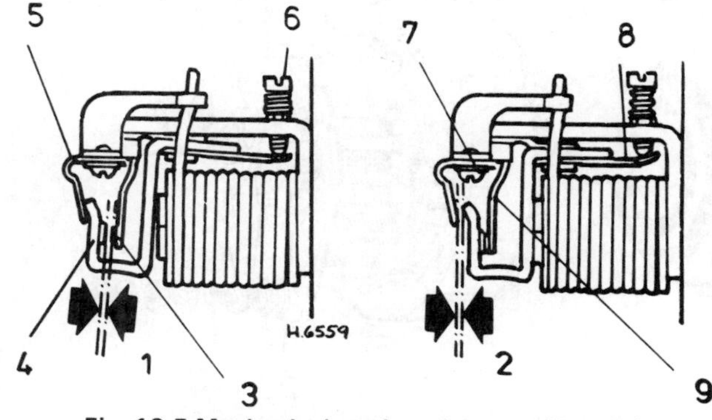

Fig. 10.5 Mechanical setting of cut-out (Sec 15)

1 *0.01 to 0.02 in (0.25 to 0.51 mm)*
2 *0.030 in (0.76 mm)*
3 *Follow through – 0.01 to 0.02 in (0.25 to 0.51 mm)*
4 *Armature tongue and moving contact*
5 *Stop arm*
6 *Output adjusting screw*
7 *Armature securing screw*
8 *Armature tension spring*
9 *Fixed contact blade*

16 Alternator – general description

Later Mini models are equipped with an alternator in place of the dynamo and control box. The Lucas 11AC alternator and separate 4TR control unit was used initially, but this has now been superseded by the 16ACR alternator with control unit incorporated.

Both types of alternator are similar in construction, comprising basically an aluminium casing, housing a three-phase star connected stator. A rotor carrying the field windings rotates within the stator and is driven by the fanbelt. The alternator output is controlled by a voltage regulator located in the separate control unit on the 11AC alternator and contained within the end housing on the 16ACR machine.

As its name implies, the alternator generates alternating current (ac) as opposed to direct current (dc) generated by the dynamo. The alternating current is rectified by diodes, located in the alternator end housing, into direct current, which is the current required for battery charging.

The main advantage of the alternator over its predecessor, the dynamo, lies in its ability to provide a high charge at low revolutions. Driving slowly in heavy traffic with a dynamo invariably means no charge is reaching the battery. In similar conditions, even with the wiper, heater, lights and perhaps radio switched on the alternator will ensure a charge reaches the battery.

17 Alternator – special procedures

In order to protect the sensitive electronic components in the alternator, the following precautions must always be observed when working on this unit or any other part of the car electrical system.

a) All alternator systems covered by this manual use a negative earth. Even the simplest mistake of connecting a battery the wrong way round could burn out the alternator diodes in a matter of seconds
(b) Never disconnect the battery when the engine is running
(c) Before disconnecting any wiring in the system, the engine ignition should be switched off. This will minimise accidental short circuits.
(d) The alternator must never be run with the output wire disconnected
(e) Always disconnect the battery from the car's electrical system if an external charging source is being used
(f) Do not use test wire connections that could move accidentally and short circuit against nearby terminals. Short circuits will not blow fuses – they will blow diodes or transistors
(g) Always disconnect the battery cables and alternator output lead before carrying out any electric welding work on the car

18 Alternator – maintenance

1 The alternator has been designed for the minimum amount of maintenance in service, the only item requiring regular attention being the fanbelt. The fanbelt should be carefully inspected every 3000 miles (5000 km) and its tension checked and, if necessary, adjusted as follows.
2 The fanbelt should be tight enough to ensure that there is no slip between the belt and alternator pulley. If a shrieking noise is heard from the engine when accelerated rapidly, then it is likely that the belt is slipping. On the other hand the belt must not be too tight, otherwise the bearings will wear rapidly. Ideally 0.5 in (12 mm) of fanbelt deflection should be felt using light finger pressure at a point midway

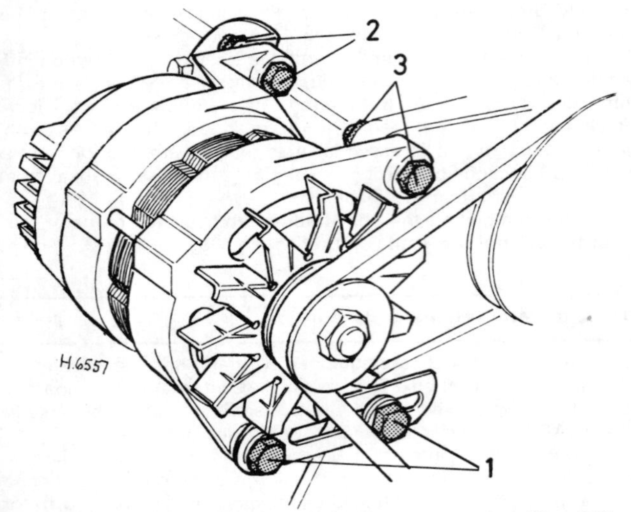

Fig. 10.6 Alternator mounting and adjustment points (Sec 18)

1 *Adjustment arm fixings*
2 *Securing nut and nut (rear)*
3 *Securing nut and bolt (front)*

between the alternator and crankshaft pulleys.

3 To adjust the tension slacken the two alternator upper mounting bolts and nuts, and the lower retaining nut on the adjustment arm slightly. Move the bottom of the alternator outwards to increase the tension and inwards to decrease it. If the tension is being increased use a large screwdriver or flat bar placed between the alternator and cylinder block to lever the unit outwards and hold it in position until the retaining nut is tightened.

19 Alternator – fault tracing and rectification

Due to the specialist knowledge and equipment required to test or repair an alternator, it is recommended that if the performance is suspect, the car be taken to an automobile electrician who will have the facilities for such work. Because of this recommendation, information is limited to the inspection and renewal of the brushes. Should the alternator not charge or the system be suspect, the following points should be checked before seeking further assistance:

(a) Check the fanbelt tension as described in Section 18
(b) Check the battery as described in Section 3
(c) Check all electrical connections for cleanliness and security

20 Alternator – removal and refitting

Note: *If the car is fitted with exhaust emission control equipment, it will be necessary to remove the air pump and drivebelt as described in*

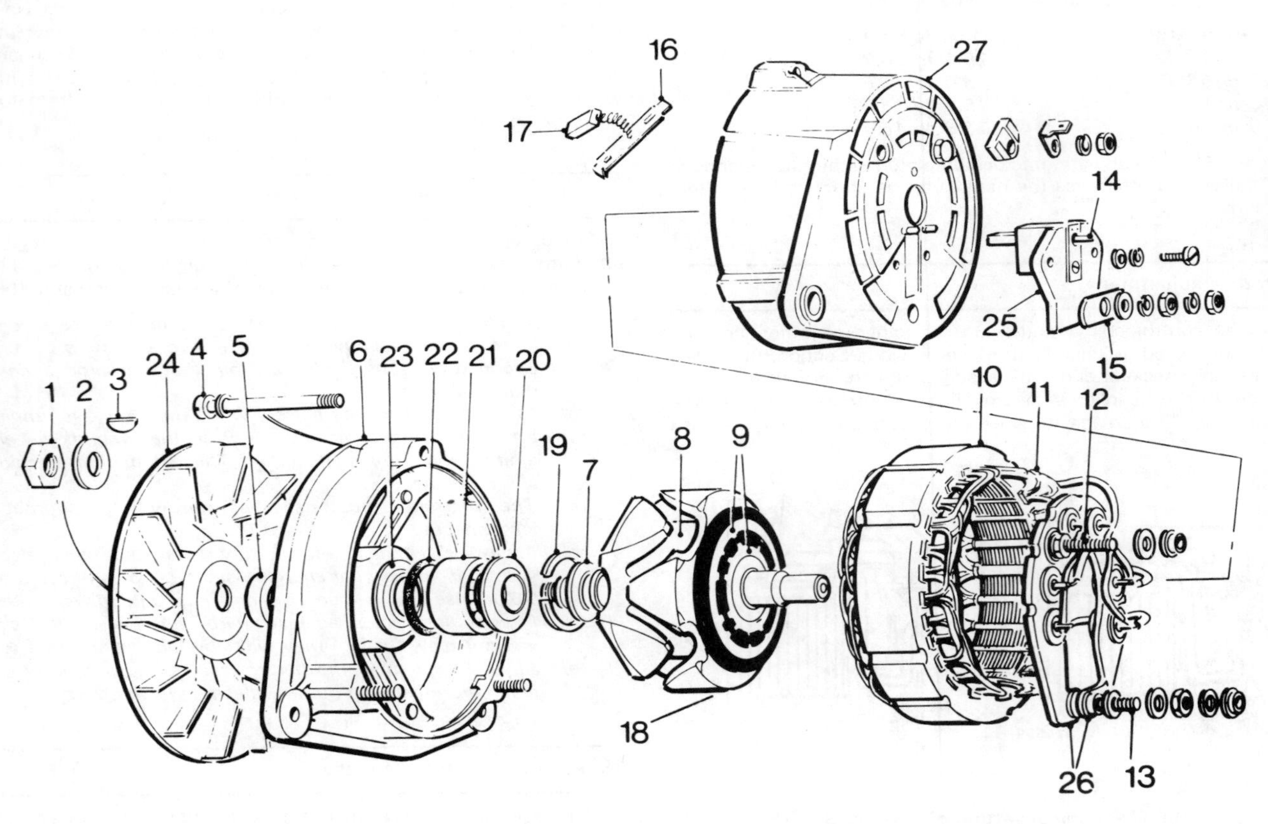

Fig. 10.7 Exploded view of the Lucas 11AC alternator (Sec 21)

1 *Shaft nut*
2 *Spring washer*
3 *Key*
4 *Through-bolt*
5 *Distance collar*
6 *Drive end bracket*
7 *Jump ring shroud*
8 *Rotor (field) winding*
9 *Slip rings*
10 *Stator laminations*
11 *Stator windings*
12 *Warning light terminal*
13 *Output terminal*
14 *Field terminal blade*
15 *Output terminal plastic strip*
16 *Terminal blade retaining tongue*
17 *Brush*
18 *Rotor*
19 *Bearing circlip*
20 *Bearing retaining plate*
21 *Ball bearing*
22 *O-ring oil seal*
23 *O-ring retaining washer*
24 *Fan*
25 *Brushbox*
26 *Heat sink assemblies*
27 *Slip ring end covers*

Chapter 3 to provide access to the alternator.

1 On models fitted with an ignition shield over the front of the engine release the three retaining lugs and lift off the shield.

2 Release the spring clip and disconnect the wiring connector from the rear of the alternator.

3 Slacken the alternator adjusting arm nut and the bolt securing the adjusting arm to the alternator.

4 Slacken the two upper mounting nuts and bolts, move the alternator toward the engine and slip the fanbelt off the pulley.

5 Remove the two upper mounting nuts and bolts and the bolt securing the adjusting arm to the alternator. Lift the alternator off the engine.

6 Refitting is the reverse sequence to removal. Ensure that the fanbelt is correctly tensioned as described in Section 18 before finally tightening the mounting and adjustment arm bolts.

21 Alternator brushes – removal, inspection and refitting

11AC alternator

1 Remove the alternator from the car as described in Section 20.

2 To remove the brushes, undo and remove the nut and spring washer. The large Lucar terminal and the plastic strip from the output terminal.

3 Undo and remove the two securing screws and withdraw the brush box. Note that there are two small washers between the brush box and end bracket.

4 Close up the retaining tongue at the root of each terminal blade and withdraw the brush, spring and terminal assemblies from the brush box.

5 With the brushes removed, measure their length, and renew them if worn to less than the minimum specified length.

6 Check that the brushes slide smoothly in their holders. Any sticking tendency may first be rectified by wiping with a petrol moistened cloth, or if this fails, by carefully polishing with a very fine file where any binding marks may appear.

7 Refitting the brushes is the reverse sequence to removal. When refitting the terminal blades to the brush box bend the retaining tongue, at the root of each blade, out slightly to retain the blade in position.

16ACR alternator

8 Remove the alternator from the car as described in Section 20.

9 Undo and remove the two retaining screws and lift off the moulded end cover.

10 Detach the cable from the terminal blade on the outer of the three rectifier plates. Also detach the cable from the blade between the middle and inner of the three rectifier plates.

11 Undo and remove the four screws securing the brush assemblies to the brush holder.

12 Undo and remove the screw securing the surge protection diode cable to the brush holder.

13 Finally undo and remove the three bolts and lift off the brush holder and regulator assembly. Note that there is a small leaf spring fitted at the side of the inner brush.

14 With the brushes and brush holder removed, measure the brush

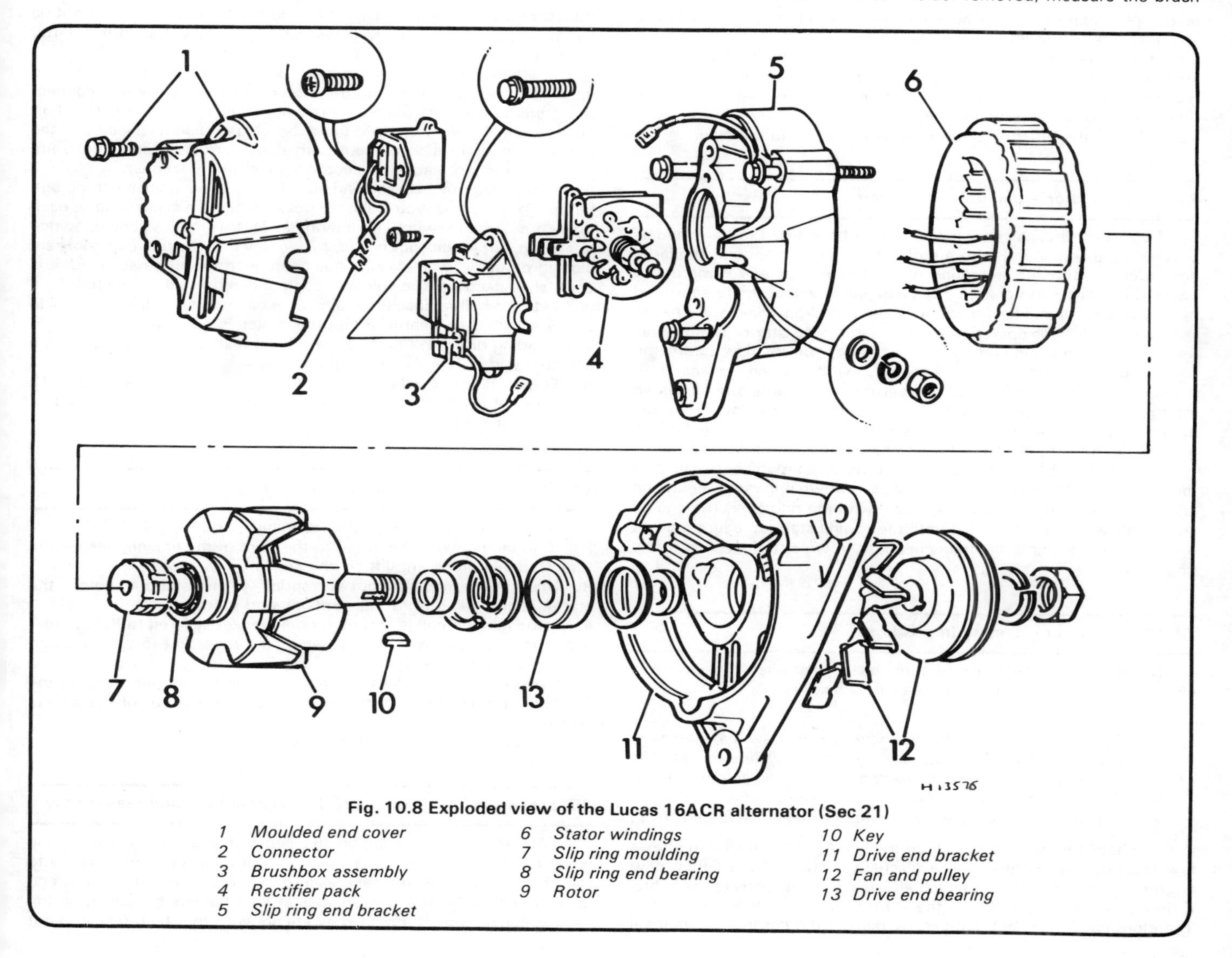

Fig. 10.8 Exploded view of the Lucas 16ACR alternator (Sec 21)

1 Moulded end cover
2 Connector
3 Brushbox assembly
4 Rectifier pack
5 Slip ring end bracket
6 Stator windings
7 Slip ring moulding
8 Slip ring end bearing
9 Rotor
10 Key
11 Drive end bracket
12 Fan and pulley
13 Drive end bearing

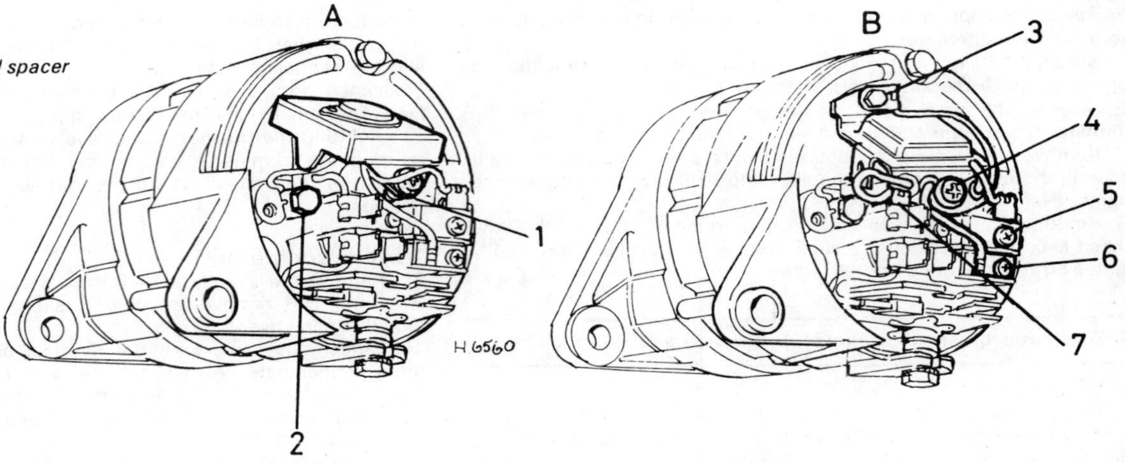

A 11TR regulator
B 8TR regulator
1 Mounting screw and spacer
2 Earth (–)
3 Earth (–)
4 Mounting screw
5 Field (F)
6 Positive (+)
7 B +

Fig. 10.9 View of the alternator regulator connections (Sec 21)

length protruding from the holder and renew the brushes if worn to less than the minimum specified length.
15 Check that the brushes slide smoothly in their holders. Any sticking tendency may first be rectified by wiping with a petrol moistened cloth, or if this fails, by carefully polishing with a very fine file where any binding marks may appear.
16 Refitting the brushes is the reverse sequence to removal.

22 Starter motor – general description

Two types of Lucas starter motor have been fitted to Mini models covered by this manual. Both are of the inertia type and are similar in construction, with the exception of the brush gear and commutator layout. The starter motors are interchangeable and both are energized by a separate solenoid switch mounted on the front inner wing panel.

The principle of operation of the inertia type starter motor is as follows: when the ignition switch is turned, current flows from the battery to the starter motor solenoid switch, which causes it to become energised. Its internal plunger moves inwards and closes an internal switch, so allowing full starting current to flow from the battery to the starter motor. This creates a powerful magnetic field to be induced into the field coils which causes the armature to rotate.

Mounted on helical splines is the drive pinion which, because of the sudden rotation of the armature, is thrown forwards along the armature shaft and so into engagement with the ring gear. The engine crankshaft will then be rotated until the engine starts to operate on its own and, at this point, the drive pinion is thrown out of mesh with the ring gear.

23 Starter motor – testing in position

1 If the starter motor fails to turn the engine when the switch is operated there are four possible reasons why:

(1) The battery is faulty
(b) The electrical connections between the switch, solenoid, battery and starter motor are somewhere failing to pass the necesary current from the battery through the starter to earth
(c) The solenoid switch is faulty
(d) The starter motor is either jammed or electrically defective

2 To check the battery, switch on the headlights. If they dim after a few seconds, the battery is in a discharged state. If the lights glow brightly, operate the starter switch and see what happens to the lights. If they dim, power is reaching the starter motor but failing to turn it. Therefore check it is not jammed by placing the car in gear (manual transmission only) and rocking it to and fro. Should the motor not be jammed, it will have to be removed for proper inspection. If the starter turns slowly when switched on, proceed to the next check.
3 If, when the starter switch is operated, the lights stay bright, insufficient power is reaching the motor. Remove the battery connections, starter/solenoid power connections and the engine earth strap and thoroughly clean and refit them. Smear petroleum jelly around the battery connections to prevent corrosion. Corroded connections are the most frequent cause of electric system malfunctions.
4 When the above checks and cleaning tasks have been carried out, but without success, you will have possibly heard a clicking noise each time the starter switch is operated. This is the solenoid switch operating, but it does not necessarily follow that the main contacts are closing properly (if no clicking has been heard from the solenoid, it is certainly defective). The solenoid contact can be checked by putting a voltmeter or bulb across the main cable connection of the starter side of the solenoid and earth. When the switch is operated, there should be a reading or lighted bulb. If there is no reading or lighted bulb, the solenoid unit is faulty and should be renewed.
5 Finally, if it is established that the solenoid is not faulty and 12 volts are getting to the starter, then the motor is faulty and should be removed for inspection.

24 Starter motor – removal and refitting

1 Disconnect the battery earth terminal.
2 If an ignition shield is fitted to the front of the engine, release the three retaining lugs and lift off the shield.
3 Undo and remove the nut and spring washer and then detach the starter motor cable from the terminal stud (photo).
4 If the ignition coil is mounted on a bracket secured to the cylinder head, undo and remove the nut securing the bracket to the head and place the coil to one side.
5 Undo and remove the two bolts securing the starter motor to the flywheel housing, then lift the motor upwards and out of the engine compartment.
6 Refitting is the reverse sequence to removal.

25 Starter motor (Lucas M35G) – dismantling and reassembly

1 With the starter motor on the bench, loosen the screw on the cover band and slip the cover band off. With a piece or wire bent into the shape of a hook, lift back each of the brush springs in turn and check the movement of the brushes in their holders by pulling on the flexible connectors. If the brushes are so worn that their faces do not

24.3 Unscrew the nut securing the starter motor cable

rest against the commutator, or if the ends of the brush leads are exposed on their working face, they must be renewed.

2 If any of the brushes tend to stick in their holders then wash them with a petrol moistened cloth and, if necessary, lightly polish the sides of the brush with a very fine file, until the brushes move quite freely in their holders.

3 If the surface of the commutator is dirty or blackened, clean it with a petrol dampened rag. Secure the starter motor in a vice and check it by connecting a heavy gauge cable between the starter motor terminal and a 12 volt battery.

4 Connect the cable from the other battery terminal to earth in the starter motor body. If the motor turns at high speed it is in good order.

5 If the starter motor still fails to function or if it is wished to renew the brushes, then it is necessary to further dismantle the motor.

6 Lift the brush springs with the wire hook and lift all four brushes out of their holders one at a time.

7 Remove the terminal nuts and washers from the terminal post on the commutator end backet.

8 Unscrew the two through-bolts which hold the endplates together and pull off the commutator end bracket. Also remove the drive end bracket, which will come away complete with the armature.

9 At this stage if the brushes are to be renewed, their flexible connectors must be unsoldered and the connectors of new brushes soldered in their place. Check that the new brushes move freely in their holders as detailed above. If cleaning the commutator with petrol fails to remove all the burnt areas and spots, then wrap a piece of glasspaper round the commutator and rotate the armature. If the commutator is very badly worn, remove the drivegear as detailed in Section 27. Then mount the armature in a lathe, and with the lathe turning at high speed, take a very fine cut out of the commutator and finish the surface by polishing with glass paper. Do not undercut the mica insulators between the commutator segments.

10 With the starter motor dismantled, test the four field coils for an open circuit. Connect a 12 volt battery with a 12 volt bulb in one of the leads between the field terminal post and the tapping point of the field coils to which the brushes are connected. An open circuit is proven by the bulb not lighting.

11 If the bulb lights, it does not necessarily mean that the field coils are in order, as there is a possibility that one of the coils will be earthing to the starter yoke or pole shoes. To check this, remove the lead from the brush connector and place it against a clean portion of the starter yoke. If the bulb lights the field coils are earthing Renewal of the field coils calls for the use of a wheel-operated screwdriver, a soldering iron, caulking and riveting operations and is beyond the scope of the majority of owners. The starter yoke should be taken to a reputable electrical engineering works for new field coils to be fitted. Alternatively, purchase an exchange Lucas starter motor.

12 If the armature is damaged, this will be evident after visual inspection. Look for signs of burning, discoloration, and for conductors that have lifted away from the commutator. Reassembly is a straight reversal of the dismantling procedure.

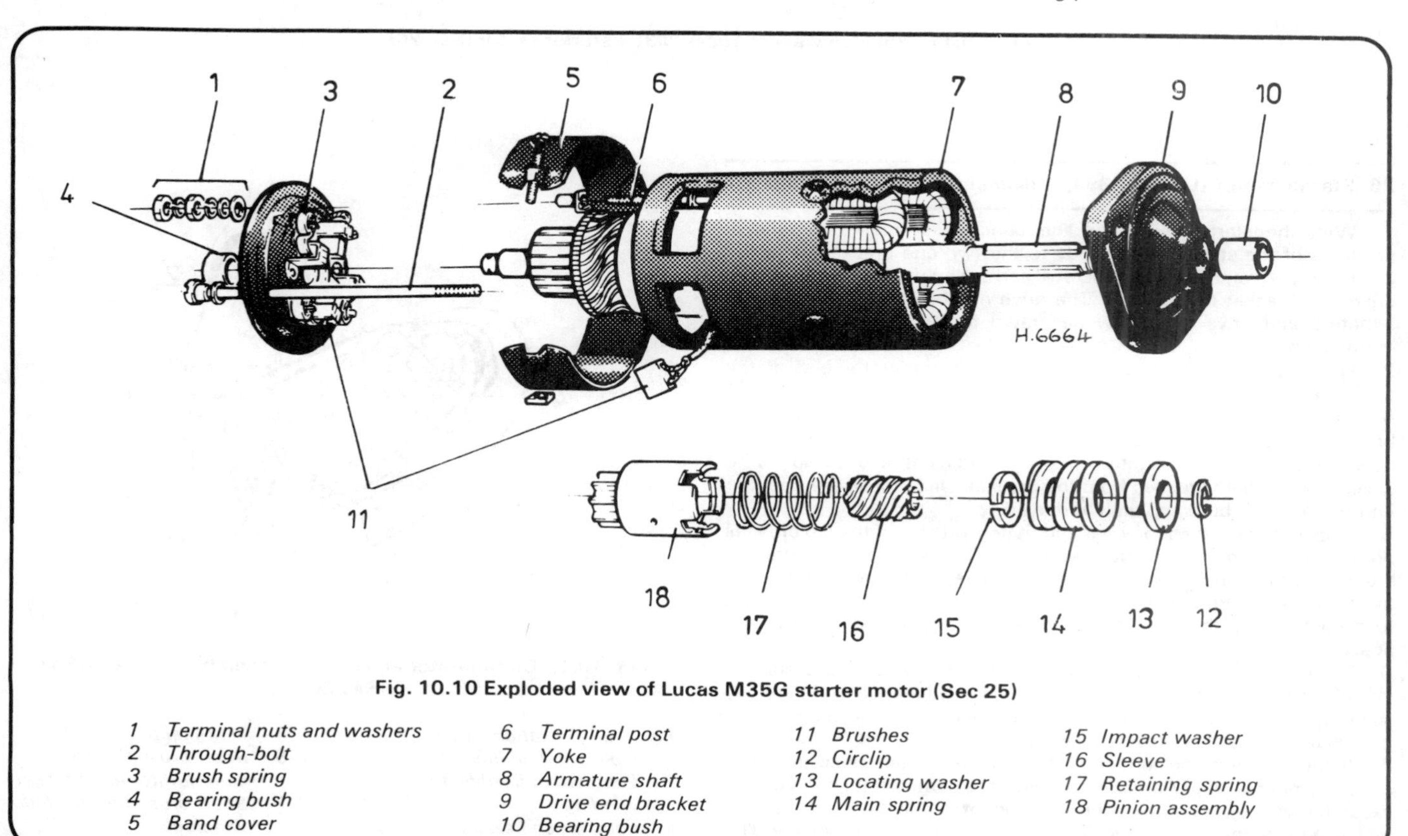

Fig. 10.10 Exploded view of Lucas M35G starter motor (Sec 25)

1 Terminal nuts and washers
2 Through-bolt
3 Brush spring
4 Bearing bush
5 Band cover
6 Terminal post
7 Yoke
8 Armature shaft
9 Drive end bracket
10 Bearing bush
11 Brushes
12 Circlip
13 Locating washer
14 Main spring
15 Impact washer
16 Sleeve
17 Retaining spring
18 Pinion assembly

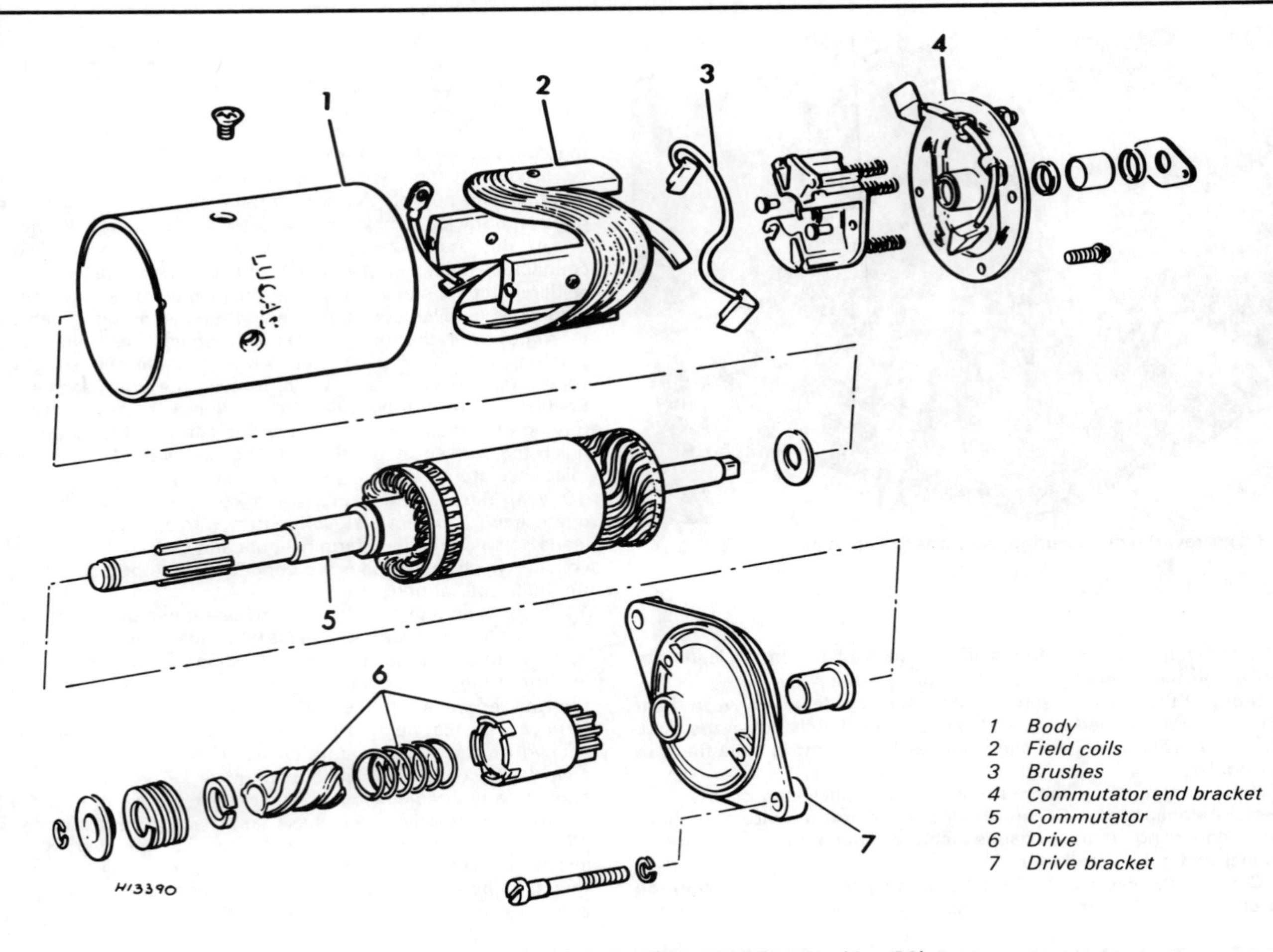

Fig. 10.11 Exploded view of Lucas M35J starter motor (Sec 26)

26 Starter motor (Lucas M35J) – dismantling and reassembly

1 With the starter motor on the bench, first mark the relative positions of the starter motor body to the two end brackets.

2 Undo and remove the two screws and spring washers securing the drive end bracket to the body. The drive end bracket, complete with armature and drive, may now be drawn forwards from the starter motor body.

3 Lift away the thrust washer from the commutator end of the armature shaft.

4 Undo and remove the two screws securing the commutator end bracket to the starter motor body. The commutator end bracket may now be drawn back slightly, allowing sufficient access so as to disengage the field brushes from the bracket. Once these are free, the end bracket can be completely removed.

5 Inspect the brushes for wear and fit new brushes if the old brushes are nearing the minimum specified length. To renew the end bracket brushes, cut the brush cables from the terminal posts and, with a small file or hacksaw, slot the head of the terminal posts to a sufficient depth to accommodate the new leads. Solder the new brush leads to the posts.

6 To renew the field winding brushes, cut the brush leads approximately 0.25 in (6 mm) from the field winding junction and carefully solder the new brush leads to the remaining stumps, making sure that the insulation sleeves provide adequate cover.

7 If the commutator surface is dirty or blackened, clean it with a petrol dampened rag. Carefully examine the commutator for signs of excessive wear, burning or pitting. If evident it may be reconditioned by having it skimmed at the local engineering works or BL dealer. The thickness of the commutator must not be less than specified. For

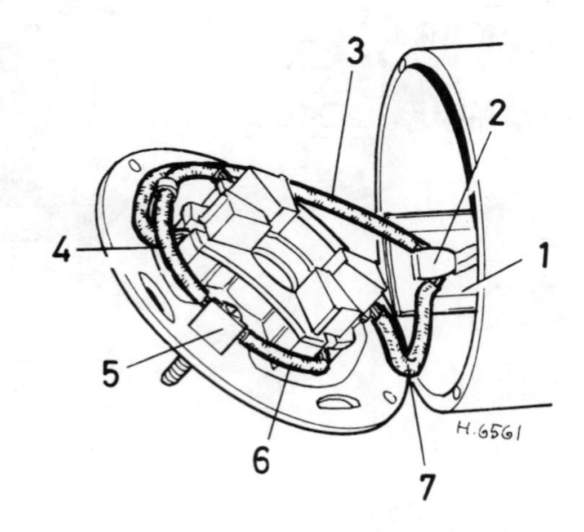

Fig. 10.12 Commutator end bracket assembly – Lucas M35J (Sec 26)

1 Yoke insulation piece
2 Field winding junction
3 Long brush flexible, field winding
4 Long brush flexible, commutator end bracket
5 Terminal post
6 Short brush flexible, commutator end bracket
7 Short brush flexible, field winding

minor reconditioning, the commutator may be polished with glass paper. **Do not undercut the mica insulators between the commutator segments.**

8 With the starter motor dismantled, test the field coils for open circuit. Connect a 12 volt battery with a 12 volt bulb in one of the leads between each of the field brushes and a clean part of the body. The lamp will light if continuity is satisfactory between the brushes, windings and body connection.

9 Renewal of the field coils calls for the use of a wheel-operated screwdriver, a soldering iron, caulking and riveting operations and is beyond the scope of the majority of owners. The starter motor body should be taken to an automobile electrical engineering works for new field coils to be fitted. Alternatively purchase an exchange Lucas starter motor.

10 Reassembly of the starter motor is the reverse sequence to removal.

27 Starter motor drive pinion – removal and refitting

1 Using a starter motor pinion compressor or similar tool, compress the mainspring until sufficient clearance exists to enable the circlip on the end of the shaft to be removed. Remove the pinion compressor and then slide off the locating washer and mainspring.

2 Slide the remaining parts off the armature shaft with a rotary action.

3 Examine the teeth of the drive pinion that engage with the flywheel ring gear. If they are badly worn on their leading edge, renew the pinion assembly. Bear in mind that if the drive pinion teeth are worn, the teeth on the ring gear are likely to be in a similar condition.

4 Inspect the remainder of the drive pinion components and renew the assembly if any are worn.

5 Reassembly of the drive pinion is the reverse sequence to removal. **Note:** *It is most important that the drive pinion components are completely free from oil, grease and dirt before reassembly. Under no circumstances should any of the parts be lubricated, as this will attract asbestos dust from the clutch which could cause the drive pinion to stick.*

28 Starter solenoid – removal and refitting

1 Disconnect the battery earth terminal.

2 Carefully ease back the rubber covers to gain access to the terminals (photo).

3 Make a note of the Lucar terminal connectors and detach these terminals.

4 Undo and remove the heavy duty cable terminal connection nuts and spring washers. Detach the two terminal connectors.

5 Undo and remove the two securing screws and lift away the solenoid.

6 Refitting is the reverse sequence to removal.

29 Direction indicator flasher unit and circuit – fault tracing and rectification

Note: *The actual flasher unit is enclosed in a small metal container located in the engine compartment or behind the instrument panel. The unit is acutated by the direction indicator switch. If the flasher unit fails to operate, or works very slowly or very rapidly, check the flasher indicator circuit as described below before assuming there is a fault in the unit itself.*

1 Examine the direction indicator bulbs front and rear for broken filaments or dirty contacts.

2 If the external flashers are working but the internal flasher warning light has ceased to function, check the filament of the warning bulb and renew as necessary.

3 With the aid of the wiring diagram, check all the flasher circuit connections if a flasher bulb is sound but does not work.

4 In the event of total direction indicator failure, check the appropriate fuse.

5 With the ignition turned on, check that current is reaching the flasher unit by connecting a voltmeter between the 'B' terminal and earth. If this test is positive, connect the 'B' terminal and the 'L' terminal and operate the flasher switch. If the flasher bulb lights up, the flasher unit itself is defective and must be renewed, as it is not possible to dismantle and repair it.

6 Should a fault develop in the hazard warning light circuit, the fault tracing procedure is the same as described above. A separate flasher unit is used for the hazard circuit and is located on the left-hand side of the engine compartment bulkhead.

30 Horn – fault tracing and rectification

1 The horn is located in the engine compartment and is attached to a bracket, which is in turn secured to the front body panel by two small nuts and bolts (photo).

2 The horn is not repairable and should not be dismantled. On early type horns an adjustment is provided to compensate for wear of the moving parts.

3 Adjustment is by means of a screw on the broad rim of the horn nearly opposite the two terminals. Do not confuse this with the large screw in the centre.

4 Turn the adjustment screw anti-clockwise until the horn just fails to sound. Then turn the screw a quarter of a turn clockwise, which is the optimum setting.

5 If the horn fails to work it may be tested with a voltmeter or 12

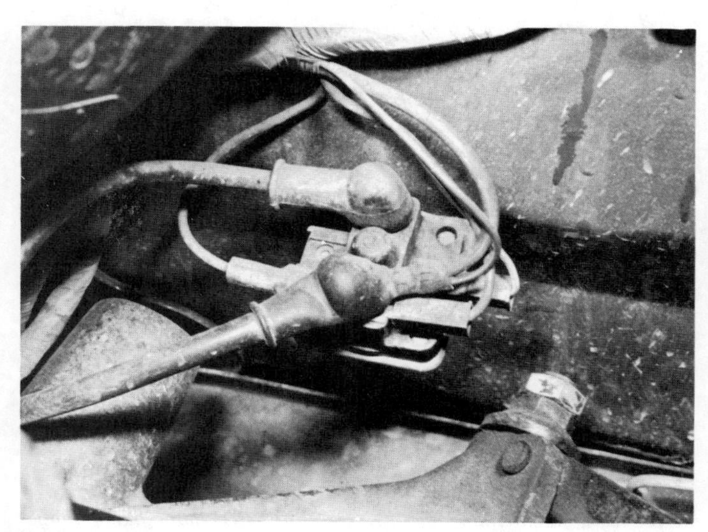

28.2 Electrical connections at the starter solenoid

30.1 Horn location showing electrical leads and mounting nuts

volt bulb and test lead as follows.

6 Detach the horn wires and connect the voltmeter leads of the bulb and test lead across them. On horns having only a single supply wire, connect the other voltmeter lead or the bulb to a good earth.

7 With the horn push depressed, there should be a reading on the voltmeter or the bulb should light. If it does the horn is faulty and should be renewed.

8 If there is no reading at the voltmeter or the test bulb does not light, check the appropriate fuse. If the fuse has not blown, the fault is likely to be in the wiring from the horn push to the horn or the horn push itself.

31 Fuses – general

1 The fuses are located in a block which is mounted on the right-hand wing valance on early models, and on the right-hand side of the engine compartment bulkhead on later models (photo). The fuse block is covered by a plastic push-on cover. Upon inspection it will be seen that there are two main fuses on early models and four main fuses on later versions. In both cases, two spare fuses are contained within the fuse block or cover.

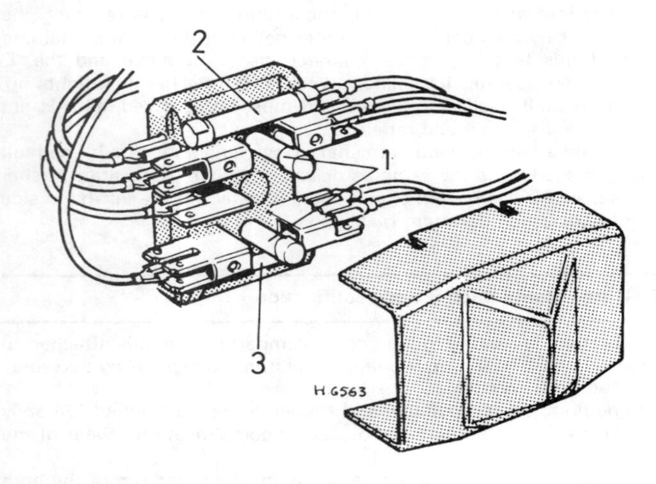

Fig. 10.13 The fuse block fitted to early models (Sec 31)

1 Spare fuses
2 35 amp fuse
3 35 amp fuse

31.1 Location of the fuse block on later models

2 Fuse failure may be diagnosed by the simultaneous failure of two or more electrical systems.

3 If a fuse blows it must be renewed with a fuse of the same rating. If the new fuse blows immediately the particular electrical service is operated, there is a fault in the system and the circuit must be carefully inspected to find the cause of the trouble.

4 To renew a fuse, simply withdraw it from the contacts in the fuse block. Before refitting a new fuse ensure that the contacts are clean and free from corrosion. If necessary the contacts may be cleaned with a fine grade emery paper.

5 The fuses and their respective circuits are as follows:

Early models

Fuse connecting	Rating	Function
1 and 2	35 amp	The auxiliary units are protected by this fuse, as are the interior light and horn which will operate without the ignition switched on. The fitting of additional accessories which are required to operate independently of the ignition circuit should be connected to the '2' terminal.
3 and 4	35 amp	This fuse protects the auxiliary units which operate only when the ignition is switched on. The units connected into the circuit are the direction indicators, windscreen wiper motor, heater blower and stop lights. The fitting of additional accessories which are required to operate only when the ignition is switched on should be connected to the '4' terminal.

Line fuses

A line fuse is fitted to protect an individual unit or circuit. To change a line fuse, hold one end of the container, press and twist off the other end. Line fuses will be found in the following positions:

Side and tail lights (8 amp)	Located adjacent to the wiring connectors on the engine bulkhead
Hazard flasher (35 amp)	Located adjacent to the fuse block

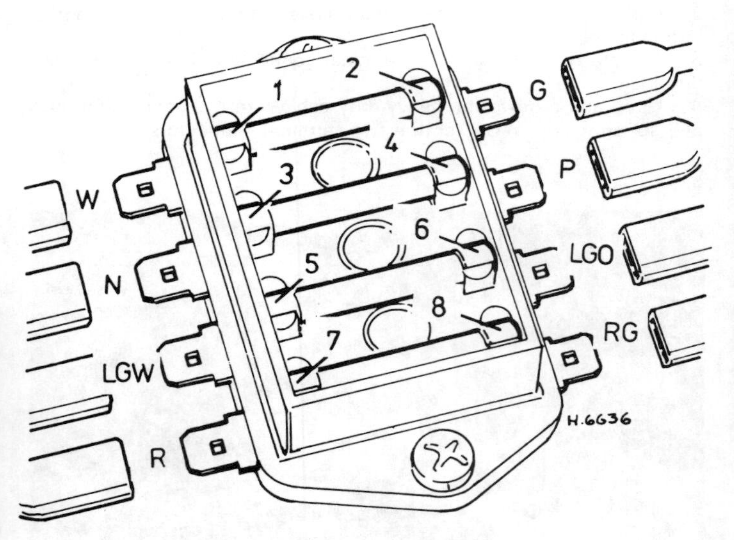

Fig. 10.14 The fuse block fitted to later models showing the wiring colour codes (Sec 31)

W – white
N – brown
LGW – light green/white
R – red
G – green
P – purple
LGO – light green/orange
RG – red/green

Later models

Fuse connecting	Rating	Function
1 and 2	35 amp	Stop lights, reversing lights, direction indicators, heated rear window. These systems will only operate with the ignition switch at II.
3 and 4	25 amp	Horn, headlight flasher, brake failure circuit. These systems operate independently of the ignition switch.
5 and 6	25 amp	Heater blower motor, windscreen wipers and washers, radio. These systems will operate with the ignition switch at I or II.
7 and 8	15 amp	Side and tail lights, panel lights.

Line fuses

Line fuses will be found in the following positions:

Hazard warning, interior light (15 amp)	Located on the engine compartment bulkhead
Radio	Located in the main feed line to the radio. The fuse rating should be as specified by the manufacturer.

32 Windscreen wiper arms and blades – removal and refitting

1 To remove the wiper blades from the arms, lift up the arms and ease back the small metal clip that secures the blade to the arm. Now slide the blade off the end of the arm (photo).

2 To refit the blade, slide in onto the arm until the retaining clip clicks into position and locks the blade in place.

3 Before removing a wiper arm, turn the windscreen wiper switch on and off, to ensure the arms are in their normal parked position with the blades parallel to the bottom of the windscreen.

4 To remove the arm, pivot the arm back and pull the wiper arm head off the splined drive, at the same time easing back the clip with a screwdriver (photo).

5 When refitting an arm, place it so it is in the correct relative parked position and then press the arm head onto the splined drive until the retaining clip clicks into place.

33 Windscreen wiper mechanism – fault tracing and rectification

1 Should the windscreen wipers fail, or work very slowly, then check the terminals for loose connections, and make sure the insulation of the external wiring is not cracked or broken. If this is in order, then check the current the motor is taking by connecting up an ammeter in the circuit and turning on the wiper switch. Consumption should be approximately 2 to 3 amps.

2 If no current is passing through, check the fuse. If the fuse has blown, renew it after having checked the wiring of the motor and other electrical circuits serviced by this fuse for short circuits. If the fuse is in good condition check the wiper switch.

3 If the wiper motor takes a very high current, check the wiper blades for freedom of movement. If this is satisfactory, check the gearbox cover and gear assembly for damage and measure the armature endfloat, which should be as shown in the specifications. The endfloat is set by the adjusting screw. Check that excessive friction in the cable guide tubes caused by too small a curvature is not the cause of the high current consumption.

4 If the motor takes a very low current and the battery is fully charged, the fault is likely to be the motor brush gear. To check this it will be necessary to remove the motor from the car for dismantling and inspection as described in the following Sections.

5 Should the wiper fail to park, or operate on only one speed where two-speed wipers are fitted, the fault will probably lie in the limit switch assembly. Renewal of this switch is described in Section 36.

34 Windscreen wiper motor – removal and refitting

1 Disconnect the battery earth terminal.

2 Remove the wiper arms from the spindles as described in Section 32.

3 Withdraw the electrical cable terminal connector from the motor, and if a separate earth wire is fitted, detach this from the wing valance.

4 Undo the nut securing the cable rack guide tube to the wiper motor gearbox (photo).

5 Undo and remove the two motor strap retaining screws and lift off the strap.

6 Carefully withdraw the motor assembly pulling the cable rack from the guide tubes.

7 To refit the motor, lightly lubricate the cable rack with a general-purpose grease.

8 Enter the cable rack into the guide tubes and carefully push it through, ensuring that it engages the wheelbox gear teeth.

9 Refit the motor retaining strap and the guide tube retaining nut.

10 Reconnect the electrical leads and the battery terminal.

11 Switch on the wipers, check the function of the motor and then turn it off. With the motor now in the 'park' position, refit the wiper blades.

35 Windscreen wiper wheelbox – removal and refitting

1 Remove the windscreen wiper motor as described in the previous Section.

2 Carefully lift back the engine compartment bulkhead insulation to provide access to the wheelboxes.

3 Undo and remove the retaining nut and spacer from each wheelbox.

4 Slacken the nuts that clamp the guide tubes between the wheelbox plates and then lift out the guide tubes.

5 The wheelboxes can now be lifted out.

6 With the wheelboxes removed, withdraw the wheelbox plates and lift out the spindle and gear. Examine the gear teeth for wear and renew as necessary.

7 Refitting is the reverse sequence to removal; bearing in mind the following points.

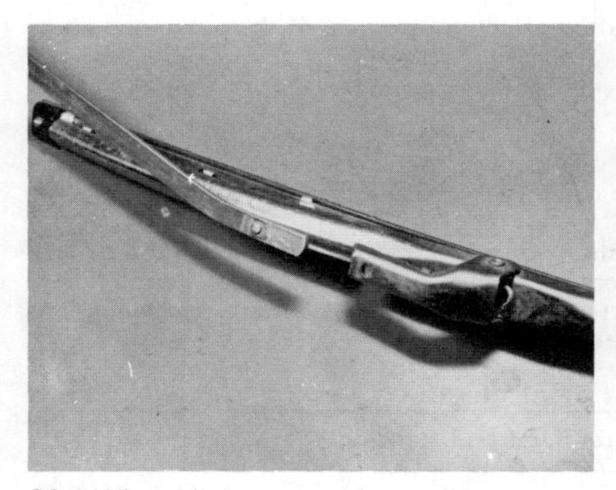

32.1 Wiper blade removal from wiper arm

32.4 The wiper arm is a push fit on the wiper spindle splines

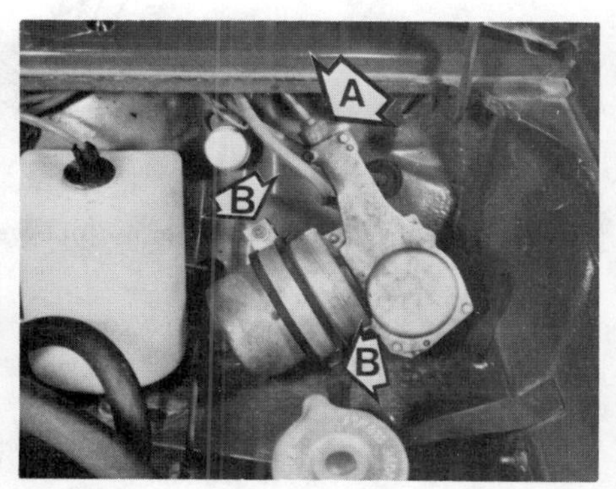

34.4 Cable rack guide tube retaining nut A and motor strap retaining screws B

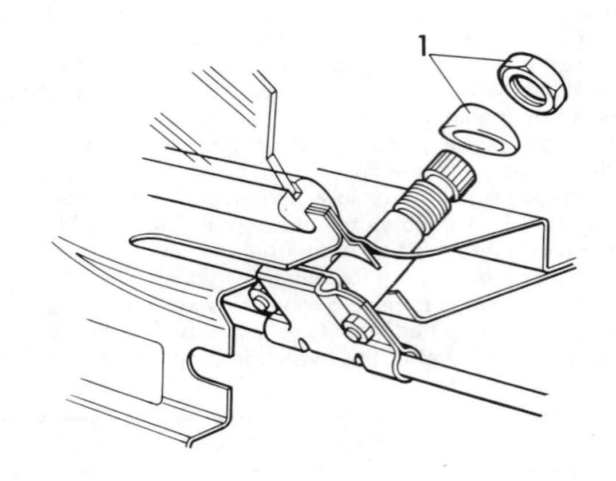

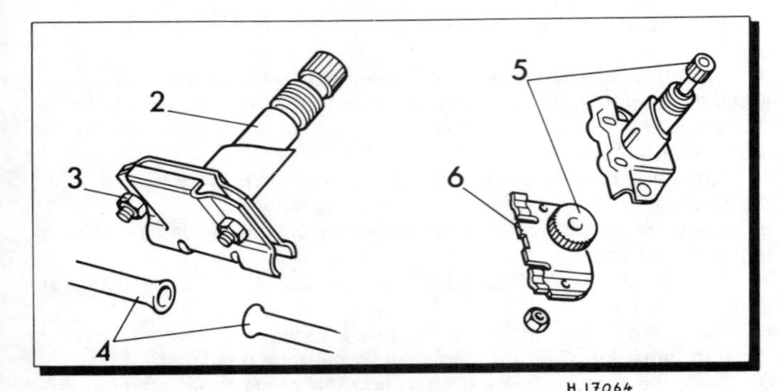

Fig. 10.15 Windscreen wiper wheelbox assembly (Sec 35)

1 Retaining nut and spacer
2 Wheelbox body
3 Wheelbox plate retaining screw
4 Wiper rack guide tubes
5 Spindle and gear
6 Lower plate

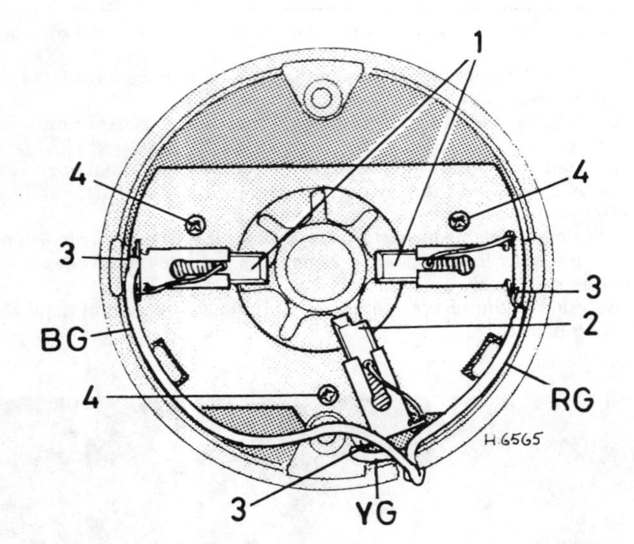

Fig. 10.16 Windscreen wiper motor brush gear (Sec 36)

1 Main brushes
2 Fast speed brush (two-speed version only)
3 Soldered brushbox connections
4 Brush gear assembly securing screws
RG – Red with green
BG – Blue with green
YG – Yellow with green

(a) Lightly lubricate the spindles and gear teeth with a general purpose grease
(b) Do not tighten the nuts that clamp the guide tubes between the wheelbox plates until the motor and cable rack have been refitted
(c) Ensure that the bend radius on the guide tube nearest to the motor is not less than 9 in (230 mm)

36 Windscreen wiper motor – dismantling, inspection and reassembly

1 Due to the limited availability of spare parts, the only repair which can be effectively undertaken on the motor is the renewal of the brushes and the limit switch. Anything more serious than this will mean exchanging the complete motor or having a repair done by an automobile electrician.
2 With the motor removed from the car, it may be dismantled as follows.
3 Undo and remove the four gearbox cover retaining screws and lift away the cover. Release the circlip and flat washer securing the connecting rod to the crankpin on the shaft and gear. Lift away the connecting rod followed by the second flat washer.
4 Raise the circlip and flat washer securing the shaft and gear to the gearbox body.
5 De-burr the gearshaft and lift away the gear, making a careful note of the location of the dished washer.
6 Scribe a mark on the yoke assembly and gearbox to ensure correct reassembly, and unscrew the two yoke bolts from the motor yoke assembly. Part the yoke assembly, including armature, from the gearbox body. As the yoke assembly has residual magnetism ensure that the yoke is kept well away from metallic dust.
7 Unscrew the two screws securing the brushgear and the terminal and switch assembly and remove both the assemblies.
8 Inspect the brushes for excessive wear. If the main brushes are worn to less than the minimum specified length, or the narrow section of the third brush is worn to the full width of the brush, fit a new brushgear assembly. Ensure that the three brushes move freely in their boxes.
9 If either the brushes or the limit switch are to be renewed on early motor assemblies, it will be necessary to unsolder the wires at the switch and then re-solder the new wires. On later types the wires are retained by Lucar connectors which are simply detached. In all cases make a note of the wire positions before disconnecting.
10 Reassembly of the windscreen wiper motor is the reverse sequence to removal.

37 Windscreen washer pump – removal and refitting

Manual pump

1 For safety reasons, disconnect the battery earth terminal.
2 Undo and remove the retaining nut at the rear of the heater and the two screws securing the front of the heater to the parcel shelf. Lower the heater to the floor.
3 Unscrew the locking ring securing the washer pump to the centre of the switch panel and pull the pump out from the rear of the panel.
4 Detach the two water hoses from the rear of the pump and lift it away.
5 Refitting is the reverse sequence to removal.

Electric pump

6 Refer to Chapter 3 and remove the air cleaner.
7 Disconnect the two electrical wires and the two water hoses from the pump.
8 Undo and remove the two securing screws and lift off the pump.
9 Refitting is the reverse sequence to removal. Make sure that the water hoses are connected to the correct outlets. Arrows on the pump body indicate the direction of water flow.

38 Headlight bulb – removal and refitting

1 Either sealed beam or renewable bulb light units are fitted to all Minis, depending on model type and year of manufacture.

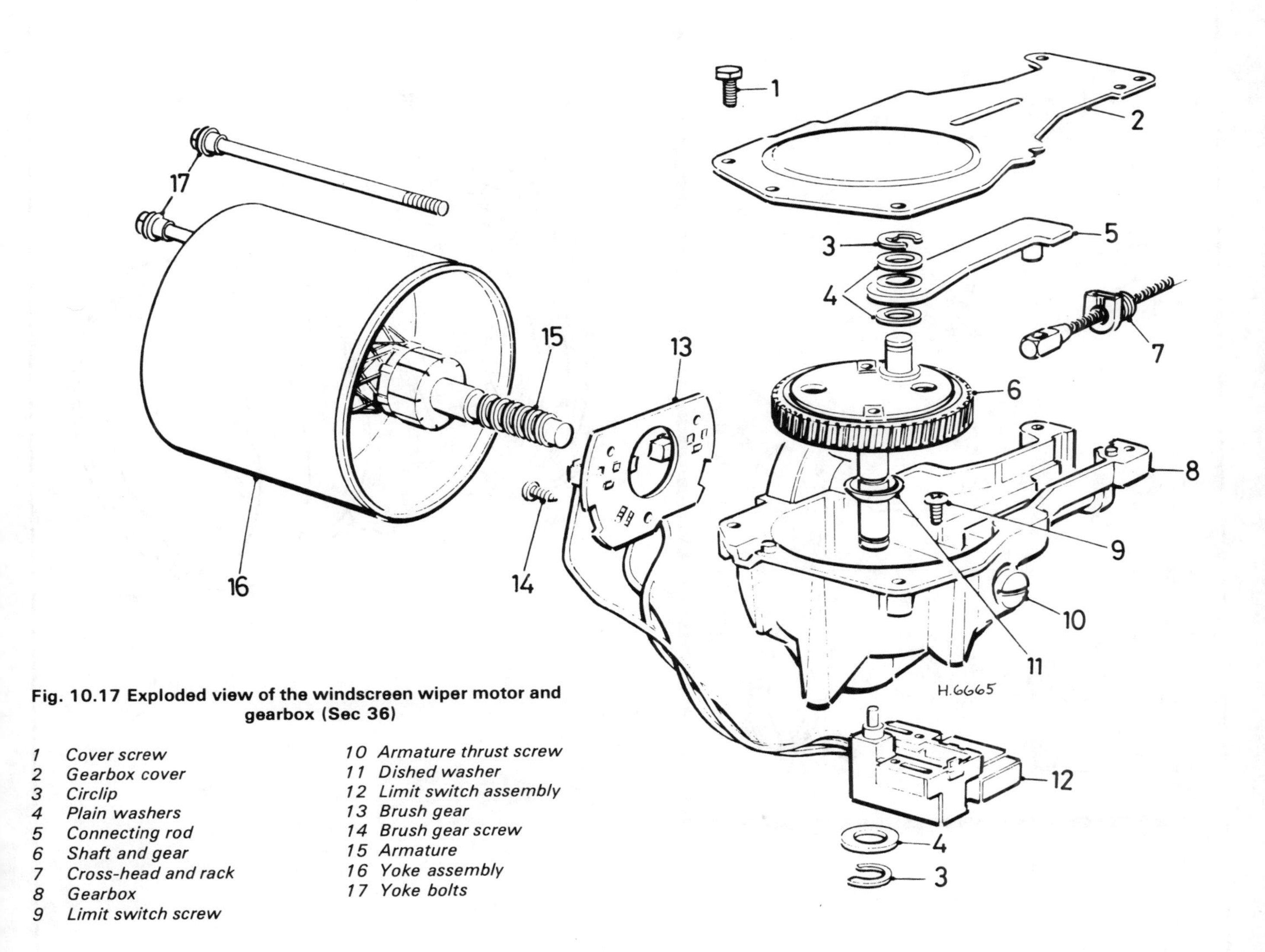

Fig. 10.17 Exploded view of the windscreen wiper motor and gearbox (Sec 36)

1 Cover screw
2 Gearbox cover
3 Circlip
4 Plain washers
5 Connecting rod
6 Shaft and gear
7 Cross-head and rack
8 Gearbox
9 Limit switch screw
10 Armature thrust screw
11 Dished washer
12 Limit switch assembly
13 Brush gear
14 Brush gear screw
15 Armature
16 Yoke assembly
17 Yoke bolts

2 To remove the headlight unit on Clubman and 1275 GT models, undo and remove the four screws and lift off the grille panel extension around the light unit. On all other models undo and remove the outer rim securing screw and ease the bottom of the outer rim forwards, lift it up and off the retaining lugs at the top of the light unit (photos).
3 Undo and remove the three small inner rim securing screws and withdraw the inner rim (photos).
4 The light unit can now be lifted out.

Sealed beam unit
5 Withdraw the three pin connector from the rear of the reflector and lift away the complete unit (photo). If it is necessary to remove the sidelight bulb, it may be detached from the holder. A bayonet or capless type bulb may be fitted, depending on year of manufacture.

Renewable bulb type
6 Withdraw the three pin connector from the rear of the reflector and disengage the spring clip from the reflector lugs. Lift away the bulb. Note the locating pip on the reflector and mating indentation in the bulb rim. If it is necessary to remove the sidelight bulb from the reflector, detach the bulb holder and then press and turn the bulb anti-clockwise. Withdraw it from the holder.

Alternative renewable bulb type
7 On certain models an alternative bulb type headlight assembly of slightly different design to the standard unit may be fitted.
8 To renew a bulb on these units, first remove the outer rim as described in paragraph 2.
9 Carefully pull the three adjusting screws one at a time out of their locations and lift out the reflector.
10 Withdraw the three pin connector from the rear of the reflector and disengage the spring clip from the reflector lugs. Lift away the bulb. Note the position of the projection on the bulb rim in relation to the bulb locator and ensure that the new bulb is fitted correctly. If it is necessary to remove the sidelight bulb from the reflector, detach the bulb holder and then press and turn the bulb anti-clockwise. Withdraw it from the holder.

All models
11 Refitting in all cases is the reverse sequence to removal. Where a bulb is fitted ensure that the locating slot in the bulb correctly registers in the reflector.

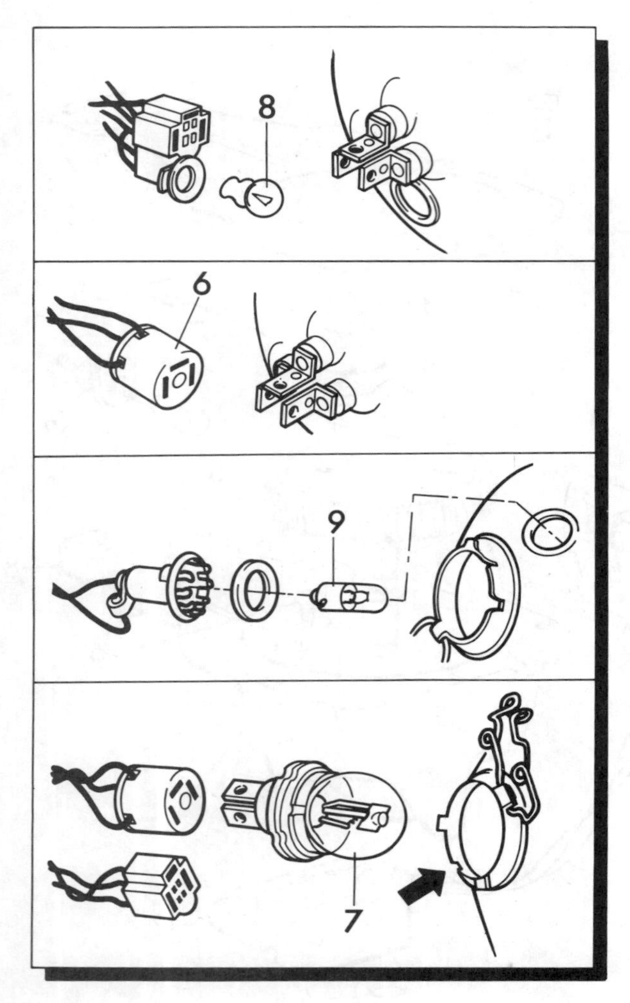

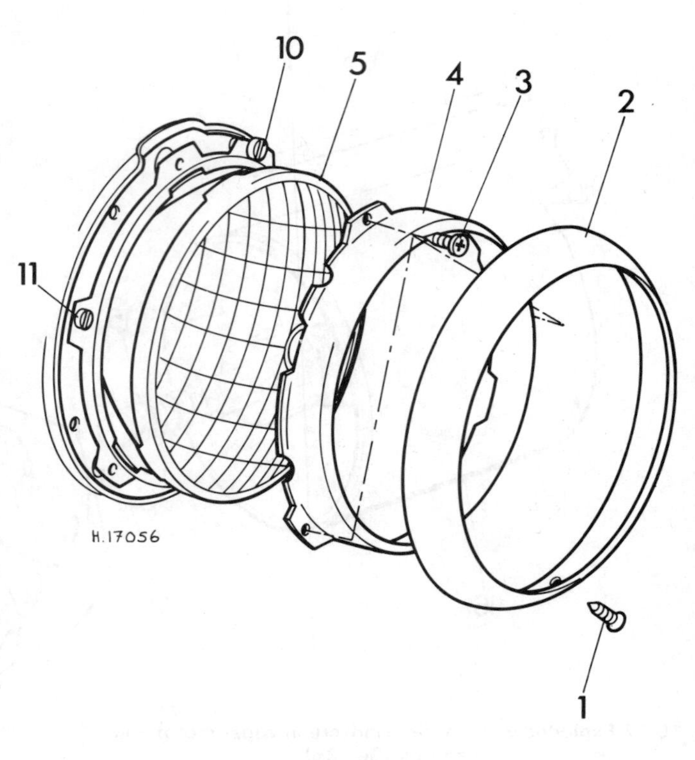

Fig. 10.18 Headlight bulb assemblies (Sec 38)

1	*Outer rim retaining screw*	*7*	*Headlight bulb*
2	*Outer rim*	*8*	*Sidelight bulb (used with sealed beam light unit)*
3	*Inner rim retaining screw*	*9*	*Sidelight bulb (used with bulb type light unit)*
4	*Inner rim*	*10*	*Vertical adjustment screw*
5	*Light unit*	*11*	*Horizontal adjustment screw*
6	*Three-pin connector*		

38.2a Undo the outer rim securing screw...

38.2b ...and lift the rim off the upper lugs

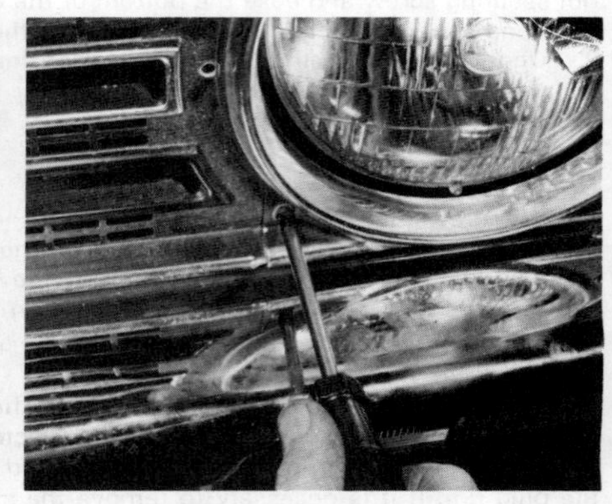

38.2c On Clubman models remove the grille panel extension

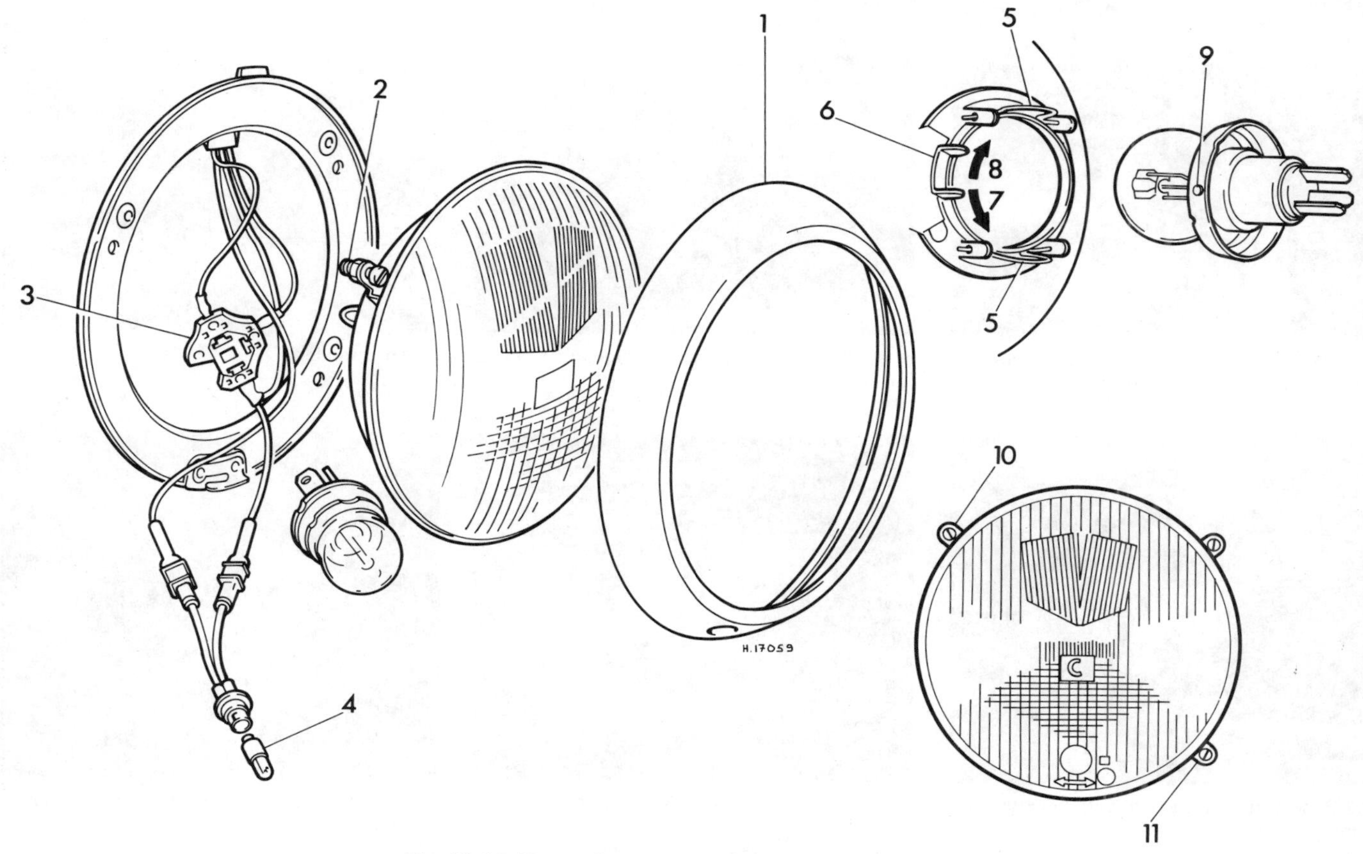

Fig. 10.19 Alternative type headlight assembly (Sec 38)

1 Outer rim
2 Adjusting screws
3 Three pin connector
4 Sidelight bulb
5 Spring clip
6 Bulb locator
7 Position of bulb locator for countries where travel is on the left-hand side of the road
8 Position of bulb locator for countries where travel is on the right-hand side of the road
9 Projection on bulb
10 Horizontal adjustment screw
11 Vertical adjustment screw

38.3a Unscrew the inner rim securing screws...

38.3b ...and lift off the inner rim

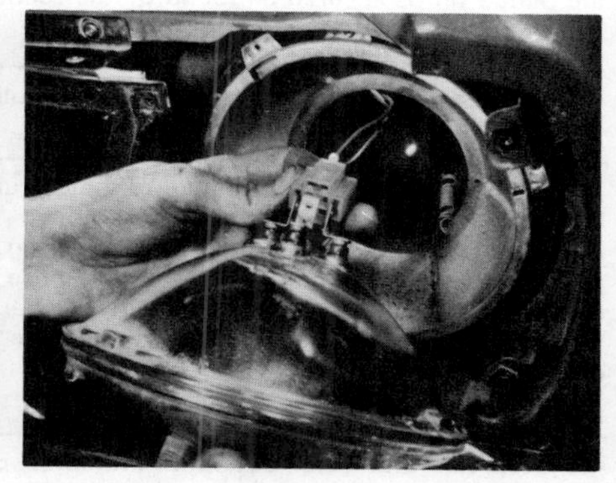

38.5 Detach the electrical connector and lift away the light unit

39 Headlight aim – adjustment

1 The headlights may be adjusted for both vertical and horizontal beam positions by means of the two adjusting screws. On the standard fitting sealed beam and bulb type headlight units, the upper spring-loaded screw adjusts the vertical position and the side spring-loaded screw adjusts the horizontal position (photo). On the alternative type headlight units, the two diametrically opposite screws are used for adjustment. The upper screw adjusts the horizontal setting and the lower screw adjusts the vertical setting.

2 The lights should be set so that on full or high beam, the beams are set slightly below parallel with a level road surface. Do not forget that the beam position is affected by how the car is normally loaded for night driving, and set the beams with the car loaded to this position.

3 Although this adjustment can be approximately set at home, it is recommended that this be left to a local garage who will have the necessary equipment to do the job more accurately.

39.1 Headlight vertical position A and horizontal position B adjusting screws

40.1a Fold back the rubber flange and remove the rim...

40.1b ...and lens

40.2 Push and turn the bulb anti-clockwise to remove

41.1 Undo the two screws and lift off the lens

42.1 Rear light cluster lens removed for bulb renewal

40 Front direction indicator bulb – removal and refitting

1 To renew a bulb, very carefully fold back the rubber flange with the aid of a screwdriver and remove the plated rim and lens (photos).
2 Push the bulb in slightly and turn it anti-clockwise to remove it (photo).
3 Refitting is the reverse of the removal procedure, but ensure that the plated rim is secured all round by the rubber flange.

41 Front sidelight and direction indicator bulb (combination type) – removal and refitting

1 Undo and remove the two screws that secure the lens to the light body. Carefully lift away the lenses (photo).
2 Either bulb is retained by a bayonet fixing, so to remove a bulb push in slightly and rotate in an anti-clockwise direction.
3 Refitting is the reverse sequence to removal. Take care not to over tighten the two lens retaining screws as the lenses can be easily cracked.

42 Stop/tail and rear direction indicator bulb – removal and refitting

1 When it is necessary to renew a bulb, withdraw the three screws to release the light lenses (photo).
2 The flashing indicator bulb is fitted in the top and the stop/tail bulb in the lower compartment (centre compartment later models).
3 The latter is of the double filament type giving a marked increase in illumination on brake application to provide a stop warning. This bulb also has offset locating pins to ensure correct fitting.
4 Both bulbs have bayonet fixings; to remove push in slightly, and rotate in an anti-clockwise direction.
5 Refitting is the reverse squence to removal. Take care not to overtighten the lens securing screws as the lenses can easily be cracked.

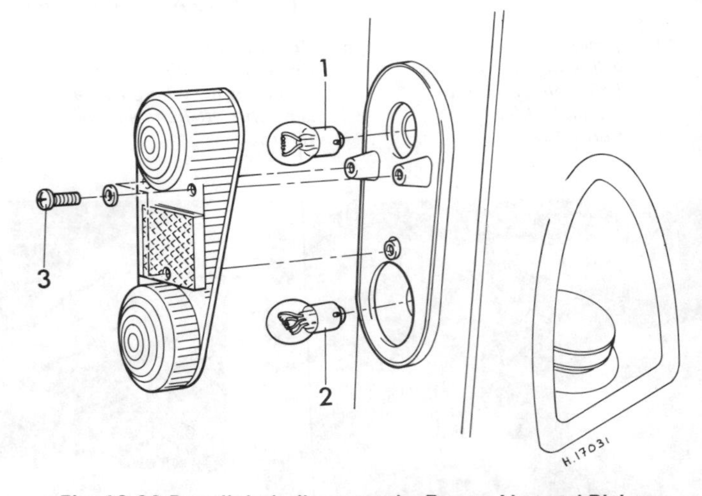

Fig. 10.20 Rear light bulb renewal – Estate, Van and Pick-up models (Sec 42)

1 *Direction indicator bulb*
2 *Stop/tail bulb*
3 *Lens securing screws*

43 Reversing light bulb – removal and refitting

1 On later models the rear light clusters are increased in size to accommodate a reversing light bulb.
2 The reversing light bulb is fitted to the lower of the three compartments and its renewal is the same as for the stop/tail and direction indicator bulbs described in the previous Section.

44.1 Removal of the number plate lens and bulb holder on Saloon models

44.4 On Estate, Van and Pick-up models lift off the cover and lens...

44.5 ..and remove the bulbs by turning them anti-clockwise

44 Number plate light bulb – removal and refitting

Saloon models

1 To renew the bulb, undo and remove the lens securing screws and carefully ease the lens and bulb holder out of the light unit. In some cases it will be found that the lens and bulb holder cannot be withdrawn due to the wires fouling the light unit. If this happens, open the boot lid, remove the three retaining screws and lift off the light unit. The lens and bulb holder can now be removed (photo).
2 The festoon type bulb is removed by simply withdrawing it from the bulb holder contacts.
3 Refitting is the reverse sequence to removal.

Estate, Van and Pick-up models

4 Undo and remove the retaining screw and lift off the cover and lens (photo).
5 Remove the bulbs by turning anti-clockwise and lifting out (photo).
6 Refitting is the reverse sequence to removal.

45 Interior light bulb – removal and refitting

1 To gain access to the bulb, carefully squeeze the two sides of the plastic lens together until the retaining lugs of the lens are clear of the sockets in the light base.
2 Draw the lens from the light base.
3 The festoon bulb may now be detached from the contact blades.
4 Refitting the bulb and lens is the reverse sequence to removal.

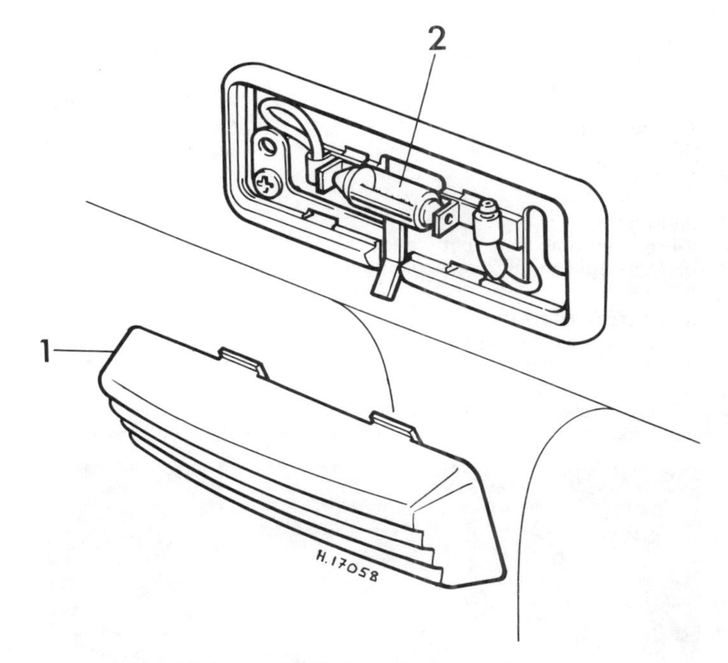

Fig. 10.21 Interior light bulb renewal (Sec 45)

1 Lens *2 Bulb*

46 Warning and panel light bulb – removal and refitting

Models with central instrument panel

1 Access to the instrument panel warning lights and panel illumination lights is gained from the engine compartment by withdrawing the push type bulb holders from the rear of the speedometer and instruments.
2 On later models it may be found helpful to remove the air cleaner assembly as described in Chapter 3 to provide greater access.

Models with offset instrument panel

4 On models having an instrument panel in front of the driver, access to the bulbs is through an access panel beneath the parcel shelf and from the side of the panel after the facia trim has been eased back.
5 The bulb holders are a push fit in the rear of the instrument panel and the capless bulbs are also a push fit in the holders.

47 Instrument panel –removal and refitting

Models with central instrument panel (except Mini 850)

1 Disconnect the battery earth terminal.
2 Carefully ease out the trim panels at the rear of the facia on either side of the instrument panel.
3 Fold back the parcel shelf cover around the front of the instrument panel.
4 Slacken the nut securing the heater unit to the rear mounting bracket. Undo and remove the two screws securing the front of the heater to the parcel shelf and lower the unit to the floor.
5 Undo and remove the screws securing the instrument panel to the facia.
6 Working in the engine compartment, remove the air cleaner as described in Chapter 3.
7 Unscrew the knurled nut securing the speedometer cable to the rear of the speedometer and withdraw the cable.
8 Remove the clip that secures the oil pressure gauge pipe to the engine compartment bulkhead.
9 From inside the car draw the instrument panel away from the facia and disconnect the wires and bulb holders from the rear of the instruments. Label each wire as it is removed to prevent confusion when refitting.
10 Unscrew the union nut and release the oil pipe from the rear of the oil pressure gauge.
11 Unscrew the knurled retaining nuts and lift out the instruments.
12 Undo and remove the two securing screws and lift out the speedometer and sealing ring.
13 If required, the fuel gauge and voltage stabilizer may be removed from the rear of the speedometer after removing the retaining screws

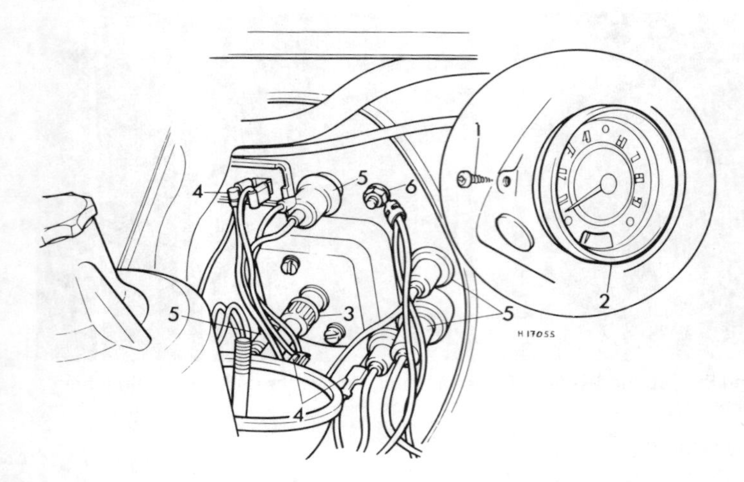

Fig. 10.22 Instrument panel removal – 850 models (Sec 47)

1 Retaining screw
2 Instrument panel
3 Speedometer cable
4 Wiring connectors
5 Bulb holders
6 Earth lead

and nuts.
14 Reassembly and refitting of the instruments and panel is the reverse sequence to dismantling and removal.

Mini 850 models

15 Disconnect the battery earth terminal.
16 Working in the engine compartment, remove the air cleaner as described in Chapter 3.
17 Withdraw the sound insulation from speedometer aperture.
18 Unscrew the knurled retaining nut and detach the speedometer cable from the rear of the speedometer.
19 Disconnect the wires from the fuel gauge and voltage stabilizer. Label each wire as it is removed to prevent confusion when refitting.
20 Note the locations of the bulb holders and remove them from the rear of the speedometer.
21 Disconnect the earth wire.
22 From inside the car undo and remove the two screws securing the speedometer to the cowling and then lift out the speedometer.
23 Refitting is the reverse sequence to removal.

Models with offset instrument cluster

24 Disconnect the battery earth terminal.
25 Hold both sides of the instrument nacelle and carefully pull it off the instrument cluster (photo).
26 Remove the upper plastic trim strip to gain access to the panel upper retaining screws.
27 Undo and remove the side and upper retaining screws securing the instrument panel to the mounting brackets (photos).
28 Draw the panel outward and detach the speedometer cable, the wiring multi-plug connector and (where fitted) the two electrical leads at the rear of the tachometer (photos).
29 Carefully lift away the instrument panel, taking care not to damage the printed circuit.
30 Refitting is the reverse sequence to removal.

48 Instrument panel – dismantling and reassembly

Note: *On models fitted with a centrally mounted panel the instruments and components are withdrawn as part of the instrument panel removal sequence (see Section 47). The following procedure is therefore applicable to models having an offset instrument panel mounted in front of the driver.*
1 Remove the instrument panel as described in Section 47.

Fuel and temperature gauge removal

2 Ease off the spring clips securing the instrument lens glass and carefully remove the glass, sealing rings and printed face plate.

47.25 Remove the instrument cluster nacelle

47.27a Undo the side...

47.27b ...and upper retaining screws

47.28a Detach the speedometer cable...

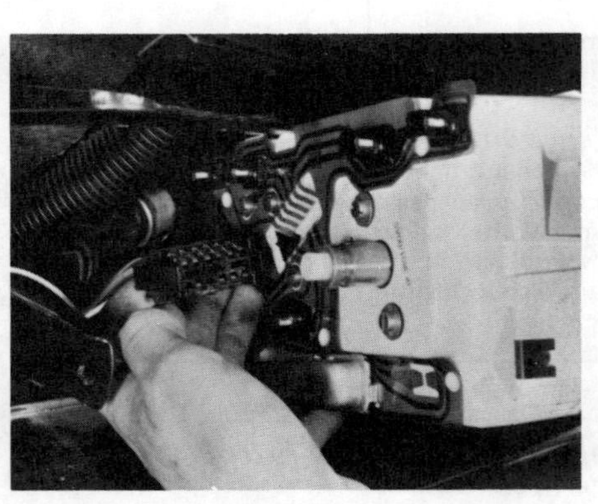

47.28b ...and the multi-plug connector, then lift away the instrument panel

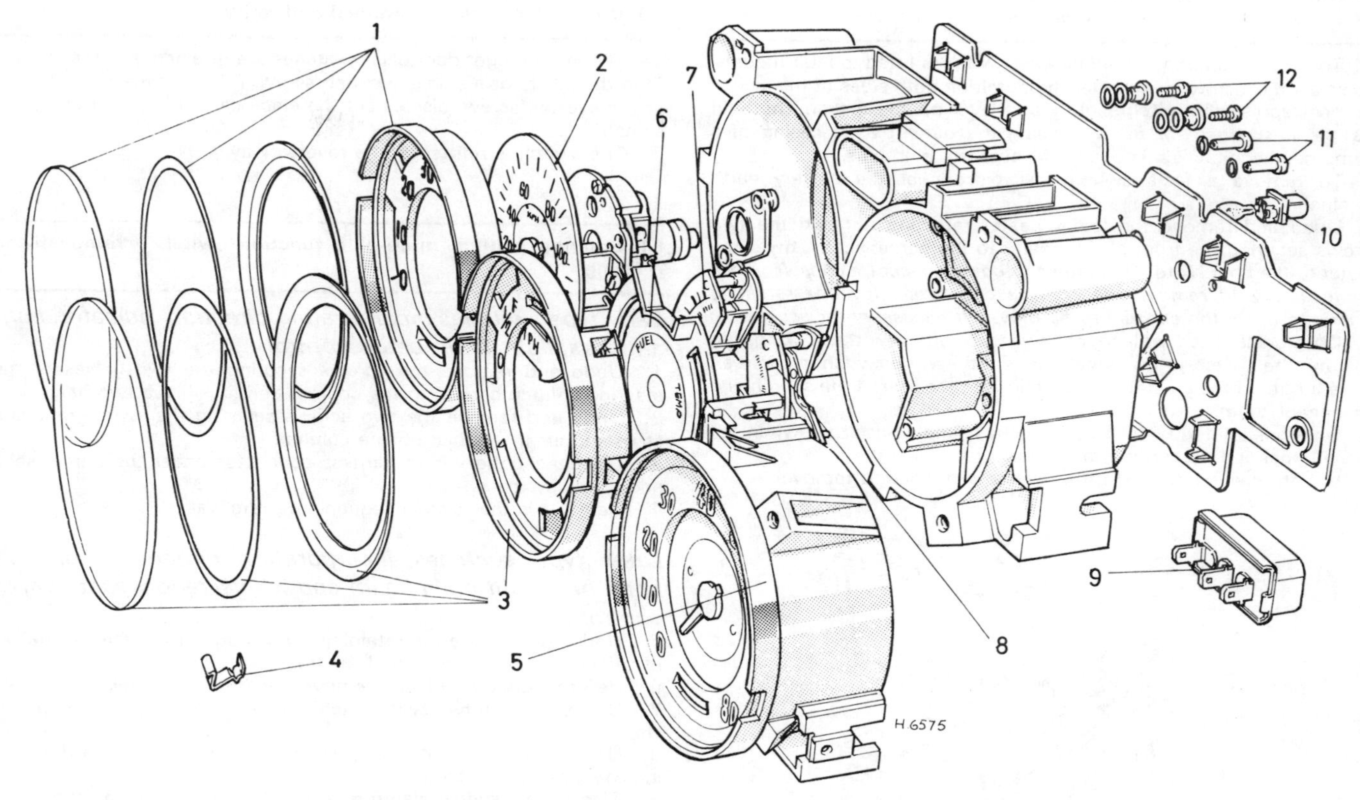

Fig. 10.23 Exploded view of the offset instrument cluster (Sec 48)

1 *Speedometer lens and faceplate assembly*
2 *Speedometer unit*
3 *Fuel/temperature gauge lens and faceplate assembly*
4 *Lens securing clips*
5 *Tachometer assembly (where fitted)*
6 *Fuel/temperature gauge facing*
7 *Fuel gauge*
8 *Temperature gauge*
9 *Voltage stabilizer*
10 *Panel lamp bulb and holder*
11 *Fuel/temperature gauge securing screws*
12 *Speedometer securing screws*

3 Undo and remove the three small screws and lift out the instrument facing.
4 At the rear of the instrument panel, undo and remove the two screws securing the gauge to the panel body and remove the gauge.

Speedometer removal

5 Ease off the spring clips securing the speedometer lens glass and carefully remove the glass, sealing rings and printed face plate.
6 At the rear of the instrument panel undo and remove the two screws securing the speedometer to the panel body and remove the speedometer.

Tachometer removal (where fitted)

7 Detach the voltage stabilizer lead and bulb holder from the rear of the tachometer.
8 Carefully prise up the pegs securing the printed circuit to the tachometer body and lift the unit away.

Printed circuit and voltage stabilizer

9 Pull the voltage stabilizer carefully out of its location in the printed circuit at the rear of the instrument panel.
10 Withdraw the panel and warning light bulb holders.
11 Where fitted, undo and remove the three screws and the voltage stabilizer tag connections for the tachometer.
12 Undo and remove the four screws securing the fuel and temperature gauges.
13 Carefully prise out the plastic pegs securing the printed circuit to the instrument panel and lift off the printed circuit.
14 In all cases reassembly is the reverse of the dismantling sequence.

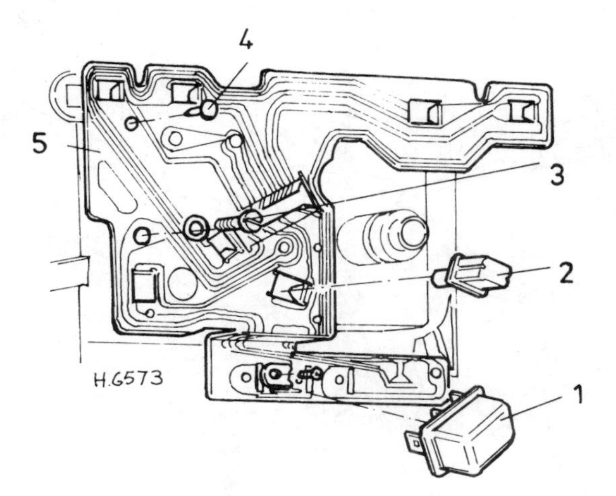

Fig. 10.24 Offset instrument panel printed circuit connections (Sec 48)

1 *Voltage stabilizer*
2 *Panel light*
3 *Fuel and temperature gauge securing screws*
4 *Printed circuit securing stud*
5 *Printed circuit*

49 Facia switches – removal and refitting

1 To renew a bulb in the illuminated switches fitted to later models, insert a small screwdriver under the notch on both sides of the switch rocker. Depress the notch slightly and lever off the rocker. The bulb may be unscrewed for renewal using the outer plastic casing of a wiring connector which is a snug fit over the bulb lens.
2 To remove a facia switch first disconnect the battery earth terminal.
3 Undo and remove the lower heater retaining nut and the two screws securing the front of the heater to the parcel shelf. Lower the heater to the floor. **Note**: *On models fitted with a centre console, it will be necessary to remove the console and facia glovebox retaining screws to allow the console to be moved if necessary for access.*
4 On models fitted with toggle switches, unscrew the locking ring securing the switch to the panel and withdraw the switch to the rear. Make a note of the electrical connections at the rear of the switch and disconnect them.
5 On models fitted with rocker switches simply push the switch out of the panel and detach the multiplug.
6 In both cases refitting is the reverse sequence to removal.

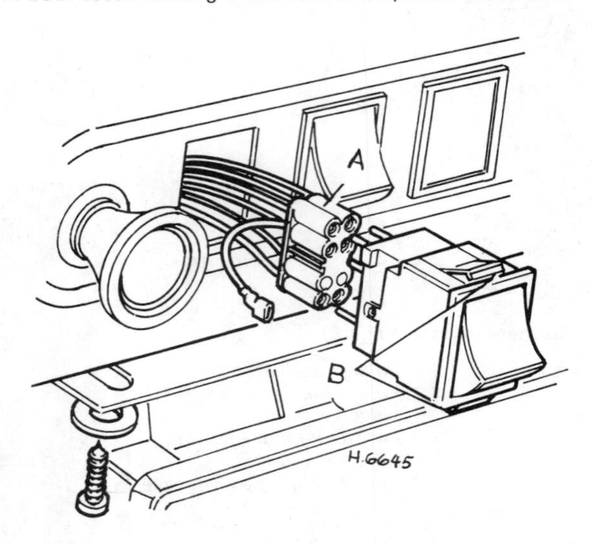

Fig. 10.25 Removal of rocker type facia switch (Sec 49)

A Multi-plug connector
B Switch retaining tabs

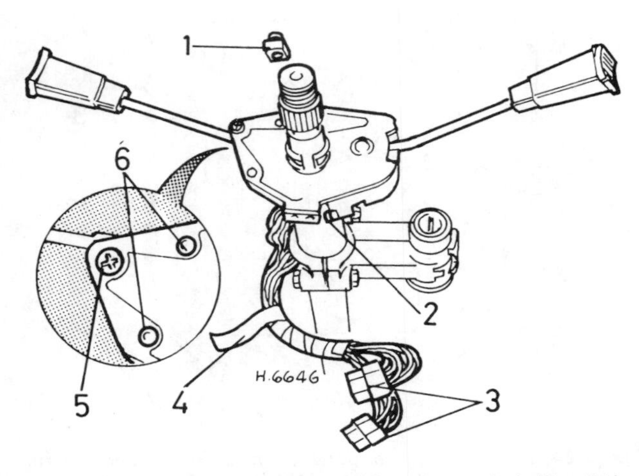

Fig. 10.26 Steering column multi-function switch (Sec 51)

1 Cancelling ring drive block
2 Clamp screw
3 Milti-plug connectors
4 Insulating tape
5 Screw
6 Rivet locations

50 Door pillar switch – removal and refitting

1 The interior light door pillar switches are retained by either a push fit in the pillars or a single securing screw. Prise out the push fit type or remove the screw, disconnect the electrical lead and lift away the switch.
2 The switch is refitted in the reverse way.

51 Steering column multi-plug function switch – removal and refitting

Early type switches incorporating direction indicator, horn and headlight main beam control

1 Undo and remove the screws securing the two halves of the steering column shroud to the column and lift off the two halves.
2 Undo and remove the two screws securing the switch retaining strap and lift the switch off the column.
3 Disconnect the wiring harness connector under the parcel shelf and lift away the switch.
4 Refitting is the reverse sequence to removal.

Later type switches incorporating direction indicator, horn, headlight main beam and windscreen washer/wiper control

5 Undo and remove the retaining screws and lift off the two halves of the steering column shroud (photos).
6 Refer to Chapter 11 and remove the steering wheel.
7 Disconnect the two switch multi-plug connectors under the parcel shelf.
8 Undo and remove the retaining screw and lift out the direction indicator cancelling block.
9 Slacken the switch clamp screw and slide the switch off the end of the steering column.
10 If it is wished to renew either of the switches they may be renewed as a complete assembly or individually. If they are to be renewed individually, it will be necessary to drill out the two rivets securing the windscreen washer/wiper switch to the mounting plate and unwrap the insulating tape securing the harness together.
11 Refitting is the reverse sequence to removal. Ensure that the striker dog on the nylon switch centre is in line with and adjacent to the direction indicator switch stalk.

52 Stop light switch – removal and refitting

Note: *The stop lights are operated either hydraulically by a pressure sensitive switch incorporated in the braking system of electrically by an on/off switch mounted above the brake pedal.*

Hydraulically operated type

1 Remove the brake master cylinder filler cap and place a piece of polythene over the filler neck. Now refit the cap. This will prevent loss of hydraulic fluid when the stop light switch is removed.
2 Lift up the rubber cover, if fitted, and disconnect the two wires from the stop light switch located on the right-hand side of the front subframe beneath the flywheel housing.
3 Using a large socket and extension bar, undo and remove the switch from the pipe connector.
4 Refitting the switch is the reverse sequence to removal. If precautions were taken to prevent fluid loss, it should not be necessary to bleed the hydraulic system. However, if the brake pedal now feels spongy, bleed the system as described in Chapter 9.

Electrically operated type

5 Disconnect the two wires at the switch, accessible from below the parcel shelf.
6 Undo and remove the locknut and then withdraw the switch from its mounting bracket.
7 Refitting is the reverse sequence to removal. Adjust the position of the switch and locknuts so that the stop lights operate after 0.25 in (6.3 mm) of brake pedal travel.

51.5a Remove the securing screws...

51.5b ...and lift off the steering column shroud

53 Ignition switch – removal and refitting

1 Undo and remove the securing screws and lift off the two halves of the steering column shroud.
2 Disconnect the ignition switch multi-plug connector.
3 Inspect the top of the ignition switch housing, and if a small screw is present, unscrew it. The ignition switch can now be withdrawn from the steering lock housing.
4 If a small retaining screw is not visible, then the ignition switch is of the sealed type and can only be removed with the steering lock housing as a complete assembly. This procedure is described fully in Chapter 11 Section 26.
5 Refitting the ignition switch is the reverse sequence to removal.

54 Reversing light switch – removal, refitting and adjustment

Note: *The following procedures apply to later Mini Saloon models having reversing lights incorporated in the rear light clusters. The switch is located in the gearchange remote control housing and is actuated by the gearchange lever when reverse is selected.*
1 To remove the switch, jack up the front of the car and support it on axle stands.
2 Working underneath the car, disconnect the two switch wires,

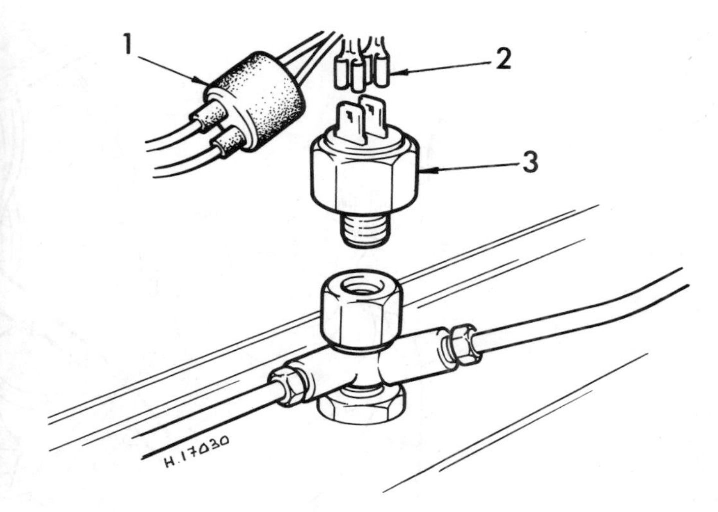

Fig. 10.27 Hydraulic stop light switch removal (Sec 52)

1 Rubber cover (where fitted)
2 Electrical leads
3 Stop light switch

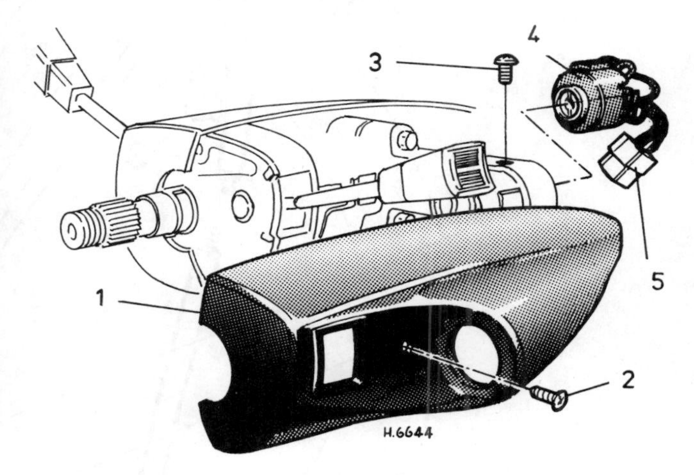

Fig. 10.28 The later type ignition/starter switch (Sec 53)

1 Steering column shroud
2 Shroud retaining screw
3 Ignition switch securing screw
4 Ignition switch
5 Multi-plug connector

slacken the locknut and unscrew the switch from the remote control housing.
3 Refitting is the reverse sequence to removal.
4 Adjustment is carried out as follows. With the wires disconnected, screw the switch into the housing until slight resistance is felt.
5 Connect the wires, select reverse gear and switch on the ignition. Continue screwing the switch in until the reversing lights just come on and then screw the switch in a further quarter of a turn.
6 Tighten the locknut and check that the reversing lights are illuminated with the gear lever in reverse and extinguished in all other gear positions.

55 Speedometer cable – removal and refitting

Models with central instrument panel

1 Disconnect the battery earth terminal.
2 Working in the engine compartment, detach the speedometer cable from the rear of the speedometer by unscrewing the knurled retaining nut and pulling the cable into the engine compartment.
3 Release the cable from the cable clip on the bulkhead.

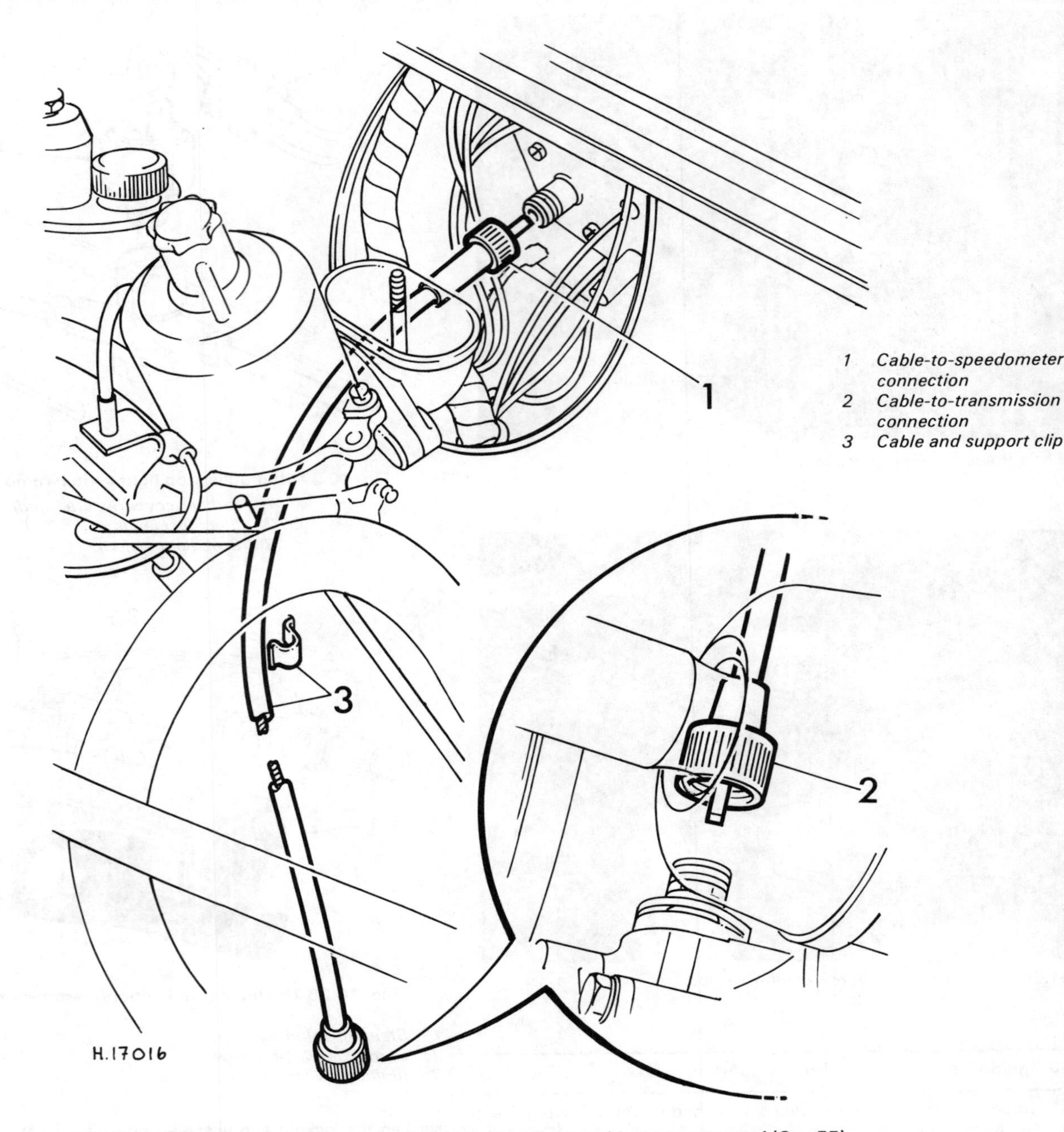

Fig. 10.29 Speedometer cable removal – models with central instrument panel (Sec 55)

Models with offset instrument panel

4 Disconnect the battery earth terminal.

5 Hold both sides of the instrument nacelle and carefully pull it off the instrument panel.

6 Remove the upper trim strip to gain access to the upper instrument panel retaining screws.

7 Undo and remove the side and upper retaining screws securing the instrument panel to the mounting brackets.

8 Draw the panel outward slightly, depress the lug on the side of the speedometer cable connector and withdraw the cable off the end of the speedometer.

9 Pull the cable through the bulkhead grommet and into the engine compartment.

All models

10 Working under the car disconnect the cable from the transmission unit. To gain access, work through the aperture above the left-hand driveshaft.

11 Should the cable securing nut be tight to turn by hand, remove the bolt that secures the speedometer drive and withdraw the cable complete with the drive assembly. The cable may then be detached from the drive assembly.

12 Refitting the speedometer cable is the reverse sequence to removal but the following additional points should be noted:

- *(a) If the speedometer drive was removed, always fit a new joint washer*
- *(b) To lubricate the inner cable, withdraw the inner cable and lightly grease it except for 8 in (200 mm) at the speedometer end. Refit the inner cable and wipe away any surplus grease*
- *(c) Ensure that there is approximately 0.75 in (10 mm) projection of the inner cable beyond the outer casing at the speedometer end*

56 Fault diagnosis – electrical system

Symptom	Reason(s)
Starter motor fails to turn engine	Battery discharged or defective Battery connections loose or corroded Engine earth strap loose or broken Pinion jammed in mesh with flywheel gear Loose or broken connections in starter motor circuit Starter motor switch or solenoid faulty Starter motor brushes worn, sticking or connections loose Commutator dirty, worn or burnt Starter motor armature faulty Field coils earthed or broken
Starter motor turns engine very slowly	Battery discharged or defective Loose or corroded connections in starter motor circuit Starter motor brushes worn, sticking or connections loose Commutator dirty, worn or burnt
Starter motor operates without turning engine	Starter motor pinion sticking Pinion or flywheel gear teeth worn or broken
Starter motor noisy or rough	Pinion or flywheel gear teeth worn or broken Starter motor mounting bolts loose
Battery will not hold charge	Fanbelt slipping or broken Electrolyte level low or electrolyte weak Dynamo or alternator defective Voltage regulator faulty or maladjusted Short circuit causing continuous drain on battery Battery defective
Ignition warning light stays on with engine running	Fanbelt broken or slack Loose connections or broken wires in charging circuit Dynamo or alternator defective Voltage regulator defective or maladjusted
Ignition warning light stays on when ignition turned off (disconnect battery at once)	Voltage regulator defective, contacts sticking or maladjusted Alternator control unit defective
Ignition warning light fails to come on	Bulb failure Loose connection or broken wire Voltage regulator defective or maladjusted Alternator control unit defective
Gauges give inaccurate readings	Voltage stabiliser defective (readings fluctuate with engine speed) Gauge sender unit defective Gauge defective
Gauges read maximum or minimum all the time	Leads disconnected, broken or earthed Voltage stabiliser defective Gauge or sender defective
Wiper motor fails to work	Loose connection or broken wire Switch defective Fuse blown Motor internal fault Wiper blades frozen to screen
Wiper motor works slowly and draws excessive current	Rack cable bent or unlubricated Wheelboxes binding or damaged Motor internal fault
Wiper motor works slowly and draws little current	Loose or dirty connections Motor internal fault
Wiper motor works but blades remain static	Rack cable or wheelbox worn Motor gearbox worn Rack cable disconnected from gearbox

Symptom	Reason(s)
Lights do not come on	Fuse blown (if applicable) Bulb blown Bulb holder or connection corroded Broken wire Switch defective Battery discharged
Lights come on but fade out	Battery discharged Loose or corroded connections
Lights very dim	If engine not running, battery discharged Loose or corroded connections Lamp lens dirty Bulb or reflector tarnished Incorrect bulb fitted
Headlights give poor illumination	Bulb or reflector tarnished Lens dirty Headlights misaligned
Horn does not work	Fuse blown Loose or corroded connections Wire broken Horn switch defective Horn defective
Horn sounds continuously	Horn switch jammed Wire to horn switch earthed
Horn tone poor	Loose or corroded connections Horn defective or in need of adjustment

Note: *When investigating electrical faults, check the fuse and the security of connections first. Remember that bulb holders and many other electrical components depend on secure mounting to the body or other metal structure to complete the circuit; loose or corroded fastenings can give rise to apparently inexplicable faults.*

Master key to wiring diagrams (Figs. 10.30 to 10.38 inclusive)

Some of the components listed in this key may not be fitted to individual models

1 *Dynamo or alternator*
2 *Control box*
3 *Battery (12 volt)*
4 *Starter solenoid*
5 *Starter motor*
6 *Lighting switch*
7 *Headlamp dip switch*
8 *RH headlamp*
9 *LH headlamp*
10 *Main beam warning lamp*
11 *RH sidelamp/parking lamp*
12 *LH sidelamp/parking lamp*
14 *Panel lamps*
15 *Number plate lamp(s)*
16 *RH stop and tail lamp*
17 *LH stop and tail lamp*
18 *Stop lamp switch*
19 *Fuse block*
20 *Interior light*
21 *RH door switch(es)*
22 *LH door switch(es)*
23 *Horn(s)*
24 *Horn push*
25 *Flasher unit*
26 *Direction indicator, headlamp flasher, and dip switch*
27 *Direction indicator warning lamp(s)*
28 *RH front flasher lamp*
29 *LH front flasher lamp*
30 *RH rear flasher lamp*
31 *LH rear flasher lamp*
32 *Heater or fresh-air blower switch*
33 *Heater or fresh-air blower*
34 *Fuel gauge*
35 *Fuel gauge tank unit*
36 *Windscreen wiper switch*
37 *Windscreen wiper motor*
38 *Ignition/starter stitch*
39 *Ignition coil*
40 *Distributor*
41 *Fuel pump*
42 *Oil pressure switch*
43 *Oil pressure gauge or warning lamp*
44 *Ignition warning lamp*
45 *Speedometer (headlamp flasher switch on Canadian Mini 1000)*
46 *Water temperature gauge*
47 *Water temperature transmitter*
49 *Reversing lamp switch*
50 *Reversing lamp*
64 *Bi-metallic instrument voltage stabilizer*
67 *Line fuse (35 amp)*
75 *Automatic transmission inhibitor switch (when fitted)*
77 *Windscreen washer motor*
78 *Windscreen washer switch*
83 *Induction heater and thermostat*
84 *Suction chamber heater*
95 *Tachometer*
110 *RH repeater flasher*
111 *LH repeater flasher*
115 *Rear window demister switch*
116 *Rear window demister unit*
139 *Alternative connections for two-speed wiper motor and switch*
150 *Rear window demist warning lamp*
152 *Hazard warning light*
153 *Hazard warning switch*
154 *Hazard warning flasher unit*
158 *Printed circuit instrument panel*
159 *Brake pressure warning lamp and lamp test switch*
160 *Brake pressure failure switch*
164 *Ballast resistor*
168 *Ignition key audible warning buzzer*
170 *RH front side marker lamp*
171 *LH front side marker lamp*
172 *RH rear side marker lamp*
173 *LH rear side marker lamp*
198 *Driver's seat belt switch*
199 *Passenger's seat belt switch*
200 *Passenger's seat switch*
201 *Seat belt warning gearbox switch*
202 *Seat belt warning lamp*
203 *Seat belt warning code*

Cable colour code

N	Brown	P	Purple	W	White
U	Blue	G	Green	Y	Yellow
R	Red	LG	Light Green	B	Black
O	Orange	K	Pink		

When a cable has two colour code letters the first denotes the main colour and the second denotes the tracer colour

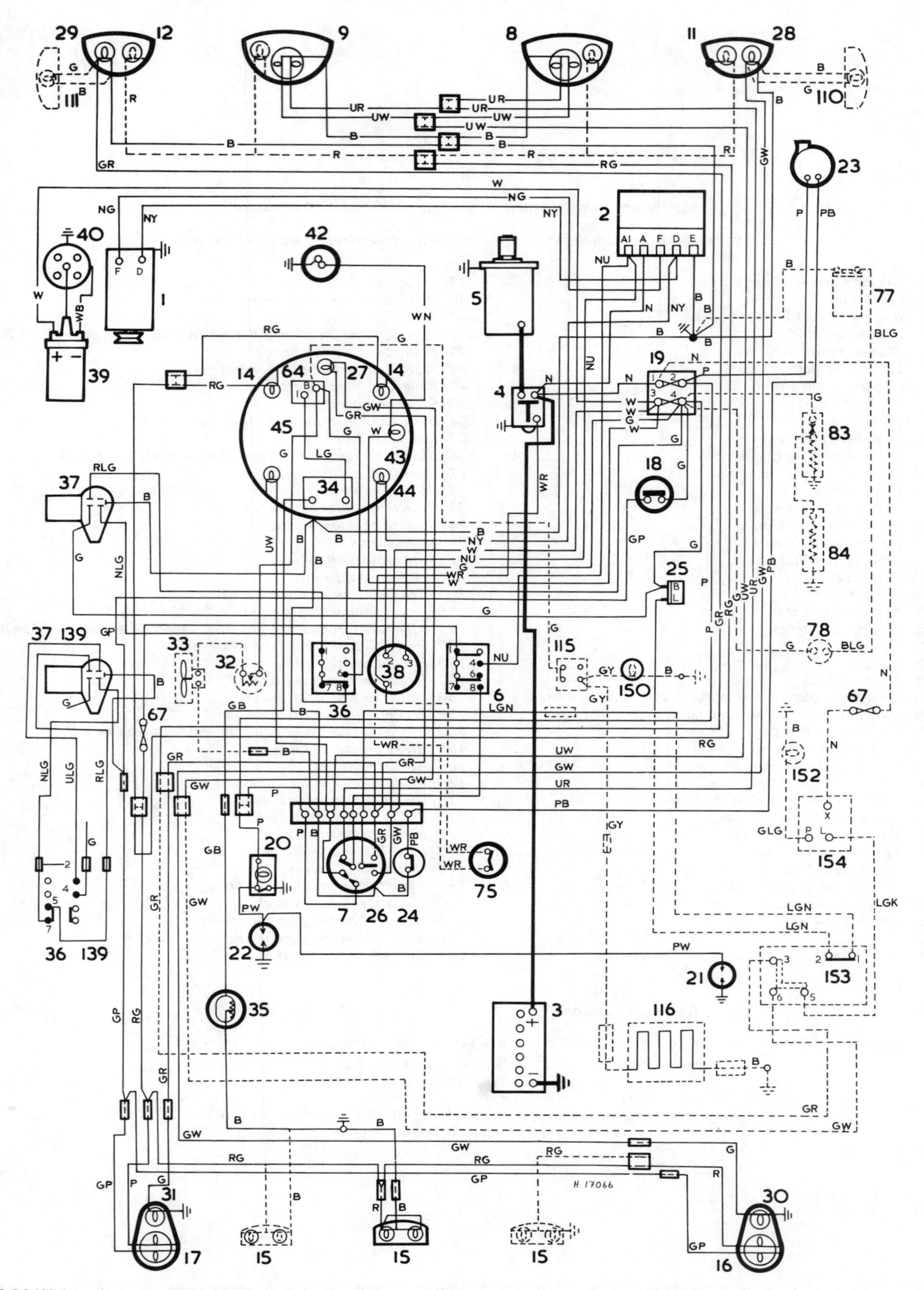

Fig. 10.30 Wiring diagram – Mini 850 De Luxe Saloon, Van and Pick-up (with dynamo and toggle type switches). For key see page 215

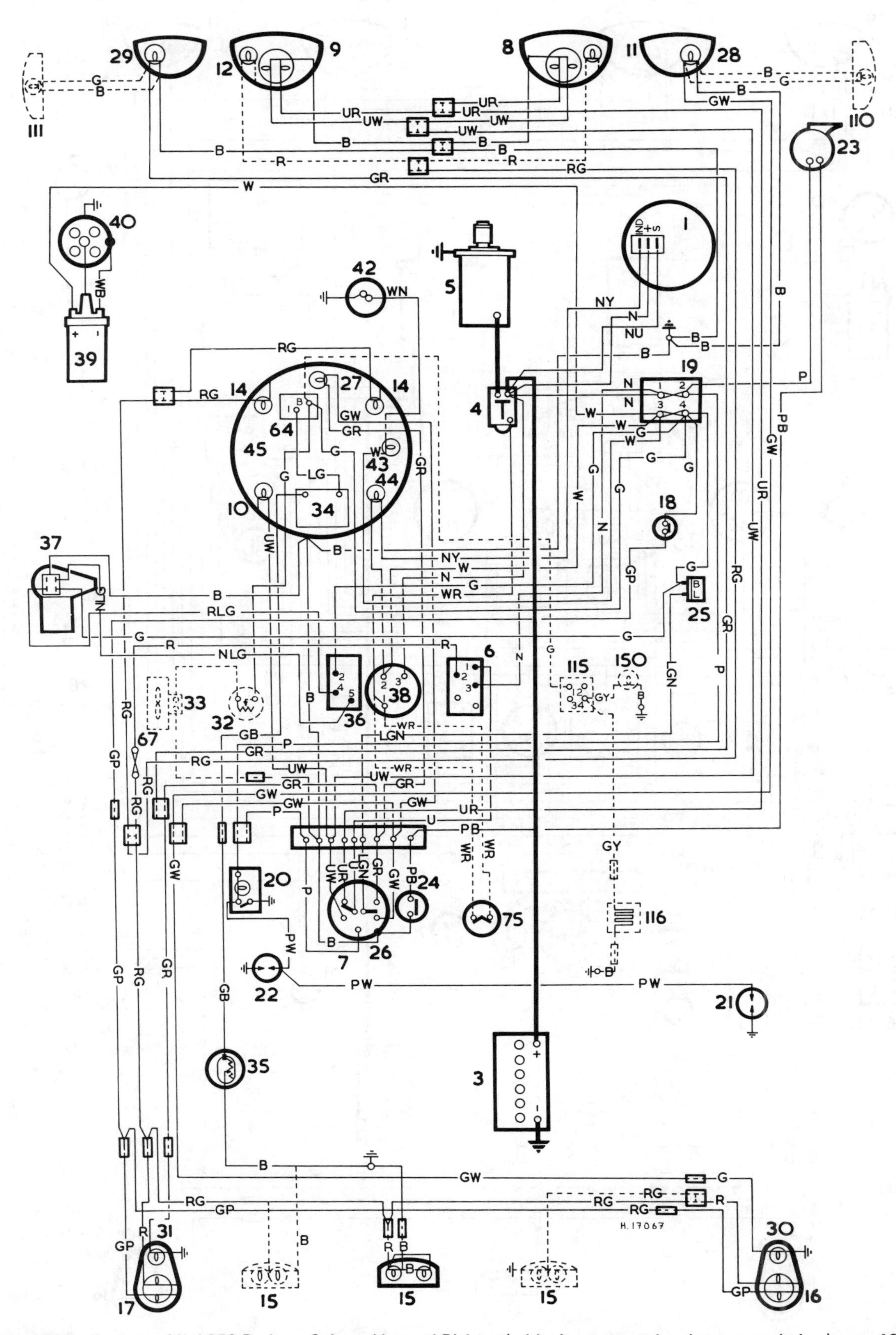

Fig. 10.31 Wiring diagram – Mini 850 De Luxe Saloon, Van and Pick-up (with alternator and rocker type switches) – pre 1976. For key see page 215

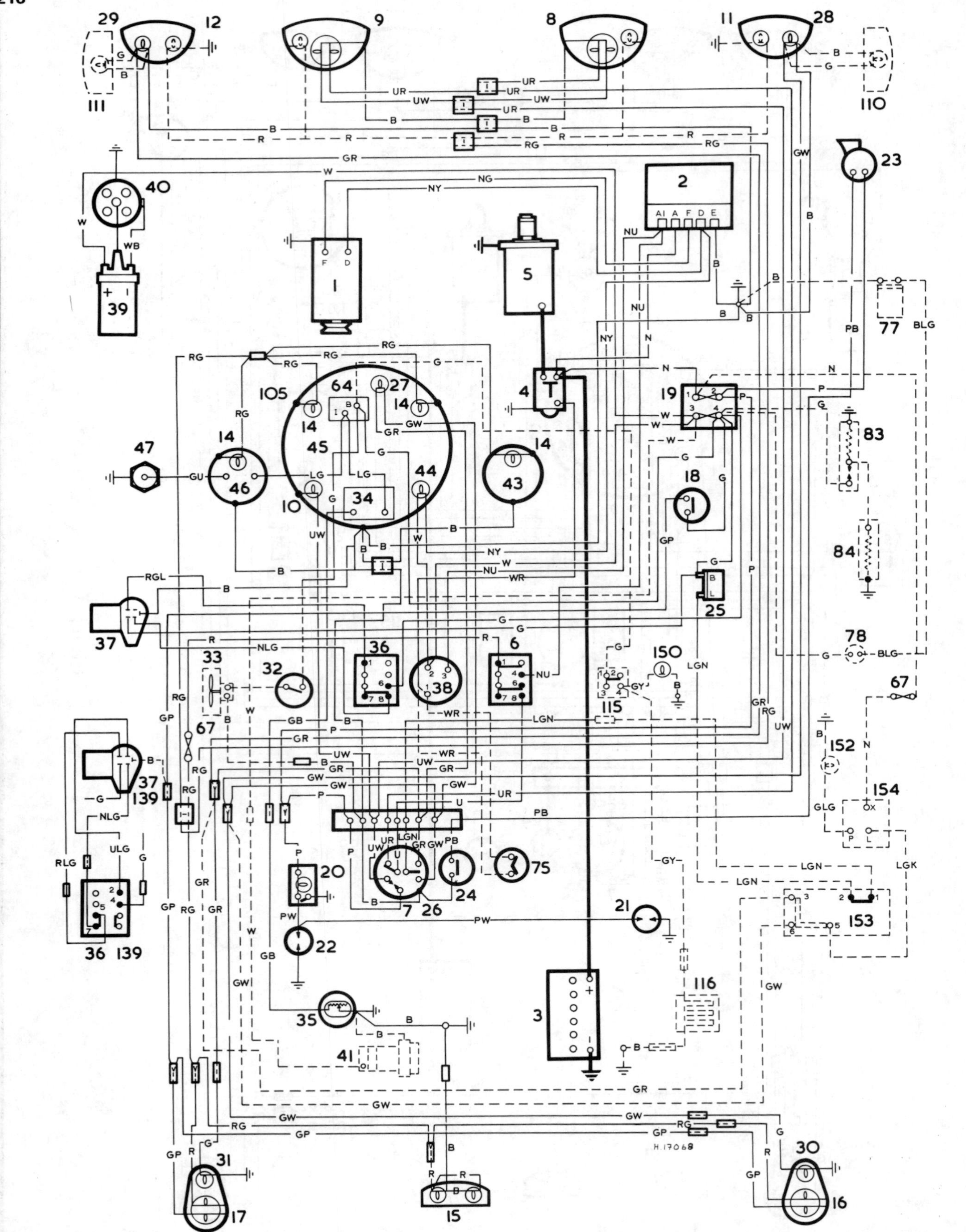

Fig. 10.32 Wiring diagram – Mini 1000 Special De Luxe Saloon and Cooper S Mk III (with dynamo and toggle type switches). For key see page 215

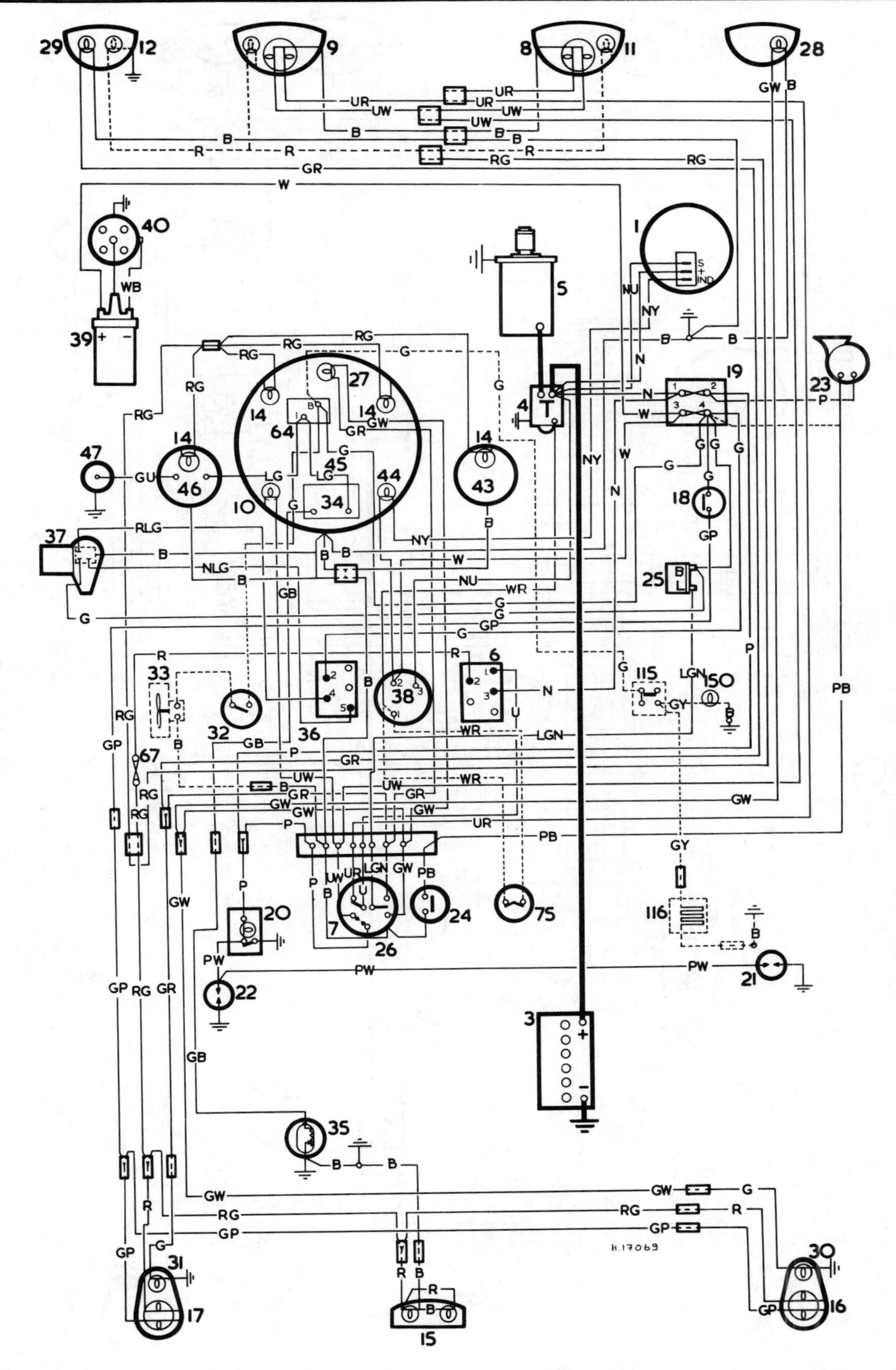

Fig. 10.33 Wiring diagram – Mini 1000 Special De Luxe Saloon (with alternator and rocker type switches) – pre 1976. For key see page 215

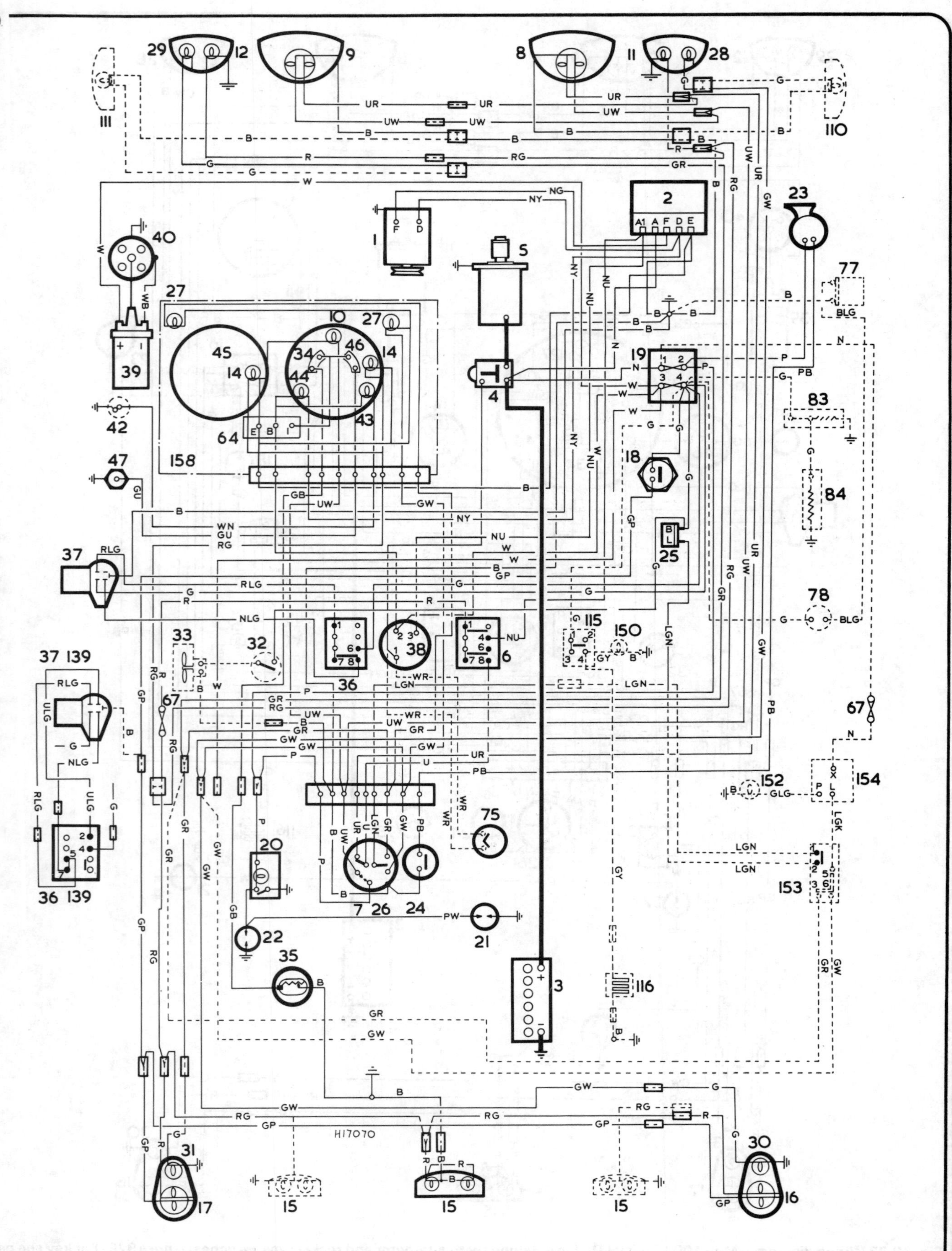

Fig. 10.34 Wiring diagram – Mini Clubman Saloon and Estate (with dynamo and toggle type switches). For key see page 215

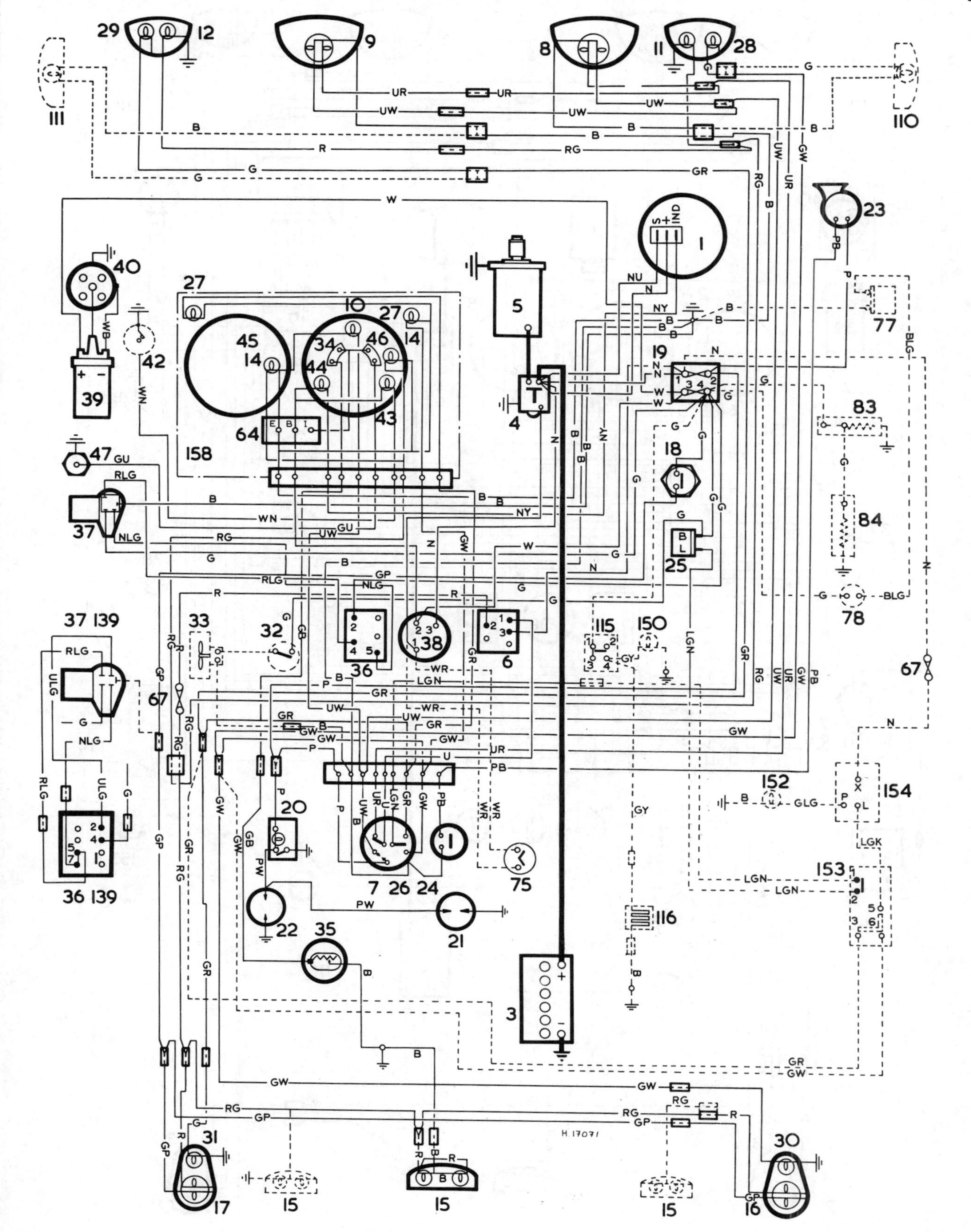

Fig. 10.35 Wiring diagram – Mini Clubman Saloon and Estate (with alternator and rocker type switches) – pre 1976. For key see page 215

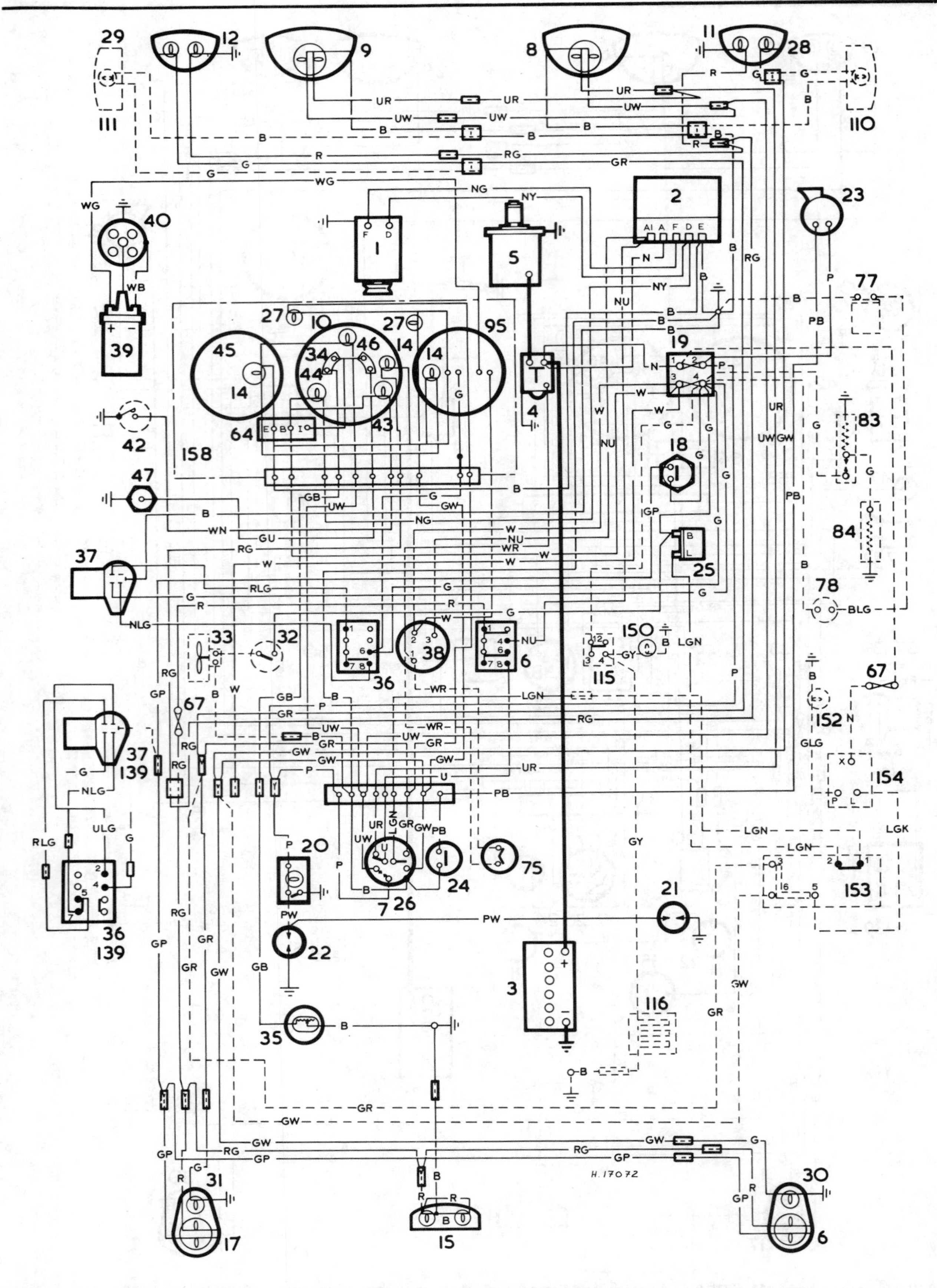

Fig. 10.36 Wiring diagram – Mini 1275 GT (with dynamo and toggle type switches). For key see page 215

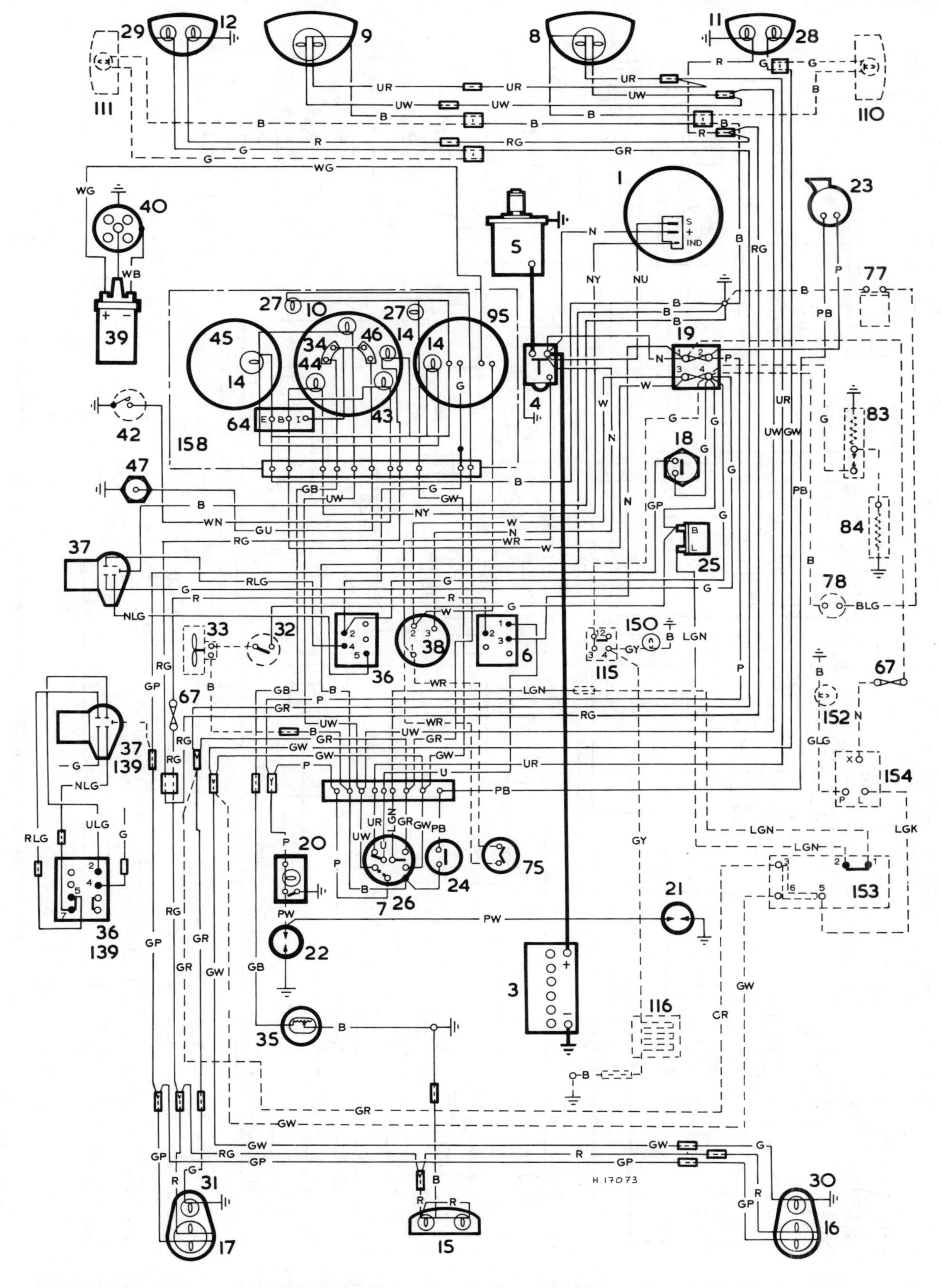

Fig. 10.37 Wiring diagram – Mini 1275GT (with alternator and rocker type switches) – pre 1976. For key to see page 215

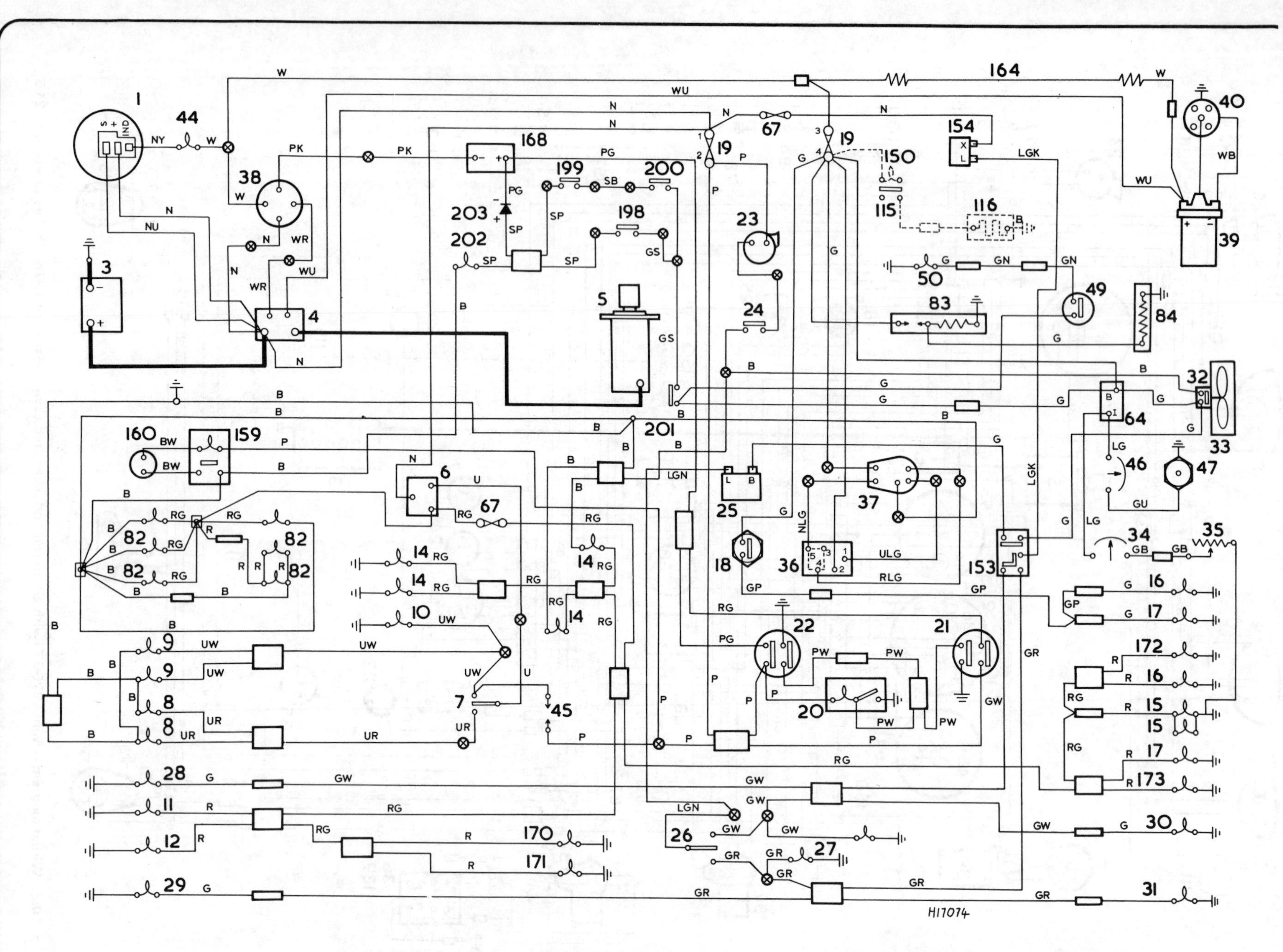

Fig. 10.38 Wiring diagram – Mini 1000 Saloon (Canada) – pre 1977. For key see page 215

Master key to wiring diagrams (Figs. 10.39 to 10.44 inclusive)

Some of the components listed in this key may not be fitted to individual models

1 Alternator
3 Battery
4 Starter solenoid
5 Starter motor
6 Lighting switch
7 Headlamp dip switch
8 Headlamp dip beam
9 Headlamp main beam
10 Main beam warning lamp
11 Sidelamp – RH
12 Sidelamp – LH
14 Panel illumination lamps
15 Number plate illumination lamps
16 Stop lamps
17 Tail lamp – RH
18 Stop lamp switch (hydraulic)
18 Stop lamp switch (mechanical)
19 Fuse box
20 Interior lamp
21 Interior lamp switch (door)
22 Tail lamp – LH
23 Horn
24 Horn-push
25 Indicator flasher unit
26 Indicator switch
27 Indicator warning lamp
28 Front indicator lamp – RH
29 Front indicator lamp – LH
30 Rear indicator lamp – RH
31 Rear indicator lamp – LH
32 Heater switch
33 Heater motor
34 Fuel level indicator
35 Fuel level indicator tank unit
37 Windscreen wiper motor
38 Ignition switch
39 Ignition coil
40 Distributor
42 Oil pressure switch
43 Oil pressure warning lamp
44 No charge warning lamp
45 Headlamp flasher switch
46 Water temperature indicator
47 Water temperature transmitter
49 Reversing lamp switch
50 Reversing lamp
56 Clock (if fitted)
57 Cigar lighter (if fitted)
60 Radio
64 Voltage stabilizer
67 Line fuse
75 Automatic transmission inhibitor switch
77 Windscreen washer motor
82 Switch illumination lamp
83 Induction heater and thermostat
84 Suction chamber heater
95 Tachometer
110 Indicator repeater lamps
115 Heated rear screen switch
116 Heated rear screen
118 Combined windscreen washer and wiper switch
132 Brake warning lamp
150 Heated rear screen warning lamp
152 Hazard warning lamp
153 Hazard warning switch
154 Hazard warning flasher unit
158 Printed circuit instrument panel
159 Brake failure test switch and warning lamp
160 Brake pressure differential switch
164 Resistive cable
165 Handbrake switch
166 Handbrake warning lamp
168 Ignition key warning buzzer
169 Buzzer door switch
170 RH front side marker lamp
171 LH front side marker lamp
172 RH rear side marker lamp
173 LH rear side marker lamp
198 Driver's seat belt switch
199 Passenger's seat belt switch
200 Passenger seat switch
201 Seat belt warning gearbox switch
202 Seat belt warning light
203 Blocking diode – seat belt warning
208 Cigar lighter illumination
210 Panel illumination rheostat
211 Heater control illumination
286 Rear fog guard switch
287 Rear fog guard warning lamp
288 Rear fog guard lamp
291 Brake warning relay
314 Clock illumination

Cable colour code

B Black
G Green
K Pink
LG Light Green
N Brown
O Orange
P Purple
R Red
U Blue
W White
Y Yellow
S Slate

When a cable has two colour code letters the first denotes the main colour and the second denotes the tracer colour.

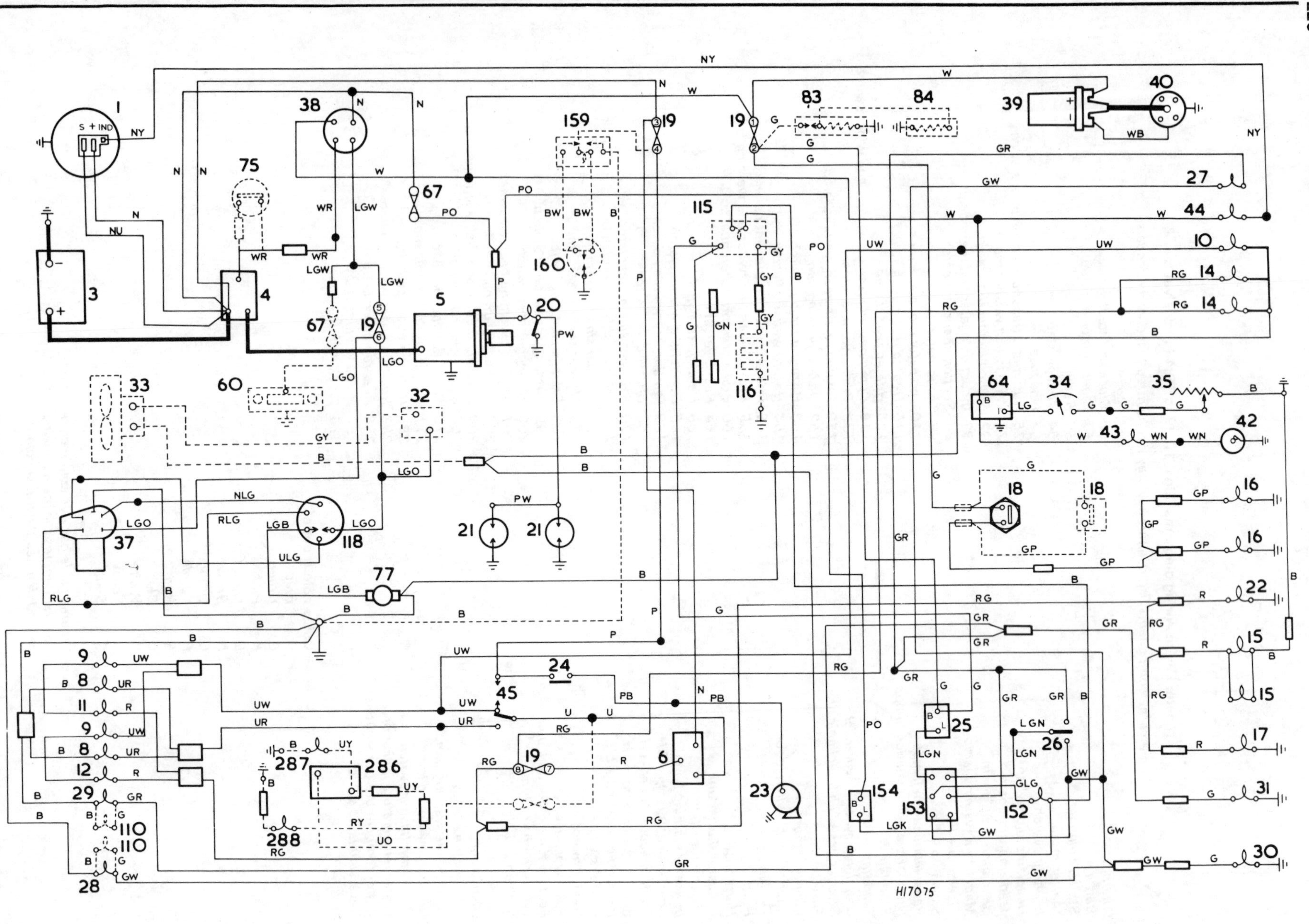

Fig. 10.39 Wiring diagram – Mini 850 Saloon, Van and Pick-up – 1976 onwards. For key see page 225

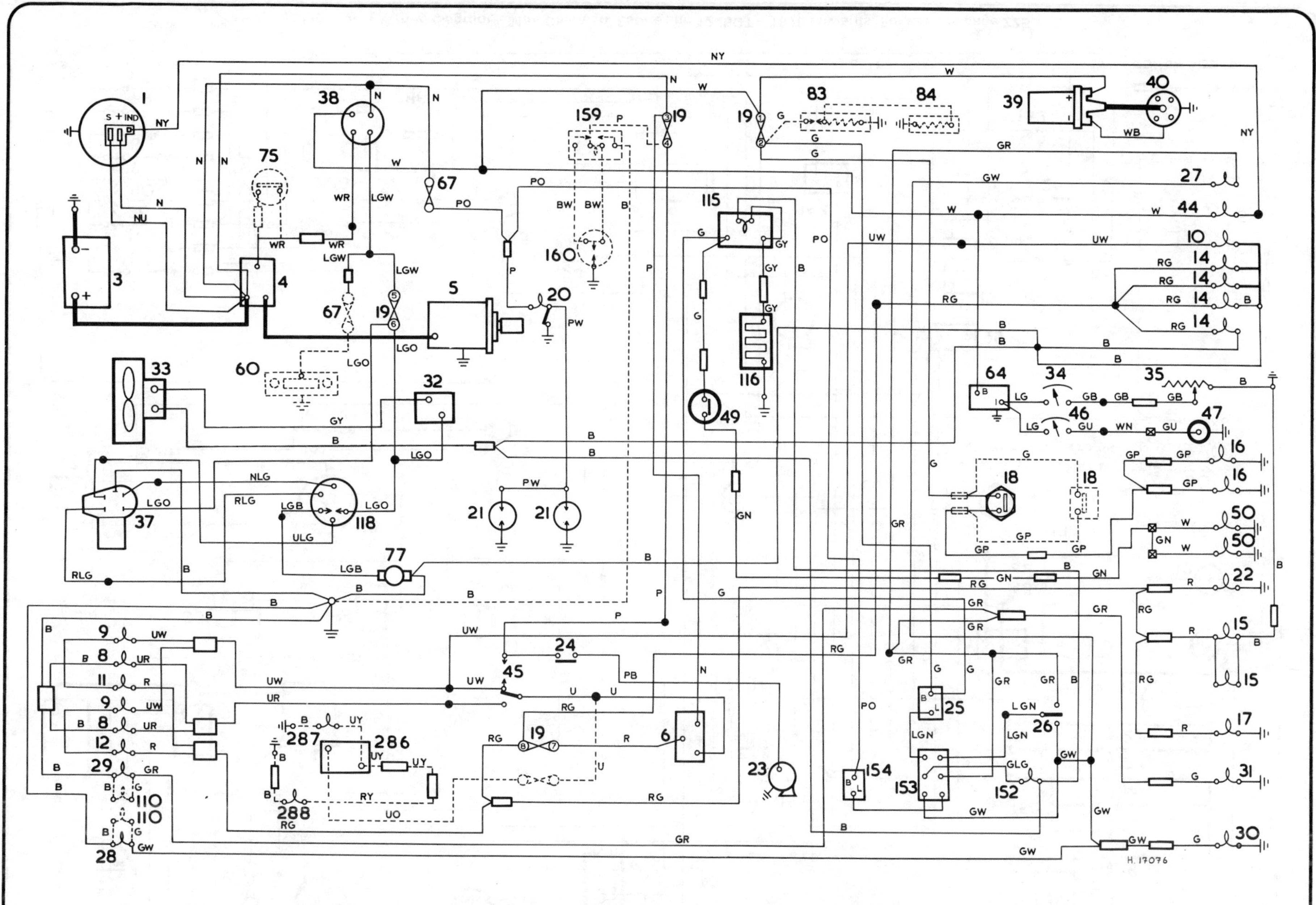

Fig. 10.40 Wiring diagram – Mini 1000 Saloon (triple instrument facia) – 1976 onwards (UK, Europe, Sweden); and Mini Special (triple instrument facia) – 1976 to 77. For key see page 225

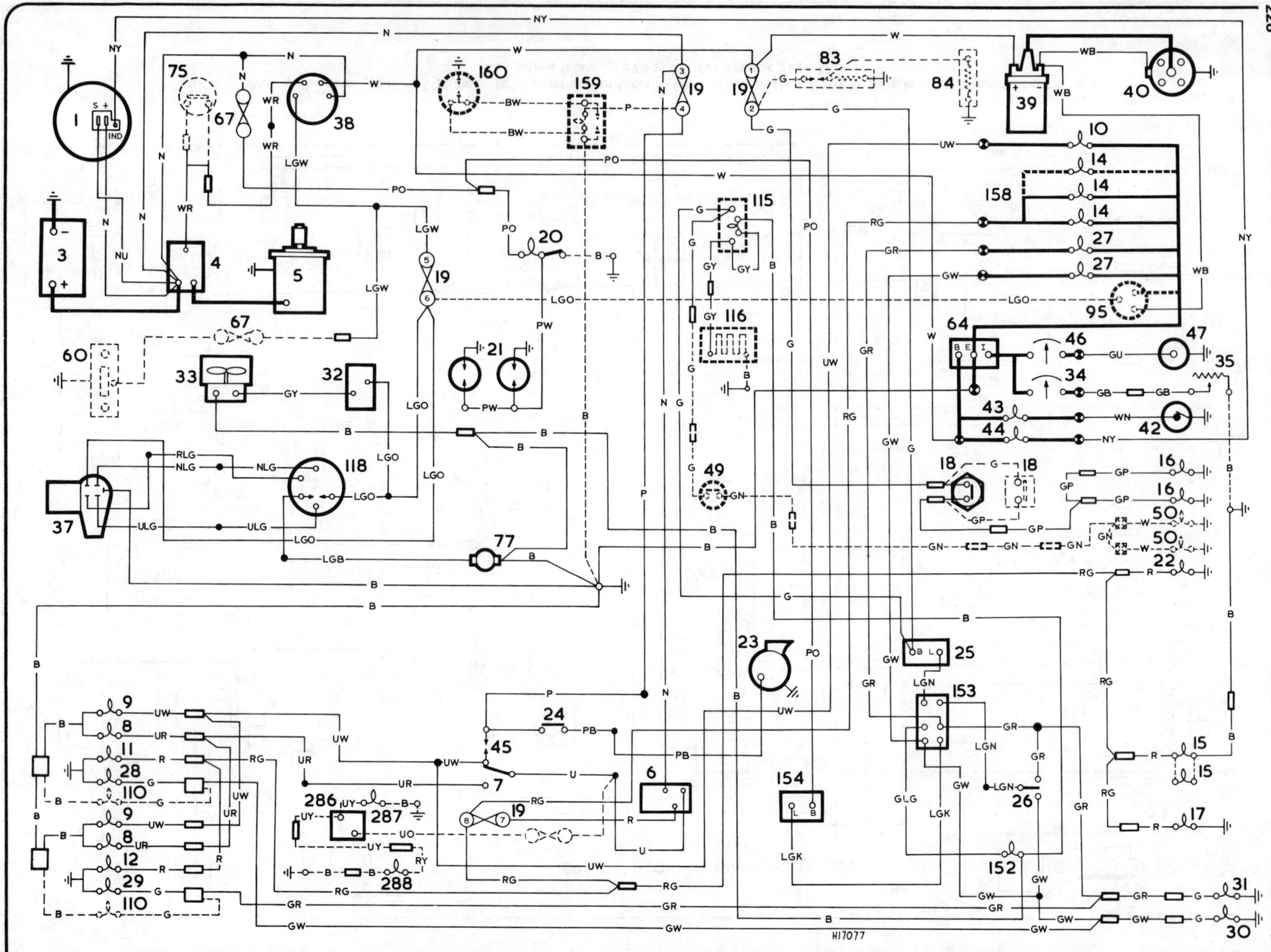

Fig. 10.41 Wiring diagram – Mini Clubman, Estate and 1275GT – 1976 onwards. For key see page 225

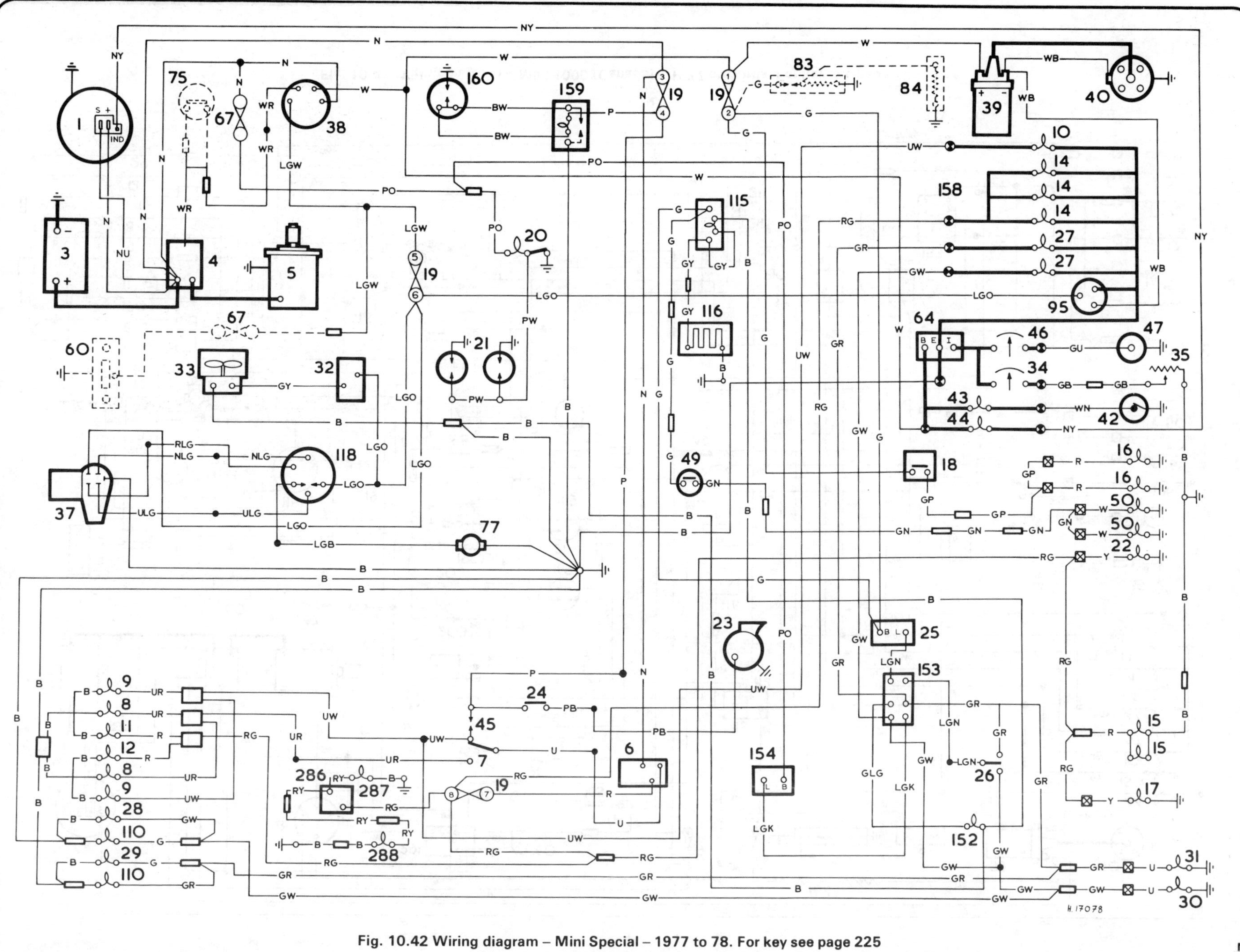

Fig. 10.42 Wiring diagram – Mini Special – 1977 to 78. For key see page 225

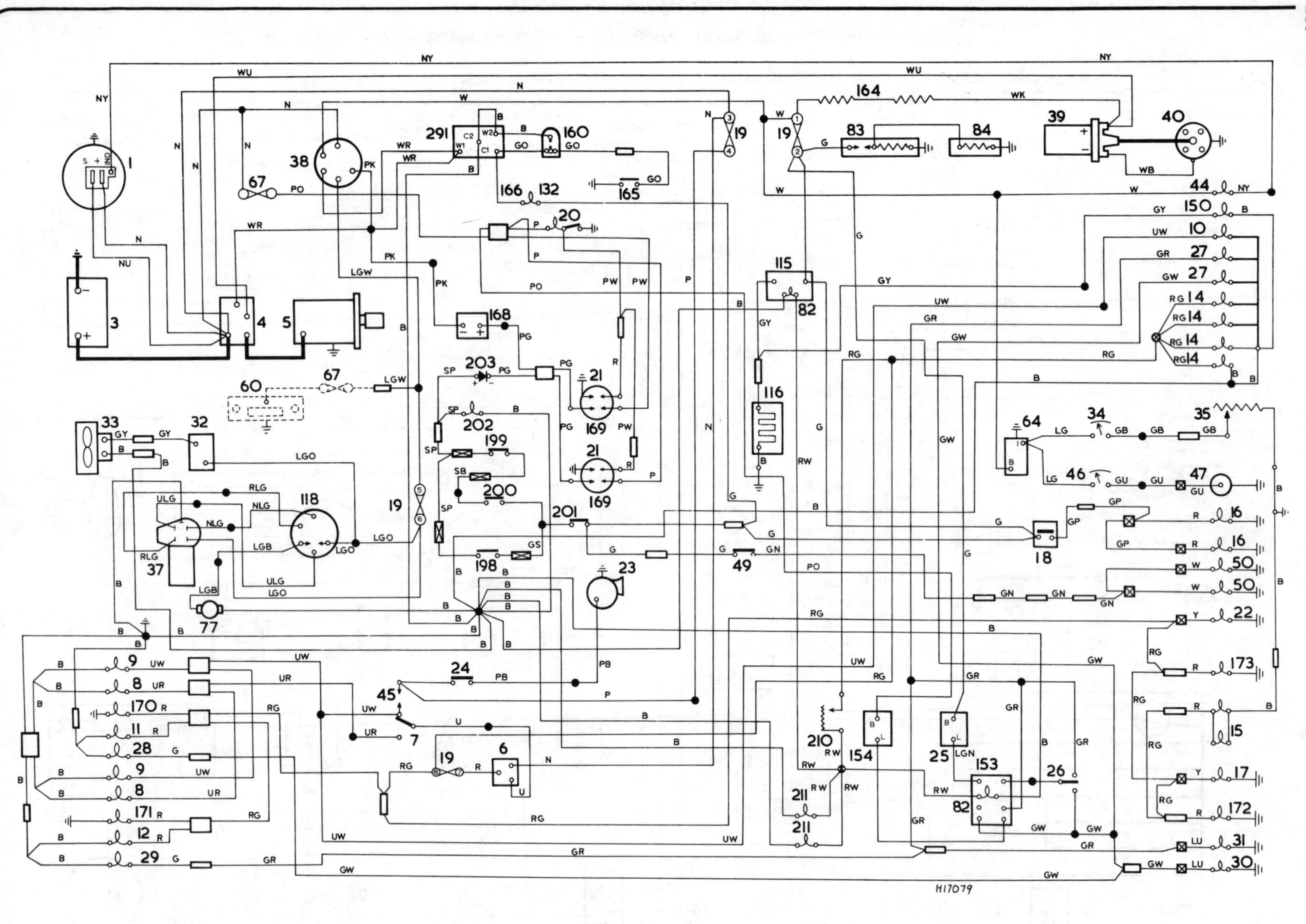

Fig. 10.43 Wiring diagram – Mini 1000 (Canada) – 1977 onwards. For key see page 225

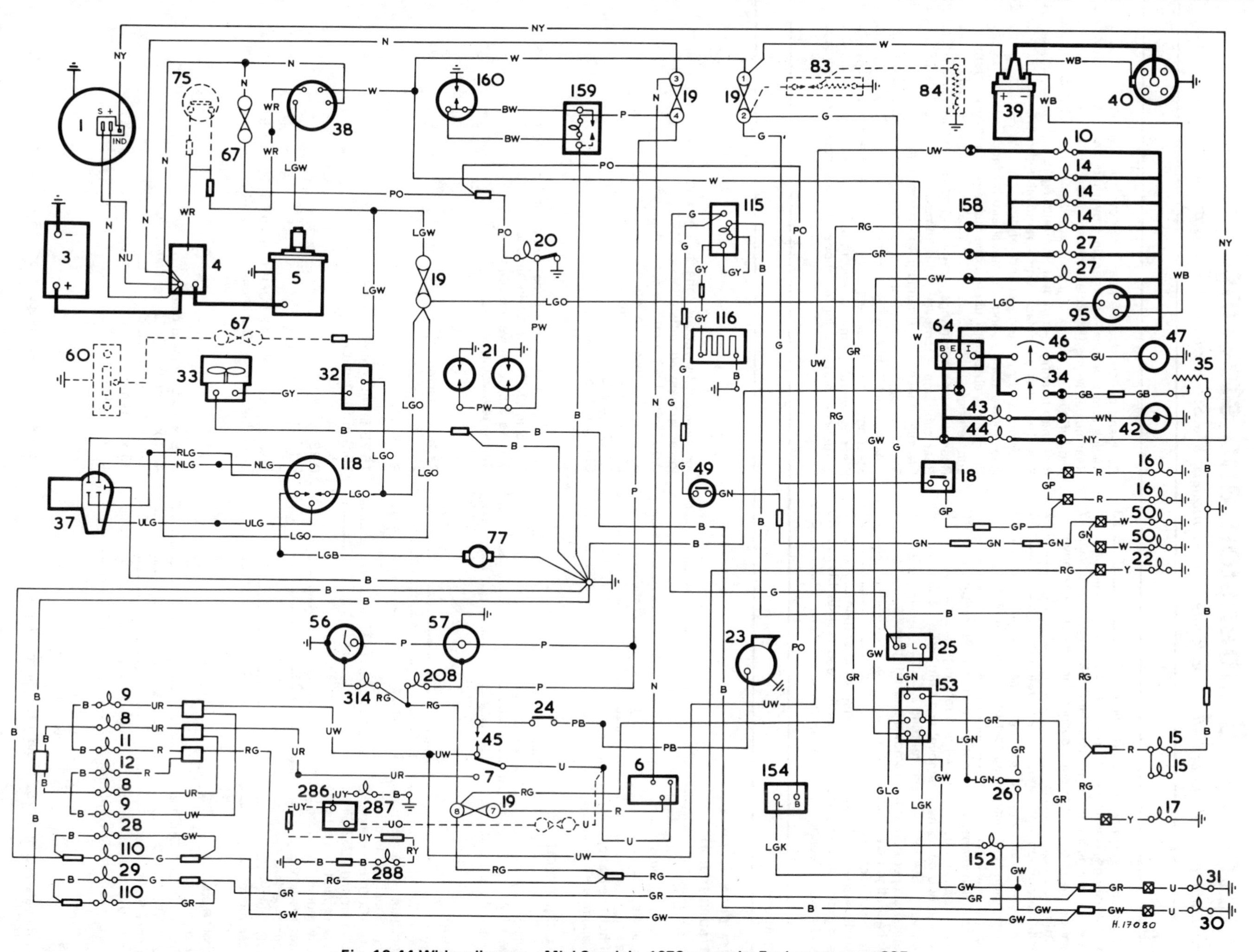

Fig. 10.44 Wiring diagram – Mini Special – 1979 onwards. For key see page 225

Chapter 11 Suspension and steering

For modifications, and information applicable to later models, see Supplement at end of manual

Contents

Specifications

Rubber cone suspension

Front suspension

Type	Independent by rubber cone springs and unequal length upper and lower suspension arms
Front wheel alignment	0.0625 in (1.58 mm) toe-out, unladen
Castor angle	3° ± 1° positive, unladen
Camber angle	2° ± 1° positive, unladen
Swivel hub inclination	9° 30', unladen
Shock absorbers	Girling telescopic

Rear suspension

Type	Independent by rubber cone springs and trailing radius arms
Rear wheel alignment	0.125 in (3.17 mm) toe-in, unladen
Camber angle	0.5° to 2.5° positive, unladen
Shock absorbers	Girling telescopic

Steering

Type	Rack-and-pinion
Turns lock-to-lock	2.7
Steering gear adjustment	Shims
Steering wheel diameter:	
850, 1000 and Cooper S	15.75 in (400 mm)
Clubman and 1275GT	15.0 in (381 mm)
Lubricant capacity (see text):	
Early models	0.33 pint (0.2 litre)
Later models	0.17 pint (0.1 litre)
Lubricant type (see text):	
Early models	Gear oil, viscosity SAE 90EP (Duckhams Hypoid 90)
Later models	Semi fluid grease (Duckhams Adgear 00)

Roadwheels

Wheel size:	
850, 1000 and Clubman	3.5B x 10 ventilated disc
1275GT	4.5J x 10 or 4.5J x 12 ventilated disc
Cooper S	4.5J x 10 ventilated disc
'Denovo' wheels	80 x 310 mm
1100 Special (alloy option)	5J x 10 alloy

Tyres

Tyre size:	
All models except 1275GT and 1100 Special (alloy option)	5.20 x 10 tubeless crossply or 145 x 10 tubeless radial ply
1275GT:	
Early models	145 x 10 tubed radial ply
Later models	145/70SR x 12 tubeless radial ply

'Denovo' fitment	155/65SF x 310 radial ply	
1100 Special (alloy option)	165/70HR x 10	
Tyre pressures	**lbf/in²**	**bar**
Crossply tyres:		
Front	24	1.7
Rear (normal load)	22	1.6
Rear (fully laden)	24	1.7
Radial tyres		
145 x 10:		
Front	28	1.9
Rear	26	1.8
145/70SR x 12:		
Front	28	1.9
Rear	28	1.9
155/65SF x 310 Denovo:		
Front	26	1.8
Rear	24	1.7
165/70HR x 10:		
Front	24	1.7
Rear	26	1.8

Hydrolastic suspension

***Note:** The suspension and steering on vehicles equipped with Hydrolastic suspension is identical to models fitted with rubber cone suspension, with the following exceptions:*

Front suspension

Type	Independent by interconnected Hydrolastic displacers and unequal length upper and lower suspension arms
Trim height (measured from the centre of the front hub to the edge of the wheel arch)	13.5 in (343 mm) ± 0.37 in (9.5 mm)

Rear suspension

Type	Independent by interconnected Hydrolastic displacers, trailing radius arms and coil hold-down springs

Torque wrench settings	**lbf ft**	**Nm**
Front hub nut (driveshaft):		
All models except Cooper S and 1275GT	60	83
Cooper S and 1275GT	150	207
Brake caliper retaining bolts	38	52
Tie-rod to subframe	22	30
Tie-rod to suspension arm	19	26
Upper suspension arm pivot shaft nut	53	72
Lower suspension arm pivot bolt nut	33	45
Roadwheel nuts	45	63
Steering column lower clamp pinch-bolt	12	16
Steering column upper clamp	14	19
Steering rack U-bolts	11	15
Tie-rod balljoint retaining nut	22	30
Swivel hub balljoint domed nut	75	102
Swivel hub balljoint to suspension arm	40	54
Steering wheel nut	35	47
Steering rack tie-rod ball housing collar	38	52
Rear hub retaining nut	60	81
Radius arm pivot shaft nut	53	72

1 General description

The front and rear suspension assemblies and associated components are mounted on subframes which are bolted to the underside of the bodyshell. The subframes are of welded all-steel construction, the front subframe also providing mounting points for the engine/transmission assembly.

The front suspension on all Mini models is of the independent type, each side consisting of a lower wishbone and single upper link. The lower wishbone is supported in rubber bushes at its inner end, while the inner end of the upper link pivots on two caged needle roller bearings. The outer ends of the two suspension arms are bolted to the tapered shanks of the upper and lower swivel hub balljoints. Fore-and-aft movement of each front suspension assembly is controlled by a tie-bar bolted at one end to the lower wishbone and mounted at the other end, via rubber bushes, to the subframe. The swivel hub contain tapered roller or ball bearings which support the outer ends of the driveshafts, and also provides mounting points for the drum brake backplate or disc brake calipers. Suspension and steering movement of the swivel hub is catered for by adjustable upper and lower balljoints.

The rear suspension on all models is also independent by means of two trailing radius arms. The forward end of each radius arm contains a needle roller bearing and bronze bush, which allows the arm to pivot on a shaft bolted to the subframe. The brake backplate is bolted to the rear end of each radius arm, as is the stub axle which carries the rear wheel hub and bearings.

While all Mini models share the same suspension component layout, two different types of springing and damping have been employed. All models are now equipped with dry suspension, whereby a rubber cone spring and telescopic shock absorber are fitted to the suspension assembly at each wheel. Early Clubman and 1275GT models were equipped with Hydrolastic suspension, whereby a displacer unit which combines the actions of both spring and shock absorber is fitted to each suspension assembly, in place of the rubber cone. The displacer units are interconnected front-to-rear on each side

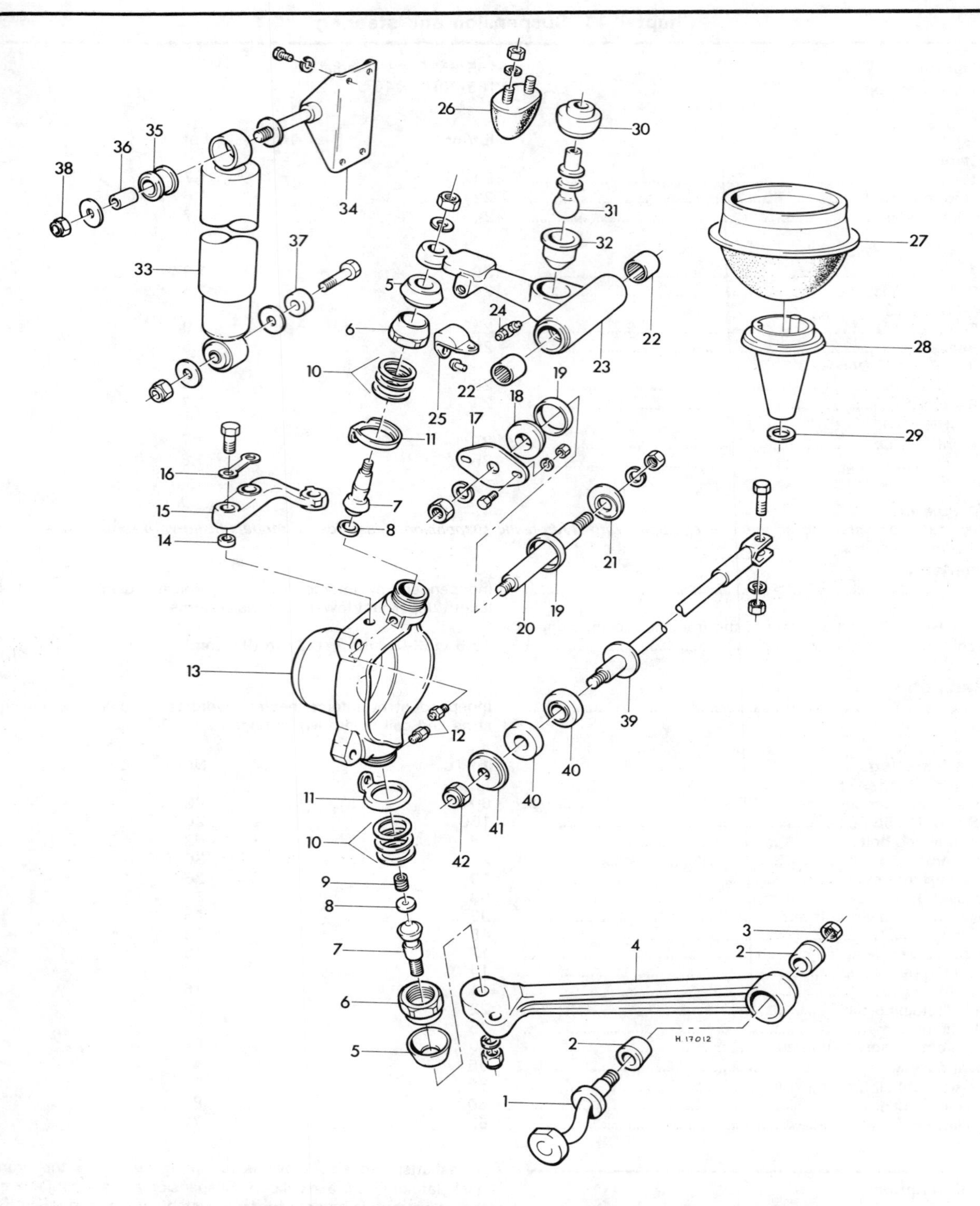

Fig. 11.1 Exploded view of the front suspension – rubber cone spring type (Sec 1)

1 Lower arm pivot pin	*12 Grease nipple*	*23 Upper suspension arm*	*33 Shock absorber*
2 Bushes	*13 Swivel hub*	*24 Grease nipple*	*34 Upper mounting bracket*
3 Locknut	*14 Ring dowel*	*25 Rebound buffer*	*35 Upper bush*
4 Lower suspension arm	*15 Steering arm*	*26 Bump buffer*	*36 Sleeve*
5 Dust cover	*16 Lockwasher*	*27 Rubber cone spring*	*37 Distance piece*
6 Ball-pin retainer	*17 Retaining plate*	*28 Cone strut*	*38 Locknut*
7 Ball-pin	*18 Thrust collar*	*29 Spacer (where fitted)*	*39 Tie-bar*
8 Ball-seat	*19 Sealing rings*	*30 Dust cover*	*40 Tie-bar bushes*
9 Spring	*20 Upper arm pivot shaft*	*31 Knuckle*	*41 Cup washer*
10 Shims	*21 Thrust washer*	*32 Ball socket*	*42 Locknut*
11 Lockwasher	*22 Needle roller bearings*		

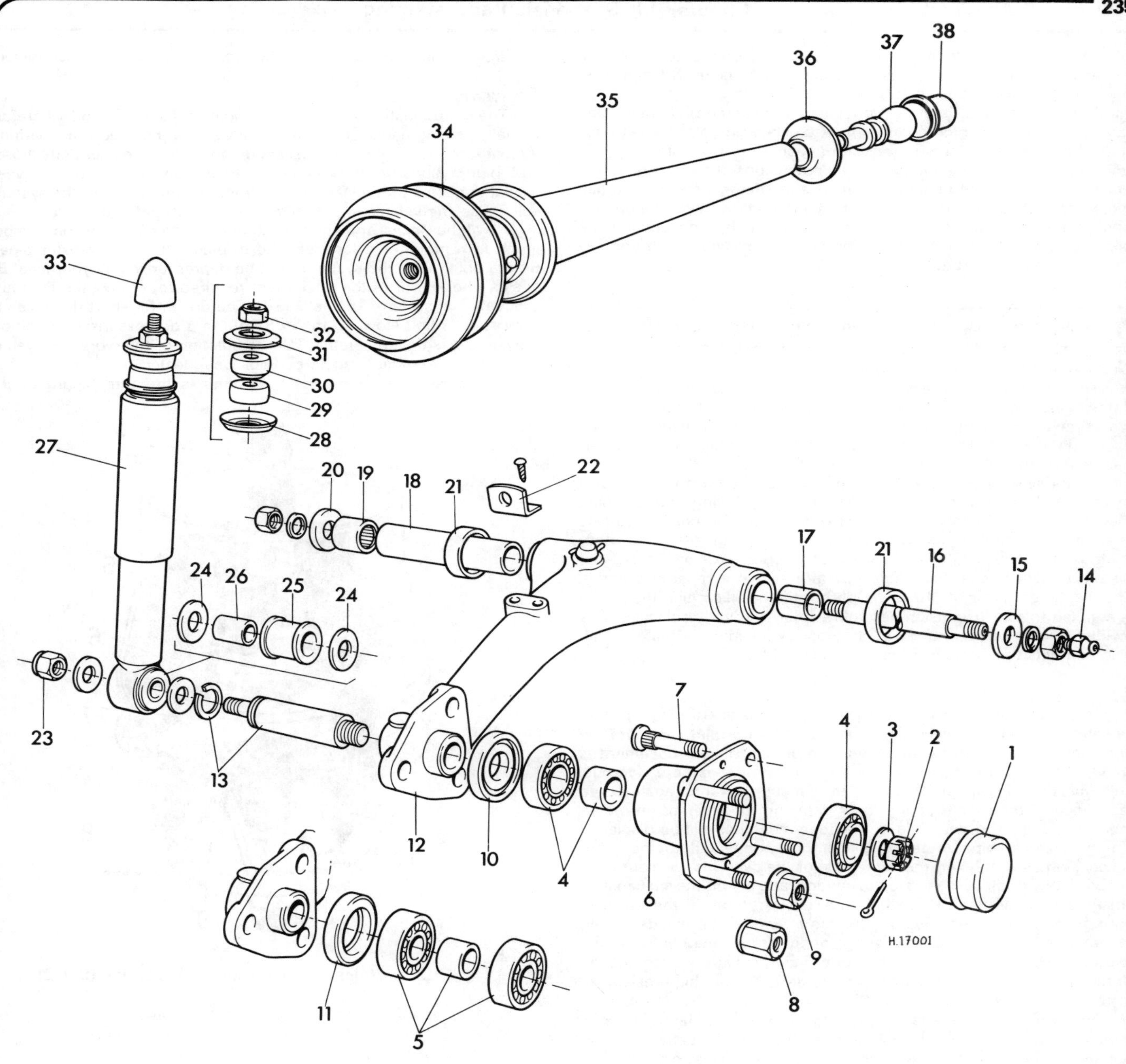

Fig. 11.2 Exploded view of the rear suspension – rubber cone spring type (Sec 1)

1 Hub cap
2 Castellated nut
3 Thrust washer
4 Bearings and spacer
5 Bearings and spacer (Cooper S and 1275GT)
6 Rear hub
7 Wheel stud
8 Wheel nut
9 Wheel nut (1275GT)
10 Oil seal
11 Oil seal (Cooper S and 1275GT)
12 Radius arm
13 Stub axle
14 Grease nipple
15 Thrust washer
16 Pivot shaft
17 Bronze bush
18 Lubricating tube
19 Needle roller bearing
20 Thrust washer
21 Sealing rings
22 Brake hose bracket
23 Locknut
24 Washers
25 Shock absorber bush
26 Sleeve
27 Shock absorber
28 Dished washer
29 Mounting rubber – plain
30 Mounting rubber – spigotted
31 Dished washer
32 Locknut
33 Rubber cap
34 Rubber cone spring
35 Spring strut
36 Dust cover
37 Knuckle joint
38 Ball socket

of the vehicle and are filled with a water-based, non-corrosive fluid under pressure. The principles of operation of the hydrolastic suspension system are described in detail in Section 2.

The steering gear is of the conventional rack-and-pinion type and is secured to the engine compartment bulkhead by a U-bolt at each end of the rack housing. Tie-rods from each end of the steering gear housing operate the steering arms, via both exposed and rubber gaiter enclosed balljoints. The upper splined end of the helically toothed pinion protrudes from the rack housing and engages with the splined end of the steering column. The pinion spline is grooved and the steering column is held to the pinion by a clamp bolt which partially rests in the pinion groove.

2 Hydrolastic suspension system – principles of operation

Component layout

The Hydrolastic suspension system consists of a Hydrolastic unit (known as a displacer) fitted to the suspension assembly at each wheel, and two metal pipes which interconnect the displacer units on each side of the vehicle, front to rear. The system is filled with a water-based, non-corrosive antifreeze fluid under pressure.

Each displacer consists of a rubber spring fitted to the upper part of the unit. This rubber spring is the actual springing and damping medium, and is shaped in such a way as to give a progressive rate characteristic similar to the rubber cone spring fitted to non-Hydrolastic Minis. At the lower end of the displacer unit a tapered piston, attached to a diaphragm operates within a tapered cylinder. The diaphragm seals off the lower part of the displacer and the piston is coupled to the suspension assembly. Internally the displacer unit is divided into an upper and lower chamber by a separator plate, which also contains the damper valves and a bleed hole.

Operation

Movement of the vehicle suspension actuates the displacer piston, causing fluid to be displaced through the separator plate and into the upper chamber either via the bleed hole, if suspension movement is small, or through the damper valve if the movement is more vigorous. This causes the upper chamber to deflect upwards against the resistance of the rubber spring, thus damping the suspension movement. In addition to this, fluid in the upper chamber will be displaced via the transfer pipe to the displacer unit connected to the other suspension assembly, on the same side of the car. This will cause the piston in this displacer to move downwards and act on the suspension, ensuring that the vehicle remains in a level attitude. In the event of both suspension assemblies on the same side of the car deflecting together (ie body roll when cornering), no fluid movement between the two displacers will occur and the entire fluid pressure will be applied simultaneously to both displacer pistons giving a very high resistance to the rolling movement.

As the relative front end weight of the Mini is high, the normal ride attitude of the car would be tail high, as the partially deflected front suspension would transfer fluid to the rear suspension, causing it to rise. To overcome this, non-adjustable coil hold-down springs are fitted between the chassis and each rear suspension arm. Thus, fluid is transfered from rear to front and a near level attitude is maintained.

Servicing

The Hydrolastic system is completely sealed, and therefore virtually maintenance free. It is advisable, however, at periodic intervals, to inspect the external condition of the displacer units, hoses and pipe unions. Any seepage of fluid from the union between displacer hose and transfer pipe, or from any other part of the system, will cause the vehicle suspension to sag on the affected side.

It will be necessary when working on certain suspension components to remove or disconnect the displacer units or transfer pipes. Before doing this, the system must be depressurised by your local BL dealer who will have the equipment required to remove the fluid and evacuate the system. The vehicle can be driven for short distances at slow speeds (ie below 30 mph/48 kph) in a depressurised condition, providing it is driven carefully. On completion of the work the system must be repressurised, again by your local dealer.

The pressure in the system determines the trim height of the

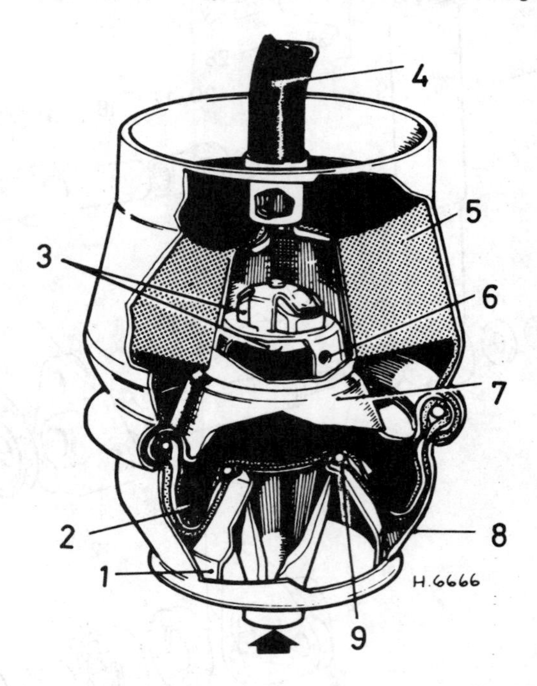

Fig. 11.3 Hydrolastic suspension displacer unit (Sec 2)

1 *Tapered piston*
2 *Diaphragm*
3 *Damper valve*
4 *Interconnecting pipe*
5 *Rubber spring*
6 *Bleed hole*
7 *Separator plate*
8 *Displacer body*
9 *Diaphragm*

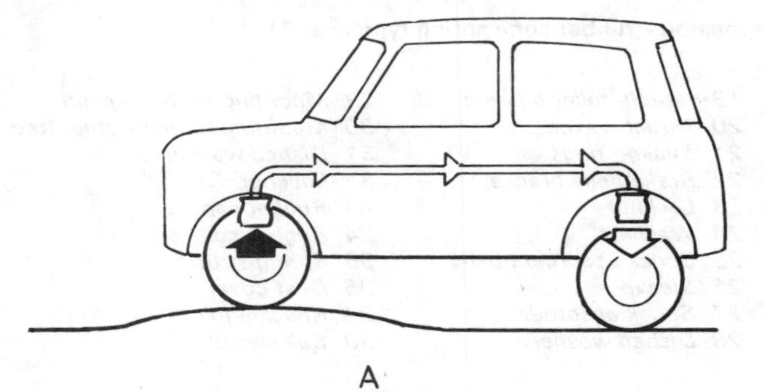

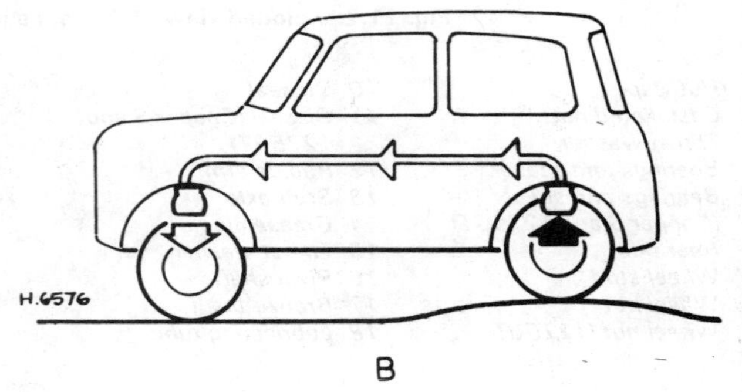

Fig. 11.4 Principles of Hydrolastic suspension (Sec 2)

A *The rear rises in response to upward motion of the front wheel*

B *The front rises in response to upward motion of the rear wheel.*

vehicle and this should also be checked periodically to ensure that it has not altered appreciably. The trim height is measured from the centre of the front wheel hub to the top of the wheel arch. It is important to ensure that the correct height is maintained otherwise the steering geometry may be affected, resulting in uneven tyre wear and insensitive handling.

3 Suspension and steering components – inspection for wear

Steering

1 First check for wear in the steering tie-rod outer balljoints. Turn the steering to left or right lock sufficiently to allow the joints to be observed. Now have an assistant turn the steering wheel back and forth slightly. If there is any side movement in the balljoint it must be renewed. Similarly place your hand over the rubber gaiter at the end of the rack housing and feel for any excess free play of the inner balljoint. If the condition of this joint is suspect, a further investigation should be carried out with the gaiter removed. If necessary, adjust as described in Section 30.

Front suspension

2 To inspect the front suspension, jack up the front of the car and support it on axle stands.
3 Grasp the roadwheel at the 12 o'clock and 6 o'clock positions and try to rock it. If any movement is felt it is likely to be in one or more of the following areas:

Wheel bearings
4 Continue rocking the wheel while your assistant depresses the footbrake. If the movement disappears or becomes less severe, then the wheel bearings in the swivel hub are at fault. If the movement felt at the roadwheel is greater than 0.25 in (6.3 mm), the bearings should be renewed.

Swivel hub balljoints
5 Wear of the swivel hub balljoints is fairly common on Minis and will be quite obvious on inspection because the whole swivel hub will appear to move in relation to the suspension arms as the wheel is rocked. If this is the case, the balljoints should be adjusted, or if badly worn, renewed as described in Section 6.

Suspension arm mountings
6 Check for wear of the lower arm inner mounting bushes where the arm is bolted to the subframe. If the bushes are worn, the arm will appear to move in and out as the wheel is rocked.
7 The upper arm inner roller bearings cannot be inspected without partially dismantling the suspension because the rubber cone spring or displacer unit holds the arm in tension and any wear will not be evident. It can be removed for closer inspection if required as described in Section 9; however, wear of the upper arm and its bearings is uncommon.
8 With the brakes still firmly applied, try to rotate the wheel back and forth. If any movement is now felt, examine the tie-bar between the lower suspension arm and subframe for wear or deterioration of the rubber bushes.

Rear suspension

9 To check the rear suspension for wear, jack up the rear of the car and support it on axle stands placed under the subframe.
10 Wear of the rear suspension components can often be felt when driving the car as a tendency for the rear of the vehicle to wander over uneven road surfaces or when cornering. To isolate the worn components, grasp the roadwheel at the 12 o'clock and 6 o'clock positions and try to rock it. If any movement is felt, it is likely to be in one of the following areas:

Wheel bearings
11 Continue rocking the wheel while an assistant depresses the footbrake. If the movement disappears or becomes less pronounced, then the wheel bearings in the rear hub are at fault. If the movement felt at the roadwheel is greater than 0.25 in (6.3 mm), the bearings should be renewed.

Radius arm bearings
12 With the footbrake still applied, continue rocking the wheel and observe the front of the radius arm. If it can be seen to move appreciably up and down, then wear has taken place in the roller or plain bearing in the radius arm, or on the pivot shaft. If this is the case, the radius arm should be removed for overhaul as described in Section 20.

4 Front swivel hub – removal and refitting

1 Remove the wheel trim and slacken the roadwheel retaining nuts.
2 Extract the split pin and then undo and remove the driveshaft retaining nut and thrust collar (photo).
3 Working under the wheel arch, undo and remove the single retaining screw and lift out the upper suspension arm rebound rubber. Insert a solid packing piece of approximately the same thickness in its place.
4 Jack up the front of the car and support it on axle stands placed under the subframe. Remove the front roadwheel.
5 On disc brake models, undo and remove the brake caliper retaining bolts. Lift off the caliper complete with brake pads, and tie it out of the way from a convenient place under the wheel arch. On models fitted with drum brakes, clamp the flexible brake hose with a proprietary brake hose clamp or a self-gripping wrench with its jaws suitably protected. Now slacken the brake hose union, at the wheel cylinder by half a turn.
6 Undo and remove the steering tie-rod outer balljoint retaining nut and then separate the taper of the balljoint shank from the steering arm, using a universal balljoint separator (photo). If a separator is not available, refit the retaining nut two turns and then firmly strike the end of the steering arm with a few sharp blows, using a medium hammer. When the shock has freed the taper, remove the retaining nut and lift off the balljoint.
7 Next undo and remove the nuts securing the upper and lower swivel hub balljoints to the suspension arms (photo), and release the balljoint shank tapers from the suspension arms, using the procedure described in the previous paragraph.
8 Carefully lift the swivel hub assembly off the two suspension arms.

4.2 Driveshaft retaining nut and split pin

4.6 Remove the steering tie-rod balljoint with a universal separator

4.7 Remove the lower swivel hub balljoint retaining nut

At the same time, tap the centre of the driveshaft, using a soft-faced mallet, until the driveshaft can be withdrawn from the rear of the swivel hub assembly.
9 On disc brake models, withdraw the swivel hub assembly and then lift off the driving flange and disc. On models fitted with drum brakes, support the flexible brake hose to avoid stetching it and then rotate the complete swivel hub assembly anti-clockwise to unscrew it from the hose (photo). The hub can now be lifted away and the end of the brake hose protected to prevent dirt ingress. Take care not to lose the copper sealing washer from the end of the hose as the hose is removed.
10 Refitting the swivel hub assembly is the reverse sequence to removal, bearing in mind the following points:

(a) *Ensure that the flexible brake hose is not twisted when refitting the swivel hub to models equipped with drum brakes, and bleed the hydraulic system at the appropriate wheel on completion of the reassembly*
(b) *Tighten all retaining nuts and bolts to the specified torque*
(c) *Finally, tighten the driveshaft retaining nut when the vehicle has been lowered to the ground (photo)*

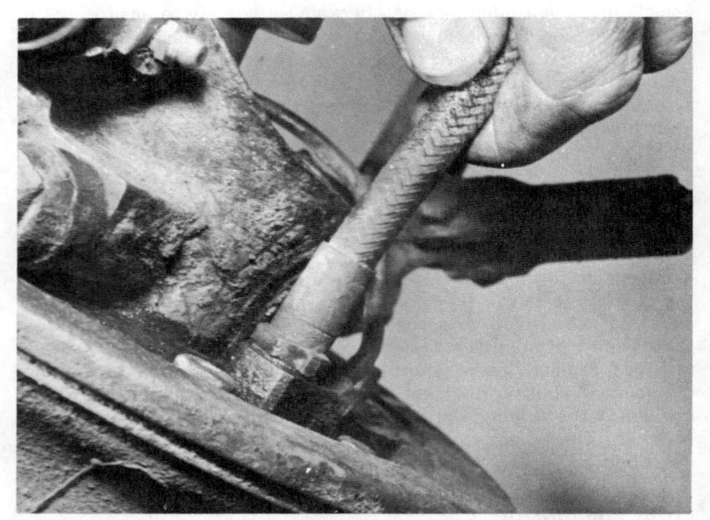
4.9 Rotate the disconnected swivel hub anti-clockwise to unscrew it from the brake hose

4.10 Tighten the driveshaft retaining nut with the weight of the car on its wheels

5 Front hub bearings – removal and refitting

Drum brake models

1 Remove the swivel hub assembly from the car as described in the previous Section.
2 With the assembly on the bench, slacken the brake adjusters, remove the two brake drum retaining screws and lift off the drum. If it is tight, tap it gently using a soft-faced mallet.
3 Arrange two robust wooden blocks approximately 10 in (250 mm) high, on the bench, far enough apart for the drive flange to lie freely between them, with the brake shoes resting on the top of the blocks. Using a tube or drift of suitable diameter, tap the drive flange out of the hub. It is likely that the inner race of the outer bearing together with the oil seal and the outer bearing distance piece will come away with the flange. If this happens, carefully remove these items from the flange with the aid of a puller.
4 Now undo and remove the four bolts securing the brake backplate to the swivel hub and lift off the backplate with brake shoes still in position.
5 Clean away any surplus grease from the centre of the hub between the bearings, and then prise out the two oil seals using a screwdriver. Note that there is a spacer fitted between the rear oil seal and the bearing outer race.
6 Using a tube or drift of suitable diameter tap out the bearing inner races away from the centre of the hub. Take care not to lose the balls which will be dislodged as the inner races are released, and recover the spacer (if fitted) between the two bearings.
7 Firmly support the swivel hub in a vice and drift out the two bearing outer races from each side of the hub.
8 Clean the bearings and swivel hub thoroughly in petrol or paraffin and dry with a lint-free rag. Remove any burrs or score marks from the hub bore with a fine file or scraper.
9 Examine carefully the bearing inner and outer races, the balls and ball cage for pitting, scoring or cracks, and if at all suspect renew the bearings. it will also be necessary to renew the oil seals as they will have been damaged during removal.
10 If the old bearings are in a satisfactory condition and are to be re-used, reassemble the balls to the ball cage, place it in the outer race and then press the inner race into position.
11 Before refitting the bearings to the hub, pack them thoroughly with a high melting-point grease. Do not fill the space between the bearings in the swivel hub with grease.
12 Place one of the bearings in position on the hub with the word THRUST or the markings stamped on the outer race facing toward the centre of the hub. **Note**: *Certain later models are fitted with bearings having lengthened inner races which butt against each other. On these assemblies the bearing spacer is omitted and the bearings are fitted with the identification markings facing* **away** *from the centre of the hub.* Using a tube of suitable diameter or a drift, press the outer race into the hub between the vice jaws or very carefully tap it into position. Ensure that the outer race does not tip slightly and bind as it is being fitted. If this happens, the outer race will crack so take great care to keep it square. Ensure that the bearing seats firmly against the shoulder in the centre of the hub when fitted.
13 Now place the bearing spacer in position and repeat the previous paragraph for the second bearing. **Note**: some makes of bearing have lengthened inner races which butt against each other. In this case the bearing spacer is no longer needed.
14 Tap a new oil seal into place over the outer bearing using a block of wood to keep it square. Note that both oil seals are fitted with their sealing lips inwards and that the inner seal has a second lip on its inner circumference.
15 Refit the split spacer against the inner bearing and tap in the inner oil seal using a tube of suitable diameter.
16 Refit the brake backplate to the swivel hub and secure with the four retaining bolts, tightened to the specified torque.
17 Place the distance piece over the driving flange with the chamfer towards the flange. With the inner race of the inner bearing suitably supported, tap the driving flange into the bearings. Ensure that the flange enters the distance piece between the two bearings squarely, otherwise the bearing inner race will be dislodged with possible damage to the oil seal.
18 The brake drum and its retaining screws can now be refitted and the complete swivel hub assembly refitted to the car as described in the previous Section. When refitting the hub assembly, ensure that the water shield on the driveshaft is packed with grease around its sealing face and positioned 0.25 in (6.35 mm) from the end of the shaft.

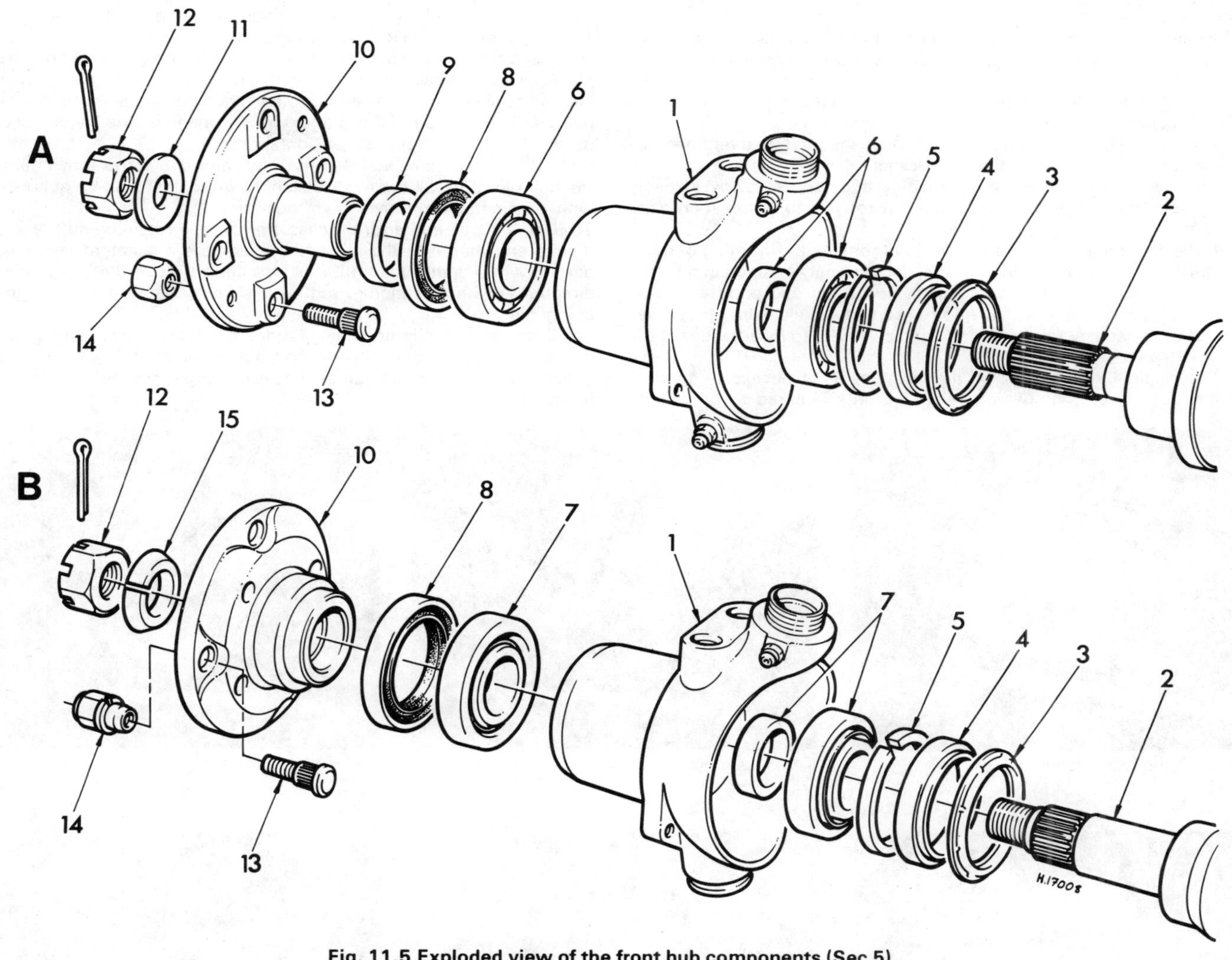

Fig. 11.5 Exploded view of the front hub components (Sec 5)

A Drum brake models *B Disc brake models*

1 Swivel hub
2 Driveshaft
3 Water shield
4 Inner oil seal
5 Oil seal spacer
6 Ball bearing and spacer set
7 Taper roller bearing and spacer set
8 Outer oil seal
9 Distance ring
10 Driving flange
11 Thrust washer
12 Castellated hub nut
13 Wheel stud
14 Wheel nut
15 Thrust washer

Disc brake models

19 Remove the swivel hub assembly from the car as described in the previous Section.

20 With the assembly on the bench, lift off the tapered collar (fitted to certain Cooper S models) from the front of the outer bearing and then prise out the two oil seals using a screwdriver. Now lift out the inner bearing spacer, the two taper roller bearings and the distance piece.

21 Using a suitable drift, tap out the two bearing outer races from each side of the hub.

22 Thoroughly clean the bearings and swivel hub in petrol or paraffin and dry with a lint-free rag. Remove any burrs or score marks from the hub bore with a fine file or scraper.

23 Carefully examine the bearing outer races, the rollers and roller cages for pitting, scoring, or cracks, and if at all suspect renew the bearings. It will also be necessary to renew the oil seals as they will have been damaged during removal.

24 Begin reassembly by refiting the bearing outer races to the hub, with their smaller diameter toward the hub centre. Press the outer races into the hub using a tube of suitable diameter and a vice, or very carefully tap them into place using a brass drift. Ensure that the race does not tip slightly and bind as it is being installed. If this happens, the outer race will crack so take great care to keep it square. The outer race must seat firmly against the shoulder in the centre of the hub when fitted.

25 Pack the two roller bearings with a high melting-point grease and position them in their outer races with the distance piece in between.

26 Install the two new oil seals with their sealing lips inwards and use a tube of suitable diameter to tap them fully home. Note that there is a spacer fitted behind the inner oil seal and that the inner seal also has a second lip on its inner circumference.

27 Position the tapered collar over the outer bearing (where fitted), and refit the swivel hub assembly to the car as described in the previous Section. When refitting the swivel hub, ensure that the water shield on the driveshaft is packed with grease around its sealing face and positioned 0.25 in (6.35 mm) from the end of the shaft.

6 Front swivel hub balljoints – removal and refitting

1 Remove the swivel hub assembly from the car as described in Section 4 and mount it firmly in a vice, with the balljoint requiring

attention uppermost.

2 Remove the rubber dust cover, tap back the lockwasher, and using a large socket or box spanner, undo and remove the domed retaining nut.

3 Lift off the ball-pin, ball-pin seat, and if working on the lower balljoint assembly, the ball-pin seat tension spring.

4 Lift off the shims located over the lockwasher and then remove the grease nipple and lift away the lockwasher.

5 Clean all the components thoroughly and then carefully inspect the ball-pin, ball-pin seat and domed nut for pitting, score marks or corrosion.

6 If the components are worn, a balljoint repair kit, consisting of new ball-pin, ball-pin seat, spring, shims, lockwasher and retaining nut should be obtained from your local dealer. If the old parts are in a satisfactory condition they may be re-used and any slackness that may have been previously felt in the joint can be taken up by adjustment of the shim sizes.

7 Before final reassembly of the balljoint, it is necessary to determine the correct number and size of shims required to provide a snug fit of the ball-pin with the domed retaining nut fully tightened. This is done in the following way.

8 Place the lockwasher in position and refit the grease nipple. Now place all the available shims over the lockwasher and then refit the ball-pin seat, the ball-pin and domed retaining nut. Assemble all the parts without grease at this stage, and if working on the lower balljoint do not fit the ball-pin seat tension spring.

9 Fully tighten the retaining nut and then check the movement of the ball-pin. With all the available shims fitted, it should be quite slack with considerable up-and-down movement.

10 Using a trial and error process, remove the retaining nut, take out a shim and then refit the nut and recheck the movement of the ball-pin. Continue doing this until it is possible to move the ball-pin in all directions, without binding, but with slight resistance to movement being felt.

11 Dismantle the joint again, lubricate all the parts with general purpose grease and finally reassemble the joint. If working on the lower assembly, the ball-pin seat tension spring should now be fitted (photos).

6.11a Fit the lockwasher...

6.11b ...spring...

6.11c ...ball-pin seat...

6.11d ...and shims

6.12a Now refit the ball-pin and nut...

6.12b ... screw in the grease nipple ...

6.12c ...and fully tighten the nut

6.12d Bend up the lockwasher...

6.13 ...and fit the dust cover

12 Tighten the retaining nut fully, check that the ball-pin still moves freely with only slight resistance, and if satisfactory bend up the lockwasher to secure the retaining nut (photos).
13 Refit the rubber dust cover to the ball-joint (photo) and then refit the swivel hub to the car as described in Section 4.

7 Front lower suspension arm – removal and refitting

1 Remove the wheel trim and slacken the roadwheel retaining nuts.
2 Working under the wheel arch, undo and remove the single retaining screw and lift out the upper suspension arm rebound rubber. Insert a solid packing piece of approximately the same thickness in its place.
3 Jack up the front of the car and support it on axle stands placed under the subframe. Remove the front roadwheel.
4 Undo and remove the nut and washer securing the swivel hub balljoint to the lower suspension arm. Release the taper of the balljoint shank using a universal balljoint separator. Alternatively refit the nut two turns to protect the threads, and then firmly strike the end of the suspension arm, using a few sharp blows from a medium hammer until the taper is released. Now remove the retaining nut.
5 Move the lower suspension arm downwards to disengage the balljoint shank.
6 Next undo and remove the nut and bolt securing the tie-bar to the suspension arm and then move the tie-bar sideways out of the way.
7 Undo and remove the nut and washer from the rear of the pivot bolt securing the lower suspension arm to the subframe (photo).
8 Lever the pivot bolt forward and off the subframe and then lift out the lower suspension arm.
9 Lift the rubber bushes off the suspension arm and inspect them carefully for swelling, cracks or deterioration of the rubber. Also inspect the pivot bolt for wear or damage. Renew any worn components.
10 Refitting the lower suspension arm is the reverse sequence to removal, bearing in mind the following points:

(a) *Ensure that the flat of the pivot bolt head locates under the tab on the subframe*
(b) *Do not fully tighten the pivot bolt retaining nut until the car has been lowered to the ground*
(c) *Ensure that all nuts and bolts are tightened to the specified torque.*

8 Front suspension tie-bar – removal and refitting

1 Remove the wheel trim, slacken the roadwheel retaining nuts, jack up the front of the car and support it on axle stands placed under the subframe. Remove the roadwheel.
2 Undo and remove the locknut securing the front end of the tie-bar to the subframe (photo). Now lift off the thrust washer and the rubber thrust bush.
3 Undo and remove the bolt, nut and spring washer securing the other end of the tie-bar to the lower suspension arm. Disengage the tie-bar from the suspension arm and subframe and then lift it off the car. Slide the remaining rubber thrust bush off the tie-bar end.
4 Carefully inspect the tie-bar thrust bushes for swelling, compression damage or deterioration of the rubber and check the tie-bar for straightness and elongation of the mounting bolt holes. Also check the securing bolt for wear of its shank. If any of the components are defective a new tie-bar kit should be obtained from your local dealer.
5 Refitting the tie-bar is the straightforward reverse of the removal sequence.

9 Front upper suspension arm – removal and refitting

Note: *Before carrying out this operation on cars fitted with Hydrolastic suspension, it will be necessary to have the system depressurised by your local BL garage. If working on cars equipped with rubber cone suspension, special tool 18G574B will be required to compress the rubber cone.*
1 Remove the wheel trim, slacken the roadwheel retaining nuts and jack up the front of the car. Place axle stands under the subframe and then remove the roadwheel.
2 Undo and remove the nut and spring washer securing the swivel hub balljoint to the upper suspension arm.
3 Using a universal balljoint separator, release the taper of the balljoint shank from the upper suspension arm. Alternatively, refit the nut two turns to protect the threads and then sharply strike the end of the suspension arm using a medium hammer until the taper is released. Now remove the nut and disengage the balljoint shank from the arm.
4 The procedure now varies slightly depending upon whether Hydrolastic or rubber cone suspension is fitted.

Hydrolastic suspension models

5 Undo and remove the single retaining screw and lift out the upper suspension arm rebound rubber.
6 Lift up the rubber dust cover around the knuckle joint located on the top of the upper suspension arm. Withdraw the ball end of the knuckle joint from its seat in the upper arm and then prise the shank of the knuckle joint out of the displacer unit using a screwdriver. The shank of the knuckle joint is a simple push fit in the displacer unit; however, corrosion may make it initially tight to remove. Recover the spacer (where fitted) from the shank.
7 Undo and remove the nut and spring washer from each end of the upper arm pivot shaft.
8 Undo and remove the two nuts, bolts and spring washers securing

7.7 Lower suspension arm inner mounting

8.2 Tie-bar front mounting

the pivot shaft thrust collar retaining plate, thrust collar and seal and then withdraw the pivot shaft forward and out of the upper suspension arm.

9 Now take out the rear thrust collar and seal and then manipulate the upper arm out of the subframe.

10 With the upper arm removed, inspect the pivot shaft and the needle roller bearings for wear, and if necessary renew them. The needle roller bearings can be removed from the upper arm by tapping them out of each side using a long thin drift inserted through the other side. Press in new bearings using a vice, or drift them in using a tube of suitable diameter or a shouldered mandrel. Ensure that the marked ends of the bearings face outwards.

11 Also carefully inspect the ball end of the knuckle joint and its plastic cup seat in the upper arm. If the ball end is corroded, worn or pitted or if the plastic cup seat is cracked or worn, renew the joint. The plastic cup seat can be removed by prising out with a screwdriver. The new knuckle joint will be supplied fully assembled and the plastic cup seat can be fitted to the arm with the joint in this condition. The rubber dust cover and ball end will then have to be removed to allow refitment of the upper arm.

9.14 Subframe tower mounting bolt fitted to later models

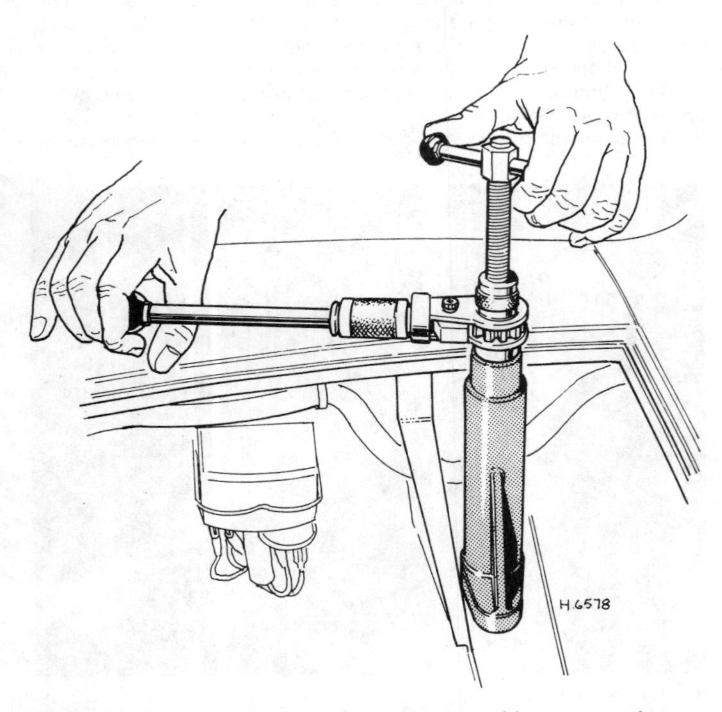

Fig. 11.6 Use of special tool to compress rubber cone spring (Sec 9)

12 Refitting the upper suspension arm is the reverse sequence to removal bearing in mind the following points:

- (a) *Lubricate all the parts with general purpose grease during reassembly*
- (b) *If the original knuckle joint is being refitted, pack the cup seat with Dextragrease Super GP available from BL dealers*
- (c) *Ensure that the dust cover is correctly located over the knuckle joint cup, when refitting, otherwise dirt and road grit will enter the joint*
- (d) *Ensure that all nuts and bolts are tightened to the specified torque*
- (e) *Do not drive the car (except to your nearest BL garage) until the suspension has been repressurised*

Rubber cone suspension models

13 Undo and remove the nut and flat washer securing the shock absorber to the upper suspension arm. Now move the shock absorber sideways until it is clear of the mounting stud.

14 Working in the engine compartment, undo and remove the two bolts (or nuts) securing the subframe tower to the bulkhead crossmember. Lift off the locking plate and then refit the bolts (or nuts). On later models undo and remove the large hexagon-headed plug that is used instead of the two bolts or nuts (photo).

15 It is now necessary to compress the rubber cone spring using service tool 18G574B as follows. Position the body of the tool over the two subframe tower retaining bolts (or nuts) and turn the tool centre screw, nine complete turns, to engage the threads in the rubber cone. Now turn the ratchet handle of the tool until it contacts the tool body. Hold the centre screw and turn the ratchet handle clockwise until all tension is removed from the strut which interconnects the rubber cone and the upper suspension arm.

16 Undo and remove the single retaining screw and lift out the upper suspension arm rebound rubber.

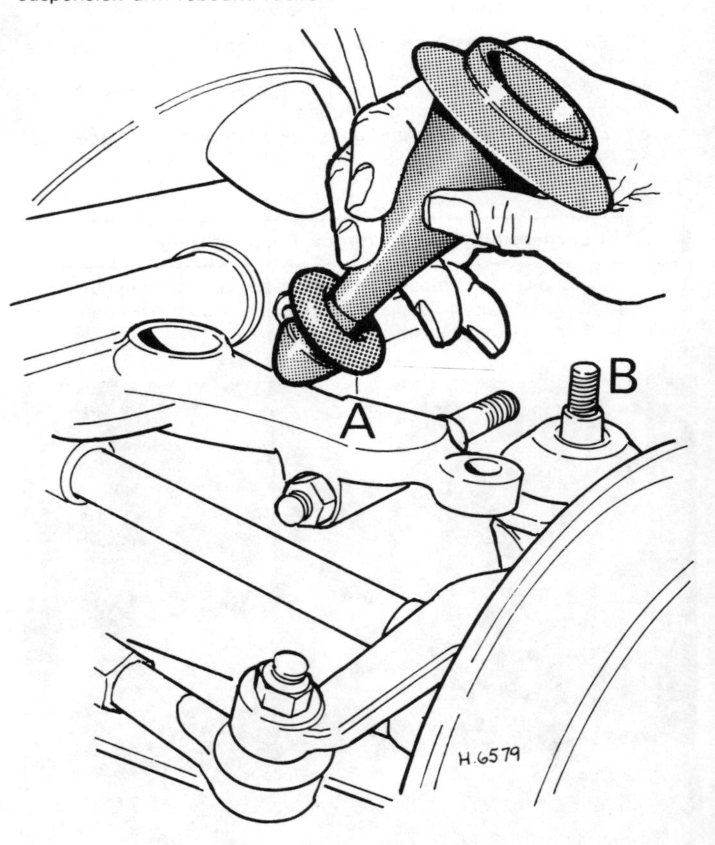

Fig. 11.7 Suspension strut removal – rubber cone spring suspension (Sec 9)

A *Upper suspension arm* B *Upper swivel hub balljoint*

17 Lift up the rubber dust cover around the knuckle joint located at the base of the spring strut.
18 Withdraw the ball end of the knuckle joint from its seat in the upper arm and then lift out the spring strut assembly from the rubber cone. If it is tight, prise it out using a screwdriver.
19 The remainder of the removal and refitting procedure is the same as described in paragraphs 7 to 12 inclusive.

10 Front suspension rubber cone spring – removal and refitting

1 Begin by removing the front upper suspension arm as described in the previous Section.
2 The service tool 18G574B that is used to compress the rubber cone must now be released by turning the ratchet anti-clockwise until all tension in the rubber cone is released.
3 Now unscrew the service tool and withdraw the rubber cone from its location in the subframe.
4 Refitting is the reverse sequence to removal.

11 Front suspension Hydrolastic displacer unit – removal and refitting

1 Begin by removing the front upper suspension arm as described in Section 9.
2 Using two large spanners, undo and remove the displacer hose from the transfer pipe union on the engine compartment bulkhead.
3 Push the displacer unit upward, undo and remove the two screws securing the displacer retaining bracket to the subframe tower.
4 Rotate the displacer anti-clockwise and withdraw it from its location on the subframe.
5 Refitting the displacer unit is the reverse sequence to removal. When installing the displacer, rotate it clockwise to engage the registers on the locating plate.

12 Front shock absorber (rubber cone suspension models) – removal and refitting

1 Remove the wheel trim, slacken the roadwheel retaining nuts and jack up the front of the car. Place axle stands under the subframe and remove the roadwheel.
2 Undo and remove the shock absorber upper and lower retaining nut and washers and lift off the shock absorber (photos).
3 Examine the shock absorber for leaks or damage of the outer casing. Hold the shock absorber upright and fully compress and extend it six times. Now slowly extend and compress it again. If 'dead' areas are apparent, if there is free travel when changing direction, or if the unit is damaged or leaking, it must be renewed.
4 Refitting is the reverse sequence to removal. Hold the shock absorber in an upright position and fully compress and extend it six times to expel any air before fitting.

13 Front subframe mountings – removal and refitting

Note: *The following information is applicable to later models equipped with bonded rubber mountings between the front subframe and vehicle underbody. The mountings can be removed with the subframe in position as follows.*

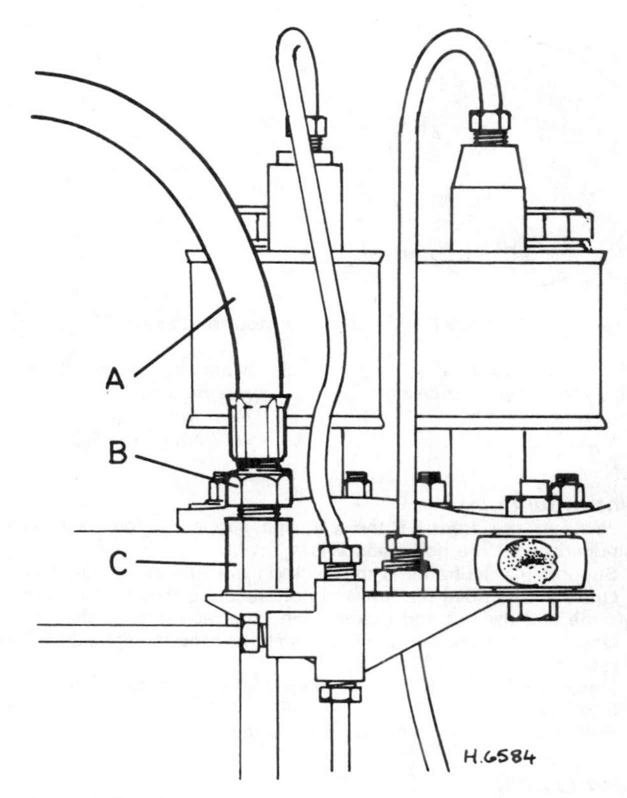

Fig. 11.8 Hydrolastic displacer hose connections (Sec 11)

A Hose
B Hose union
C Connector

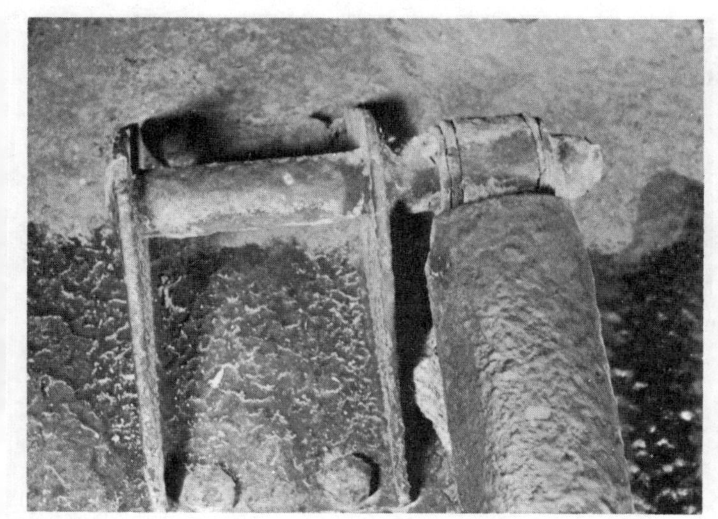

12.2a Shock absorber upper...

12.2b ...and lower mounting

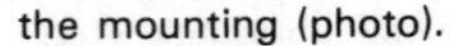

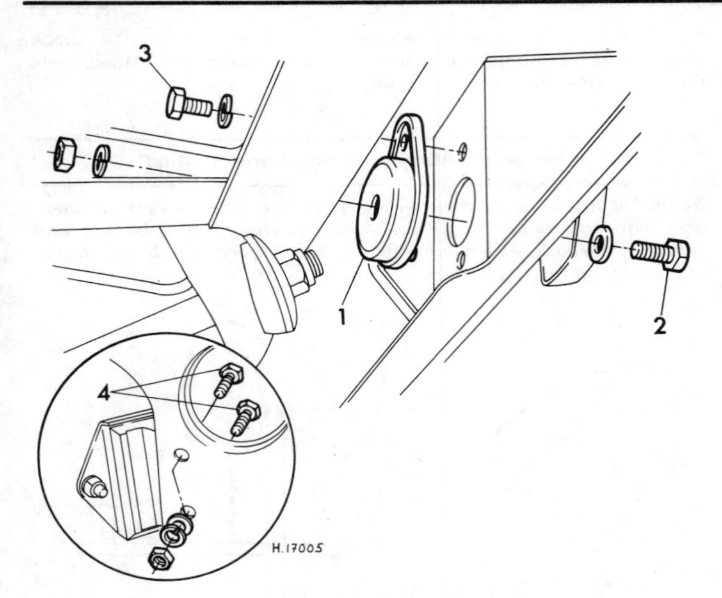

Fig. 11.9 Front subframe mountings (Sec 13)

1 Front mounting
2 Mounting-to-subframe retaining bolt
3 Mounting-to-body retaining bolt
4 Rear mounting-to-subframe retaining bolts

Front mountings

1 Jack up the front of the car and support it on axle stands positioned under the body side sills.
2 Support the subframe with a jack on the side to be released.
3 Undo and remove the nut and bolt securing the mounting to the subframe and the nut and bolt securing the mounting to the body.
4 Undo and remove the two nuts and bolts securing the subframe to the rear mounting.
5 Lower the jack slightly, lever the subframe rearwards, and extract the front mounting.
6 Refitting is the reverse sequence to removal.

Rear mounting

7 Jack up the front of the car and support it on axle stands positioned under the body side sills.
8 Support the subframe with a jack on the side to be released.
9 Undo and remove the two nuts and bolts securing the subframe to the mounting (photo).
10 Lift up the carpets inside the car and have an assistant hold the two bolts securing the mounting to the body. Undo and remove the nuts from below and lift off the mounting.
11 Refitting is the reverse sequence to removal.

14 Front subframe – removal and refitting

The front subframe, complete with engine/transmission unit and all suspension components still in position, can be removed from the car using the procedure described in Chapter 1. With the engine/transmission unit lifted off, the suspension components can then be withdrawn by referring to the relevant Section of this Chapter.

15 Rear hub bearings – removal and refitting

1 Jack up the rear of the car and support it on axle stands placed under the rear subframe. Withdraw the wheel trim and remove the appropriate roadwheel.
2 Slacken off the brake adjuster, unscrew the two brake drum retaining screws and lift off the drum. If it is tight, tap it gently using a soft-faced mallet.
3 By judicious tapping and levering, extract the hub cap and withdraw the retaining split pin from the hub securing nut (photo).
4 Using a large socket, undo and remove the hub securing nut and thrust washer. Note that the left-hand hub nut has a left-hand thread and the right-hand hub nut has a right-hand thread.
5 Withdraw the hub from the stub axle using a hub puller. Alternatively, lever it off using two stout screwdrivers or flat bars.
6 With the hub assembly removed from the car, prise out the rear oil seal and then tap out the two bearing inner races using a brass drift. Take care not to lose the balls which will be released as the inner races are removed. On Cooper S and 1275GT models, taper roller bearings are fitted and the inner races are simply lifted out.
7 Withdraw the distance piece (if fitted) located between the two bearings and then drive out the two outer races away from the hub centre.
8 Thoroughly clean all the parts in petrol or paraffin and dry with a lint-free cloth.
9 Carefully examine the bearing inner and outer races, and the ball cage and balls for scoring, pitting or wear ridges; renew as necessary. The hub oil seal must be renewed as it will have been damaged during removal. If the bearings are in a satisfactory condition, reassemble the balls and ball cage to the outer race and then press the inner race back into position.
10 Before refitting the bearings remove any burrs that may be present in the bore of the hub. Use a fine file or scraper.
11 Pack the bearings using a general purpose lithium based grease and fit the inboard bearing to the hub with the narrow edge of the

13.9 Front subframe rear mounting

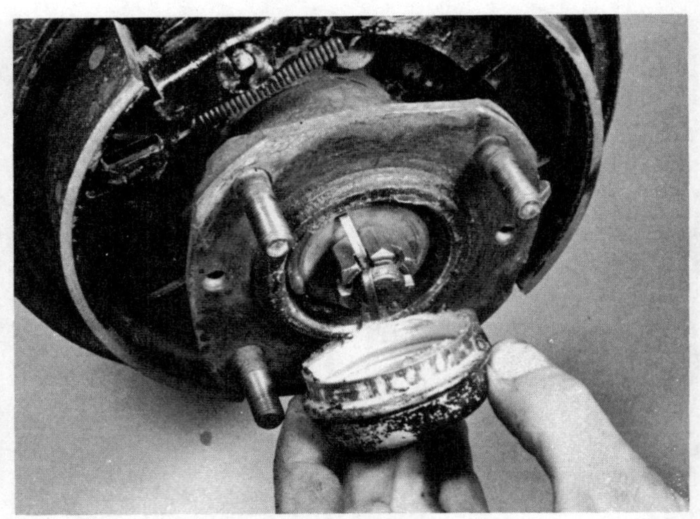

15.3 Rear hub cap, retaining nut and split pin

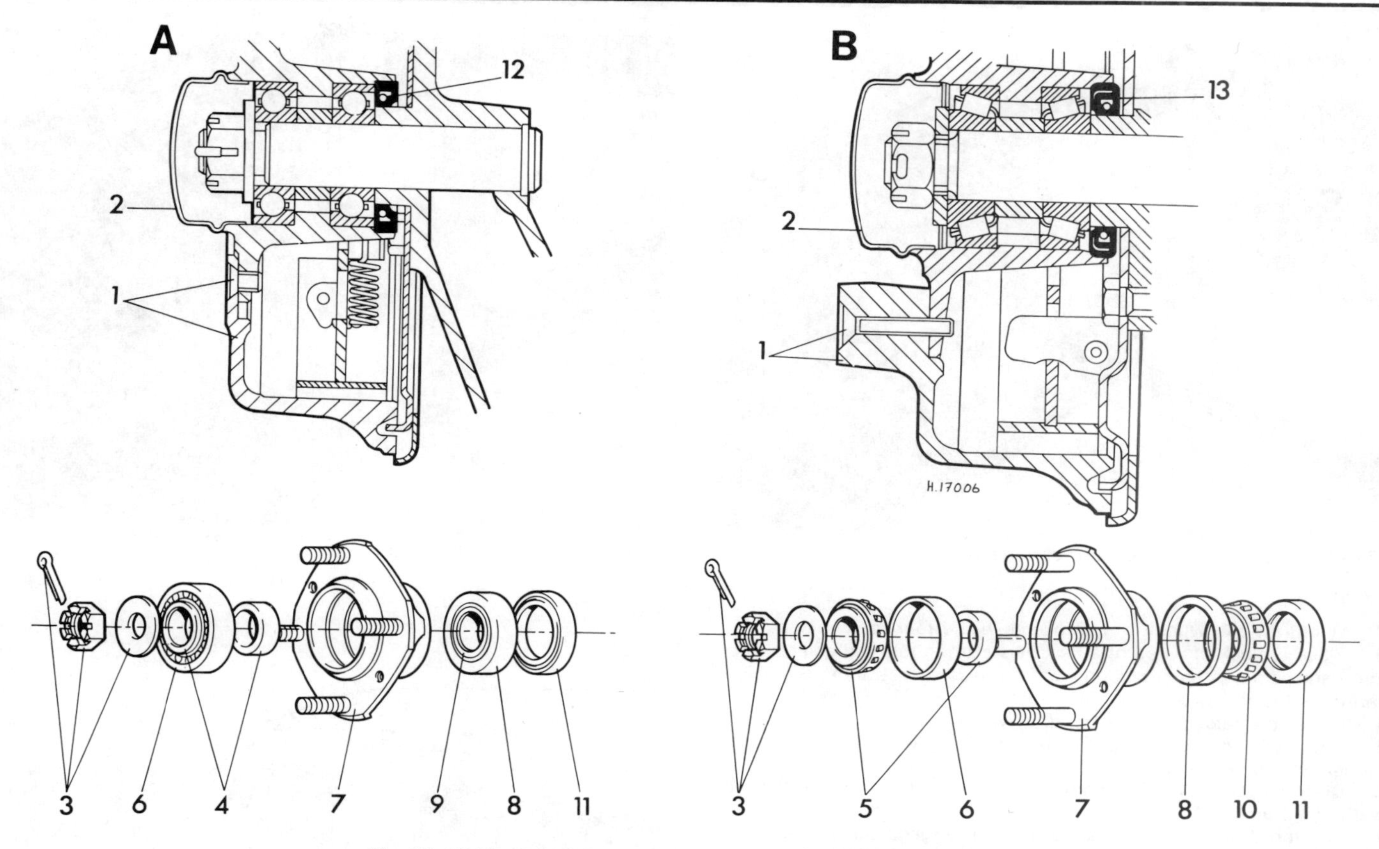

Fig. 11.10 Exploded view of the rear hub components (Sec 15)

A All models except Cooper S and 1275GT *B Cooper S and 1275GT*

1 *Brake drum and retaining screw*
2 *Hub cap*
3 *Hub retaining nut assembly*
4 *Outer ball bearing inner race and spacer*
5 *Outer taper roller bearing inner race and spacer*
6 *Outer bearing outer race*
7 *Rear hub*
8 *Inner bearing outer race*
9 *Inner ball bearing inner race*
10 *Inner taper roller bearing inner race*
11 *Oil seal*
12 *Oil seal installed with lips facing inwards*
13 *Oil seal installed with lips facing outwards*

bearing outer race facing away from the hub centre (see Fig. 11.10A). Press or tap the bearing into position, using the outer race only, with a tube of suitable diameter until the bearing abuts the shoulder in the hub. Take great care to keep the bearing square as it is installed, otherwise it will jam in the hub bore, and could cause the outer race to crack.

12 Fit a new oil seal to the rear of the hub with its lip facing *towards* the bearing. On models fitted with taper roller bearings, the oil seal lip faces *away* from the bearing.

13 Place the distance piece in position and fit the outboard bearing into the hub, again ensuring that the narrow edge of the bearing outer race faces away from the hub centre. **Note**: some makes of plain ball-bearings have lengthened inner races which butt against each other. In this case the bearing distance piece is no longer needed.

14 With the bearings installed, refit the hub to the stub axle and gently tap it home using a soft-faced mallet. Ensure that the stub axle squarely enters the distance piece between the two bearings.

15 Place the thrustwasher over the stub axle, chamfered side toward the bearing, then refit the securing nut and tighten it to the specified torque. Align the next split pin hole and fit a new split pin.

16 Refit the hub cap, brake drum and roadwheel, readjust the brake adjuster and then lower the car to the ground.

16 Rear rubber cone spring – removal and refitting

1 Jack up the rear of the car and place axle stands under the subframe. Withdraw the wheel trim and remove the roadwheel.

2 Place a block of wood or a jack beneath the radius arm and then remove the rear shock absorber as described in Section 18.

3 With the shock absorber removed, lower the radius arm as far as it will go.

4 Using a screwdriver or thin flat bar, prise the rear end of the spring strut out of the rubber cone (photo). Now disengage the ball end of the knuckle joint at the front of the spring strut from its seat and lift the strut off the car.

5 The rubber cone spring can now be levered off its location in the subframe and withdrawn from the car (photo).

6 Before refitting the rubber cone spring, drift the ball end of the knuckle joint out of its location in the spring strut; examine it and its seat in the radius arm for scoring, corrosion and damage. Renew the complete knuckle joint if worn. If the joint is in a satisfactory condition, pack the cup seat with Dextragrease GP (available from your local dealer) and then refit the ball end of the knuckle joint to the cup seat. Ensure that the rubber dust cover is correctly located, otherwise water and grit will enter the joint.

7 The remainder of the refitting procedure is the reverse sequence to removal. When refitting the shock absorber, be sure that the spring strut and knuckle joint are properly engaged as the radius arm is raised.

17 Rear Hydrolastic displacer unit – removal and refitting

Note: *To enable the displacer unit to be removed it will first be necessary to have the Hydrolastic system depressurised by your local BL garage.*

1 Jack up the rear of the car and support it on axle stands placed under the rear subframe.

16.4 Remove the rear rubber cone spring strut...

16.5 ...and rubber cone spring

2 Withdraw the wheel trim and remove the rear roadwheel.
3 Place a block of wood or a jack beneath the rear radius arm, then undo and remove the nut, spring and flat washers securing the helper spring to the radius arm.
4 Lower the radius arm as far as it will go.
5 Undo and remove the single retaining screw and lift the bump rubber off the subframe.
6 Disconnect the flexible Hydrolastic hose from its union at the rear of the subframe.
7 Pull the displacer strut rearwards to disengage the knuckle joint ball from its seat and then withdraw the strut from the displacer unit.
8 Rotate the displacer anti-clockwise and lift it from its location on the subframe.
9 Before refitting the displacer unit examine the knuckle joint ball end (assuming that it was released from its seat as the strut was removed) and seat for scoring, pitting or corrosion. Renew the complete knuckle joint if worn. If the joint is in a satisfactory condition, pack the cup seat with Dextragrease GP, available from your local dealer, and then refit the ball end of the knuckle joint to the cup seat. Ensure that the rubber dust cover is correctly located, otherwise water and grit will enter the joint.
10 The remainder of the refitting procedure is the reverse sequence to removal, bearing in mind the following points:

(a) *When installing the displacer, turn it clockwise to lock it into the registers on the subframe locating plate*
(b) *As the radius arm is lifted to refit the helper spring, ensure that the strut correctly locates in the knuckle joint and displacer*
(c) *When refitting is complete, have the system repressurised at your nearest BL garage*

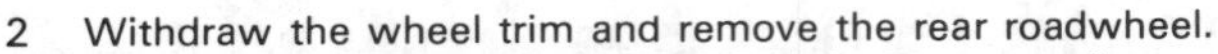

18 Rear shock absorber (rubber cone suspension models) – removal and refitting

1 Jack up the rear of the car and support it on axle stands. Withdraw the rear wheel trim and remove the roadwheel.
2 If removing the left-hand shock absorber on Saloon models, or either of the rear shock absorbers on Cooper S models equipped with twin fuel tanks, it will first be necessary to remove the fuel tank(s) as described in Chapter 3.
3 Support the radius arm using a jack or block of wood, then undo and remove the shock absorber retaining locknut and washers from the radius arm (photo).
4 Working inside the car or luggage compartment, lift off the protective rubber cap, then undo and remove the two locknuts from the upper end of the shock absorber (photo).
5 Lift off the thrust washer and rubber bush, and then withdraw the shock absorber from under the car.

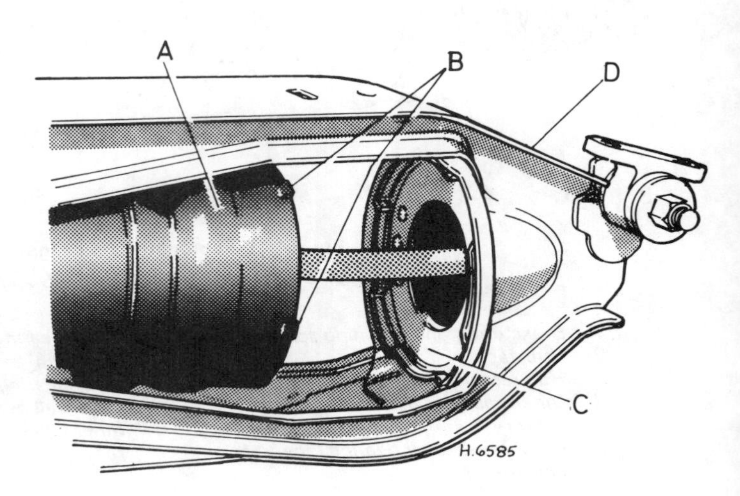

Fig. 11.11 Rear Hydrolastic displacer unit separated from locating plate (Sec 17)

A Displacer unit
B Locating lugs
C Locating plate
D Subframe

6 Examine the shock absorber for leaks or damage to the outer casing. Hold the shock absorber upright, and fully compress and extend it six times. Now slowly compress and extend it once more. If 'dead' areas are apparent, if there is free travel when changing direction, or if the unit is damaged or leaking, it must be renewed.
7 Refitting is the reverse sequence to removal. Hold the shock absorber in an upright position and fully compress and extend it six times to expel any air before installing.

19 Rear helper spring (Hydrolastic suspension models) – removal and refitting

The procedure is the same as described in the previous Section for removal and refitting of the shock absorbers.

20 Rear radius arm – removal and refitting

Note: *On models fitted with Hydrolastic suspension it will be necessary to have the system depressurised by your local BL dealer before proceeding with the removal sequence.*

18.3 Remove the shock absorber lower...

18.4 ...and upper mounting

20.8 The small distance piece is fitted to the handbrake moving sector

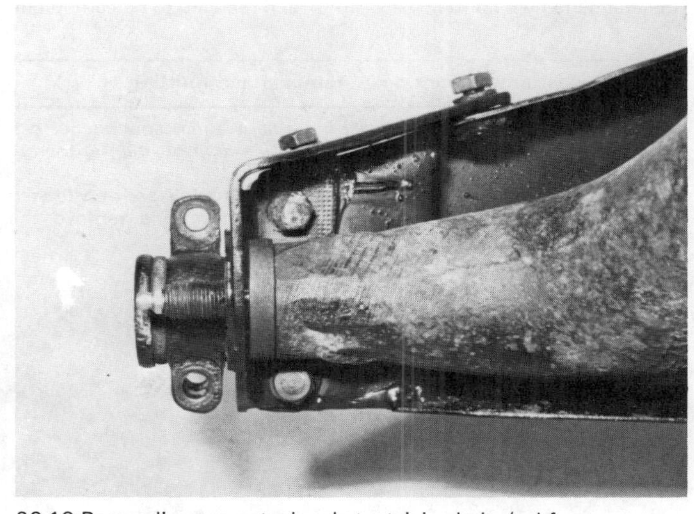
20.10 Rear radius arm outer bracket retaining bolts (subframe removed in this photo)

1 Jack up the rear of the car and support it on axle stands placed under the subframe. Withdraw the wheel trim and remove the roadwheel.
2 Remove the rear shock absorber as described in Section 18 if working on vehicles fitted with rubber cone suspension, or the rear helper spring (Section 19) if Hydrolastic suspension is fitted.
3 Lower the radius arm as far as it will go. When working on vehicles fitted with rubber cone suspension, extract the spring strut from the cone spring. Then pull the strut rearwards, to disengage the ball end of the knuckle joint from its cup seat in the radius arm. If Hydrolastic suspension is fitted, pull the displacer strut rearwards to disengage the strut from the knuckle joint (or the ball end of the knuckle joint from its seat) and then move the strut forwards and out of the displacer unit.
4 Undo and remove the retaining screws and lift off the finisher panel from the end of the body side sills (where fitted).
5 On models fitted with Hydrolastic suspension, undo and remove the retaining screw and lift off the bump rubber from the subframe.
6 Clamp the flexible brake hose, located over the top of the radius arm, with a brake hose clamp or self-gripping wrench with jaws suitably protected. Now undo the union nut securing the metal pipe to the hose and undo and remove the nut securing the hose to its bracket. Plug the ends of the hose and pipe after removal to prevent dirt ingress.
7 Extract the split pin and withdraw the clevis pin securing the end of the handbrake cable to the brake operating lever. Detach the cable and tension spring from the bracket at the rear of the brake backplate.
8 The handbrake cable moving sector is secured to the front of the radius arm either by a through-bolt and lower locknut, or by an upper retaining spire clip, thrust washer and spring washer. In the case of the through-bolt, undo and remove the lower locknut and then remove the sector from the bolt. Take care not to lose the small distance tube from the centre of the sector (photo). If the sector is retained by a spire clip, prise the clip off the upper end of the pivot pin, lift off the washers and then withdraw the sector and pivot from the radius arm.
9 From underneath the car undo and remove the radius arm pivot shaft inner retaining nut and spring washer. Undo and remove the pivot shaft outer retaining nut and washer.
10 Undo and remove the four bolts securing the radius arm outer bracket to the subframe. Note that two of these bolts can only be removed using a socket and extension or box spanner inserted between the radius arm and subframe or bracket (photo). Lift away the bracket.

11 Carefully lift the radius arm off the subframe, taking care not to lose the thrust washers and rubber seal fitted at each end of the radius arm pivot shaft.

12 Refitting the radius arm is the reverse sequence to removal, bearing in mind the following points:

- *(a) When refitting the ball end of the knuckle joint to the seat in the radius arm, pack the cup seat with Dextragrease GP available from your local dealer*
- *(b) When installation is complete, bleed the hydraulic system at the disconnected side, referring to Chapter 9 if necessary*
- *(c) Have the Hydrolastic system repressurised at your nearest BL garage on completion of reassembly*

21 Radius arm bearings – dismantling, overhaul and reassembly

1 With the radius arm removed from the car, as described in the previous Section, lift off the rubber seal and thrust washer from each end of the pivot shaft and then slide the pivot shaft out of the bearings (photos).

2 Wipe away all traces of grease from the pivot shaft and the bearings, and carefully inspect these components. Signs of wear will be most obvious on the pivot shaft in the form of scoring, pitting, wear, ridges or deterioration of the surfice hardening. If any of these conditions are apparent, the shaft and bearings require renewal (photo).

3 The removal and refitting of both the bearings, and the line reaming of the bronze bearing to suit the outside diameter of the pivot shaft, entails the use of several special tools. As there is no other way of satisfactorily carrying out this work, it is strongly recommended that once the radius arm is removed it is taken to your local BL garage for the complete bearing removal, refitting and reaming to be carried out.

22 Rear subframe mountings – removal and refitting

Note: *The subframe front and rear mountings and rubber bushes can be removed and refitted with the subframe still in position in the car as described below.*

1 Jack up the rear of the car and support it on axle stands positioned under the side sills. Withdraw the wheel trim and remove the appropriate rear wheel.

Front mounting

2 Remove the radius arm assembly from the car as described in Section 20.

3 Undo and remove the nut and washer securing the support bolt to the subframe.

4 Undo and remove the two bolts and spring washers securing the mounting to the body.

5 Lever the subframe down slightly and lift off the mounting assembly (photo).

6 The support bolt and rubber bushes can now be removed from the mounting.

7 Refitting is the reverse sequence to removal, noting that the step in the mounting and the short bolt must be at the top (where applicable).

Rear mounting

8 Undo and remove the nut and washer securing the mounting to the subframe.

9 On Estate, Van and Pick-up models, undo and remove the two bolts securing the mounting to the body. On Saloon models, have an assistant hold the bolts from inside the luggage compartment while the retaining nuts are removed from below.

10 Lever the subframe down slightly and slide the mounting assembly sideways and off the subframe.

11 The rubber bushes can now be removed from the mounting.

12 In all cases, refitting is the reverse sequence to removal, noting that the step in the mounting and the short bolt must be at the front.

23 Rear subframe – removal and refitting

Note: *Corrosion of the rear subframe is a common occurrence on Minis, particularly older models, and is one of the main causes of MOT test failure on these cars (photo). Where corrosion has reached an advanced stage, renewal of the subframe is the only satisfactory cure. Despite its reputation for being an extremely difficult task, removal of the rear subframe is in fact a fairly straightforward operation. Before*

21.1a Lift off the radius arm bearing rubber seal...

21.1b ...and thrust washer...

21.1c ...then slide out the pivot shaft

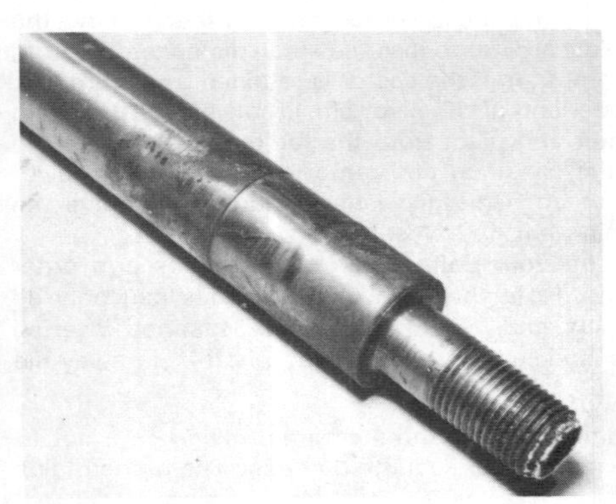

21.2 A badly ridged radius arm pivot shaft

22.5 Removing a rear subframe front mounting (subframe removed in this photo)

23.0 Advanced stage of corrosion on rear subframe sidemember

carrying out this work on cars fitted with Hydrolastic suspension, it will be necessary to have the system depressurised by your local BL dealer.

1 Jack up the rear of the car and securely support it on axle stands positioned under the rear body side sills. Where the battery positive lead is routed through the subframe, disconnect the negative and then the positive lead from the battery terminals and pull the positive lead clear of the frame, noting its routing for reference when refitting.

2 On early models undo and remove the two adjusting nuts securing the ends of the two handbrake cables to the trunnion on the handbrake lever (photo). Pull the cables out of the trunnion and then slide off the washers and tension spring. **Note:** *On later models a single front cable is used and the tension springs are omitted.*

3 Lift up the carpets to expose the cable guide plates located at the point where the cable passes through the floor.

4 Engage the help of an assistant to hold the nuts from underneath the car while the cable guide retaining screws are removed from above (photos). Lift off the guides and sealing pads, and from underneath the car, pull the ends of the cable through the opening in the floor and out of the passenger compartment.

5 Remove the brake master cylinder reservoir filler cap and place a piece of polythene over the filler neck, then refit the cap. This will help prevent fluid loss when the rear pipes are disconnected.

6 From underneath the rear of the car, undo and remove the brake hydraulic pipe union from the centre of the pressure regulating valve

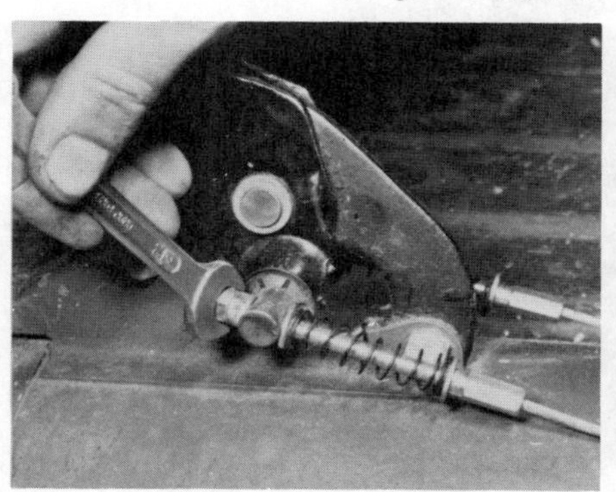

23.2 Remove the handbrake cable adjusting nuts

23.4a Hold the cable guide retaining nuts from below...

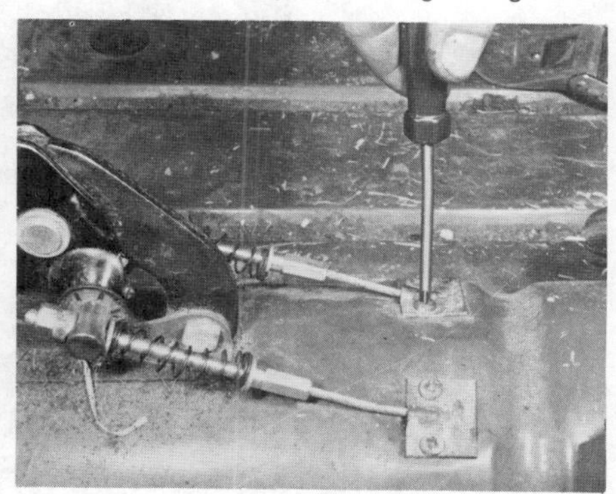

23.4b ...and unscrew from above

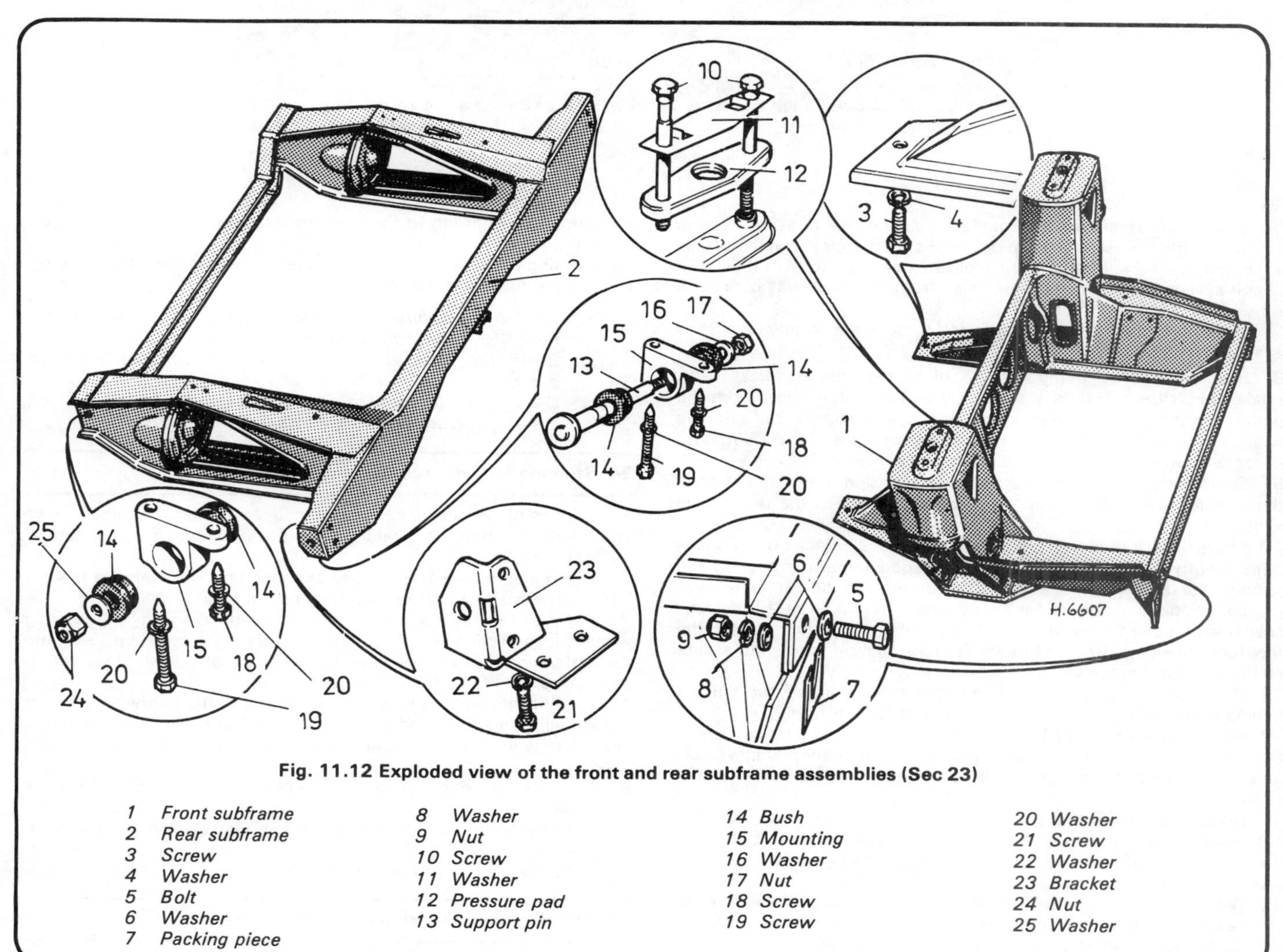

Fig. 11.12 Exploded view of the front and rear subframe assemblies (Sec 23)

1 Front subframe
2 Rear subframe
3 Screw
4 Washer
5 Bolt
6 Washer
7 Packing piece
8 Washer
9 Nut
10 Screw
11 Washer
12 Pressure pad
13 Support pin
14 Bush
15 Mounting
16 Washer
17 Nut
18 Screw
19 Screw
20 Washer
21 Screw
22 Washer
23 Bracket
24 Nut
25 Washer

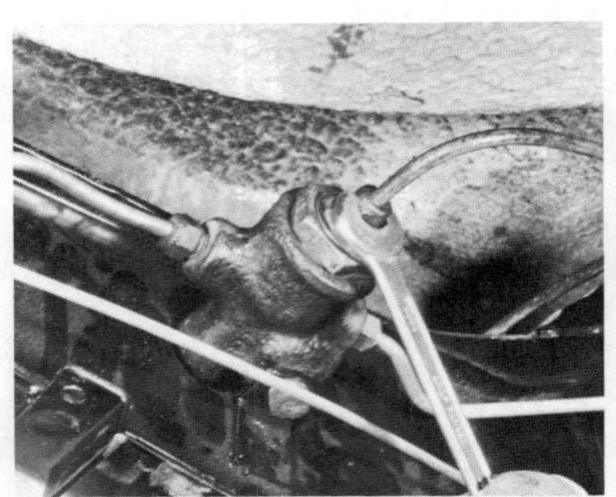
23.6a On early models remove the hydraulic pipe from the regulating valve

23.6b On later models unscrew the hydraulic pipe union at the pipe connector...

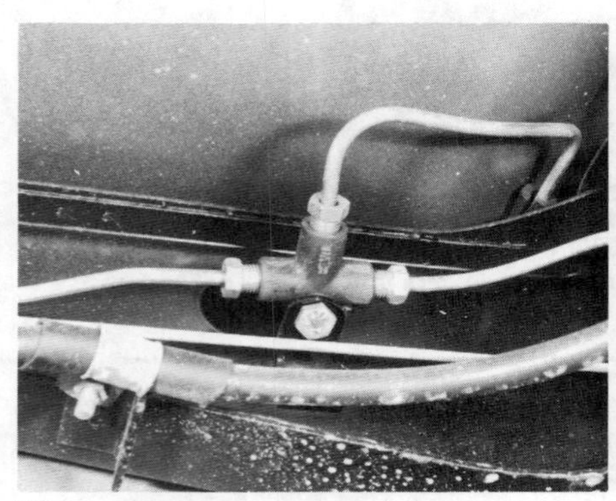
23.6c ...or three-way connector

23.13 Rear subframe mounting

on early models (photo). On models equipped with a dual circuit braking system, unscrew the pipe unions at the pipe connectors on each side of the subframe front crossmember (photo). On later dual circuit systems unscrew the pipe union from the three-way connector on the rear subframe (photo).

7 Refer to Chapter 3 if necessary and remove the complete exhaust system from the car.

8 If an electric fuel pump is fitted, disconnect the electrical leads, slacken the clips and detach the fuel inlet and outlet hoses from the pump. During this operation, clamp the hoses using a self-gripping wrench with suitably protected jaws to prevent loss of fuel. Plug both hoses with a bolt or suitable metal rod upon removal.

9 On models fitted with Hydrolastic suspension, undo and remove the transfer pipe unions from the pressure valves at the rear of the subframe.

10 Place a block of wood under the rear wheels or jack up the radius arms slightly. From inside the car or luggage compartment, undo and remove the shock absorber upper mounting, on rubber cone suspension models, or the helper spring upper mounting on Hydrolastic suspension models. On Saloon cars, it will be necessary to detach the fuel tank retaining strap and move the tank slightly to provide access to the left-hand mounting.

11 Undo and remove the retaining screws and lift off the finisher panels from each end of the body side sills (where fitted).

12 Place a jack under each side of the subframe, or a trolley jack in the centre, with a substantial plank of wood running transversely across the subframe, and *just* take the weight of the frame on the jacks.

13 Undo and remove the two bolts securing each of the four subframe mountings to the body (photo). If the bolts are tight, use liberal amounts of penetrating oil on them and allow time for the oil to soak.

14 With the mounting bolts removed, engage the help of an assistant to steady the subframe and then slowly lower the jacks until the subframe can be withdrawn from the rear of the car.

15 With the subframe removed from the car it can now be completely dismantled by referring to the relevant Sections and Chapters of this manual.

16 Refitting the subframe is the reverse sequence to removal, bearing in mind the following points:

- (a) *Line up the subframe mountings and fit all the bolts finger tight first, before progressively tightening*
- (b) *Bleed the complete hydraulic system on completion as described in Chapter 9*
- (c) *On models fitted with Hydrolastic suspension, have the system repressurised at your nearest BL garage*

24 Steering wheel – removal and refitting

1 Depending on model, either undo and remove the retaining screws and lift off the trim, or carefully prise up the steering wheel central motif (photos).

2 Using a suitable socket or box spanner, undo and remove the nut which retains the wheel on the steering column.

3 Recover the retaining nut lockwasher and then lift the steering wheel off the splines on the column. If it is tight, tap it up using the palm of your hand, or very carefully use a rubber mallet. Make sure it doesn't come off suddenly and cause injury!

4 To refit the steering wheel, make sure that the roadwheels are in the straight-ahead position and that the small triangle on the direction indicator switch bush is pointing toward the horn push (later models only).

5 Refit the steering wheel to the column with the wheel spokes centralised.

6 Refit the lockwasher and retaining nut, then tighten the nut to the specified torque.

7 Refit the trim or central motif.

25 Steering column – removal and refitting

1 Disconnect the battery earth terminal.

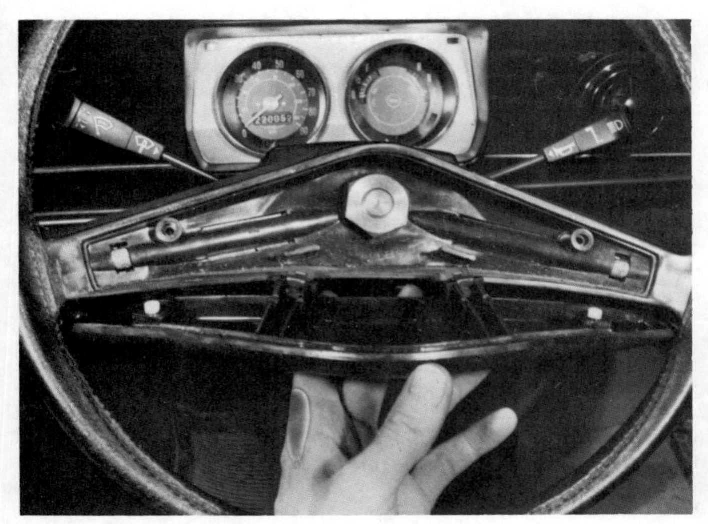

24.1a Remove the screws and lift off the trim...

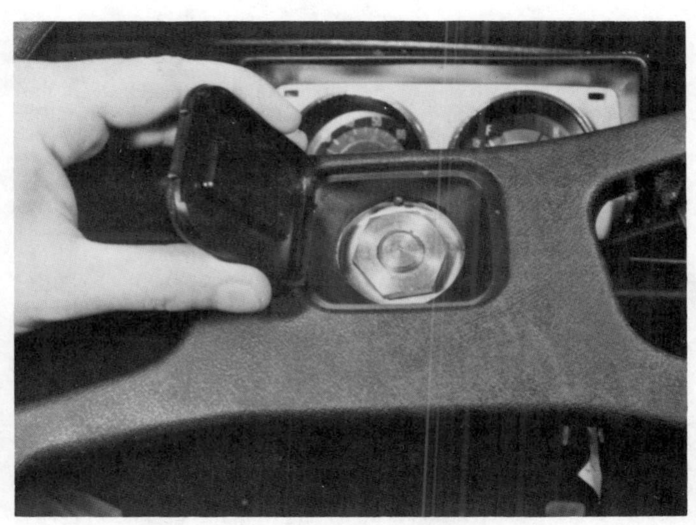

24.1b ...or prise up the central motif according to model

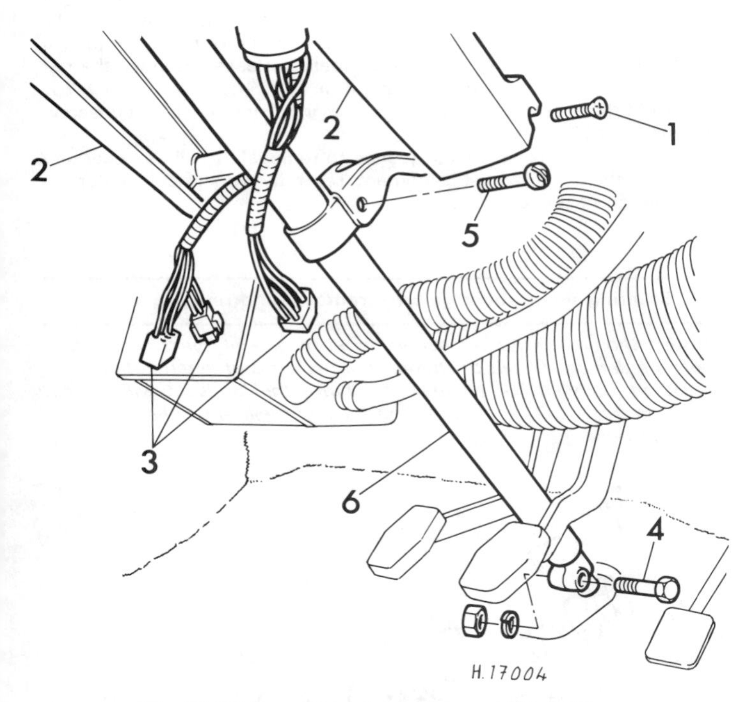

Fig. 11.13 Steering column removal (Sec 25)

1 Column shroud retaining screw
2 Column shroud halves
3 Multi-plug connectors
4 Pinch-bolt
5 Upper column support clamp bolt
6 Steering column

2 Undo and remove the screws securing the two halves of the steering column shroud to the column and lift off the shroud.
3 Disconnect the electrical wiring multi-plug connectors located under the parcel shelf.
4 At the base of the column, undo and remove the pinch-bolt securing the inner column clamp to the pinion shaft.
5 Undo and remove the upper column support clamp bolt at the parcel shelf. On later models where a shear bolt is used, cut a slot in the bolt and use a screwdriver to unscrew it, or drill a small hole and remove it with a stud extractor.
6 Position the roadwheels in the straight-ahead position, pull the column upwards and remove it from the car.

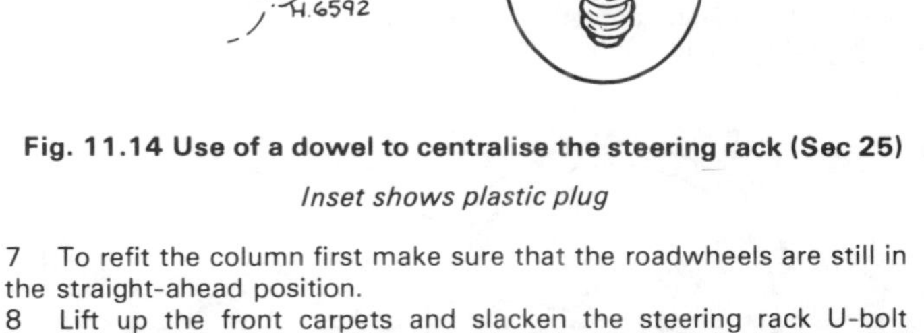

Fig. 11.14 Use of a dowel to centralise the steering rack (Sec 25)

Inset shows plastic plug

7 To refit the column first make sure that the roadwheels are still in the straight-ahead position.
8 Lift up the front carpets and slacken the steering rack U-bolt locknuts sufficiently to allow sideways movement of the rack housing.
9 Slacken the upper column support clamp mounting bracket bolts, to allow movement of the bracket.
10 Lift out the rubber grommet in the passenger side floor and then remove the plastic plug from the rack housing. Insert a centralising pin into the hole of 0.25 in (6 mm) diameter. A bolt or $\frac{1}{4}$ in (6 mm) drill are ideal for this purpose. Move the rack sideways slightly until the pin fully engages with the hole in the rack thus centralising the assembly. Engage the steering inner column clamp with the pinion shaft ensuring that the steering wheel spokes are horizontal/centre spoke vertical.
11 Refit the column clamp bolt and then remove the centralising pin. Refit the plastic plug and grommet.
12 Refit the upper column support clamp bolt, using a new shear bolt on later models. Ensure that there is no twist or strain on the column as the bolt is inserted. Reposition the clamp and bracket if necessary.
13 The remainder of the refitting procedure now varies according to model year as described below.

Models with single stalk multi-function switch

14 Tighten the steering column clamp and bracket retaining bolts and the steering rack U-bolt locknuts to the specified torque.
15 Reconnect the electrical multi-plugs under the parcel shelf.

16 If the steering column has been dismantled, adjust the direction indicator switch cancelling stud so that it just trips the switch levers as the wheel is turned.
17 With the roadwheels in the straight-ahead position and the steering column installed, the direction indicator stalk should be at 20° to the horizontal (Fig. 11.15), with the cancelling levers of the switch. If this is not the case, slacken the steering column support bracket clamp and rotate the column as necessary.
18 Finally refit the steering column shrouds and the carpets.

Models with twin stalk multi-function switch

19 Position the outer column to give 0.06 in (2 mm) clearance between the steering wheel hub and the boss of the multi-function switch, then tighten the shear bolt until the head breaks off.
20 Reconnect the electrical multi-plugs under the parcel shelf.
21 Refit the steering column shrouds and the carpets.

26 Steering column – dismantling and reassembly

1 With the steering column removed from the car as described in the previous Section, begin dismantling by removing the steering wheel as described in Section 24.
2 Undo and remove the retaining screws and withdraw the multi-function switch from the column.
3 On early models, undo and remove the direction indicator cancelling stud and locknut from the inner column.
4 The inner column can now be withdrawn from the lower end of the outer column tube. Before doing this insert the ignition key into the switch and turn it to the I position. This will release the steering lock and allow the inner column to be removed.
5 Prise the top bush out of the column if necessary using a screwdriver. The lower felt bush is removed by simply sliding it out of the outer column.
6 To remove the steering lock/ignition switch, drill out the shear bolt heads, or alternatively drill a hole in the shear bolts and unscrew them using a stud extractor. The clamp plate and lock/switch assembly can then be removed.
7 With the steering column assembly dismantled, check the inner and outer column for straightness by rolling them on a flat surface. Renew the parts if distortion is obvious.
8 Begin reassembly by lubricating the upper polythene bush with graphite grease. Insert the bush into the top of the outer column, chamfered end first. Tap the bush fully into position, ensuring that the shouldered slot engages with the detent in the outer column.
9 Insert the inner column into the lower end of the outer column and slide it in approximately half way.
10 Soak the lower felt bush in engine oil and then wrap it around the inner column until its ends are butted together. Now carefully slide the inner column fully home.
11 Refit the multi-function switch assembly, and on early models the direction indicator cancelling stud and locknut.
12 Refit the steering lock/ignition switch using new shear bolts. Do not shear the heads off the bolts until the steering column has been refitted and the operation of the steering lock tested.
13 Refit the steering column to the car as described in Section 25 and then, when the column is correctly positioned in relation to the steering gear, refit the steering wheel.

27 Steering tie-rod outer balljoint – removal and refitting

Note: *If any side movement is present in the outer balljoint, it will be necessary to renew the complete joint as it cannot be dismantled or repaired*

1 Withdraw the wheel arm, slacken the roadwheel retaining nuts and jack up the front of the car. Position axle stands under the subframe and remove the roadwheel.
2 Slacken the locknut on the steering tie-rod a quarter of a turn.
3 Undo and remove the balljoint shank locknut and separate the taper of the shank using a universal balljoint separator. Alternatively, refit the nut two turns and sharply strike the end of the steering arm with a medium hammer. When the taper is released, remove the nut and lift the balljoint off the steering arm.
4 Hold the steering tie-rod with a self-gripping wrench and unscrew the balljoint from the tie-rod.
5 Refitting is the reverse sequence to removal. It will be necessary to have the front wheel alignment reset by your local dealer on completion of this operation.

28 Steering rack rubber gaiter – removal and refitting

Note: *Should the rubber gaiters at each end of the steering rack become damaged, split or show any other signs of deterioration, they must be renewed immediately, otherwise the lubricant will be lost from the rack unit, and water and road grit will enter the assembly, causing rapid internal wear.*

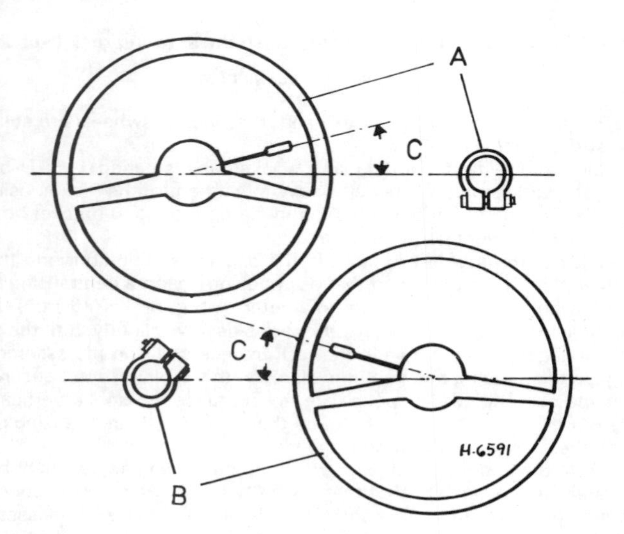

Fig. 11.15 Correct position of clamp bolt and direction indicator lever when refitting the early type steering column (Sec 25)

A RHD models
B LHD models
C = 20°

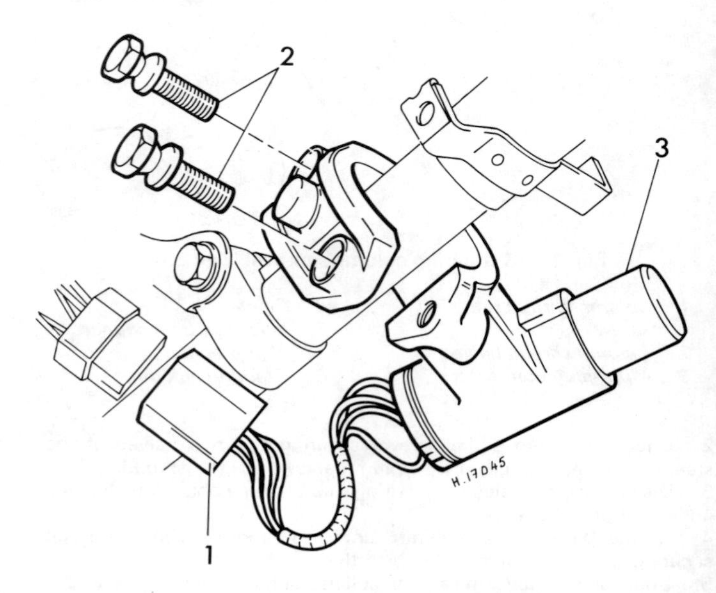

Fig. 11.16 Steering lock/ignition switch assembly (Sec 26)

1 Multi-plug connector
2 Shear bolts
3 Steering lock/ignition switch

1 Begin by removing the steering tie-rod outer balljoint as described in the previous Section.
2 Mark the position of the locknut on the tie-rod so that it can be refitted in the same place and then unscrew it from the tie-rod.
3 Place a suitable container beneath the rubber gaiter to catch any oil that may spill from the rack (early models only).
4 Now undo and remove the two retaining clips or cut off the wire clips and then slide the gaiter off the rack housing and tie-rod.
5 Refitting the rubber gaiter is the reverse sequence to removal. With the gaiter in position refill the rack with the appropriate lubricant as described in Section 31 before refitting the retaining clips or wire.

29 Rack-and-pinion steering gear – removal and refitting

Note: *The rack-and-pinion steering gear is secured to the front floor of the car by U-bolts and locknuts. To enable the steering gear to be removed, it will be necessary to lower the rear of the front subframe by approximately 3 in (76 mm) to provide the necessary working clearances.*
1 Working in the engine compartment, remove the air cleaner assembly, referring to Chapter 3 if necessary.
2 Undo and remove the nuts and bolts securing the exhaust pipe-to-manifold clamp. Lift off the clamp. On Cooper S models, remove the complete exhaust system as described in Chapter 3.
3 Undo and remove the bolt securing the engine tie-rod to the side of the cylinder block.
4 Detach the clutch operating lever return spring, and then undo and remove the two bolts securing the clutch slave cylinder to the flywheel housing. Tie the slave cylinder out of the way from a convenient place on the bulkhead.
5 Undo and remove the two bolts (or nuts) each side securing the subframe towers to the bulkhead crossmember. On later models undo and remove the large hexagon-headed plug used in place of the bolts or nuts.
6 Working inside the car undo and remove the securing screws and lift off the two halves of the steering column shroud.
7 Undo and remove the nut and bolt securing the inner column clamp to the steering gear pinion shaft.
8 Slacken the upper column clamp bolt at the parcel shelf bracket. To do this cut a slot in the shear bolt head and unscrew it with a screwdriver.
9 Lift the complete steering column upwards until the inner column clamp is disengaged from the pinion shaft.
10 Lift up the carpets and then undo and remove the four steering rack U-bolt locknuts.
11 Jack up the front of the car and support it on axle stands positioned under the body side sills. Remove both front roadwheels.
12 From underneath the car, undo and remove the nut and bolt securing the exhaust pipe support to the bracket on the side of the gearbox.
13 On manual transmission models fitted with a remote control gearchange, undo and remove the bolts securing the rear of the remote control housing to the floor. On automatic transmission models it should be possible to lower the subframe sufficiently for removal of the steering gear without disconnecting the gear selector cable. However, if during subsequent operations the cable appears to be under tension, disconnect it from the transmission as described in Chapter 6, Section 24.
14 On models fitted with rubber cone suspension, disconnect the front shock absorbers from the upper suspension arms.
15 Undo and remove the locknuts securing the steering outer balljoint shanks to the steering arms on the swivel hubs. Release the tapers using a universal balljoint separator or shock them free by striking the steering arms with a medium hammer.
16 Support the subframe securely on jacks and then undo and remove the nuts and bolts securing the subframe to the rear mountings or to the floor.
17 Slacken the bolt securing the front of the subframe or subframe mountings to the body.
18 Carefully lower the jacks, allowing the subframe to drop by approximately 3 in (76 mm) at the rear.
19 Lift off the rack-and-pinion retaining U-bolts and clamp pads and then manoeuvre the rack assembly out from between the subframe and body on the driver's side.
20 Refitting the steering gear is the reverse sequence to removal bearing in mind the following points.

(a) *Do not tighten the U-bolt locknuts until the upper column is fitted and secure*
(b) *When refitting the upper column to the pinion shaft and mountings, refer to the procedure described in Section 25*

30 Rack-and-pinion steering gear – dismantling and reassembly

Note: *It is not possible to make any adjustments to the rack-and-pinion steering gear unless it is removed from the car. With it removed, it is as well to dismantle and examine the whole unit before making any adjustments. This will save having to remove the unit again later because of initial non-detection of wear. If wear is very bad it is advisable to fit an exchange reconditioned unit. It must be pointed out that dismantling and reassembly of the steering gear is rather involved and may be beyond the scope of the average DIY enthusiast. Read through the complete Section first to familiarise yourself with the procedure and ensure that the necessary tools and equipment are available before proceeding.*
1 Mark the position of the locknuts on the tie-rods so that the toe-out is approximately correct on reassembly.
2 Slacken the locknuts and, gripping the tie-rods firmly with a self-gripping wrench, unscrew the tie-rod balljoints. Now unscrew the locknuts also.
3 If the steering gear is fitted with black rubber gaiters, it will be filled with oil. If it is fitted with transparent rubber gaiters it will be filled with grease. If working on the oil-filled type ensure that a container is available before proceeding further.
4 Unscrew the clips or cut the wires that secure the rubber gaiters to the rack housing and tie-rods. Carefully remove the gaiters, and on oil-filled types, drain the oil from the housing.
5 On inspection it will be seen that the ball housing at the inner end of each tie-rod is secured to the rack by a locking collar. The locking collar is then peened into a groove in the ball housing on early models, or retained by a grooved pin on later types.
6 On early models punch or prise up the peening and then unlock the ball housing and collar using BL special tool No 18G1278. Alternatively, use two small Stilson wrenches, but take care not to damage the housing and collar faces.
7 On later models, it is first necessary to drill out the grooved pin. To do this use a 0.156 in (3.97 mm) drill, and drill to a depth of 1.6 in (4 mm). Now unlock the ball housing and collar using the procedure described in the previous paragraph.
8 Unscrew the ball housing and then lift off the tie-rod, ball seat and spring from the end of the rack. The locking collar can now be removed.
9 Repeat this procedure for the other tie-rod, noting that if these components are to be re-used they must be refitted to the same side of the rack from which they were removed.
10 At the base of the pinion housing, undo and remove the two rack damper cover bolts and spring washers. Lift off the damper cover together with its shims, and then withdrw the thrust spring, yoke, and O-ring seal from the rack housing.
11 Undo and remove the two bolts and lift off the pinion end cover together with its gasket and shims.
12 Carefully push out the pinion and lower bearing.
13 Withdraw the rack from the pinion end of the housing. **Note:** *If the rack is withdrawn from the plain end of the housing the rack teeth will damage the support bush.*
14 Extract the pinion upper bearing from the rack housing, followed by the oil seal.
15 From the plain end of the rack housing, undo and remove the small retaining screw and then withdraw the rack support bush. **Note:** *On some models a rivet is used instead of a screw and this must be carefully drilled out.*
16 Thoroughly clean all the parts with paraffin. Carefully inspect the teeth on the rack and the pinion for chipping, roughness, uneven wear, hollows, or fractures. Renew both components if either is badly worn.
17 Carefully inspect the component parts of the inner balljoints for wear or ridging, and renew as necessary.
18 The outer tie-rod joints cannot be dismantled, and if worn must be renewed as a complete assembly. Examine the component parts of the damper and renew any that show signs of wear. Pay particular attention to the oil seals; as a precautionary measure it is always best to renew them.

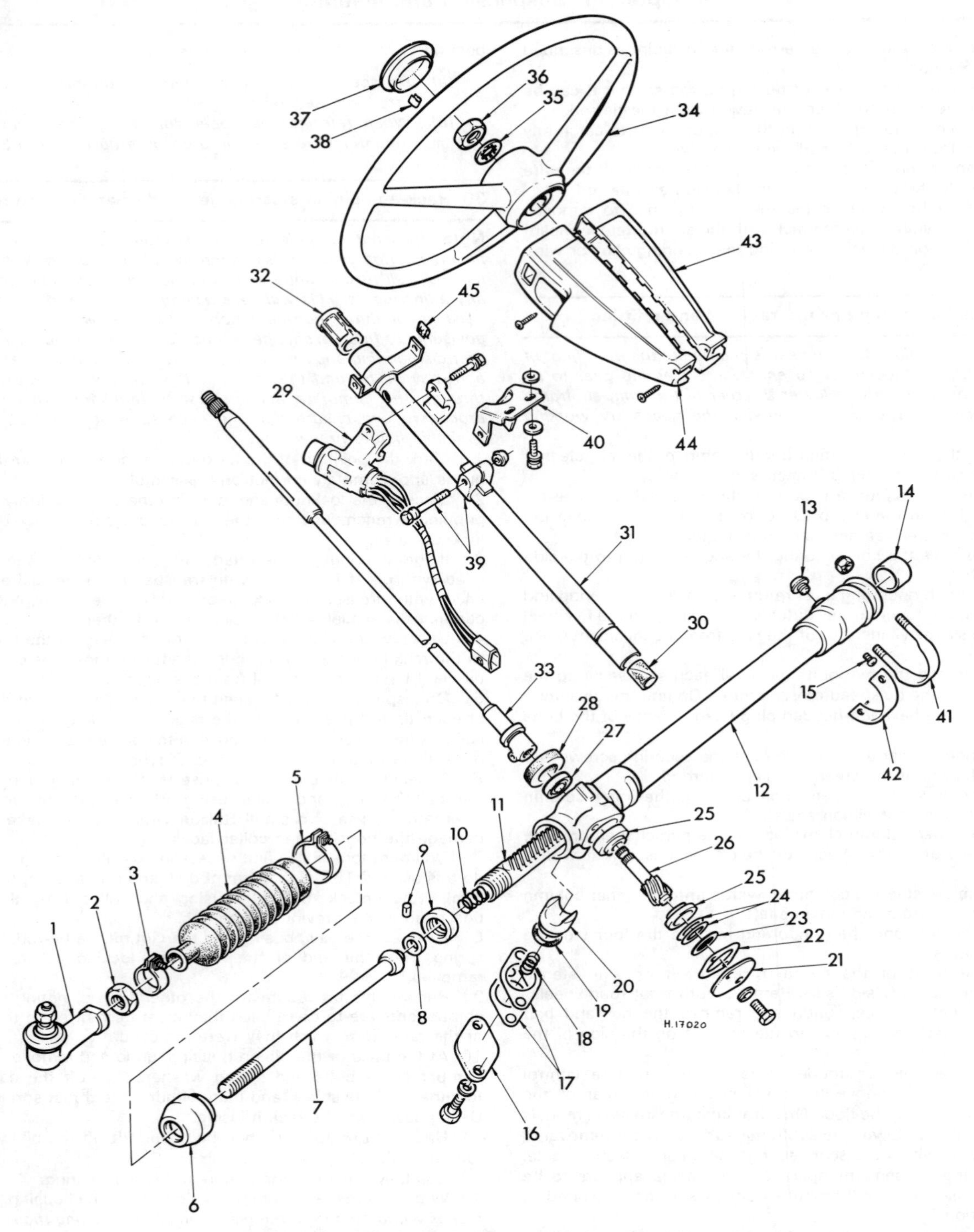

Fig. 11.17 Exploded view of the steering gear (Sec 30)

1 Balljoint
2 Locking nut
3 Retaining clip
4 Rubber gaiter
5 Retaining clip
6 Ball housing
7 Tie-rod
8 Ball-seat
9 Locknut and grooved pin
10 Thrust spring
11 Rack
12 Rack housing
13 Rack centring hole plug
14 Rack bearing
15 Bearing retaining screw
16 Damper cover plate
17 Shims
18 Thrust spring
19 O-ring seal
20 Rack support yoke
21 Pinion end cover
22 Gasket
23 Shim – standard
24 Shims
25 Pinion bearings
26 Pinion
27 Pinion seal
28 Sealing washer
29 Ignition switch and steering lock with shear bolts
30 Lower felt bush
31 Steering column – outer
32 Upper bush
33 Steering column – inner
34 Steering wheel
35 Locking washer
36 Nut
37 Hub cover
38 Retaining clip
39 Column clip and shear bolt
40 Clamp plate
41 U-bolt
42 Anti-friction strip
43 Left-hand shroud
44 Right-hand shroud
45 Spring nut

19 The rubber gaiters are particularly prone to damage and it is advisable to renew them as a matter of course.
20 Begin reassembly by refitting the rack support bush to the plain end of the rack housing. If the original bush is being refitted, align the screw holes in the bush and rack housing.
21 If a new rack support bush is being fitted, drill a 0.109 in (2.7 mm) hole, into the bush, through the retaining screw hole, to a depth of 0.142 in (10.5 mm).
22 Apply jointing compound to the threads of the support bush retaining screw. Refit and tighten the screw, then check that the bush bore has not distorted. Make sure that the screw does not break right through the bush into the bore.
23 Lubricate the upper pinion bearing and fit it into place in the housing. Use the pinion to push the bearing fully into position.
24 Insert the rack into the housing from the pinion end and then refit the pinion, splined end first.
25 Lubricate the lower pinion bearing and place it in position on the lower end of the pinion shaft.

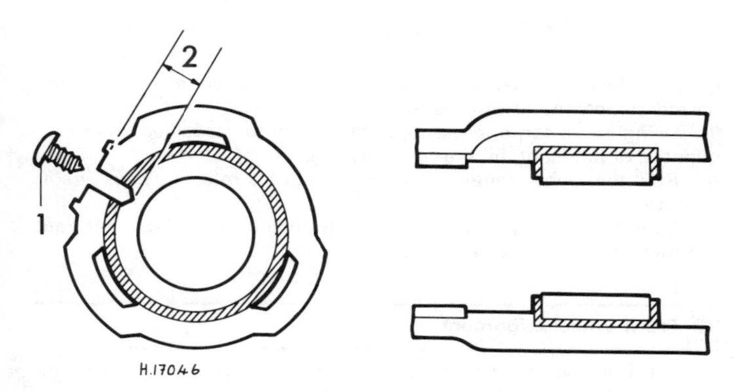

Fig. 11.18 Refitting the rack support bush (Sec 30)

1 Retaining screw 2 Drill to a depth of 0.142 in (10.5 mm)

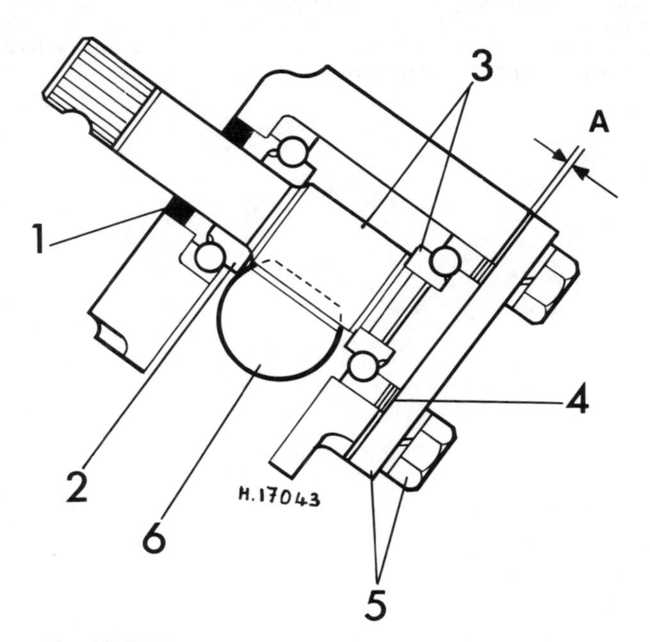

Fig. 11.19 Reassembly of the pinion housing (Sec 30)

1 Oil seal
2 Upper pinion bearing
3 Pinion and lower bearing
4 Preload shims
5 End cover and retaining bolt
6 Rack
A = 0.011 to 0.013 in (0.28 to 0.33 mm)

26 Refit the preload shims, using additional shims if necessary, until the shim pack stands proud of the pinion housing.
27 Refit the end cover and retaining bolts and tighten the bolts lightly and evenly until all pinion endfloat is taken up.
28 Using feeler gauges, measure the gap between the end cover and the pinion housing. Now take off the end cover and remove the appropriate number of shims until a gap of 0.011 to 0.013 in (0.28 to 0.33 mm) still remains.
29 With the correct shims in position, refit the end cover using a new gasket, and with the bolt threads lightly coated in jointing compound, tighten them fully.
30 Place a new oil seal over the pinion and insert it into the housing. The seal must be fitted with the seal lips toward the pinion bearing and with its top face flush with the end of the housing.
31 Lubricate the rack damper yoke and slide it into the housing. Refit the cover plate and retaining bolts, but do not fit the spring at this stage.
32 Tighten the cover plate bolts evenly until the rack is lightly clamped by the yoke. Turn the pinion two or three turns in either direction and check that the rack is not binding in any position. If necessary, slacken the cover plate bolts slightly to achieve this.
33 Take a feeler gauge measurement of the gap between the damper cover plate and the housing and then remove the cover plate.
34 Fit a new O-ring seal to the damper yoke and place the spring in position. Add shims equal to the gap measured between the cover plate and housing plus 0.002 to 0.005 in (0.05 to 0.13 mm). Refit the cover plate and tighten down the bolts. Turn the pinion through 180° in each direction from the centre and make sure there is no tightness or binding.
35 Screw one of the tie-rod ball housing locking collars onto the rack as far as it will go. If the original components are being re-used, make sure that the collar is being refitted to the end of the rack from which it was removed.
36 Lubricate the thrust spring and ball seat and then locate them in the end of the rack. Lubricate the tie-rod balljoint and the ball housing and refit these components.
37 Tighten the ball housing until the tie-rod ball is clamped and will not move without binding.
38 Now slacken the ball housing slightly (approximately $\frac{1}{8}$ of a turn) until the tie-rod is just free to move. **Note**: *The tie-rod will still feel stiff to move because of the tension of the thrust spring, but there should be no trace of binding or endfloat.*
39 Hold the ball housing in this position and screw the locking collar into contact with it. Tighten the locking collar using the same procedure used for removal, making sure that the position of the ball

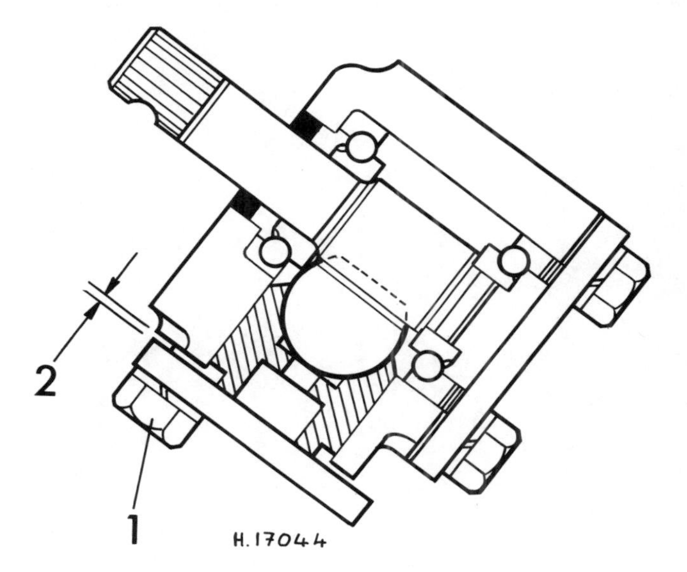

Fig. 11.20 Reassembly of the rack damper (Sec 30)

1 Damper cover plate retaining bolts
2 Measured gap plus 0.002 to 0.005 in (0.05 to 0.13 mm) – see text

housing does not alter.
40 If working on early type racks, peen the edge of the locking collar into the groove of the ball housing using a small punch.
41 On later type racks, protect the rack housing from swarf and drill a 0.156 in (3.97 mm) diameter hole, 0.312 in (8.0 mm) deep, between the locking collar and ball housing. The hole must be drilled on the side facing away from the rack teeth and at least 90° away from any previous hole. **Note**: *The rack may be drilled a maximum of three times only. With the hole drilled, drive in a new grooved pin and retain it by peening over the edge of the hole.*
42 Repeat the above procedure for the other tie-rod and ball housing.
43 Refit the rubber gaiter and retaining clips or wire to the plain end of the rack assembly.
44 Stand the assembly upright and fill it through the pinion end of the housing with the correct quantity and type of lubricant as shown in the Specifications.
45 Refit the remaining rubber gaiter and its retaining clips or wire.
46 If the original tie-rods have been refitted, screw on the tie-rod outer balljoint locknuts to the positions marked during dismantling. Now screw on the balljoints and tighten the locknuts.
47 If new tie-rods have been fitted, screw on the locknuts and then screw on the balljoints, by an equal amount each side, until the dimension between their centres is as shown in the Specifications. Tighten the locknuts.
48 The steering gear can now be refitted to the car as described in Section 29. It will be necessary to have the front wheel alignment checked and reset as described in Section 32 after refitting.

31 Rack-and-pinion steering gear – lubrication

1 The steering gear is filled with lubricant during manufacture and then sealed. Additional lubricant will only be required in service if a leak develops, either from the rubber gaiters or from any of the joints, or if the steering gear has been dismantled.
2 The steering gear fitted to early models, identified by black rubber gaiters, is filled with oil. The equipment fitted to later models, identified by transparent rubber gaiters is filled with grease. The grade and quantity of lubricant for both types is given in the Specifications.
3 Should it be necessary to refill the rack, proceed as follows.
4 Jack up the driver's side of the car, suitably support it on stands, and remove the front roadwheel.
5 Centralise the steering gear so that the wheels are in the straight-ahead position.
6 Slacken the retaining clips or remove the wire securing the rubber gaiter to the rack housing and tie-rod. Slide the rubber gaiter down the tie-rod sufficiently to provide access.
7 Using an oil can or grease gun filled with the specified grade and quantity of lubricant, fill the rack housing.
8 Refit the rubber gaiter and secure it with the retaining clips or soft iron wire.
9 Turn the steering from lock to lock to distribute the lubricant, refit the roadwheel and lower the car to the ground.

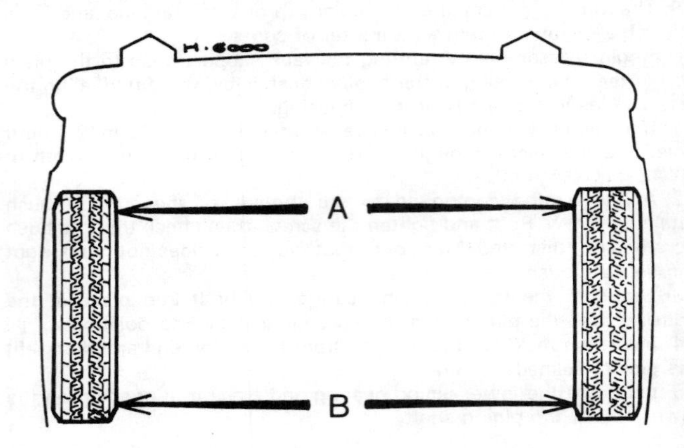

Fig. 11.21 Front wheel alignment (Sec 32)
Dimension A must be 0.0625 in (1.6 mm) greater than B

32 Front wheel alignment

1 The front wheels are correctly aligned when they turn out at the front (toe-out) by the specified amount with the vehicle unladen. Adjustment is carried out by loosening the locknut securing each tie-rod balljoint, and the outer clips on the gaiters, then turning both tie-rods equally until the adjustment is correct.
2 Accurate adjustment and setting of the front wheel alignment involves the use of optical aligning equipment or scuff plates, and it is strongly recommended that this work be entrusted to your local dealer.
3 If the front wheels are not in alignment, tyre wear will be heavy and uneven, and the steering will be unresponsive.

33 Fault diagnosis – suspension and steering

Note: *Before diagnosing steering or suspension faults, be sure that trouble is not due to incorrect tyre pressures, mixture of tyre types, binding or maladjusted brakes, or distortion of the body or subframe.*

Symptom	Reason/s
Vehicle pulls to one side	Wheel alignment incorrect Wear in front suspension or steering components Accident damage to steering or suspension components
Steering stiff or heavy	Steering gear requires lubricating Swivel hub balljoints dry or damaged Steering rack or column bent or damaged Wheel alignment incorrect
Excessive play in steering	Worn steering or suspension joints Worn rack-and-pinion assembly
Wheel wobble and vibration	Wheels needs balancing Wheel nuts loose Roadwheel buckled or distorted Hub bearings badly worn Worn steering or suspension joints Worn rack-and-pinion assembly
Tyre wear uneven	Steering geometry incorrect Worn steering or suspension components Wheels out of balance Accident damage
Clonks and rattles from steering or suspension	Lack of lubrication (where applicable) Worn, damaged or loose components

Chapter 12 Bodywork and fittings

For modifications, and information applicable to later models, see Supplement at end of manual

Contents

1 General description

Although the Mini has been produced in many forms since its introduction, the principle of construction has remained the same. The body and floor pan are of a monocoque all-steel, welded construction creating a very strong and torsionally rigid shell. The front and rear suspension assemblies are mounted on subframes, bolted to the underside of the bodyshell. The front subframe also provides mounting points for the engine/transmission unit.

The body has been designed to provide as much interior space as possible and all models except the Van and Pick-up have a seating capacity of four adults. The sides of the car have been curved to give extra width at elbow and shoulder height and the doors, although rather low, provide ample room for entry and exit. A considerable amount of storage space, in the form of handy side pockets and full width parcel shelf, is also provided inside the car.

Although the Mini bodyshell is extremely strong, it is likely to have suffered to some degree, particularly on older models, from the effects of rust and corrosion. Common problem areas are the front wings, body side sills and the rear subframe. Particular attention should be paid to the rear subframe and areas around its mountings, as well as the side sills, as these are load bearing areas; corrosion here, if left unchecked, could seriously affect the roadworthiness of the vehicle. The subframes are covered in detail in Chapter 11 and full information regarding the treatment of rust and corrosion and body repairs will be found in subsequent Sections of this Chapter.

2 Maintenance – bodywork and underframe

The general condition of a vehicle's bodywork is the one thing that significantly affects its value. Maintenance is easy but needs to be regular. Neglect, particularly after minor damage, can lead quickly to further deterioration and costly repair bills. It is important also to keep watch on those parts of the vehicle not immediately visible, for instance the underside, inside all the wheel arches and the lower part of the engine compartment.

The basic maintenance routine for the bodywork is washing – preferably with a lot of water, from a hose. This will remove all the loose solids which may have stuck to the vehicle. It is important to flush these off in such a way as to prevent grit from scratching the finish. The wheel arches and underframe need washing in the same way to remove any accumulated mud which will retain moisture and tend to encourage rust. Paradoxically enough, the best time to clean the underframe and wheel arches is in wet weather when the mud is thoroughly wet and soft. In very wet weather the underframe is usually cleaned of large accumulations automatically and this is a good time for inspection.

Periodically, except on vehicles with a wax-based underbody protective coating, it is a good idea to have the whole of the underframe of the vehicle steam cleaned, engine compartment included, so that a thorough inspection can be carried out to see what minor repairs and renovations are necessary. Steam cleaning is available at many garages and is necessary for removal of the accumulation of oily grime which sometimes is allowed to become thick in certain areas. If steam cleaning facilities are not available, there are one or two excellent grease solvents available such as Holts Engine Cleaner or Holts Foambrite which can be brush applied. The dirt can then be simply hosed off. Note that these methods should not be used on vehicles with wax-based underbody protective coating or the coating will be removed. Such vehicles should be inspected annually, preferably just prior to winter, when the underbody should be washed down and any damage to the wax coating repaired using Holts Undershield. Ideally, a completely fresh coat should be applied. It would also be worth considering the use of such wax-based protection for injection into door panels, sills, box sections, etc, as an additional safeguard against rust damage where such protection is not provided by the vehicle manufacturer.

After washing paintwork, wipe off with a chamois leather to give an unspotted clear finish. A coat of clear protective wax polish, like the many excellent Turtle Wax polishes, will give added protection against chemical pollutants in the air. If the paintwork sheen has dulled or oxidised, use a cleaner/polisher combination such as Turtle Extra to restore the brilliance of the shine. This requires a little effort, but such dulling is usually caused because regular washing has been neglected. Care needs to be taken with metallic paintwork, as special non-abrasive cleaner/polisher is required to avoid damage to the finish. Always check that the door and ventilator opening drain holes and pipes are completely clear so that water can be drained out. Bright work should be treated in the same way as paint work. Windscreens and windows can be kept clear of the smeary film which often appears, by the use of a proprietary glass cleaner like Holts Mixra. Never use any form of wax or other body or chromium polish on glass.

3 Maintenance – upholstery and carpets

Mats and carpets should be brushed or vacuum cleaned regularly to keep them free of grit. If they are badly stained remove them from the vehicle for scrubbing or sponging and make quite sure they are dry before refitting. Seats and interior trim panels can be kept clean by wiping with a damp cloth and Turtle Wax Carisma. If they do become stained (which can be more apparent on light coloured upholstery) use a little liquid detergent and a soft nail brush to scour the grime out of the grain of the material. Do not forget to keep the headlining clean in the same way as the upholstery. When using liquid cleaners inside the vehicle do not over-wet the surfaces being cleaned. Excessive damp could get into the seams and padded interior causing stains, offensive odours or even rot. If the inside of the vehicle gets wet accidentally it is worthwhile taking some trouble to dry it out properly, particularly where carpets are involved. *Do not leave oil or electric heaters inside the vehicle for this purpose.*

4 Minor body damage – repair

The photographic sequences on pages 262 and 263 illustrate the operations detailed in the following sub-sections.

Repair of minor scratches in bodywork

If the scratch is very superficial, and does not penetrate to the metal of the bodywork, repair is very simple. Lightly rub the area of the scratch with a paintwork renovator like Turtle Wax New Color Back, or a very fine cutting paste like Holts Body+Plus Rubbing Compound, to remove loose paint from the scratch and to clear the surrounding bodywork of wax polish. Rinse the area with clean water.

Apply touch-up paint, such as Holts Dupli-Color Color Touch or a paint film like Holts Autofilm, to the scratch using a fine paint brush; continue to apply fine layers of paint until the surface of the paint in the scratch is level with the surrounding paintwork. Allow the new paint at least two weeks to harden: then blend it into the surrounding paintwork by rubbing the scratch area with a paintwork renovator or a very fine cutting paste, such as Holts Body+Plus Rubbing Compound or Turtle Wax New Color Back. Finally, apply wax polish from one of the Turtle Wax range of wax polishes.

Where the scratch has penetrated right through to the metal of the bodywork, causing the metal to rust, a different repair technique is required. Remove any loose rust from the bottom of the scratch with a penknife, then apply rust inhibiting paint, such as Turtle Wax Rust Master, to prevent the formation of rust in the future. Using a rubber or nylon applicator fill the scratch with bodystopper paste like Holts Body+Plus Knifing Putty. If required, this paste can be mixed with cellulose thinners, such as Holts Body+Plus Cellulose Thinners, to provide a very thin paste which is ideal for filling narrow scratches. Before the stopper-paste in the scratch hardens, wrap a piece of smooth cotton rag around the top of a finger. Dip the finger in cellulose thinners, such as Holts Body+Plus Cellulose Thinners, and then quickly sweep it across the surface of the stopper-paste in the scratch; this will ensure that the surface of the stopper-paste is slightly hollowed. The scratch can now be painted over as described earlier in this Section.

Repair of dents in bodywork

When deep denting of the vehicle's bodywork has taken place, the first task is to pull the dent out, until the affected bodywork almost attains its original shape. There is little point in trying to restore the original shape completely, as the metal in the damaged area will have stretched on impact and cannot be reshaped fully to its original contour. It is better to bring the level of the dent up to a point which is about ⅛ in (3 mm) below the level of the surrounding bodywork. In cases where the dent is very shallow anyway, it is not worth trying to pull it out at all. If the underside of the dent is accessible, it can be hammered out gently from behind, using a mallet with a wooden or plastic head. Whilst doing this, hold a suitable block of wood firmly against the outside of the panel to absorb the impact from the hammer blows and thus prevent a large area of the bodywork from being 'belled-out'.

Should the dent be in a section of the bodywork which has a double skin or some other factor making it inaccessible from behind, a different technique is called for. Drill several small holes through the metal inside the area – particularly in the deeper section. Then screw long self-tapping screws into the holes just sufficiently for them to gain a good purchase in the metal. Now the dent can be pulled out by pulling on the protruding heads of the screws with a pair of pliers.

The next stage of the repair is the removal of the paint from the damaged area, and from an inch or so of the surrounding 'sound' bodywork. This is accomplished most easily by using a wire brush or abrasive pad on a power drill, although it can be done just as effectively by hand using sheets of abrasive paper. To complete the preparation for filling, score the surface of the bare metal with a screwdriver or the tang of a file, or alternatively, drill small holes in the affected area. This will provide a really good 'key' for the filler paste.

To complete the repair see the Section on filling and re-spraying.

Repair of rust holes or gashes in bodywork

Remove all paint from the affected area and from an inch or so of the surrounding 'sound' bodywork, using an abrasive pad or a wire brush on a power drill. If these are not available a few sheets of abrasive paper will do the job just as effectively. With the paint removed you will be able to gauge the severity of the corrosion and therefore decide whether to renew the whole panel (if this is possible) or to repair the affected area. New body panels are not as expensive as most people think and it is often quicker and more satisfactory to fit a new panel than to attempt to repair large areas of corrosion.

Remove all fittings from the affected area except those which will act as a guide to the original shape of the damaged bodywork (eg headlamp shells etc). Then, using tin snips or a hacksaw blade, remove all loose metal and any other metal badly affected by corrosion. Hammer the edges of the hole inwards in order to create a slight depression for the filler paste.

Wire brush the affected area to remove the powdery rust from the surface of the remaining metal. Paint the affected area with rust inhibiting paint like Turtle Wax Rust Master; if the back of the rusted area is accessible treat this also.

Before filling can take place it will be necessary to block the hole in some way. This can be achieved by the use of aluminium or plastic mesh, or aluminium tape.

Aluminium or plastic mesh or glass fibre matting, such as the Holts Body+Plus Glass Fibre Matting, is probably the best material to use for a large hole. Cut a piece to the approximate size and shape of the hole to be filled, then position it in the hole so that its edges are below the level of the surrounding bodywork. It can be retained in position by several blobs of filler paste around its periphery.

Aluminium tape should be used for small or very narrow holes. Pull a piece off the roll and trim it to the approximate size and shape required, then pull off the backing paper (if used) and stick the tape over the hole; it can be overlapped if the thickness of one piece is insufficient. Burnish down the edges of the tape with the handle of a screwdriver or similar, to ensure that the tape is securely attached to the metal underneath.

Bodywork repairs – filling and re-spraying

Before using this Section, see the Sections on dent, deep scratch, rust holes and gash repairs.

Many types of bodyfiller are available, but generally speaking those proprietary kits which contain a tin of filler paste and a tube of resin hardener are best for this type of repair, like Holts Body+Plus or Holts No Mix which can be used directly from the tube. A wide, flexible plastic or nylon applicator will be found invaluable for imparting a smooth and well contoured finish to the surface of the filler.

Mix up a little filler on a clean piece of card or board – measure the hardener carefully (follow the maker's instructions on the pack) otherwise the filler will set too rapidly or too slowly. Alternatively, Holts No Mix can be used straight from the tube without mixing, but daylight is required to cure it. Using the applicator apply the filler paste to the prepared area; draw the applicator across the surface of the filler to achieve the correct contour and to level the filler surface. As soon as a contour that approximates to the correct one is achieved, stop working the paste – if you carry on too long the paste will become sticky and begin to 'pick up' on the applicator. Continue to add thin layers of filler paste at twenty-minute intervals until the level of the filler is just proud of the surrounding bodywork.

Once the filler has hardened, excess can be removed using a metal plane or file. From then on, progressively finer grades of abrasive paper should be used, starting with a 40 grade production paper and finishing with 400 grade wet-and-dry paper. Always wrap the abrasive paper around a flat rubber, cork, or wooden block – otherwise the surface of the filler will not be completely flat. During the smoothing of the filler surface the wet-and-dry paper should be periodically rinsed in water. This will ensure that a very smooth finish is imparted to the filler at the final stage.

At this stage the 'dent' should be surrounded by a ring of bare metal, which in turn should be encircled by the finely 'feathered' edge of the good paintwork. Rinse the repair area with clean water, until all of the dust produced by the rubbing-down operation has gone.

Spray the whole repair area with a light coat of primer, either Holts Body+Plus Grey or Red Oxide Primer – this will show up any imperfections in the surface of the filler. Repair these imperfections with fresh filler paste or bodystopper, and once more smooth the surface with abrasive paper. If bodystopper is used, it can be mixed with cellulose thinners to form a really thin paste which is ideal for filling small holes. Repeat this spray and repair procedure until you are satisfied that the surface of the filler, and the feathered edge of the paintwork are perfect. Clean the repair area with clean water and allow to dry fully.

The repair area is now ready for final spraying. Paint spraying must be carried out in a warm, dry, windless and dust free atmosphere. This condition can be created artificially if you have access to a large indoor working area, but if you are forced to work in the open, you will have to pick your day very carefully. If you are working indoors, dousing the floor in the work area with water will help to settle the dust which would otherwise be in the atmosphere. If the repair area is confined to one body panel, mask off the surrounding panels; this will help to minimise the effects of a slight mis-match in paint colours. Bodywork fittings (eg chrome strips, door handles etc) will also need to be masked off. Use genuine masking tape and several thicknesses of newspaper for the masking operations.

Before commencing to spray, agitate the aerosol can thoroughly, then spray a test area (an old tin, or similar) until the technique is mastered. Cover the repair area with a thick coat of primer; the thickness should be built up using several thin layers of paint rather than one thick one. Using 400 grade wet-and-dry paper, rub down the surface of the primer until it is really smooth. While doing this, the work area should be thoroughly doused with water, and the wet-and-dry paper periodically rinsed in water. Allow to dry before spraying on more paint.

Spray on the top coat using Holts Dupli-Color Autospray, again building up the thickness by using several thin layers of paint. Start spraying in the centre of the repair area and then work outwards, with a side-to-side motion, until the whole repair area and about 2 inches of the surrounding original paintwork is covered. Remove all masking material 10 to 15 minutes after spraying on the final coat of paint.

Allow the new paint at least two weeks to harden, then, using a paintwork renovator or a very fine cutting paste such as Turtle Wax New Color Back or Holts Body+Plus Rubbing Compound, blend the edges of the paint into the existing paintwork. Finally, apply wax polish.

5 Major structural damage or corrosion – general

1 Because the body is built on the monocoque principle and is integral with the underframe, major damage must be repaired by specialists with the necessary welding and hydraulic straightening equipment.

2 Although subframes are used front and rear, they act in the main as supports and locations for the power units and suspension systems.

3 If the damage is severe, it is vital that on completion of the repair and body and subframes are in correct alignment. Less severe damage may also have twisted or distorted the body or subframes, although this may not be visible immediately. It is therefore always best on completion of repair to check for twist and squareness to make sure all is well.

4 To check for twist, position the car on a clean level floor, place a jack under each jacking point, raise the car and take off the wheels. Raise or lower the jacks until the sills are parallel with the ground. Depending where the damage occurred, using an accurate scale, take measurements at the suspension mounting points and if comparable readings are not obtained it is an indication that the body is twisted.

5 After checking for twist, check for squareness by taking a series of measurements on the floor. Drop a plumb line and bob weight from various mounting points on the underside of the body and mark these points on the floor with chalk. Draw a straight line between each point and measure and mark the middle of each line. A line drawn on the floor starting at the front and finishing at the rear should be quite straight and pass through the centres of the other lines. Diagonal

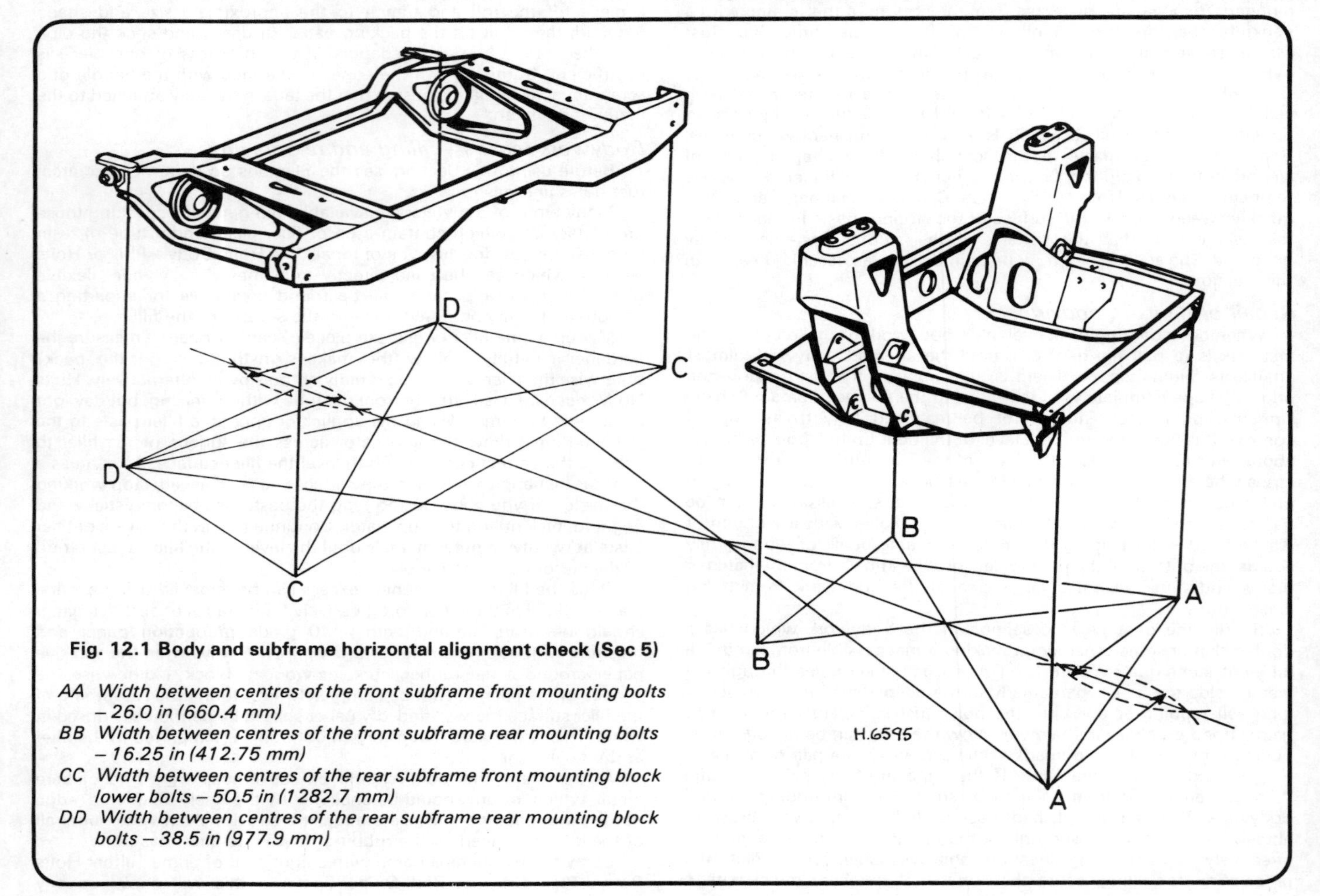

Fig. 12.1 Body and subframe horizontal alignment check (Sec 5)

AA Width between centres of the front subframe front mounting bolts – 26.0 in (660.4 mm)
BB Width between centres of the front subframe rear mounting bolts – 16.25 in (412.75 mm)
CC Width between centres of the rear subframe front mounting block lower bolts – 50.5 in (1282.7 mm)
DD Width between centres of the rear subframe rear mounting block bolts – 38.5 in (977.9 mm)

measurements can also be made as a check for squareness.
6 On older Minis, rust or corrosion of the vehicle underframe is a common occurence and, if the corrosion has reached an advanced state, may be grounds for failure of the annual MoT test.
7 Where serious rust or corrosion has affected a load bearing area, it will be necessary to have this repaired immediately either by fitting a new body section or, in less serious cases, by plating over the affected area. The load bearing areas of the Mini consist of the subframe, the side sills (inner and outer) and any area of the vehicle structure within 12 in (305 mm) of a suspension, steering, subframe, or seat belt anchorage point.
8 Repairs of this nature are best left to a body repair specialist, as any new section or plating that may be necessary must be welded in place to restore the original structural rigidity of the bodyshell. The repair of corrosion to structural areas using fibreglass, body filler, or the retention of new sections with pop rivets, or screws, is not acceptable to MoT requirements.

6 Maintenance – locks and hinges

Once every 6000 miles (10 000 km) or 6 months the door, bonnet and boot hinges should be lubricated with a few drops of engine oil from an oil can. The door striker plates should also be given a thin smear of grease to reduce wear and ensure free movement.

7 Door rattles – tracing and rectification

The most common cause of door rattles is a loose, misaligned or worn door striker plate, but other causes may be:

(a) Loose door handles or door hinges
(b) Loose, worn or misaligned door lock components
(c) Worn sliding window channels or sliding window catches (Van and Pick-up models)

8 Front door interior trim panel (Saloon and Estate models) – removal and refitting

1 Undo and remove the two screws and lift off the interior pull handle (photo).
2 Undo and remove the retaining screws and lift away the door lock remote control handle followed by the window regulator handle and surround (photos).
3 Carefully ease off the interior lock control surround (photo).
4 On later models undo and remove the retaining screws and lift away the storage bin.
5 Using a wide-bladed screwdriver or flat strip of metal inserted between the trim panel and the door, carefully detach the trim panel clips from the door panel (photo).
6 When all the clips are released, the panel can be withdrawn.
7 If it is wished to gain access to the internal door components, carefully peel off the waterproof covering.
8 Refitting is the reverse sequence to removal, but ensure that the waterproof covering is in position before refitting the panel.

9 Doors – removal and refitting

All models except Van and Pick-up

1 Refer to Section 32 and remove the fresh air valve assembly (if fitted), from the facia.
2 Gently ease the door sealing rubber from the door pillar around the area where it retains the facia inner trim panel.
3 Undo and remove the retaining screws (if fitted), and then carefully fold back the facia inner trim to give access to the door check strap aperture.
4 Extract the split pin and clevis pin from the door check strap.
5 Support the weight of the door on blocks, or engage the help of an assistant. Undo and remove the four nuts and two washer plates, accessible from inside the front wheel arch.
6 Carefully lift the door assembly, complete with hinges, off the

8.1 Remove the interior pull handle retaining screws and handle

8.2a Remove the door lock remote control handle...

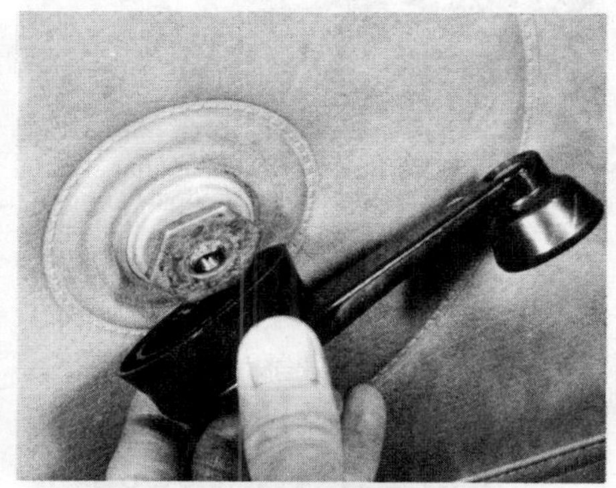
8.2b ...and the window regulator handle

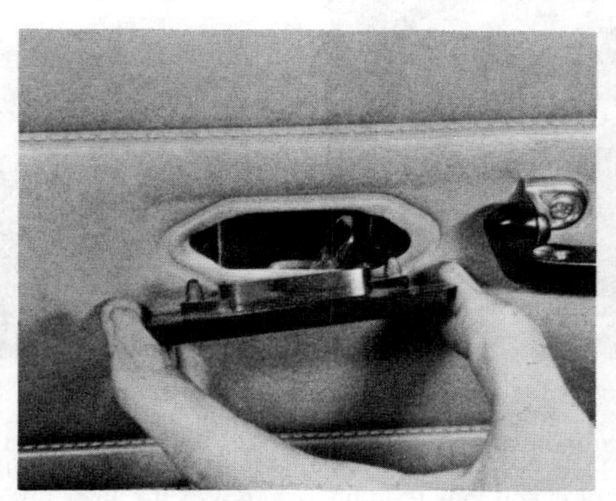
8.3 Ease off the interior lock control surround...

8.5 ...then detach the panel clips and withdraw the trim panel

This photographic sequence shows the steps taken to repair the dent and paintwork damage shown above. In general, the procedure for repairing a hole will be similar; where there are substantial differences, the procedure is clearly described and shown in a separate photograph.

First remove any trim around the dent, then hammer out the dent where access is possible. This will minimise filling. Here, after the large dent has been hammered out, the damaged area is being made slightly concave.

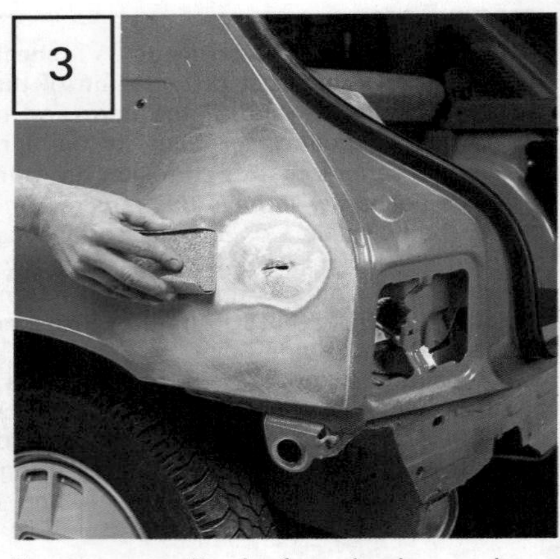

Next, remove all paint from the damaged area by rubbing with coarse abrasive paper or using a power drill fitted with a wire brush or abrasive pad. 'Feather' the edge of the boundary with good paintwork using a finer grade of abrasive paper.

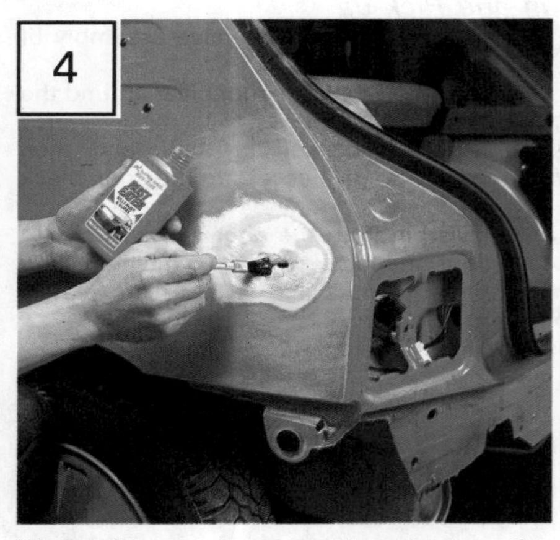

Where there are holes or other damage, the sheet metal should be cut away before proceeding further. The damaged area and any signs of rust should be treated with Turtle Wax Hi-Tech Rust Eater, which will also inhibit further rust formation.

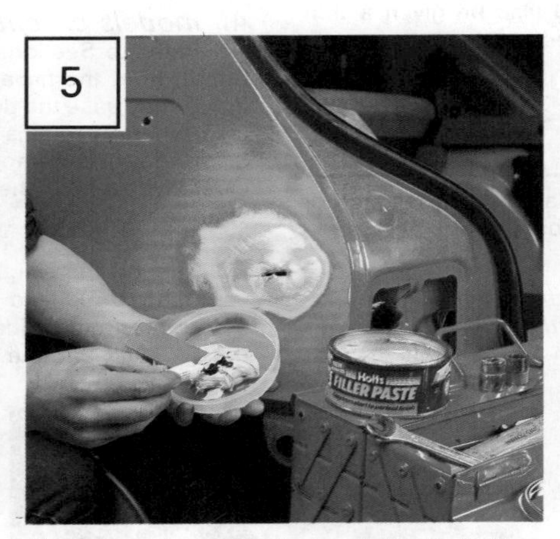

For a large dent or hole mix Holts Body Plus Resin and Hardener according to the manufacturer's instructions and apply around the edge of the repair. Press Glass Fibre Matting over the repair area and leave for 20-30 minutes to harden. Then ...

... brush more Holts Body Plus Resin and Hardener onto the matting and leave to harden. Repeat the sequence with two or three layers of matting, checking that the final layer is lower than the surrounding area. Apply Holts Body Plus Filler Paste as shown in Step 5B.

For a medium dent, mix Holts Body Plus Filler Paste and Hardener according to the manufacturer's instructions and apply it with a flexible applicator. Apply thin layers of filler at 20-minute intervals, until the filler surface is slightly proud of the surrounding bodywork.

For small dents and scratches use Holts No Mix Filler Paste straight from the tube. Apply it according to the instructions in thin layers, using the spatula provided. It will harden in minutes if applied outdoors and may then be used as its own knifing putty.

Use a plane or file for initial shaping. Then, using progressively finer grades of wet-and-dry paper, wrapped round a sanding block, and copious amounts of clean water, rub down the filler until glass smooth. 'Feather' the edges of adjoining paintwork.

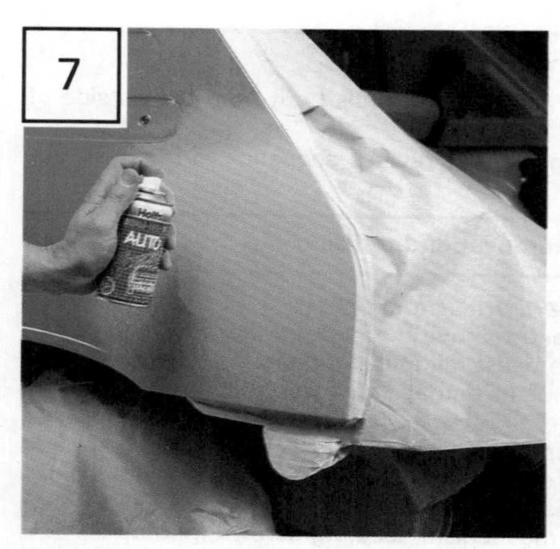

Protect adjoining areas before spraying the whole repair area and at least one inch of the surrounding sound paintwork with Holts Dupli-Color primer.

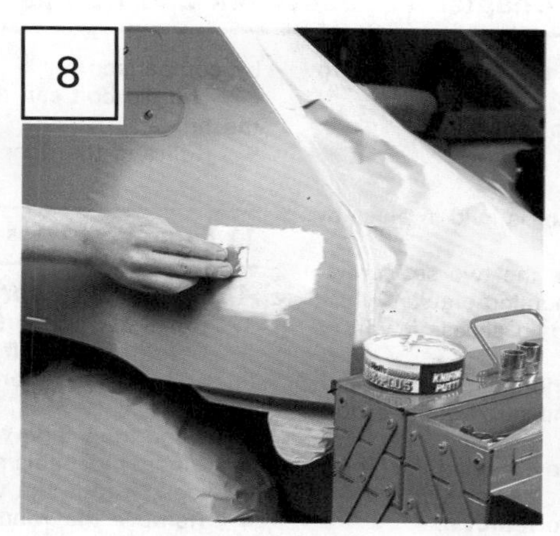

Fill any imperfections in the filler surface with a small amount of Holts Body Plus Knifing Putty. Using plenty of clean water, rub down the surface with a fine grade wet-and-dry paper – 400 grade is recommended – until it is really smooth.

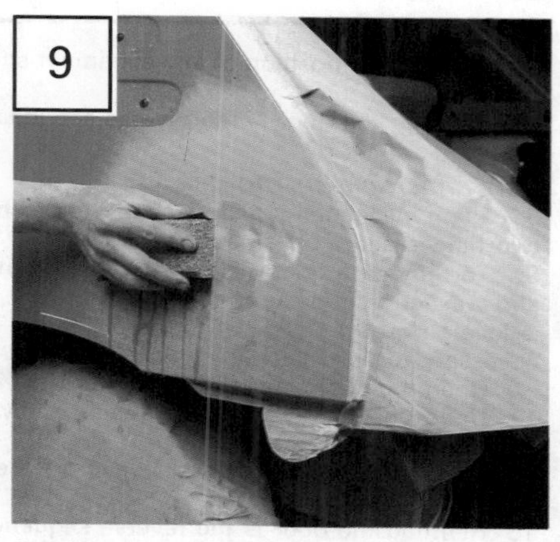

Carefully fill any remaining imperfections with knifing putty before applying the last coat of primer. Then rub down the surface with Holts Body Plus Rubbing Compound to ensure a really smooth surface.

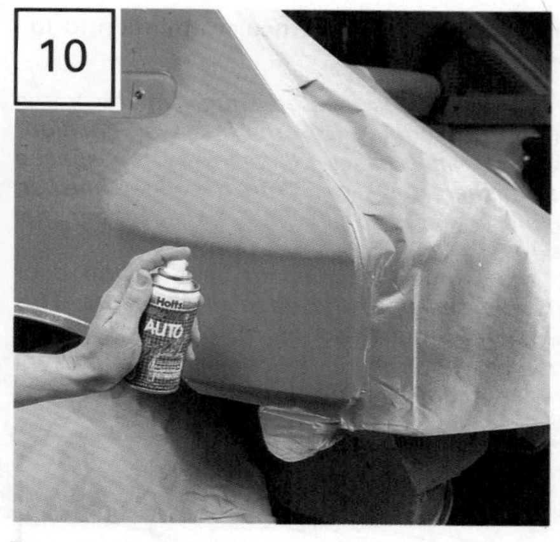

Protect surrounding areas from overspray before applying the topcoat in several thin layers. Agitate Holts Dupli-Color aerosol thoroughly. Start at the repair centre, spraying outwards with a side-to-side motion.

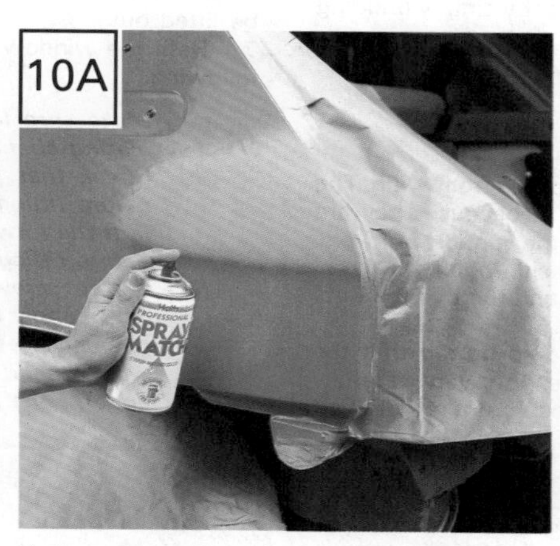

If the exact colour is not available off the shelf, local Holts Professional Spraymatch Centres will custom fill an aerosol to match perfectly.

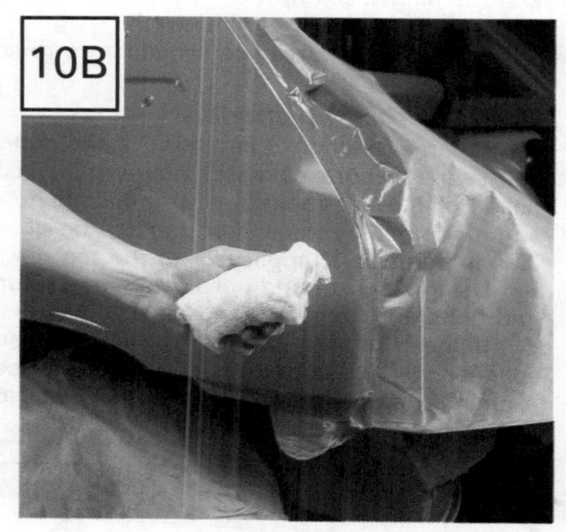

To identify whether a lacquer finish is required, rub a painted unrepaired part of the body with wax and a clean cloth.

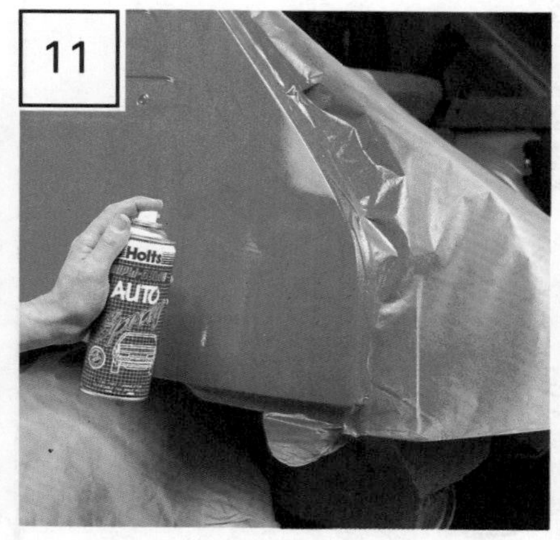

If *no* traces of paint appear on the cloth, spray Holts Dupli-Color clear lacquer over the repaired area to achieve the correct gloss level.

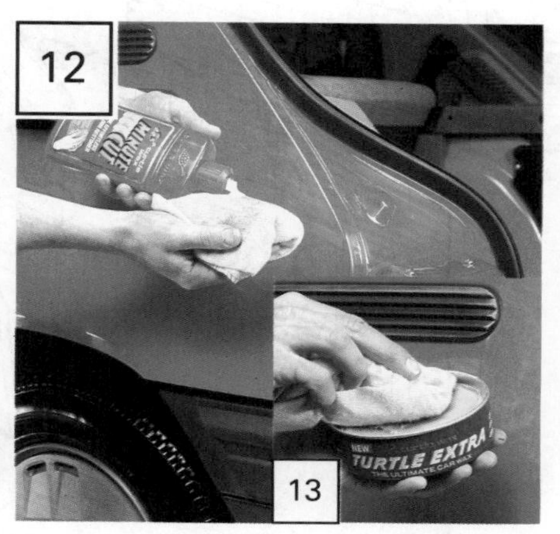

The paint will take about two weeks to harden fully. After this time it can be 'cut' with a mild cutting compound such as Turtle Wax Minute Cut prior to polishing with a final coating of Turtle Wax Extra.

When carrying out bodywork repairs, remember that the quality of the finished job is proportional to the time and effort expended.

body, noting the position of any alignment shims that may be fitted to the hinges.
7 Refitting the door is the reverse sequence to removal.

Van and Pick-up models

8 Upon inspection it will be seen that each door is held in place by two hinges and a check strap.
9 To remove a door, first unscrew and remove the two set screws and washers that secure the door check strap coupling bracket which is located on the inside of the door pillars. To gain access it will be necessary to ease back the side trim first.
10 Open the door carefully and pull out the interior lining of the door.
11 Undo and remove the cross-head screw and nut from the door side of each of the two hinges.
12 The door can now be lifted away from the body, leaving the hinges still attached to the body.
13 Refitting the door is the reverse sequence to removal.

10 Door hinge – removal and refitting

All models except Van and Pick-up

1 Remove the door as described in Section 9.
2 The hinges can now be removed from the door by simply undoing the retaining screws and lifting off.
3 Refitting is the reverse sequence to removal.

Van and Pick-up models

4 Refer to Section 9 and remove the door.
5 Two nuts/bolts hold each hinge to the inside of the front wing. The heads of the nuts/bolts are very difficult to get at because they are surrounded at the top and bottom by the sides of the support brackets. This is particularly applicable to the top hinge, inside bolt.
6 Using a socket and universal coupling, undo and remove the nuts and bolts and lift away the hinge.
7 If the head on one of the bolts has become so burred that the spanner will no longer fit and provide a positive grip, very carefully examine a new hinge and decide on the exact position of the old bolt by comparison.
8 The old bolt can then be carefully drilled out from the outside of the hinge.
9 Refitting the door hinge is the reverse sequence to removal.

11 Front door glass – removal and refitting

All models except Van and Pick-up

1 Refer to Section 8, and remove the door interior trim panel.
2 Carefully ease off the waist rail finisher strips from the top of the door edge, taking care not to damage them as they are lifted away from the clips.
3 Wind the window approximately half-way so that the two arms of the winder mechanism are as near vertical as they can be. With a piece of wood, wedge the window glass at the sill in this position.
4 Remove the winder mechanism securing screws (photo).
5 Pull the regulator away from the door panel enough to move it forwards so that the rear arm comes out of the window channel. Then move the mechanism back to release the arm from the front channel and take it away.
6 Support the glass with one hand, remove the wedge and tilt the forward edge down into the door so that the top rear corner of the glass comes inside the top of the window frame. The glass can then be lifted out.
7 Refit the window in reverse order with particular attention to the following.

(a) Make sure that the window is located snugly in the frame glazing channels before wedging it in the half-way position
(b) Check that the waist rail finisher clips are evenly spaced before fitting the finishers back on. With the inner finisher, butt the forward end against the glazing channel rubber seal before fitting the rest
(c) Before screwing the winder mechanism back to the door panel apply a suitable sealer to the edge of the plate. This compensates for any irregularities in the panel stamping which could cause rattles. Ensure that the lip on the front edge of the plate is engaged inside the panel

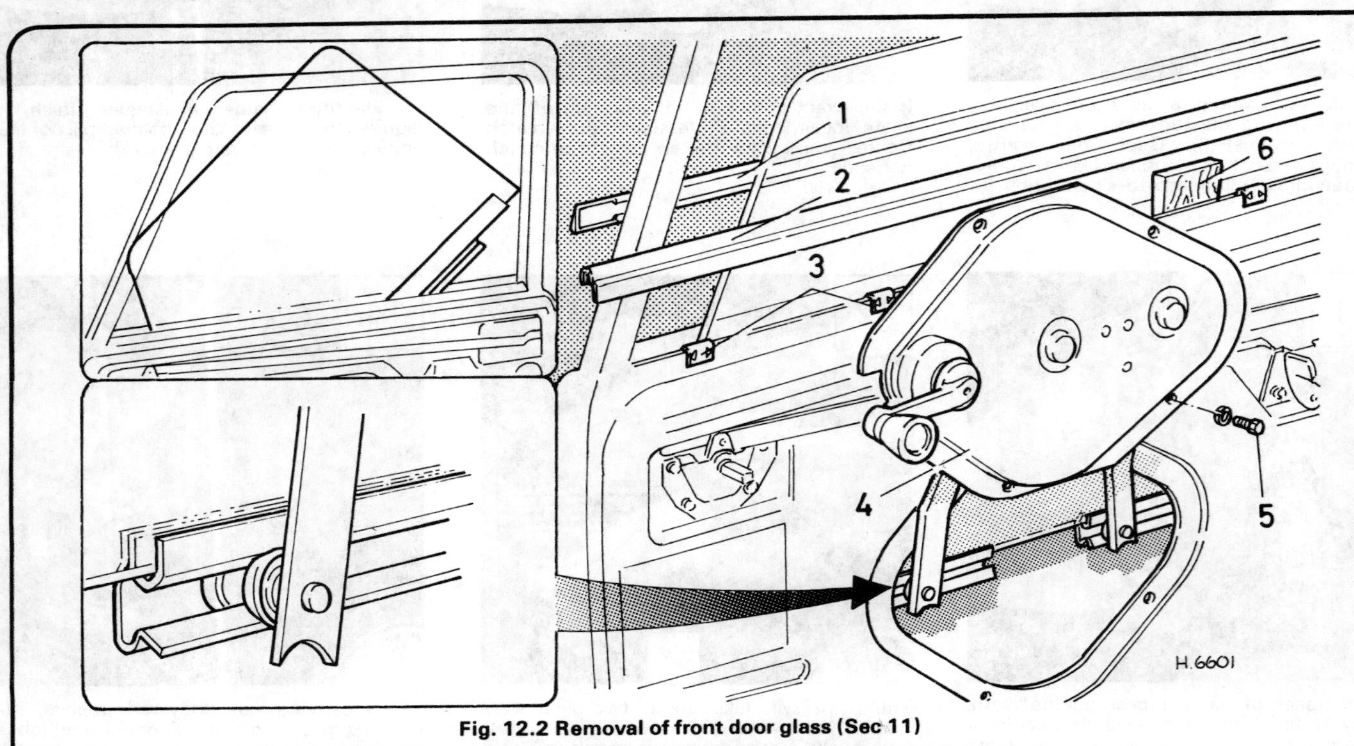

Fig. 12.2 Removal of front door glass (Sec 11)

Inset shows regulator arm and position of door glass ready for removal

1 *Waist rail finisher (outer)*
2 *Waist rail finisher (inner)*
3 *Securing clips for finishers*
4 *Window winder regulator*
5 *Regulator securing screws*
6 *Wedge (to hold glass)*

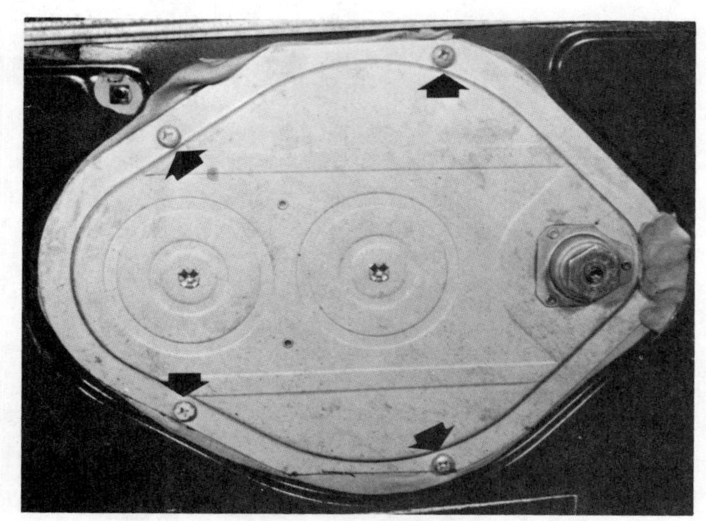
11.4 The window winder mechanism securing screws

(d) *Put the adhesive sealing strips back where they came from using a good impact adhesive*

Van and Pick-up models

8 Undo and remove the retaining screw, boss and washer securing the catches to the glass. Lift off the catches and sealing rubbers.
9 Slide the front glass rearwards and then undo and remove the screw securing the lower channel to the door. If the screw is very tight or badly corroded, apply liberal amounts of penetrating oil to the screw and allow it to soak in. Give the screw a sharp tap with a hammer and drift to break the corrosion. It should now be possible to unscrew it.
10 Move both glasses forward and repeat the above procedure, if necessary, on the other lower channel retaining screw.
11 Ease the glasses, lower channel, and glass catch strip towards the centre of the car at the bottom and then lift the assembly off the door. The two sliding glasses can then be removed from the lower channel.
12 Refitting is the reverse sequence to removal.

12 Front door lock assembly – removal and refitting

All models except Van and Pick-up

1 Refer to Section 8 and remove the inner trim panel.
2 Undo and remove the screws securing the door inner remote control handle to the door panel (photo).
3 Undo and remove the screws securing the interior lock control to the door panel (photo).
4 Undo and remove the screws securing the door lock to the side of the door (photo).
5 Slide the door lock out of its location in the door and carefully

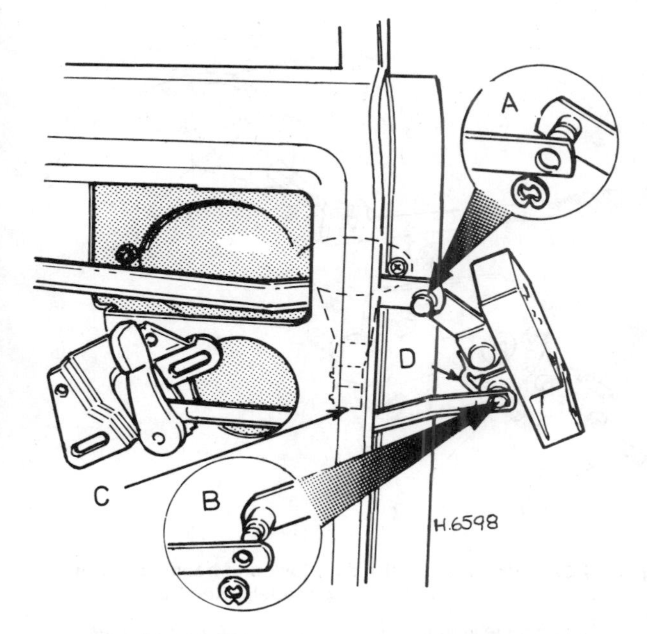

Fig. 12.3 Front door lock removal (Sec 12)

A Remote control handle operating rod
B Interior lock operating rod
C Exterior handle lock link
D Latch lock rod

release the two small circlips securing the remote control handle and interior lock operating rods to the door lock assembly.
6 Lift away the door lock, and then withdraw the remote control and interior lock control from the door panel.
7 Refitting is the reverse sequence to removal. Ensure that the small link rod on the lock assembly is engaged with the operating link of the exterior door handle.

Van and Pick-up models

8 Undo and remove the three screws that secure the lock body to the inner door panel (photo).
9 Undo and remove the screw located at the end of the locking handle spindle.
10 Slacken the inner handle clamp screw (where fitted) and slide out the outer handle and escutcheon. Now lift off the lock body.
11 Refitting is the reverse sequence to removal.

13 Front door exterior handle (Saloon and Estate models) – removal and refitting

1 Refer to Section 8 and remove the interior trim panel.

12.2 Remove the door inner remote control handle retaining screws...

12.3 ...the interior lock control retaining screws...

12.4 ...and the door lock retaining screws

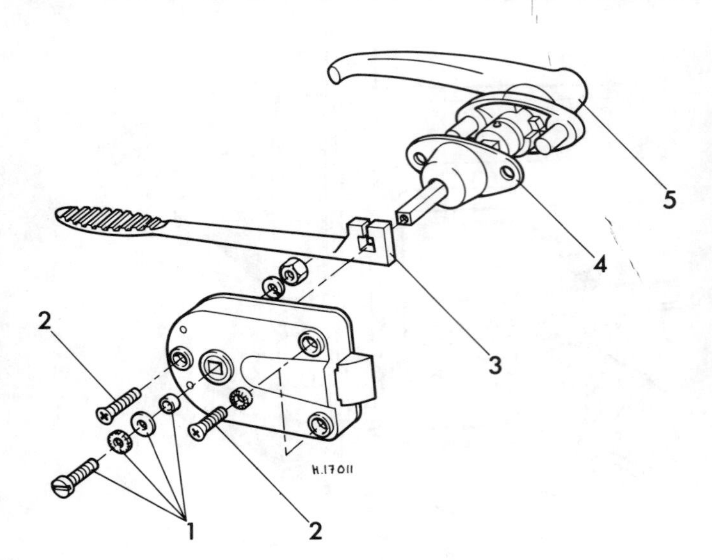

Fig. 12.4 Exploded view of the door lock and handle assembly fitted to Van and Pick-up models (Sec 12)

1 *Lock handle spindle fixings*
2 *Lock body retaining screws*
3 *Interior handle*
4 *Seal*
5 *Exterior handle*

12.8 The lock body retaining screws on Van and Pick-up models

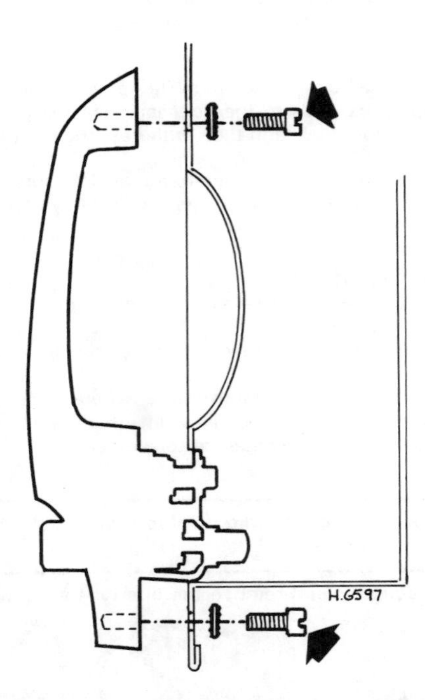

Fig. 12.5 Exterior door handle securing screws (arrowed) – Saloon and Estate models (Sec 13)

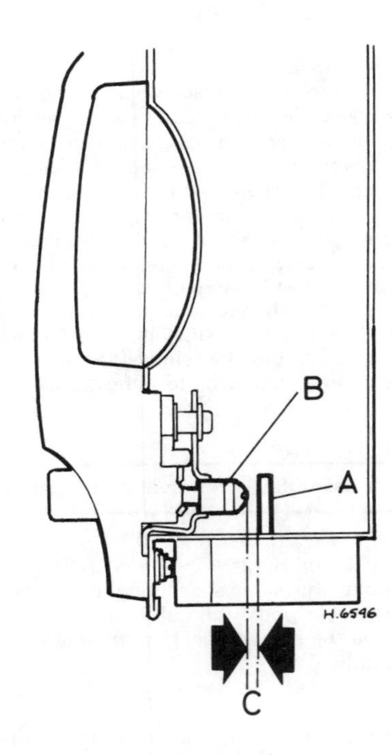

Fig. 12.6 Door handle push button plunger adjustment (Sec 13)

A *Lock release lever*
B *Plunger cap*
C = 0.031 to 0.062 in (1.0 to 1.5 mm)

2 Undo and remove the screws securing the interior lock control to the inner door panel.
3 Undo and remove the screws securing the door lock assembly to the side of the door, and move the lock up at the bottom and away from the door.
4 Undo and remove the screws securing the exterior handle to the door and lift the handle off.
5 With the handle removed, the lock barrel and push button can be withdrawn as follows.
6 Prise off the retaining clip securing the lock barrel to the handle.
7 Insert the key into the lock and withdraw the lock barrel.
8 Undo and remove the screw securing the retaining plate to the exterior handle.
9 Lift off the retaining plate, operating link, washer, and spring. Now withdraw the push button.
10 Reassembly and refitting of the exterior handle is the reverse sequence to removal. On the earlier type door handle the push button plunger incorporates an adjustable nylon cap over the plunger. The adjustment of this cap is set during manufacture, but if necessary it can be screwed in or out slightly to give 0.03 to 0.06 in (1 to 1.5 mm) of free play before contacting the door lock release lever.

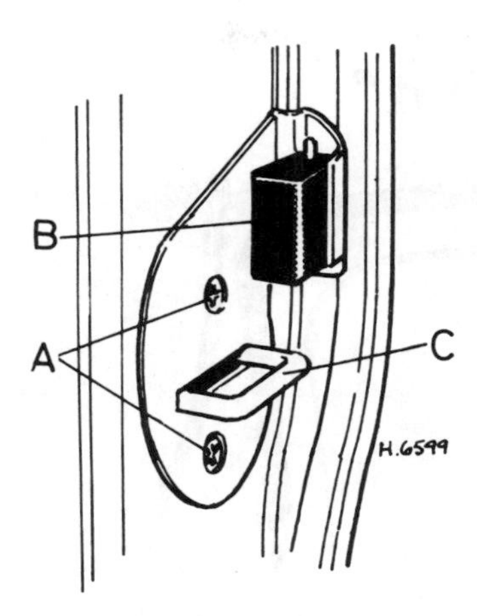

Fig. 12.7 The front door striker plate fitted to Saloon and Estate models (Sec 14)

A Securing screws
B Over travel stop
C Striker loop

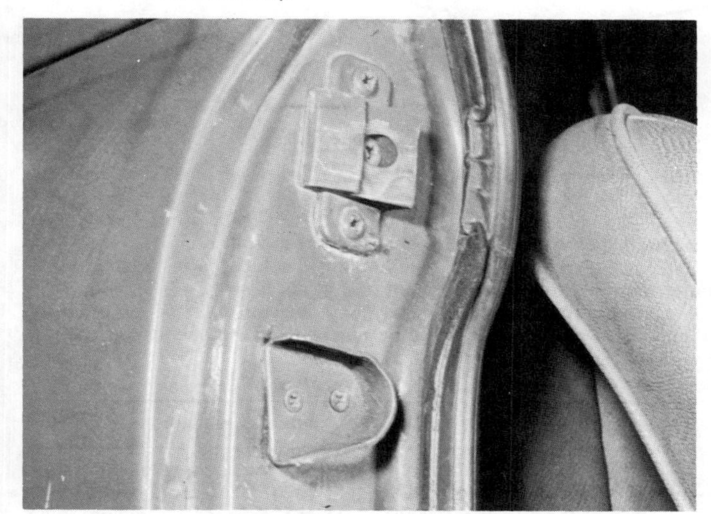

14.4 Front door striker and guide plate on Van and Pick-up models

14 Front door striker plate – removal and refitting

All models except Van and Pick-up

1 Remove the striker plate cover from the body pillar.
2 Undo and remove the striker plate retaining screws, lift out the striker lock and remove the striker plate.
3 Refitting is the reverse sequence to removal. Adjust the striker plate so that as the door is closed, the striker lock passes through the door lock without fouling. It should also be possible to push the door in slightly against compression of the sealing rubber when the door is closed.

Van and Pick-up models

4 To remove the striker on these models, simply undo and remove the retaining screws and lift off (photo).
5 When refitting the striker plate, adjust it so that the door sealing rubber is just compressed and the door is flush with the adjoining bodywork when closed.

15 Bonnet – removal and refitting

1 Open the bonnet and support on its stay.

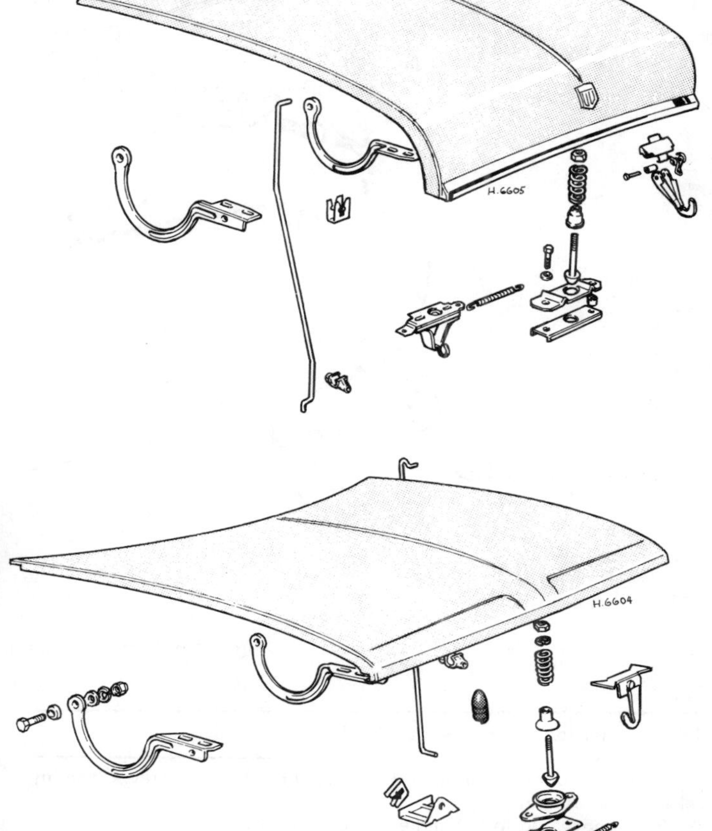

Fig. 12.8 Bonnet hinge and lock assemblies (Sec 15)

2 With a pencil, mark the outline of the hinge on the bonnet to assist correct refitting.
3 An assistant should now take the weight of the bonnet. Undo and remove the bonnet-to-hinge retaining nuts, spring and plain washers at both hinges. Carefully lift away the bonnet over the front of the car.
4 Refitting is the reverse sequence to removal. Alignment in the body may be made by leaving the securing nuts slightly loose and repositioning by trial and error.

16 Bonnet lock – removal and refitting

1 Open the bonnet and support it on its stay.
2 On models having an ignition shield attached to the body front panel, undo and remove the retaining screws and withdraw the shield.
3 Detach the slider catch return spring.
4 Undo and remove the two screws securing the lock assembly to the front panel and lift off the lock and guide plate.
5 Refitting is the reverse sequence to removal.

17 Boot lid – removal and refitting

1 Open the boot lid and disconnect the number plate light electrical leads from their connectors in the boot compartment wiring harness.
2 Support the boot lid and undo and remove the screws securing the two stays to the sides of the boot lid.
3 Undo and remove the nuts, spring and plain washers securing the hinges to the boot lid and lift off the boot lid.
4 Refitting is the reverse sequence to removal.

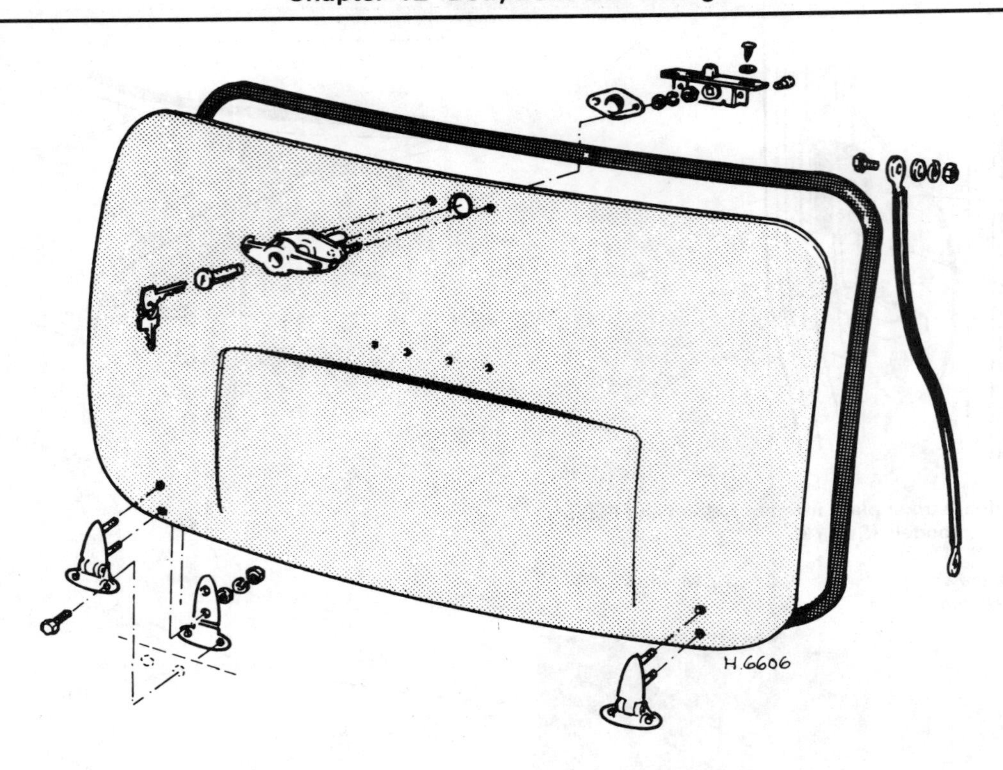

Fig. 12.9 Boot lid hinge and lock assemblies (Sec 17)

18 Boot lid lock – removal and refitting

1 Open the boot lid, undo and remove the retaining screws, and lift off the lock assembly.
2 To remove the lock handle, undo and remove the two nuts and washers and lift off the handle and joint washer.
3 If it is wished to remove the lock barrel from the handle, extract the spring clip and slide off the flat and wavy washers from the end of the handle.
4 Take out the small lock barrel retaining pin and then slide out the barrel. Recover the locking pin from the end of the handle.
5 Reassembly and refitting of the lock is the reverse sequence to removal. When reassembling the lock barrel, position the small retaining pin in the slot of the locking pin before refitting.

19 Rear doors (Estate and Van models) – removal and refitting

1 Open both doors and disconnect the door support stays by undoing the nut, washer and bolt at the end of each stay.
2 Preferably have an assistant hold the door, or place a support under it, and then bend down the tab washer on each door hinge.
3 Undo and remove the nut, tab washer, hinge centre bolt, and the spherical bush from each of the door hinges in turn.
4 Refitting is a straightforward reversal of this operation.

20 Rear door lock (Estate and Van models) – removal and refitting

1 Undo and remove the screws securing the lock to the door.
2 Disengage the lock assembly from the handle, lift it up to release the lower stay from its guide, lower it to release the upper stay, and then withdraw the complete assembly.
3 Slacken the nuts securing the stays to the lock and then unscrew the stays.
4 To remove the door handle, release the door seal retaining clips from the hole in the door panel.
5 Undo and remove the nuts and washers securing the door handle to the door. Lift off the handle and recover the joint washer.
6 To remove the lock barrel, first remove the retaining circlip and slide off the cover, spring washer and brass washers.
7 Withdraw the handle yoke, extract the lock barrel retaining pin, and remove the lock barrel and locking pin.
8 Reassembly and refitting is the reverse sequence to removal. When refitting the stays note that the cranked stay is refitted to the top with the crank to the right.

21 Tailgate (Pick-up models) – removal and refitting

1 Undo and remove the number plate light cover retaining screw and lift off the cover and lens.
2 Detach the electrical leads from the number plate light bulb holders and withdraw the leads from the tailgate.
3 Support the tailgate in the open position, and then undo and remove the tailgate stays securing screws.
4 Undo and remove the screws securing the tailgate hinges to the tailgate and carefully lift away the tailgate.
5 Refitting is the reverse sequence to removal.

22 Windscreen – removal and refitting

1 Remove the wiper arms from their spindles by using a screwdriver to ease them up, and then lift off.
2 Using a small screwdriver, carefully ease up one end of the finishing strip from its groove in the windscreen sealing rubber and then pull the entire length of the strip out of the rubber.
3 If an undamaged windscreen is being removed, from inside the car firmly push the screen outwards, starting at one of the top corners. Carefully remove the complete windscreen from the sealing rubber and lift if off the car. Withdraw the sealing rubber from the windscreen aperture in the body.
4 If a shattered windscreen is being removed, lay some old blankets or sheets over the bonnet and in the car interior, making sure that the demister vents are well covered. Break the remaining glass onto the blankets or sheets, and then withdraw the sealing rubber from the windscreen aperture. Discard the shattered glass and clean up any fragments using a vacuum cleaner. Operate the heater in all positions with the fan motor running to dislodge any trapped glass, but watch out for flying fragments which may be blown out of the ducting.

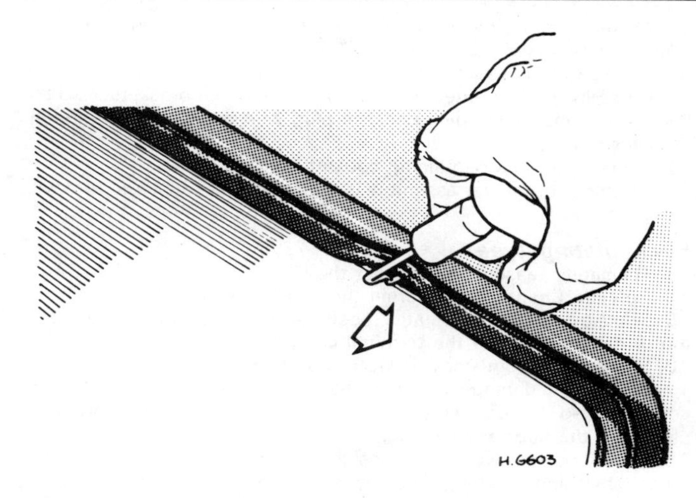

Fig. 12.10 Using a service tool to ease the rubber window channel lip over the glass (Sec 22)

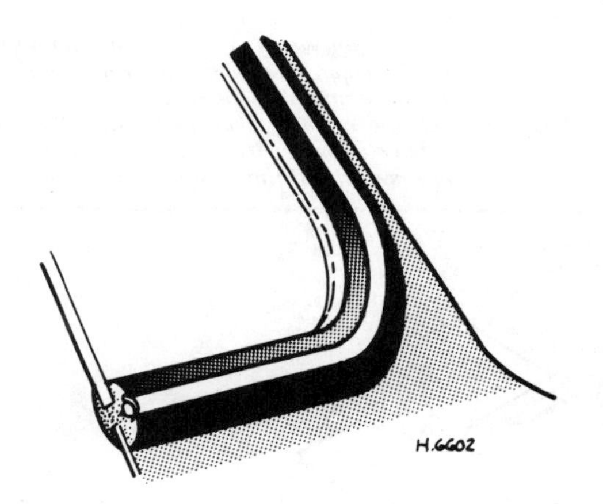

Fig. 12.11 The outside finishing strip in position (Sec 22)

5 To fit the windscreen, first inspect the sealing rubber for hardness or deterioration and renew if necessary.
6 Position the sealing rubber over the windscreen, and then insert a length of string, around the circumference of the rubber, ensuring that it seats into the body flange groove of the rubber. Position the string so that the two ends protrude by at least 12 in (300 mm) at the bottom centre of the screen.
7 Mix a concentrated soap and water solution and apply it liberally to the flange of the windscreen aperture.
8 Place the windscreen and rubber seal in position on the car, and engage the help of an assistant to apply firm pressure to the outside of the screen. From inside the car use the string to pull the rubber lip over the body flange, working slowly around the screen until the string has been fully withdrawn.
9 Starting at the top centre of the rubber seal, use a wide-bladed screwdriver to spread the lips of the seal, while at the same time pressing the finishing strip into place. Work around the entire circumference of the windscreen in this way.
10 With the screen in position and the finishing strip fitted, the wiper arms can now be refitted to their spindles.

23 Rear window (Saloon and Pick-up models) – removal and refitting

The removal and refitting procedure for the rear window or its sealing rubber is the same as described in Section 22 for the windscreen. On later models, it will also be necessary to disconnect the electrical supply and earth leads to the heated rear window element before removal.

24 Rear door window (Estate and Van models) – removal and refitting

The removal and refitting procedure for the rear door window or its sealing rubber is the same as described in Section 22 for the windscreen. Note, however, that the sealing rubber does not incorporate a finishing strip.

25 Rear quarterlight glass (Saloon models) – removal and refitting

Hinged type

1 Open the window and then undo and remove the screws securing the catch to the body.
2 With the window supported, undo and remove the screws securing the hinge(s) to the body pillar.
3 Lift away the window, and if required undo and remove the retaining screw and window glass surround.
4 Refitting is the reverse sequence to removal.

Fixed type

5 Removal and refitting of the fixed type window follows the same procedure as described in Section 22. Note, however, that the sealing rubber does not incorporate a finishing strip.

26 Rear side screen window (Estate models) – removal and refitting

1 Carefully remove the trim panel from above the windows.
2 Undo and remove the screw securing the fixed window locking peg and withdraw the peg.
3 Undo and remove the screws securing the front, upper, and rear glazing channels and lift out the front and rear channels.
4 Slide the windows toward the front of the car and then pull down the rear of the upper channel to release it from the window frame.
5 Now slide the windows and upper channel rearwards to release the front of the upper channel, and then carefully remove the channel and windows.
6 Refitting is the reverse sequence to removal.

27 Heater water valve control cable – removal and refitting

1 Open the bonnet and support it on its stay.
2 Slacken the inner cable trunnion screw and the outer cable clamp screw at the water valve, and release the cable from the valve.
3 From inside the car, undo and remove the screws, securing the centre console (where fitted). This will enable the console to be moved slightly as necessary to provide access to the control cable and heater.
4 Slacken the nut securing the rear of the heater unit to its mounting bracket.
5 Undo and remove the two screws securing the heater unit to the parcel shelf and lower the heater.
6 Detach the heater switch wire from the rear of the switch.
7 Undo and remove the two nuts securing the switch panel to the bracket under the parcel shelf.
8 Pull the switch panel forward slightly, undo the control cable retaining nut, and pull the complete cable through into the car. Recover the nut and washer from the end of the cable as it is pulled through.
9 Refitting the cable is the reverse sequence to removal.

28 Heater assembly – removal and refitting

Fresh air type

1 For safety reasons, disconnect the battery earth terminal.
2 Refer to Chapter 2 and drain the cooling system.
3 On models fitted with a centre console, remove the console and the facia glovebox securing screws. This will enable the console to be moved as necessary for greater access to the heater.
4 Remove tthe front floor covering to avoid any damage through cooling water spillage as the pipes are disconnected.

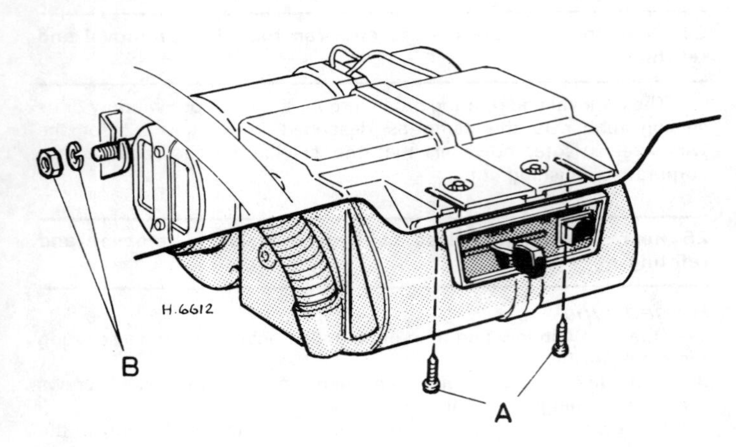

Fig. 12.12 Fresh air heater securing points (Sec 28)

A Securing screws – heater to parcel shelf
B Nut and spring washer – heater to rear bracket

5 Carefully pull the demister and air intake tubes out of the heater unit.
6 Undo and remove the two screws that secure the front of the heater to the parcel shelf.
7 Slacken the nut that secures the rear of the heater to the body mounted bracket.
8 Make a note of the electrical connections to the blower motor and switch, and detach.
9 Slacken the clips and disconnect the heater water hoses.
10 Carefully lift the heater unit from the slotted rear brackets, hold the fingers over the matrix pipe ends (or plug with corks) and lift the unit from the car.
11 Finally drain any remaining coolant from the unit.
12 Refitting the heater assembly is the reverse sequence to removal.

Recirculating type

13 For safety reasons, disconnect the battery.
14 Refer to Chapter 2 and drain the cooling system.
15 Make a note of their relative positions, then disconnect the heater motor electric leads at the terminal connectors.
16 Slacken the demister and water hose clips.
17 To prevent damage to the carpets or upholstery caused by rust contaminated water, place polythene sheeting in the appropriate places on the floor and seating.
18 Undo and remove the screws that secure the heater unit to the parcel shelf and carefully lift away the heater unit.
19 Refitting the heater unit is the reverse sequence to removal, but the following additional points should be noted:

(a) Open the heater tap on the rear of the engine and slowly refill the cooling system
(b) If the heater does not warm up, it is an indication that there is an air lock. To clear, disconnect the return hose from the lower radiator hose and plug the hole. Now extend the return hose to reach the radiator filler neck. Start the engine and observe the flow of water from the return hose. When the bubbles cease, switch off the engine and reconnect the hose

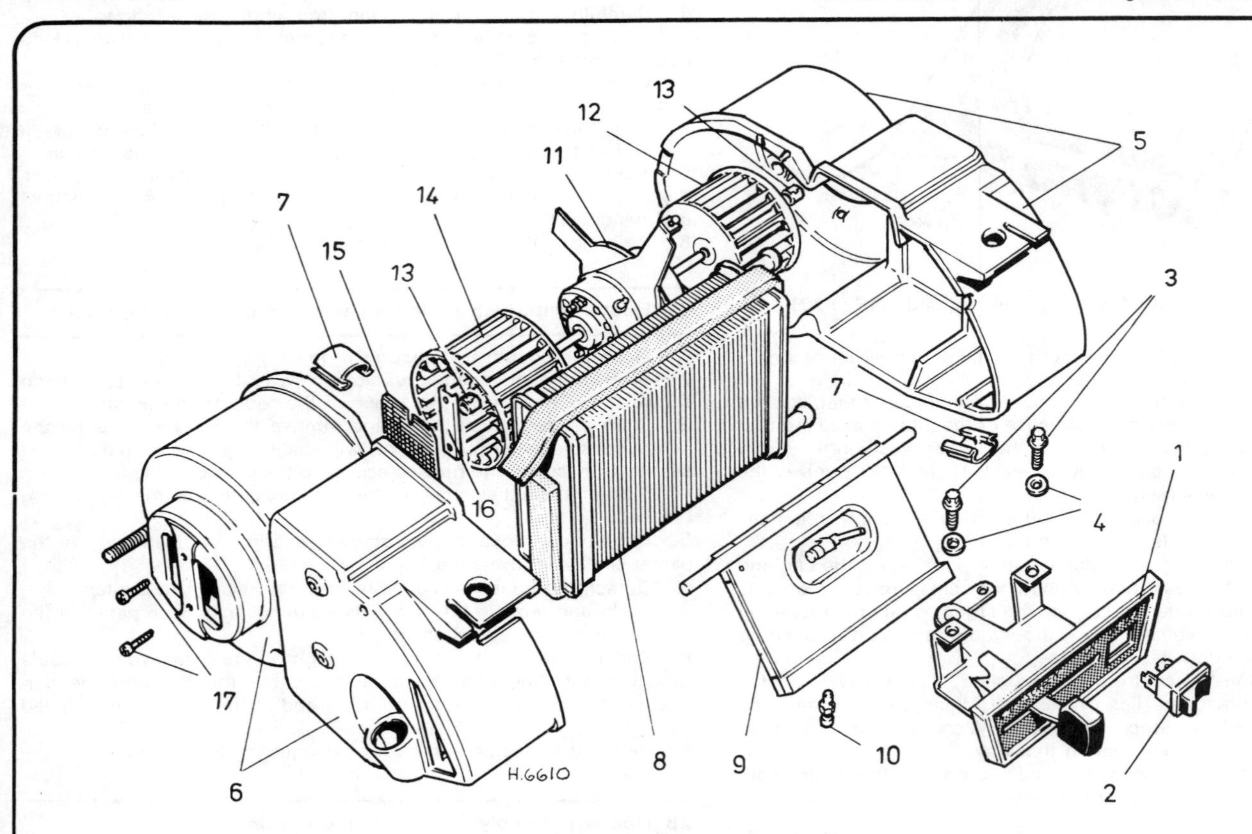

Fig. 12.13 Exploded view of the early type fresh air heater (Sec 29)

1 Control panel
2 Fan switch
3 Control panel securing screws
4 Washer
5 Heater casing
6 Heater casing
7 Retaining clip
8 Matrix
9 Air distribution flap
10 Trunnion screw
11 Fan motor
12 Air intake fan
13 Retaining clips
14 Recirculating fan
15 Flap valve
16 Valve securing plate
17 Valve securing screws

29 Heater assembly – dismantling and reassembly

Early fresh air type

1 With the heater assembly removed from the car, undo and remove the two screws securing the control panel to the heater casing and lift off the panel.

2 Carefully prise off the spring retaining clips and separate the two halves of the casing.

3 Withdraw the motor assembly and then lift out the heater matrix.

4 The two rotors may be removed from the blower motor by releasing the retaining clips and sliding off the rotors.

5 Clean all traces of rust and dirt from the matrix, and carefully inspect it for leaks or signs of excessive corrosion. If it is leaking, renewal is recommended as repairs are seldom successful unless done professionally.

6 Reassembly of the heater is the reverse sequence to the dismantling.

Later fresh air type

7 With the heater removed from the car, detach the wire from the fan motor at the rear of the fan switch.

8 Undo and remove the three screws and lift off the heater control mounting plate.

9 Undo and remove the nine screws securing the right-hand end cover and lift off the cover.

10 Carefully slide out the heater matrix.

11 Undo and remove the screws securing the fan motor to the main casing, release the motor wires and grommet, and withdraw the motor assembly.

12 If necessary, remove the two fans from the motor spindle.

13 With the heater dismantled, clean off all traces of rust and dirt from the matrix and carefully inspect it for leaks or signs of excessive corrosion. If it is leaking, renewal is recommended, as repairs are seldom successful unless done professionally.

14 Reassembly of the heater is the reverse of the dismantling procedure.

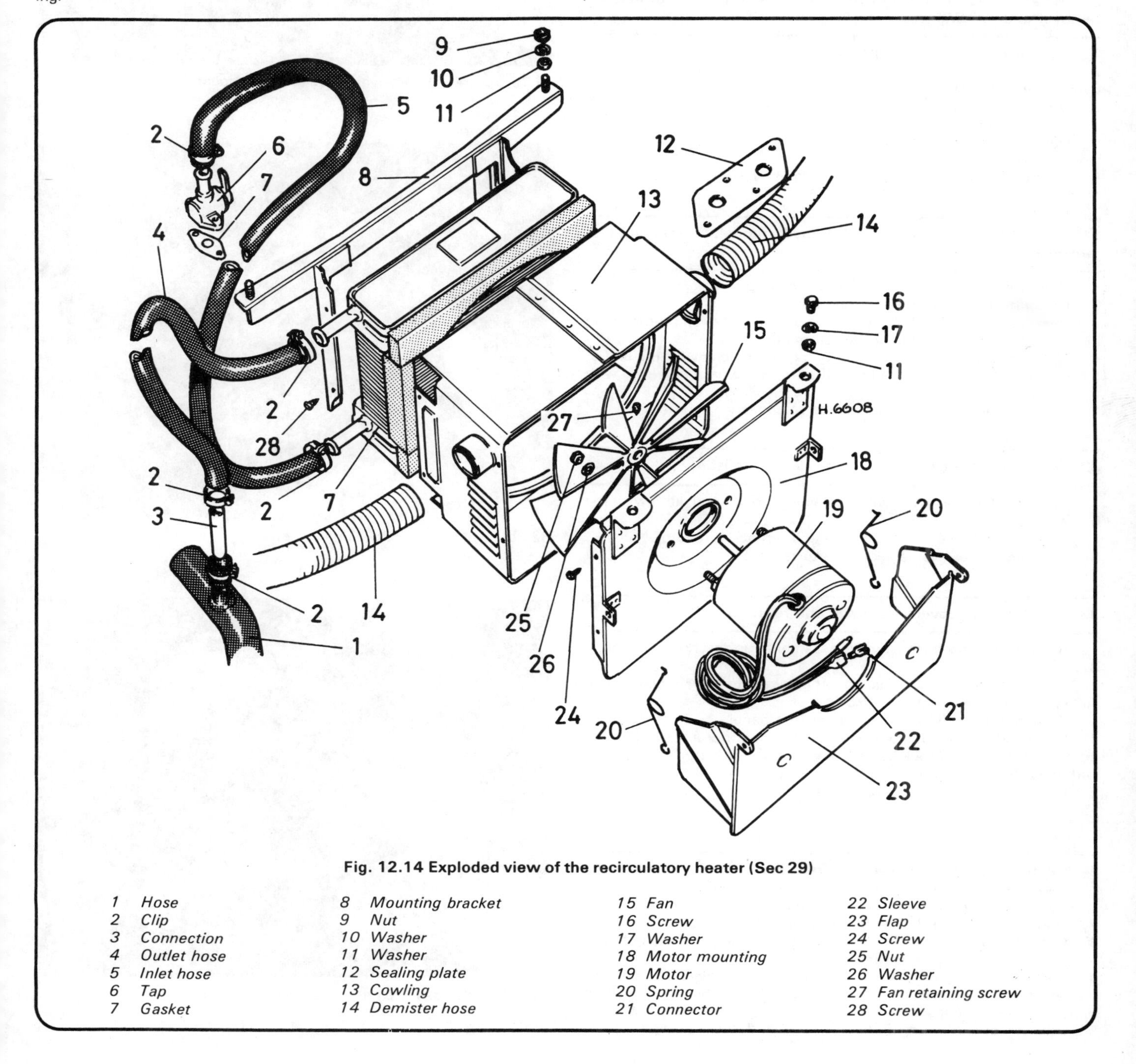

Fig. 12.14 Exploded view of the recirculatory heater (Sec 29)

1 Hose
2 Clip
3 Connection
4 Outlet hose
5 Inlet hose
6 Tap
7 Gasket
8 Mounting bracket
9 Nut
10 Washer
11 Washer
12 Sealing plate
13 Cowling
14 Demister hose
15 Fan
16 Screw
17 Washer
18 Motor mounting
19 Motor
20 Spring
21 Connector
22 Sleeve
23 Flap
24 Screw
25 Nut
26 Washer
27 Fan retaining screw
28 Screw

Recirculatory type

15 With the heater assembly removed from the car, detach the spring clips securing the demister flap to the cover plate and lift off the flap.
16 Undo and remove the screws securing the cover plate to the cowling and lift off the cover plate and motor assembly.
17 Prise the fan off the motor spindle, undo and remove the retaining nut and washer, then lift away the motor.
18 Undo and remove the screws securing the mounting bracket to the cowling, lift off the mounting bracket and withdraw the heater matrix.
19 With the heater dismantled, clean off all traces of rust and dirt from the matrix and carefully inspect it for signs of excessive corrosion. The matrix should be renewed if it is badly corroded, or if it is leaking.
20 Reassembly of the heater unit is the reverse of the dismantling procedure.

30 Heater assembly (Mini 1000 Canada models) – removal and refitting

1 Open the bonnet and support it on its stay.
2 From underneath the right-hand front wing, undo and remove the two blower assembly retaining nuts.
3 Undo and remove the bolt securing the support bracket to the front body panel.
4 Detach the fan motor wires and the air ducts, then lift away the blower assembly.
5 Refitting is the reverse sequence to removal.

31 Heater fan motor (Mini 1000 Canada models) – removal and refitting

1 Open the bonnet and support it on its stays.
2 Disconnect the fan motor wiring connector.
3 Undo and remove the three screws securing the fan motor to the blower housing, and withdraw the fan motor.
4 To remove the fan from the motor, prise it carefully off the end of the spindle. Ensure that the fan is refitted with the rotor hub level with the end of the motor spindle.
5 Refitting the fan motor is the reverse sequence to removal.

32 Fresh air valve assembly – removal and refitting

1 Unscrew the fresh air valve retaining collar and lift away the binnacle (photos).
2 Turn the air valve anti-clockwise and remove it (photo).
3 Refitting is the reverse sequence to removal.

32.1a Unscrew the fresh air valve retaining collar...

32.1b ...and lift away the binnacle

32.2 Turn the air valve anti-clockwise to remove

33 Facia top rail cover – removal and refitting

1 Remove the two fresh air valve assemblies as described in Section 32.
2 Pull the door rubber sealing strip away from the body pillar sufficiently to clear the top rail cover.
3 Withdraw the left-hand facia inner trim panel.
4 Undo and remove the four nuts securing the top rail cover, lift the front of the cover upwards to release the four studs, and then withdraw the cover from the car.
5 Refitting the facia top rail cover is the reverse sequence to removal.

34 Centre console – removal and refitting

1 For safety reasons, disconnect the battery earth terminal.
2 Undo and remove the centre console retaining screws.
3 Carefully ease off the radio knobs and finishers, and then undo and remove the radio securing wing nuts.
4 Engage fourth gear, while at the same time moving the console rearwards. Undo and remove the radio retaining screws and ease the radio clear of the console.
5 Disconnect the wiring from the clock and cigarette lighter, and

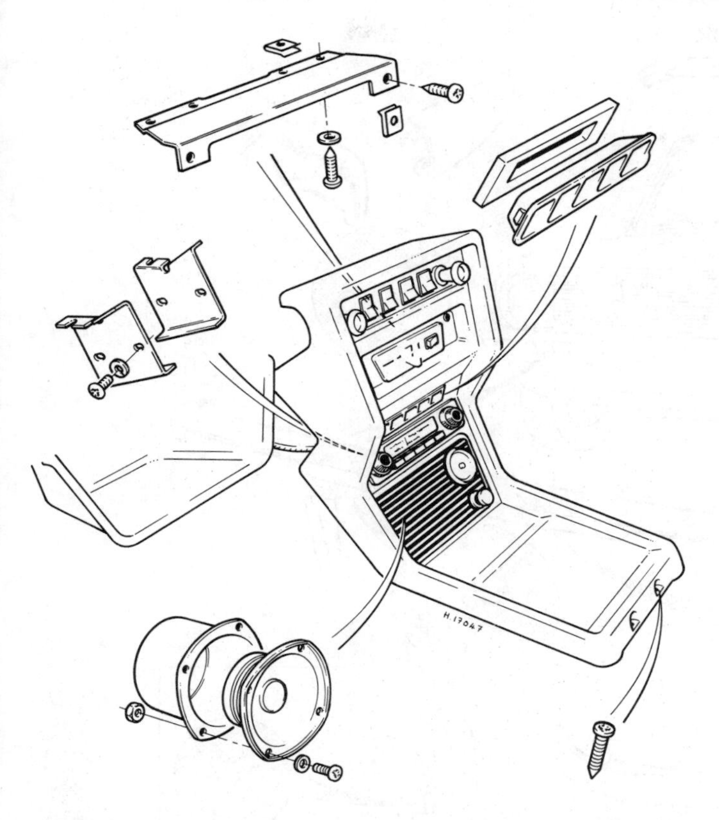

Fig. 12.15 Centre console components and attachments (Sec 34)

detach the speaker plug from the radio.

6 Release the gear lever grommet and then remove the centre console from the car.

7 With the console removed, release the clamp and lift out the cloth. Unscrew the cigarette lighter body and withdraw it. Unclip and remove the speaker grille, and then lift out the speaker after undoing the retaining screws.

8 Refitting the components to the console and the console to the car is the reverse sequence to removal.

35 Front grille – removal and refitting

All models except Clubman and 1275 GT

1 Undo and remove the self-tapping screws securing the edge trim to each side of the grille and lift off the trim.

2 Undo and remove the remaining screws securing the centre panel of the grille and withdraw the panel.

3 Refitting is the reverse sequence to removal.

Clubman and 1275GT models

4 Undo and remove the self-tapping screws securing the grille panel and the headlight extension panels (photo).

5 Lift off the extension panels, disengage the lugs on the lower edge of the grille from the grommets in the lower body panel, and lift off the grille (photo).

6 Refitting is the reverse sequence to removal.

36 Bodywork seam trim strips – removal and refitting

1 The welded seams on the exterior of the Mini bodywork are covered by protective metal and push-fit trim strips which are either chromium plated or sprayed to match the exterior colour scheme. Additionally, a chrome or black trim strip is used to cover the wheel and edges and side sill seams. This is a one piece plastic moulding running the full length of the car.

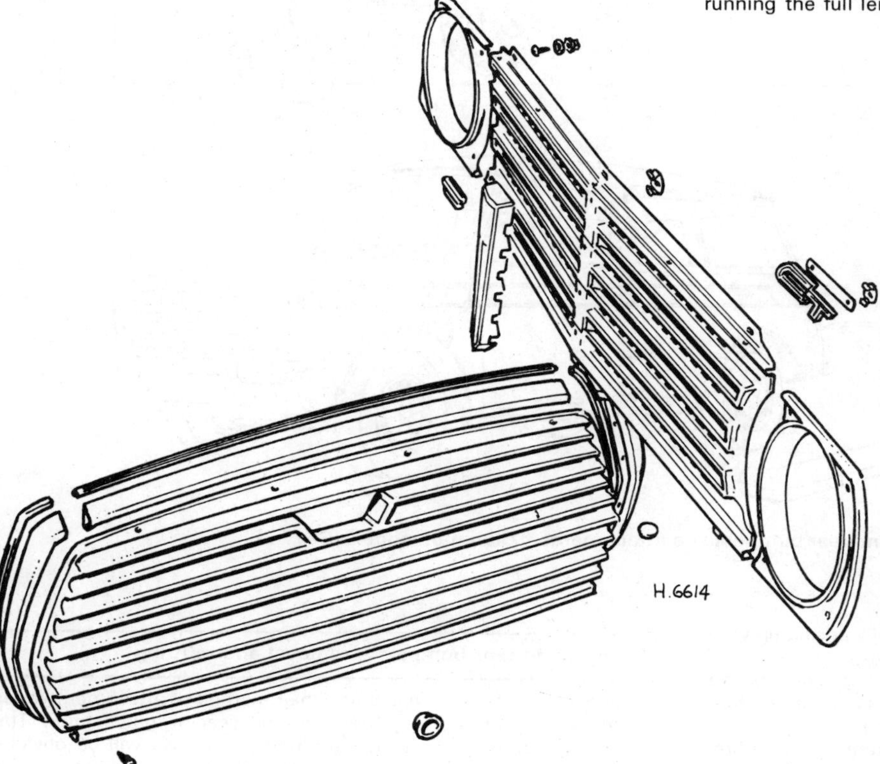

Fig. 12.16 Front grille panels and attachments (Sec 35)

35.4 Remove the grille panel retaining screws...

35.5 ...and disengage the lugs from the grommets in the body panel

Fig. 12.17 Front and rear bumpers and attachments – Clubman models (Sec 37)

2 The side seam trim strips are removed by carefully prising up with a screwdriver and lifting off.

3 To refit the strips, ensure that the small retaining clips are in sound condition and simply push the trim into place, giving it a firm push with the palm of your hand to ensure that it is fully home.

4 The wheel arch and side sill plastic moulding is removed after first drilling out the pop rivet that retains each end of the trim to the wheel arch.

5 Before fitting a new trim, heat it slightly in a warm oven until it is pliable and then carefully position it over the wheel arch edges and side sill seams. Secure each end with a pop rivet or self tapping screw.

37 Front and rear bumpers – removal and refitting

The layout of the bumpers and their method of attachment varies considerahly according to model type and year of manufacture. The location and type of retaining nuts, bolts or screws will be obvious after a visual inspection, and no problems should be encountered. On models with a full width wrap-around bumper, it is helpful to engage the aid of an assistant to support the bumper, thus ensuring that the paintwork is not scratched as it is removed.

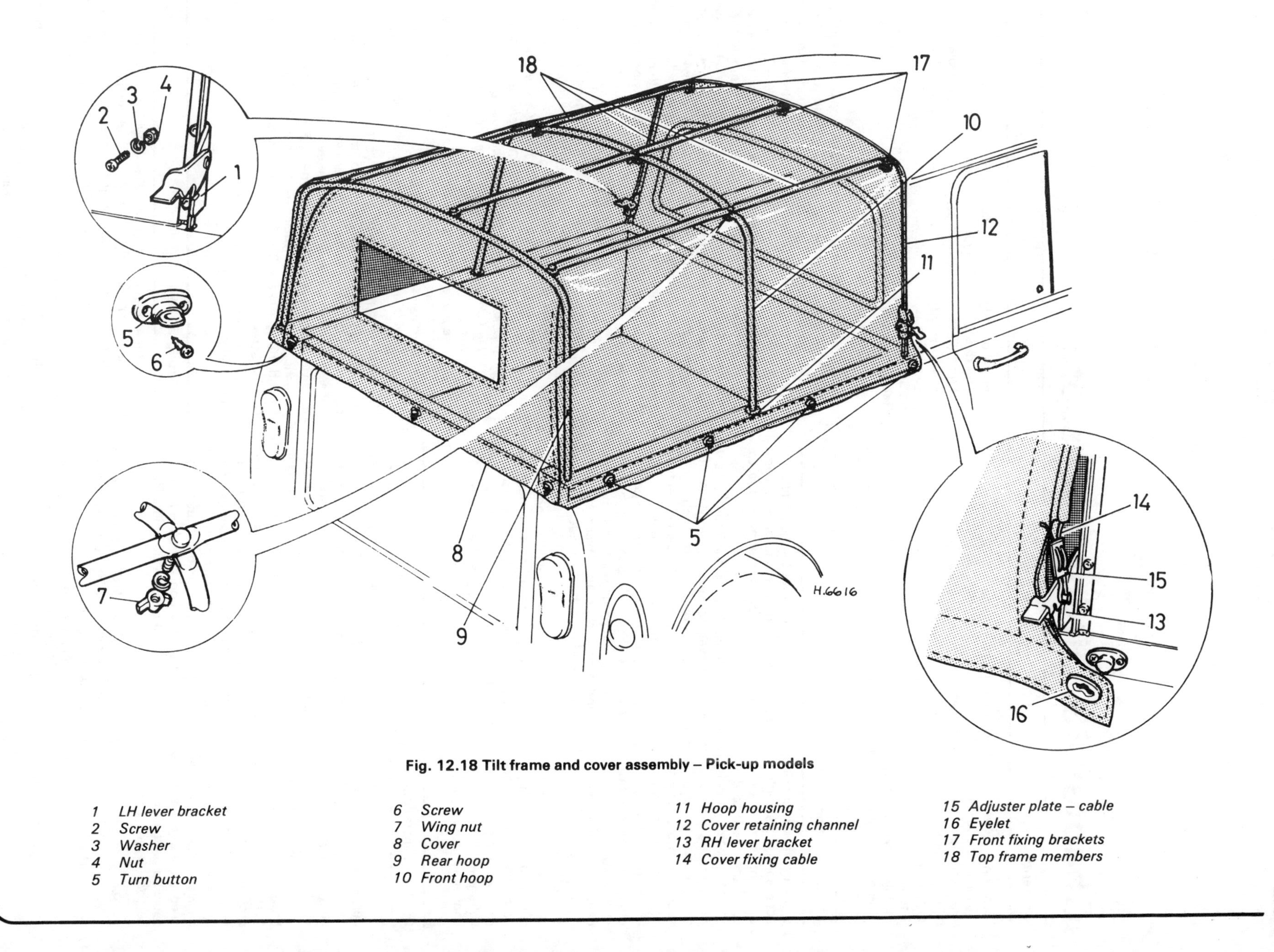

Fig. 12.18 Tilt frame and cover assembly – Pick-up models

1 LH lever bracket
2 Screw
3 Washer
4 Nut
5 Turn button
6 Screw
7 Wing nut
8 Cover
9 Rear hoop
10 Front hoop
11 Hoop housing
12 Cover retaining channel
13 RH lever bracket
14 Cover fixing cable
15 Adjuster plate – cable
16 Eyelet
17 Front fixing brackets
18 Top frame members

Chapter 13 Fitting accessories

Contents

1 Introduction

All cars, whether new or old, can be improved by the addition of accessories. As well as adding a touch of personalisation, some accessories have a practical value in as much as they make the car safer and easier to drive.

Most Mini models provide considerable scope for improvement. Although later versions are reasonably well equipped, early Minis offer the minimum of instrumentation and creature comforts. The range of accessories available is virtually limitless, but the following Sections describe the installation of some of the more popular items.

Plan the fitting of each accessory carefully, and with regard to others that may be fitted at a later date. Also make sure that you have all the special connectors and plugs, crimping tool and the correct gauge of wire. Inferior results and poor performance will result from a unit that is not properly fitted and has badly made electrical connections.

Always take great care when fitting any electrical accessory. Make sure that the polarity of the accessory concerned is set for negative earth and always disconnect the battery before starting. Take special care when fitting or working on electronic ignition systems, as the voltages produced by these units are often far higher than those of a conventional system.

2 Radio installation – general

A radio is an expensive item to buy and will only give its best performance if fitted properly. It is useless to expect concert hall performance from a unit that is suspended from the dash panel on a string with its speaker resting on the back seat or parcel shelf!

Make sure the unit is of the same polarity as the car, and ensure that units with adjustable polarity are correctly set before commencing fitting. Most radios are a standard size of 7 in (178 mm) wide by 2 in (51 mm) deep. This ensures that they will fit into the radio aperture provided in most cars. As the Mini does not have such an aperture, the radio should be fitted in a suitable position beneath the parcel shelf. Alternatively, a special console can be purchased which will fit between the parcel shelf and the floor. These consoles can also be used for additional switches and instrumentation if required. Before deciding on the exact location of the radio, the following points should be considered:

(a) *The unit must not be mounted in close proximity to an electronic tachometer, the ignition switch and its wiring, or the flasher unit and associated wiring*
(b) *The unit must be mounted within reach of the aerial lead, and in such a place that the aerial lead will not have to be routed near the components detailed in the preceding paragraph (a)*
(c) *The unit must be fitted really securely*

Some radios will have mounting brackets provided, together with instructions; others will have to be fitted using drilled and slotted metal strips, bent to form mounting brackets – these strips are available from most accessory shops. The unit must be properly earthed, by fitting a separate earthing lead between the casing of the radio and the vehicle frame.

The type of aerial used, and its fitted position, is a matter of personal preference. In general the taller the areial, the better the reception. It is best to fit a fully retractable aerial – especially if a mechanical car-wash is used or if you live in an area where cars tend to be vandalised. In this respect electric aerials, which are raised and lowered automatically when switching the radio on or off, are convenient, but are more likely to give trouble than the manual type. When choosing a site for the aerial the following points should be considered:

(a) *The aerial lead should be as short as possible – this means that the aerial should be at the front of the car*
(b) *The aerial must be mounted as far away from the distributor and HT leads as possible*
(c) *The part of the aerial which protrudes beneath the mounting point must not foul the roadwheels, or anything else*
(d) *If possible, the aerial should be positioned so that the coaxial lead does not have to be routed through the engine compartment*
(e) *The plane of the panel on which the aerial is mounted should not be so steeply angled that the aerial cannot be mounted vertically (in relation to the 'end-on' aspect of the car). Most aerials have a small amount of adjustment available*

Positioning and fitting of the speaker depends mainly on its type. Generally, the speaker is designed to fit directly in the aperture provided in the panel behind the rear seats. If this is the case it will be necessary to cut a hole in the trim panel and obtain a protective grille to cover the speaker. If a pod type speaker is being used the best acoustic results will normally be obtained by mounting it on a shelf behind the rear seats. The pod can be secured to the panel with self-tapping screws.

A typical radio installation, bearing in mind the foregoing points, is shown in the next Section.

3 Fitting a radio

1 The Mini is an extremely easy car in which to fit a radio, due to its small instrument panel and large parcel shelf. For the following installation, the space beneath the parcel shelf was chosen for the radio location, with a pod type speaker mounted on the panel behind the rear seats. To keep the cable run as short as possible, the aerial has been fitted to the nearside front wing.

2 Mark out the aerial location, and then centre punch and drill a pilot hole. To prevent damage to the wing if the drill slips, cover the surrounding area with masking tape.

3 Using a drill of suitable diameter, enlarge the hole until it is big

enough for the aerial to pass through. Alternatively, use a round file (photo).

4 Pass the aerial up through the hole in the wing, and then fit the plastic and domed washers, followed by the retaining nut (photos). With the aerial fully extended, position it so that it is vertical when viewed from the front and leaning back slightly when viewed from the side. Now tighten the retaining nut fully.

5 Drill another hole in the inner wing panel and pass the aerial lead into the engine compartment. Use the grommet supplied with the aerial, or one of a similar size, to prevent the lead chafing on the wing panel.

6 It should now be possible to feed the aerial lead through an existing grommet behind the facia panel and into the passenger compartment (photo). Pull the lead through and position it ready for connecting to the radio.

7 To mount the speaker pod, drill suitable holes in the panel behind the rear seats and secure the pod with self-tapping screws (photo).

8 Most speakers are provided with spade terminals which accept Lucar connections. To attach the connectors to the speaker wires it is advisable to use a crimping tool (photo). If one cannot be borrowed or hired, they can be purchased from accessory shops or electrical suppliers.

9 Drill a final hole in the rear panel beneath the pod and pass the speaker wires up from inside the boot compartment. Connect the wires to the speakers and then secure the speaker to the pod with the screws provided (photos).

10 It is now necessary to pass the speaker wiring through an existing hole in the rear bulkhead and into the passenger compartment. Run the wires along the floor under the carpets, but make sure they will not be trapped under the seats (photo).

11 Having decided on the radio location, mark the position of the mounting bracket holes in the parcel shelf. Drill suitable holes in the shelf panel and secure the brackets with small nuts and bolts (photo).

12 All that now remains is to connect the wiring to the radio and secure the unit to its mounting brackets. Join the speaker leads from the radio with the wires from the speaker using cable joiners (photo).

3.3 Enlarge the radio aerial hole using a round file as necessary

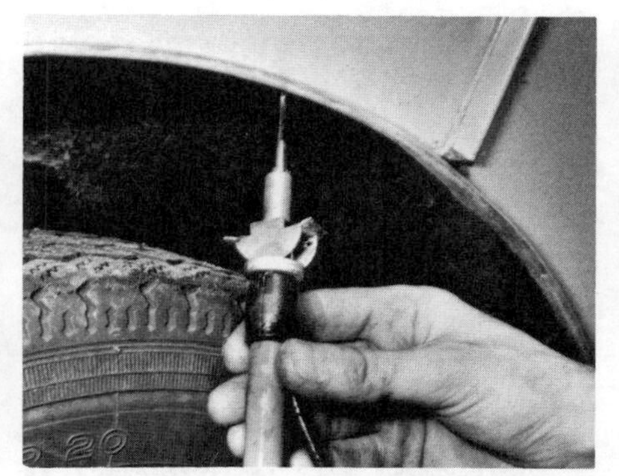

3.4a Pass the aerial up through the wing from below...

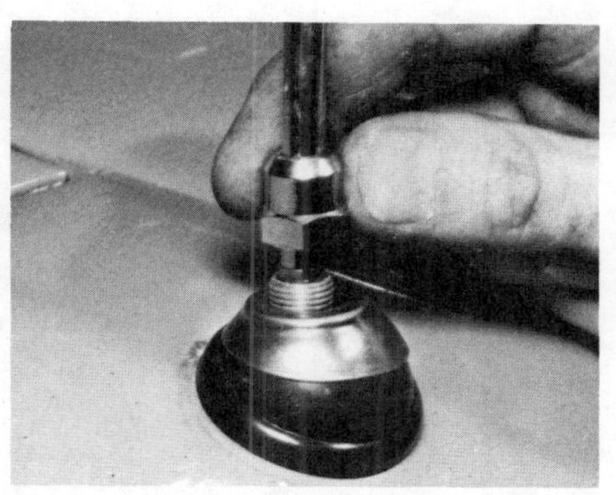

3.4b ...and fit the washers and retaining nut

3.6 Pull the aerial lead through an existing bulkhead grommet

3.7 Secure the speaker pod in place with self-tapping screws

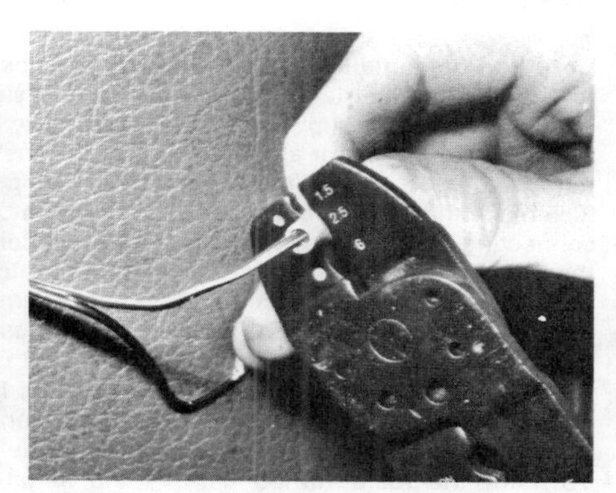

3.8 Using a crimping tool to attach Lucar connectors

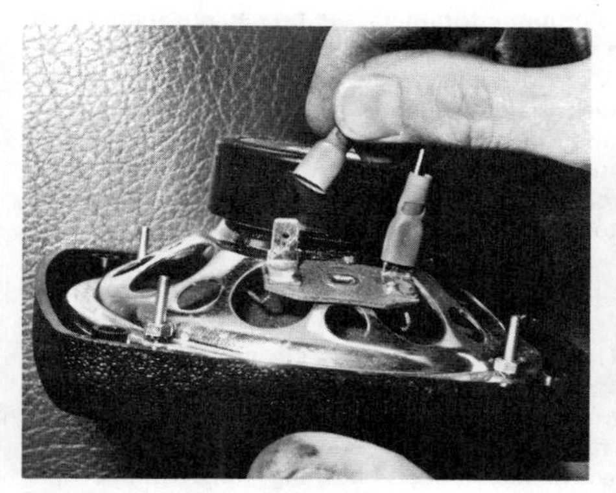

3.9a Connect the speaker wires...

3.9b ...and mount the speaker in the pod

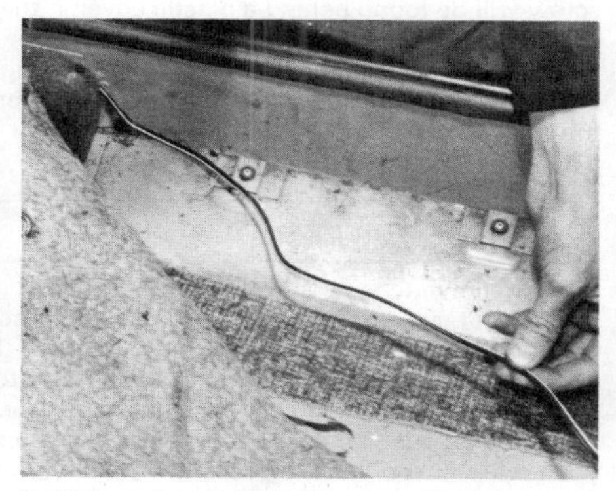

3.10 Run the speaker wires along the floor under the carpets

3.11 Radio mounting brackets in position

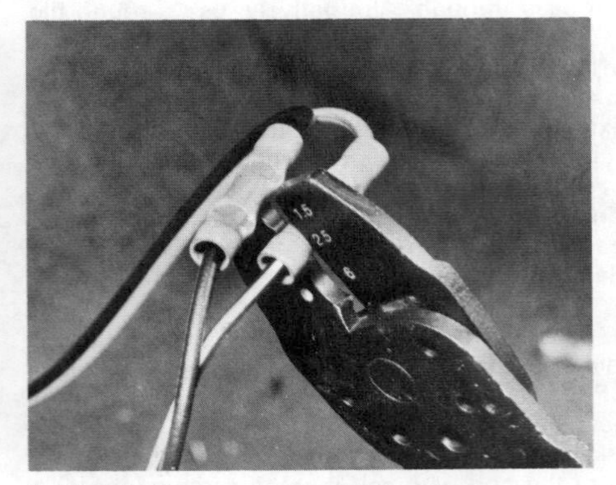

3.12 Join the speaker leads together...

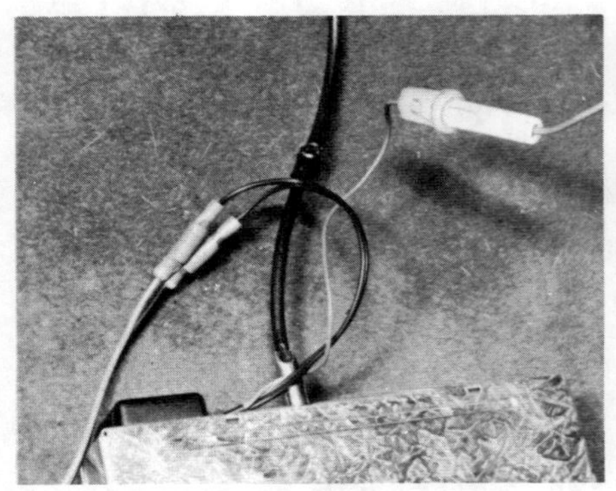

3.14a ...connect the leads to the radio...

3.14b ...and secure the unit in its brackets

3.15 The set can then be trimmed to suit the aerial

Note that on some sets a plug and socket joins the wires from radio to speaker together, and if this is available it should be used.

13 The electrical supply for the radio may be taken from any convenient live feed, or as in the case of this installation, directly from the fuse box. If working on early models having only two fuses in the fuse block the supply should be taken from the '2' terminal of the fuse connecting '1' and '2'. If working on later models having four fuses in the block, the supply should be taken from terminal '6'. In all cases, the radio supply wire must incorporate a 1 to 2 amp in-line fuse.

14 Feed the radio supply wire into the passenger compartment through an existing grommet in the bulkhead. Connect the supply to the radio, plug in the aerial and speaker leads if this has not already been done, and then secure the radio to its mountings (photos). Ensure that all surplus wiring is tucked neatly out of the way behind the radio.

15 With the radio turned on and the aerial fully extended, it is necessary to trim the set to suit the aerial. To do this, tune in to a weak station and, using a small screwdriver, turn the trimming screw until the loudest volume is obtained (photo). On many radios the trimming screw will be found behind a plastic cover in the vicinity of the volume control knob.

16 With the installation completed, run the engine. If any interference is heard, it will be necessary to fit suitable suppressors as described in the following Section.

4 Radios – suppression of interference

To eliminate buzzes and other unwanted noises costs very little and is not as difficult as sometimes thought. With a modicum of common sense and patience, and following the instructions in the following paragraphs, interferences can be virtually eliminated.

The first cause for concern is the generator. The noise this makes over the radio is like an electric mixer and the noise speeds up when you rev up (if you wish to prove the point, you can remove the fanbelt and try it). The remedy for this sample; connect a 1.0μ f – 3.0μ f capacitor between earth, probably the bolt that holds down the generator base, and the *large* terminal on the dynamo or alternator. **This is most important**: *If you connect it to the small terminal, you will probably damage the generator permanently (see Fig. 13.1).*

A second common cause of electrical interference is the ignition system. Here a 1.0μ f capacitor must be connected between earth and the 'SW' or '+' terminal on the coil (see Fig. 13.2). This may stop the 'tick-tick-tick' sound that comes over the speaker. Next comes the spark itself.

There are several ways of curing interferences from the ignition HT system. One is to use carbon film HT leads but these have a tendency to 'snap' inside, and you don't know, then, why you are firing on only half your cylinders. So the second, and more successful, method is to use resistive spark plug caps (see Fig. 13.3) of about 10 000 ohm to 15 000 ohm resistance. An alternative is to use 'in-line' suppressors (Fig. 13.3) – if the interference is not too bad, you may get away with only one suppressor in the coil to distributor line. If the interference does continue (a 'clacking' noise) then doctor all HT leads.

At this stage, it is advisable to check that the radio is well earthed, also the aerial, and to see that the aerial plug is pushed well into the set and that the radio is properly trimmed (see preceding Section). In addition, check that the wire which supplies the power to the set is as short as possible and does not wander all over the car. At this stage, it is a good idea to check that the fuse is of the correct rating. For most sets this will be about 1 to 2 amps.

At this point the more usual causes of interference have been suppressed. If the problem still exists, a look at the cause of interference may help to pinpoint the component generating the stray electrical charges.

The radio picks up electromagnetic waves in the air; now some are made by radio stations and other broadcasters and some, not wanted are made by the car. The home-made signals are produced by stray electrical discharges floating around the car. Common producers of these signals are electric motors; ie, the windscreen wipers, electric screen washers, heater fan or an electrical aerial if fitted. Other sources of interference are electric fuel pumps, flashing turn signals, and instruments. The remedy for these cases is shown in Fig. 13.4 for an electric motor whose interference is not too bad, and Fig. 13.5 for instrument suppression. Turn signals are not normally suppressed. In

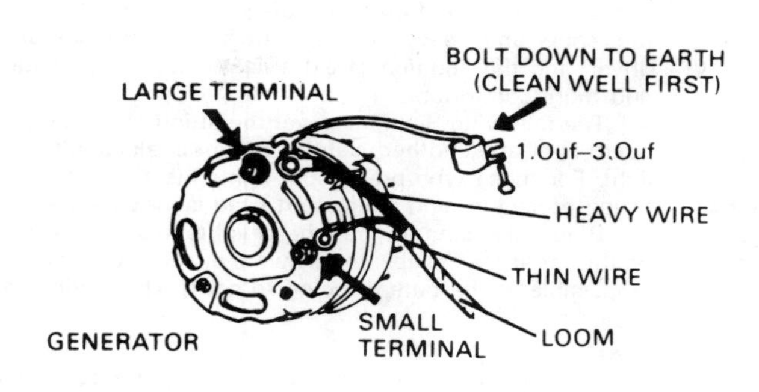

Fig. 13.1 Connecting a capacitor to the alternator (Sec 4)

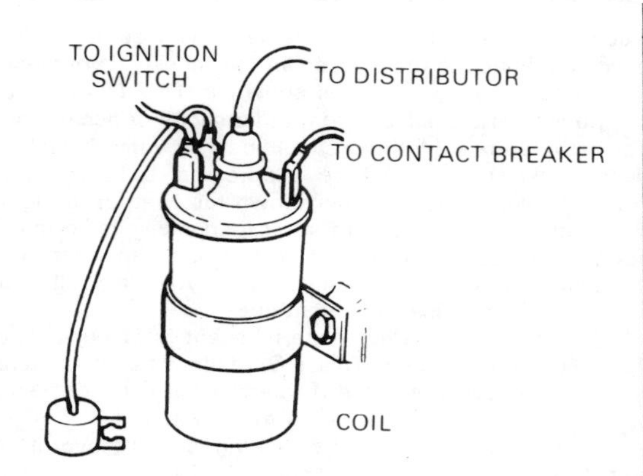

Fig. 13.2 Connecting a capacitor to the coil (Sec 4)

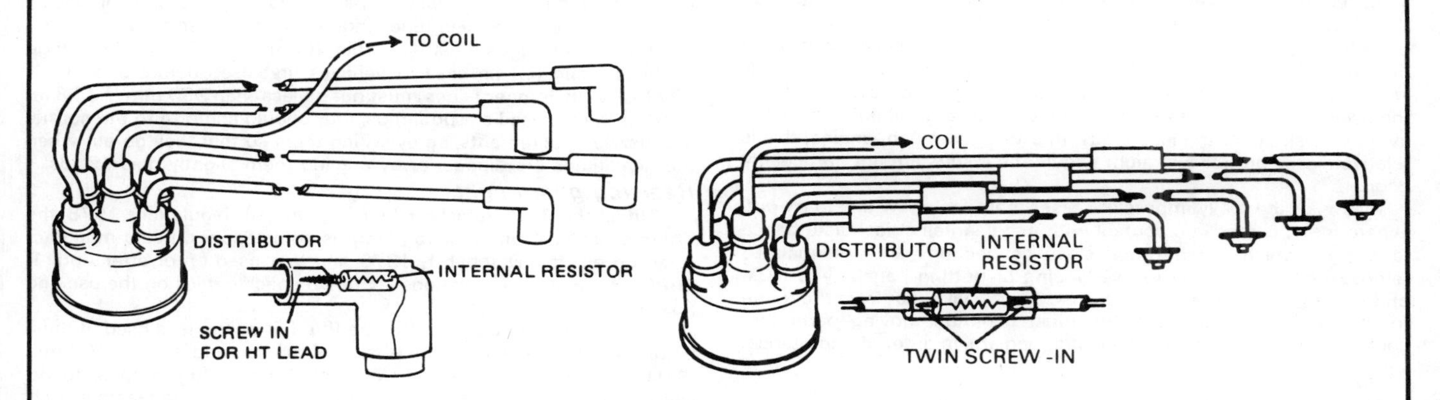

Fig. 13.3 Ignition HT lead suppression (Sec 4)

Resistive spark plug caps (left)
In-line suppressors (right)

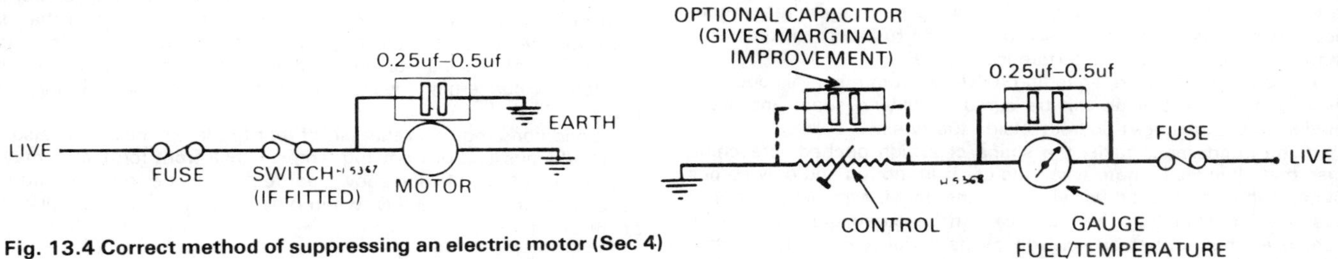

Fig. 13.4 Correct method of suppressing an electric motor (Sec 4)

Fig. 13.5 Method of suppressing instruments (Sec 4)

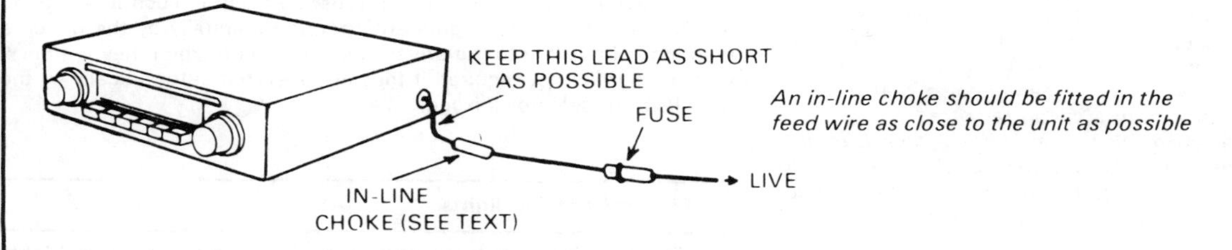

An in-line choke should be fitted in the feed wire as close to the unit as possible

Fig. 13.6 Fitting an in-line choke (Sec 4)

recent years,radio manufacturers have included in the line (live) of the radio, in addition to the fuse, an 'in-line' choke. If your installation lacks one of these, put one in as shown in Fig. 13.6. All the foregoing components are available from radio shops or accessory shops. For a transistor radio, a 2A choke should be adequate. If you have an electric clock fitted, this should be suppressed by connecting a 0.5 μf capacitor directly across it as shown for a motor in Fig 13.4.

If, after all this, you are still experiencing radio interference, first assess how bad it is, for the human ear can filter out unobtrusive unwanted noises quite easily. But if you are still adamant about eradicating the noise, then continue.

As a first step, a few 'experts' seem to favour a screen between the radio and the engine. This is OK as far as it goes, literally! – for the whole set is screened, and if interference can get past that, then a piece of aluminium is not going to stop it.

A more sensible way of screening is to discover if interference is coming down the wires. First, take the live lead; interference can get between the set and the choke (hence the reason for keeping the wires short). One remedy here is to screen the wire and this is done by buying screened wire and fitting that. The loudspeaker lead could be screened also to prevent 'pick-up' getting back to the radio – although this is unlikely.

Without doubt, the worst source of radio interference comes from the ignition HT leads, even if they have been suppressed. The ideal way of suppressing these is to slide screening tubes over the leads themselves. As this is impractical, we can place an aluminium shield over the majority of the lead areas. In a V- or twin-cam engine, this is relatively easy but for a straight engine the results are not particularly good.

Now for the really impossible cases, here are a few tips to try out. Where metal comes into contact with metal, an electrical disturbance is caused, which is why good clean connections are essential. To remove interference due to overlapping or butting panels, you must bridge the join with a wide braided earth strap (like that from the frame to the engine/transmission). the most common moving parts that could create noise and should be strapped are, in order of importance:

(a) Silencer to frame
(b) Exhaust pipe to engine block and frame
(c) Air cleaner to frame
(d) Front and rear bumpers to frame
(e) Steering column to frame
(f) Bonnet and boot lids to frame

The faults are most pronounced when the engine is either idling or labouring under loads. Although the moving parts are already connected with nuts, bolts, etc, these do tend to rust and corrode, thus creating a high resistance interference source.

If you have a 'ragged' sounding pulse when mobile, this could be wheel or tyre static. This can be cured by buying some anti-static powder and sprinkling it liberally inside the tyres.

If the interference takes the shape of a high pitched screeching noise that changes its note when the car is in motion and only comes now and then, this could be related to the aerial, especially if it is of telescopic or whip type. This source can be cured quite simply by pushing a small rubber ball on top of the aerial (yes, really!) as this breaks the electric field before it can form; but it would be much better to buy yourself a new aerial of a reputable brand. If, on the other hand, you are getting a loud rushing sound every time you brake, then this is brake static. This effect is most prominent on hot dry days and is cured by fitting a special kit, which is quite expensive.

In conclusion, it is pointed out that it is relatively easy, and therefore cheap, to eliminate 95 per cent of all noises, but to eliminate the final 5 per cent is time and money consuming. It is up to the individual to decide if it is worth it. Please remember also, that you will not get concert hall performance from a cheap radio.

Note: *If your car is fitted with electronic ignition, then it is not recommended that either the spark plug resistors or the ignition coil capacitor be fitted as these may damage the system. Most electronic ignition units have built-in suppression and should, therefore, not cause interference.*

5 Additional lights and lighting regulations – general

In standard form the Mini is certainly not blessed with the ultimate in lighting equipment, and any additions will go a long way towards improving both the looks and safety of the car. Winter driving with its fog, snow and heavy rain can put heavy demands on both car and driver, and the addition of extra lights can make winter driving safer and more comfortable.

The following Sections cover the fitting of front fog lights, rear fog guard light and another useful rear light in all conditions – a reversing light. For those who prefer spot lights instead of front fog lights, the fitting procedure and equipment used is virtually identical.

Before deciding on the type of lights to be fitted and their location on the car, it is advisable to be aware of current UK lighting regulations (applicable at the time of going to print) which briefly are as follows:

Spot and fog lights

It's illegal to mount these with the upper edge of the illuminating surface more than 1200 mm (47.24 in) from the ground. Any lamps that are mounted with the lower edges of the illuminating surface less than 500 mm (19.69 in) above the ground may only be used in fog or falling snow. In conditions where the law requires headlamps to be used, eg at night on an unlit road, a single lamp may be used only in conjunction with the headlamps. In these conditions the lamps must always be mounted and used in pairs (two fog, two spot or one of each) if they're to be used independently of the headlamps.

Their outer edges must be within 400 mm (15.75 in) of the edge of the car and (in the case of vehicles first used before January 1, 1971 only) their inner edges must not be less than 350 mm (13.78 in) apart. If they're used as spotlamps, they should conform to the normal anti-dazzle requirements, eg by wiring them so that they go out when the headlamps are dipped, or by angling them slightly downwards.

Rear fog guard lights

Under the Road Vehicles (Rear Fog Lamps) Regulations 1978, the fitting of at least one rear fog lamp is compulsory on cars manufactured on or after October 1, 1979 and first used on or after April 1, 1980. These same regulations lay down specific rules on the use and positioning of such lamps.

Either one or two lamps may be fitted. If only one is used, it must be on the centre line or to the offside of the car, and at least 100 mm (3.94 in) from the nearest brake light. No rear fog lamp is to be illuminated by the braking system of the car. The rear fog lamp switch must have a warning light to indicate to the driver when the lamps are switched on, and this switch must be wired in such a way that the rear fog lamp(s) cannot be used without either headlights, sidelights or front fog lamps also being on.

Any rear fog lamp fitted to a car manufactured from October 1, 1979 must also bear the appropriate 'E-mark' signifying conformity with EEC standards. If your car was manufactured prior to that date then you need not fit rear fog lamps at all; but if you do (and it obviously makes sense to do so) they must comply with the above regulations concerning positioning and independence of the brake lights.

Conditions requiring the use of rear fog lamps obviously also call for headlamps and/or front fog lamps. While front fog lamps may be used only in fog or falling snow, rear fog lamps are to be permitted in conditions of 'poor visibility' when only headlamps may be allowable at the front.

Reversing lights

A maximum of two reversing lights fitted to the rear of the car is permitted. The lights must show a white light to the rear and the total power of both lights together must not exceed 24 watts. They must only be used when reversing, and must be fitted in such a way as to not cause dazzle. If the lights are operated manually by the driver, a warning light visible to the driver must illuminate when they are on. A warning light is not required if they are operated automatically by the gear lever or selector linkage.

6 Fitting front fog lights

1 The following installation shows the fitting of two front fog lights with their associated wiring and switches, using the components listed below:

(a) Fog lights and mountting brackets
(b) Lucas 6RA relay
(c) Switch and switch panel

(d) Suitable lengths of 28/0.012 in (28/0.30 mm) cable
(e) Connectors, screws, drills and grommets as required

With all the necessary items at hand, begin by selecting a suitable mounting position for the lights, bearing in mind the regulations referred to in the previous Section. On the Mini the best place to mount the lights is on the grille panel using special brackets designed for this purpose (photo).

2 Position the brackets on the grille and tighten the retaining bolts so that the brackets are rigid, but the grille is not distorted (photo).

3 With the brackets in place, the fog light body can be fitted (photo).

4 The switch panel is next. If you already have other accessories fitted, you may have a spare space in an existing switch panel, or you may prefer to mount the switch in a different place altogether. For the purpose of this installation, a three hole panel has been used with space for future switches when required. The panel is positioned under the parcel shelf on the driver's side and secured with small self-tapping screws (photo).

5 Before fitting the switch into the panel, it is useful to prepare the two cables that will be connected to it. In this case one cable supplies a live feed to the switch, and the other cable takes that live feed to the relay to activate it when the switch is operated. The live feed may be taken from any suitable circuit, and if you are familiar with electrical circuitry, you may wish to consult the wiring diagram and take the feed from somewhere close to the switch. The alternative, and probably the easiest approach for the less experienced, is to take a feed directly off the fuse box. If working on early models with two fuses in the fuse block, use the '2' terminal. On later four fuse models use the '4' terminal.

6 Cut the two switch cables to approximately the correct length and then feed them through a suitable grommet in the bulkhead, so that one end of the cables is in the passenger compartment and the other end in the engine compartment.

7 At the passenger compartment end, attach a Lucar connector using a suitable crimping tool, to each end of the two cables. The cables can now be connected to the switch and the switch fitted to the panel (photo).

8 Decide on a suitable place in the engine compartment for the relay location (the stiffener panel on the offside inner wing panel is ideal). Mark their positions and then drill two suitable holes for the relay securing screws. Do not fit the relay at this stage.

9 Attach Lucar connectors to the other end of the two wires coming from the switch. Connect one of these wires to terminal 'WI' on the relay (photo) and the other wire to the live feed at the fusebox or other place of your choice.

10 It is now necessary to take another live feed to the relay which, when the relay is activated by the switch, will supply power to the fog lights. As the relay is mounted in close proximity to the fuse box, this again is the obvious choice. The same terminals are used as before, ie the '2' terminal (early models) or the '4' terminal (later models).

11 Cut a length of wire to run from the fuse box to the relay and attach a Lucar connector to one end. At the other end, attach a 'piggy-back' connector to the wire. This is a standard type Lucar connector. with a spade terminal attached to it. A second wire can be attached to the spade terminal and then the two wires together may be attached to a single terminal. By doing this, both the live wires, one to the switch and one to the relay, can be taken from a single fuse box terminal.

12 Having attached the appropriate connectors to the wires, connect the wire with the 'piggy-back' connector to the fuse box and connect the wire from the switch to the 'piggy-back' spade. Now connect the other end of the 'piggy-back' wire to the terminal 'C2' on the relay.

13 Measure and cut two suitable lengths of wire to run from the relay to each of the fog lights. Attach a Lucar connector to each one and connect both of them to terminal 'C1' on the relay. Route the wires neatly along the wiring loom that runs along the front of the car, and position their other ends adjacent to the fog lights ready for subsequent connection.

14 One final connecton is necessary at the relay, and this is an earth wire from terminal 'W2' to the relay mounting screw. Cut a suitable length of wire and attach a Lucar connector to one end and a screw tag to the other end. With all the wires connected to the relay (photo)

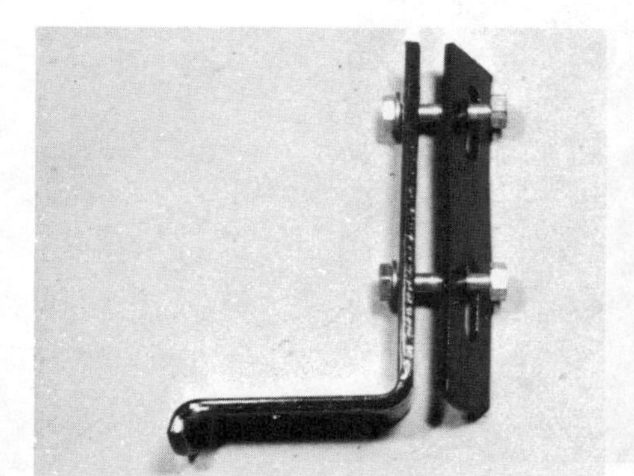

6.1 Fog light mounting brackets for grille panel installation

6.2 With the bracket in position...

6.3 ...fit the fog light body

6.4 Fitting the switch panel under the parcel shelf

6.7 With the wires connected the switch can be fitted

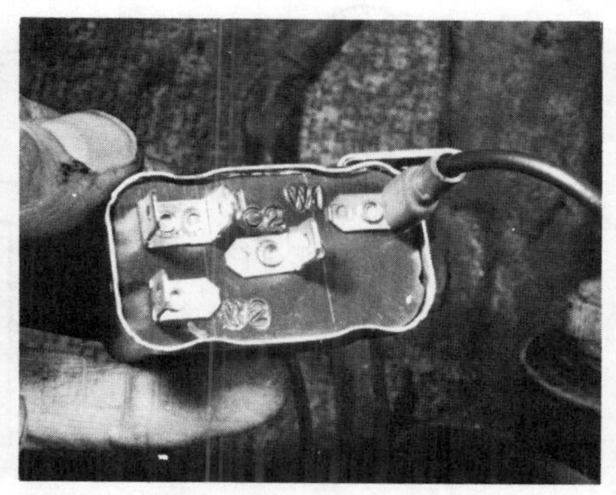

6.9 One of the switch wires is connected to relay terminal W1

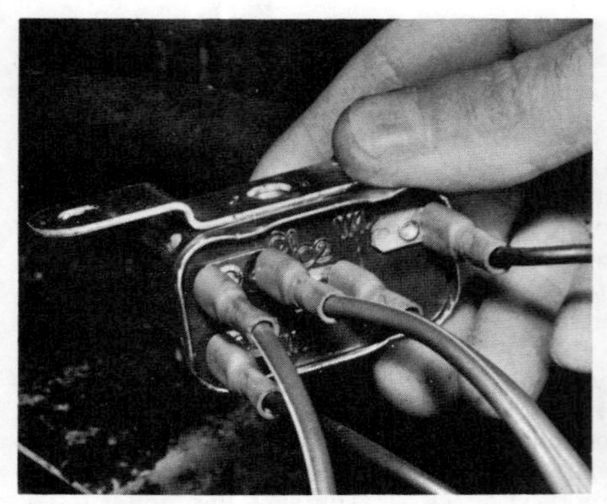

6.14a With all the wires connected...

6.14b ...the relay can be mounted. Note the earth wire under the retaining screw head

6.15a Install the bulb in the light unit...

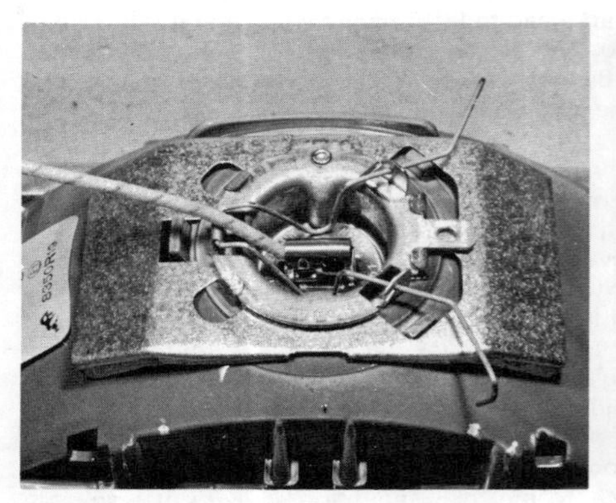

6.15b ...and secure with the wire clip

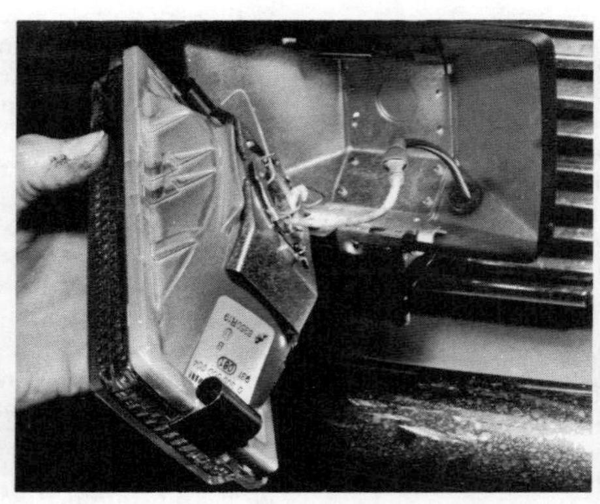

6.15c Pass the wire through the grommet and connect it to the bulb wire

6.15d The light unit can then be secured to the light body

6.16a Connect an earth lead to the light body retaining bolt...

6.16b ...and a suitable earthing point such as the horn bracket

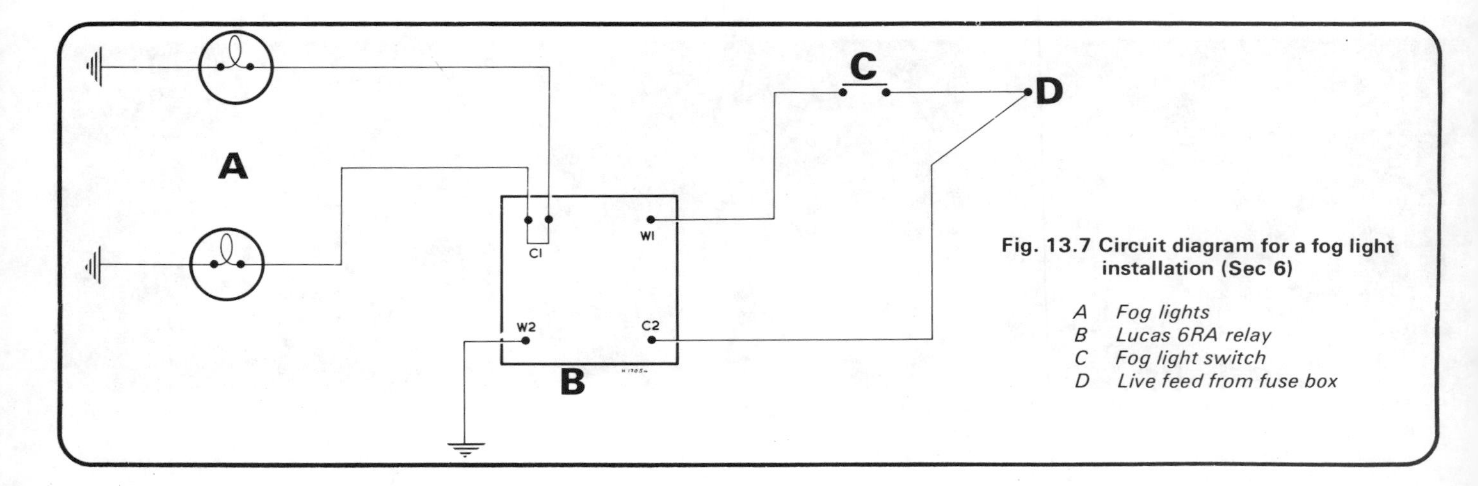

Fig. 13.7 Circuit diagram for a fog light installation (Sec 6)

A Fog lights
B Lucas 6RA relay
C Fog light switch
D Live feed from fuse box

the unit can be secured using self-tapping screws and the previously drilled holes. Make sure that the tag of the relay earth lead is fitted under one of the retaining screw heads (photo).

15 All that remains now is to connect the two feed wires to the lights and install the lights in the light bodies. This procedure will of course vary according to make of fog light being fitted. On the installation shown, the bulbs were supplied separately and required fitting to the light units (photos). Having done that, the end of the feed wire can be inserted through the grommet in the light body and connected to the small wire attached to the bulb holder (photo). The light unit can then be secured to the body (photo)..

16 To be on the safe side, an additional earth wire with a screw tag at each end connects the fog light mounting bolt with a suitable earthing point under the bonnet, such as the horn bracket retaining screws (photos).

17 With the installation complete, make sure that all connections are sound and properly made, that all wires run neatly alongside existing looms if possible, and that where necessary grommets are used to prevent chafing.

18 Adjustment of the fog light beam height and position is a matter of personal preference, but do bear in mind that the lights must not dazzle oncoming traffic.

7 Fitting a rear fog guard light

1 To install a rear fog guard light, the following items will be needed:

(a) Fog guard light
(b) Switch and switch panel
(c) Suitable lengths of 28/0.012 in (28/0.30 mm) cable
(d) Connectors, screws, drills, clips and grommets as required

2 Begin by selecting a suitable place at the rear of the car to mount the light. The most obvious place on the Mini is the body panel below the rear bumper, but any suitable place will do.

3 Drill a hole in the panel to accept the light unit retaining stud, insert the stud into the hole and screw on the nut and washer from behind. Tighten the nut securely (photo).

4 The feed wire for the light must run along the underside of the car, up into the passenger compartment and then along to the switch. Cut a suitable length of wire, and then feed one end of it through one of the vacant holes that will be found in the rear body panel. Slip a grommet over the wire and engage it with the hole to prevent chafing. The wire can now be passed into the light unit, and with the Lucar connector attached to the end, connect the wire to the bulb holder (photo).

5 Jack up the rear of the car and support it on axle stands, or alternatively run the back wheels up a pair of ramps.

6 Run the feed cable to the light neatly along the rear subframe and secure it with suitable cable clips (photo). The tags on the underbody that are used to support the fuel and brake pipe can also be used to support the cable (photo).

7 The cable must enter the passenger compartment somewhere along the underbody and it will be necessary to drill a small hole to allow the cable to enter. The point at which this happens is a matter of personal preference, but do make sure that a tight fitting grommet is used, otherwise water will find its way into the car.

8 Run the cable under the carpets and toward the front of the car. Take it up behind the heater where it will not be seen and along to the site chosen for the switch panel. A suitable connector can now be fitted and the cable attached to one of the switch terminals.

9 It is now necessary to take a live feed to the switch from a convenient live terminal under the parcel shelf or from the fuse box. If the fuse box is being used, connect the wire to terminal '4' on early models or terminal '2' on later cars. In the installation shown the live feed has been taken from a spare terminal on one of the multi-plug connectors beneath the parcel shelf (photo).

10 Connect the other end of the feed wire into the remaining switch terminal and then fit the switch into the switch panel (photo). The switch panel can be mounted in any convenient place within easy reach of the driver, and in this case a panel mounted under the parcel shelf from a previous installation has been used.

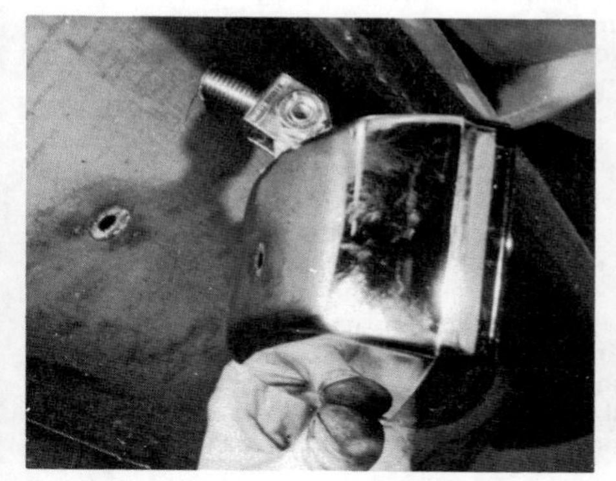

7.3 Fitting the rear fog guard light to the lower body panel

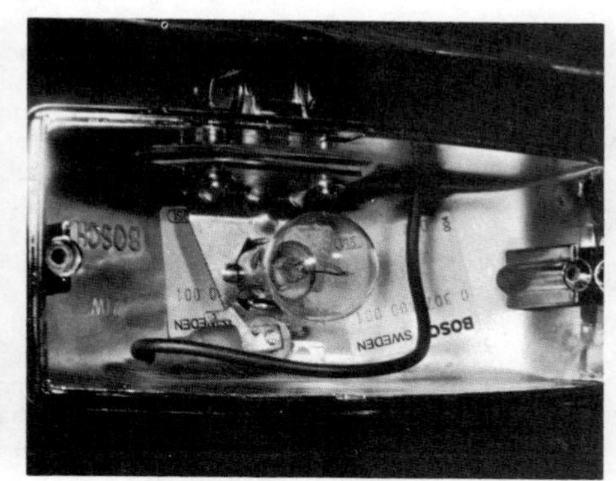

7.4 Feed the wire through and connect it to the bulb holder

7.6a Secure the cable to the subframe with clips...

7.6b ...and also use the fuel pipe retaining tags for support

7.9 A live feed for the switch may be taken from a spare terminal in a multi-plug connector

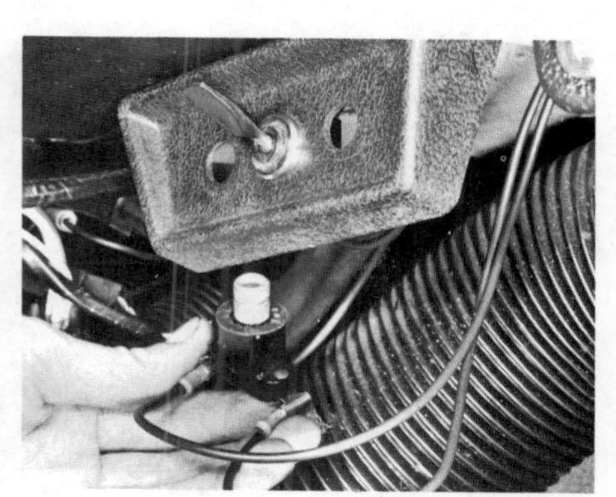

7.10 With the wires connected fit the switch into the panel...

7.11 ...and with the switch in position fit the warning light bulb and cover

8.6a Remove the plastic plug from the side of the remote control housing...

8.6b ...and screw in the reversing light switch

11 All that now remains is to fit the switch warning bulb and cover and to test the fog guard light (photo).

8 Fitting a reversing light

1 On Mini models a reversing light can be activated in one of two ways. Either a manually operated switch controlled by the driver and containing a warning light may be used, or a special switch can be obtained from a BL dealer enabling the light to be operated automatically by the gear lever or selector mechanism. On early models the switch is screwed into the front of the transmission casing below the dynamo, in place of the large hexagonal plug that must first be removed. On later models the switch is screwed into a tapped hole in the gear lever remote control housing. The following procedure relates to this type of switch.
2 If the light is to be operated by an illuminated switch, the fitting procedure is identical to that described in the previous Section for the rear fog guard light.
3 If the reversing light is to be operated automatically by a switch on the gear linkage, refer to the previous Section and fit the reversing light body and cable, but only run the cable as far as the remote control housing under the centre of the floor.
4 The live feed to the switch can be taken from the fuse box '2' terminal or from a convenient spare live terminal under the parcel shelf, such as one of the multi-plug connectors in the vicinity of the steering column.
5 With the Lucar connector attached to a suitable length of wire, connect the wire to the fuse box terminal or the vacant live terminal, and then run the wire under the carpet to a point just behind the gear lever gaiter retaining plate. Drill a hole in the floor, slip a close fitting grommet over the cable and pass the cable through the floor. Make sure that the grommet fits snugly into the hole in the floor otherwise water will enter the car.
6 From underneath the car, observe the right-hand side of the remote control housing and you will see a plastic plug inserted into a hole in the housing side (photo). Remove the plug and screw in the reversing light switch until the resistance is just felt and then screw it in one more turn (photo).
7 Attach a bullet connector to the live feed wire, and also to the wire from the reversing light. Connect the two wires to the reversing light wires using connector sleeves.
8 The adjustment of the switch is a trial and error process which can only be done satisfactorily with the battery connected and the ignition switched on. Begin by selecting reverse gear and then turn the switch body until the reversing light just comes on. Now turn it one further turn and check that it goes out in all other gear positions, When satisfactory, tighten the locknut. When doing this it will probably be necessary to stop after each turn of the switch, disconnect the wires, untangle them and then reconnect.
9 On completion make sure that the wires are properly supported under the car and are not likely to come adrift or tangle in any of the gear linkage.

9 Auxiliary instruments – general

Most Mini models are equipped with only three or four basic instruments – a speedometer, fuel gauge, water temperature gauge, and in some cases an oil pressure gauge. Other information regarding the condition of the engine or its ancillary components is relayed to the driver by warning lights.

By nature of their design, warning lights are only activated by major changes such as a lack of charge from the dynamo or alternator, or near total loss of oil pressure. Often the driver receives this information too late to prevent serious and sometimes expensive damage occuring. Instruments, however, give an accurate record of what is happening under the bonnet at all times and can give an early indication of anything amiss. For instance, an instrument showing a slight fall in oil pressure when a higher steady reading is usually indicated will allow the driver to investigate and avoid possible major mechanical trouble.

The selection of instruments available to the motorist is vast, but for the purpose of the following Sections an oil pressure gauge and battery condition indicator have been selected.

10 Fitting an oil pressure gauge

1 Oil pressure gauges fall into two distinct categories; those which are operated directly by the engine oil pressure itself via a small pipe connected in place of the warning light transmitter, and those which are electrically operated by a special sending unit. The electrically operated type is dealt with below.
2 Most instruments are quite easy to fit and the oil pressure gauge is no exception The hardest part is choosing a location for the gauge. As with all accessories, this is purely a matter of personal preference, but for the purpose of this installation the space below the parcel shelf on the driver's side was chosen.
3 Having decided on a site for the gauge, offer up the auxiliary instrument and mark the positions of the retaining screw holes. Now drill two holes of suitable diameter in the parcel shelf to accept the auxiliary panel retaining screws. The panel can now be fitted if desired, but in many cases it is easier to mount the instrument in the panel complete with wiring and then fit the complete assembly.
4 If it is wished to retain the function of the oil pressure warning light it will be necessary to obtain a T-piece, as both the warning light transmitter and the sending unit of the gauge share the same outlet connection in the cylinder block. In many of the oil pressure gauge kits currently available a T-piece is supplied as part of the kit.
5 Unscrew the existing oil pressure gauge transmitter from the cylinder block. The transmitter is located just above the starter motor to the left of the distributor.
6 Screw the gauge T-piece adaptor into place followed by the T-piece. If the oil pressure warning light is not to be used, the T-piece may be omitted.
7 Now screw the gauge sending unit into one end of the T-piece and the transmitter into the other end (photo).
8 The wire supplied in the kit can now be screwed into the terminal on the end of the sending unit (photo).
9 Run the wire neatly along the existing wiring loom and through one of the wiring grommets in the engine compartment bulkhead. Route the wire down behind the parcel shelf ready for connection to the gauge.
10 It is now necessary to bring a live feed down to the gauge, and this can be done in a number of ways. Either connect a wire to the fuse box terminal, find a spare live connector under the parcel shelf in the vicinity of the heater or ignition multi-plugs, or use a special joining connector to tap into an existing live wire. If the feed is being taken from the fuse box use the '4' terminal on early two fuse models, or the '2' terminal on later four fuse models. If a live feed is being sought under the parcel shelf, make sure that it is one that is only live when the ignition is switched on.
11 The only other electrical connection necessary is for the instrument illuminating light, and a live feed for this can be taken from any of the wires in the panel light circuit. The easiest way is to tap into a panel light wire using a joining connector.
12 With all the wires at hand, the gauge can be connected. In this installation the wire from the sending unit is attached to the gauge 'U' terminal and the live feed is connected to the 'I' terminal.
13 With the gauge in position in the auxiliary panel and the wires connected, mount the panel and secure it in position using self-tapping screws in the previously drilled holes.
14 Tuck all the wires neatly out of the way and then start the engine and check the operation of the gauge. Be prepared for a shock if the oil pressure is not as high as you thought it was going to be!

10.7 Fit the oil pressure gauge sending unit to the T-piece...

10.8 ...and connect the wire supplied to the terminal

11 Fitting a battery condition indicator

1 The fitting of this gauge is simplicity itself, and all that needs to be done is to find a suitable site to locate the gauge and make three electrical connections.
2 The site chosen for the gauge in the project car was alongside the oil pressure gauge described in the previous Section, in a two-instrument auxiliary panel. The panel was then mounted beneath the parcel shelf on the driver's side.
3 Having chosen a suitable location for the gauge, the electrical connections can now be made. Connect one end of a suitable length of wire to the '4' terminal of the fuse box on early two fuse types or the '2' terminal on the later four fuse type. Alternatively the wire can be connected to any terminal of an instrument wired through the ignition circuit. Connnect the other end of this wire to either of the terminals on the rear of the battery condition indicator.
4 The live feed for the instrument illuminating bulb can be taken from any spare live wire or terminal in the lighting circuit, or connected to one of the panel light wires using a special joining connector.
5 The other terminal on the gauge is an earth terminal and a short length of wire should be connected from this terminal to the stud on the rear of the instrument used for mounting it in the switch panel. It is a good idea to take an additional earth wire from the mounting stud to one of the auxiliary panel retaining screws.
6 With all the connections made at the rear of the instrument, and with it mounted in the switch panel, the panel can now be fitted into the chosen site under the parcel shelf (photos).
7 Make sure all the wires are tucked neatly out of sight and then start the engine and observe the readings on the gauge.

12 Electronic ignition systems – general

Electronic ignition systems fall into two main groups, those that replace the conventional contact breaker points with an alternative system, such as the photo-electric cell or a trigger unit sensitive to magnetic variations, and those that use all the existing ignition equipment and supplement it with spark boosting circuitry. Many

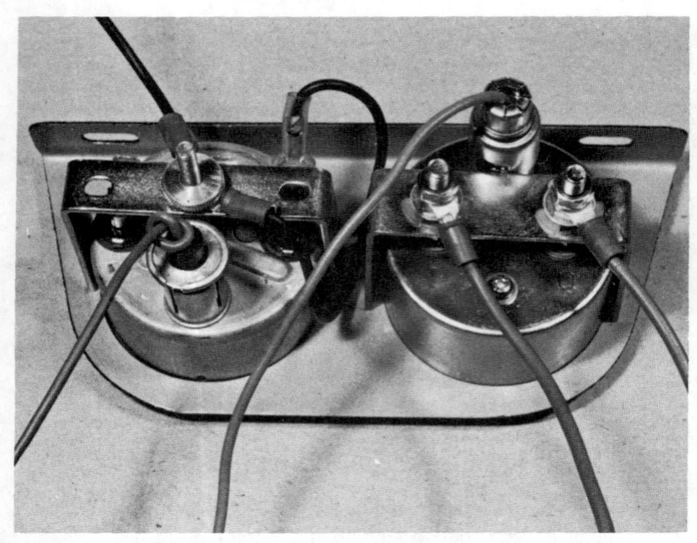

11.6a The wiring connections on the rear of the oil pressure gauge (right) and battery condition indicator (left)

11.6b Mounting the auxiliary instruments and panel under the parcel shelf

exaggerated claims have been made for both types concerning the improvements in performance and fuel economy gained after fitting an electronic ignition system. Some of the claims are true, many are false.

The biggest gains in performance and economy will be obtained from the systems that do away with the contact breaker points, and what these systems *will* do is reduce variations in dwell angle and ignition timing due to worn distributor components and dirty or badly adjusted contact breaker points. This is obviously going to improve the performance of the ignition system to some extent, which in turn will allow the engine to run more smoothly, efficiently and economically. Any improvements in performance and economy will be gained mainly from these reasons alone. What these systems will *not* do is turn your car into a high performance racing machine that pays you to drive it.

The biggest gains in performance and economy with the other group of systems are made during the tune-up you do as part of the installation procedure. All the system itself does is to improve the spark available at the spark plugs, nothing more. However, some improvement is obviously to be expected with a larger spark, but a lot of it will depend on the actual design of the engine combustion chamber and the driver's imagination.

There is one major drawback associated with systems that do away with with the contact breaker points, and that is component failure. Once the system is installed it is not an easy task to convert back to conventional ignition, and if it lets you down miles from anywhere, the only solution is to substitute each item with a new part, (always assuming that you carry a complete spare system in the boot) or walk home. However, to be fair these systems are extremely reliable and a breakdown is quite rare. Most of the spark assist (contact breaker assisted) systems incorporate a switch which isolates the unit and allows the car to run on the conventional ignition system in the event of a fault, which is one point in their favour.

The following Sections cover the fitting of the Mobelec Magnum electronic ignition system, which is an example of the breakerless type, and the Euro 90 Surefire, which is an example of the contact breaker assisted (spark assist) type. The fitting of other brands of electronic ignition systems will follow similar lines.

13 Fitting the breakerless type of electronic ignition system

Note: *The Mobelec Magnum electronic ignition system was used to illustrate fitting of the breakerless type of kit. The Mobelec Magnum kit comes with general fitting instructions. Study these instructions and the contents of this Section before starting the installation to familiarise yourself with the procedure. Also make sure that you have the correct distributor adaptor plate kit for your car.*

1 Remove the front grille to provide easier access to the distributor.

2 Remove the distributor cap, rotor arm, contact breaker points and the condenser. Disconnect the LT leads from the distributor and tape it up. If a radio suppressor is fitted to the coil, this should be removed.

3 Fit the appropriate adaptor plate where the points and condenser used to be (photo). Use the existing screws or the screws supplied in the kit to secure the adaptor plate in position. Make sure that the screws do not foul the automatic advance mechanism below the distributor baseplate.

4 Fit the timing disc over the cam. Two discs are provided for Lucas distributors, one slightly smaller that the other (photo). If even the smallest disc is a loose fit on the cam due to wear or manufacturing tolerances, Mobelec recommend that it be glued in position on the cam. Before doing this, however, stop to consider what is going to happen if for any reason you wish to revert back to conventional ignition – the disc will have to be removed from the cam, which may present problems if the glue is any good! A piece of masking tape, wrapped once around the lower part of the cam, should be adequate to ensure a snug fit and will not be difficult to remove. Push the timing disc fully into position using the rotor arm.

5 Fit the triggerhead to the adaptor plate using the screws and washers supplied. Select a grommet to fit in the slot in the distributor where the LT connector block used to be and slide the grommet over the triggerhead leads. Fit the grommet to the slot and adjust the lead length to that there is sufficient slack inside to allow for movement of the distributor baseplate, but not so much that the leads will foul the cam or rotor arm.

6 Turn the engine over until one of the pins in the timing disc is aligned with the arrow on the triggerhead. Using the plastic feeler gauges supplied in the kit, set the gap between the pin and the triggerhead to that specified by the makers – typically 0.015 in (0.38 mm) – by slackening the mounting screws slightly and moving the triggerhead as necessary. Tighten the screws and recheck the gap (photo).

7 Choose a suitable place within the engine compartment to mount the ignition unit, mark the position of the retaining screw holes, and then drill three holes of suitable diameter. Secure the unit in position using the screws provided (photo). Drill an additional hole and secure the earth lead with a separate screw, or use an existing earthing point if there is one handy.

8 Connect the red lead from the ignition unit to the '+' or 'SW' terminal on the coil. Disconnect the existing coil '–' or 'CB' lead and connect the blue lead from the ignition unit in its place. Tape up the disconnected lead from the coil, or if it is not part of the wiring loom, remove it altogether. Connect the triggerhead leads to the remaining leads from the ignition box, making sure that the protective sleeving is properly in position (photo). Position any excess cable neatly out of the way.

9 Refit the rotor arm and the distributor cap. With the battery reconnected, start the engine. Assuming that it runs satisfactorily, check the ignition timing using a stroboscopic timing light as described in Chapter 4.

10 If the engine will not start, remove the coil HT lead from the

13.3 Fit the adaptor plate to the distributor baseplate

13.4 The two timing discs supplied for Lucas distributors

13.6 Using the plastic feeler gauge to check the gap between the timing disc and triggerhead

13.7 The ignition unit in position

13.8 Ensure that the insulating sleeve is properly fitted to the triggerhead leads

distributor cap and hold the end (with insulated pliers) about $\frac{1}{4}$ in (6 mm) from the cylinder block, while an assistant cranks the engine on the starter motor. If a spark is not apparent, check all connections for correctness and electrical continuity, then commence the makers, fault-finding procedure. Assuming that a spark is obtained, it is probably only the timing which is at fault; slacken the distributor and turn it approximately 15°. Refit the HT lead and try again. If that fails, move the distributor approximately 30° the other way and try once more. Make sure that the rotor arm is fitted to the distributor and not in your pocket. When the engine is running adjust the ignition timing using a stroboscopic timing light as described in Chapter 4.

11 If the distributor has been removed from the engine and the timing has been lost (eg during engine overhaul), a rough static timing procedure may be carried out as follows.

12 Turn the engine over until No 1 piston is at TDC on the firing stroke. Temporarily fit the rotor arm to the distributor and turn it so that it points to where No 1 spark plug segment would be were the cap fitted, then fit the distributor to the engine. Turn the distributor slightly if necessary to align a timing disc pin with the triggerhead as described in paragraph 6, bearing in mind that the rotor arm should still be pointing to No 1 segment. This should permit the engine to run well enough for a stroboscopic timing check to be carried out.

14.3 The Surefire control unit in position

14.4 Connect the yellow wire from the control unit to the coil (–) or (CB) terminal

14 Fitting the contact breaker assisted type of electronic ignition system

Note: *The Euro 90 Surefire electronic ignition system was used to illustrate the fitting of the contact breaker assisted (spark assist) type of kit.*

1 The fitting of one of these systems to a Mini is quite a simple task, but read the manufacturer's instructions and the contents of this Section to familiarise yourself with the procedure before starting.

2 First decide upon a suitable site for the control unit in the engine compartment. A suitable place is the right-hand side inner wing panel, but there are a number of equally good positions. Bear in mind that the unit must be located in as cool a place as possible.

3 Offer up the unit, mark the position of the retaining screw holes and drill three holes of suitable diameter to accept the self-tapping screws provided. The unit can now be secured in position (photo). Make sure that the black wire is well fitted under the head of one of the securing screws.

4 Disconnect the wire(s) at the ignition coil '–' or 'CB' terminal and reconnect the wire(s) to the green wire from the control unit. Connect the yellow wire from the unit to the coil '–' or 'CB' terminal (photo).

5 Connect the red wire from the control unit to the spare tag on the coil '+' or 'SW' terminal.

6 Before starting the engine, remove, clean, and adjust the spark plugs as described in Chapter 4, but set the gaps to 0.035 in (0.90 mm). Now refit the plugs.

7 It is also advisable to check the condition of the contact breaker points and clean, adjust or renew them as described in Chapter 4.

8 With the installation complete, set the position switch on the control unit to the 'CONV' position and start the engine. When the engine is running move the switch to the 'ELEC' position; if the engine keeps running, all is satisfactory.

9 If poor starting or misfiring occurs, first make sure that the fault is not associated with the conventional side of the ignition system. Check the system thoroughly using the fault diagnosis chart at the end of Chapter 4. If this fails to cure the fault, it may be associated with one or more of the items listed below:

(a) Spark plug gaps set too wide
(b) Unit not earthing properly
(c) Radio suppressor connected to coil '–' or 'CB' terminal
(d) Red wire not receiving a satisfactory 12 volt supply

If, after checking all these items, the fault persists, it is possible that the unit is at fault and the manufacturers should be contacted.

Chapter 14 Supplement: Revisions and information on later models

Contents

1 Introduction

This Supplement contains information which is additional to, or a revision of, material in the preceding Chapters. It includes the new 1275 cc Mini Cooper fitted with a catalytic converter and introduced in July 1990, but it does not include the John Cooper Performance Conversion Kit which was available for fitment to 998 cc manual gearbox models only from February 1989 and did not include a catalytic converter. The John Cooper kit included twin SU HS2 carburettors, whereas the production Cooper is fitted with a single SU HIF 44 carburettor.

The Sections in this Supplement follow the same order as the Chapters to which they relate. The Specifications are all grouped together for convenience, but they follow Chapter order.

It is recommended that before any particular operation is undertaken, reference be made to the appropriate Section(s) of the Supplement. In this way any changes to procedure or components can be noted before referring to the main Chapters.

2 Specifications (1982 and later models)

The specifications below are supplementary to, or revisions of, those at the beginning of the preceding Chapters

1000 engine (manufacturer's type 99H)

Compression ratio

Manual gearbox models (1983 to 1987 inclusive)	10.3:1
Automatic transmission models	8.9:1
1988 on (category C)	9.6:1
1989 on (low compression)	8.3:1
1989 on (high compression)	9.6:1

Camshaft and camshaft bearings

Bearing inside diameter (reamed after fitting):	
Centre	41.225 to 41.267 mm
Rear	34.912 to 34.925 mm
Bearing running clearance:	
Front, centre and rear	0.025 to 0.051 mm

Valve timing (engine prefixes 99HD80, 99HD92 and 99HC20) – valve clearance 0.53 mm

Inlet opens	9° BTDC
Inlet closes	41° ABDC
Exhaust opens	49° BBDC
Exhaust closes	11° ATDC

1100 engine (manufacturer's type 10H)

Camshaft and camshaft bearings

Bearing inside diameter (reamed after fitting):	
Centre	41.225 to 41.267 mm
Rear	34.912 to 34.9255 mm

1275 engine (manufacturer's type 12A) – Cooper 1990 on

The engine specifications are identical to the 12H engine except for the differences listed below

Compression ratio	10:1

Connecting rods and big-end bearings

Bearing running clearance	0.0381 to 0.0813 mm

Crankshaft and main bearings

Main journal diameter:	
No colour code	50.83 to 50.84 mm
Red colour code	50.81 to 50.82 mm
Green colour code	50.82 to 50.83 mm
Yellow colour code	50.83 to 50.84 mm
Main bearing wall thickness:	
Red colour code	1.831 to 1.841 mm
Green colour code	1.821 to 1.831 mm
Yellow colour code	1.811 to 1.821 mm
Main bearing running clearance	0.017 to 0.058 mm
Minimum main journal regrind diameter	50.32 mm
Minimum crankpin regrind diameter	43.93 mm
Crankshaft endfloat	0.051 to 0.076 mm

Cylinder block and pistons

Piston-to-bore clearance:	
Top of skirt	0.074 to 0.114 mm
Bottom of skirt	0.023 to 0.064 mm
Piston ring gap:	
Top	0.25 to 0.45 mm
Second	0.20 to 0.33 mm
Oil control ring	0.38 to 1.04 mm

Valves and springs

Valve head diameter:	
Inlet	35.58 to 35.71 mm
Exhaust	29.25 to 29.38 mm
Valve lift	8.08 mm
Valve clearance (inlet and exhaust)	0.33 to 0.38 mm (0.013 to 0.015 in)
Valve guide length	42.85 mm
Valve guide height above head	13.72 mm
Valve spring free length	49.53 mm
Valve timing (at valve clearance of 0.53 mm):	
Inlet opens	16° BTDC
Inlet closes	56° ABDC
Exhaust opens	59° BBDC
Exhaust closes	29° ATDC

All engines

Torque wrench settings

	lbf ft	Nm
Upper tie-bar (Nyloc nut)	15 to 20	20 to 28
Engine mountings:		
⅜ in UNC screws	30	40
M8 screws	22	30
M10 screws	33	45
M12 bolts	53	72

Cooling system (1275 engine – Cooper 1990 on)

Auxiliary electric cooling fan

Thermostatic switch:	
Switches on at	98° C
Switches off at	93° C

Fuel, exhaust and emission control systems

Carburettor data

1000 engine (99H):	
1983 on:	
Needle	AAC
Exhaust emission (% CO)	2.5 ± 1.0 at idle
Idle speed	750 ± 50 rpm
Fast idle speed	1100 ± 50 rpm
1989 on (low compression):	
Needle	ADE
Exhaust emission (% CO)	1.5 to 3.5 at idle
Idle speed	750 ± 50 rpm
Fast idle speed	1100 ± 50 rpm
1989 on (high compression):	
Needle	AAC
Exhaust emission (% CO)	1.5 to 3.5 at idle
Idle speed	750 ± 50 rpm
Fast idle speed	1100 ± 50 rpm
1275 engine (12A) Cooper 1990 on:	
Carburettor type	SU HIF 44
Piston spring	Red
Jet size	0.100 in
Needle	BFY
Exhaust emission (% CO)	1.6 to 3.0 (measured at the sampling point)
Idle speed	900 rpm
Fast idle speed	1200 ± 50 rpm
Fuel type	Unleaded 95 RON minimum

Ignition system

Spark plugs

1000 engine (99H) 1987 on	Champion N12YCC or N12YC
Electrode gap:	
Champion N12YCC	0.8 mm (0.032 in)
Champion N12YC	0.6 mm (0.024 in)

Ignition coil

1000 engine (99H):	
1982 on:	
Type	AC Delco 9977230 or Ducellier 520035A
Primary resistance at 20°C	1.2 to 1.5 ohms
Consumption (engine idling)	4.5 to 5.0 ohms
Ballast resistance	1.3 to 1.5 ohms

Ignition coil (continued)

1983 on:	
Type	GCL 144
Primary resistance at 20°C	1.4 ± 0.1 ohms
Consumption (engine idling)	2.6 ± 0.2 amps
Ballast resistance	1.5 ohms
1275 engine (12A) Cooper 1990 on:	
Type	GCL 143
Primary resistance at 24°C	0.78 ± 0.08 ohms

Distributor

1000 engine (99H) 1982 on:	
Type	Lucas 59D4 or Ducellier
Dwell angle:	
Lucas	54° ± 5°
Ducellier	57° ± 2° 30′
Serial numbers:	
Lucas	41882
Ducellier	525389
1275 engine (12A) Cooper 1990 on:	
Type	Lucas 65DM4 – Electronic
Ignition amplifier	Lucas 9EM
Suppression capacitor	1 mf

Ignition timing

Stroboscopic (vacuum pipe disconnected)

1000 engine (99H):	
1983 to 1987	8° + 0° – 2° BTDC at 1500 rpm
1988 (category C)	10° + 0° – 2° BTDC at 1500 rpm
1989 on (low compression)	8° + 0° – 2° BTDC at 1500 rpm
1989 on (high compression)	10° + 0° – 2° BTDC at 1500 rpm
1275 engine (12A) Cooper 1990 on	5° ± 1° BTDC at 1500 rpm

Clutch

General

Type	Verto/Valeo diaphragm spring, hydraulically operated
Disc diameter	180.90 mm
Master cylinder bore diameter	15.88 mm
Slave cylinder bore diameter	22.22 mm
Throw-out stop clearance	6.50 mm

Torque wrench setting	lbf ft	Nm
Pressure plate-to-flywheel bolts	18	25

Manual gearbox

Clearances

Primary gear endfloat	0.10 to 0.18 mm
Idler gear endfloat	0.10 to 0.18 mm

Differential unit

Final drive ratio	10 in roadwheels	12 in roadwheels
Manual gearbox models	2.95:1	3.105:1 (Except Checkmate and Racing/Flame 1990 on) 3.44:1 (Checkmate and Racing/Flame 1990 on)
Automatic transmission models	2.76:1	3.272:1

Braking system

Front disc brakes

Maximum run-out	0.15 mm
Minimum pad thickness	3.0 mm (0.125 in)
Disc diameter (1989 on)	213.4 mm

Rear brakes

Minimum lining thickness	3.0 mm (0.125 in)

Electrical system

Alternator

1982 to 1985:	
Type	Lucas A115

Alternator (continued)

Output at 14 volts and 6000 rpm (alternator speed)	45 amps
Minimum brush length	10.0 mm
1986 on:	
Type	Lucas A127/45 or A127/55
Output at 6000 rpm (alternator speed)	45 amps or 55 amps
Minimum brush length	5.0 mm

Starter motor (1986 on)

Type	Lucas M79 pre-engaged
Minimum brush length	3.5 mm
Minimum commutator diameter	28.82 mm

Fuses

Continuous current rating comparison . . .

Fuse connecting	Fuse blow rating	Continuous current rating
1 and 2	35 amp	17 amp
3 and 4	25 amp	12 amp
5 and 6	25 amp	12 amp
7 and 8	15 amp	8 amp

Bulbs

	Wattage
Rear foglamp	21
Side repeater lamp	5

Suspension and steering

Bearing endfloat

Front hub taper bearing (permissible tolerance)	0.0 to 0.076 mm
Rear hub taper bearing (permissible tolerance)	0.025 mm preload to 0.050 mm endfloat

Roadwheels and tyres

Wheels:	Tyres
Steel:	
3.50 x 10	145 SR x 10*
4.50 x 12	145/70 SR x 12*
Alloy:	
5J x 10	165/70 x 10
4.50B x 12	145/70 SR x 12

**The low rolling resistance tyres must only be replaced with items of the same type and specification*

Tyres pressures

	lbf/in^2	bar
Steel roadwheel (145 SR x 10):		
Front	28	2.0
Rear	26	1.8
Steel roadwheel (145/70 SR x 12):		
Front	28	2.0
Rear	28	2.0
Alloy roadwheel (165/70 x 10):		
Front	24	1.7
Rear	26	1.8
Alloy roadwheel (145/70 SR x 12):		
Front	28	2.0
Rear	28	2.0

Torque wrench settings

	lbf ft	Nm
Driveshaft nut:		
Taper bearing hub*	150	203
Single split pin hole*	188 to 200	255 to 270

**continue to tighten until nut aligns with split pin hole*

3 Routine maintenance

For vehicles manufactured after 1985 the service intervals for engine oil renewal have been extended and are as follows:

Manual transmission models – renew the engine oil and oil filter every 12 000 miles (20 000 km) or 12 months, whichever comes first.

Automatic transmission models – renew the engine oil and oil filter every 6000 miles (10 000 km) or 6 months, whichever comes first.

Your dealer will advise on service intervals if any doubt exists.

4 Engine

Engine mounting – upper tie-bar 1986 on

1 From 1986 a Nyloc retaining nut is used in place of the standard plain nut and washer.

2 These nuts may be used on older engines, noting the new torque loading figure for Nyloc nuts given in the Specifications.

Inlet valve oil seals

3 In order to reduce oil consumption, valve stem oil seals are now being fitted to the inlet valves. Fitting of the seals has required the

incorporation of modified valves with cotter grooves nearer the end of the stem. The valve spring seats have also been raised by 1.2 mm.

4 New type valves and seals can be fitted to old type cylinder heads in complete sets only, with the addition of a shim 1.2 mm thick underneath each spring. These shims may also be found already fitted to engines which left the factory with the new type valves and seals in unmodified heads.

Cylinder head blanking plug – oil leakage

5 Persistent oil leakage from the cylinder head oil gallery blanking plug, situated just below the thermostat housing, may be corrected by the application of Loctite 572 prior to fitment of the brass blanking plug.

6 Alternatively, a 'Tuckers sealed rivet' which can be fitted using a blind rivet gun, is available from dealers.

7 This 'Tuckers sealed rivet' may be used on all models except the 1275 cc versions, and must also be coated with Loctite 572. On the 1275 cc engines the blanking plug is used with red Hermetite.

Crankshaft main bearings – 1985 on

8 Improved lead indium main bearings are now being fitted to all A-series engines.

9 These new bearings may only be fitted to engines with plain bottom shells in the main bearing caps.

Rear main bearing

10 When fitting the rear main bearing, it will be found that the cylinder block oilway is offset from the corresponding hole in the bearing shell. This condition is acceptable as long as 2.3 mm diameter steel rod can be inserted into the exposed section of the hole.

Front main bearing cap seal

11 When renewing this seal, apply a bead of RTV sealant to all of its mating surfaces. Doing this will ensure an oiltight seal.

Flywheel-to-crankshaft retaining bolts – refitting

12 Where the bolt which retains the flywheel to the crankshaft has been secured with thread-locking compound or an encapsulated type of bolt is used, then prior to refitting all threads in the crankshaft must be thoroughly cleaned.

13 This should be done, preferably, by using a tap of the appropriate size.

14 Discard the old retaining bolt and use only a new encapsulated bolt incorporating a thread-locking compound patch on refitting.

Timing cover

15 When fitting the timing cover, a bead of RTV sealant should be applied on each side of the new gasket on the lower half of the gasket only. After applying the sealant the timing cover should be fitted to the engine and the bolts tightened without delay before the sealant dries. This procedure provides a better seal against oil leaks.

Engine/transmission oil

16 The recommended grade of oil for the engine/transmission unit has been changed from SAE 20W/50 to SAE 10W/40 or, where the ambient temperature does not exceed 30°C (86°F), to SAE 10W/30.

Pistons (998 cc engine)

17 From VIN 331600 new pistons are used. The gudgeon pins are no longer retained with circlips, but are an interference fit in the connecting rods. Both the gudgeon pins and connecting rods are now of the same type as fitted to the 1275 cc engine.

18 Gudgeon pin removal is as given for 1275 cc engines in Chapter 1.

19 Pistons of different types are not interchangeable.

Front subframe mountings

20 When refitting the pear-shaped front mountings of the front subframe, or the subframe itself, it is important to measure the gap between the rear of the mountings and the subframe and then to select an appropriate number of shims of the same thickness for fitting in the gap. The shims are slotted and square in shape, and are 1.32 mm thick. They are located over the mounting bolt shanks.

Main bearings (Cooper 1990 on)

21 Selective main bearings are now fitted to the 1275 cc Cooper engine. Red (R), Green (G) or Yellow (Y) codes are used to identify the bearings, and the colours or 'RGY' stamp will be found on the main bearing caps and the corresponding web of the crankshaft. The bearing shells are also identified in the same way.

22 The applicable journal dimensions are given in the Specifications at the beginning of this Supplement.

Oil cooler (Cooper 1990 on) – removal and refitting

23 Disconnect the battery negative lead.

24 Remove the front grille as described in Chapter 12.

25 Place a suitable container below the oil cooler, then unscrew the banjo union bolt on the top of the oil cooler and recover the two sealing washers. Cover the oil cooler inlet with tape to prevent entry of dust and dirt.

26 Unscrew the side mounting bolts and withdraw the oil cooler sufficient to unscrew the lower banjo union bolt. Recover the two sealing washers.

27 Refitting is a reversal of removal, but top up the engine oil level as necessary.

Fig. 14.1 Oil cooler fitted to the Cooper (1990 on) (Sec 4)

1 Upper banjo connection
2 Oil cooler mountings
3 Lower banjo connection

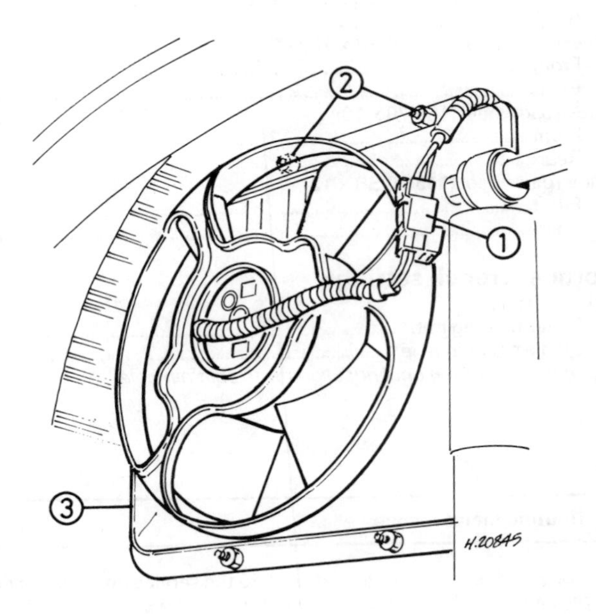

Fig. 14.2 Auxiliary electric cooling fan fitted to the Cooper (Sec 5)

1 Multi-plug
2 Mounting nuts
3 Cooling fan assembly

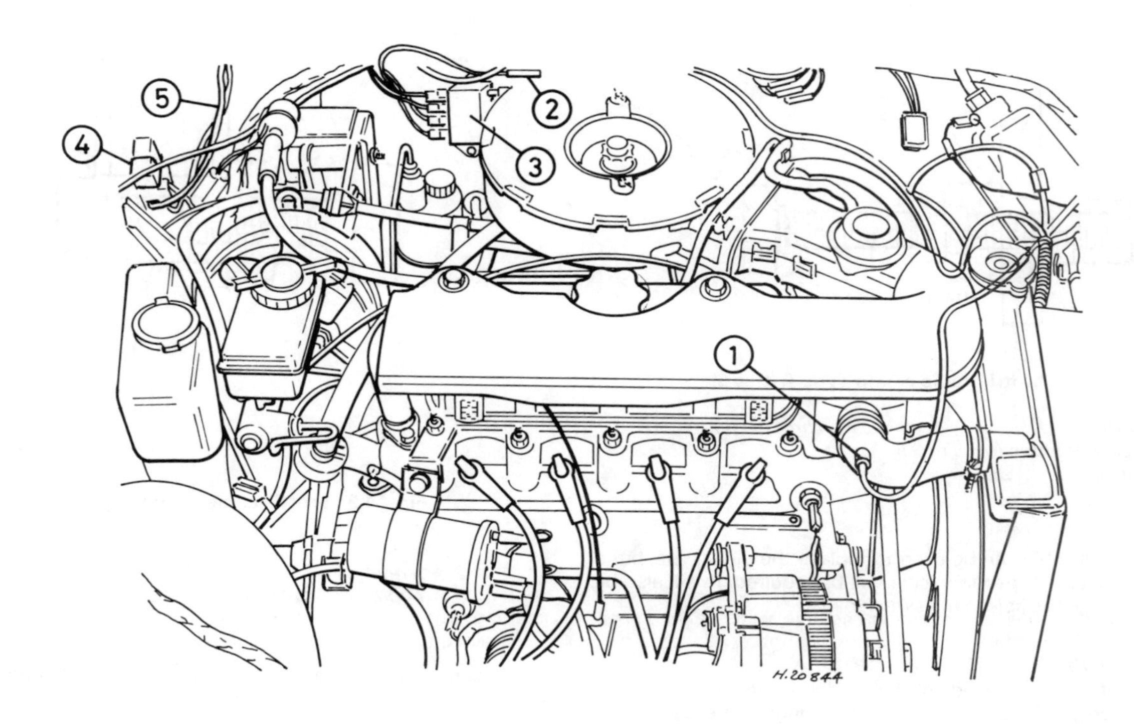

Fig. 14.3 Auxiliary electric cooling fan wiring (Sec 5)

1 Thermostatic switch
2 In-line fuse (15 amp)
3 Fusebox
4 Driving light relay
5 Driving light supplementary wiring harness

5 Cooling system

Auxiliary electric cooling fan (Cooper 1990 on)

General description

1 An auxiliary electric cooling fan is fitted to the Cooper 1275 cc engine. It is located beneath the left-hand front wheel arch and provides cooling for the radiator in addition to that provided by the belt-driven fan on the water pump.

2 The auxiliary cooling fan is switched on and off by a thermostatic switch located on the thermostat housing on the front left-hand side of the cylinder head. The operating temperatures are given in the Specifications, and the fan operates only when the ignition is switched on.

Removal and refitting

3 Apply the handbrake, then jack up the front of the car and support on axle stands. Remove the left-hand front roadwheel.

4 Disconnect the air duct from the adaptor beneath the front left-hand headlamp.

5 Disconnect the fan multi-plug from under the wheel arch.

6 Unscrew the four mounting nuts and withdraw the electric cooling fan assembly from under the wheel arch. Recover the rubber washers and clamp plates.

7 Refitting is a reversal of removal.

Auxiliary electric cooling fan thermostatic switch – removal and refitting

8 Disconnect the wiring from the switch located beneath the top hose.

9 Either drain the cooling system as described in Chapter 2, or position a suitable container beneath the thermostatic switch.

10 If the cooling system was not drained, have ready a suitable bolt or old switch for fitting in the cylinder head.

11 Unscrew the switch from the thermostat sandwich plate.

12 If the old switch is to be refitted, clean its threads thoroughly.

13 Apply suitable sealant to the threads of the switch, then refit it and tighten to the specified torque.

14 Re-connect the wiring. Top up or refill the cooling system with reference to Chapter 2.

6 Fuel, exhaust and emission control systems

Carburettor dashpot oil

1 The grade of oil for the carburettor dashpot has been changed following the change of engine/transmission oil described in Section 4. Use the same oil as used in the engine/transmission unit.

Throttle cable attachment clamp

2 There are two types of throttle cable clamp in use.

3 Type A (Fig. 14.4) is a free fit in the throttle lever. The body has a 4 BA hexagon and the screw is 5 BA.

4 To prevent distortion of the cable on fitting, hold the hexagon of the body with a 4 BA spanner whilst tightening the screw.

5 Type B (Fig. 14.5) has the body riveted to the throttle lever, and both body and screw are 7 BA.

6 Tighten in the same way as for Type A, using 7 BA spanners.

7 Both types of clamp should be tightened to the torque loading values shown in Figs. 14.4 and 14.5 to avoid undue distortion of the throttle cable.

Choke cable – failure to lock

8 Failure of the choke cable to lock can normally be traced to incorrect fitting of the cable inner to its outer. Positioning the word LOCK on the cable knob at the top during assembly will ensure that the spring clip on the cable outer is set to lock the cable inner once the knob is turned.

Choke cable – later (push-pull) type

9 The later type choke control remains at predetermined positions. It does not need to be rotated to lock or unlock it.

10 Removal of the push-pull type of cable is essentially as given in Chapter 3, Section 26, except that the control knob is retained by a clip, rather than a nut. The clip pulls free.

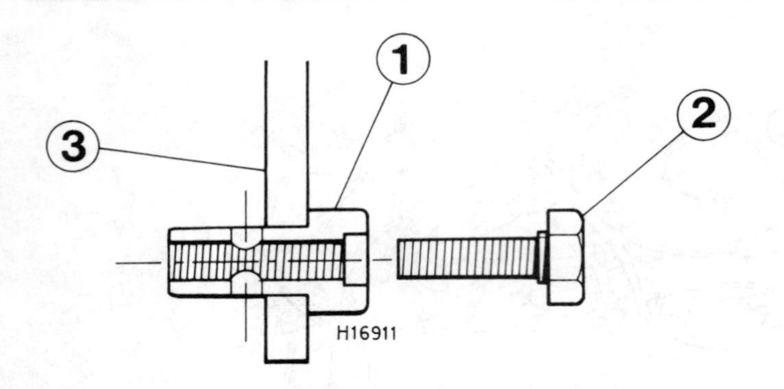

Fig. 14.4 Throttle cable clamp Type A (Sec 6)

1 Body
2 Screw (tighten to 7.5 to 8.5 lbf in)
3 Throttle lever

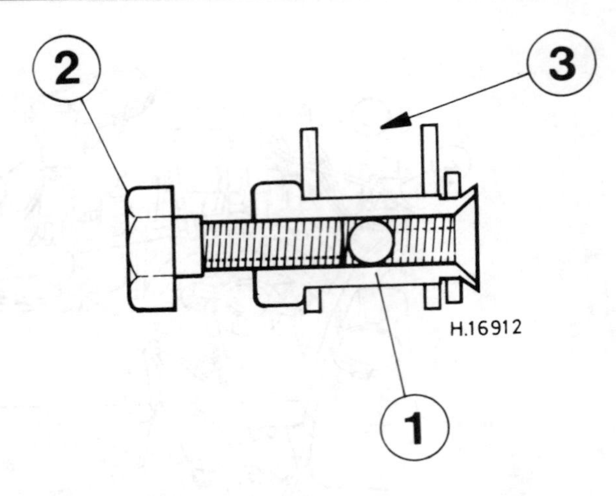

Fig. 14.5 Throttle cable clamp Type B (Sec 6)

1 Body
2 Screw (tighten to 9 to 10 lbf in)
3 Throttle lever

11 The push-pull cable can be used to replace the older type, but a different auxiliary switch panel bracket will be required. It will also be necessary to enlarge the hole in the switch panel.

Fuel pump – 1985 on

12 The mechanical pump used on later models is different in appearance to those used previously, but is fully interchangeable, except that a modified kickdown rod will be required if a new mechanical pump is fitted to older vehicles with automatic transmission.
13 Details of the rod fitment should be obtained from your dealer.

Fuel pump – removal and refitting

14 The fuel pump insulator block fitted to the early 700 series single turret fuel pump is different from the insulator block fitted to later twin turret fuel pumps. It is important to fit the correct type insulator block (see Fig. 14.6).
15 The early 700 series fuel pump requires an insulator block with a large inner aperture, whereas the later 800 series and AZX fuel pumps require an insulator block with a small aperture in order to retain the pump lever pivot. If the later type pump is fitted with an early type insulator block, there is a possibility of the pivot and lever dropping into the sump/gearbox.
16 As the fuel pumps are fully interchangeable it is important to check that the correct type insulator block is fitted.

Exhaust system

17 Before positioning the bellmouth of the exhaust front pipe over the manifold flange, smear its mating surface with sealing paste. Doing this will obviate any risk of leakage.

Exhaust manifold – Cooper S (up to 1971)

18 Before removing the LCB (long centre branch) exhaust manifold fitted to Cooper S models, partially disconnect the right front suspension and driveshaft.
19 Refer to Chapter 3 and remove the carburettor(s), inlet manifold and exhaust system.
20 Refer to Chapter 7 and detach the right-hand driveshaft at the inboard end.
21 Refer to Chapter 11 and remove the right-hand front roadwheel, disconnect the steering tie-rod, the swivel hub at its upper and lower

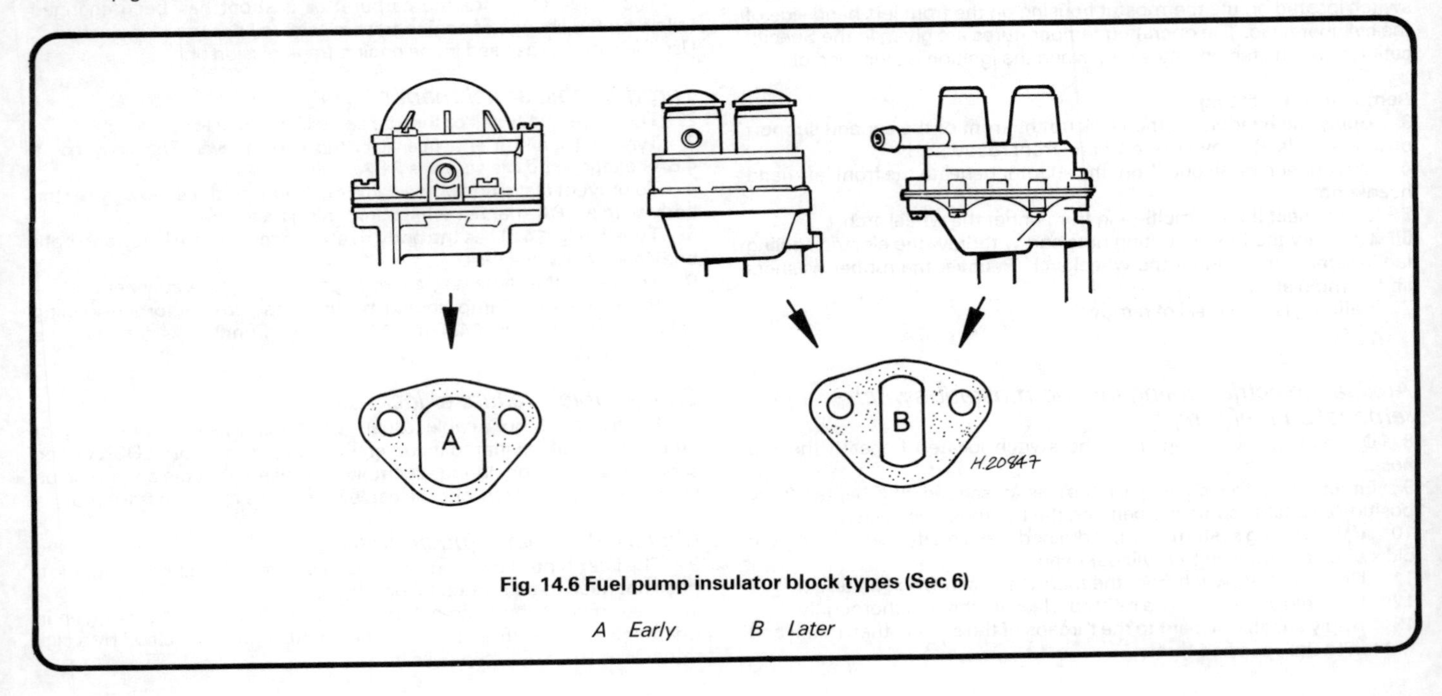

Fig. 14.6 Fuel pump insulator block types (Sec 6)

A Early
B Later

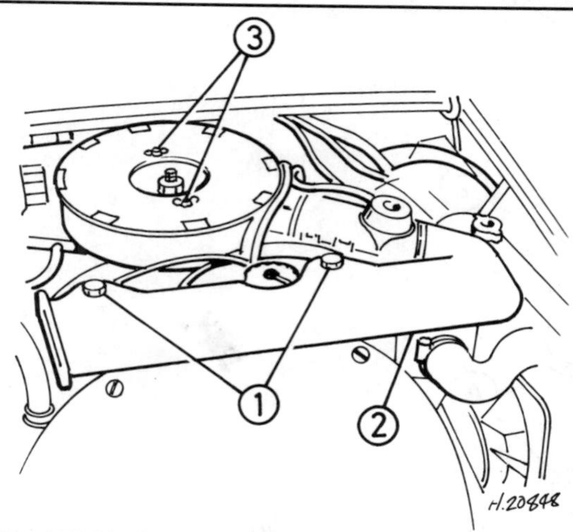

Fig. 14.7 Air cleaner and inlet duct fitted to the 1990 on Cooper (Sec 6)

1 Inlet duct mounting nuts *3 Air cleaner mounting bolts*
2 Inlet duct

joints and partially withdraw the hub and driveshaft. Do not allow the assembly to hang from the brake hose.
22 Turn the differential driving flange so that it is upright. Release the exhaust manifold from the cylinder head, manoeuvre it to the right to clear the subframe and transmission casing before easing it upwards.
23 Refitting is the reverse sequence to removal, taking note of the instructions given in the main text.

Air cleaner and inlet duct (Cooper 1990 on) – removal and refitting

24 Unscrew the two nuts securing the air inlet duct to the rocker cover studs, then release the clip and disconnect the duct from the air cleaner (Fig. 14.7).
25 Unscrew and remove the nuts and washers, then lift the air cleaner from the carburettor and disconnect the hot air hose.
26 Refitting is a reversal of removal, but check that the air cleaner bottom seal is correctly located.

SU HIF carburettor (Cooper 1990 on)

Description

27 The SU HIF carburettor fitted to the Cooper operates in a similar way to the SU HS4 carburettor described in Chapter 3, but the float chamber has been incorporated into the main body of the carburettor and a bi-metal strip is fitted to the jet adjusting (mixture) screw mechanism in order to compensate for the varying fuel densities resulting from varying fuel temperatures.

Removal and refitting

28 Disconnect the battery negative lead.
29 Remove the air cleaner and inlet duct as described previously.
30 Remove the carburettor heat shield.
31 Disconnect the choke cable and throttle cable.
32 Disconnect the vacuum pipe from the carburettor flange.
33 Loosen the clip then disconnect the fuel supply hose from the carburettor. Plug the hose.
34 Loosen the clip and disconnect the float chamber vent pipe.
35 Unscrew the mounting nuts and withdraw the carburettor from the inlet manifold together with the throttle cable bracket and spacer.
36 Refitting is a reversal of removal, but fit new gaskets and tighten the nuts evenly to prevent distortion. The throttle cable should be adjusted to give approximately 4 mm slack, and the choke cable should be adjusted to give approximately 2 mm slack.

Overhaul

37 With the carburettor removed, clean the exterior surfaces thoroughly and wipe dry.
38 Mark the float chamber cover in relation to the carburettor body. Remove the screws and withdraw the cover and sealing ring.
39 Unscrew and remove the mixture screw and spring and withdraw the seal.
40 Unscrew the jet retaining screw and remove the spring.
41 Withdraw the jet and bi-metal lever assembly. Disengage the lever from the jet.
42 Unscrew and remove the float pivot and seal.
43 Withdraw the float and the needle valve.
44 Unscrew and remove the needle valve seat.
45 Unscrew and remove the piston damper and drain the oil.
46 Mark the suction chamber in relation to the carburettor body. Remove the screws and withdraw the suction chamber together with the piston.
47 Prise the clip from the top of the piston rod then withdraw the piston and spring from the suction chamber.
48 Unscrew the needle retaining grub screw. Remove the needle, guide and spring from the piston.
49 From beneath the main body, unscrew the jet bearing nut and withdraw the bearing.
50 Note how the spring is attached to the fast idle cam lever, then bend back the locktabs, unscrew the nut and remove the washer.
51 Hold the return spring against the main body, and use a screwdriver to prise the cam lever from the end of the cold start spindle. Remove the spring.
52 Remove the end cover and spindle seat.
53 Remove the two screws and withdraw the retaining plate, cold start body and gasket.
54 Remove the O-ring from the end of the cold start spindle, and withdraw the spindle from the main body. Remove the cold start seal.
55 Dismantling of the throttle spindle is not recommended unless the components are damaged or excessively worn. If they are, first note how the return spring is attached to the throttle lever.
56 Mark the throttle valve in relation to the spindle and main body.
57 Remove the throttle valve screws while supporting the spindle with a block of wood if necessary.
58 Open the throttle and withdraw the valve disc.
59 Remove any burrs from the spindle screw holes with a fine file.
60 Bend back the locktabs and unscrew the spindle nut. Remove the lockwasher, plain washer, throttle lever, and return spring.
61 From the opposite end of the spindle, loosen the nut and bolt and remove the throttle damper lever.
62 Check the threaded end of the spindle and main body in relation to each other, then withdraw the spindle. Remove the two seals.
63 Clean all the components in fuel and allow to dry. Thoroughly examine the components for damage and excessive wear. In particular check the throttle spindle and bearings for wear. If excessive, renewal of the spindle may be sufficient, but if the bearings are worn it may be necessary to renew the complete carburettor, as new bearings are not always available. Check the needle valve and seating for excessive ridging. Examine the main body for cracks and for security of the brass fittings and piston key. Check the tapered needle, jet and jet bearing for wear. Shake the float and listen for any trapped fuel which may have entered through a small crack or fracture. Renew the components as necessary and obtain a complete set of gaskets and seals, and two new throttle valve screws if necessary.
64 Clean the inside of the suction chamber and the periphery of the piston with methylated spirit. *Do not use any form of abrasive.* Lubricate the piston rod with engine oil and insert it into the suction chamber. Hold the two components horizontal and spin the piston in several positions. The piston must spin freely without touching the suction chamber.
65 Commence reassembly by fitting the throttle spindle and two seals to the main body. The seals must be slightly recessed in their housings.
66 Locate the return spring and throttle lever on the end of the spindle, and fit the plain washer, lockwasher, and nut. Tighten the nut while holding the lever, and bend over the locktabs to lock.
67 Engage the return spring with the throttle lever and main body, and tension the spring.
68 Fit the throttle valve disc to the spindle in its original position, and insert the new screws, tightening them loosely (coat the threads with thread-locking fluid).
69 Open and close the throttle several times to settle the disc, then tighten the screws while supporting the spindle on a block of wood. Using a small chisel, spread the ends of the screws to lock them.
70 Locate the throttle damper lever loosely on the end of the spindle.
71 Locate the cold start seal in the main body with the cut-out uppermost.

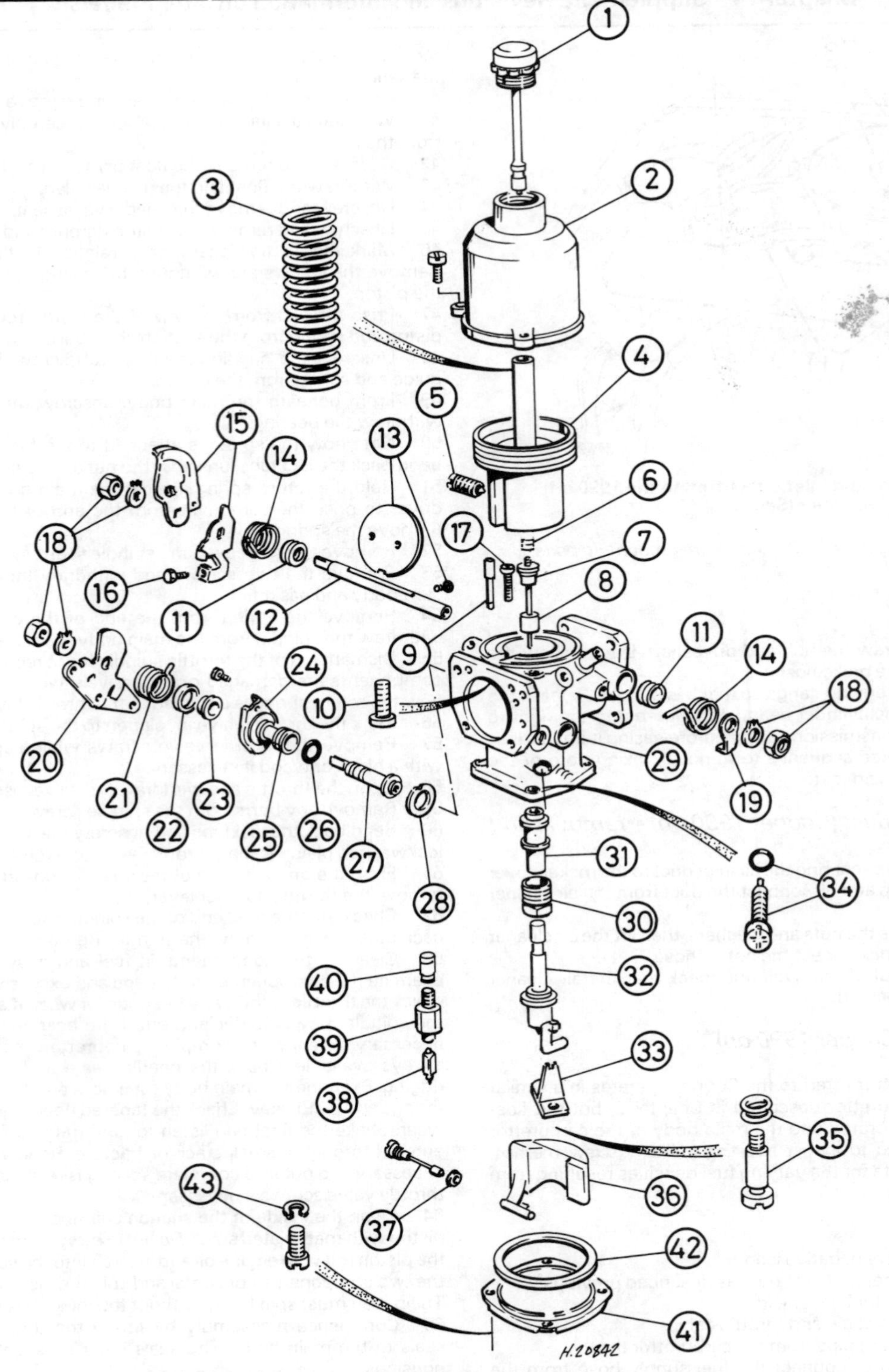

Fig. 14.8 SU HIF carburettor fitted to the 1990 on Cooper (Sec 6)

1 Piston damper
2 Suction chamber
3 Piston spring and clip
4 Piston
5 Needle retaining screw
6 Spring
7 Jet needle
8 Guide
9 Lifting pin
10 Lifting pin spring and circlip
11 Spindle seal
12 Throttle spindle
13 Throttle valve and screw
14 Return springs
15 Throttle lever and progressive throttle cam
16 Fast idle adjustment screw
17 Throttle adjustment screw
18 Spindle nuts and tab washers
19 Return spring lever
20 Mixture control lever and fast idle cam
21 Return spring
22 Dust cap
23 Seal
24 Retaining plate
25 Cold start body
26 O-ring
27 Cold start spindle
28 Cold start seal
29 Main body
30 Jet bearing
31 Jet bearing nut
32 Jet assembly
33 Bi-metal jet lever
34 Jet adjusting screw and seal
35 Jet retaining screw and spring
36 Float
37 Float pivot and seal
38 Needle valve
39 Needle valve seat
40 Fuel strainer
41 Float chamber cover
42 Cover seal
43 Screw and spring washer

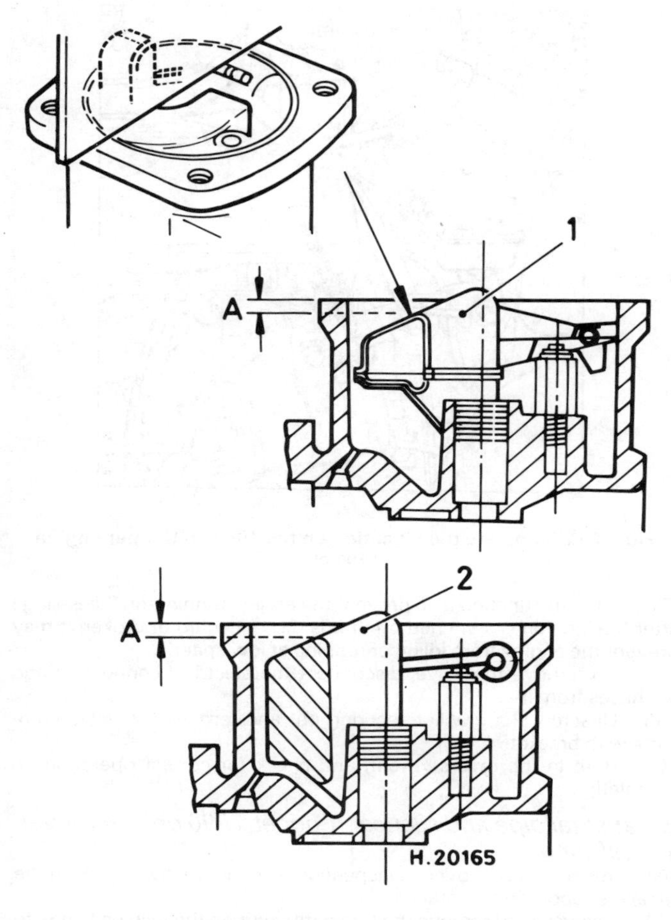

Fig. 14.9 Float level adjustment 'A' (Sec 6)

1 Type 1 float 2 Type 2 float

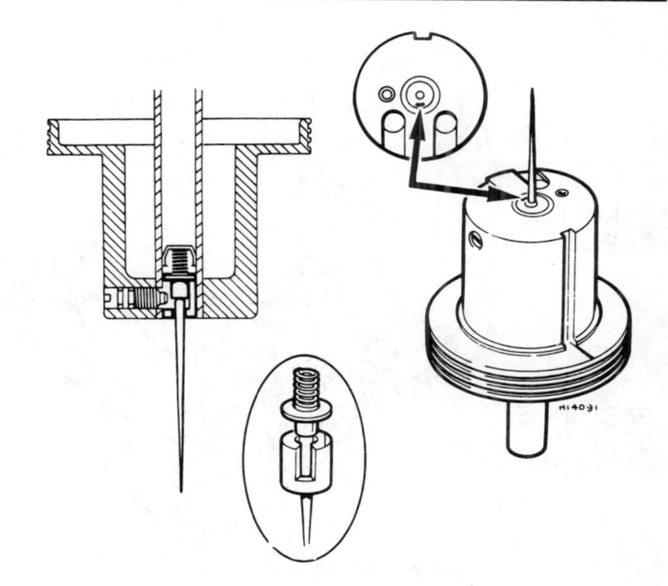

Fig. 14.10 Tapered needle installation (Sec 6)

Arrows indicate etch mark location

72 Insert the cold start spindle (hole uppermost), and fit the O-ring.
73 Fit the cold start body with the cut-out uppermost, and the retaining plate with the slotted flange facing the throttle spindle. Use a new gasket, then insert and tighten the retaining screws.
74 Fit the spindle seat and end cover, followed by the spring, cam lever, lockwasher, and nut. Make sure that the spring is correctly engaged, then tighten the nut and bend over the locktabs to lock.
75 Insert the jet bearing and nut, and tighten the nut.
76 Connect the bi-metal lever with the fuel jet, making sure that the jet head moves freely in the cut-out.
77 Insert the mixture screw and seal into the main body. Fit the jet to the bearing, and at the same time engage the slot in the bi-metal lever with the small diameter of the mixture screw.
78 Insert the jet retaining screw with the spring, and tighten the screw.
79 Adjust the mixture so that the top of the jet is flush with the venturi bridge.
80 Insert and tighten the needle valve seat, and with the carburettor inverted, insert the needle valve.
81 Position the float, then insert the pivot and seal through the body and float and tighten.
82 To check the float level adjustment, hold the carburettor inverted, with the float keeping the needle valve shut. Refer to Fig. 14.9 and, using a straight edge and feeler blade, check that the centre portion of the float is 1.0 ± 0.5 mm below the surface of the float chamber face for the type 1 float, or 2.0 ± 0.5 mm below the surface of the float chamber face for the type 2 float. If not, bend the tab which contacts the needle valve as necessary.
83 Fit the float chamber cover in its original position together with a new sealing ring. Tighten the screws in diagonal sequence.
84 Insert the spring, needle, and guide into the piston with the guide etch marks facing the suction transfer holes, and with the bottom face of the guide flush with the bottom face of the piston (Fig. 14.10).
85 Insert and tighten the guide retaining grub screw.
86 Lower the piston and needle assembly into the main body, at the same time engaging the slot with the piston key.
87 Locate the spring over the piston rod.
88 Hold the suction chamber directly over the piston with its location mark aligned with the mark on the body, then lower it over the spring and piston rod. It is important not to tension the spring by twisting the suction chamber.
89 Insert and tighten the suction chamber retaining screws. Lift the piston with the finger, then release it and check that it returns to the venturi bridge without any assistance. If not, it may be necessary to loosen the retaining screws and slightly reposition the suction chamber.
90 Hold the piston fully up, then fit the clip to the top of the piston rod.
91 Pour clean engine oil into the top of the suction chamber until the level is 13 mm above the top of the hollow piston rod. Refit and tighten the piston damper.

Idle speed and mixture adjustments

92 Check that the valve clearances and ignition timing are correct and that the spark plugs are in good serviceable condition. Also check the following points:

- *(a) The air cleaner element is clean*
- *(b) The crankcase ventilation hoses are secure and in good condition*
- *(c) The choke cable is correctly adjusted*
- *(d) The piston damper is topped up with engine oil, and the piston moves freely*
- *(e) The accelerator cable is correctly adjusted*
- *(f) The fast idle screw is correctly adjusted so that there is clearance between the screw and the cam with the choke control off*

93 Run the engine to normal operating temperature. Driving the car on the road for approximately 4 miles will achieve this.
94 The adjustments should be completed within two minutes of the engine reaching normal temperature, *before* the electric cooling fan operates. If the adjustments are not completed within the two minutes or if the cooling fan operates, wait for the fan to switch off then increase the engine speed to 2000 rpm for approximately 30 seconds. The adjustments can then be resumed.
95 Check that all electrical components are switched off.
96 Connect a tachometer to the engine.
97 Allow the engine to idle and check that the idle speed is as given in the Specifications. If adjustment is necessary, turn the screw located on the dashpot base.

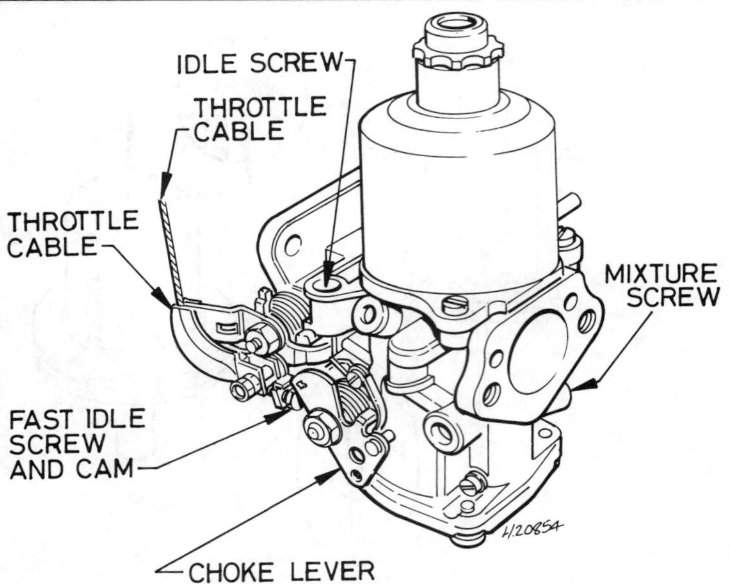

Fig. 14.11 Adjustment location points on the SU HIF carburettor fitted to the Cooper (Sec 6)

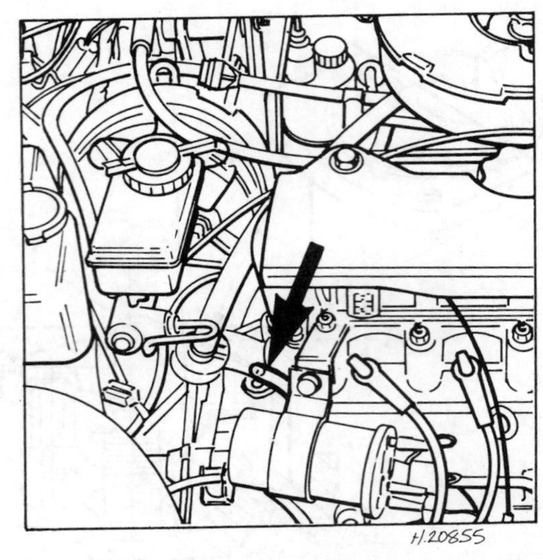

Fig. 14.12 Sampling pipe location on the 1990 on Cooper engine (Sec 6)

98 Unscrew the plug from the sampling pipe located on the right-hand side of the cylinder head (Fig. 14.12), and connect an exhaust gas analyser to the pipe.

99 With the engine idling, check that the CO % is as given in the Specifications. If not, turn the adjustment screw located on the side of the carburettor body. Turn the screw by small increments and allow the reading to stabilise between adjustments.

100 If necessary re-adjust the idling speed as described in paragraph 97.

101 Note that if the CO % is adjusted near the 3.0 % upper limit, the efficiency of the catalytic converter will be reduced. If the CO reading is then taken from the exhaust tailpipe, there may be little difference between the two readings, though this does not mean that the catalytic converter is not functioning correctly and will not adversely affect the unit.

102 Check the fast idling speed by pulling out the choke until the arrow on the carburettor fast idle cam is aligned with the adjustment screw. If adjustment is necessary, turn the fast idle screw.

103 Stop the engine and disconnect the tachometer and exhaust gas analyser. Refit the plug to the sampling pipe.

Anti run-on valve (Cooper 1990 on) – removal and refitting

104 The anti run-on valve is mounted on a bracket on the bulkhead (Fig. 14.13). Its function is to prevent the engine running-on ('dieseling') after the ignition is switched off. If it is disconnected or broken it may prevent the engine from idling or running at low speeds.

105 To remove the valve, disconnect the electrical connectors and the hoses from it.

106 Unscrew the bracket securing nut and remove the valve complete with bracket.

107 Refit in the reverse order, and check for correct operation on completion.

Exhaust tailpipe and silencer (Cooper 1990 on) – removal and refitting

108 Position the car over an inspection pit or alternatively jack up the car and support on axle stands.

109 Unscrew and remove the two nuts securing the tailpipe flange to the catalytic converter studs.

110 Unscrew the two nuts from the tailpipe mounting brackets.

111 Withdraw the tailpipe and recover the flange gasket.

112 Refitting is a reversal of removal, but clean the flanges and fit new gaskets.

Catalytic converter (Cooper 1990 on) – removal and refitting

113 Remove the exhaust tailpipe and silencer as described previously.

114 Unscrew the two nuts securing the exhaust front pipe to the catalytic converter studs.

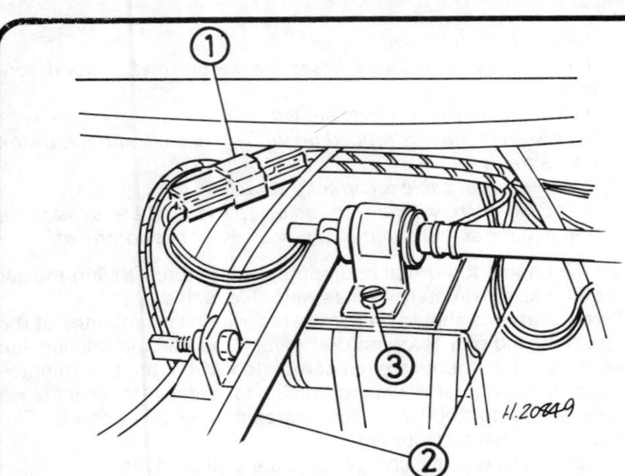

Fig. 14.13 Anti run-on valve location (Sec 6)

1 Multi-plug connector
2 Hoses
3 Anti run-on valve and bracket

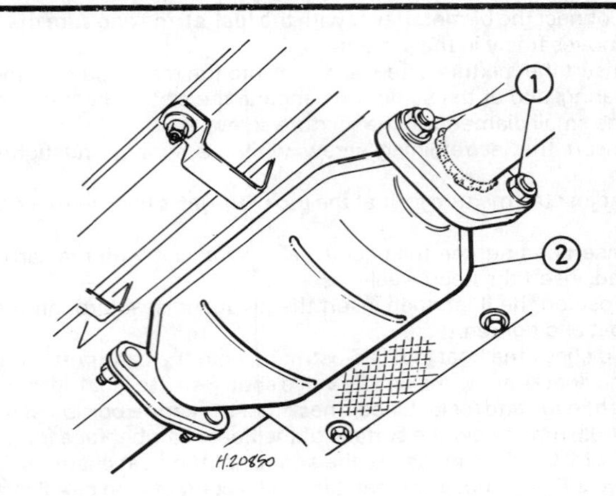

Fig. 14.14 Catalytic converter fitted to the 1990 on Cooper (Sec 6)

1 Flange mounting nuts
2 Catalytic converter

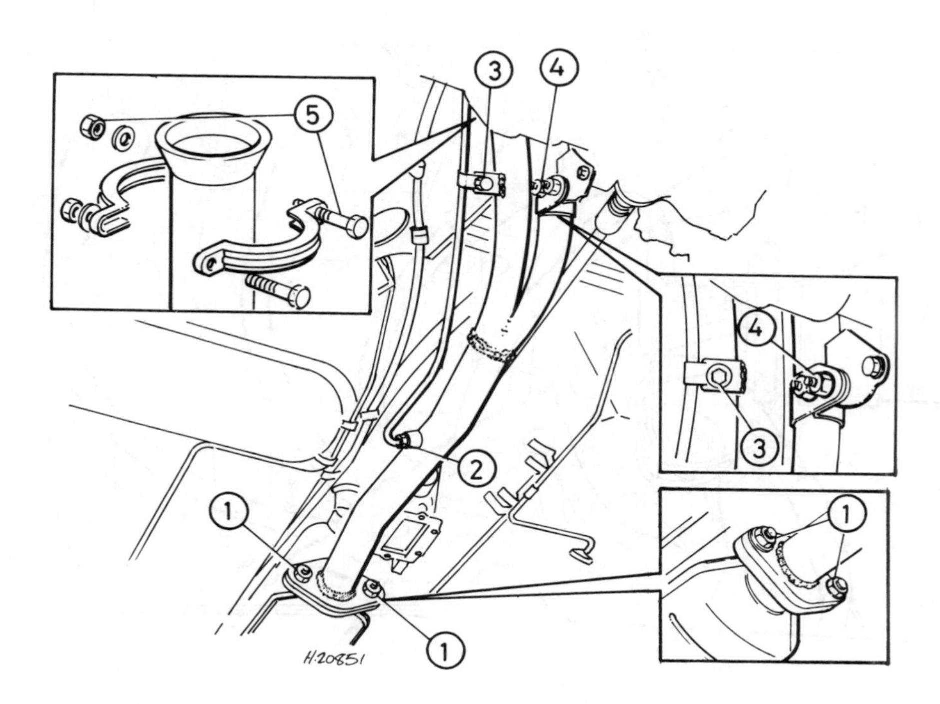

Fig. 14.15 Exhaust front pipe fitted to the 1990 on Cooper (Sec 6)

1 Catalytic converter flange mounting nuts
2 Sampling pipe union nut
3 Sampling pipe mounting bolt
4 Front pipe mounting
5 Front pipe-to-manifold clamp and bolts

115 Withdraw the catalytic converter and recover the flange gasket.
116 Refitting is a reversal of removal, but clean the flanges and fit new gaskets.

Exhaust front pipe (Cooper 1990 on) – removal and refitting

117 Remove the air cleaner assembly as described previously.
118 Remove the catalytic converter as described previously.
119 Unscrew the union nut securing the CO sample pipe to the exhaust front pipe, then unbolt the sample pipe from the front pipe.
120 Unscrew the mounting bolt from the bracket on the differential housing.
121 Unbolt the exhaust manifold clamps and withdraw the front pipe from under the car.
122 Refitting is a reversal of removal, but on completion check that the manifold-to-front pipe joint is not leaking.

7 Ignition system

Ballasted ignition system

Identification and warning

1 To determine if a vehicle is equipped with a ballasted ignition system, check for the presence of a supplementary wiring harness, incorporating the white/pink ballast resistor lead, between the fuse block and the ignition coil LT terminal.
2 The ballast resistor lead replaces the original coil feed. The original lead is colour-coded white and is retained in the harness to accommodate vehicles not fitted with a ballasted system. Do not connect this white lead to the ignition coil, it must remain taped to the harness.
3 Failure to observe this warning will result in coil overheating and premature contact breaker point failure. Similar damage will occur if a coil designed for use with a ballasted system is fitted to a non-ballasted system, this being due to the excessive primary current produced. Check any replacement coil is of the correct type.

General description and testing

4 The ballasted ignition system improves ignition performance, particularly when starting the engine. Ballast is provided by a low resistance lead incorporated in the supply from the ignition switch to the ignition coil positive (+) terminal. The starter solenoid circuit is wired so that, upon operation of the starter, the ballast resistance is bypassed. This has the effect of slightly increasing coil primary voltage which in turn temporarily increases HT output to improve starting.
5 To test the system, first obtain a multimeter and a test lead fitted with crocodile clips at each end. Turn over the engine until the contact breaker points are closed. Connect the meter between the ignition coil positive terminal and earth and then set it on its 0 to 20 volts dc scale. Disconnect the coil HT lead and then turn on the ignition; the meter should read approximately 6.5 volts.
6 Leave the ignition on and connect the test lead between the coil negative (–) terminal and earth. The meter reading should not exceed 1.0 volt. If it does this indicates a high resistance across the contact breaker points. Clean or renew the points, as necessary.
7 Leave the test lead connected and turn the engine over until the contact breaker points are open. The meter reading should now increase to indicate approximately 12.0 volts.
8 Transfer the test lead to the coil positive terminal and spin the engine with the starter. The meter should read between approximately 9.5 and 11.5 volts. If not check the starter solenoid to coil wiring.
9 On completion of testing, remove all equipment from the car and check all connections are correctly made. Do not inadvertently connect the coil positive terminal to earth whilst the ignition is on; this will result in full battery voltage flowing through the ballast resistor causing it to overheat and become damaged.

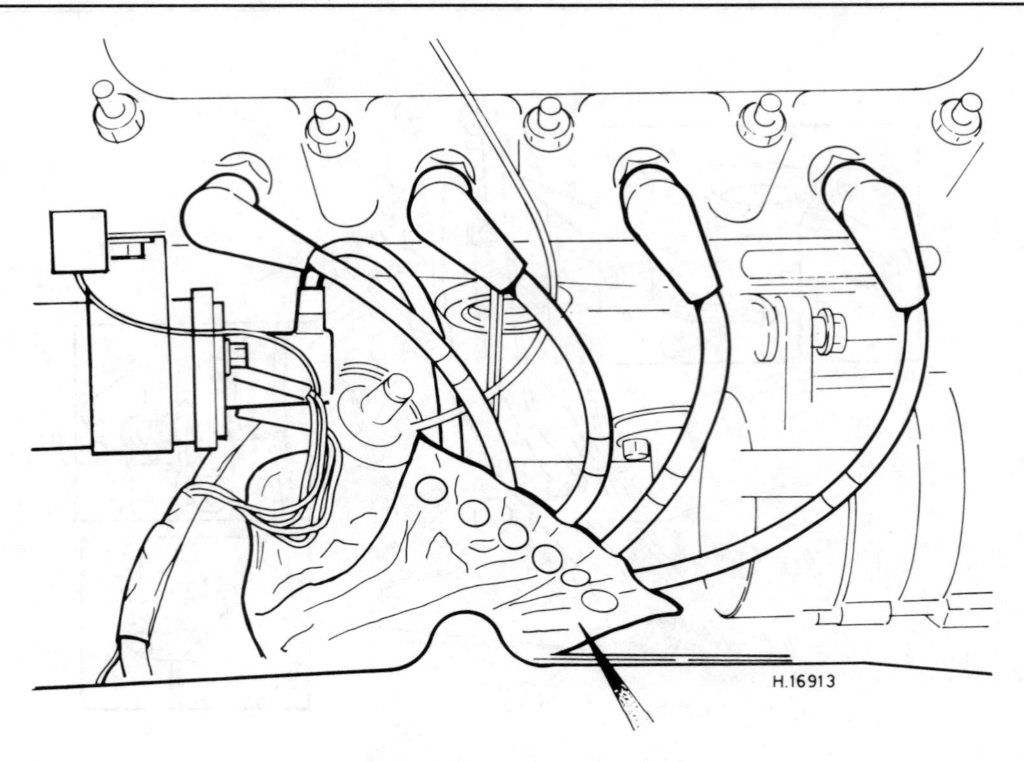

Fig. 14.16 Distributor plastic cover (arrowed) (Sec 7)

Distributor – plastic cover

10 From 1985, the distributor has been fitted with a plastic cover to prevent water ingress causing misfiring in wet conditions.

11 These covers may be obtained from your dealer and fitted to earlier models, as follows.

12 Disconnect the HT leads from the coil and spark plugs.

13 Fit the cover over the leads and distributor cap, ensuring that the elasticated end of the sleeve covers the distributor cap clips and lower edge of the cap.

14 Fasten the six press studs, so that the five HT leads are separated, and reconnect the HT leads to the coil and spark plugs.

Contact breaker points

15 When examining the contact breaker points, disregard any blue discoloration which may be apparent on their faces. This is due to the formation of tungsten oxide and has no detrimental effect on ignition performance; it is not indicative of condenser failure.

Spark plugs

16 The spark plugs listed in Chapter 4 are no longer fitted and are replaced by other types (see Specifications).

Transmission controlled ignition advance system

General description

17 Some models are fitted with a transmission controlled ignition advance system.

18 The system consists of a vacuum line connected to the distributor-to-inlet manifold vacuum hose which runs to an inhibitor switch located behind the gearchange remote control housing.

19 A solenoid valve, operated by the inhibitor switch is mounted in this vacuum line.

20 When fourth gear is selected, the inhibitor switch energises the solenoid valve, and increased vacuum is applied to the advance mechanism of the distributor.

21 When anything other than fourth gear is selected, the system is de-energised and vacuum is vented to atmosphere, the vacuum line to the distributor is sealed, and the system reverts to normal operation.

Checking and adjusting

22 To check the operation of the system, chock the front wheels, apply the handbrake and start the engine.

23 Increase engine speed to approximately 2500 rpm.

24 Depress and hold the clutch pedal down while selecting fourth gear.

25 With fourth gear selected, engine speed should increase by 300 to 400 rpm.

26 Disengage fourth gear, release the clutch pedal and stop the engine.

27 To adjust the inhibitor switch, place the front of the vehicle on axle stands, apply the handbrake and select neutral.

28 Disconnect the electrical leads from the inhibitor switch and loosen the locknut securing the switch to its mounting bracket.

29 Connect a self-powered test lamp to the terminals of the inhibitor switch, and screw the switch out of its mounting bracket until the lamp lights.

30 Now screw the switch in until the lamp goes out.

31 Screw the switch in a further $1\frac{1}{2}$ to 2 flats, then tighten the locknut.

32 Check that the lamp lights only when the fourth gear is selected.

33 Remove the test lamp, reconnect the electrical leads, and carry out the test procedure previously described.

Removing and refitting

34 Remove the switch as described for adjusting, but screw the switch right out from its bracket, after disconnecting the leads and loosening the locknut.

35 Refit in the reverse order, and carry out the adjustment and checking procedure.

Solenoid valve – removal and refitting

36 Pull the vacuum hoses from the solenoid valve.

37 Disconnect the electrical leads.

38 Remove the mounting screw, noting the earth lead, and remove the valve.

39 Refit in the reverse order, ensuring that the earth lead is fitted under the mounting bolt.

Electronic ignition system (Cooper 1990 on)

General description

40 The Lucas electronic ignition system consists of a distributor, an amplifier module and a coil. Externally, the distributor resembles a conventional type, but internally a reluctor and a pick-up unit take the place of the cam and contact breaker points.

41 Each time one of the reluctor arms passes through the magnetic field of the pick-up coil, an electrical signal is sent to the amplifier module which then triggers the coil in the same way as the opening of the points in a conventional system. Both centrifugal and vacuum advance are used in the accustomed manner.

42 Because there are no contact breaker points to wear out, the electronic ignition system is extremely reliable. As long as the distributor is lubricated and the spark plugs inspected or renewed at the specified intervals, and leads and connections are kept clean and dry, it is very unlikely that trouble will be experienced.

43 Because of the high voltages generated, *care should be taken to avoid receiving personal electric shocks from the HT system.* This is particularly important for anyone fitted with an artificial cardiac pacemaker.

Static timing

44 The only suitable method of ignition timing for road use is using a stroboscopic lamp. However, for initial setting-up purposes (eg after engine overhaul, or if the timing has been completely lost) the following procedure will enable the engine to be run in order to undertake dynamic timing.

45 Pull off the HT lead and remove No 1 spark pug (nearest the crankshaft pulley).

46 Place a finger over the plug hole and turn the engine in the normal direction of rotation (clockwise from the crankshaft pulley end) until pressure is felt in No 1 cylinder. This indicates that the piston is commencing its compression stroke. The engine can be turned with a socket and bar on the crankshaft pulley bolt.

47 Continue turning the engine until the timing marks (see Chapter 4) are correctly aligned.

48 Remove the distributor cap and check that the rotor arm is pointing towards the No 1 spark plug HT lead segment in the cap.

49 If the rotor arm is not pointing towards the No 1 spark plug HT lead segment in the cap, slacken the distributor clamp bolt and turn the distributor body as necessary, then tighten the bolt. It is not possible to align the reluctor arms as they are totally enclosed within the distributor.

50 Refit the distributor cap, No 1 spark plug and the HT lead.

51 It should now be possible to start and run the engine, enabling the ignition timing to be checked accurately using a stroboscopic timing light.

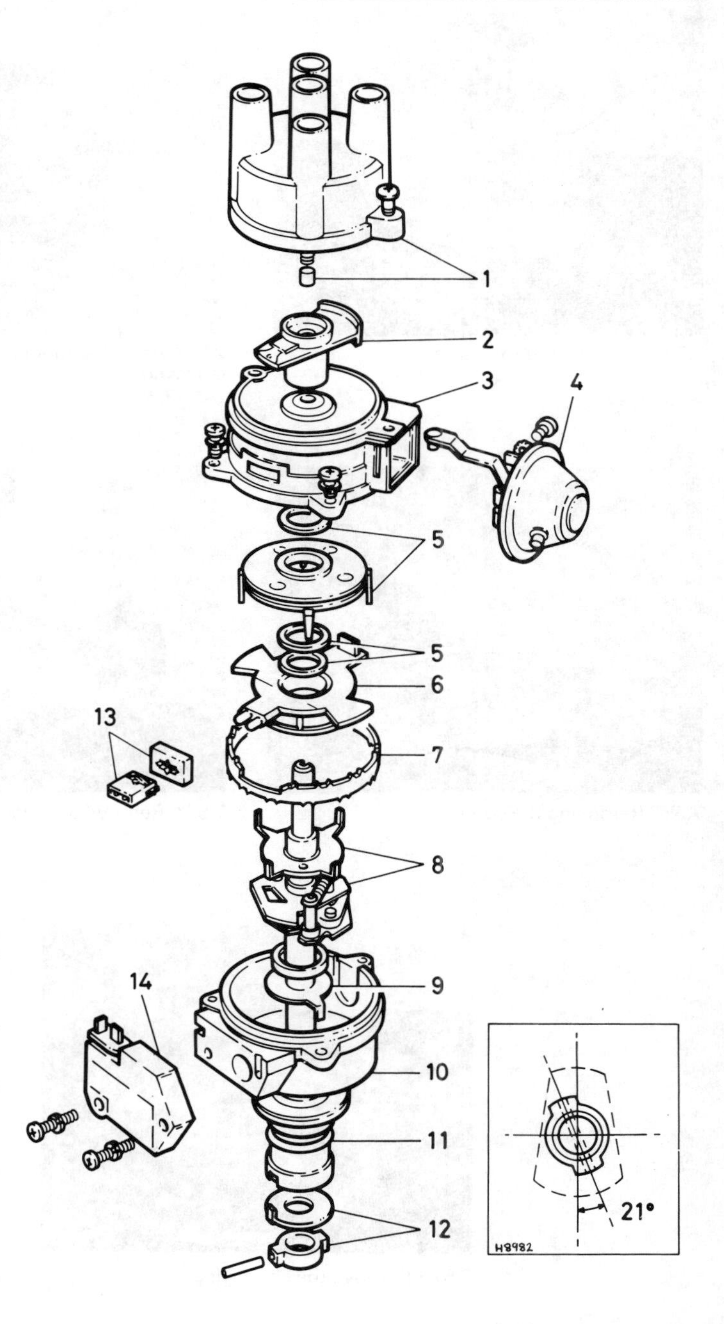

Fig. 14.17 Exploded view of the electronic ignition distributor fitted to the 1990 on Cooper (Sec 7)

1 *Distributor cap, carbon brush and spring*
2 *Rotor arm*
3 *Upper housing*
4 *Vacuum unit*
5 *Stator pack, thrustwashers and circlip*
6 *Pick-up winding*
7 *Clamp ring*
8 *Reluctor, centrifugal advance mechanism, and shaft assembly*
9 *Thrustwasher*
10 *Lower housing*
11 *O-ring*
12 *Drive dog and thrustwasher*
13 *Connector and gasket*
14 *Amplifier module*
Inset indicates correct rotor arm-to-drive dog offset

Electronic ignition distributor (Cooper 1990 on)

Removal and refitting

52 The procedure is similar to that described in Chapter 4, except that the distributor cap is retained with two screws instead of spring clips, and it will be necessary to disconnect the amplifier multi-plug instead of the single low tension lead.

Dismantling and reassembly

53 Remove the distributor, as described previously.

54 Pull off the rotor arm (photo).

55 Remove the two screws and pull the amplifier module from the connector, then remove the gasket and pull off the connector (photos).

56 Remove the screws and separate the upper housing from the lower housing (photos).

57 Remove the clamp ring and pick-up winding from the upper housing (photos).

58 Remove the vacuum unit retaining screw, then extract the circlip and thrustwasher, withdraw the stator pack from the link arm, and remove the vacuum unit. Recover the remaining thrustwasher from the upper housing (photos).

59 Further dismantling is not normally necessary. However, the shaft assembly may be removed from the lower housing by driving the roll pin from the drive dog after marking the drive dog in relation to the shaft (photos).

7.54 Removing the rotor arm

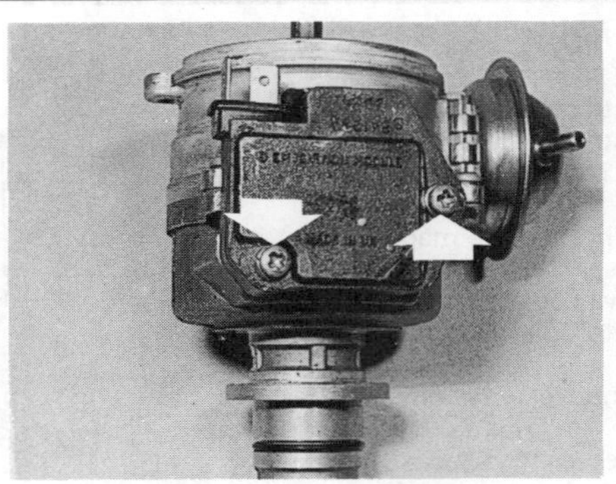
7.55A Amplifier module retaining screws (arrowed)

7.55B Removing the amplifier module

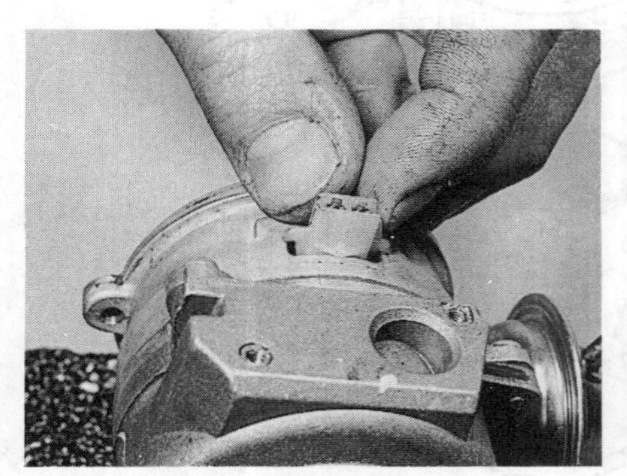
7.55C Removing the connector

7.56A Remove the screws ...

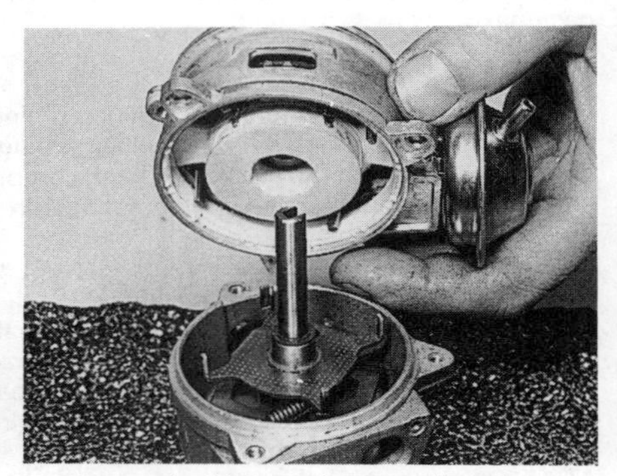
7.56B ... and withdraw the upper housing

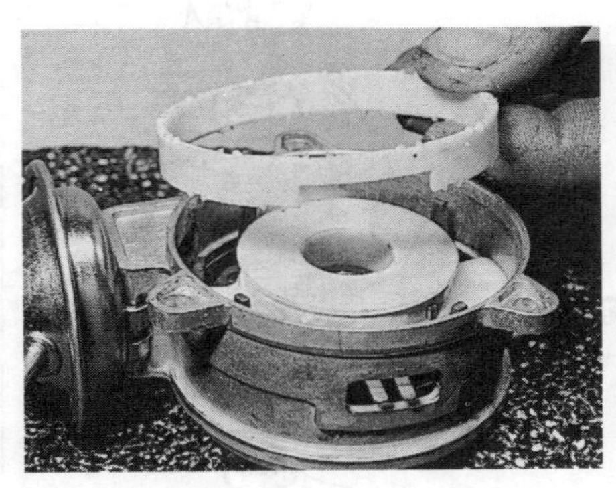
7.57A Remove the clamp ring ...

7.57B ... and pick-up winding

60 Clean and examine all the components, and renew them as required.
61 Refit the shaft assembly if removed, locate the drive dog and drive in the roll pin. Check that the drive dog offset is positioned correctly in relation to the rotor arm by referring to Fig. 14.17.
62 Lubricate the shaft bearing with a little engine oil. Also lubricate the centrifugal advance mechanism.
63 Locate the thrustwasher in the upper housing.
64 Grease the end of the link arm then insert the vacuum unit in the upper housing and engage the stator pack with the link arm. Retain the stator pack with the thrustwasher and circlip, and fit the vacuum unit retaining screw (photo).
65 Insert the pick-up winding in the upper housing and centralise the terminals in the aperture, then fit the clamp ring with the cut-out over the aperture.
66 Fit the lower housing to the upper housing and insert the screws finger tight. Rotate the shaft several times then fully tighten the screws.
67 Check that the reluctor arms do not touch the stator pack arms as they can easily be bent inadvertently.
68 Fit the connector and gasket.
69 Apply heat conducting silicone grease to the mounting face of the amplifier module then fit the module and tighten the screws.
70 Refit the rotor arm.
71 If necessary, renew the O-ring on the shank of the distributor, then refit the distributor, as described in Chapter 4.

Electronic ignition amplifier (Cooper 1990 on) – general

72 If, after carrying out the test procedure described at the end of this Section, the amplifier module is diagnosed as being faulty, make sure that the wiring is intact and secure.

7.58A Vacuum unit retaining screw (arrowed)

7.58B Remove the circlip ...

7.58C ... followed by the thrustwasher ...

7.58D ... stator pack ...

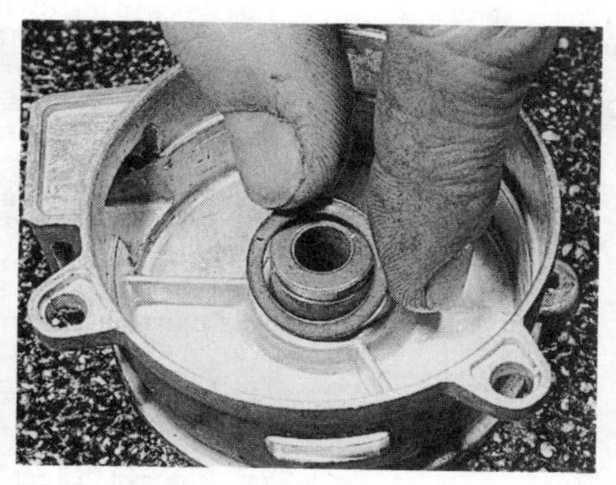

7.58E ... and thrustwasher

7.59A Centrifugal mechanism in the distributor lower housing

73 As a double-check remove the module, gasket and connector, and lightly squeeze together the terminals inside the connector. Clean the terminals in the module and distributor before refitting the module, and remember to apply heat-conducting silicone grease to the mounting face on the distributor.

74 Disconnect the wiring from the module, clean the terminals, and lightly squeeze together the terminals inside the connector before refitting it. Make sure that the connector is fully located over the base.

75 Check that the LT leads are correctly fitted to the ignition coil.

Fault diagnosis – electronic ignition

76 Electronic ignition is normally very reliable; if it does fail, such failure tends to be complete. In cases of misfiring, or other intermittent faults, it is probably best to check the HT system first (as described in Chapter 4) before proceeding to the table below.

77 An electrical multi-meter which can measure voltage and resistance (ohms) will be required for testing purposes. Such a meter need not be very expensive and is a useful addition to the electrically-minded mechanic's tool kit.

7.59B Roll pin (arrowed) in the distributor drive dog

7.64 Stator pack fitted in the upper housing

Electronic ignition system test procedure

Test	Remedy
1 Is the battery voltage greater than 11.7 volts?	Yes: Proceed to Test 2 No: Recharge the battery
2 Is the voltage at the coil '+' terminal within 1 volt of battery voltage?	Yes: Proceed to Test 3 No: Faulty wiring or connector between ignition switch and coil, or faulty ignition switch
3 Is the resistance between the ignition coil '+' and '–' terminals between 0.4 and 0.9 ohms?	Yes: Proceed to Test 4 No: Renew the ignition coil
4 Is the resistance between the ignition coil '+' and HT terminals between 5.0 and 15.0 k ohms?	Yes: Proceed to Test 5 No: Renew the ignition coil
5 Connect a low-wattage bulb across the ignition coil '+' and '–' terminals and spin the engine on the starter. Does the bulb flash?	Yes: Proceed to Test 6 No: Proceed to Test 10
6 Is the resistance of any HT lead greater than 20 k ohms?	Yes: Renew the HT lead No: Proceed to Test 7
7 Are there any signs of tracking on the ignition coil, distributor cap or rotor arm?	Yes: Renew the component as necessary No: Proceed to Test 8
8 Is the ignition timing correct?	Yes: Proceed to Test 9 No: Adjust ignition timing
9 Are the spark plugs in good condition?	Yes: Check carburettor settings and engine mechanical condition No: Renew the spark plugs
10 Are the module connections good?	Yes: Proceed to Test 11 No: Refer to paragraphs 72 to 75 of this Section.
11 With the module removed, is the resistance of the distributor pick-up coil between 950 and 1150 ohms?	Yes: Refer to paragraphs 72 to 75 of this Section No: Renew the distributor pick-up coil

8 Clutch

Verto clutch

General description

1 The Verto clutch differs from all previous Mini clutches in that the pressure plate and friction plate are both on the 'outside' of the flywheel, ie on the side furthest from the pistons.

2 The operation principle of the Verto clutch is the same as that of previous types. The friction plate is sandwiched firmly between the flywheel and pressure plate friction surfaces when the clutch pedal is released; when the pedal is depressed, the release components cause the diaphragm spring to flex and the grip of the pressure plate is relaxed.

3 The clutch is self-adjusting in use. Adjustment of the throw-out stop should only be necessary after dismantling has taken place.

Removal, overhaul and refitting

4 Special tools will be required to undertake this operation. They should be available from your BL dealer or tool hire agent; details are as follows:

- *(a) Spanner 18G 1303, or a deep socket (1½ in AF), to undo the flywheel centre bolt*
- *(b) Puller 18G 1381, or its equivalent (available from most major accessory outlets), to remove the flywheel/clutch assembly from the crankshaft taper*
- *(c) Clutch centering tool 18G 684. This tool is not essential and a way of avoiding its use is described in the text.*

5 With the handbrake applied, disconnect the battery and, if greater access to the engine bay is required, remove the bonnet.

6 Disconnect the wiring from the starter solenoid. Detach the solenoid from the wing valance and carefully place it to one side. Disconnect the starter motor cable and remove the motor.

7 Remove the exhaust pipe-to-manifold clamp. Detach the clutch slave cylinder mounting plate from the flywheel housing, taking care to retain the spacer. Place the slave cylinder and mounting plate to one side.

8 Position a jack beneath the gearbox casing. Use a piece of wood to protect the casing from the jack and take the weight of the engine/gearbox assembly.

9 Remove the right-hand engine mounting-to-subframe securing bolts. Raise the right-hand end of the engine so that access can be gained to the clutch cover securing bolts. Remove the cover, noting the fitted position of the carburettor drain pipe. Remove the thrust bearing sleeve.

10 Make sure that the slots in the end of the crankshaft hub are horizontal (3 o'clock and 9 o'clock). Lock the flywheel by jamming a wide-bladed screwdriver between the starter ring gear and the flywheel housing.

11 Relieve the lockwasher from the slots, then undo the flywheel centre bolt using spanner 18G 1303 or equivalent. Make sure the spanner fits well as the bolt is very tight.

12 Remove the bolt and the keyplate from the crankshaft, then fit puller 18G 1381 or equivalent to the flywheel. Do not tighten the puller-to-flywheel studs/bolts fully or the clutch driven plate may be damaged.

13 Screw in the puller centre bolt until the flywheel/clutch assembly is released from the crankshaft taper. If the unit seems reluctant to come off, strike the centre bolt sharply with a hammer to help to release the taper.

14 Remove the flywheel/clutch unit. Unscrew the pressure plate bolts, half a turn at a time in a criss-cross sequence, and remove the pressure plate and driven plate from the flywheel.

15 Inspect the components for wear and damage. The driven plate should be renewed as a matter of course unless it is nearly new. It must certainly be renewed if the linings are burnt, contaminated or badly worn, or if the centre splines are worn. The source of any contamination must be dealt with.

16 The flywheel and pressure plate are not sold separately, but must

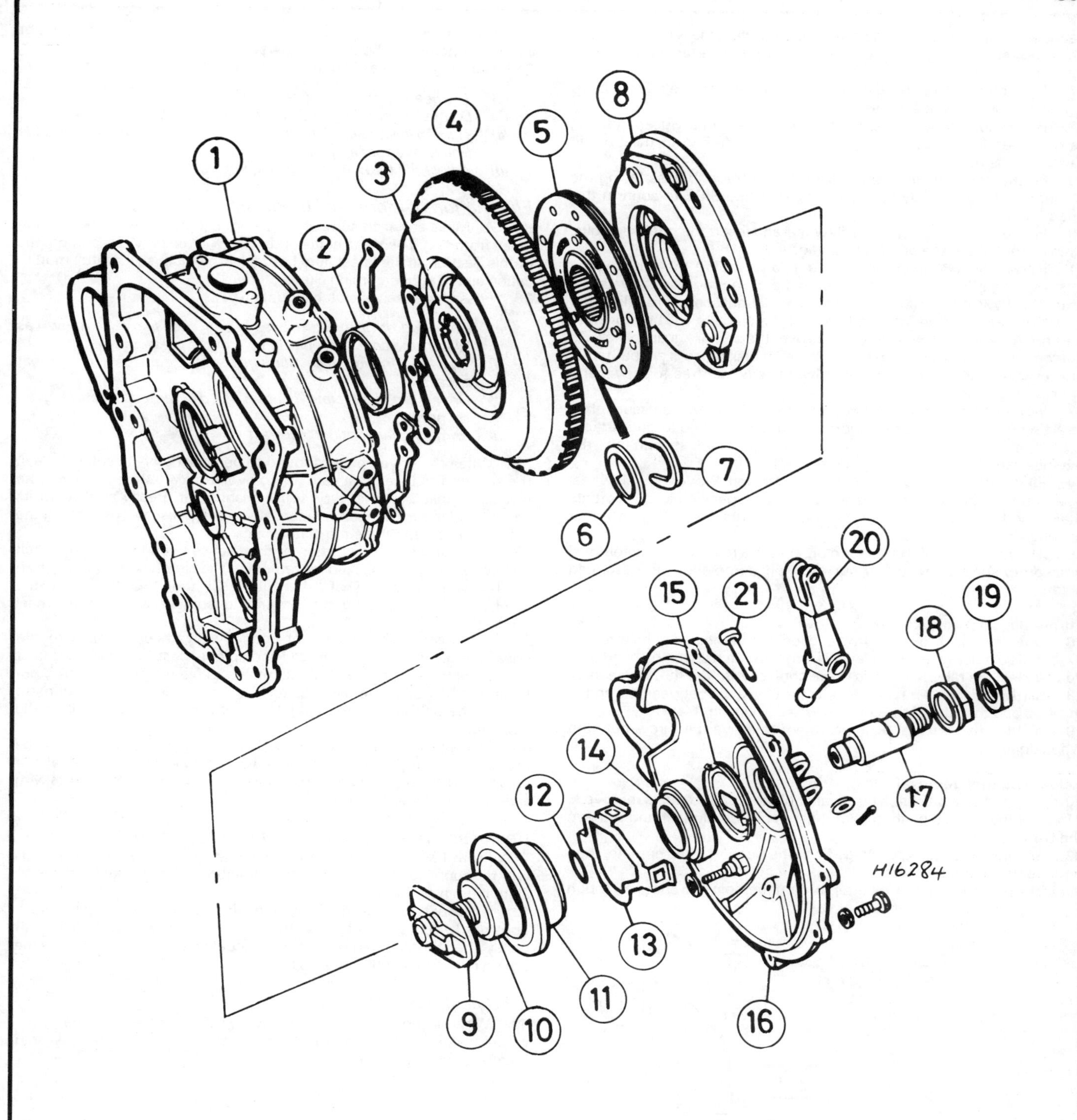

Fig. 14.18 Exploded view of Verto clutch (Sec 8)

1 *Flywheel housing*
2 *Oil seal (primary gear)*
3 *Dust shield*
4 *Flywheel*
5 *Driven plate*
6 *Primary gear locking ring*
7 *C-shaped thrustwasher*
8 *Pressure plate*
9 *Keyplate*
10 *Flywheel retaining bolt*
11 *Thrust sleeve*
12 *O-ring*
13 *Spring clip*
14 *Release bearing*
15 *Retainer plate*
16 *Clutch cover (release bearing housing)*
17 *Plunger*
18 *Throw-out stop*
19 *Locknut*
20 *Release lever*
21 *Pivot pin*

be renewed as a matched assembly if wear or damage is evident. Deep grooving, cracks or crazing of the friction surfaces are grounds for renewal.
17 Consideration should also be given to renewing the release bearing whilst it is easily accessible.
18 Before commencing reassembly, check the primary gear endfloat, as described in Chapter 6, Section 11, whilst referring to the Specifications at the beginning of this Chapter.
19 Fit the driven plate to the flywheel with the hub boss facing the flywheel. (The plate may be marked FLYWHEEL SIDE to confirm this orientation.)
20 Fit the pressure plate to the flywheel and insert the retaining bolts. Only finger tighten the bolts at this stage.
21 If tool 18G 684 is available, use it to centralize the driven plate relative to the flywheel and pressure plate. If the tool is not available, offer the flywheel/clutch assembly to the crankshaft. Providing the pressure plate bolts are not too tight, the driven plate will be moved to the correct central position as it passes over the primary gear splines. Do not force the assembly onto the crankshaft if resistance is encountered, but remove it and check that the drive plate is just free to move, and approximately central.
22 When centralisation has been achieved, tighten the pressure plate retaining bolts in a criss-cross sequence to the specified torque setting.
23 If a centralisation tool was used, remove it and fit the flywheel/clutch assembly to the crankshaft.
24 Fit the keyplate and the flywheel centre bolt. Prevent the flywheel from rotating and tighten the centre bolt to the specified torque setting. Stake the lockwasher into the slots of the clutch hub. Fit the thrust bearing sleeve.
25 The remainder of the refitting process is a reversal of the removal procedure. Adjust the throw-out stop on completion as described below.

Throw-out stop adjustment
26 Unscrew the throw-out stop and locknut to the end of its thread.
27 Pull the release lever out (away from the clutch cover) by hand until you can feel the release bearing make contact with the thrust sleeve.
28 Screw the throw-out stop in until the clearance between the end of the stop and the face of the cover is as shown in Fig. 14.19.
29 Tighten the locknut, taking care not to move the throw-out stop when doing so.

Release bearing removal and refitting
30 Proceed as with clutch removal until the clutch cover is removed.
31 Pull the release bearing components off the plunger and retrieve the O-ring.
32 Separate the spring clip legs from the bearing retainer plate, then remove the bearing.
33 Examine the bearing for external damage, spin it to check for rough running and inspect it for grease leakage. If there is the slightest doubt as to its condition it should be renewed.
34 Refitting is a reversal of removal, but note the following points:

(a) The bearing seal faces away from the retainer plate
(b) Do not forget to fit the O-ring on the plunger
(c) Tighten fasteners to their specified torques, where applicable (see relevant Chapters)
(d) Adjust the throw-out stop on completion

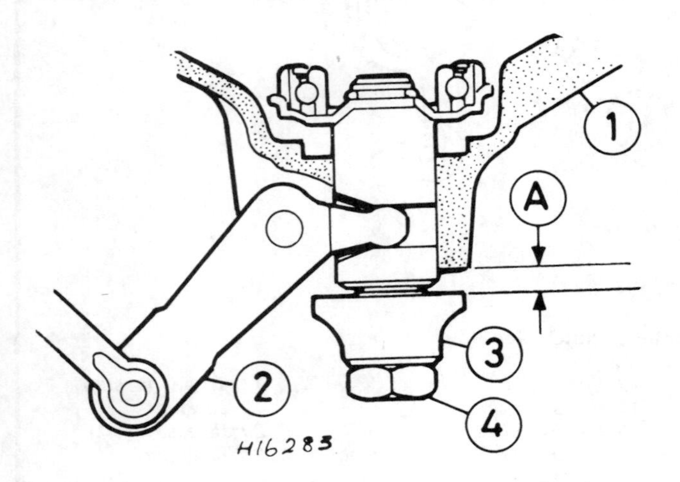

Fig. 14.19 Verto clutch throw-out stop adjustment (Sec 8)

1 Clutch cover
2 Release lever
3 Throw-out stop
4 Locknut
A = 6.5 mm

Elimination of judder (all models)
35 All Minis suffer to some extent from clutch judder when moving away from rest. The Verto clutch, referred to in the previous paragraphs of this Section, is the latest (and hopefully the most successful) modification aimed at overcoming clutch judder.
36 Possible causes of clutch judder are:

(a) Damaged or distorted release bearing housing (also known as 'clutch end cover'), diaphragm spring or pressure plate
(b) Flywheel friction face damaged, taper damaged, or run-out excessive
(c) Driven (friction) plate contaminated, warped or sticking on splines
(d) Primary gear endfloat incorrect

37 When the driven plate is found to be sticking on its splines, clean the splines, but take great care not to over lubricate them. A new plate will be supplied with a very small quantity of grease applied to its splines and this is all that is needed; any more grease will only fly off the splines and contaminate the plate linings.
38 Misalignment or distortion of the release bearing housing (clutch end cover) may be checked by removing the clutch components from the housing and crankshaft, then fitting BL tool 18G 1247 onto the crankshaft before sliding the cover into contact with the flywheel housing.
39 If the cover spigot will not enter the flywheel housing, then a misalignment problem exists and the spigot must be relieved until it enters the housing freely. It is acceptable to file the spigot to size, but this must be done carefully; use a lathe if possible. Correct alignment will not be achieved if the spigot is a firm or interference fit in the housing.
40 In view of the number of modifications already made, and the possibility of more to come, you are advised to consult your BL dealer or reputable parts supplier before purchasing any clutch components with a view to eliminating judder.

Replacement clutch covers – timing apertures
41 From 1986, all replacement clutch end covers for A-series engines will be supplied with the timing inspection hole blanked off by an aluminium membrane.
42 If one of these new covers is to be fitted to an earlier engine which does not have timing marks on the timing chain cover and crankshaft pulley, then the aluminium membrane should be broken out to allow the timing marks on the flywheel to be seen.

Modifications – 1989 on
43 When removing the clutch slave cylinder or the clutch and flywheel assembly, it is necessary to first remove the windscreen washer fluid reservoir and pump.

9 Manual gearbox

Third motion shaft bearing
1 It has been found that in some instances failure of the third motion shaft bearing has been caused by the first speed gear rubbing against the plastic ball bearing cage, resulting in the cage breaking up. Therefore, when renewing the bearing, or when removing the transmission for any other reason, it is worthwhile checking the condition of the plastic cage.
2 Where the plastic cage has been worn the first speed gear should be renewed, together with the bearing.

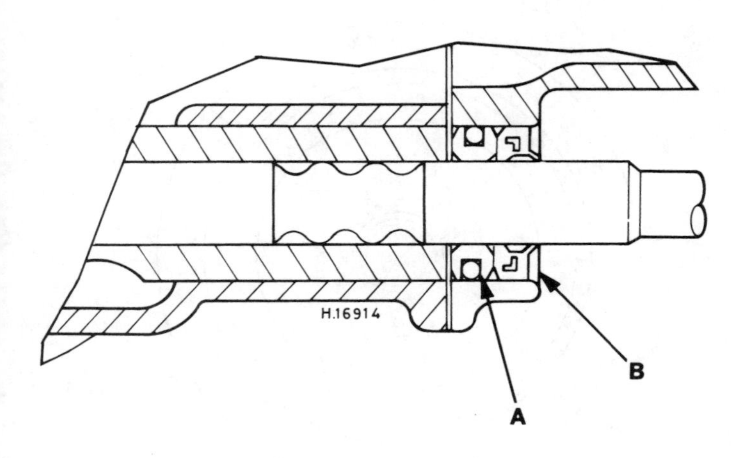

Fig. 14.20 Selector shaft seal and bush (Sec 9)

A Bush B Seal

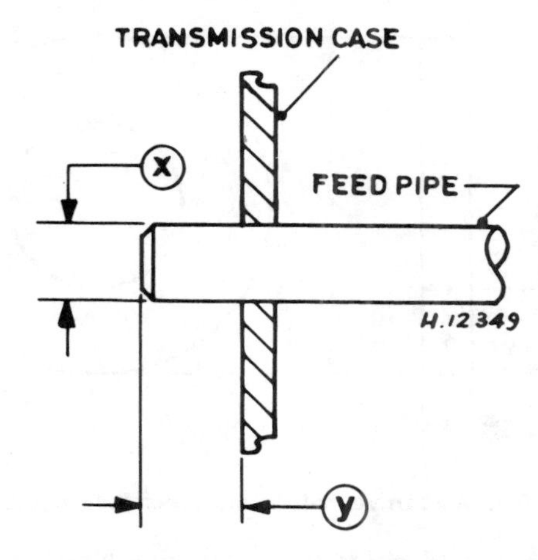

Fig. 14.21 Automatic transmission feed pipe dimensions (Sec 10)

X = Pipe diameter 8.692 to 8.717 mm
Y = End clearance 9.525 to 11.099 mm

Mainshaft – modification 1985 on

3 Later models have a modified mainshaft with a larger threaded portion and larger locknut.

4 This should be taken into account if the mainshaft is renewed because of breakage.

Selector shaft – oil leakage

5 Oil leakage from the gear selector shaft oil seal may be cured by fitting a nylon bush and O-ring seal, obtainable from your dealer, behind the seal (Fig. 14.20).

6 The bush will align the shaft centrally in the seal, making the seal more effective.

7 Later gearboxes are fitted with a larger type of nylon bush during production and should not need modifying.

8 This later bush is not suitable for use on any gearbox to which it has not been fitted as standard.

9 After fitting a nylon bush to the selector shaft, check selection of all gears; any stiffness evident will indicate that the gearbox is not suitable for modification, and the bush should be removed.

Fault diagnosis

10 Should gear selection prove difficult, then suspect the roll pin of the remote control assembly of becoming displaced from the rod yoke. If this fault has occurred, then refer to your BL dealer or a reputable parts supplier for advice on preventing recurrence of the problem.

11 In the event of the gearchange remote control reverse gear stop plate becoming detached, again refer the problem to your BL dealer who will have information on relevant modifications.

12 Should reverse gear engagement be difficult on 1000 models, especially when the engine is hot, the primary drive gear may be sticking to the crankshaft due to carbon 'bleeding' from the inner bush. A modified bush has been introduced from approximately VIN 412928 and this may be fitted to earlier models. When fitting the bush, adjust the primary gear endfloat to the maximum given in the Specifications in Chapter 6.

10 Automatic transmission

Fault diagnosis

1 It is possible that a condition known as 'tie-up' (more than one gear selected) on light throttle 3rd to 4th upshifts with D selected will be experienced. This problem will be due to pressure loss between the top/reverse clutch feed pipe and governor housing.

2 Should this fault occur, it will be necessary to remove the governor assembly and check the feed pipe end-to-transmission casing clearance. The pipe must also be examined for signs of damage or distortion and renewed if necessary.

3 Consult your BL dealer if you think it necessary to carry out these checks; the operation is beyond the scope of this manual. For information, the pipe diameter and end clearance are shown in the accompanying figure (Fig. 14.21). If end clearance is not sufficient, remove the transmission front cover and carefully lever the pipe towards the governor. Take great care not to distort the pipe when refitting the governor; retain the pipe in position with a suitable lever to prevent it from being pushed back into the casing.

4 If, with N or P selected and the engine at idle, a buzzing noise is heard from the transmission casing, then suspect a faulty torque converter feed pipe valve and refer the problem to your BL dealer who will have the relevant information on modified valves.

Torque converter removal – special tool

5 The instructions given in Chapter 1, Section 13 for removing the torque converter include the use of a special tool.

6 A suitable puller may be made up as follows.

7 Cut a disc 96 mm in diameter from a mild steel sheet 15 mm thick.

8 Drill and tap a hole in the centre of the disc which will accept a suitable size bolt, which will enter the threaded crankshaft and is long enough to bottom in the crankshaft when in use, but will not engage in the thread.

9 A shorter bolt and suitable spacer may be used. Ensure it is possible to remove the spacer before inserting it into the crankshaft.

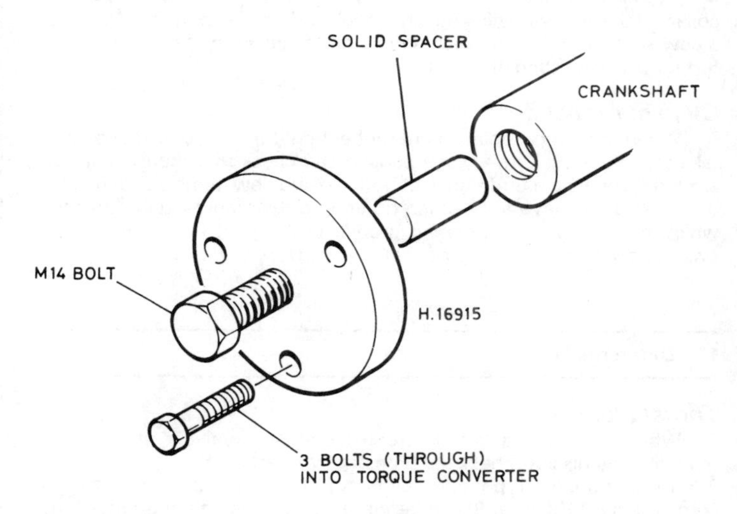

Fig. 14.22 Showing locally manufactured puller for removing the torque converter (Sec 10)

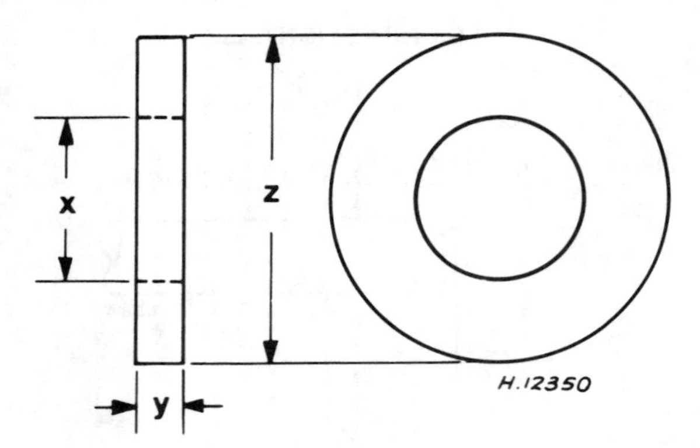

Fig. 14.23 Driveshaft fitting special washer (Sec 11)

X = 25 mm *Z = 50 mm*
Y = 6.5 mm

10 Drill a further three holes equidistant from the centre, which will line up with the three bolt holes in the torque converter.
11 By using three bolts of the same size as the torque converter bolts, but approximately 12 mm longer, the 'puller' can be bolted to the torque converter and the taper seat 'broken' by screwing in the central bolt.
12 The internal threaded portion of the crankshaft should be protected during this operation.

11 Driveshafts and universal joints

Driveshaft fitting – Cooper S (up to 1971) and 1275 GT

1 The following procedure must be observed during fitting of the driveshafts to Mini 1275 GT and Cooper S models, otherwise it is possible that the split collar fitted beneath the shaft to hub retaining nut will become clamped to the shaft before the shaft is fully home in the hub bearings, resulting in noise and excessive wear of the bearing spacer, shaft splines and associated component parts.
2 Insert the driveshaft through the swivel hub, but do not fit the split collar. Obtain a plain washer of the dimensions shown in the accompanying figure (Fig. 14.23). If necessary, make the washer from mild steel.
3 Fit the plain washer over the driveshaft end. Fit the shaft retaining nut and tighten it to 150 lbf ft (203 Nm) to seat the shaft in the hub bearings. Remove the nut and washer. Smear engine oil over the driveshaft threads.
4 Examine the split collar and renew it if damaged or worn. Fit the collar. Fit the shaft retaining nut and retighten it to 150 lbf ft (203 Nm). Fit a new split pin to lock the nut in position. If necessary, tighten the nut further to allow fitting of the pin.

CV joint rubber boot

5 When ordering a replacement rubber boot for a CV joint, if possible take along the old item for comparison and check that the mouldings around the inner circumference of both old and new items are identical.
6 Later boots have a V-section rib around their inner circumference which fits into a corresponding groove in the joint body. *Under no circumstances fit a new type of boot to an old type joint.*

12 Differential unit

Thrust block

1 When overhauling the differential unit of a vehicle fitted with manual transmission, check the type of driveshaft joint.
2 If offset sphere type inner joints are fitted, then the thrust block (item 7, Fig 8.1, Chapter 8) can be discarded as it is no longer fitted to differential units in production. If Hardy-Spicer joints are fitted, then the thrust block must be retained.

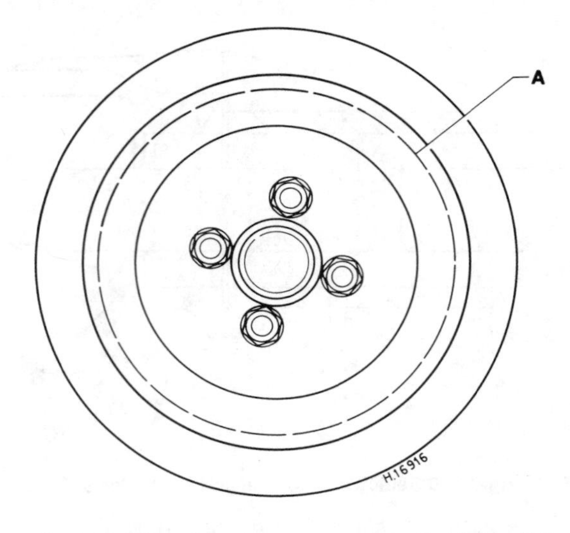

Fig. 14.24 Disc run-out measurement point A (Sec 13)

13 Braking system

Disc brakes

1 The disc brakes fitted to the Mini 25 and all models with 12 inch wheels are the same as those fitted to the 1275 GT described in Chapter 9.

Front brake – run-out check

2 The procedure for checking the front brake disc run-out is given in Chapter 9, but it should be noted that the measurement of disc run-out should be taken at the point shown in Fig. 14.24.
3 This is best achieved by using a dial test indicator clamped to a suitable part of the suspension members.
4 Also, when attempting to rectify run-out by repositioning the disc, the disc and drive flange assembly should be removed together and rotated through 45 degrees on the driveshaft splines.
5 This procedure may be repeated until the tolerance given in the Specifications Section of this Supplement is achieved.
6 If the tolerances cannot be met, renew the brake disc.

Front disc brakes – brake pad squeal

7 To alleviate the problem of brake pad squeal from front brake pads, dismantle the brake pads, shims and anti-rattle springs, as described in Chapter 9.
8 Thoroughly clean all brake dust from the calipers and pistons, particularly in the brake pad backing plate locating area. **Note:** *Asbestos dust can be harmful if inhaled. Wipe away the dust carefully in a well-ventilated area if possible. Do not use compressed air and do not inhale the dust.*
9 Smear a small amount of high temperature, lead-free, anti-seize grease onto the edges of the pad backing plates which contact the calipers, and onto both sides of the shims.
10 Do not allow any grease onto the friction material of the brake pads.
11 Reassemble and test the front brake disc assembly as described in Chapter 9.

Brake master cylinder – revised front/rear split

12 From November 1985, a new type of brake master cylinder with a revised front/rear split was introduced. This new cylinder has a stepped bore and the primary and secondary circuits have been reversed.
13 Should an older type brake master cylinder require renewing, then one of these new type cylinders will be supplied.
14 To fit the new cylinder to pre November 1985 vehicles two modified brake pipes will be required and, on vehicles without a brake fluid reservoir level indicator light, a conversion wiring loom is also required.
15 These should be available from your dealer.
16 For identification purposes, the new cylinder has a yellow plastic

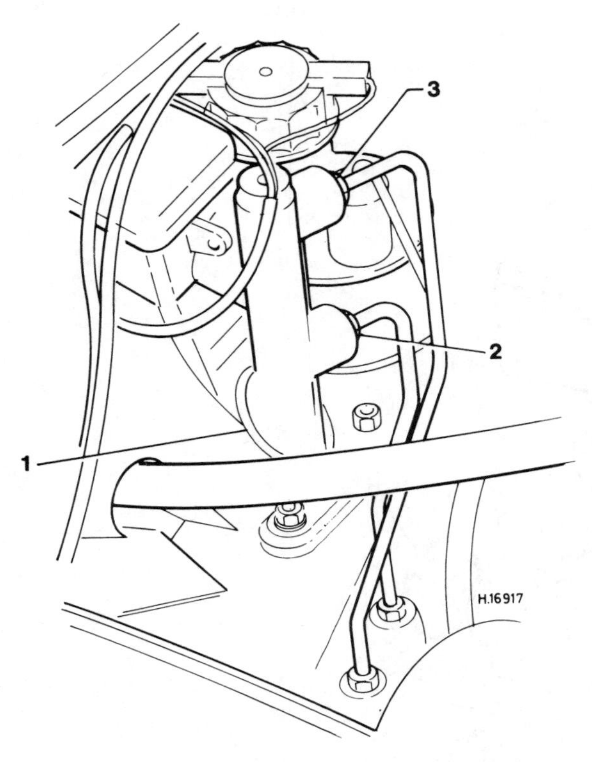

Fig. 14.25 Later type master cylinder (Sec 13)

1 Yellow band
2 Larger union
3 Smaller union

band around its body Fig. 14.25, and the lower union nut is larger than the upper (on earlier cylinders, these were the same size).
17 A vehicle with front/rear split may be identified by the pressure reducing valve mounted on the bulkhead crossmember (Fig. 14.26).
18 To fit a new type master cylinder to pre November 1985 vehicles, proceed as follows.
19 Remove the brake master cylinder, as described in Chapter 9 (Note: on vehicles equipped with a fluid level indicator, disconnect the wiring connectors from the switch on the cylinder cap).
20 Remove the existing pipelines from the pressure reducing valve (which run to the brake master cylinder).
21 Fit the new pipelines to the pressure reducing valve.
22 Fit the new brake master cylinder, which is a reversal of removing, then connect the new pipelines to it.
23 To fit the wiring conversion loom, first cut the connector from the end of the two black and white wires removed from the brake warning switch on the old cylinder (Fig. 14.27).
24 Join the two wires together, fit a Lucar connector, and connect it to one terminal of the float level switch on the new master cylinder.
25 Using black cable, make up an earth lead with a Lucar connector at one end and an eyelet at the other.
26 The earth lead should be 533 mm (21 in) long, and is connected to the other connector on the brake master cylinder switch and routed along the wiring loom in the engine bay to the existing earth screw.
27 Fill and bleed the hydraulic system, as described in Chapter 9, and check the operation of both the brake warning light and the low level warning light.

Braking system (1989 on) – description

28 As from 1989 models the brake master cylinder is of the horizontal type with a servo unit fitted directly behind it.

Tandem master cylinder (1989 on) – removal and refitting

29 Position the car over an inspection pit or alternatively jack up the car and support on axle stands.

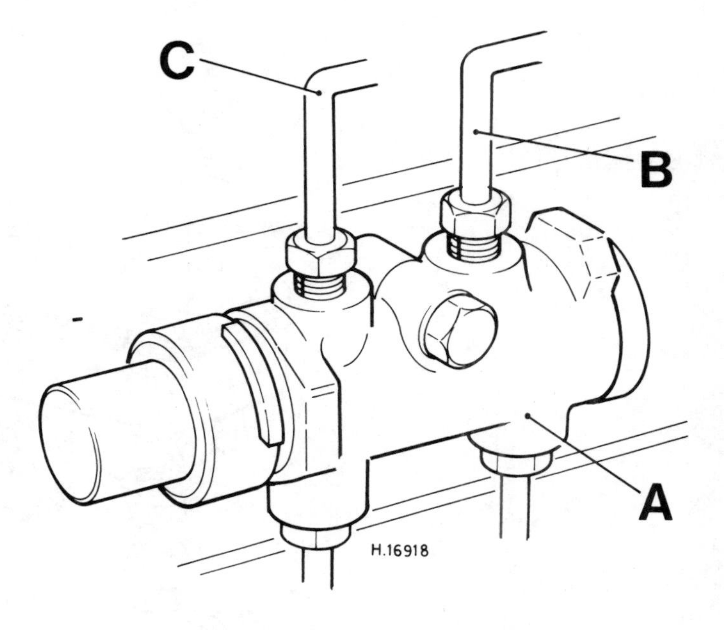

Fig. 14.26 Pressure reducing valve (Sec 13)

A Valve body
B Larger union
C Smaller union

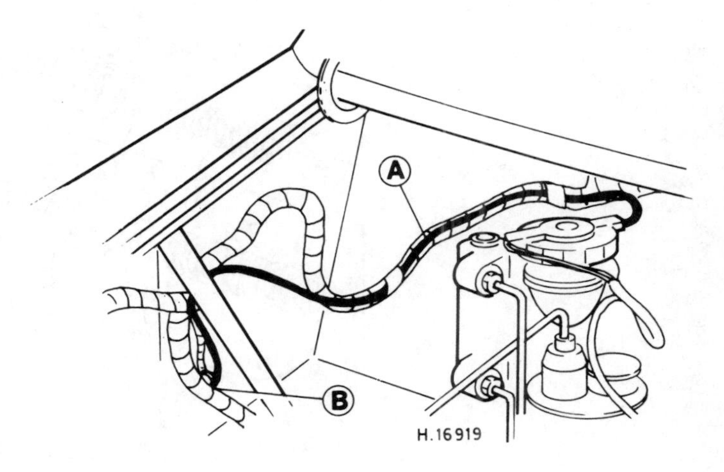

Fig. 14.27 Braking system conversion wiring loom location (Sec 13)

A Loom　*B Earth screw*

30 Connect a bleed tube to both the front caliper and rear wheel cylinder on the right-hand side and place the ends of the tubes in suitable containers.
31 Open both bleed screws and depress the brake pedal until the master cylinder is completely empty, then tighten the bleed screws.
32 Disconnect the low fluid warning wiring from the brake fluid reservoir filler cap.
33 Place a container or cloth rags beneath the master cylinder to catch spilled fluid.
34 Unscrew the union nuts and disconnect the hydraulic lines from the master cylinder. Stick tape over the outlet ports to prevent the ingress of dust and dirt.
35 Unscrew the mounting nuts securing the master cylinder to the vacuum servo unit, then withdraw it from the engine compartment taking care not to spill any brake fluid on the bodywork.
36 Remove the O-ring from the recess in the master cylinder.

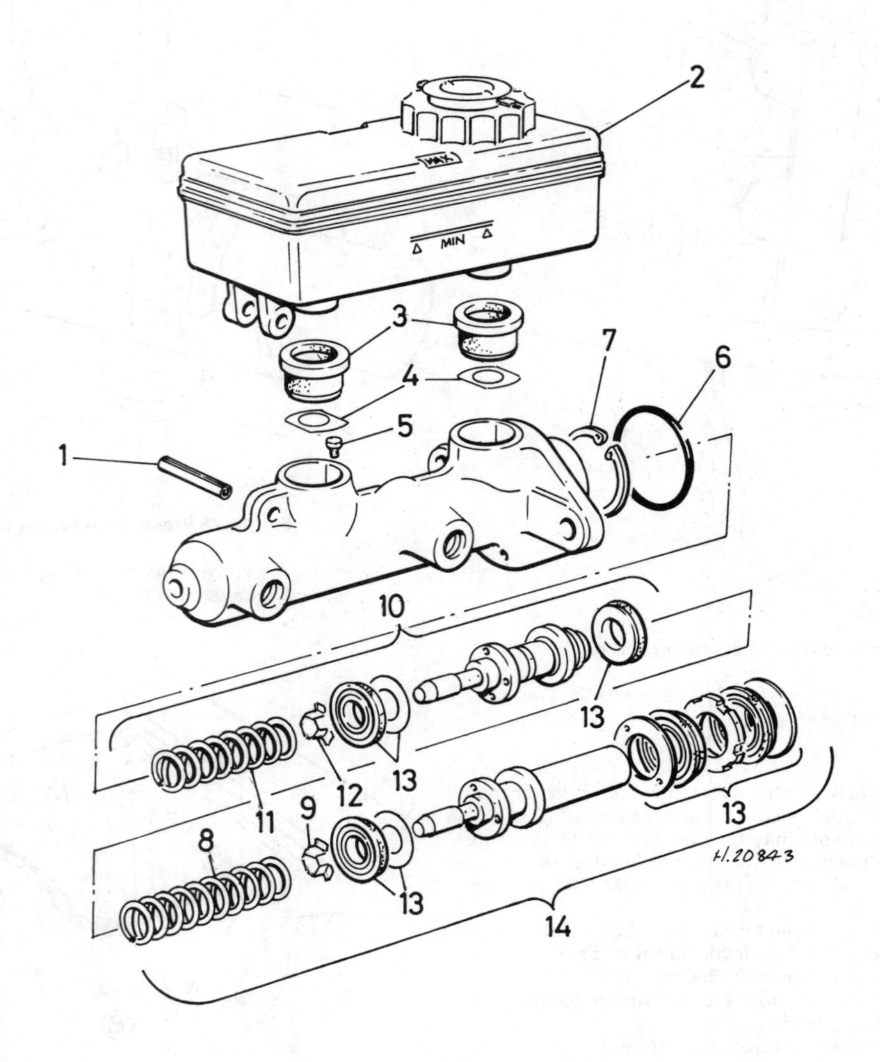

Fig. 14.28 Exploded view of the brake master cylinder fitted to 1989 on models (Sec 13)

1 Roll pin
2 Brake fluid reservoir
3 Sealing washers
4 Metal seating washers
5 Secondary piston stop pin
6 O-ring
7 Circlip
8 Primary spring
9 Spring retainer
10 Secondary piston components
11 Secondary spring
12 Spring retainer
13 Seal and washer
14 Primary piston components

37 Refitting is a reversal of removal, but note the following additional points:

(a) *Smear the O-ring with clean brake fluid before fitting it in the recess*
(b) *Make sure that the pushrod is correctly located in the cylinder*
(c) *Tighten all nuts and bolts to the specified torque. Do not over-tighten the hydraulic line unions*
(d) *On completion, bleed the hydraulic system as described in Chapter 9*
(e) *Check that the low fluid warning system is functioning correctly*

Vacuum servo unit (1989 on) – removal and refitting

38 Disconnect the low brake fluid warning system wiring from the fluid reservoir filler cap.
39 Unscrew the master cylinder mounting nuts from the servo unit.
40 Position a container beneath the master cylinder, then loosen only the hydraulic line union nuts to prevent damage to the lines when the master cylinder is moved from the servo unit. Move the master cylinder from the servo unit, then retighten the union nuts.
41 Disconnect the vacuum hose from the servo unit and release it from the clip.

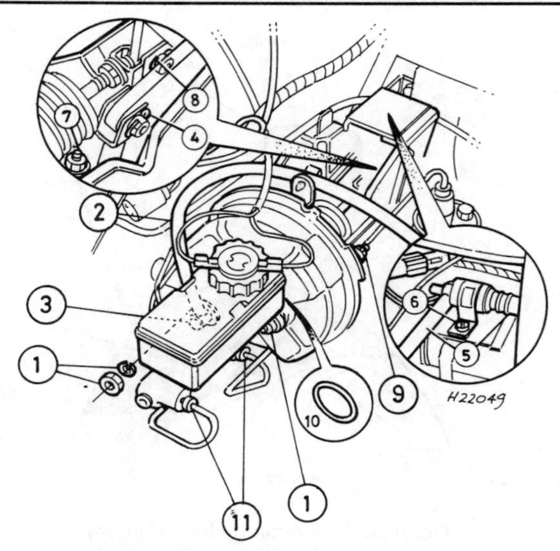

Fig. 14.29 Brake master cylinder and servo unit fitted on 1989 models on (Sec 13)

1 *Master cylinder mounting nuts*
2 *Vacuum hose retaining clip*
3 *One-way vacuum valve*
4 *Brake pedal clevis pin*
5 *Anti run-on valve hoses*
6 *Anti run-on valve mounting nuts*
7 *Servo mounting bracket nuts*
8 *Servo pushrod clevis pin*
9 *Servo-to-mounting bracket nuts*
10 *O-ring*
11 *Brake pipe union nuts*

42 Extract the split pin, and withdraw the clevis pin securing the pushrod to the brake pedal.
43 Disconnect the anti run-on valve hoses and plug them.
44 Unscrew the bolt securing the anti run-on valve to the servo mounting bracket.
45 Unscrew the mounting nuts and bolts and withdraw the servo unit and bracket assembly from the engine compartment.
46 Separate the servo unit from the bracket by disconnecting the clevis and unscrewing the nuts. Prise the O-ring from the recess in the master cylinder.
47 Refitting is a reversal of removal but note the following additional points:

(a) *Smear the O-ring with clean brake fluid*
(b) *If necessary, on completion bleed the hydraulic system with reference to Chapter 9*

Vacuum servo unit air filter (1989 on) – renewal

48 Working in the engine compartment, prise back the rubber boot from the rear of the servo and slide it along the push rod (Fig. 14.30).
49 Prise the air filter from inside the servo body.
50 Cut the new air filter in one place with a sharp knife, then locate it over the pushrod and push it into the servo body.
51 Refit the rubber boot.

14 Electrical system

Starter motor – 1986 on

General

1 At the beginning of 1986 a Lucas M79 pre-engaged starter motor was fitted in place of the inertia type used on earlier models. Removal and refitting procedures for the motor and solenoid are given in the following paragraphs but at the time of writing information on repair and overhaul was unavailable.

Removal and refitting

2 Disconnect the battery negative lead.

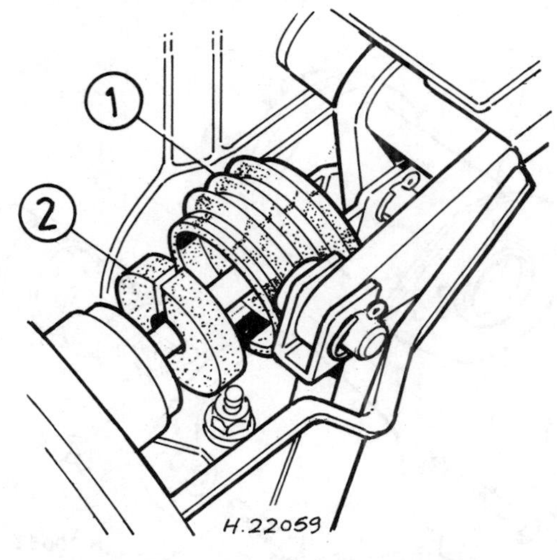

Fig. 14.30 Vacuum servo unit air filter (Sec 13)

1 *Rubber boot* 2 *Air filter*

3 From within the engine compartment release the horn and horn bracket and move them to one side.
4 Undo the nut and disconnect the leads at the upper terminal on the solenoid.
5 Disconnect the leads at the two solenoid spade terminals after identifying their positions.
6 Undo the two starter retaining bolts and remove the unit from the car.
7 Refitting is the reversal of removal.

Solenoid removal and refitting

8 Remove the starter as previously described.
9 Undo the nut and disconnect the lead at the lower terminal on the solenoid.
10 Undo the two bolts and remove the solenoid yoke (Fig. 14.32).
11 Withdraw the plunger spring, unhook the plunger from the starter operating lever and remove the plunger.
12 Refitting is a reversal of removal.

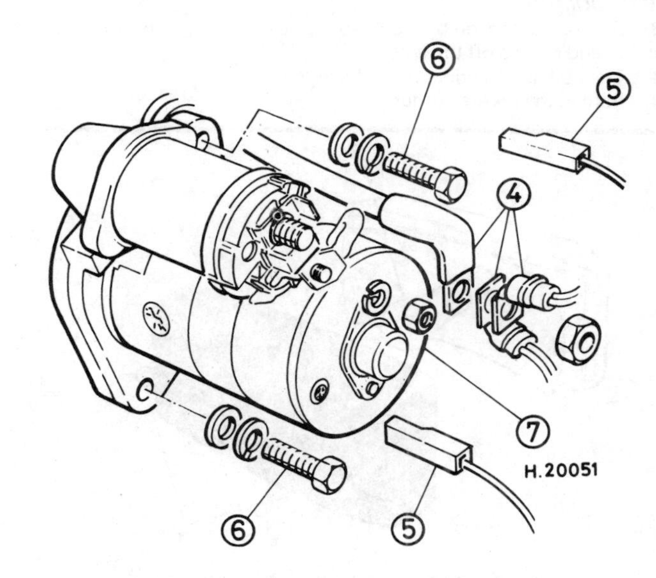

Fig. 14.31 Pre-engaged starter motor attachments (Sec 14)

4 *Solenoid upper terminal leads*
5 *Solenoid spade terminal leads*
6 *Retaining bolts*
7 *Starter motor*

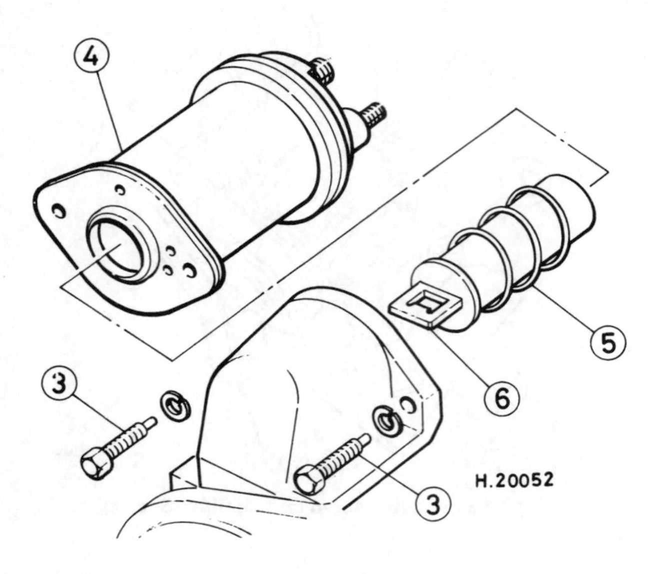

Fig. 14.32 Pre-engaged starter solenoid removal (Sec 14)

3 *Retaining bolts*
4 *Solenoid yoke*
5 *Plunger spring*
6 *Plunger*

Alternator

13 When overhauling or replacing an alternator, check that the spring washer is fitted beneath the pulley retaining nut. Failure to fit this washer can result in separation of the pulley halves with the resulting loss in fanbelt drive.

Side repeater light

14 Access to the rear of the light and the bulbholder is gained through the front wheel arch (Fig. 14.33).

15 Push the bulbholder in and rotate it, this will release it from the rear of the light unit and allow the holder and electrical lead to be drawn down out of the wheel arch.

16 The bulb is a push-fit in the holder.

17 Refit in the reverse order.

Rear foglight

18 Access to the bulb is gained by removing the two lens cover screws and pulling off the lens.

19 The bulb is a bayonet fix in the holder.

20 Refit in the reverse order.

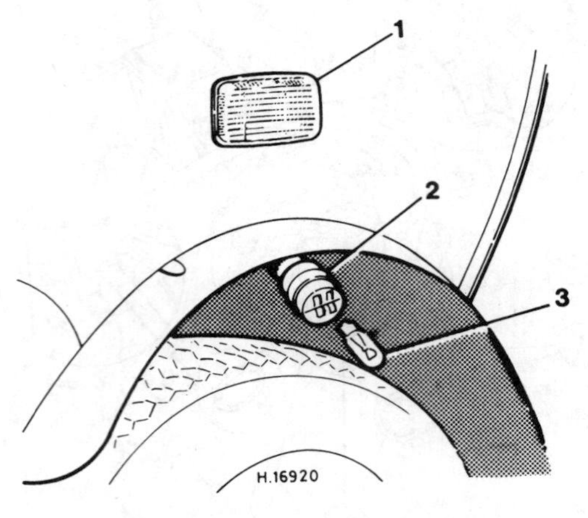

Fig. 14.33 Side repeater light (Sec 14)

1 *Light* 2 *Holder* 3 *Bulb*

Dim-dip unit – removal and refitting

21 Remove the instrument panel as described in Chapter 10.

22 Disconnect the dim-dip unit from the wiring loom connector.

23 Refitting is a reversal of removal.

Dim-dip resistor – removal and refitting

24 Disconnect the battery negative lead.

25 Open the bonnet, and unclip the wiring loom connector on the right-hand side of the engine compartment.

26 Pull the resistor plug from the connector, and release the wiring loom.

27 Unscrew the mounting bolt and withdraw the resistor and mounting plate.

28 Refitting is a reversal of removal.

Radio (1989 on) – removal and refitting

29 Disconnect the battery negative lead.

30 Prise the side covers from the radio, then loosen the two small screws.

31 Press the two screws in to release the radio securing clips.

32 Push the radio out from behind the facia and disconnect the wiring connectors and aerial lead.

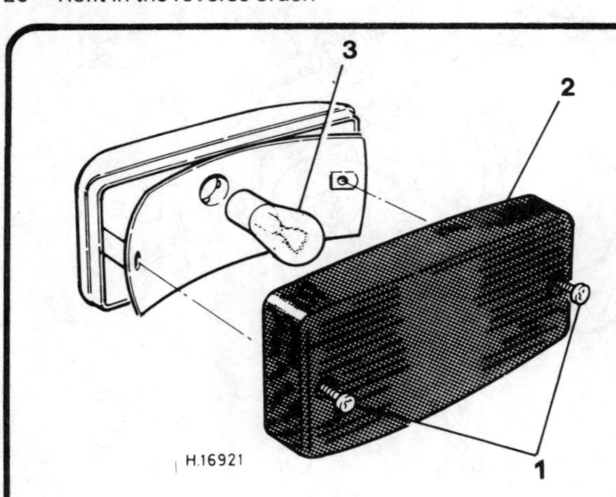

Fig. 14.34 Rear foglight (Sec 14)

1 *Lens retaining screws*
2 *Lens*
3 *Bulb*

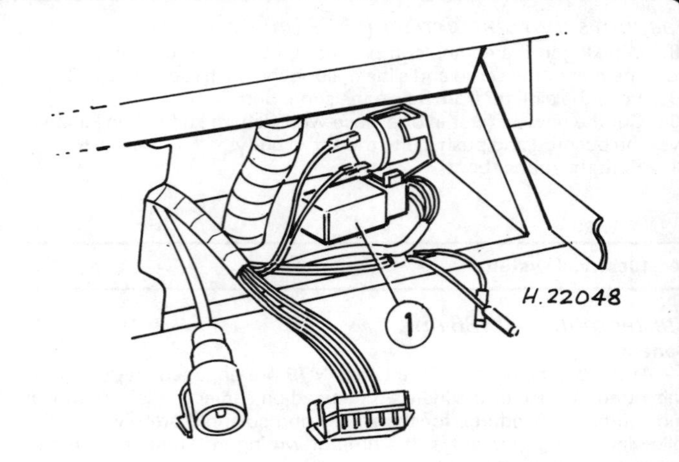

Fig. 14.35 Dim-dip unit (1) located behind the instrument panel (Sec 14)

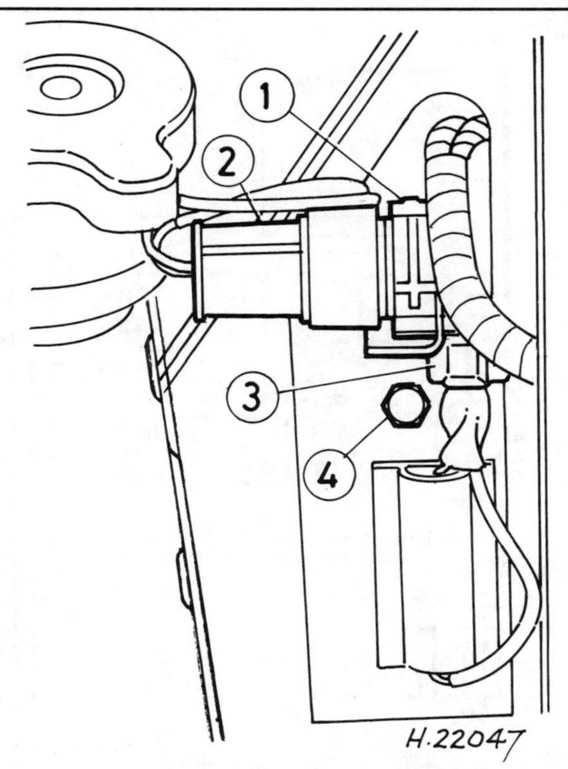

Fig. 14.36 Dim-dip resistor (Sec 14)

1 *Wiring loom connector*
2 *Resistor plug*
3 *Wiring loom clip*
4 *Mounting plate bolt*

33 Refitting is a reversal of removal, but make sure that the radio is fully engaged with the clips.

Mobile radio equipment – interference-free installation

VHF/FM broadcasts

Reception of VHF/FM in an automobile is more prone to problems than the medium and long wavebands. Medium/long wave transmitters are capable of covering considerable distances, but VHF transmitters are restricted to line of sight, meaning ranges of 10 to 50 miles, depending upon the terrain, the effects of buildings and the transmitter power.

Because of the limited range it is necessary to retune on a long journey, and it may be better for those habitually travelling long distances or living in areas of poor provision of transmitters to use an AM radio working on medium/long wavebands.

When conditions are poor, interference can arise, and some of the suppression devices described previously fall off in performance at very high frequencies unless specifically designed for the VHF band. Available suppression devices include reactive HT cable, resistive distributor caps, screened plug caps, screened leads and resistive spark plugs.

For VHF/FM receiver installation the following points should be particularly noted:

(a) *Earthing of the receiver chassis and the aerial mounting is important. Use a separate earthing wire at the radio, and scrape paint away at the aerial mounting.*
(b) *If possible, use a good quality roof aerial to obtain maximum height and distance from interference generating devices on the vehicle.*
(c) *Use of a high quality aerial downlead is important, since losses in cheap cable can be significant.*
(d) *The polarisation of FM transmissions may be horizontal, vertical, circular or slanted. Because of this the optimum mounting angle is at 45° to the vehicle roof.*

Citizens' Band radio (CB)

In the UK, CB transmitter/receivers work within the 27 MHz and 934 MHz bands, using the FM mode. At present interest is concentrated on 27 MHz where the design and manufacture of equipment is less difficult. Maximum transmitted power is 4 watts, and 40 channels spaced 10 kHz apart within the range 27.60125 to 27.99125 MHz are available.

Aerials are the key to effective transmission and reception. Regulations limit the aerial length to 1.65 metres including the loading coil and any associated circuitry, so tuning the aerial is necessary to obtain optimum results. The choice of a CB aerial is dependent on whether it is to be permanently installed or removable, and the performance will hinge on correct tuning and the location point on the vehicle. Common practice is to clip the aerial to the roof gutter or to employ wing mounting where the aerial can be rapidly unscrewed. An alternative is to use the boot rim to render the aerial theftproof, but a popular solution is

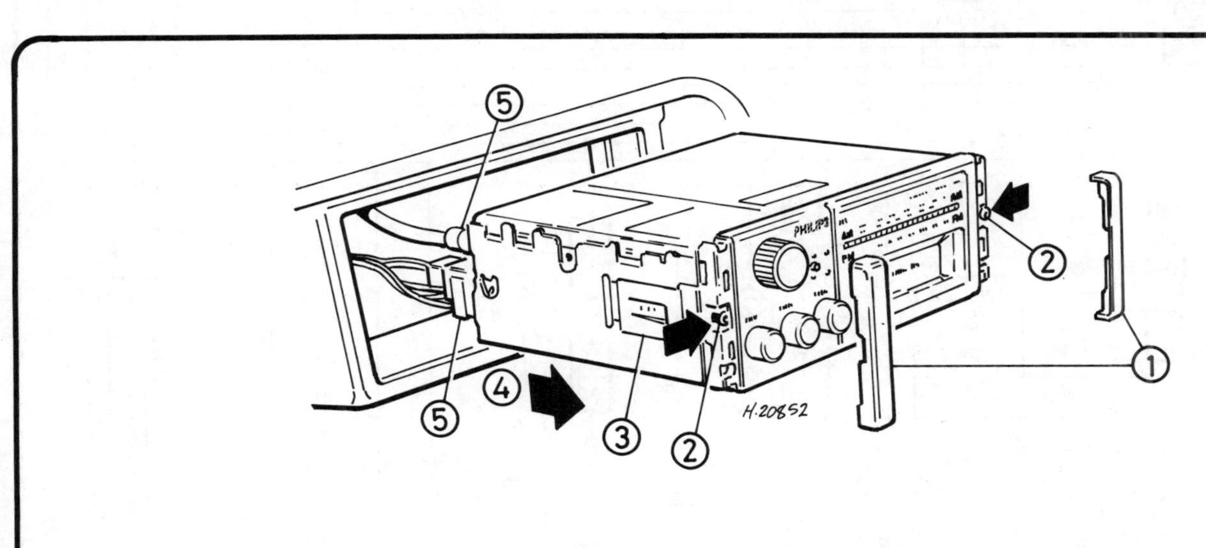

Fig. 14.37 Radio mountings for 1989 on models (Sec 14)

1 *Side covers*
2 *Securing screws*
3 *Holding clips*
4 *Direction of removal*
5 *Multi-plug and aerial lead*

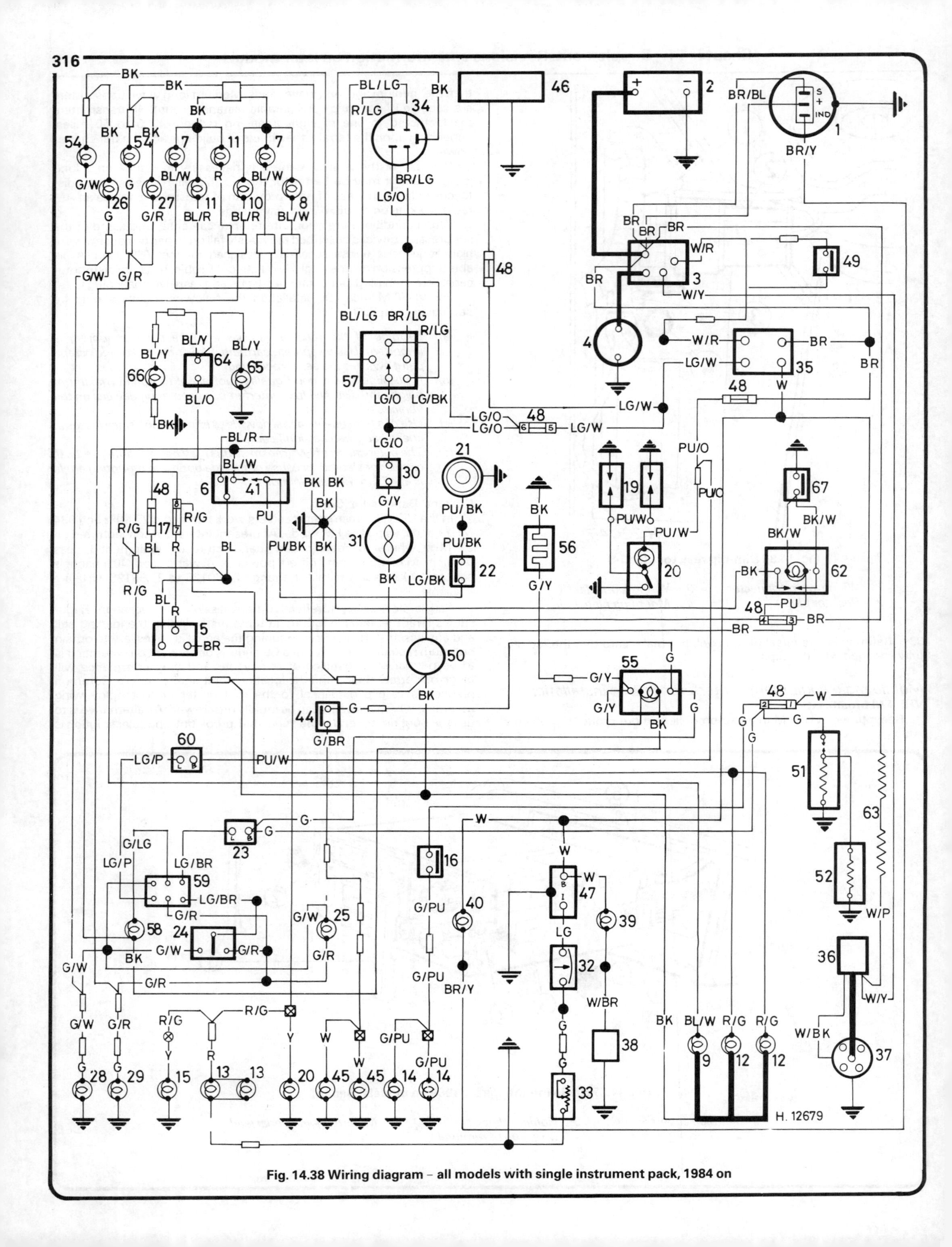

Fig. 14.38 Wiring diagram – all models with single instrument pack, 1984 on

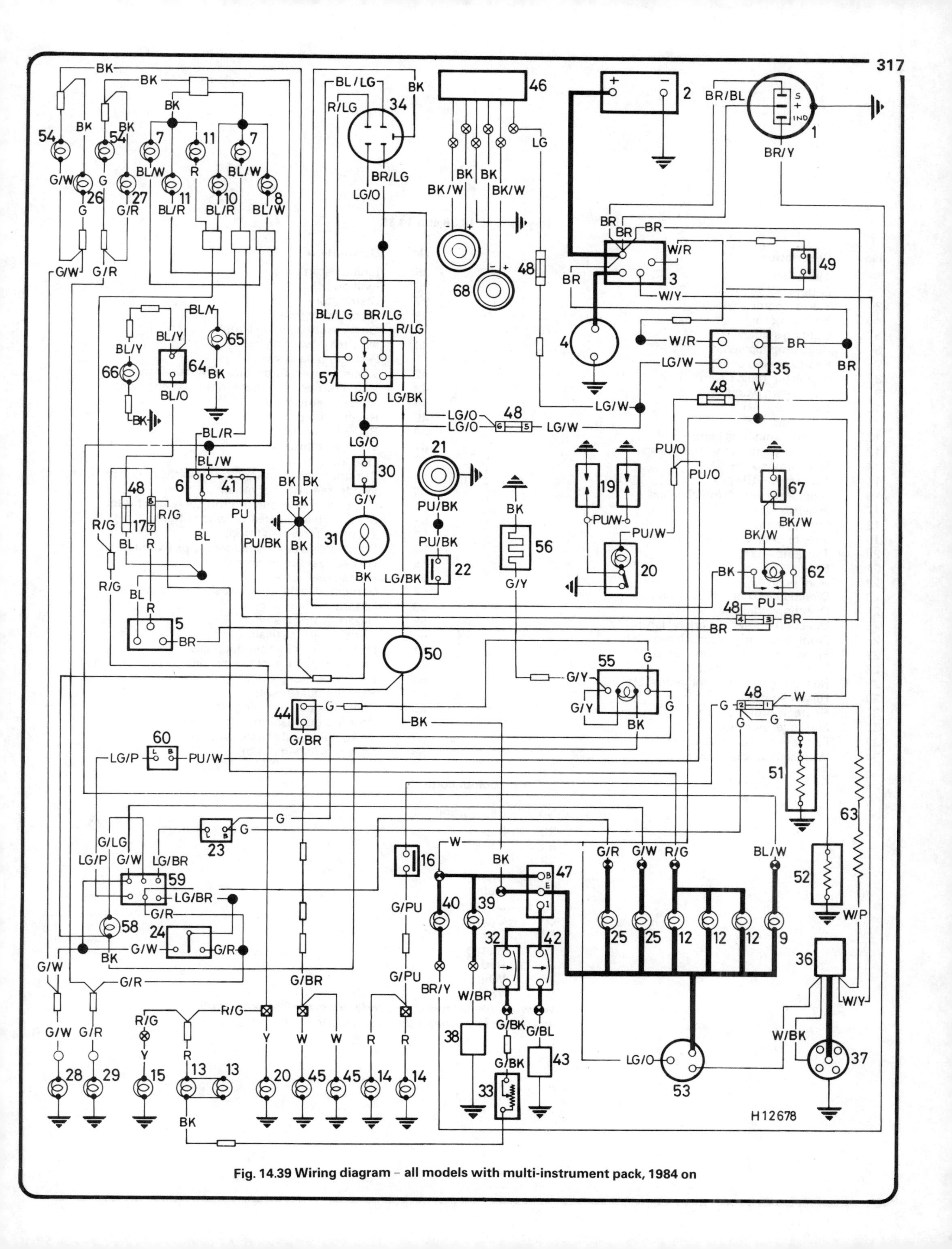

Fig. 14.39 Wiring diagram – all models with multi-instrument pack, 1984 on

Key to Figs. 14.38 and 14.39

No	Description
1	Alternator
2	Battery
3	Starter motor solenoid
4	Starter motor
5	Lighting switch
6	Headlamp dip switch
7	Headlamp dip beam
8	Headlamp main beam
9	Main beam warning lamp
10	Sidelamp – RH
11	Sidelamp – LH
12	Panel illumination lamps
13	Number plate illumination lamps
14	Stop-lamps
15	Tail lamps – RH
16	Stop-lamp switch (mechanical)
17	Fusebox
18	Interior lamp
19	Interior lamp switch (door)
20	Tail lamp – LH
21	Horn
22	Horn push
23	Direction indicator flasher unit
24	Direction indicator switch
25	Direction indicator warning lamp
26	Front direction indicator lamp – RH
27	Front direction indicator lamp – LH
28	Rear direction indicator lamp – RH
29	Rear direction indicator lamp – LH
30	Heater switch
31	Heater motor
32	Fuel level indicator
33	Fuel level indicator tank unit
34	Windscreen wiper motor

No	Description
35	Ignition/start switch
36	Ignition coil
37	Distributor
38	Oil pressure switch
39	Oil pressure warning lamp
40	No charge warning lamp
41	Headlamp flash switch
42	Water temperature indicator (when fitted)
43	Water temperature transmitter (when fitted)
44	Reverse lamp switch
45	Reverse lamp
46	Radio (when fitted)
47	Voltage stabilizer
48	Line fuse
49	Automatic gearbox ignition inhibitor switch (when fitted)
50	Windscreen washer motor
51	Induction heater and thermostat (when fitted)
52	Suction chamber heater (when fitted)
53	Tachometer (when fitted)
54	Direction indicator repeater lamps (when fitted)
55	Heated rear screen switch
56	Heated rear screen
57	Combined windscreen washer and wiper switch
58	Hazard warning lamp
59	Hazard warning switch
60	Hazard warning flasher unit
61	Printed circuit instrument panel
62	Brake low fluid level warning lamp and test switch
63	Ballast resistor (cable)
64	Rear fog-guard switch
65	Rear fog-guard warning lamp
66	Rear fog-guard lamp
67	Brake fluid level sensor switch
68	Speakers (when fitted)

Colour code

No	Description
BL	Blue
BK	Black
BR	Brown
G	Green
GR	Slate
LG	Light green
O	Orange
P	Pink
PU	Purple
R	Red
W	White
Y	Yellow

When a cable has two colour code letters the first denotes the main colour and the second denotes the tracer colour.

Key to Fig. 14.40

No	Description
1	Direction indicator unit
2	Direction indicator switch
3	Hazard warning switch
4	Hazard warning unit
5	Hazard warning light
6	RH front direction indicator
7	RH side repeater lamp
8	RH rear direction indicator
9	LH front direction indicator
10	LH side repeater lamp
11	LH rear direction indicator
12	Automatic transmission inhibitor switch
13	Distributor
14	Ignition coil
15	Starter relay
16	Ignition switch
17	Starter motor solenoid
18	Ballast resistor
19	In-line fuse
20	Fusebox
21	Stop lamp switch
22	Dim/dip resistor
23	Heated rear window switch
24	Heater motor
25	Reversing lamp switch
26	Interior light
27	RH front door switch
28	Fuel tank sender unit
29	Radio – single speaker
30	Radio/cassette player
31	RH stop light
32	RH sidelamp
33	LH sidelamp
34	Headlamp main beam
35	Headlamp dip beam
36	Brake failure light test switch
37	Ignition warning light
38	LH indicator warning light
39	RH indicator warning light

No	Description
40	Main beam warning light
41	Coolant temperature gauge
42	Fuel gauge
43	Rear fog lamp warning lamp
44	Panel lights
45	Heater switch
46	Horn switch
47	Voltage stabilizer
48	Battery
49	Lighting switch
50	Headlamp dipswitch
51	Number plate illumination lamps
52	RH tail lamp
53	LH tail lamp
54	Horn
55	Windscreen wiper motor
56	Headlamp flasher switch
57	Rear fog lamp switch
58	Windscreen washer motor
59	Heated rear window element
60	LH front door switch
61	Wash/wipe switch
62	Alternator
63	Coolant thermistor
64	Oil pressure switch
65	Brake fluid level switch
66	Oil pressure warning light
67	Tachometer
68	RH/single door speaker
69	LH front door speaker
70	LH stop light
71	Rear fog lamp
72	Dim/dip relay
73	LH reversing lamp
74	RH reversing lamp
75	Emission control valve switch
76	Heated rear window warning light
77	Vacuum solenoid valve

Colour code

BK	Black
BL	Blue
BR	Brown
G	Green
GR	Slate
LG	Light green
O	Orange
P	Pink
PU	Purple
R	Red
W	White
Y	Yellow

When a cable has two colour code letters, the first denotes the main colour and the second the tracer colour

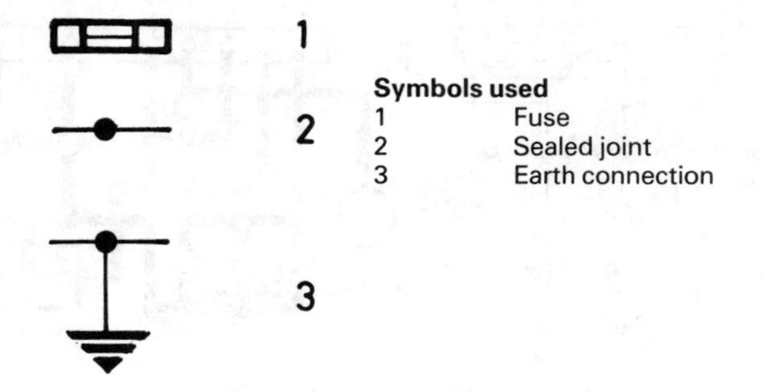

Symbols used

1	Fuse
2	Sealed joint
3	Earth connection

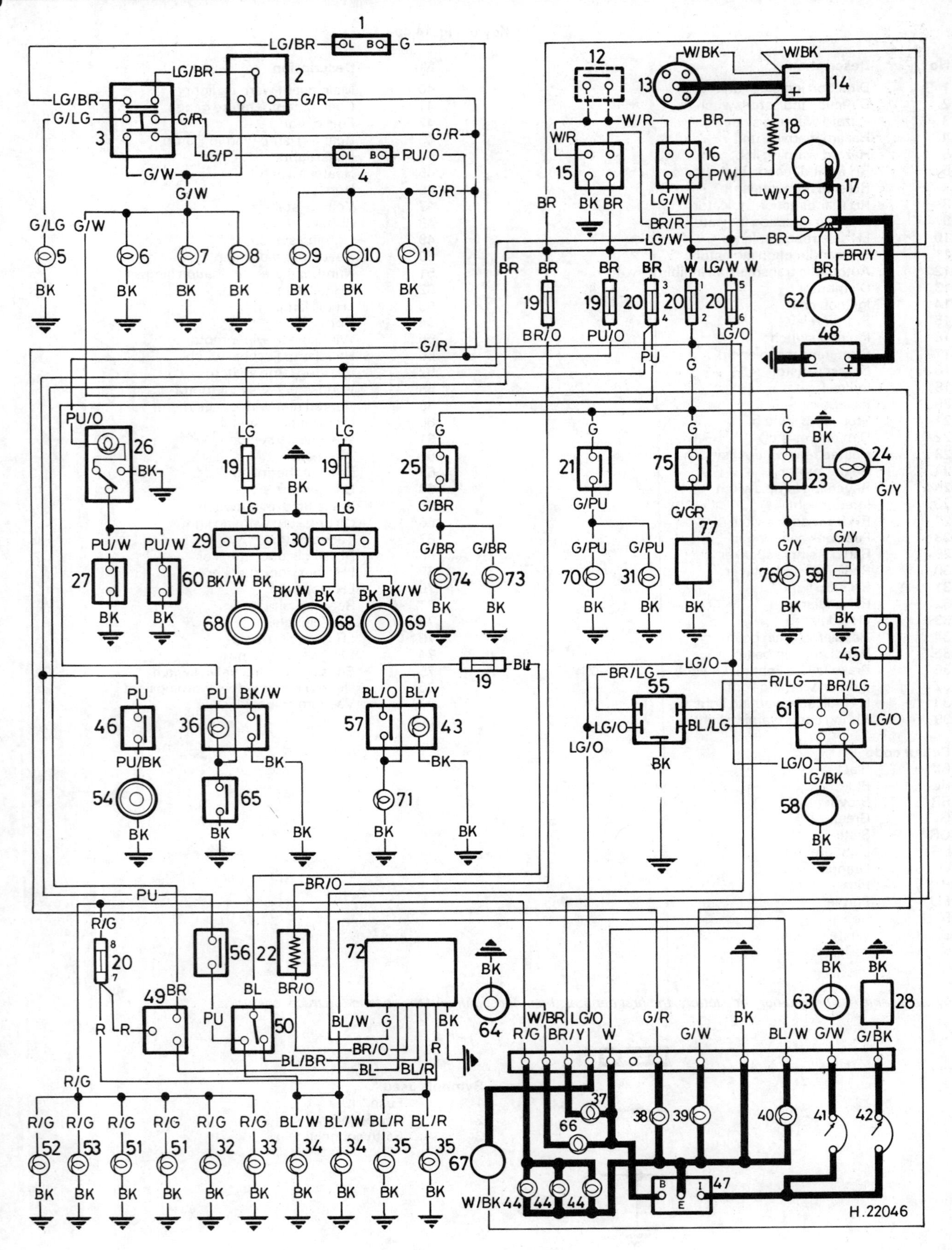

Fig. 14.40 Wiring diagram – 1988 on

to use the 'magmount' – a type of mounting having a strong magnetic base clamping to the vehicle at any point, usually the roof.

Aerial location determines the signal distribution for both transmission and reception, but it is wise to choose a point away from the engine compartment to minimise interference from vehicle electrical equipment.

The aerial is subject to considerable wind and acceleration forces. Cheaper units will whip backwards and forwards and in so doing will alter the relationship with the metal surface of the vehicle with which it forms a ground plane aerial system. The radiation pattern will change correspondingly, giving rise to break-up of both incoming and outgoing signals.

Interference problems on the vehicle carrying CB equipment fall into two categories:

(a) *Interference to nearby TV and radio receivers when transmitting.*
(b) *Interference to CB set reception due to electrical equipment on the vehicle.*

Problems of breakthrough to TV and radio are not frequent, but can be difficult to solve. Mostly trouble is not detected or reported because the vehicle is moving and the symptoms rapidly disappear at the TV/radio receiver, but when the CB set is used as a base station any trouble with nearby receivers will soon result in a complaint.

It must not be assumed by the CB operator that his equipment is faultless, for much depends upon the design. Harmonics (that is, multiples) of 27 MHz may be transmitted unknowingly and these can fall into other user's bands. Where trouble of this nature occurs, low pass filters in the aerial or supply leads can help, and should be fitted in base station aerials as a matter of course. In stubborn cases it may be necessary to call for assistance from the licensing authority, or, if possible, to have the equipment checked by the manufacturers.

Interference received on the CB set from the vehicle equipment is, fortunately, not usually a severe problem. The precautions outlined previously for radio/cassette units apply, but there are some extra points worth noting.

It is common practice to use a slide-mount on CB equipment enabling the set to be easily removed for use as a base station, for example. Care must be taken that the slide mount fittings are properly earthed and that first class connection occurs between the set and slide-mount.

Vehicle manufacturers in the UK are required to provide suppression of electrical equipment to cover 40 to 250 MHz to protect TV and VHF radio bands. Such suppression appears to be adequately effective at 27 MHz, but suppression of individual items such as alternators/dynamos, clocks, stabilisers, flashers, wiper motors, etc, may still be necessary. The suppression capacitors and chokes available from auto-electrical suppliers for entertainment receivers will usually give the required results with CB equipment.

Other vehicle radio transmitters

Besides CB radio already mentioned, a considerable increase in the use of transceivers (ie combined transmitter and receiver units) has taken place in the last decade. Previously this type of equipment was fitted mainly to military, fire, ambulance and police vehicles, but a large business radio and radio telephone usage has developed.

Generally the suppression techniques described previously will suffice, with only a few difficult cases arising. Suppression is carried out to satisfy the 'receive mode', but care must be taken to use heavy duty chokes in the equipment supply cables since the loading on 'transmit' is relatively high.

15 Suspension and steering

Front hub bearings

1 Where front hub bearings have become noisy or generally worn, examine the oil seal spacer and driveshaft bearing journals. In certain circumstances, fretting between the drive flange and spacer can occur, leading to bearing contamination. Renew any parts as necessary.

Rear hub bearings – water contamination

2 If the rear hub bearings have become contaminated by water, then remove the brake backplate from the suspension arm (see Section 7, Chapter 9), clean the mating surfaces of each component and apply a jointing compound to one of the surfaces before fitting the components back together.

Front and rear hub bearings (disc brake models)

3 Models with disc brakes may have taper roller bearings in both the front and rear hubs. The removal, refitting and torque settings are as given in Chapter 11 for disc brake models.

4 The endfloat tolerances are given in the Specifications and are measured at the hub circumference with the wheel removed. There is no need to change the bearings until the maximum endfloat has been exceeded.

Rear hub oil seal (disc brake models)

5 When fitting the rear hub oil seal on disc brake models ensure it is positioned with its open end facing *away* from the bearing.

Rear suspension – Saloon

6 With the car in motion a knocking noise from the left-hand rear corner is likely to be caused by a build-up of tolerances in the suspension, leading to fouling between the top stud of the left-hand rear shock absorber and the fuel tank.

7 To obviate this noise, regain sufficient clearance by making up two steel spacers; each one 55 mm x 10 mm x 3 mm in size, and fit them between the tank flange and floor panel as shown in the accompanying figure (Fig. 14.41).

Steering lock – warning

8 Do not, under any circumstances, attempt to improve lock operation by introducing oil into it. Should oil find its way into the ignition switch it will create a fire hazard. Oil will also cause inefficient operation by attracting dirt into the mechanism.

Wheel size

9 As from October 1984 all models are fitted with 12 inch wheels as listed in the Specifications.

Rear wheel toe-in – excessive tyre wear

10 Too much toe-in of the rear wheels can cause excessive wear of the rear tyres.

11 Where this is found to be the case then a spacer, available from your dealer, may be fitted between the radius arm outer bracket and the subframe.

12 In some cases the bolt holes on the lower side of the outer bracket may need to be elongated.

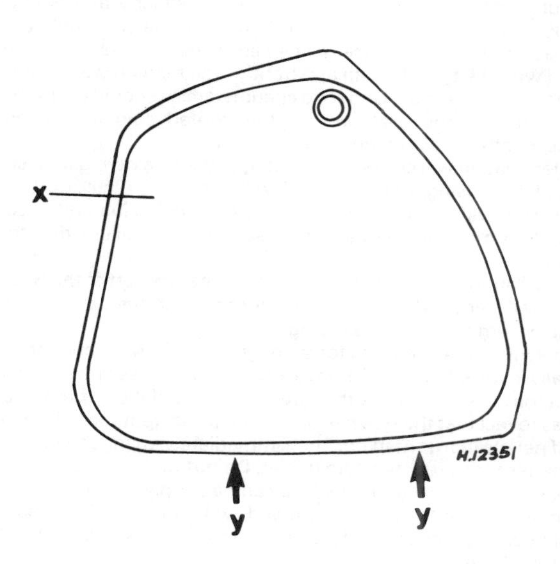

Fig. 14.41 Position of fuel tank-to-floor panel spacers (Sec 15)

X Fuel tank Y Spacer

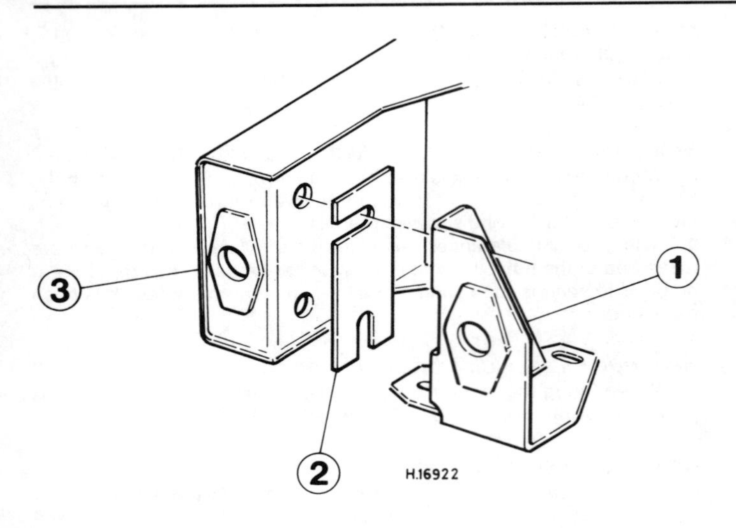

Fig. 14.42 Radius arm outer bracket spacer (Sec 15)

1 *Bracket* 3 *Subframe*
2 *Spacer*

13 Where only one tyre is affected, it is permissible to fit a spacer to that side only.

Driveshaft hub nuts – 1986 on

14 Some later driveshafts only have one split pin hole for locking the hub nut.

15 When refitting a hub nut to one of these driveshafts, tighten the nut to the specified torque (see Specifications) and then continue tightening the nut to align the split pin hole.

Wheels and tyres – general care and maintenance

Wheels and tyres should give no real problems in use provided that a close eye is kept on them with regard to excessive wear or damage. To this end, the following points should be noted.

Ensure that tyre pressures are checked regularly and maintained correctly. Checking should be carried out with the tyres cold and not immediately after the vehicle has been in use. If the pressures are checked with the tyres hot, an apparently high reading will be obtained owing to heat expansion. Under no circumstances should an attempt be made to reduce the pressures to the quoted cold reading in this instance, or effective underinflation will result.

Underinflation will cause overheating of the tyre owing to excessive flexing of the casing, and the tread will not sit correctly on the road surface. This will cause a consequent loss of adhesion and excessive wear, not to mention the danger of sudden tyre failure due to heat build-up.

Overinflation will cause rapid wear of the centre part of the tyre tread coupled with reduced adhesion, harsher ride, and the danger of shock damage occurring in the tyre casing.

Regularly check the tyres for damage in the form of cuts or bulges, especially in the sidewalls. Remove any nails or stones embedded in the tread before they penetrate the tyre to cause deflation. If removal of a nail *does* reveal that the tyre has been punctured, refit the nail so that its point of penetration is marked. Then immediately change the wheel and have the tyre repaired by a tyre dealer. **Do not** drive on a tyre in such a condition. In many cases a puncture can be simply repaired by the use of an inner tube of the correct size and type. If in any doubt as to the possible consequences of any damage found, consult your local tyre dealer for advice.

Periodically remove the wheels and clean any dirt or mud from the inside and outside surfaces. Examine the wheel rims for signs of rusting, corrosion or other damage. Light alloy wheels are easily damaged by 'kerbing' whilst parking, and similarly steel wheels may become dented or buckled. Renewal of the wheel is very often the only course of remedial action possible.

The balance of each wheel and tyre assembly should be maintained to avoid excessive wear, not only to the tyres but also to the steering and suspension components. Wheel imbalance is normally signified by vibration through the vehicle's bodyshell, although in many cases it is particularly noticeable through the steering wheel. Conversely, it should be noted that wear or damage in suspension or steering components may cause excessive tyre wear. Out-of-round or out-of-true tyres, damaged wheels and wheel bearing wear/maladjustment also fall into this category. Balancing will not usually cure vibration caused by such wear.

Wheel balancing may be carried out with the wheel either on or off the vehicle. If balanced on the vehicle, ensure that the wheel-to-hub relationship is marked in some way prior to subsequent wheel removal so that it may be refitted in its original position.

General tyre wear is influenced to a large degree by driving style – harsh braking and acceleration or fast cornering will all produce more rapid tyre wear. Interchanging of tyres may result in more even wear, but this should only be carried out where there is no mix of tyre types on the vehicle. However, it is worth bearing in mind that if this is completely effective, the added expense of replacing a complete set of tyres simultaneously is incurred, which may prove financially restrictive for many owners.

Front tyres may wear unevenly as a result of wheel misalignment. The front wheels should always be correctly aligned according to the settings specified by the vehicle manufacturer.

Legal restrictions apply to the mixing of tyre types on a vehicle. Basically this means that a vehicle must not have tyres of differing construction on the same axle. Although it is not recommended to mix tyre types between front axle and rear axle, the only legally permissible combination is crossply at the front and radial at the rear. When mixing radial ply tyres, textile braced radials must always go on the front axle, with steel braced radials at the rear. An obvious disadvantage of such mixing is the necessity to carry two spare tyres to avoid contravening the law in the event of a puncture.

In the UK, the Motor Vehicles Construction and Use Regulations apply to many aspects of tyre fitting and usage. It is suggested that a copy of these regulations is obtained from your local police if in doubt as to the current legal requirements with regard to tyre condition, minimum tread depth, etc.

16 Bodywork and fittings

Front door lock – Saloon and Estate

1 If problems are experienced with lock operation, suspect incorrect positioning of the handle inner remote control mechanism (see Section 12, Chapter 12).

2 If the handle fails to lock, loosen the three mechanism retaining screws and move it forwards to correct operation. If the handle fails to unlock, move the mechanism rearwards.

Windscreen mirror

3 If attempting to remove a self-adhesive interior mirror from the windscreen, avoid possible damage to the screen by gently warming the mirror base and area of screen around it. Use a hair drier or rag soaked in warm water as a heat source.

Heater – poor performance

4 Where poor heater performance is experienced, it may be due to the foam liner in the inlet duct being too long and causing a partial blockage of the air inlet duct.

5 Where this is so, remove the inlet duct and cut approximately 75.0 mm of foam liner from the liner rear end.

6 Refit the liner, ensuring it is now clear of the air box and refit the air duct.

7 Check the operation of the heater on completion.

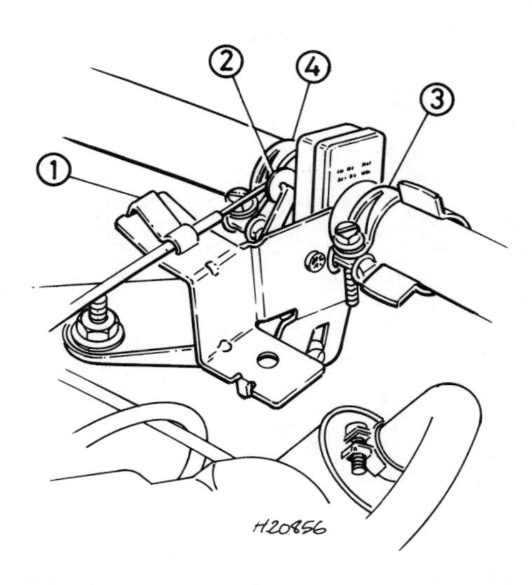

Fig. 14.43 Heater valve for 1989 on models (Sec 16)

1 Outer cable securing clip
2 Inner cable fixing
3 and 4 Coolant hose clips

Heater matrix – modification

8 To overcome difficulty in fitting, the diameter of the pipe-to-matrix hose has been increased and the length of the inlet hose has also been increased.

9 If a heater matrix on an early vehicle (pre 1986) is changed for any reason, it is important that a longer hose is fitted.

10 The hose length should be 1005.0 mm.

Heater valve (1989 on) – removal and refitting

11 Drain the cooling system with reference to Chapter 2.

12 Disconnect the coolant hoses and control cable, and withdraw the heater valve from the bulkhead.

13 Refitting is a reversal of removal, but check that the valve can be moved through its full range of travel. If necessary adjust the cable.

General repair procedures

Whenever servicing, repair or overhaul work is carried out on the car or its components, it is necessary to observe the following procedures and instructions. This will assist in carrying out the operation efficiently and to a professional standard of workmanship.

Joint mating faces and gaskets

Where a gasket is used between the mating faces of two components, ensure that it is renewed on reassembly, and fit it dry unless otherwise stated in the repair procedure. Make sure that the mating faces are clean and dry with all traces of old gasket removed. When cleaning a joint face, use a tool which is not likely to score or damage the face, and remove any burrs or nicks with an oilstone or fine file.

Make sure that tapped holes are cleaned with a pipe cleaner, and keep them free of jointing compound if this is being used unless specifically instructed otherwise.

Ensure that all orifices, channels or pipes are clear and blow through them, preferably using compressed air.

Oil seals

Whenever an oil seal is removed from its working location, either individually or as part of an assembly, it should be renewed.

The very fine sealing lip of the seal is easily damaged and will not seal if the surface it contacts is not completely clean and free from scratches, nicks or grooves. If the original sealing surface of the component cannot be restored, the component should be renewed.

Protect the lips of the seal from any surface which may damage them in the course of fitting. Use tape or a conical sleeve where possible. Lubricate the seal lips with oil before fitting and, on dual lipped seals, fill the space between the lips with grease.

Unless otherwise stated, oil seals must be fitted with their sealing lips toward the lubricant to be sealed.

Use a tubular drift or block of wood of the appropriate size to install the seal and, if the seal housing is shouldered, drive the seal down to the shoulder. If the seal housing is unshouldered, the seal should be fitted with its face flush with the housing top face.

Screw threads and fastenings

Always ensure that a blind tapped hole is completely free from oil, grease, water or other fluid before installing the bolt or stud. Failure to do this could cause the housing to crack due to the hydraulic action of the bolt or stud as it is screwed in.

When tightening a castellated nut to accept a split pin, tighten the nut to the specified torque, where applicable, and then tighten further to the next split pin hole. Never slacken the nut to align a split pin hole unless stated in the repair procedure.

When checking or retightening a nut or bolt to a specified torque setting, slacken the nut or bolt by a quarter of a turn, and then retighten to the specified setting.

Locknuts, locktabs and washers

Any fastening which will rotate against a component or housing in the course of tightening should always have a washer between it and the relevant component or housing.

Spring or split washers should always be renewed when they are used to lock a critical component such as a big-end bearing retaining nut or bolt.

Locktabs which are folded over to retain a nut or bolt should always be renewed.

Self-locking nuts can be reused in non-critical areas, providing resistance can be felt when the locking portion passes over the bolt or stud thread.

Split pins must always be replaced with new ones of the correct size for the hole.

Special tools

Some repair procedures in this manual entail the use of special tools such as a press, two or three-legged pullers, spring compressors etc. Wherever possible, suitable readily available alternatives to the manufacturer's special tools are described, and are shown in use. In some instances, where no alternative is possible, it has been necessary to resort to the use of a manufacturer's tool and this has been done for reasons of safety as well as the efficient completion of the repair operation. Unless you are highly skilled and have a thorough understanding of the procedure described, never attempt to bypass the use of any special tool when the procedure described specifies its use. Not only is there a very great risk of personal injury, but expensive damage could be caused to the components involved.

Conversion factors

Length (distance)					
Inches (in)	X 25.4	= Millimetres (mm)	X 0.0394	= Inches (in)
Feet (ft)	X 0.305	= Metres (m)	X 3.281	= Feet (ft)
Miles	X 1.609	= Kilometres (km)	X 0.621	= Miles
Volume (capacity)				
Cubic inches (cu in; in³)	X 16.387	= Cubic centimetres (cc; cm³)	X 0.061	= Cubic inches (cu in; in³)
Imperial pints (Imp pt)	X 0.568	= Litres (l)	X 1.76	= Imperial pints (Imp pt)
Imperial quarts (Imp qt)	X 1.137	= Litres (l)	X 0.88	= Imperial quarts (Imp qt)
Imperial quarts (Imp qt)	X 1.201	= US quarts (US qt)	X 0.833	= Imperial quarts (Imp qt)
US quarts (US qt)	X 0.946	= Litres (l)	X 1.057	= US quarts (US qt)
Imperial gallons (Imp gal)	X 4.546	= Litres (l)	X 0.22	= Imperial gallons (Imp gal)
Imperial gallons (Imp gal)	X 1.201	= US gallons (US gal)	X 0.833	= Imperial gallons (Imp gal)
US gallons (US gal)	X 3.785	= Litres (l)	X 0.264	= US gallons (US gal)
Mass (weight)				
Ounces (oz)	X 28.35	= Grams (g)	X 0.035	= Ounces (oz)
Pounds (lb)	X 0.454	= Kilograms (kg)	X 2.205	= Pounds (lb)
Force				
Ounces-force (ozf; oz)	X 0.278	= Newtons (N)	X 3.6	= Ounces-force (ozf; oz)
Pounds-force (lbf; lb)	X 4.448	= Newtons (N)	X 0.225	= Pounds-force (lbf; lb)
Newtons (N)	X 0.1	= Kilograms-force (kgf; kg)	X 9.81	= Newtons (N)
Pressure				
Pounds-force per square inch (psi; lbf/in²; lb/in²)	X 0.070	= Kilograms-force per square centimetre (kgf/cm²; kg/cm²)	X 14.223	= Pounds-force per square inch (psi; lbf/in²; lb/in²)
Pounds-force per square inch (psi; lbf/in²; lb/in²)	X 0.068	= Atmospheres (atm)	X 14.696	= Pounds-force per square inch (psi; lbf/in²; lb/in²)
Pounds-force per square inch (psi; lbf/in²; lb/in²)	X 0.069	= Bars	X 14.5	= Pounds-force per square inch (psi; lbf/in²; lb/in²)
Pounds-force per square inch (psi; lbf/in²; lb/in²)	X 6.895	= Kilopascals (kPa)	X 0.145	= Pounds-force per square inch (psi; lbf/in²; lb/in²)
Kilopascals (kPa)	X 0.01	= Kilograms-force per square centimetre (kgf/cm²; kg/cm²)	X 98.1	= Kilopascals (kPa)
Millibar (mbar)	X 100	= Pascals (Pa)	X 0.01	= Millibar (mbar)
Millibar (mbar)	X 0.0145	= Pounds-force per square inch (psi; lbf/in²; lb/in²)	X 68.947	= Millibar (mbar)
Millibar (mbar)	X 0.75	= Millimetres of mercury (mmHg)	X 1.333	= Millibar (mbar)
Millibar (mbar)	X 0.401	= Inches of water (inH_2O)	X 2.491	= Millibar (mbar)
Millimetres of mercury (mmHg)	X 0.535	= Inches of water (inH_2O)	X 1.868	= Millimetres of mercury (mmHg)
Inches of water (inH_2O)	X 0.036	= Pounds-force per square inch (psi; lbf/in²; lb/in²)	X 27.68	= Inches of water (inH_2O)
Torque (moment of force)				
Pounds-force inches (lbf in; lb in)	X 1.152	= Kilograms-force centimetre (kgf cm; kg cm)	X 0.868	= Pounds-force inches (lbf in; lb in)
Pounds-force inches (lbf in; lb in)	X 0.113	= Newton metres (Nm)	X 8.85	= Pounds-force inches (lbf in; lb in)
Pounds-force inches (lbf in; lb in)	X 0.083	= Pounds-force feet (lbf ft; lb ft)	X 12	= Pounds-force inches (lbf in; lb in)
Pounds-force feet (lbf ft; lb ft)	X 0.138	= Kilograms-force metres (kgf m; kg m)	X 7.233	= Pounds-force feet (lbf ft; lb ft)
Pounds-force feet (lbf ft; lb ft)	X 1.356	= Newton metres (Nm)	X 0.738	= Pounds-force feet (lbf ft; lb ft)
Newton metres (Nm)	X 0.102	= Kilograms-force metres (kgf m; kg m)	X 9.804	= Newton metres (Nm)
Power				
Horsepower (hp)	X 745.7	= Watts (W)	X 0.0013	= Horsepower (hp)
Velocity (speed)				
Miles per hour (miles/hr; mph)	X 1.609	= Kilometres per hour (km/hr; kph)	X 0.621	= Miles per hour (miles/hr; mph)
Fuel consumption*				
Miles per gallon, Imperial (mpg)	X 0.354	= Kilometres per litre (km/l)	X 2.825	= Miles per gallon, Imperial (mpg)
Miles per gallon, US (mpg)	X 0.425	= Kilometres per litre (km/l)	X 2.352	= Miles per gallon, US (mpg)

Temperature

Degrees Fahrenheit = (°C x 1.8) + 32

Degrees Celsius (Degrees Centigrade; °C) = (°F - 32) x 0.56

**It is common practice to convert from miles per gallon (mpg) to litres/100 kilometres (l/100km), where mpg (Imperial) x l/100 km = 282 and mpg (US) x l/100 km = 235*

Index

F

G

H

T

U

V

W